CARIBBEAN HISTORY

CARIBBEAN HISTORY

FROM PRE-COLONIAL ORIGINS TO THE PRESENT

Tony Martin

Emeritus Professor of Africana Studies
Wellesley College

PEARSON

Boston   Columbus   Indianapolis   New York   San Francisco   Upper Saddle River
Amsterdam   Cape Town   Dubai   London   Madrid   Milan   Munich   Paris   Montréal   Toronto
Delhi   Mexico City   São Paulo   Sydney   Hong Kong   Seoul   Singapore   Taipei   Tokyo

Editorial Director: Craig Campanella
Editor in Chief: Dickson Musslewhite
Executive Editor: Jeff Lasser
Editorial Project Manager: Rob DeGeorge
Editorial Assistant: Julia Feltus
Director of Marketing: Brandy Dawson
Senior Marketing Manager: Maureen E. Prado Roberts
Marketing Assistant: Samantha Bennett
Senior Managing Editor: Ann Marie McCarthy
Senior Project Manager: Debra A. Wechsler
Senior Operations Supervisor: Mary Fischer
Operations Specialist: Alan Fischer
Cover Designer: Bruce Kenselaar
Cover Photo: National Academy for the Performing Arts, Port of Spain, Trinidad. Photo by Tony Martin, 2011.
Full-Service Project Management: Moganambigai Sundaramurthy
Composition: Integra Software Services Pvt. Ltd.
Printer/Binder: R. R. Donnelley/Harrisonburg
Cover Printer: R. R. Donnelley/Harrisonburg
Text Font: 10/12 Times

Credits and acknowledgments borrowed from other sources and reproduced, with permission, in this textbook appear on the appropriate page within the text or on page 347.

Many of the designations by manufacturers and seller to distinguish their products are claimed as trademarks. Where those designations appear in this book, and the publisher was aware of a trademark claim, the designations have been printed in initial caps or all caps.

Library of Congress Cataloging-in-Publication Data
Martin, Tony
  Caribbean history : from pre-colonial origins to the present/Tony Martin.
    p. cm.
  Includes bibliographical references and index.
  ISBN-13: 978-0-13-220860-4 (alk. paper)
  ISBN-10: 0-13-220860-1 (alk. paper)
  1. Caribbean Area—History. 2. Caribbean Area—Race relations. I. Title.
  F2175.M28 2012
  972.9—dc23

                          2011032034

10 9 8 7 6 5 4 3 2 1

ISBN 10:   0-13-220860-1
ISBN 13: 978-0-13-220860-4

To SHABAKA,

Beloved Son,

Constant companion

Through the writing of this book.

Baby, this one can only be for you,

In whom I am well pleased.

CONTENTS

PREFACE

In this text I have attempted to overhaul, as it were, the approach to a survey of Caribbean history. I have tried to reframe the way in which some, at least, of the subject is viewed and presented. I have tried to manage the delicate balancing act of a readable undergraduate narrative which nevertheless avoids the temptation of degenerating into a series of bland sound bites, some accurate, some not. I have tried to present a greater depth of information than is often the case in surveys. There is a modest sprinkling of new information here that has not appeared elsewhere, whether in monographs or in other surveys. There is also a fair amount of "virtually" new material, that is, material gleaned from a new look at old sources that have been around, sometimes for hundreds of years, but which have not been reexamined in depth for a long time. I have also benefitted, as all survey text writers must, from very recent scholarship.

Within the modest confines of Chapter 1, "Original Peoples," I have still tried to present a fuller account of the indigenous people than is customary in surveys. I have continued this endeavor into Chapter 2. Access to recent scholarship has enabled me to correct an occasional misconception of earlier surveys. Here, as elsewhere throughout the book, I have not been afraid to stop to savor a quotation for its sheer literary beauty. It might be Columbus waxing lyrical (even in translation) over the natural beauty of the islands, or English poet Wordsworth praising Toussaint L'Ouverture in exquisite verse, or John G. Stedman in Suriname breaking into poetry when his excellent-enough prose could not adequately express his anguish at the loss of his concubine Joanna and their son.

In Chapter 2, "The Coming of Columbus," I have naturally not entertained any notion of Columbus as a "discoverer" of people who were just waiting around for millennia for him to discover them. I have acknowledged his role as a conduit for enslavement and genocide. After all is said and done, however, Columbus remains a towering figure in the history of the Caribbean and the world. While some of the realities discussed here clearly tarnish his reputation, they cannot objectively diminish his impact. Columbus' first voyage represented a watershed in world history, whether for good or ill, like few events have ever done.

I have given a fuller consideration to the question of pre-Columbian Old World visitors to the New World than has been attempted in any previous survey. This brief discussion takes us back to Ancient Egypt and Plato, for which I make no apologies. If modern survey textbook writers have largely ignored this fascinating aspect of Caribbean history, their venerable precursor, Bartolomé de Las Casas, writing in the sixteenth century, did not. He speculated on the similarity between the Egyptian and Central American pyramids.

The whole "Columbian exchange" of everything from animals and plants to syphilis has also received more focus here than in earlier surveys. I have also highlighted Columbus' African connections which, though obscurely known, have not hitherto been the subject of much interest.

I have been more forthright in calling what Columbus initiated "genocide" than is usual in survey texts. These have mostly preferred euphemisms concerning the "disappearance" of the indigenous population. I have also addressed the vexed question of the number of victims of this Caribbean genocide. It has been fashionable in some quarters to dismiss the elevated indigenous population estimates of Las Casas as part of a grossly exaggerated "Black Legend." Now, however, comes recent scholarship, noted here, which suggests that Las Casas may, if anything, have underestimated the indigenous population at the time of Columbian contact. While these new conclusions are not universally accepted, their consideration materially changes the tenor of the debate concerning just how many people the Spaniards exterminated in the first half century or so after Columbus.

The traditional notion of the Arawaks as "docile," though not totally without foundation, has nevertheless tended to obscure the desperate resistance they offered to Spanish aggression. This is especially strange since Las Casas and other contemporary Spanish historians documented it. In this text I have tried to restore this aspect of the first indigenous–Spanish encounter to its rightful importance.

The Northern European challenge to Spain (Chapter 3) is well known and well covered in most earlier surveys. Here too, however, I have tried to flush out some aspects that are often mentioned but mostly only in passing. These include the search for El Dorado, the campaigns of English pirates Francis Drake and John Hawkins and the largely forgotten adventures of Robert Dudley, including his claiming of Trinidad for Queen Elizabeth I of England in 1595, an incident which will surprise most readers of this book, including many mature historians. Equally surprising will be the revelation that Dudley had two apparently enslaved East Indians with him, one of whom remained in Trinidad, becoming, in 1595, the first Indian immigrant in the Caribbean.

In this chapter, as in earlier and subsequent chapters, I have tried to present a vivid picture of the "micro" aspects of Caribbean history in addition to the traditional big "macro" overview. Henry Whistler's narrative was very helpful here, in providing a real sense of what it was like to be a soldier in Oliver Cromwell's grand "Western design" against Jamaica in 1655. Far from the glorious English victory of the sound bites, this came close to being a pyrrhic victory for the English. The campaign against Santo Domingo, which preceded the attack on Jamaica, was a comprehensive Spanish rout of the English invaders. Whistler is known to Caribbean historiography. Historians seem to have used him but rarely, however, save for his famous reference to Barbados as the "dunghill whereon England doth cast forth its rubbish."

In this chapter I have also tried to provide a full listing of all the European colonizers, including some such as the Swedes, Latvians, Roman Catholic Knights of Malta, Sephardic Jews and German bankers of the House of Welser (in Venezuela), who are only sporadically mentioned.

My extensive treatment of the period of African enslavement (Chapters 4–9) reflects the reality, seemingly sometimes forgotten, that for the 384 years from 1502 to 1886, most of the period since Columbus, Africans were enslaved somewhere or other in the Caribbean. There is no getting around the fact that this represents a major reality of Caribbean history. I have tried to restore to this unfortunate period the importance it deserves.

Here again, I have tried to convey a vivid sense of the "micro" reality—what it was like to be an enslaved person. The historiography of enslavement is probably the most extensive of any aspect of Caribbean history, and yet in three and a half decades of teaching Caribbean history and lecturing to lay audiences about it, I was always struck by the seeming inability of that vast literature to convey to the public a full sense of the savagery of the institution, the struggle of the enslaved to live some approximation of normal lives in spite of it and the ferocity of African retaliation when the opportunity presented itself. In the process I have had to treat forthrightly those aspects of the institution which some, in a latter-day Victorian-like squeamishness, might consider too lurid to be told.

I argue here that the response of the enslaved approximated something akin to perpetual war, especially in the late eighteenth and early nineteenth centuries. Eric Williams, as far back as 1944 in *Capitalism and Slavery,* indicated that the enslaved through their rebelliousness played a great part in securing their own emancipation. He showed that attributing exaggerated weight to the work of the metropolitan abolitionist "saints" was misguided. Yet he did not probe the rebellious activity of the enslaved sufficiently to *demonstrate* what he had correctly postulated.

I present the history of Caribbean African enslavement here as a great epic of persistent, protracted and eventually successful struggle against great odds. The enslaved were hampered by enforced lack of access to literacy; brutish punishments; restricted mobility; limited access to arms, ammunition, military reinforcements and diplomatic support; and the absence of the kind of state industrial apparatus that would normally sustain a war. They were also fighting the most powerful nations on the face of the earth. Yet they persisted bravely and eventually won their freedom.

In examining the armed struggles against enslavement waged in Suriname, Dominica, St. Vincent, Jamaica and elsewhere, I have again tried to restore to importance episodes that are often relegated to sound bites or not mentioned at all. Yet it is clear from this work that these were real wars waged by enslaved people who for tens, sometimes for hundreds of years simply could not be defeated by European forces. In the process they perfected techniques of guerilla warfare that would have been at home in the Vietnamese and other guerilla wars of the twentieth century.

To say that too much credit has been given to the "saints" in the past is not, however, to say that European abolitionists did not play an important role. However belated their appearance, they provided a crucial element, in the British empire especially, as the struggle against enslavement neared its climax. They provided the enslaved with an international support group, as it were, in the belly of the beast. Whether their motives were pure and whether they loved Africans sufficient to want to live next door to them after Emancipation and whether they would let their daughter marry a freedman are matters of at best secondary significance.

Few of the twentieth century's great liberation struggles—the Vietnam War, the Irish struggle against the British, the antiapartheid struggle in South Africa and Zimbabwe, the struggle for Civil Rights and Black Power in the United States, the liberation struggles against the Portuguese in Angola and Mozambique, the Indian struggle against British rule—succeeded without mobilizing international support. The Caribbean enslaved were not in a position to establish their own lobbies in the metropolis but the metropolitan abolitionists fulfilled that function.

In my enslavement chapters I have utilized what may perhaps be a novel device in letting some key representatives of the enslaved population act as narrators and commentators. I return to them again and again to provide corroborative first-person evidence from the enslaved themselves, for facts gleaned partially from other sources. The fact that the Caribbean does not have an established literary genre of slave narratives as does African America, may have obscured the reality that some of the most important narratives of the enslaved came out of the Caribbean. The three authors I utilize here for ongoing commentary and corroboration are Olaudah Equiano, Mary Prince and Esteban Montejo. Equiano, enslaved in both the Caribbean and the United States, wrote the first blockbuster narrative coming out of the Americas. Mary Prince's was the first ever by a woman. Montejo narrated his in 1963 when he was 103 years old, making his the final narrative by a freedman in the Americas. Together these three narrators cover a wide and representative swath of the Caribbean and environs—Barbados, Montserrat, Bermuda, Turks Island, Antigua and Cuba. In addition, Equiano most valuably begins his narrative with capture in Africa and brings us through the Middle Passage. He also traveled all over the Caribbean and to ports in the United States as an enslaved seaman. He was also enslaved in Virginia—altogether a first-person account of immense value.

I have used in a similar way another self-described "narrative," that of Scottish-Dutch soldier of fortune John G. Stedman, who spent five years fighting the Maroons of Dutch Suriname in the 1770s. Accounts of European travelers in the enslaved Caribbean are numerous, though curiously not celebrated as a literary genre, which they should be. Stedman's is arguably the best of them all. As a commissioned officer he moved in the highest echelons of white

Surinamese society. As a confirmed liberal he mixed easily with his black troops and with the enslaved people who supported his troops as porters and laborers. He experienced Suriname like few others, visiting plantations, doing tours of military duty in the jungles and dining with governors. He wandered the streets, ever ready to remonstrate or even pick a fight with those, black or white, who offended him for whatever reason. In his celebrated love affair with the fifteen-year-old enslaved Joanna, he elevated an objectively sordid business into one of the great love stories of Caribbean history. He was an extraordinarily incisive observer of a wide gamut of plantation society. Even though he was fighting the Maroons, he respected them as worthy opponents and was able to provide unequalled detail concerning the military campaigns against them, as well as their military strategies and tactics. He was also a very literate person and well read. He could place what he observed in Suriname in wider contexts when he needed to.

Stedman's observations extend to drawings later made into woodcuts by William Blake, the celebrated English poet and artist. These drawings are classics by themselves and have been used in all manner of Caribbean books often, unfortunately, without attribution, and creating a false impression that the drawings relate to Santo Domingo or Jamaica or wherever else the offending books were about.

Some other writers serve as first-person narrators and corroborators, though mostly to a lesser extent than those named above. The exception is Thomas Thistlewood in eighteenth-century Jamaica, who documented in sordid detail, in his own hand, many of the worst excesses of plantation society, from giving venereal diseases to his enslaved people to, most infamously, using defecation and rape as forms of punishment.

Thistlewood and Stedman were miles apart in their attitudes toward the enslaved population. Yet they had much in common. They were both dedicated diarists. In the midst of his jungle campaigns Stedman would retire to his hammock to document the day's happenings. On one occasion when his home was threatened with destruction, Thistlewood ran back to the house to save his diaries, for which historical scholarship is profoundly grateful.

Both men were commissioned officers, Thistlewood in the militia. They were both British and were exact contemporaries. The fact that they were based in opposite ends of the Caribbean highlights the historical unity of the Caribbean experience. Both men were exceedingly literate, Thistlewood perhaps surprisingly so, given his depravity. Stedman's diaries are interspersed with classical allusions and quotations and poems of his own composition. Thistlewood maintained a library, constantly augmented with works from England, often obtained immediately upon publication, on a wide variety of scholarly and other subjects, and including children's books for his son, Mulatto John. Adam Smith and Rousseau are among the authors he read in the midst of his depraved depredations against his enslaved Africans.

Thistlewood and Stedman both had colored sons named John. Both Johns died tragically in the bloom of their early manhood. Both diarists suffered the loss of loved ones to poison, Joanna for Stedman and Mulatto John for Thistlewood. The available published version of Thistlewood's diaries is only Douglas Hall's abridgement of a longer original. Yet despite this and other shortcomings, including the fact that they inevitably view slavery through the eyes of an enslaver, still, as Hall says, "There is no other document known to us which by daily record over thirty-six years, allows us to find *people,* rather than names, among the [enslaved] work force of the time."

In Chapter 10, "After Emancipation," I try to show the savagery that descended upon the newly freed immediately after Emancipation. This included the floggings and banishments of those long suffering Africans who misguidedly thought that Emancipation meant immediate freedom. I have also examined the flagrant official disregard for the ameliorative aspects of the British Emancipation Act, as modest as they were. The continued flogging of women was arguably the worst of these official infractions.

I also discuss the continuing post-apprenticeship campaign to thwart African progress through immigration, oppressive laws and other means. I also address here, in a more focused way than other surveys, the remarkable progress of the formerly enslaved, even in the face of great obstacles.

In Chapter 11, "Immigration in the Nineteenth and Twentieth Centuries," I have tried to give a much fuller account of nineteenth- and twentieth-century immigration than is to be found in any other survey. (Some earlier popular histories largely ignored this topic, in at least one outstanding case, totally so.) I have greatly expanded coverage of two of the most important immigrant groups, Chinese and Indians. I have also fleshed out somewhat coverage of such groups as the Portuguese, African Americans and post-Emancipation Africans. I have elevated intra-Caribbean immigration to its rightful position as one of the most significant of all immigrant streams. I have included Lebanese-Syrians and Jews, two important groups of immigrants who normally receive no treatment in surveys and perfunctory treatment elsewhere.

Chapter 12, "The Caribbean and Africa through the Early Twentieth Century," is new to survey texts. Caribbean interest in Africa was a major factor in African progress and exerted a tremendous influence on the entire Pan-African world, well into the late twentieth century and beyond. Many of the major early intellectuals, political activists and newspaper publishers were involved in the Pan-African activity emanating from the Caribbean in the nineteenth century and later.

United States–Caribbean relations (Chapter 13) are widely covered in survey texts. I have added a section on the Caribbean–African American aspect of that connection, an element of overwhelming importance for the histories of both the Caribbean and African America.

Some earlier surveys have tended to begin to fizzle out early in the twentieth century. Even Eric Williams, a major participant himself in much of the century's historical developments, had little to say on much of this in his survey, *From Columbus to Castro*, though it remains an important book. Here (Chapters 14 and 15) I have looked at the twentieth century in much more detail than hitherto. Many of the topics covered here are absent from earlier surveys or receive too little attention. These include the 1912 racial massacre in Cuba, World War I, the postwar upheaval and more, including Audrey Jeffers, the most important Caribbean women's leader of the period. Marcus Garvey, sometimes given adequate treatment in African American texts, is usually glossed over or worse in Caribbean texts. Yet he was just as important a figure in the Caribbean as he was in African America. I have remedied this neglect here. In considering the rise of the Afro-Caribbean middle class in the interwar years, I have again explored a subject as often neglected as it is important. The manner of this group's rise in business may surprise some.

Survey textbook writers on the Caribbean have all grappled with the problem of what to do as the narrative approaches contemporary times. It is usually more difficult to take the entire region as a single entity the nearer one gets to the present. This has usually meant a country-by-country or region-by-region approach as the text gets into the twentieth century. In at least one important earlier text, the twentieth-century region-by-region discussion consumed over half the entire book.

I tried in Chapter 15 to avoid this approach, which I consider dreary and boring, but I have not been able to avoid it altogether. In this chapter I have also provided more information than hitherto on a variety of subjects, including the British West Indies federation, Black Power, British Guiana's troubles in the 1950s and 1960s and Indian consciousness.

A NOTE ON USAGE

Since at least the early twentieth century, Civil Rights activists in African America and the Caribbean have been calling for the capitalization of the word "Negro." Marcus Garvey's Universal Negro Improvement Association demanded capitalization at its 1920 International Convention in New York. Just as this campaign was beginning to bear fruit in the 1960s, the word "Negro" itself became unacceptable. It was replaced by "Black," "Afro-American" and eventually "African American" and "African." The term "Negro" nevertheless lingered longer in the Caribbean, even in its noncapitalized form. Most of the direct quotes in this text did not capitalize "Negro" in the originals. I took the liberty to capitalize it throughout, in order to avoid an unacceptable overuse of the term "sic."

In the Caribbean the prefix "Afro" came into increased use in the late twentieth century, though its use actually dated back to the nineteenth. Some people also began to reject the term "West Indian," among them Amy Jacques Garvey, Marcus Garvey's wife, from as early as the 1940s. Such persons preferred the presumed indigenous and at least less Columbus-driven term "Caribbean," though "Caribbean" has problems of its own, being derived from "Carib," which was for the early Spaniards synonymous with "cannibal." I have nevertheless tended to prefer "Caribbean" to "West Indian," though the latter still intrudes in instances of necessity.

In the late twentieth century the word "slave" likewise joined the politically incorrect lexicon. "Enslaved" became the acceptable term for people who were not slaves by nature but simply forced into an enslaved status. The intent was fine, but the result can at times be stylistically challenging. In some contexts it takes a whole convoluted phrase to replace "slave." In this text I mostly use "enslaved" but sometimes, for stylistic simplicity, I use "African," "black" or some other designation. It is obvious from the context when I mean "African" to denote someone of African birth or descent, whether living in the Caribbean or anywhere else. In a few instances, as with the derivatives "slavemaster," "slave trade," "slave narrative" and "slavery," I have remained with the old forms.

I do not use "mulatto" and "colored" in present-day contexts, though it is not always possible to totally get around them for the historical period. The "coloreds" (sometimes "mulattoes") of the Caribbean, like those of South Africa, early became for officialdom a separate and distinct segment of society. Special laws applied to them. They were conscripted into separate militias. They were separately enumerated in censuses, and they were emancipated as a class separately from the great mass of enslaved. I have continued to use "colored" in historical contexts, especially where the term would have indicated persons legally distinct from "blacks."

I am very aware of the racist roots of the term "mulatto," which I myself describe in these pages. I have nevertheless felt it necessary to keep the term in some special circumstances within quotation marks, or where it formed part of someone's informal name, such as Thomas Thistlewood's son, "Mulatto John." Suggested alternatives such as "mixed race" (which I sometimes use) and "bi-racial" (which I have not used) are not without problems of their own. Both of these alternatives came into vogue in the late twentieth century in the context of some hostility to darker folk. For many of their proponents these terms actually represented a desire to return to the official differentiation between light and dark, which had increasingly eroded in the twentieth century.

"Further Reading" references are not intended to be exhaustive bibliographies. Rather they are simply suggestions. They usually indicate sources that I found especially helpful. Thanks to the wonderful world of the Internet, sources that may on their face seem obscure are now rendered accessible, sometimes even more so than recent scholarship. Google Books and other entities have digitized many of the rare books of Caribbean history. They have rendered them easily downloadable, often for free. JSTOR and others have done the same for journal articles. University students and patrons of public libraries can now access free, thanks to the subscriptions of their host institutions, thousands of articles from hitherto difficult to obtain journals.

ACKNOWLEDGMENTS

I would like to thank thirteen of the fourteen anonymous peer reviewers who commented on this work at various stages during its development. I was initially unaware of their identities, but I subsequently learned that some consented to the mention of their names. These were Fitzroy Andre Baptiste of the University of the West Indies, Trinidad; Edward L. Cox of Rice University; Graciella Cruz-Taura, Florida Atlantic University; Laurent Dubois, Michigan State University; Felix Germain, St. John's University; Alto A. Lauria-Santiago, Rutgers University; and Bert J. Thomas, Brooklyn College. I thank also those who preferred to remain anonymous. These scholars approached their task with a commendable application. They will see evidence of my receptiveness to many of their suggestions.

A few reviewers were extraordinarily fulsome in their praise. Even less enthusiastic reviews were nevertheless helpful, for they contained suggestions that I could use. There were occasions, even in the most positive of reviews, when a reviewer confidently signaled as wrong a fact of mine which was actually correct, though little known. My assertion of a Bahamian ancestry for W. E. B. DuBois is a case which comes to mind. In such instances I tried to revisit and strengthen what I had to say to forestall, I hope, similar misunderstandings by future reviewers.

Original Peoples

THE ISLANDS

The term "Caribbean" is normally understood to embrace the thousands of islands, large and small, which stretch like stepping-stones from Florida in the north to the northern shores of South America. To their west the islands are washed by the waters of the Caribbean Sea, which is itself enclosed by the Caribbean coasts of Central and South America. The waters of the mighty Atlantic Ocean lap the eastern shores of most of the islands. Further east is West Africa. There is practically nothing between the islands' eastern shores and Africa.

In English-language history texts of the Caribbean, it has been customary to include Belize in Central America and the Guianas (Guyana, Suriname and Cayenne) in South America. This is because these mainland territories were traditionally closely tied administratively to Caribbean islands. Similar considerations to a lesser extent apply to Bermuda which, though geographically isolated far into the Atlantic, nevertheless shares much historically with Caribbean islands. The Bahamas are technically a separate entity from the Caribbean but are historically very much a part of the area.

The term "Greater Caribbean" can be used to describe the islands together with the mainland countries which border them. This textbook will follow the traditional practice of focusing primarily on the islands, the Guianas and Belize (though much more on the former than the latter). It is impossible, however, to ignore entirely the Greater Caribbean area. The larger area has always interacted with the islands.

The Caribbean islands are subdivided into three major geographical areas. The Greater Antilles comprise the four largest islands of Cuba, Hispaniola (shared between Haiti and the Dominican Republic), Puerto Rico and Jamaica. The Bahamas are the myriad islands that extend from Florida to the Greater Antilles. The Lesser Antilles consist of a string of smaller islands from the vicinity of Puerto Rico to Trinidad in the south. These Lesser Antilles are further subdivided into the Leeward Islands in the north and the Windward Islands in the south. Both these terms are leftovers from the days of sailing ships.

It has been customary, especially in the Lesser Antilles, to consider these islands "mere specks in the ocean," insignificant to world affairs and lacking all potential to someday become world leaders. While it is true that some islands are little more than uninhabited rocks, it is also true that some at least of the islands are not nearly as small as their own inhabitants have been led to believe.

The problem lies partly in the Mercator projection map which has been the standard way of visualizing the world since the sixteenth century. This map, one of the great hoaxes of the colonial era, shows the Northern Hemisphere (especially Europe and North America), much larger in relation to the rest of the world than they really are. Areas in the Southern Hemisphere (e.g., the Caribbean, Africa and South America) are drawn much smaller than they are in reality.

These distortions have been remedied in the Peters maps, which will be preferred in this book. One glance at the Peters maps will establish how big or small areas are in relation to one another. It will be readily apparent that Cuba, for example, is nearly as big as England. Columbus recognized this fact immediately in 1492—in fact he thought that Cuba was larger than England and Scotland put together.

The islands are all within the tropical or subtropical zones and form a single cultural unit. Similarities far outweigh differences in topography, flora and fauna, local foodstuffs, lifestyle and cultural expressions. The broad sweep of history has similarly touched all the islands, at every stage of their development.

Today, for reasons which will become apparent in this book, the islands are home to a variety of racial and linguistic groups. Most territories are now independent, though some still remain attached, via one political device or another, to their French, Dutch, British or U.S. overlords.

FIRST NATIONS

The written history of the Caribbean began abruptly with Christopher Columbus' European incursion of 1492. The people Columbus met were not literate and therefore did not document their history in writing. The picture available to us today of the pre-Columbian period is far from complete, but scholars have been steadily piecing together information on the lives of the first Caribbean nations. Information on these original people comes from three main sources, namely

1. The work of archaeologists. These have unearthed skeletal remains, remains of settlements and artifacts of all kinds. Archaeologists have also worked closely with scholars in other disciplines such as linguistics, geography and ethnography to try to reconstruct the lives of the original peoples.

2. The study of First Nations people who survived outside the Caribbean. The first inhabitants of the islands migrated primarily from South and Central America. Some of their distant relations, as it were, still live in places such as Guyana and Venezuela. It is possible by observing the languages and cultures of these survivors to catch an occasional glimpse of their earlier Caribbean counterparts.

3. The observations of the first Europeans. It is unfortunate to have to rely heavily on the testimony of Columbus and his compatriots since, however useful their observations, they were still outsiders looking in on cultures they did not always understand. Still we are greatly indebted to the early European historians, conquerors, priests, administrators and travelers for documenting the lifestyles of the original inhabitants. They thereby provided at the very least, a body of material to sift through and analyze, if even all of it cannot always be uncritically accepted as self-evident truth.

It was not long after 1492 before a few native peoples were born and raised in Spanish colonialism, complete with literacy in the Spanish language. In an ideal situation, these should have been a perfect group to record in writing the history and culture of their people. Unfortunately, however, as will soon be shown, by the time they came along, their people were already being rapidly exterminated. This extermination was virtually complete before there was time for a stable literate native community to emerge in the islands, with the facilities and leisure to document the history of their own people.

An obvious place for a literate class of indigenous historians to start would have been the *areytos* (or *arietos*), which survived the early years of the Spanish invasion. *Areytos* were songs accompanied by dance, in which people sang of the history and genealogies of their community. These ceremonies could go on for days and were reminiscent of the

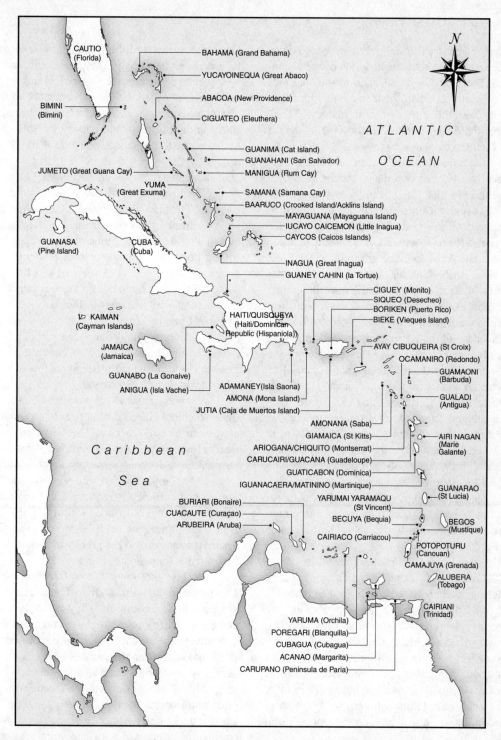

Map 1-1 Indigenous Names for the Caribbean *Source:* Based on Sued-Badillo, Jalil, Ed.
General History of the Caribbean, Volume 1: Autochthonous Societies. London: Palgrave Macmillan;
Paris: UNESCO, 2003.

recitations of the traditional *griots* of West Africa who likewise memorized the histories of their communities. Bartolomé de Las Casas, most illustrious of the pioneer Spanish historians of the area, enthused over this form of oral history. "They remember these songs better," he observed, "than if they had written them down in books."

It has traditionally been asserted that Columbus in 1492 met two major groups of indigenous people in the Caribbean. These were the Arawaks (usually called Tainos in the Spanish-speaking territories) and the Island Caribs (so named to distinguish them from their Carib cousins in South America). The Arawaks lived primarily, though not exclusively, in the Greater Antilles, the Bahamas and parts of Trinidad. The Caribs lived mainly, though not exclusively, in the Lesser Antilles. The Caribs were relative newcomers to the islands. The Arawaks and their predecessors had inhabited the islands for perhaps 7,000 years or thereabouts.

Archaeologists have argued among themselves as to whether the terms "Arawak" and "Taino" are appropriate for the Caribbean in 1492. Some argue that the alleged Island Arawaks were in fact far removed from their distant Arawak forebears from South America. They argue that the term "Arawak" is a catch-all for a variety of Caribbean peoples who were, in 1492, at differing stages of development. Some suggest that the term "Taino" is less inappropriate than "Arawak" since it connotes a common linguistic tradition, rather than a homogenous cultural grouping.

Those who challenge the suitability of the terms "Arawak" and "Taino" have come up with a bewildering welter of alternative designations. Instead of a single Arawak or Taino population, they propose a fragmented assortment of Huecoids, Ortoiroids, Casimiroids, Saladoids, Barrancoids, Troumassoids and others, all defined by styles of pottery found at various archaeological locations. Some of these groups are said to have been extinct, at least as culturally unique groups, in 1492. Others were assimilating into a newly developing Taino culture.

For reasons of convenience, this text will continue to designate as Arawaks and Tainos the indigenous people who greeted Columbus in the Greater Antilles and the Bahamas. The terms will be used interchangeably. The Caribs will continue to be considered a separate group. Columbus is said to have encountered the last remnants of a third group, the Siboneys, in Western Cuba. The existence of these people is also a matter of dispute among archaeologists. Some suggest that if the Siboneys did exist they should more properly be termed "Guanahatabeys" or "Guanahacabibes."

The first known human beings in the islands lived in Trinidad about 6,000 BC. Archaeologists have examined their remains at the Banwari Trace site in Trinidad. Their pioneering presence may be linked both to Trinidad's closeness to the South American mainland, from whence these first arrivals came, and to the fact that Trinidad was joined to that mainland at various times in the past. People were living in Cuba by around 5,000 BC.

These early Trinidadians were part of a so-called Archaic immigrant group who continued into the Leeward and Windward Islands. They eventually merged with later immigrants.

A subsequent wave of new immigrants, among them so-called Huecoids and Saladoids, entered the area from South America. The Saladoids reached Puerto Rico by at least 430 BC. They continued into Hispaniola.

By around 400 AD, the various immigrant groups had sufficiently interacted to form the basis of a developing Caribbean culture. This process was well underway in 1492 when the invading Spaniards interrupted the process and destroyed the first Caribbean peoples.

Despite the inevitable differences over time and between locations, all of these communities shared much in common. They cultivated cassava and corn (maize), relied heavily on the sea for food and travel, traded with others in the region, fashioned implements and jewelry of stone, bone, wood, shell and mother of pearl, inhaled tobacco or other drugs, lived in wooden houses (*bohíos*) around a plaza and manufactured pottery. By the time that the Europeans came along, they met a Caribbean community which had been evolving for a long time. In its more advanced areas, most notably Hispaniola and Puerto Rico, this community was on the verge of developing powerful states.

The first Spanish observers described hundreds of political leaders or caciques. As in Africa of the same period, or indeed Europe itself, the most powerful caciques ruled over less powerful ones in a sort of confederacy. What the Spaniards called the *caciques majores* were akin to paramount chiefs in Africa or kings and emperors in Europe. The caciques under them would correspond roughly to the barons and earls of Europe and the lesser chiefs of Africa.

There were five major kingdoms (*cacicazgos*) in Hispaniola in 1492. They were Jaragua, ruled by the cacique Behechio, Maguana, ruled by Caonabo, Marién ruled by Guacanagari, Maguá under Guarionex and possibly a fifth, Higüey, under the cacica (female cacique) Iguanama. Hispaniola was also divided into five geographical regions, which did not necessarily coincide with political jurisdictions.

Caciques held tremendous power and combined both religious and political authority. Like African chiefs they sat on a *duho* or ceremonial stool. They wore various emblems of office. They alone were allowed more than one wife, having on occasion as many as twenty or thirty. There were no standing armies, but in time of war caciques could, according to Spanish reports, mobilize as many as 15,000 soldiers in Hispaniola and 11,000 in Puerto Rico. The islands lacked iron and steel. The most potent weapon at their disposal was therefore the poison-tipped arrow. Spanish armor provided some protection, but Oviedo in the 1520s reported that the Spaniards had still not found an antidote to this poison.

Caciques could order soldiers into suicide missions. The early Spanish historian Gonzalo Fernandez de Oviedo claimed that caciques on the Greater Caribbean mainland would occasionally themselves commit suicide in order to induce some of their subjects into the act.

Caciques lived with their extended families in large dwellings. They also maintained a *caney*, a spacious building for receiving important dignitaries. They constructed and maintained such public works as roads, ballparks and irrigation schemes. Succession was matrilineal. This meant that neither the cacique's son nor his wife inherited. Instead, inheritance passed to the cacique's mother's children, that is, to the ruler's brother or sister, or thence to the mother's nieces or nephews. If there were no heirs, then elections determined a successor. When caciques died, their possessions were distributed among mourners. Food was buried with them, to sustain them on their journey through the afterlife.

Most of the indigenes in the Greater Antilles and the Bahamas spoke the same language. The only exceptions were western Cuba, presumed home of the Siboneys/Guanahatabeys/Guanahacabibes and two isolated areas in northeast Hispaniola.

The Caribbean people were expert mariners. They had plied their waters for thousands of years. They knew the wind and ocean current patterns and were intimately familiar with the geography of the region. Here, as in Africa, Asia and elsewhere, local mariners were of invaluable assistance to European explorers. The Lucayos of the Bahamas showed Columbus how to get to Cuba. The indigenes told him that Martinique was one of the most easterly of the islands and therefore a convenient departure point for the journey back to Spain. In the Azores on the way back from Columbus' first voyage, two captured Arawaks drew him a map of the islands using beans. Native mariners such as these were the largely unsung heroes of European exploration. Columbus did, however, acknowledge them in a letter written at the end of his first voyage. "They are of a very keen intelligence," he wrote, "and men who navigate all those seas, so that it is marvelous the good account they give of everything. . . ."

The local vessels were dugout canoes of various sizes, made from the trunk of a single tree. After his first voyage, Columbus reported seeing canoes with as many as 70–80 people in them, each with an oar. Historian Las Casas reported canoes with up to a hundred on board.

On his fourth voyage in 1502, Columbus reported the biggest canoe he had ever seen, in the Bay Islands off the coast of Honduras. It contained a cabin for passengers and was laden with beer, cacao, cotton and other goods for trading. Columbus was so impressed that he kidnapped the canoe's captain for use as a guide. The natives' navigational skills were matched by their expertise as swimmers.

The sea also provided much of their food. Fish protein was supplemented by *hutías* and *coríes,* two

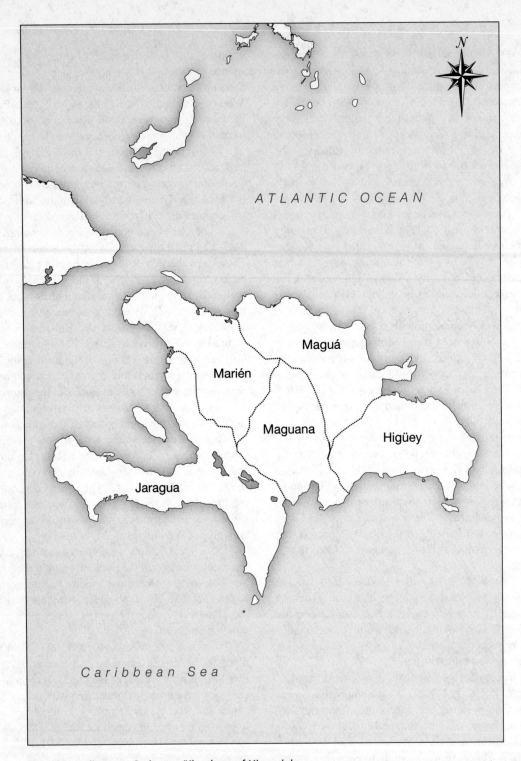

Map 1-2 Indigenous *Cacicazgos*/Kingdoms of Hispaniola

PIRRAVGVE·DE·LA·MARGERITE

PIRRAVGVE·DE·LA·TRENITE

Indigenous pirogues from Margarita and Trinidad in battle, ca. 1590. Women rowed while their husbands fought. Anyone taken prisoner remained a captive for life.

small animals which the indigenes hunted. They also ate the iguana, "a kind of serpent that is very fierce and fearful to look upon but is entirely harmless," as historian Oviedo noted. It was "better to eat than to see" he concluded.

A nonbarking dog was the only domesticated animal. The indigenes grew cotton and cultivated their staple food crop, cassava. Many of the staples and fruits they ate are still staples today. These included sweet potatoes, tannias, topee tambu, avocadoes, guavas, hog plums, mammee apples, bird peppers and others.

The local people made bread from both corn and cassava. Columbus proclaimed the cassava bread tasty and nutritious. The Spaniards generally adopted both corn and cassava bread. Cassava bread lasted for months and Spanish sailors used it for ship's rations.

Roasting was the preferred means of cooking corn in the islands. On the South American mainland, people ground corn to make a dough which they placed on a leaf and baked. Oviedo liked it this

way in the 1520s and many people on the mainland and in Trinidad still do. The Spaniards did not only adopt indigenous bread. They also adopted the indigenous methods of cultivating corn and cassava.

Indigenous houses (*bohíos*) were substantial structures, usually arranged around a plaza. Oviedo described the construction of *bohíos* in Hispaniola. The walls were made of canes tied with lianas and then plastered with earth. Roofing material was straw or long grass. The result, said Oviedo, was a house impervious to rain and with a roof as good as its tiled counterpart in Spain. On his second voyage in 1493, Columbus was impressed by a village in Puerto Rico. The houses were constructed of straw and wood. A clean, straight street ran from the village plaza to the sea. Walls made of woven reeds lined the street. Above them grew a pleasant spectacle of greenery which reminded Columbus of the orange and cedar groves of Valencia and Barcelona in Spain.

The beauty of the islands in general astounded the Spaniards. Columbus, in a famous letter written after his first voyage, waxed ecstatic about the exquisite beauty of the Hispaniola that he would soon devastate:

> [The mountains] are most beautiful, of a thousand shapes, and all accessible and filled with trees of a thousand kinds and tall, and they seem to touch the sky; and I am told that they never lose their foliage, which I can believe, for I saw them as green and beautiful as they are in Spain in May, and some of them were flowering, some with fruit, and some in another condition, according to their quality. And there were singing the nightingale and other little birds of a thousand kinds in the month of November, there where I went. There are palm trees of six or eight kinds, which are a wonder to behold on account of their beautiful variety, and so are the other trees and fruits and herbs; therein are marvelous pine groves, and extensive champaign country; and there is honey, and there are many kinds of birds and a great variety of fruits. Up-country there are many mines of metals, and the population is innumerable. [Hispaniola] is marvelous, the sierras and the mountains and the plains and the champaigns and the lands are so beautiful and fat for planting and sowing, and for livestock of every sort, and for building towns and cities. The harbors of the sea here are such as you could not believe in without seeing them, and so the rivers, many and great, and good streams, the most of which bear gold.

Although much of Spanish officialdom considered the indigenous people idolaters (Columbus did not) and tried at least in theory to convert them to Christianity, some Spaniards acknowledged the indigenes' belief in life after death and in the equivalents of heaven and hell. The indigenes recognized many spirits and venerated zemis, triangular figures which proliferate in their archaeological sites.

To the very early Spanish observers, the pace of life in the islands seemed relaxed. Las Casas noted that the islanders lacked the European drive for incessant accumulation of wealth. Some Spaniards saw this as evidence of their lack of civilization. For recreation, Las Casas wrote, they danced, sang and played the ball game *batey* in their ballparks, also called *bateyes*.

According to Spanish observers, the indigenes treated their women well. Apart from the caciques, men were content with one wife. The same could not be said for Spaniards, Las Casas was careful to point out. Divorce was rare but easy to accomplish. Failure to have children was one ground for divorce. There was a division of labor similar to many other societies. Men hunted, fished and cleared the land. Women cooked, gathered fruits, weeded the fields and reaped the harvest.

Childbirth was relatively easy. Pregnant women worked to the last minute and gave birth "almost painlessly," as the explorer Amerigo Vespucci claimed for Paria, Venezuela, in 1499. They were up in a day and proceeded to the river to take a bath. Oviedo, also writing of women on the mainland, said that after delivery they went to the river for a bath and then rested for a few days. In the process, he claimed, their sexual organs returned to a near-virginal state. He cited as authority the testimony of Spaniards who had been intimate with local women.

Oviedo suggested that well-to-do women were more concerned with their appearance and more likely to be sexually liberated than their more humble counterparts. Writing in the 1520s when many of the women he described had grown up in the new world of Spanish exploitation, he claimed that "high born" women avoided contact with commoners, except for Spaniards, all of whom they considered to be nobility, even though they recognized differences of rank among the Spaniards. He described a situation not unlike the forced sexualization of colored women in the later era of African slavery.

Many of these women, Oviedo claimed, would eat special herbs to induce abortion. This was because they wanted to have a good time and did not want their breasts to become flabby through child rearing. When their breasts did become saggy, they wore a device that sounded very much like a brassiere. Oviedo described it thus:

> When the principal women see that their breasts are sagging, they support them with a rod of elaborately wrought gold about a palm and a half long. Some of these rods weigh more than two hundred *castellanos.* A small hole is drilled through each end through which are fastened cotton cords. One end of the cord goes over the shoulder and the other under the arm pit, where the two ends are tied.

Women of the Island of Giants (Curaçao) and the Bahamas were, like their men, taller than elsewhere in the region. Spaniards noted, with some surprise, the physical prowess and martial qualities of many of these women. Like their men, they were exceptional swimmers. The Spaniard Hojeda met natives at Paria, and especially the women among them, he said, who could swim two leagues in one go. Columbus' first serious fight in the islands was with a small party of male and female Caribs in the waters of St. Croix. They could fire their arrows just as easily from the water as they could from their canoes. J.G. Stedman's late eighteenth-century portrait of an Arawak girl in Suriname complete with bow and arrows suggests that the female use of that weapon was widespread and endured for centuries after Columbus.

The fighting qualities of island women led to the legend of Matinino (Martinique), reported by Columbus after his first voyage. The island was said to be inhabited only by women. Men visited them periodically for purposes of procreation, but did not stay. The women were reputedly expert archers. On one occasion, Columbus did indeed encounter a body of women on Guadeloupe, armed with bows and arrows. Their men were away hunting.

The matrilineal descent for caciques gave women access to considerable power and many of them became caciques themselves. The female cacique Anacaona was one of the major paramount chiefs in Hispaniola in the time of Columbus. A partial compilation of caciques at the time of European incursion showed several females in Hispaniola and Puerto Rico but none in Cuba, Jamaica or Trinidad.

As in Europe and elsewhere, political alliances were often cemented through royal marriages. Spanish commanders Ponce de Leon and Cristobal de Sotomayor in Puerto Rico partook of such relationships with the sisters of caciques. In their cases, however, their liaisons stopped short of marriage.

Such then were the indigenous people who greeted Columbus in 1492. Their society had been evolving in the islands for thousands of years. They were comfortable with their environment and could have learnt from new European arrivals the way they had learned from new South and Central American arrivals in the past. But nothing in their past could have prepared them for the coming of the Spaniards. In short shrift their islands would be transformed forever. They, the original inhabitants, would however not survive in any significant way to reap the rewards of technological change. Their own destruction would be the price of material progress that a harsh history would exact from them.

Further Readings

Morison, Samuel Eliot. *Christopher Columbus, Mariner.* Boston: Little, Brown and Company, 1955.

Oviedo, Gonzalo Fernandez de. *Natural History of the West Indies.* Translated and edited by Sterling A. Stoudmire. Chapel Hill: University of North Carolina Press, 1959.

Sued-Badillo, Jalil, Ed. *General History of the Caribbean. Volume I: Autochthonous Societies.* London: Macmillan and Paris: UNESCO, 2003.

Williams, Eric. *Documents of West Indian History.* Port of Spain: PNM Publishing Company, 1963.

2

The Coming of Columbus

Christopher Columbus landed at Guanahani (now Watlings Island in the Bahamas) on Friday October 12, 1492. His little fleet of three small ships had taken only thirty-three days to cross the Atlantic, quite a feat for tiny sailing vessels whose commanders had only an imprecise idea of where they might be going and whether they would even eventually strike land. Many other people from Africa, Europe, Asia and the Pacific had undoubtedly preceded Columbus to the Americas, but none with the major consequences that would quickly follow from Columbus' voyage.

BEFORE COLUMBUS

Human beings have always traveled long distances. The first humans emigrated out of Africa millions of years ago and populated the whole world. Ancient Egyptians circumnavigated Africa in the fourth century BC. Neither land nor sea nor desert has ever impeded the human urge to explore our universe. Both Columbus and his many predecessors to the Americas belong in this context.

The ancient Greek philosopher Plato in his *Timaeus*, around 360 BC, told of the lost civilization of Atlantis, possibly on an island in the ocean which now bears its name. He said the Atlanteans invaded Athens in ancient Greece but their civilization was later destroyed in a deluge. Plato cited ancient Egyptians as his authority. He himself, like other early Greek philosophers, had studied in Egypt. Various possible locations were proposed for Atlantis over the years. As late as 1500, in the midst of Columbus' Caribbean adventures, an English map listed the island of Atlantis near Barbados. Some thought the Azores and the Cape Verde Islands, from which Columbus sailed to the Caribbean on his third voyage, were remnants of sunken Atlantis.

Various other islands were thought to occupy the unexplored Atlantic Ocean, among them the Fortunate Islands and Antilia (which gave its name to the Antilles). Columbus was on the lookout for Antilia in 1492.

The presence of Egyptian-style pyramids in Central America has also long stimulated speculation of early contact with Egypt. Historian Las Casas, who missed little, noted the similarities. In the 1960s, the Norwegian explorer Thor Heyerdahl demonstrated that Egyptian vessels could easily have made it to the Americas. He found fisherman at Lake Chad in Central Africa who were still building boats similar to ancient Egyptian ships. He commissioned them to build a replica of an Egyptian vessel.

The Caribbean and the Americas, according to an English map of 1500. Many of the old myths survive, but already, a remarkable eight short years after Columbus, knowledge of the emerging New World has diffused significantly throughout Europe. Florida and Barbados have been named, though the latter is off the Florida coast. The Greater Antilles are identified as the King of Spain's dominions. Gold and flying fish are correctly noted. The Caribs have already become cannibals. Columbus is given his due. Codfish, still a Caribbean staple, are correctly located in their Newfoundland habitat.

On the other hand, the Greater Caribbean is full of savage men, some of whom worship devils. The mermaids, also known as sirens, who Columbus was on the lookout for, still lurk seductively in Caribbean waters. Central America still gives way to Asia, land of China, elephants, apes, pepper, and spices. Asia is approached through a Great Strait south of Florida. Antarctica squats in South America's space.

The influence of ancient authorities (with whom Columbus was very familiar) persists. Antilia is associated with Plato's Atlantis and is not far from Barbados. Marco Polo is not named, but his influence is felt through the continuing identification of Cuba with Japan (Cipangu or Cipango) and in the attribution of China's leadership to the Great Khan. Ptolemy is cited as reference for India's location.   *Source:* Wiener, Leo. *Africa and the Discovery of America*, Vol. 2. Philadelphia: Innes and Sons, 1922.

Heyerdahl set sail from Morocco. The ship's rudder soon broke and the ocean currents, without benefit of engine, sail, or rudder, took the boat to Barbados.

If ocean currents alone can transport vessels across the Atlantic, this raises the possibility of accidental voyages before Columbus. Many such have been documented. Las Casas was aware of such occurrences. Alvares Cabral, the Portuguese "discoverer" of Brazil, was actually blown off course while traveling along the West African coast in 1500. He ended up in Brazil and decided that since he was already there he might as well discover it. When the Viking Leif Ericsson became the first known European in the Americas in 1000 AD, he was thought to be retracing the steps of a compatriot who was blown off course in 986 and sighted the North American coast.

Angolans fleeing their war-torn land in the 1970s were, like Alvares Cabral nearly 500 years earlier, blown across the Atlantic to Brazil. In a tragic case of 2006, the bodies of eleven men, probably Senegalese, were found in a small boat off the eastern coast of Barbados. They may have been trying to reach Europe before being blown across the Atlantic. In 1493, Columbus found a ship's beam in the house of a local inhabitant in Guadeloupe. He surmised that it must have drifted to Guadeloupe either from Hispaniola or the Canary Islands off the coast of Africa. West Africa is actually the nearest point in the "Old World" to the Caribbean and such accidental contact is in no way far-fetched.

Several researchers now argue for the presence of Africans in the New World before Columbus. They point to indigenous legends of black traders, the presence of corn (maize) in West Africa and the Caribbean, the use of blue and white cowrie shells as currency in both places, traditions among the Caribbean people and the fact that ocean currents can facilitate travel in either direction. There is also speculation based on ambiguous ancient European references that Caribbean people may have accidentally reached Europe.

The most celebrated event in the history of such speculation concerns Abubakari II, a Muslim African king of the Mali empire from 1305 to 1307. This story is documented in histories of Mali written in the fourteenth century AD by Arab Muslim historians Al-Umari and Al-Qalqashandi. Abubakari is said to have dispatched 200 canoes down the Senegal River to explore the Atlantic Ocean. Only one returned, with tales of the others being swept away in a "river" (current) within the ocean. Abubakari thereupon equipped another 2,000 canoes, half filled with provisions, and personally led this new expedition into the ocean. He never returned but could conceivably have reached the New World, as his hapless successors did 700 years later. West African canoes were as large as those in the Caribbean, with early sixteenth-century Europeans reporting as many as 120 in a single canoe.

Much of the enhanced European navigational knowledge of Columbus' time was actually learned from Moors (Muslims) of North Africa who ruled Spain (or parts of it), from 711 to 1492 AD. In 1600, a Moroccan delegation to London suggested a joint Moroccan-English attack on Spain's New World empire. A Moorish navigator in occupied Spain, Khashkhash Ibn Saeed Ibn Aswad, is said to have traversed the Ocean of Darkness and Fog (Atlantic) and returned to Spain in 889 AD. Another one, Ibn Farrukh of Granada, Spain, is said to have made a similar round trip in 999 AD.

Irish lore had it that St. Brendan journeyed to the Americas in the sixth century. In 1291, just a few years before Abubakari II, the Vivaldi brothers sailed from Venice, Italy, in search of a western route to the east. They never returned.

DNA evidence on chicken bones found in Chile suggests that some Polynesians made it to South America a hundred years before Columbus.

The Chinese sailor Zheng He is thought by some to have reached the Americas in 1421.

FIRST ENCOUNTER

The indigenous people who greeted Columbus would have been surprised to learn that he had "discovered" them, as is traditionally alleged. This does not, however, detract from the monumental achievement of Columbus' visit. This encounter changed the world forever. Others from far away had undoubtedly happened upon the islands before. Columbus, however, with his consummate navigational skills, was able to return to Spain whence he had come. He was able to return at will, to chart and map the newly encountered areas, to initiate ethnographic, cultural, botanical and linguistic observations concerning the newly encountered people, to assess the economic value to Europe of this "New World," and altogether to initiate the process that would in a few short centuries shift the focus of world superpower from Europe and Asia to the Americas.

Columbus thanked God for his good fortune, claimed the new territory for the king and queen of Spain, renamed it San Salvador (Holy Savior) and wrote down the first of his many impressions of the native people. He immediately adopted the two contrasting attitudes toward these people that would continue to characterize him. On one hand, he praised their cleanliness, generosity and well-formed figures. On the other hand, he coldly assessed them to be timid people, naked, with neither beasts of burden nor iron and steel, ineffective in weaponry, practically defenseless against Spanish arms and therefore easily enslaved. They were timid and liable to run away until coaxed by curiosity and Spanish trinkets to come forward. Unfortunately for them, as it was to turn out, they had access to gold, for which, as they would shortly discover, the invading Spaniards were willing to commit genocide.

The Arawaks had a boundless capacity for generosity. They provided food, shelter, fresh water, help in salvaging wrecked Spanish vessels, just about anything they could to welcome the white strangers. Indeed, reported Las Casas, they thought the Spaniards were gods come from heaven.

In some of the early encounters with the Arawaks, Columbus, anxious to win their confidence

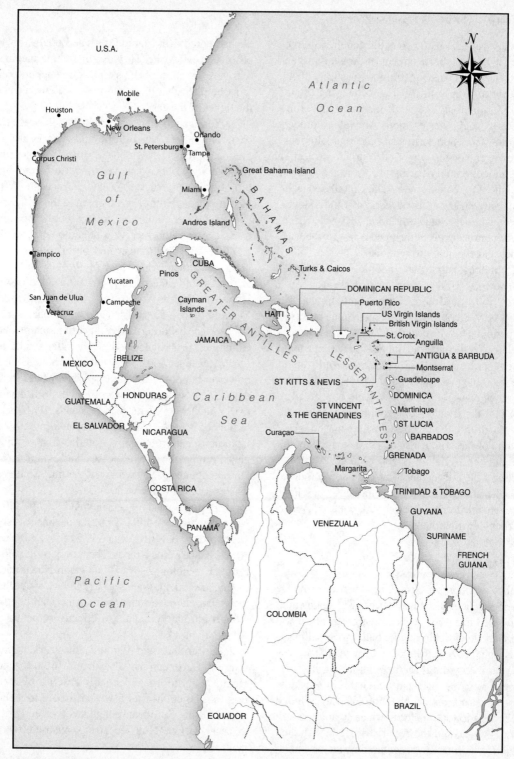

U.S.A.

Mobile

Houston

New Orleans

Orlando

St. Petersburg
Tampa

Corpus Christi

Gulf

of

Mexico

Great Bahama Island

Miami

BAHAMAS

Andros Island

Tampico

CUBA

Pinos

Turks & Caicos

Yucatan

GREATER ANTILLES

San Juan de Ulua

Campeche

Cayman
Islands

DOMINICAN REPUBLIC

Puerto Rico

US Virgin Islands

British Virgin Islands

St. Croix

Anguilla

HAITI

Veracruz

JAMAICA

ANTIGUA & BARBUDA

Montserrat

MEXICO

BELIZE

ST KITTS & NEVIS

Guadeloupe

GUATEMALA

HONDURAS

Caribbean

DOMINICA

Martinique

ST VINCENT
& THE GRENADINES

Sea

ST LUCIA

EL SALVADOR

NICARAGUA

Curaçao

BARBADOS

LESSER ANTILLES

GRENADA

Margarita

Tobago

COSTA RICA

TRINIDAD & TOBAGO

GUYANA

PANAMA

VENEZUALA

SURINAME

FRENCH
GUIANA

Pacific

Ocean

COLOMBIA

Atlantic

Ocean

N

BRAZIL

EQUADOR

Map 2-1 The Caribbean

13

in the short run, the better to exploit their resources later, professed embarrassment at Arawakan generosity. He had to remonstrate with some of his sailors not to overdo things by exchanging bits of broken glass and similar junk for bales of cotton, gold jewelry and other precious Arawak commodities. These were short-term strategies on Columbus' part, however, for his very first journal entry after landfall noted, ominously, that the Arawaks seemed ideally suited for enslavement. Their intelligence, he thought, only enhanced their value as future slaves. As the Portuguese had long done in West Africa, Columbus immediately kidnapped a few, to be used as guides and eventual interpreters.

Columbus called these people Indians, rather than Arawaks. His voyage was in search of a western route to India, China and Japan. He deduced correctly from his navigational research and experience that he could sail west to reach eastern countries. Of course he did not know that a huge continent and a vast Pacific Ocean would stand astride his route to Asia. Long after 1492 and subsequent voyages to the New World, he continued to believe that the islands he encountered were in the vicinity of India, that Cuba was Cipango (Japan), that China of the "Great Khan" (as described by the thirteenth-century Italian traveler Marco Polo) was just around the corner and that the people indigenous to the area were Indians. "Indians" they have largely remained up to the present, even if "West" rather than "East" Indians.

COLUMBUS

Columbus was born in Genoa, now part of Italy. He was well-educated and a mariner of great distinction. He explained in a 1501 letter to King Ferdinand and Queen Isabella of Spain that he had started sailing at an early age, had sailed for over forty years (twenty-three years according to the journal of his first Caribbean voyage), and had traveled all the waters known to Europeans of his time. These included experience in Europe as far north as Iceland, North and West Africa, and the Americas. He had studied all available writings on cosmography, history, navigation, geography, philosophy and other related subjects, whether by ancient Greeks, Arabs or others.

He had pored over Marco Polo's accounts of his travels in Asia and Africa. He was a master mariner and he was sure, in spite of the skeptics he encountered in large number, that there had to be a western route to the riches of the east.

Spain and Portugal were locked in a race to the east. Trade between Europe and Asia in precious metals, spices, silks, cotton, drugs and perfumes was lucrative but expensive. It had to be conducted largely overland across western Asia and Africa, passing through many middlemen in the process.

Whoever could find a direct route from Europe to Asia first could receive a huge bonanza for their trouble. The Portuguese in Columbus' time were busily exploring the coast of West Africa. Their efforts would take them around the Cape of Good Hope in South Africa in 1487 and thence to Mozambique in East Africa and on to Asia.

Spanish-Portuguese competition, intensified by Columbus' first voyage, led to arbitration mediated by Pope Alexander VI of the Roman Catholic Church, a powerful temporal as well as spiritual leader in those days. The pope chose a line of longitude 100 leagues (318 miles) west of the Azores islands. By papal bull (edict) of May 4, 1493, less than two months after Columbus' return to Spain from his first voyage, he gave Portugal the right to possess and exploit any new lands encountered to the east of the line. Spain could take everything to the west.

Portugal was not satisfied and the arrangement was renegotiated in 1494. This time the line was shifted westward, to 370 leagues (1,175 miles) west of the African Cape Verde Islands. The new line later allowed Portugal to colonize Brazil and claim Newfoundland in Canada. Spain, thanks to Columbus, would eventually lay claim to most of the American continent, though ultimately unable to effectively occupy and defend all of it.

Columbus had labored for years trying to interest European royal patrons in his scheme. He made an informed scholarly case for his conviction that he could find a western route to Asia. He reminded his European potentates (correctly, it was to turn out) that untold riches awaited whoever would invest in his ideas.

Columbus remained fourteen years in Portugal lobbying the country's king. The latter tried to double cross him. While keeping Columbus waiting, he secretly sent a vessel to explore Columbus' proposed western route. Luckily for Columbus, the Portuguese ship was buffeted by a storm and had to turn back. Columbus learnt of this treachery and decided to look elsewhere. He left Portugal for Castile (Spain) in 1484 or early 1485. Here his lobbying would achieve success after about seven more years of effort. He also sent his brother Bartolomé to lobby King Henry VII of England. Bartolomé was captured by pirates, resulting in a series of adventures, including a possible trip to the Cape of Good Hope with the Portuguese navigator Bartolomé Diaz. Bartolomé Columbus finally made it to England in late 1488 or early 1489. He eventually succeeded in interesting Henry VII in the scheme, but by the time he did so Columbus had already returned to Spain from his first trip to the Caribbean.

In Castile, meanwhile, Columbus won the patronage of King Ferdinand and Queen Isabella of the Spanish kingdoms of Castile and Aragon. The monarchs had been busy waging war against Granada, the last of the Moorish (Muslim) kingdoms that had ruled Spain for nearly 800 years, ever since they invaded from Africa in 711. Columbus sailed for the Caribbean in 1492, the same year in which the Moors were defeated. Before leaving, he extracted various promises from the king and queen. In the event of success he would be granted the noble title of Admiral of the Ocean Sea. He would be viceroy and governor of all newly encountered lands. Ten percent of all gold and other riches procured would belong to him, tax free. These privileges would pass to his heirs forever.

FIRST VOYAGE, 1492–1493

Columbus left Spain on August 2, 1492. His small but famous fleet consisted of his flagship, the *Santa Maria*, together with the *Pinta* and the *Niña*. There were about ninety men on board. As he would do for all of his four voyages, Columbus first sailed south toward Africa before heading across the Atlantic. His prior experience sailing with the Portuguese to Guinea (West Africa) had taught him that wind and other conditions would be favorable there to sailing

ships venturing across the Atlantic. His actual point of departure for the Atlantic crossing was the Spanish colony of the Canary Islands, off the coast of northwest Africa. He departed Gomera, most westerly of the Canary Islands on September 6, 1492, but did not clear the islands and enter the open ocean until September 9.

No one in the certain memory of Columbus' European era had ever ventured west into the unknown. Portuguese sailors traveling in Africa usually remained in sight of land. In order to allay the justified fears of his men, Columbus therefore kept two logs, one accurate to the best of his knowledge and the other a false one, indicating that a lesser distance had been traveled than he thought to be the case. The shorter the distance traveled, the less would be the sailors' apprehensions of never returning home.

Columbus, experienced sailor that he was, eventually began to see signs, such as the appearance of certain birds, which he interpreted to mean that land could not be too far away. After thirty-three days, he made landfall at Guanahani. In a letter to the Spanish monarchs at the end of this first voyage, Columbus was full of praise for the nautical expertise of the local people. It was these local people who showed him how to get from the Bahamas to Cuba. On all his voyages he would rely on the maritime expertise of these indigenous people.

Columbus explored much of the Cuban coastline on this trip, before going to the island the Arawaks called Haiti, but which he characteristically renamed "La isla española" ("The Spanish Island," or Hispaniola). This island is now shared by modern day Haiti and the Dominican Republic. In Cuba the Spaniards encountered tobacco, the use of which was deeply entrenched in Arawak culture. In Hispaniola, Columbus' insistent queries for gold were answered. As indicated by Arawaks on other islands, there were substantial deposits of gold to be found here.

Since the desire for gold was preeminent among the Spaniards, Hispaniola seemed an appropriate location for Columbus' first attempted European settlement in the New World. This was Navidad. Thirty-nine of Columbus' men stayed behind to become its first inhabitants when the admiral, as he now was, returned to Spain in 1493.

The men constructed a fort from the timbers of the *Santa Maria*, which had been wrecked in the area. Columbus left Navidad for home on January 4, 1493, but made some intermediate stops along the coast of Hispaniola. He would have arrived home in twenty-eight days, he later wrote, had he not encountered the worst winter storms in memory, which detained him twenty-three days. In the Azores, many of his crew were arrested by the Portuguese authorities, who thought that Columbus had made an illicit visit to Africa in contravention of the Portuguese monopoly.

Columbus was back in Palos, Spain, on March 15, 1493, after a trip of 224 days. It was a triumphant return, with parades featuring six captured Arawaks, parrots, gold, masks made from precious stones and other exotic objects. He was warmly welcomed by king, queen and populace.

SECOND VOYAGE, 1493–1496

Six months later, on September 25, 1493, Columbus left Spain on his second trip to the Caribbean. He again sailed first to the Canary Islands. The trip from the Canaries to Dominica took twenty-one or twenty-two days. Columbus commanded seventeen vessels with approximately 1,200 sailors, soldiers and would-be colonists on board, together with plants, seeds, animals and tools to equip a European settlement. This was Europe's largest expedition of exploration to date.

From Dominica, Columbus made his way up through the Leeward Islands—Marie Galante, Les Saintes, Guadeloupe, Antigua, Nevis, St. Eustatius, St. Croix and the other Virgin Islands, and on to Vieques and Puerto Rico. He encountered some twenty large and forty small islands altogether.

In Guadeloupe, he kidnapped two boys and twelve teenage girls from an otherwise deserted house. In St. Croix, he had his first serious fight in the islands when four Carib men and two girls put up a fierce resistance, killing one Spaniard before being overwhelmed.

Back in Hispaniola Columbus discovered that his Navidad garrison had been completely wiped out by the cacique Caonabó. The Spaniards' aggressive demands for gold and women had pushed the Arawaks beyond the point of endurance. In January

1494, Columbus therefore founded the new outpost of Isabella, the first white permanent settlement in the Caribbean and the entire American continent. Columbus hoped to use Isabella as a trading post like the Portuguese post of Elmina in West Africa (modern Ghana), which he had visited. Columbus next sent back twelve of his seventeen ships, which arrived in Spain on March 7, 1494, after a voyage of twenty-five days. In the meantime, he explored the south coast of Cuba and made his way to Jamaica, where he reached St. Ann's Bay on May 5. He killed and wounded some Arawaks at Rio Bueno before returning to Cuba and Hispaniola.

Columbus as viceroy and governor was still an explorer, but conquest, colonization, and the accumulation of wealth now became priorities as well. The hard face of Spanish tyranny now increasingly confronted the local people. By 1496, Columbus had totally subjugated Hispaniola. In the process he had killed and enslaved many. Several hundred enslaved Arawaks were shipped to Spain, in emulation of the Portuguese shipment of enslaved Africans to Europe, which had been going on for about half a century. Las Casas in his *History of the Indies* accused Columbus of using this Arawak slave trade as a principal source of income.

Columbus remained in the islands for two years and nine months this time around. He sailed from Guadeloupe on April 20, 1496, and arrived back in Cadiz, Spain, on June 11. On board were many enslaved Arawaks and Caribs.

THIRD VOYAGE, 1498–1500

Columbus persuaded Ferdinand and Isabella to sponsor a third voyage, which began in 1498. An advance party of Spaniards and supplies sailed in January 1498. Columbus himself departed Spain around the end of May. This time Columbus first sailed further down the African coast than on his previous voyages. He passed the Canary Islands and proceeded south to the vicinity of the Cape Verde Islands, off the coast of Senegal, before turning west. This more southerly route took him to Trinidad, roughly in the same latitude as this part of West Africa.

Columbus landed at Erin Bay, Trinidad, on August 1, 1498. He thought he was in West Africa, when he noticed local people in canoes wearing cotton bandanas similar to ones which Portuguese had obtained in Sierra Leone. He tried to entice them with the usual worthless items of trade but these Trinidadians were not impressed with his junk. They let fly with a volley of arrows, which, happily for Columbus, missed their mark. He therefore decided to leave them alone for the time being.

On his way back to Hispaniola, Columbus sighted or explored Tobago, Chacachacare Island, Margarita and Grenada. He became the first known European to set foot in South America (Venezuela). He arrived in Hispaniola on August 31 to a multitude of troubles. The Isabella colonists had removed to a new settlement at Santo Domingo. Some were in open rebellion. Some had complained about Columbus to the sovereigns in Spain, who now began to allow interlopers to flaunt Columbus' theoretical viceroyalty over all of the New World. Columbus himself intensified the enslavement of the native people. To crown matters, the sovereigns sent out Francisco de Bobadilla on a fact-finding mission. Bobadilla shipped Columbus and his two brothers off to Spain in chains. They arrived back in Cadiz in October 1500.

FOURTH VOYAGE, 1502–1504

Though Columbus again received royal authorization for this, his last voyage, he was still officially banned from visiting Hispaniola. He once again sailed via Africa, as he had done on all three previous trips. This time he stopped at Morocco and the Canary Islands, from where he reached Martinique in twenty-one days.

He revisited islands encountered on his second voyage and showed up at Santo Domingo, where he was duly refused permission to land by Governor Don Nicolas de Ovando. He thereupon ranged the Central American Caribbean coasts of Honduras, Nicaragua, Costa Rica and Panama, in search of a passage through the landmass. He killed and kidnapped more native people along the way. His two remaining ships became so unseaworthy that Columbus had to abandon them in St. Ann's Bay, Jamaica, where he remained marooned for a year and five days, kept alive by Arawak solicitude,

before being rescued by Spaniards from Santo Domingo. He arrived back in Spain on November 7, 1504, after an absence of two and a half years.

Columbus died a year and a half later at Valladolid, Spain, in May 1506. In 1509, his son Diego was allowed to become governor of Hispaniola and resume his father's hereditary titles. Columbus would eventually be revered by Europeans for opening up a New World of unprecedented power and riches, but at the time of his death he was a somewhat saddened figure, struggling with a somewhat ungrateful Spain for full implementation of all the promises contracted with him in 1492.

GLOBALIZATION

The world had long been a global place. Ancient Nile Valley conquests in Africa, Europe and Asia thousands of years earlier, Hannibal of North Africa's campaigns in Spain and Italy in the third century BC, East African Swahili and Chinese trading visits to each others' countries in the first millennium AD, the Muslim near 800 year occupation of Spain, the thirteenth-century travels of Marco Polo and Portuguese explorations along the West African coast had all testified to this.

By opening up the Americas to outside influence, Columbus, as it were, completed the circle of globalization and ensured Europe's dominance in the new scheme of things. Thanks to Columbus Europe, Asia and Africa now became inextricably intertwined with his New World.

The connection to Europe was the most obvious. Spain, on the authority of the papal bull of 1493, as amended by the Treaty of Tordesillas in 1494, claimed hegemony over most of the American continent. Beginning with the abortive Navidad settlement of 1493, she moved to consolidate her claims with effective occupation on the ground. Spain would in time prove ineffective in occupying and defending so vast a territory, but other European nations would aggressively fill the breach.

Asia too was immediately incorporated into the New World. Columbus' term "Indies" eloquently spoke to this fact. It was the quest for a new trade route to the east that brought Columbus to the Caribbean in the first place. And he went to his deathbed still thinking that he had opened up lands in the vicinity of China.

Millions of Europeans would eventually follow Columbus to replace the native peoples exterminated by the Spanish and their successors. Centuries later, substantial numbers of Chinese and Indians would also immigrate to the Caribbean.

The transformation of the Caribbean into a region of many predominantly African nations was, however, the most dramatic and unexpected result of Columbus' opening up of the area. Although he could not have foreseen the Africanization of much of the Caribbean, Columbus himself began the process of incorporating a strong consciousness of Africa into his New World adventure. He often used Africa as a familiar point of reference to evaluate his new Caribbean experiences.

His study of Marco Polo and the Bible both made him conscious of the ancient glory of the East African kingdom of Ethiopia and its fabled Christian king, Prester John, a very popular figure in the European imagination. Just as the cotton bandanas of Trinidad led him to believe he might have been encountering West Africans, an unsubstantiated report of native people wearing white tunics in Cuba led him to surmise that he might have reached Prester John's country of Ethiopia.

Long before Prester John, the biblical Queen of Sheba was also thought to have come from Ethiopia. Columbus imagined himself in Ophir, land of the Queen of Sheba, while in Costa Rica. When he realized that Hispaniola was not Cipango (Japan), he thought that it, too, might be Ophir.

Nor did Columbus have to look very far for familiarity with real Africans. He had sailed with the Portuguese to West Africa, at least once and possibly twice, probably between 1482 and 1484. There, in modern day Ghana, he visited Elmina Castle and probably witnessed its construction. The Portuguese had been bringing enslaved Africans to the Iberian Peninsula since 1441. These would in fact later provide the first enslaved Africans brought to the Caribbean. Columbus' son and biographer Ferdinand Columbus cited the Italian Agostino Giustiniani as a reference for the contention that it was as a result of discussions with Portuguese who sailed to Elmina that Columbus decided to sail west.

The philologist Leo Wiener suggested in 1922, in *Africa and the Discovery of America*, that African merchants, probably Portuguese-acculturated *pombeiros*, traded to the New World before Columbus. Citing J. B. Thacher's *Christopher Columbus* (Vol. II, 1903) as his authority, Wiener said that prominent persons in Santiago, Cape Verde Islands, told Columbus of canoes trading between Guinea and points west.

By the sixteenth century, Africans of some prominence could be found in the Iberian Peninsula. Afonso Alvares was a Portuguese-born writer in Lisbon. In 1557, the famous African-born Juan Latino became a faculty member at the University of Granada. The Moorish invasion of 711–1492 also brought many Africans to Spain and environs, some from as far as West Africa, much of which was Muslim. Columbus may have suspected that these Muslim Africans of North and West Africa had preceded him to the Caribbean. On his first voyage, he brought along an Arabic speaker and a sailor who had met a West African king.

Columbus' West African connection was strengthened by the fact that all four of his voyages began from the African islands of the Canaries and Cape Verde. There were two reasons for this. First, as seen, his earlier African maritime experience convinced him that sailing conditions would make a crossing easier from Africa than directly from Spain. Second, he believed with the ancient Greek philosopher Aristotle that the same latitudes would produce the same conditions worldwide. So if people in Sierra Leone wore cotton bandanas, it would be no surprise if those in Trinidad did the same. If gold existed in abundance in West Africa, then it ought to be found in the similar latitudes of the Caribbean. Columbus may have expected to find darker skinned people in the Caribbean as well. He seemed surprised to discover that the Arawaks had straight hair and were generally not as dark as Africans.

SLAVERY AND GENOCIDE

The globalization of the Caribbean was made easier by the extermination of the native population, which made more urgent the need to find new peoples to take their place. Columbus himself, and all the early

Spanish chroniclers, noted the great multitude of people living in the islands. Spanish activity was concentrated in the Greater Antilles and the Bahamas. Trinidad and Margarita were later added to this list. Writing in 1493 at the end of his first voyage, Columbus described "an infinite number of small villages and people without number" in Cuba. Bartolomé de Las Casas, an eyewitness to this genocide, put the population of Hispaniola in 1492 at 3–4,000,000. In his *Very Brief Account of the Destruction of the Indies* (also translated as *The Devastation of the Indies*), published in 1552, he put the remaining native people in Hispaniola at 200. Cuba, he said, was by then almost totally depopulated of its original inhabitants. Jamaica and San Juan (Puerto Rico) were deserted and laid waste. The Lucayos (Bahamas) did not have a single survivor from among the 500,000 who Columbus met there.

Islands near Puerto Rico had been depopulated and destroyed. Las Casas thought that the Spaniards had killed 12–15,000,000 on the mainland of Central and South America as well. Archaeologists have corroborated the eyewitness impressions of Columbus, Las Casas and others. The islands were some of the most densely populated areas in the New World in 1492. Some modern historians have nevertheless reduced drastically the estimates for numbers of Arawaks in 1492. Estimates for Hispaniola have gone as low as 60,000, though Sherburne F. Cook and Woodrow Borah, using mathematical models, in the 1970s raised the estimate for Hispaniola alone to 8,000,000, nearly three times Las Casas' estimate in *Devastation*. David Henige summarizes Cook and Borah's findings as follows:

> Briefly, Cook and Borah conclude that about 8 million Indians were probably living on Hispaniola when Columbus landed there; that this population was halved during the next four years; that it was reduced to some 30,000 Indians by 1514; and that there were almost no Indians alive by the middle of the sixteenth century.

Whether there were 60,000 or 8,000,000 Arawaks in Hispaniola in 1492, the fact is that by the time the Spaniards did their first censuses in the sixteenth century, the Arawaks were almost all dead. They did not "disappear," as some historians are wont to say. They were the victims of genocide.

One school of thought nevertheless prefers to blame European-introduced epidemics, especially of smallpox, rather than wanton brutality, for the decimation of the indigenes. Cook and Borah are among those proffering an epidemic explanation. The first recorded smallpox epidemic in Hispaniola is variously dated at 1507 or 1518–1519. If Cook and Borah (and others) are correct in positing a cataclysmic and practically immediate decimation of the indigenes not long after 1492, then genocide induced by war, enslavement and wanton aggression has to be a more reasonable explanation. The evidence of widespread early Spanish brutality is unassailable and contemporary observers did not mention epidemics as a cause of the early extermination of the indigenes. It would have been inconceivable for persons living through such epidemics not to have mentioned them if they were in fact the main cause of the devastation of the indigenous people. Genocide was clearly already well underway before epidemics came along to accelerate the process of extermination. When, on January 22, 1518, Alonso de Zuazo, a Spanish judge in Hispaniola, bemoaned the extermination of the Arawaks in a letter to Carlos de Chievres, adviser to Spanish king Charles V, he did not blame epidemics. Their extermination, he said, "is the result of the repartimientos [a device for enslaving the indigenes, to be discussed shortly], from the time of the old Admiral to today." He estimated Hispaniola's indigenous population in 1492 at 1,130,000. "Today," he said, "their number does not exceed 11,000. Judging from what has happened, there will be none of them left in three or four years time unless some remedy is applied." Zuazo was writing only a few years after the suggested epidemic of 1507 and on the eve of the 1518–1519 epidemic. He was also writing just after the first large-scale Spanish contract for the importation of Africans (the *asiento*) made necessary, as the settlers saw it, by the decimation of the indigenes and consequently of the settlers' labor force. This decimation had brought forth a royal assent to the importation of Africans in 1501, six years before the first claimed epidemic.

Captain Juan Melgarejo, governor of Puerto Rico, reported in 1582 that there were no indigenous people left, save for 12–15 brought in from the mainland. This time he attributed their demise to measles, colds, smallpox and ill-treatment. But this was very late in the day, long after the indigenes had been near totally wiped out.

A 1508 census in Hispaniola counted 60,000 native people, but these included enslaved Arawaks brought in from the Bahamas. The contemporary historian Gonzalo Fernandez de Oviedo estimated in 1548 only 500 left of the original inhabitants of 1492 and their offspring. Their numbers had been augmented by enslaved compatriots brought in from other islands and the mainland. By the middle of the sixteenth century, therefore, the genocide against the native people in the Greater Antilles and the Bahamas was more or less complete.

This process of extermination began in earnest on Columbus' second voyage. On the first voyage, he had assessed the people's strengths and weaknesses and, most important, had confirmed the area's economic potential, especially the presence of gold in Hispaniola.

By 1494, the reign of terror in Hispaniola had begun. Columbus and his subordinates were cutting off ears, dismembering people, capturing and killing caciques, taking Arawaks' wives and daughters by force and devising novel and cruel ways to slaughter the native people. Las Casas reported Arawaks beheaded for fun. Spaniards, he said, would lay bets on who could decapitate an Arawak or cut him in half with one blow of the sword. On one occasion, he said, the Spaniards put about 700 Arawaks in a large building and stabbed them all to death in retaliation for the killing of eight Spaniards. They tricked the female cacique Anacaona and eighty of her chiefs into a large building when they came to welcome the Spaniards. The Spaniards burnt them to death and killed as many of the Arawaks still outside the building as they could. They spared Anacaona the flames and hanged her instead as a special favor.

They hanged Arawaks thirteen at a time, in honor of Jesus Christ and his twelve apostles. "My eyes have seen these acts so foreign to human nature," wrote Las Casas in his *History of the Indies*, "and now I tremble as I write. . . ." He explained further to Emperor Charles V in 1519, "I am one of the oldest immigrants to the Indies, where I have spent many years and where, I have not read in histories, that sometimes lie, but saw with my own eyes. . . ."

Slavery was a major vehicle for the extermination of the native people. On Friday October 12, 1492, the day he first set foot in the Caribbean, Columbus confided to his journal that the Arawaks ought to make good slaves. He seized seven of them right away, as the Portuguese with whom he sailed to West Africa were wont to do. By this act of kidnapping, Columbus in effect initiated the transatlantic slave trade. Before long that trade would be associated with the forced transportation of Africans to the Caribbean, first from Europe and then direct from Africa. The trade started, however, in the reverse direction, with Columbus' Caribbean captives transported to Europe.

Columbus thought, based on his West African experience, that males would be more amenable to enslavement if they had some female companionship from among their own race. He therefore ordered the seizure of some women and children. He explained in his journal, "I afterwards sent to a house on the western side of the river, and seized seven women, old and young, and three children. I did this because the men would behave better in Spain if they had women of their own land, than without them. For on many occasions the men of Guinea have been brought to learn the language of Portugal," but being unencumbered by family relationships, they simply disappeared when they were taken back home. Despite Columbus' precautions, at least one of these first enslaved Arawaks emulated the West Africans by promptly disappearing when they brought him back to Hispaniola in 1493. Another, baptized and renamed "Don Diego," served Columbus well as an interpreter.

In early 1495, Columbus enslaved 1,500 Arawaks for shipment to Spain. Only 500 could be packed into the departing vessels, so he allowed resident Spaniards in Hispaniola to help themselves to the rest. About 200 of those transported died at sea and half of the survivors arrived in Spain ill. They were put on the auction block naked. Almost all of them perished shortly afterwards.

In 1496, Columbus assured the sovereign that he could send over 4,000 native people. They would

Spaniards hanging Arawaks thirteen at a time in honor of Jesus Christ and his twelve apostles. This is one of the classic engravings done by Theodorus de Bry (1528–1598) for Las Casas' *Devastation of the Indies.   Source:* Las Casas, Bartolomé de. *Narratio regionum indicarum per Hispanos*, a 1598 Latin version of his *Devastation of the Indies*, published by his illustrator Theodorus de Bry. Accessed at: http://lcweb2.loc.gov/service/rbc/rbc0001/2008/2008kislak20219/2008kislak20219.pdf.

be worth more than three times as much as West Africans, he promised. He had noticed on a recent trip to the slave-trading Cape Verde Islands that there was a great unsatisfied demand for enslaved people in Castile, Portugal, Aragon, Italy, Sicily and the Canary Islands.

When he himself returned to Spain in 1496, Columbus took a further thirty enslaved indigenes. The sale of enslaved people transported in 1496 helped finance Columbus' third voyage. Transatlantic slavery was now in full swing. It was slavery at home in the Caribbean, however, rather than the export of native peoples to Spain, which would quickly bring untold suffering and rapid extermination to the native peoples. For "into this

sheepfold," lamented Las Casas in his *Devastation of the Indies*, "into this land of meek outcasts there came some Spaniards who immediately behaved like ravening wild beasts, wolves, tigers, or lions that had been starved for many days . . . killing, terrorizing, afflicting, torturing, and destroying the native peoples, doing all this with the strangest and most varied new methods of cruelty, never seen nor heard before. . . ."

The military subjugation of Hispaniola during Columbus' second trip further intensified the enslavement of the native peoples. Columbus exacted a gold tribute which forced every Arawak in Hispaniola to periodically produce a certain amount of gold or be killed. The amount of gold demanded was inevitably onerous, and many Arawaks committed suicide or went into hiding and died of starvation as a result. A reduction in the amount of tribute did not help and Columbus introduced in its place, the *repartimiento* (literally "distribution" of natives) or *encomienda* (a "grant" of indigenous forced laborers). According to this system, Spaniards were granted land together with native people to work it. Historian Oviedo, writing between 1535 and 1557, thought that Columbus' introduction of the *repartimiento* or *encomienda* system was a virtual sentence of death on one million or more native people.

The term *encomienda* appeared in official directives from the Spanish monarchs as early as 1500 and 1503. As customary the forced relocation and forced labor of this prelude to extermination was justified both by the need for labor to extract wealth for the Spaniards and by the need to win native souls for Christendom.

The reign of terror visited upon the hapless natives provided a pilot program for the fate that would later befall enslaved Africans. The indigenes were branded like cattle with hot irons. Las Casas described natives under the table foraging like animals for bones and scraps of food thrown by eating Spaniards. With rations running low on Columbus' return trip to Spain in 1496, the Spaniards debated eating the captive natives or throwing them overboard to conserve supplies. Columbus on this occasion tried to restrain his colleagues from such drastic action. Unexpected landfall in Portugal ended the still unresolved debate.

In Hispaniola meanwhile, husbands and wives were separated for eight to twelve months at a time, while the men worked the mines and women labored on farms. When reunited they were too exhausted to procreate normally, or at all. There were mass suicides involving as many as a hundred people at a time. They died in large numbers and infant mortality was appalling. The Franciscan friar Pedro de Cordoba reported to King Ferdinand II of Spain in 1517 that "The women, exhausted by labor, have shunned conception and childbirth . . . many, when pregnant, have taken something to abort and have aborted. Others after delivery have killed their children with their own hands, so as not to place or leave them in such oppressive slavery."

When natives became sick in the mines, Spaniards killed or beat them and turned them loose to make their way home. Most died along the way, said Las Casas, who himself saw some of them dead along the roads. Many who did not die from wanton cruelty succumbed to smallpox and other European diseases, to which they had not been exposed before and to which they had no immunity.

The Arawaks of Hispaniola bore the brunt of early enslavement, but Caribs were enslaved very early as well. As early as 1494, Columbus told his sovereign that the Caribs might make better slaves than the Arawaks, since they were intelligent and well-built. The allegation of cannibalism which the Spaniards pinned on the Caribs, together with their spirited resistance to Spanish aggression and proselytizing, provided the Spaniards with convenient pretexts to enslave them, even during moments of royal vacillation on the policies leading to extermination of the Arawaks. For as far as Spanish theologians were concerned, Carib traits placed them outside any strictures which natural law might have provided against the enslavement of other people.

And as the Arawaks in Hispaniola died out, the Spaniards turned increasingly to neighboring islands and to Mexico and elsewhere on the mainland. They thus developed a thriving intraregional slave trade. One of the first places to be depopulated in the search for replacements for Hispaniola was the Lucayos Islands (Bahamas). In a statement that could easily have been written of the later "Middle Passage" from Africa to the Caribbean, Las Casas described up to 500 Bahamians crammed into the holds of Spanish vessels with insufficient light, air, food, or water. Up to a third might be thrown overboard after dying along the way. Las Casas thought that a ship without a compass might navigate from the Bahamas to Hispaniola by simply following the trail of dead bodies in the water.

The natives of Trinidad received an unusual respite from these cruelties when King Ferdinand I suggested in 1510 that the pearl trade they facilitated was too valuable to the Spaniards to risk the disruption that attempted enslavement might cause.

Like their enslaved African counterparts later, the indigenous women bore an extra burden on account of their sex. As already seen, they were worked actually or practically to death like the men and as a result often could not produce milk for their babies or were too weak to maintain interest in sex. When they did procreate, they sometimes induced abortions rather than giving birth to children in a world of genocidal Spanish cruelty. Like their men, they committed suicide.

Columbus' first voyage took approximately ninety males away from home. Columbus and the majority of the crew returned home after 224 days. Thirty-nine stayed behind to found the Navidad settlement. Some 1,200 males comprised Columbus' second voyage. They did not all return together, but those who came back with Columbus were gone for two years and nine months.

The first white women to the islands were probably the thirty on Columbus' third voyage in 1498, though some may have come with Antonio de Torres in 1495. The total absence of white women, augmented by Columbus' precedent of simply kidnapping native people for whatever purpose, led inevitably to widespread rape and abuse of the local women. In Guadeloupe on the second voyage, Columbus himself sanctioned the kidnapping of two boys and twelve teenage girls.

Las Casas detailed many of the indignities heaped upon these unfortunate women. A Spaniard raped the wife of the powerful Hispaniola cacique Guarionex, in the ruler's presence. "The Spaniards broke up marriages," he reported, "separating husbands and wives, robbed couples of their children, took for themselves the wives and daughters of the people, or gave them to the sailors and soldiers as consolation, and the sailors bore them away on their vessels. . . . "

On one occasion in neighboring Yucatan, Las Casas reported, the Spanish authorities assembled 150 "maidens" and 100 or 200 "comely" boys. Spaniards were allowed to choose a girl or boy according to their preference, in exchange for wine, oil, vinegar or pigs.

Columbus' Genoese friend Michele de Cuneo himself described his encounter with a beautiful Carib girl warrior he captured in St. Croix waters on the second voyage. Columbus gave him the girl as his personal slave. He tried to rape her but she resisted fiercely and scratched him with her

fingernails. He thereupon beat her very badly with a piece of rope. After having his way with her he called her a harlot. Las Casas described an incident in Guatemala where a Spaniard dragged away a girl from her mother and cut off her hands with his sword when she resisted. She continued to resist and he killed her. Some Spaniards lived in open polygamous concubinage.

Despite his own culpability in helping unleash this misfortune on the native people, Columbus by 1500 seemed as disgusted as Las Casas by what he witnessed. Upset at the Spanish treachery which now had him imprisoned, he complained bitterly to a governess at the Spanish court. A class of Spanish pimps had arisen in Hispaniola, he wrote, who specialized in procuring girls and women for the Spaniards. Nine- and ten-year-old girls were especially prized, he complained, but any woman could fetch a good price, regardless of age.

One by-product of the Spanish debauchery of the native women was syphilis, the AIDS of its day. It sprang suddenly on the Spanish population, caused excruciating suffering and death, spread rapidly and was incurable.

Since syphilis made its appearance in Europe soon after Columbus' return, Europeans were not slow to make the connection. They blamed the Caribbean people for its appearance, even as, 500 years later, many North Americans would seek to blame Haiti for the origin of AIDS.

Various theories have been suggested over the years for the origin of syphilis. Some think it may have been a relatively benign European disease which suddenly mutated and turned virulent. Others think that it may have been endemic but not lethal in the islands. It would then have turned deadly for the Spaniards who had no immunities to it. Some think that it may have been a sudden mutation of a universal disease such as yaws. One thing, however, is certain. It was the Europeans who spread it from Spain to the rest of Europe, Africa, Asia and the Pacific. In many countries, it came to be known by the name of whichever country was thought to have introduced it to a given place——French disease to the Italians and English, Spanish disease to the English, German disease to Poles, disease of the Europeans to Indians, Portuguese disease to the Japanese and so on. Columbus' son, Ferdinand, called it the French disease.

Samuel Eliot Morrison, exceptionally among major historians of Columbus, admitted in 1955 that "The cruel policy initiated by Columbus and pursued by his successors resulted in complete genocide." Spanish policy to the indigenes also falls easily within the definition of genocide enshrined in the Convention on the Prevention and Punishment of the Crime of Genocide adopted by the United Nations General Assembly in 1948:

> In the present Convention, genocide means any of the following acts committed with intent to destroy, in whole or in part, a national, ethnical, racial or religious group, as such:
>
> (a) Killing members of the group;
> (b) Causing serious bodily or mental harm to members of the group;
> (c) Deliberately inflicting on the group conditions of life calculated to bring about its physical destruction in whole or in part;
> (d) Imposing measures intended to prevent births within the group;
> (e) Forcibly transferring children of the group to another group.

THE REQUISITION

In the midst of this debauchery and slaughter, it may have taken some effort to be reminded that proselytizing and the winning of souls to Christianity were the professed aim of many Spaniards, including Columbus, King Ferdinand and Queen Isabella. Columbus actually at one time wanted his New World profits to go toward equipping a crusade to wrest Jerusalem from the Muslims. He left money in his will for such a purpose.

Yet after Columbus' second voyage absolutely no converts had been made, except for a handful of captives who survived the journey and were baptized in Spain.

When conversion was attempted in the islands, it was sometimes a crude business, with armed Spaniards proclaiming from a distance in Spanish, which the local people did not understand, that they must convert in a short period of time or be enslaved or worse. This was the notorious "requisition" (*requerimiento*) which Spanish commanders read on approaching native settlements.

A 1509 version of this remarkable document informed the natives that since God created the world 5,000 years earlier, people had multiplied and nations had gone their separate ways. God had subsequently given St. Peter and succeeding popes authority over all these diverse peoples until the end of time. He had chosen Rome as an appropriate place from which the pope might rule the world. One of St. Peter's papal successors had made a donation of the islands and adjacent mainland territories (*tierra firme*) to the sovereigns of Spain, which meant that the indigenes were now subjects of Spain. If they submitted to this new arrangement, they would be treated well, exempted from enslavement and would not even have to convert to Christianity, though, according to the document, most who had heard this requisition had so converted.

"But, if you do not do this," the requisition warned,

> and maliciously make delay in it, I certify to you that, with the help of God, we shall powerfully enter into your country, and shall make war against you in all ways and manners that we can, and shall subject you to the yoke and obedience of the Church and of their Highnesses; we shall take you and your wives and your children, and shall make slaves of them, and as such shall sell and dispose of them as their Highnesses may command; and we shall take away your goods, and shall do you all the mischief and damage that we can, as to vassals who do not obey, and refuse to receive their lord, and resist and contradict him; and we protest that the deaths and losses which shall accrue from this are your fault. . . .

Abolitionist priests, Las Casas especially, feared that the Spanish approach to the native people was squandering a great opportunity given the Spaniards by God to bring these numerous peoples to a knowledge of Christianity.

CRIMINALS, MONSTROSITIES, FABLED PLACES AND LITTLE MEN

The quality of the early Spanish settlers also made a humane approach to the native people more difficult than it might otherwise have been. A seventeenth-century Englishman famously said of Barbados that it was the dunghill whereon England cast forth its rubbish. Georgia in the southern United States and Australia began as penal colonies for English criminals. The Portuguese exiled criminals to Guinea-Bissau in West Africa. In Hispaniola, these criminal outposts found an unhappy precedent, though it must be remembered that the dregs of Spanish society who made their way to the New World were still operating within parameters set by their ruling classes.

It was none other than King Ferdinand and Queen Isabella who on April 30, 1492, set the scene by pardoning up front any criminals who wished to accompany Columbus. Such criminals were to be exempt from punishment of any kind, for crimes committed up to the date of this royal decree. They were also pardoned in advance for any crimes they might commit during the voyage or for two months after returning home.

In 1497, in between Columbus' second and third voyages, the sovereigns issued a proclamation of amnesty to all murderers and other criminals willing to help establish Spanish settlements in Hispaniola. The only criminals excepted from the amnesty were heretics, counterfeiters, sodomites, persons guilty of treason and a few others. Murderers would have to remain two years in the Caribbean to obtain their full pardons. Lesser criminals would have their criminal records expunged after a year in Hispaniola. By 1500, even Columbus could describe the Spanish settlers on Hispaniola as mostly a bunch of vice-ridden vagabonds, fearful of neither God nor sovereign.

There was a widespread notion in Europe that "monstrosities" inhabited parts of the earth as yet unexplored by Europeans. Columbus therefore kept a sharp eye out for human or near-human monsters. He reported on the first voyage that he had seen mermaids, though they were not as beautiful as alleged. He was referring to manatees. (Almost 300 years later, European soldier of fortune John G. Stedman in Suriname was expressing skepticism at accounts from some European contemporaries of the existence of mermaids in the area.) On the same voyage Columbus reported hearing, though he was careful to say that he could not confirm this information, that people in western Cuba were born with tails. He also heard of an island where people had no hair. He heard of men with one eye and some with dogs' noses, who indulged in cannibalism. He admitted at the end of the voyage, however, that he found no monstrosities. Quite to the contrary, the Arawaks were handsome people who held good looks in high esteem.

The accusations of cannibalism leveled against Caribs can also be viewed as a variant of the monstrosity stories. The word "Carib" is itself derived from a word meaning "cannibal." When Columbus' famished crew debated eating their Caribbean captives in 1496 they proposed eating the Caribs first, since they were supposedly cannibals themselves. While some, Las Casas included, could matter-of-factly refer to the Caribs as cannibals, others traced these charges to the preservation of skulls and other body parts of beloved ancestors. Natives of New Granada in Central America thought that the Spaniards were cannibals. According to Las Casas, Spaniards in New Granada kept butcher shops where corpses of natives were hung up for sale as fodder for Spanish dogs.

More serious than the foregoing were the Spanish attempts to portray the Caribbean people as inferior beings—"half devil and half child" as Rudyard Kipling, "poet laureate of British imperialism," wrote in his infamous nineteenth-century "White Man's Burden." As they did with the Africans later, the Spaniards sought to justify their treatment of the native population by demonizing them. According to historian Oviedo, the native people were "by nature idle and vicious, disinclined to work, of a melancholy disposition, cowardly, base, prone to evil, liars, forgetful, and inconsistent." For the sixteenth-century jurist Juan Gines de Sepulveda, the native people were "little men in whom you will scarcely find even vestiges of humanity. . . ." Why, he exclaimed, they did not even have private property. They were as inferior to the Spaniards "as children are to adults, as women are to men. They are as different from Spaniards as cruel people are from mild people, as monkeys from men."

In a practice run for the notion of "arrested development" later applied to Africans, Oviedo thought the native people capable of a spark of intelligence just before adolescence, after which they regressed mentally. In his *General and Natural History of the Indies,* Oviedo first blamed Columbus for introducing the *repartimiento* and *encomienda,* thereby assuring the extermination of the native people. He then argued that, these facts notwithstanding, the natives had made things worse by poisoning and hanging themselves for fun and in order to avoid work. In addition, they were sodomites and idolaters, and deserved to die. God permitted the natives to be wiped off the face of the earth, Oviedo reassured, partly because of the sins of the Christians in not converting them and partly because of their own abominations. Of the Caribbean peoples, Oviedo explained, God may well have said, "It repenteth me that I made them."

Las Casas was outraged by Oviedo's commentary. The natives were not sodomites, he said. He again unwittingly anticipated the experience of the Africans to come when he explained that they believed they would go to heaven when they died. Suicide hastened that process and relieved them of their present suffering.

Fray Tomas Ortiz heaped more scorn on the native people in a speech to the Spanish Council of the Indies (which oversaw Spain's new colonies) in 1512. "They were like stupid asses," he said,

> half-witted and without feeling. . . . They gloried in being drunk, and made wine from different fruits, nuts and grains; they got drunk on fumes and on certain herbs, which made them lose their senses. . . . They were incapable of learning the doctrines of the faith [and were] of little intelligence. . . . They lacked human art and skill; and when they forgot the teachings of the faith which they had learned, they said that those things were for Castile and not for them, and that they wished to change neither their customs nor their gods.

In the midst of all this devastation of the indigenous people a few voices could be heard pleading for their preservation, but they were few and far between, too little and too late. Various Spanish monarchs made intermittent calls for humane treatment of the indigenous people in between aiding and abetting their extinction. In 1493, Ferdinand and Isabella suggested treating the natives well, all the better to Christianize them. In 1500, they emancipated Caribbean natives enslaved in Spain and ordered them repatriated home. Isabella even sent out detailed suggestions for preservation of the natives. Las Casas pointed out that Nicolas de Ovando, first royal governor of Hispaniola, ignored her suggestions and, from 1502 on, made matters worse via the *encomienda.*

Yet Isabella in 1503 ordered Ovando to force the natives to work for the Spaniards, though as free persons rather than as enslaved persons, a seeming contradiction in terms. In the same year, she equally contradictorily contracted with one Cristobal Guerra to enslave native people "as nearly as possibly with their consent" and also to seize monsters, animals, serpents and fishes, subject to a 25 percent tax to the crown. In the same year, Isabella proclaimed open season on allegedly cannibalistic Caribs, who had presumed to reject the Catholic faith and even defended themselves militarily against Spanish invasion. She ordered that they should be sold into slavery and forced to accept Christianity.

In 1516, a reform commission of Hieronymite (Jeronimite) fathers was sent out to see what could be done to ameliorate the condition of the oppressed indigenous people. They were charged to gather up the remaining natives and group them into new villages closer to the places of their forced labor. Caciques could maintain some authority over their subjects, but they themselves would now be subordinate to a Spanish administrator and priest. This was in fact an early example of the indirect rule later practiced by European conquerors in Africa and elsewhere. Spaniards would be encouraged to marry daughters of caciques. This seemingly curious device would ensure, under native customary law, that the Spaniards would inherit cacique status.

Caciques would be pressured to adopt habits of dress, matrimonial arrangements and a general lifestyle closer to that of "civilized" Europeans. Like enslaved Africans later on, they must not carry arms except when hunting. Natives would be obliged to work, with men serving two month shifts in mines. Hospitals and orphanages were to be built, and Christianization was to be aggressively pursued.

King Ferdinand II appointed Las Casas "Protector of the Indians" at this time and bade him assist the Jeronimites. Las Casas had only recently (1514) realized the error of his ways as a prosperous recipient of an *encomienda* in Cuba. He was preparing a sermon for Pentecost in 1514 when he came upon the following biblical exaltation that changed his life: "The poor man has nothing but a little bread; whoever deprives him of it is a murderer. Whoever does not give the worker his wages is a bloodhound. . . ." Las Casas henceforth preached against the enslavement and mistreatment of the indigenous peoples. He wrote many major books with that end in view and lobbied tirelessly on both sides of the Atlantic. He did not succeed in preserving the native peoples but we are indebted to him for his historical and cultural research. He was the first great abolitionist in the Caribbean and the Americas.

Las Casas had no military power at his disposal, but he used the moral suasion that he could muster as a bishop, a man of letters and a confessor. No amount of amelioration missions could save the natives, he said, unless the whole *encomienda* system was dismantled. He accused Columbus of breaking international law by kidnapping the local people. He said that the oppressed natives had a natural right to wage just war against those who had invaded their lands and despoiled their countries. He invoked divine retribution on the heads of these Spaniards, whose wars and rapine had made much more difficult the task of winning souls for Christianity.

Sometimes, he said, God had already punished Spaniards by letting whole families perish at sea on the way home to Spain, and all their ill-gotten gold with them. Because of the suffering they visited on the poor natives in pursuit of that damned gold, he said, God had consumed it all and no man ever grew rich from it. For Columbus himself to die in poverty and disgrace was for Las Casas the ultimate expression of God's divine retribution.

All of this negativity was partially balanced by stories of wonderful places in the area. Ponce de

Leon became the first European to land in the future United States when he stopped in Florida in 1513. He was on his way from Puerto Rico in search of the Bahamian island of Bimini, reputed home of the Fountain of Youth. Several Europeans searched in the sixteenth century for El Dorado, the fabled South American city of gold.

ARAWAK RESISTANCE

The Arawaks who Columbus characterized as timid, and who initially thought that the Spaniards were angels from heaven, were quickly forced to defend themselves. With invasion, conquest, enslavement and extermination descending upon them, they faced the stark choice of resisting or dying.

The wiping out of the 1493 Spanish garrison at Navidad was their first decisive counterattack to Spanish invasion. Luckily for them, Navidad contained a limited number of Spaniards with no reinforcements available. Caciques on Hispaniola and other neighboring islands could muster large armies of several thousands, but these eventually proved ineffective against the superior military hardware and technology of the Spaniards.

Once confronted with the harsh reality of their impending extermination, the Arawaks fought desperately and valiantly, but eventually to no avail. Their weapons were no match for the crossbows, muskets, lances, swords and most terrible of all in the view of Las Casas, the ferocious greyhounds of the invading Spaniards. Each dog, Las Casas estimated, could tear to pieces twenty naked Arawaks in an hour. Spanish swords could cut an Arawak in half. Ten mounted Spaniards fighting on nonmountainous terrain, said Las Casas, could kill 100,000 Arawaks with their lances. The Arawaks had never seen horses and, it was said, originally believed that horse and rider were one.

Yet they fought back so courageously, said Las Casas, "That, even though they had their bellies ripped open by swords, were tripped by the horses and speared by men on horseback (each one of them killed 10,000 of them in an hour), lions or the bravest men in history could not have shown greater courage. . . . Their misfortune was that they lacked guns and horses. . . ."

The first large-scale battle between Arawaks and Spaniards took place in 1495 ending in the defeat of the cacique Guatiguaná. A large force assembled by the cacique Mayobanex was shortly afterward defeated when he gave asylum to his colleague Guarionex who was being sought by the Spaniards.

When large-scale resistance failed, and with extermination already a reality, some surviving Arawaks turned to guerrilla warfare. One of the most celebrated of these was Enrique (also called Enrequillio), the last surviving cacique in Hispaniola. He grew up in a Franciscan Roman Catholic monastery, could read and write Spanish, and was conversant with Spanish ways. A Spaniard raped his wife, stole his mare and put him in prison. After his release, Enrique vainly sought redress from the Spanish authorities on Hispaniola. Enrique eventually gathered a band of about 100 men and waged guerilla warfare against the invaders. He defeated Spanish patrols sent against him but refrained from killing Spaniards except in battle, even sparing the lives of retreating Spanish soldiers.

As in the case of African Maroons later on, freedom-seeking indigenes sought out and joined Enrique's forces. Enrique, also, like his African successors in Suriname, Jamaica and elsewhere developed sophisticated techniques for surviving in the bush. He cultivated the land. He had procedures in place for removing women, children, the elderly and the sick to safety in times of conflict. He became very adept at the use of the Spanish arms which his fighters liberated from defeated Spanish soldiers and elsewhere. Enrique developed a network of spies and scouts who could provide early warning against hostile Spanish intruders.

Enrique won every armed encounter against the Spaniards. Eventually no Spaniard would volunteer for action against him. Only those conscripted for the purpose would go. After fourteen years of this, a Spanish Franciscan friar attempted to negotiate a deal with Enrique. He had himself rowed ashore in an area where he thought Enrique might be. Like the Cubans at the Bay of Pigs in 1961, Enrique's local forces mobilized immediately and intercepted the friar when he landed. Under strict orders not to kill Spaniards except in battle, they ripped off his

robes, tore them to shreds and left him in his underwear while they repaired to Enrique for instructions.

Enrique himself emerged to speak with the friar, who assured him that he would be treated well if he made peace. Enrique informed the friar that the Spaniards had killed his father and grandfather, slaughtered the rulers and people of his Xaragua province, raped his wife and decimated the entire island of Hispaniola. Nothing that any Spaniard could say to him could persuade him to willingly risk the fate of his people.

Enrique's efforts were independently complemented by the freedom fighters Ciguayo and Tamayo. Ciguayo secured a Spanish lance and possibly a sword as well. With a band of ten to twelve men, he terrorized the mines and plantations killing any Spaniards he came upon. He was killed in an encounter with a Spanish force, fighting with superhuman bravery even after being run through with a lance. Ciguayo was followed by Tamayo who amassed Spanish weapons and clothing and killed as many Spaniards as he could. Enrique persuaded Tamayo to join forces with him and become one of his captains.

Las Casas considered it miraculous and a manifestation of divine judgment that Ciguayo and Tamayo with a handful of followers would have brought fear and paranoia to all Hispaniola at a time when only two natives were left for every twelve to fifteen Spaniards. It was a far cry from the time when 300 Spaniards had devastated the initial Arawak population that he now estimated to have been three to four million. "If only the [original inhabitants] had weapons like ours," Las Casas lamented, "and horses and arquebuses, they would not have been exterminated from the surface of the earth as we exterminated them." Unable to defeat Enrique, the Spaniards eventually left him alone and after many years made peace as other Europeans would later do with the Surinamese and Jamaican Maroons whom they could not defeat.

The most enduring symbol of resistance continues, however, to be the cacique Hatuey. Five hundred and more years after Columbus, his name still resonates through the islands. Hatuey fled Hispaniola for Cuba with as many of his followers as he could take. He wished to avoid the death and destruction brought by the Spaniards. In 1511, however, the

Spaniards moved in strength to Cuba and began the same round of outrages they had perpetrated in Hispaniola. Hatuey tried to stay one step ahead of the Spaniards and defended himself wherever he encountered them.

When Hatuey realized that the Spaniards were now really in Cuba to stay, he gathered his followers. He reminded them of the atrocities the Spaniards had committed in Hispaniola. "Do you know why they do this?" he asked rhetorically. "We do not know," his people replied. "But," they ventured, in one of the saddest statements in all of Caribbean history, "it may be that they are by nature wicked and cruel."

This was only part of the answer, Hatuey assured them. He showed them a basket filled with gold. This, he explained, was the god the Spaniards worshipped, for which they were willing to decimate and ravage the islands. Maybe, he suggested, his people should dance for this god and then maybe Christians would do them no harm. They danced until they were exhausted. "Now if we try to keep this gold," Hatuey warned, "the Christians will find it. If even we hide it in our intestines they will extract it. Let us therefore throw it in the river."

The Spaniards eventually captured Hatuey. They burned to death the cacique and as many of his followers as they could find. After they tied Hatuey to the stake and before applying the torch, a Franciscan friar offered him a chance to convert to Christianity, be baptized and go to heaven. "Is that where Christians go?" Hatuey wanted to know. "Yes," was the reply, "and if you do not accept the faith you'll go to hell."

Death of Hatuey. Engraving by Theodorus de Bry (1528–1598).   *Source:* Las Casas, Bartolomé de. *Narratio regionum indicarum per Hispanos*, a 1598 Latin version of his *Devastation of the Indies*, published by his illustrator Theodorus de Bry. Accessed at: http://lcweb2.loc.gov/service/rbc/rbc0001/2008/2008kislak20219/2008kislak20219.pdf.

"I'd rather go to hell," said Hatuey, "than go to any place where the Christians are."

As in every place the Europeans conquered, they were able to exploit rivalries and animosities among local groups, in order to divide and conquer. Their outstanding ally in Hispaniola was the cacique Guacanagarí who had befriended Columbus on his first voyage.

CARIB RESISTANCE

The Caribs are traditionally reputed to have been more "warlike" than the Arawaks. They certainly appeared to have been initially less welcoming to the Spaniards. Columbus' first fight in the Caribbean was with a small Carib party of four men and two women (one woman in some accounts). This was on November 14, 1493, off the coast of St. Croix. The Spaniards had just kidnapped four Carib women and two children when a canoe came into view and engaged the Spaniards. Columbus' ships rammed and capsized the canoe but its occupants kept firing their arrows as easily from the water as if they had been on dry land. One of the women's arrows pierced a Spanish shield and one Spaniard was killed. The outnumbered and outgunned Caribs fought bravely. The Spaniards threw one of the men overboard with his intestines ripped apart and hanging out. He swam for shore holding his intestines in one hand. They caught him again, bound him hand and feet, and again threw him into the sea. He somehow managed to free himself and began swimming once more. This time the Spaniards shot him up with their crossbows until he died.

Women continued to figure among Carib fighters. In 1496, Columbus was met in Guadeloupe by a contingent of women armed with bows and arrows. Their men were away hunting. As usual, Columbus kidnapped three boys and ten women. He used them as hostages to extort free food from the Caribs.

A 1503 proclamation from Queen Isabella complained that the Caribs were killing Spaniards and resisting Christianization. So enslave them, she ordered. As the sixteenth century wore on, debates intensified among Spanish intellectuals as to whether indigenous peoples could justifiably be enslaved. These debates were of little more than

academic interest to the Arawaks who were already dead or well on the way to extermination. The jurists and theologians nevertheless seemed to agree that the Caribs because of their alleged cannibalism, resistance to Spanish aggression and unwillingness to convert, thereby made themselves just subjects for enslavement. One result of such thinking was a sort of open season on Caribs. And whoever the Spaniards wished to enslave could be the more easily warred against and subjugated if they were defined rightly or wrongly as Caribs.

In San Juan Bautista (Puerto Rico) in 1511, Caribs and Arawaks joined in the most serious rebellion to date against the Spanish invasion. In 1593, the Spanish authorities in Trinidad were desperately requesting help to control the Caribs who were killing Spaniards and their native allies. Caribs suffered greatly at the hands of Spanish slave raiders and later other European conquerors. They nevertheless consolidated their forces and regrouped in a few islands, principally Dominica, Grenada and St. Vincent. In St. Vincent, as will be seen later, they remained, as the miscegenated Black Caribs, a formidable force until the end of the eighteenth century.

On the whole, however, the Caribs shared the fate of the Arawaks. They, too, were eventually exterminated, with a few racially mixed remnants remaining in Trinidad, Dominica and St. Vincent. The quasi-official British-Vincentian *St. Vincent Handbook* of 1938 sought to put the final touches on their extermination. "As in North America so in the West Indies too," it said, "the ousted natives have deteriorated instead of advancing alongside their superiors. At present there are very few pure Caribs for the greater part . . . have intermarried with the East Indians, Creoles and Negroes and now are indistinguishable from the general population."

COLUMBIAN EXCHANGE

The interaction of cultures, however unequal, brought with it a variety of cultural exchanges. As already noted, some have tried to place syphilis within this category. Tobacco is probably the most famous European borrowing from the native peoples. Oviedo describes the indigenous people inhaling through two tubes placed in their nostrils. They would smoke until they lay stretched out on the ground bereft of their senses. The Arawaks used tobacco for medicinal purposes and for religious and other ceremonies. After entering into a tobacco-induced trance during religious ceremonies they would sometimes do something akin to the "speaking in tongues" of Christianity and other religions. Some commentators, both contemporary and modern, and including Fernando Ortiz in *Cuban Counterpoint*, have suggested that the extreme narcotic effect of Arawak tobacco may have been due to an admixture of a ground substance, *cohoba*. Some have suggested that *cohoba* was simply an Arawak word for "tobacco." The term *cohoba* was also used for the ceremonies attending its use. By the late sixteenth century, in any event, American tobacco had securely entered European pharmacopeia as a remedy for a wide array of maladies.

The enslaved Africans also were soon growing and using tobacco to ease the fatigue of their hard toil. They became so addicted to the substance that the Spanish slave masters tried to deny them access to it.

Whether New World tobacco in fact introduced smoking to the Old World and whether the word "tobacco" was of Amerindian derivation have long been topics of uncertainty. Leo Wiener noted that various substances were smoked, mainly for medicinal purposes, in Europe, Africa and the Arab countries since antiquity. Old World smoking, like its New World counterpart, was facilitated by the use of reeds and pipes. Wiener suggested that the word "tobacco" came from the Arabic word *tubbaq*, introduced into European languages by the Arabs and rendered *tobbaqah* in Spanish. He thought that African traders brought tobacco to the New World before Columbus.

The presence of smoking in pre-Columbian Europe need not, however, nullify the fact of exposure to New World smoking as a catalyst for the "new" popularity of smoking in Europe from the sixteenth century. And it seems that the word "tobacco," despite its Arabic derivation, then reentered Arabic via its post-Columbian European forms.

From as early as 1493, Columbus brought livestock and a variety of botanical specimens, including fruit trees. He also collected botanical specimens to be taken to Spain. Indigenous staples such as cassava and corn were incorporated into Spanish diets. Several Caribbean words were incorporated into European languages. They include "cacique," "hurricane," "hammock," and "canoe." Despite Columbus' propensity for renaming the places he encountered, several local geographical names survived, including Jamaica and Cuba. In the case of Haiti, the victorious Africans of the Haitian Revolution (1791–1803) abandoned the Saint Domingue designation of the defeated French. In a remarkable gesture of solidarity with the original inhabitants, they named their new nation Haiti, its original Arawak name.

The most important Spanish economic introduction was sugarcane, which Columbus brought from the Canary Islands in 1493. By 1518, it was being extensively cultivated in Hispaniola. It spread to Jamaica, Cuba, Puerto Rico and later to parts of Central and South America. By the mid-seventeenth century, larger sugar plantations were already employing as many as 120 people. Sugar would in time dominate the economy of the entire region for centuries.

ENRICHMENT OF SPAIN

In his years of lobbying for royal patronage, Columbus assured his would-be benefactors that untold riches awaited them. His letter at the end of his first voyage emphasized the profits which he was now sure would accrue to Spain and all Christendom as a result of his endeavors. Imprisoned in 1500, Columbus reminded the seemingly ungrateful sovereigns that he had transformed Spain, a poor country, into the richest country in the world.

Las Casas pointed out that New World gold came to dominate international markets. Up to 1518, most of that gold came from Hispaniola. Pearls gathered from the "Pearl Coast" near Margarita are said to have exceeded all sources of wealth from the New World prior to the 1545 contributions from Peru. When in 1517 Spain began selling licenses (*asientos*) to foreign merchants to supply its colonies with enslaved Africans, this opened up another source of enormous state wealth. The famous alcazars (palace-fortresses) of Madrid and Toledo were constructed in the 1530s from profits of the *asiento*.

The Spaniards in due course exhausted the gold of Hispaniola, but the gold and silver of Peru and Mexico were by then ready to replace and exceed Hispaniola's output. By then the Caribbean had also become a staging ground for the even vaster wealth generated by Spanish conquest and exploitation of the rest of the Americas. Hernán Cortes invaded Mexico from Cuba in 1519. Ponce de Leon invaded Florida from Puerto Rico in 1521, after briefly stopping there in 1513. Francisco Pizarro, eventual conqueror of Peru, began his career as a conquistador by sailing from Hispaniola in 1510. Vasco Nuñez de Balboa sailed from Hispaniola on the voyages that made him in 1513 the first European at the Pacific Ocean.

Spain sought to maximize the wealth of the Caribbean and environs by instituting a series of monopolistic practices. All gold and precious metals belonged to the monarchs. Individuals required permits to mine for precious minerals and had to pay a royalty to the monarchs. Stringent administrative practices enforced the monopoly.

From 1493, all shipping to and from the Caribbean had to pass through the Spanish port of Cadiz, in order for permits, cargoes and the like to be inspected. Elaborate records were kept. To streamline these procedures, Spain erected a House of Trade (*Casa de la Contratación de las Indias*) in Seville in 1503, 70 miles up the Guadalquivir River. The wealth congregated there was said to be enough to pave the streets of Seville with silver and gold. Seville then supplanted Cadiz as the sole port of entry and exit for Caribbean destinations. A branch of the House of Trade was established in each colony.

French, English, Dutch and other European pirates were quickly attracted to the enormous wealth being shipped to Spain. They became a major threat and so from 1521 the Spanish crown introduced armed convoys to escort the booty home. Havana, Cuba, was strategically best suited as a collection point for these *flotas* and helped Cuba eclipse Hispaniola as the most important of the Spanish island colonies.

By the end of the sixteenth century, the islands, though still very important, had lost ground to Mexico, Peru and elsewhere as generators of Spanish wealth. It would not be long, however, before other European nations would challenge Spanish monopoly and eventually supersede Spanish preeminence in the islands.

They would all, however, whether in the Caribbean or elsewhere in the Americas, mostly follow the precedents that Spain had established. Like Spain, they would decimate the indigenous populations, transplant European populations into the area, enslave indigenes and Africans, spread Christianity, and establish monopolies over their colonial possessions.

Further Readings

Cook, Sherburne F., and Woodrow Borah. "The Aboriginal Population of Hispaniola," in Cook and Borah, *Essays in Population History: Mexico and the Caribbean*, Vol. I. Berkeley: University of California Press, 1971–1974, pp. 376–410.

Crosby, Alfred W., Jr. *The Columbian Exchange: Biological and Cultural Consequences of 1492*. Westport, CT: Greenwood Press, 1972.

Hair, P. E. H. "Columbus from Guinea to America." *History in Africa*, 17, 1990, 113–129.

Henige, David. "On the Contact Population of Hispaniola: History as Higher Mathematics." *Hispanic American Historical Review*, 58, 2, 1978, 217–237. Reprinted in Verene Shepherd and Hilary McD. Beckles, Eds., *Caribbean Slavery in the Atlantic World*. Kingston: Ian Randle Publishers, 2000.

Las Casas, Bartolomé de. *History of the Indies*. Translated and edited by Andree M. Collard. New York: Harper and Row, 1971.

Las Casas, Bartolomé de. *The Devastation of the Indies: A Brief Account*. Baltimore: Johns Hopkins University Press, 1992. First pub. 1542.

Morison, Samuel Eliot. *Christopher Columbus, Mariner*. Boston: Little, Brown and Company, 1955.

Oviedo, Gonzalo Fernandez de. *Natural History of the West Indies*. Chapel Hill: University of North Carolina Press, 1959.

Wiener, Leo. *Africa and the Discovery of America*, Vol. 2. Philadelphia: Innes and Sons, 1922.

Williams, Eric. *Documents of West Indian History*. Port of Spain: PNM Publishing Company, 1963.

3

The Northern European
Challenge to Spain

STATE OF THE SPANISH CARIBBEAN

By 1500, when the Portuguese accidentally encountered and claimed Brazil, the entire American continent was nominally (at least as far as Europeans were concerned) in the hands of the Southern European nations of Spain and Portugal. Spain, Portugal and its southern counterpart, Italy, had been forerunners in European expansion overseas, in the years leading up to Columbus. Perhaps their close proximity to Africa and its islands (Madeira, Cape Verde, the Canaries, Sao Thome and Prinicipe and others) may have been a partial explanation. Spanish and Portuguese conquest and settlement of these islands in the fourteenth and fifteenth centuries were a prelude to Columbus' western adventures.

Information diffused rapidly throughout Europe and the vastness and enormous wealth of Spain's new empire became quickly apparent. The earliest surviving map of the Caribbean islands was drawn in 1500 by the Spaniard Juan de La Cosa, who may have accompanied Columbus on his second voyage. It was already very accurate. Early maps of the area were quickly available across Europe, fueled by a printing industry dominated by Germany, Italy and the Netherlands.

It was therefore only a matter of time before Spain's northern rivals (principally England, France and the Netherlands) would issue a challenge to Spain's claimed monopoly. The sixteenth century in the Caribbean quickly became a race between Spanish efforts to consolidate their control and Northern European efforts to encroach on Spain's new empire.

Hispaniola remained throughout the sixteenth century the seat of Spanish administration in the area. Columbus, according to the terms of his contract with the Spanish monarchs, was the first Spanish viceroy and admiral. The former position gave him administrative and judicial power and the latter jurisdiction over maritime matters. In 1499 the monarchs sent out Francisco de Bobadilla to investigate complaints against Columbus. Bobadilla, as already seen, shipped Columbus home in chains and exercised administrative control until 1502. Columbus was allowed to keep his maritime jurisdiction and monies due him under his contract, until his death in 1506. Fray Nicolas de Ovando (governor from 1502 to 1508) arrived in Hispaniola with 30 ships and 2,500 settlers, to begin the task of repopulating and island, whose indigenous inhabitants were already well on the way to extinction. Diego Colon, Columbus' son, succeeded Ovando. Under these men, Hispaniola rapidly developed into a prototype of sorts for the expanding Spanish American empire.

Spain would soon find herself with the largest empire since the Nile Valley, Greek, Roman and other huge empires of antiquity. The principal administrative agency for coordinating and consolidating this empire was the *Casa de la Contratación de las Indias(House of Trade for the Indies.)*. The *Casa* became a vast and efficient regulatory agency overseeing most aspects of Spain's American colonies. Almost all ships sailing to and from the Caribbean had to pass through Seville. The work of the *Casa* fell into four broad categories:

1. *Fiscal duties.* The *Casa* was a customs house. It collected customs duties, especially the crown's share of gold and precious metals. It inspected cargoes.
2. *Regulatory duties.* It recorded and licensed all passengers to the Caribbean.
3. *Technical duties.* It inspected private ships for seaworthiness and itself fitted out government ships. It established the position of *piloto mayor* (chief pilot) in 1508, with Amerigo Vespucci, after whom America was subsequently named, the first incumbent. The *Casa de Contratación* established Europe's first school of navigation. As European geographical knowledge of the Americas expanded, the *Casa* kept an up-to-date record of new information. It maintained a constantly updated standard chart, the *padrón real,* which ships sailing to the Caribbean had to be up-to-date with.
4. *Judicial matters.* The *Casa* exercised judicial powers in civil and criminal matters pertaining to the Indies.

Ultimate authority over Spain's Caribbean colonies resided initially in the crown of Castile, advised by the Council of Castile, which combined the functions of a supreme court and a cabinet. This council drafted laws and decrees for the colonies. The Council of Castile evolved into the informal committee which by 1519 was being referred to as the Council of the Indies, with Juan Rodríguez de Fonseca in charge. It was formalized by Charles V in 1524 and existed until 1834.

Communication between Spain and the islands was frequent and efficient. Writing in 1525, historian Oviedo described an outward voyage as almost as predictable and uneventful as one centuries later might have been. "The customary course from Spain to the West Indies begins at Seville," he wrote, "the location of your Majesty's Board of Trade. . . . There the captains and first officers . . . receive their clearance papers. . . ."

The ships then followed the route pioneered by Columbus. A week's sail brought them to the Canary Islands and a fresh supply of food, water and other items. About twenty-five days out of the Canaries the ships were in the Caribbean. The first islands sighted, according to Oviedo, might be any one of the following—The Saints, Marie-Galante, Desirade, Martinique, Dominica, Guadeloupe, St. Kitts or others in that vicinity.

Occasionally, in the hands of an inexperienced navigator, the ships might first sight one of the Greater Antilles or bypass the islands altogether and land on the mainland. The average voyage from Seville to Hispaniola took thirty-five to forty days. "The voyage is very safe and uneventful over this route," wrote Oviedo. The return trip took an average of fifty days, though Oviedo knew of two ships that did the trip back in twenty-five days in 1525. Sixty-six Spanish ships crossed the Atlantic in 1508, either outbound or homeward bound. Seventy-seven crossed in 1514 and 108 in 1520.

Santo Domingo, capital city of Hispaniola, served as administrative hub for the area. In 1511 this was formally recognized by the creation of the *audiencia* or administrative region of Santo Domingo. This included the islands and *Tierra Firme* or northern coast of South America. Other *audiencias* were established later. *Audiencias* also administered appeals courts which were independent of governors. Founded in 1494, Santo Domingo had a population of 3,000 in 1527. It served as the initial major base for exploration and conquest of the expanding Spanish empire. Puerto Rico and Cuba increasingly shared these roles from the early sixteenth century, with Cuba eventually superseding Hispaniola in this regard.

In 1499 Alonso de Ojeda began exploration of *Tierra Firme* as he sailed along the Venezuelan coast from Margarita Island to Maracaibo. Amerigo Vespucci sailed with him. In 1499 also, Vicente Yáñez Pinzón, former captain of the *Niña* of

Columbus' first voyage, sailed along the coast of Northern Brazil and the "Wild Coast" of Guiana.

The Spaniards realized in 1512, unfortunately for the indigenous people, that the oysters they fished around Cubagua Island were rich in pearls. Cubagua and Margarita quickly became the "Pearl Coast." The oyster beds in Cubagua were nearly exhausted by 1540 and new beds were opened up off Margarita. The center of pearl fishing later shifted to the Gulf of Panama. The town of New Cadiz was established in Cubagua and for about twenty-five years was one of the most prosperous places in the Caribbean.

Interest in *Tierra Firme* and the Pearl Coast led to further exploration of nearby Trinidad and Orinoco in Venezuela. Ponce de León did a preliminary reconnaissance of Puerto Rico in 1508. In 1508 Governor Ovando sent Sebastian de Ocampo to circumnavigate Cuba, which Columbus had partially explored during his first voyage. In 1511 Diego Velázquez invaded Cuba from Hispaniola. The conquest was completed in 1512. Bartolomé de Las Casas traveled with the invading party. The conquest of Jamaica was completed by Juan de Esquivel in 1509.

Gold extraction initially dominated economic activity in three of these four islands of the Greater Antilles. By 1510, 4.9 million grams of gold had been extracted from Hispaniola. Between 1511 and 1520 another 9.1 million grams were extracted in Hispaniola, Puerto Rico and Cuba. As the gold became exhausted in the Greater Antilles, other forms of economic activity emerged to take its place. Between 1500 and 1520 there were large cassava plantations in Hispaniola and Puerto Rico, worked by indigenous labor.

Cattle ranching (for the export of hides) became important in Hispaniola, Puerto Rico and Cuba. Much of the meat was discarded since it greatly exceeded the demand of the small populations. From 1506 until its decline circa 1575–1600, sugar also became a major agricultural product, first for domestic consumption and later for export, both in Hispaniola and Puerto Rico. The first production was from seeds Columbus brought from the Canary Islands in 1493.

Sugar estates, called *ingenios,* became major centers of population, with the former *encomenderos* often the new sugar barons. Thousands of enslaved

Africans (of whom more in Chapter 4) were brought in to work them. They were joined by the few surviving indigenes in the early years. Sugar technicians were also brought in from the Canary Islands, Sicily and Portugal. In 1535 there were 200 Portuguese workers on the plantations of Hispaniola, with smaller numbers from the Canary Islands and Sicily.

Sugar plantations relied either on water-powered mills called *ingenios*, or *trapiches,* drawn by horses and oxen. In 1527 there were nineteen *ingenios* and six *trapiches* in Hispaniola. In 1548 there were thirty-five sugar plantations in Hispaniola and eleven in Puerto Rico.

Spanish consolidation was impressively reflected in the rapid growth of new towns and cities. After the failed Hispaniola settlements of Navidad (1493) and Isabella (1493), Santo Domingo (1494) became the first European city in the New World to endure. There were five Spanish towns in Hispaniola by 1503. Seven more were incorporated in 1507. There were fifteen all told in 1508. San Juan, Puerto Rico, was founded in 1508, Santiago de Cuba in 1514 and Havana, Cuba, in 1515.

Acla in Panama was founded in 1516 and abandoned in 1559. Panama City was founded in 1519. Other important mainland towns and cities included Nombre de Dios (Panama) in 1520; Coro (Venezuela), 1527; Nueva Córdoba (later Cumaná in Venezuela), 1562; Caracas (Venezuela), 1567; Santa Maria de la Antigua del Darién (Panama), 1571; and Portobello (Panama), 1597. By 1571 there were over 200 extant Spanish towns and cities in the Americas.

These towns and cities were typically carefully planned and sometimes quite imposing. Oviedo gave an engaging description of Santo Domingo in 1525:

> There are a number of small towns on [Hispaniola]. . . . Concerning Santo Domingo, the principal city, I wish to point out that with regard to the buildings, no town in Spain—unless it is Barcelona, which I have seen many times—is superior in general. The houses in Santo Domingo are for the most part of stone

like those in Barcelona, and the walls are strong and beautiful, constructed of wonderful masonry. The general layout of the city is much better than that of Barcelona, because the many streets are more level and wide and incomparably straighter. Since the city was founded in our own time, there was opportunity to plan the whole thing from the beginning. It was laid out with ruler and compass with all the streets being carefully measured. Because of this, Santo Domingo is better planned than any town I have seen. . . . There must be some seven hundred citizens in this city, living in such houses as I have already described. Some of the private homes are so luxurious that any grandee in Spain would find himself most comfortable there. Admiral Diego Columbus, your Majesty's Viceroy, has such a magnificent house that I cannot remember one in Spain a quarter as good. It is well constructed of stone and located on the port. It has many fine rooms and commands a beautiful view of both land and sea.

Santo Domingo was a real modern city catering to the manifold needs of its residents. In 1526 a legal brothel was established, with the needs of the European bachelors working in the *ingenios* in mind. The Franciscan order established a monastery in 1502. By 1525 Oviedo could report three monasteries, one Dominican (founded in 1520), one Franciscan and one founded in 1514, belonging to the order of St. Mary of Mercy. They all had "handsome but modest buildings," he reported, "which are not so grotesque as some of those in Spain." In all three, moreover, "God is worshipped most devoutly because they are inhabited by holy and exemplary monks." Female convents came later.

The religious community founded the first European schools in Hispaniola, and therefore in the Americas. A Franciscan school, established in 1505, was the first. In 1538 the College of the Dominican Order in Santo Domingo was accredited as St. Thomas Aquinas University. In 1540 in Santo Domingo the University of Santiago de la Paz y Gorjón was founded. These were the first institutions of tertiary education in the Americas, 200 years before Harvard University, 400 and more years before the University of the West Indies in Jamaica.

Oviedo reported a "fine hospital" in 1525 where the indigent were accepted and well cared for. Here, as in so many other areas, Hispaniola provided a precedent that would be followed for centuries to come. Like French Algeria, British Australia and British-Boer South Africa in subsequent centuries, Hispaniola was fast becoming a settler colony which many Europeans would make their permanent homes. To the benefits of Old World technology and know-how they would add the advantages of enslaved subject peoples, upon whom they could build a lifestyle not often equaled in Europe.

Though Santo Domingo maintained its administrative preeminence well into the seventeenth century, it increasingly, and of necessity, had to share its prominence with new centers of Spanish activity. An *audiencia* of Castilla del Oro (Golden Castile, the name given to the Isthmus of Panama) was set up in 1513.

Castilla del Oro was earlier settled from Hispaniola. Rodrigo de Bastidas and Juan de la Cosa visited the Gulf of Darien in 1500, with de la Cosa carrying out further explorations in 1504. In 1509 Alonso de Ojeda took hundreds of settlers to northern Columbia, while Diego de Nicuesa took hundreds to Veragua. Most of these, including de la Cosa, were killed by indigenes or otherwise died, resulting in Spain's greatest losses in the Americas to date. Reinforcements were sent from Hispaniola and leadership of both communities eventually devolved on Vasco Núñez de Balboa. Balboa founded the city of Darién. Following information provided by indigenous informants, he marched across the Isthmus of Panama to become, in 1513, the first European to see the Pacific Ocean, near the town which subsequently bore his name.

Castilla del Oro was rich, as its name implied, in gold and other products. But even more fabulous wealth awaited the Spanish as their restless, ruthless and gold-hungry *conquistadores* (conquerors) fanned out from Hispaniola and the newer bases.

Two of the richest prizes of all awaited them in Mexico and Peru. Expeditions from Cuba reconnoitered Mexico in 1517 and 1518. Hernando Cortés finally invaded Mexico from Cuba in 1519. The conquest was complete in 1521. Mexico became a new starting point for expeditions into Central and North America. Spaniards from Mexico invaded Guatemala and Honduras in 1524. There they encountered and almost came to blows with other Spaniards pushing north from Darién in the Castilla del Oro.

The second major development after Mexico was the conquest of Peru in 1532 and 1533. The gold of Peru and silver of Mexico (found in 1550) soon eclipsed the riches flowing to Spain from the rest of its American empire.

The main Spanish island settlements outside of the Greater Antilles were Cubagua, Margarita and Trinidad. All three are close together off the *Tierra Firme* coast of Venezuela. Cubagua and Margarita were from the beginning treated as appendages of *Tierra Firme,* rather than as parts of the islands. Trinidad, the largest of the Lesser Antilles, got an "island" identity, though itself often connected administratively to Venezuela.

Antonio de Berrio y Oruña attacked Trinidad's indigenes around 1584 with the help of the governor of Margarita. In 1592 he established San José de Oruña as Trinidad's first European capital. The Spaniards also set up the port settlement of Puerto de los Hispanioles (Port of Spain), known to the indigenes as Conquerabia. Trinidad, like Jamaica, remained sparsely populated by Spaniards. Caribs and Arawaks remained the bulk of the population for some time after de Berrio. Hispaniola for a while suffered significant Spanish population loss, as its residents emigrated to the newly opened up Spanish colonies.

The Spaniards also expended considerable energy in the sixteenth century trying unsuccessfully to locate El Dorado, the fabled city of gold. It was thought to be somewhere in the Wild Coast area of Guiana, between the Orinoco and Amazon rivers. In this endeavor they were later joined by French adventurers and notably by the Englishman Sir Walter Raleigh.

Raleigh studied assiduously all the documentary and oral evidence he could extract from Spanish sources and summarized it in his book, *The Discoverie of the Large, Rich and Bewtiful Empyre of Guiana, With a Relation of the Great and Golden Citie of Manoa (which the Spanyards call El Dorado). . . . (1596).*

El Dorado was, in Raleigh's account, the imperial city of Manoa, ruled over by the Emperor Inga, a relative of Atabalipa, a ruler of Peru at the time of the Spanish conquest. When the Spaniards executed Atabalipa, Raleigh said, some of his relatives and their supporters fled east across South America, conquering new territories along the way. They then founded the empire of Guiana, between the Amazon and Orinoco rivers. Guiana, wrote Raleigh,

> is directly east from Peru towards the sea . . . and it hath more abundance of gold than any part of Peru, and as many or more great cities than ever Peru had when it flourished most: it is governed by the same laws, and the emperor and people observe the same religion, and the same form and policies in government as was used in Peru . . . and as I have been assured by such of the Spaniards as have seen Manoa the imperial city of Guiana, which the Spaniards call El Dorado, that for the greatness, for the riches and for the excellent [situation], it far exceedeth any of the world, at least of so much of the world as is known to the Spanish nation: it is founded upon a lake of salt water. . . .

Raleigh then proceeded to quote a Spanish description of the court of Guaynacapa, an ancestor of the current emperor of Guiana:

> All the vessels of his house, table, and kitchen were of gold and silver, and the meanest of silver and copper for strength and hardness of the metal. He had in his wardrobe hollow statues of gold which seemed giants, and the figures in proportion and bigness of all the beasts, birds, trees and herbs, that the earth bringeth forth. . . .

There was in addition, Raleigh reported, an infinite quantity of unwrought gold and silver which the Peruvians hid from the Spaniards. These reports might appear unbelievable, Raleigh said, but they were in fact very plausible when viewed against the golden millions being taken daily out of Peru into Spain.

The first, or possibly the second, European to see Manoa, according to Raleigh, was one Johannes Martines, member of a Spanish expedition to Guiana circa the 1540s. Martines negligently allowed all his expedition's gunpowder to be lost and was condemned to death by the commander, Diego de Ordás. His sentence was commuted to being set adrift in a canoe with his arms but no food. Martines was fortunately captured that same evening by indigenous people. He was taken, blindfolded, on a journey of fourteen or fifteen days to Manoa. There they removed his blindfold. Two whole days of further travel through Manoa itself remained until he was brought to the palace of Inga, ruler of Manoa.

Martines remained at Inga's palace for seven months, sufficient to begin learning the local language. Inga gave him the option to remain in Manoa or return to his people and he elected to leave. On his departure Inga made him a gift of an enormous quantity of gold objects, and an escort to accompany him to the Orinoco River, there to obtain passage to the islands.

Neighboring peoples robbed Martines and his escorts of all his gold, save two calabashes his robbers thought contained food, but which were actually "filled with beads of gold curiously wrought."

The indigenes conveyed Martines down the Orinoco River to Trinidad. From there he traveled to Margarita and then to Puerto Rico where he died. He told his story in Puerto Rico. "This Martines was he," said Raleigh, "that christened the city of Manoa, by the name of El Dorado."

Raleigh considered Guianese "marvelous great drunkards, in which vice I think no nation can compare with them." During royal feasts the officials participating were stripped naked and anointed with a white substance called *curucai*. Servants then blew fine gold dust through hollow canes, onto the naked bodies, "until they be all shining," as Raleigh explained, "from the foot to the head." They sat around like this drinking for up to six or seven days. It was because of this and the abundance of gold he saw in Manoa, including religious objects and implements of war, that Martines called Manoa El Dorado.

The Guianese of El Dorado traded extensively over a wide swath of South America and the islands. Whether among the "cannibals" of Dominica, the "Indians" of Trinidad, or the indigenes of Paria, plates of Guiana gold were standard apparel among the leading men of society. This was true all the way from Dominica to the Amazon in modern-day Brazil.

Among the Spaniards who attempted to find the source of this El Dorado gold was Antonio de Berrio, before he became Trinidad's first Spanish governor in 1592. Others had attempted to approach El Dorado by sea from the Atlantic coast. Some had even explored by river from Peru. De Berrio set out overland in the early 1580s from Nuevo Reygno de Granada with 700 horses, 1,000 head of cattle and "many women, Indians, and slaves." In a year he penetrated 1,500 miles via land and river.

He fought as he went. One indigenous nation, the Amapaia, living along the Orinoco River, inflicted severe losses killing, among others, sixty of de Berrio's best soldiers. He eventually made peace with them and was allowed to sojourn for six months among them. By this time he had only 120 troops left, and no horses or cattle. Swift flowing uncharted rivers and illness had also taken their toll.

Despite his eventual peace with the Amapaians, they remained reticent about information concerning El Dorado. They were themselves rich in gold, and presented de Berrio with "curiously wrought" gold plates and other objects, the exquisiteness of which could not, de Berrio thought, be matched by anything in Europe.

None of this prevented de Berrio from claiming the Orinoco area for Spain. On April 23, 1593, while he was governor of Trinidad, de Berrio's official, Domingo de Vera, claimed Guiana/Orinoco on de Berrio's behalf, for Spain, as de Berrio had previously done about a decade earlier.

By the end of the sixteenth century then, Spanish insular settlements centered on Hispaniola, Cuba, Puerto Rico, Jamaica and Trinidad. Margarita and Cubagua were administratively closely integrated with the Venezuela mainland of *Tierra Firme.* Trinidad and Jamaica remained sparsely populated by Spaniards. The Lucayos (Bahamas), *Tierra Firme* and Central America had all been raided extensively and their people enslaved and transported to the Greater Antilles. By the end of the sixteenth century, Northern European encroachment had also become an inescapable reality.

CHALLENGING SPAIN

News of Columbus' voyage brought an almost immediate response from Northern Europe. Columbus had sought sponsorship from both England and France before turning to Ferdinand and Isabella in Spain. The enormity of Columbus' achievement brought instant awareness in England and France of the profound opportunity that had been lost. The Englishman Thomas Gage, in *The English American, A New Survey of the West Indies (1648),* dealt harshly with his King Henry VII for squandering this opportunity. For this "narrow hearted" monarch, "abounding in riches," rejected Columbus (as Gage saw it), while the cash-strapped Ferdinand, despite his war against the Moors of Granada, "was compelled to borrow with some difficulty a few crowns of a very mean man [Luis Santángel] to set forth Columbus upon so glorious an expedition."

Henry VII wasted no time in trying to recover lost ground, however. On March 5, 1496, with Columbus still in the Caribbean on his second voyage, Henry VII granted John Cabot a patent to search for new lands to the east, west, or north.

Cabot was a Genoese like Columbus and had previously worked for Ferdinand and Isabella in Spain. He may have met Columbus when the latter passed through Valencia in April 1493, on his way to a royal audience after his successful first trip to the Caribbean.

Cabot's journey was to be a direct challenge to Columbus, and therefore to Spain. He hoped to find a northern westerly route to Asia, as opposed to Columbus' southerly route, what would later be referred to as a north-west passage.

Cabot made the English seaport of Bristol his home. Bristol's sailors had been exploring the Atlantic from possibly as early as 1480. In recent years they had concentrated their efforts on finding the "island of Brazil" and the seven cities of Cibola. Some believed that Bristol men may have made a transatlantic landfall before 1465.

Cabot's 1496 trip was aborted. He sailed again on May 20, 1497, and hit Newfoundland in thirty-five days. He planted English and papal flags, sighted and named various places, and was back in Bristol in August 1497. He made no contact with indigenous people, though seeing evidence of their presence.

Like Columbus, he thought he had encountered the land of the Great Khan and looked forward to a follow-up trip to Cipango (Japan). He sailed again from Bristol in May 1498 but was apparently lost at sea. Columbus was in the midst of his third voyage. The race to a New World was on.

King Henry's 1496 patent allowed Cabot, his three sons and their heirs and assigns the right to claim lands anywhere belonging to "heathens" and "infidels," and as yet unknown to Christians. In so doing Henry began the implicit articulation of Northern Europe's case for rights to the New World. The principal arguments, as enunciated by Henry and his Northern counterparts and successors, were as follows:

1. *Rejection of the papal donation.* Henry's patent was a de facto rejection of the pope's granting to Spain, finalized in the Treaty of Tordesillas (1494), of all non-Christian lands from the North to the South Pole, west of a certain line of longitude. Ferdinand and Isabella certainly read Henry's action this way and warned him in 1496 not to do it.

Over the next century, Northern European leaders waxed eloquent on their disdain for Spain's presumed pope-derived right. Queen Elizabeth I of England said that the papal donation could not bind rulers who did not acknowledge the pope's authority. Sir William Cecil, the queen's principal secretary, told the Spanish ambassador in 1562 that the pope had "no right to partition the world and to give and take kingdoms to whomsoever he pleased." "The sun shines on me as well as on others," reasoned Francis I of France in 1526. "I should be very happy to see the clause in Adam's will which excluded me from my share when the world was being divided."

2. *Effective occupation.* In confining his patent to John Cabot to "heathen" and "infidel" lands not already occupied by Christians, Henry VII was tacitly accepting the international law principle of effective occupation. If Spain had effectively established a Christian presence in a place, he would leave it alone.

Conversely, however, explained Queen Elizabeth I, "prescription without possession is of no avail." She could not recognize any Spanish "imaginary proprietorship" over unoccupied lands. The mere fact that Spaniards "have touched here and there, have erected shelters, have given names to a river or promontory," did not mean a thing without effective occupation. Thomas Gage in 1648 elaborated picturesquely on Queen Elizabeth's point—"to me it seems as little reason that the sailing of a Spanish ship upon the coast of India should entitle the King of Spain to that country, as the sailing of an Indian or English ship upon the coast of Spain should entitle either the Indians or English unto the dominion thereof."

However sound in the abstract, these were of course mere arguments of convenience. When their opportunities arose, as they soon would, the Northern Europeans would prove themselves no less capable than the Spaniards of forcible colonization and genocide, whether in South Africa, Australia, Tasmania, North America or anywhere else.

3. *Might is right.* As the sixteenth century wore on, and Northern Europeans became even more disdainful of Spanish claims; some argued that Spain had obtained her colonies by force, and so could legally and morally be dislodged by greater force. International law and God were on the side of whoever won the war.

Some, even such English slave traders and cutthroats as Francis Drake and John Hawkins, could argue with a straight face that Spain had committed genocide against its indigenes and therefore had no moral right to posses such ill-gotten territories. Thomas Gage cited Bartolomé de Las Casas as his authority.

4. *Spanish wealth a cause of mischief.* Spain's threatened hegemony in Europe and its "vast ambitious desire of universal monarchy," as an English parliamentarian put it in 1623, were directly attributable to the vast treasure extracted from the New World. The only way to stop the Spaniard would be to "cut him up at root . . . in the West Indies." "It is his Indian gold that endangereth and disturbeth all the nations of Europe," said Sir Walter Raleigh in 1596.

These elaborate arguments in the mouths of influential people became *casi belli*, reasons for war. By 1559 at the Treaty of Cateau-Cambrésis, France and Spain could formally agree to a state of perpetual war, "no peace beyond the line," in the Caribbean. Whether they were at war or peace in Europe, the Caribbean, defined as west of the prime meridian and south of the Tropic of Cancer, was declared a permanent free-fire zone, where "violence done by either party to the other side shall not be regarded as in contravention" of any peace treaties existing between them. This situation of extraordinary violence lasted for over a hundred years, until 1684, when France and Spain reestablished peace beyond the line at the Treaty of Ratisbon.

By 1520, twenty years after the Portuguese claimed Brazil, Portuguese ships were using the Lesser Antilles as rest stops on their way to South America. English and French ships began to appear by the late 1520s. In 1528 Charles V of Spain expressed great upset at the authorities in Santo Domingo for allowing an English ship to land and leave unmolested.

The main initial challenge to Spain in the Caribbean was through what the Spaniards considered "contraband" trade. Spain, like its European successors in the Caribbean, asserted an exclusive right to trade with its colonies. Trade with these colonies was extremely lucrative, and the Northern Europeans sought to cash in. Spain was unable to build merchant marine capacity fast enough to supply the needs of its rapidly expanding and far-flung western empire.

The Northern Europeans, led by the Dutch, were eager and able to fill the breach. Much of the sixteenth and seventeenth centuries in the Caribbean therefore resolved itself into a kind of undeclared "war" among Holland, England, France and Spain for Caribbean commerce. A Spanish official writing to the King of Spain in 1604 estimated that the Dutch maritime towns of Holland and Zealand had more than 2,000 ships in their merchant marine alone. He estimated over 100 Dutch ships to be in the Caribbean as he wrote.

Spanish colonists were often willing to trade with the Northern Europeans, who represented a reliable supply of European goods. Tobacco was early an important item traded by the colonists. Spain countered the contraband trade by banning cultivation in Panama in 1586. In 1606, the government put a ten-year ban on tobacco cultivation in Puerto Rico, Hispaniola, Cuba, Margarita, and Cumaná (Venezuela), among other places.

In 1691, when three English ships arrived back home with Trinidad tobacco valued at well over a million ducats, the Spanish ambassador suggested to his king that the governor of Trinidad should be punished. In 1612 the governor of Margarita suggested a ban on tobacco cultivation in Trinidad.

From 1502 Spain began importing enslaved Africans to replace the exterminated indigenes. As the number of imports escalated Spain in 1517 regularized the process through the *asiento*, a contract whereby a designated supplier would be given a monopoly for the supply of enslaved Africans for a set number of years. Since the papal bull had excluded Spain from Africa, the Spanish had to rely on suppliers of other nationalities. In time the *asiento,* for the supply of Africans to islands and mainland, became one of the most coveted prizes in international trade, and on occasion the cause of wars.

The supply of Africans also became an important element in contraband trade. Sir John Hawkins initiated the English slave trade to the Caribbean in 1562–1563. He captured 300 or more Africans, "partly by the sword, and partly by other means" at Sierra Leone. From there he visited several ports in Hispaniola, where he exchanged them for hides, sugar, ginger and pearls. The locals were willing to turn a blind eye to the illegality of Hawkins' trade. The authorities in Spain, however, forfeited hides which he unwisely sent there.

Hawkins was followed closely by four English ships which traded 234 Africans in Hispaniola in May 1563. In 1565 seven more English ships arrived with 400 Africans to trade. Hawkins himself was back in 1565 with more enslaved Africans. This time the Hispaniola authorities were hesitant and Hawkins resorted to threats. A refusal to grant a trading license

might "move me to aught that I should not do," he warned. He expressed willingness to pay whatever the normal duties were. If they refused him a license, however, he would have to hurt them and it would be all their own fault for being so obtuse.

Hawkins was essentially a pirate, and pirates figured largely in the contraband trade and the general lawlessness and violence that the Europeans brought to the Caribbean. Reggae singer Bob Marley, in "Redemption Song," one of his most loved compositions, remembers:

> *Old pirates, yes they rob I*
> *Take I from the merchant ships. . . .*

Twentieth-century African American leader Malcolm X, son of a Grenadian mother, recalled the bitter irony of Sir John Hawkins setting out on a slave raiding and pirating expedition on his flagship, the good ship *Jesus of Lubeck.*

Pirates went by a variety of names in the Caribbean. The French called them corsairs. The upper echelon of pirates were often members of the European nobility, sometimes with connections at court. Some were knighted or similarly honored, either before or as a reward for their piratical efforts. These were often called, in English, "privateers"; the term buccaneers evolved in the mid-sixteenth century for gangs of pirates, based especially in Port Royal, Jamaica and in Tortuga, an island off Hispaniola. The name emerged from the "boucans" on which they barbequed meat.

Piracy had been a part of European life for a long time and entered the Caribbean landscape with Columbus. Columbus himself encountered French pirates on his first voyage and had to change course to avoid a French pirate fleet on his third voyage home.

From individual operators pirates quickly evolved into, very often, instruments of national policy. Countries would often use pirates to attack the possessions of rival nations. Monarchs like Queen Elizabeth I might invest in the raiding and plundering expeditions of such upscale pirates as Sir John Hawkins and Sir Francis Drake. Pirate Henry Morgan was knighted and made lieutenant governor of Jamaica.

As early as 1522 the Florentine pirate Juan Verrazano, in the employ of the king of France, captured three Spanish treasure ships from Mexico. Pirates were no respecters of nations, but Spain bore the brunt of their attacks. Spanish Caribbean residents complained to the king of Spain in 1568 that for every Spanish vessel in the area there were twenty corsairs. Pirate attacks on Spain eventually weakened Spain enough to make it easier for Northern Europeans to gain a foothold in the area.

Most of the pirates were French and English, usually criminals on the run from the law. They were mostly men, but two female buccaneers, Mary Read and Annie Bonny, were captured in 1721. In addition to seizing "prize" ships on the high seas, pirates regularly raided the port towns of the Greater Caribbean. They raided Portobello in 1668; Maracaibo in 1669; Santa Marta, Rió de la Hacha, Portobello and Panama in 1670; Trinidad in 1673; Vera Cruz in 1683; San Juan de Ulúa in 1683; and Campeche (Yucatán) in 1685—hundreds of towns and villages in the late seventeenth century alone.

The pirates eventually became a headache even for their sponsors, who eventually moved to co-opt or suppress them. From the 1670s to the 1690s European nations negotiated various treaties aimed at suppressing the pirates. By the treaty of Ryswyck in 1697 Spain ceded Saint Domingue, the western part of Hispaniola, to France. This included the buccaneer nest of Tortuga Island. The French used pirates in their capture of Cartagena that year, the last time that a European government used pirates this way in the Caribbean.

Possibly the most celebrated pirate of all was the Dutchman Piet Heyn, an admiral in the Dutch West India Company who overwhelmed a Spanish treasure fleet in Cuban waters in 1628. Heyn captured 4,000,000 ducats in gold and silver, including 34 tons of silver alone, together with other valuable trading goods such as indigo and cochineal. He remained for centuries a national hero of Holland. The Spanish had their commander, Admiral Benavides, beheaded for cowardice. His second-in-command, Don Juan de Loez, was sentenced to life imprisonment. In 1624 Heyn had briefly captured Bahia (San Salvador) in Portuguese Brazil and unsuccessfully assaulted Portuguese Luanda in Angola.

England also produced a fair share of notorious pirates. Robert Dudley arrived in Trinidad via Cape Blanco, West Africa, in January 1595. He bore a special license from Queen Elizabeth I to visit Trinidad and explore Guiana, land of the elusive El Dorado, to which he dispatched an exploring party while he stayed in Trinidad. During the six-month trip Dudley's fleet captured or destroyed nine Spanish ships. On the way home they laid in wait in the Greater Antilles for stragglers from a Spanish treasure fleet, but found none.

In Spanish-ruled but sparsely populated Trinidad, Dudley was able to land soldiers in battle formation and march halfway across the island without encountering any Spaniards. He proclaimed Trinidad an English colony, in the name of his queen, Elizabeth I. Trinidad thereby became the first Caribbean island officially claimed by a European nation other than Spain.

According to Dudley he got together seven or eight of the "cheife Indians of Trinidado" and they volunteered allegiance to

> our most gracious sovereign, who is a Queene milde and gentle and the onlie Christian prince that doth withstande the crueltie of the tyranous Spaniarde, the which maketh her gratiousnes to be more than admired throughout all the face of the earth, not onlie by Christians but allsoe by pagans, infidles and salvages. . . .

Dudley affixed a leaden plaque to a tree proclaiming English jurisdiction and repeated the process almost three weeks later, on February 18, 1595, shortly after the Spaniards made a first, tentative appearance. Dudley, however, fell into the same trap of "imaginary proprietorship" that Queen Elizabeth had laughed to scorn in the Spaniards. He could not make his occupation real, and it was to be 202 years later, in 1797, before the English would effectively wrest Trinidad from Spain.

The two best known of the English sixteenth-century pirates were the upscale privateers and cousins, Sir John Hawkins and Sir Francis Drake.

For over thirty years, from 1562 to 1596, both of them, together and separately, traded enslaved Africans in the Caribbean, generally flouted Spain's laws against contraband trade, seized Spanish ships on the high seas and launched attacks, major and minor, against Spanish settlements and treasure convoys. They both died and were buried at sea on their joint last Caribbean expedition. They were not always successful by any means, and sometimes suffered heavy defeats. Drake lost two brothers on a single expedition. When they were successful, however, they were able to inflict severe damage on Spanish interests.

Drake first sailed to the Caribbean in 1566 on an expedition organized by Hawkins, though Hawkins stayed home. He captured some Africans in West Africa and sold them at Margarita, Curaçao, Rio de la Hacha and elsewhere. In 1567 Hawkins and Drake sailed together on a similar triangular trip to Africa, the Caribbean and back to Europe. Four of the fleet's nine ships were supplied by Queen Elizabeth I, regular supporter of privateering expeditions. Her most important ship on this trip was the *Jesus of Lubeck*, of which Malcolm X spoke so bitterly 300 years later. Hawkins, the expedition's leader, made the *Jesus* his flagship. This time Hawkins attacked Africans in the Cape Verde Islands. The Africans fought back with poisoned arrows and wicker shields. They inflicted heavy losses on Hawkins' men, but Hawkins was nevertheless able to capture 150 of them. Hawkins almost died from his wounds in the encounter, but an African saved his life by showing him how to apply a clove of garlic to the wound. The garlic drew out the poison. In Sierra Leone Hawkins and company captured a Portuguese ship which they renamed the *Grace of God*.

With Hawkins despairing of procuring sufficient Africans for his trip, an African collaborationist chief came to his rescue in January 1568. The chief requested Hawkins' help in hostilities with a local rival. Hawkins contributed 120 men, of whom 6 were killed and 40 wounded. They burnt the rival's town and Hawkins obtained a few hundred more enslaved prisoners, though not as many as promised by the victorious chief, who double-crossed him. Hawkins now had about 500 Africans. He disposed

of them, and miscellaneous merchandise, along the Spanish Main.

The culmination of this voyage was supposed to be an English attack on a Spanish treasure fleet at the port of San Juan de Ulúa in the Gulf of Mexico. Instead the Spanish defenders inflicted a crushing defeat on Hawkins' forces. They captured or destroyed all but two of Hawkins' ships. The good ship *Jesus,* which carried all the profits of the trip, was lost to the Spaniards. Hawkins barely managed to flee the *Jesus.*

Among the people and items lost on the *Jesus* were 57 remaining Africans, who the English planned to sell at Vera Cruz in Mexico; 29,743 gold pesos; cash in English currency; at least 30 bales of English linen; 30 gilt rapiers with their daggers and girdles, which the English had taken at Cartagena; and quintals of wax, taffeta, pewter and pearls. Hawkins even lost his fancy velvet and silk suits with their gold and pearl buttons.

There were too many English survivors for the two ships that were able to escape the rout. Hawkins was therefore forced to put 100 of his men ashore in Mexico. The indigenes promptly killed some of them. The Spaniards captured the rest. They were made galley slaves on Spanish ships. Some spent time in Seville jails or were killed by the Spanish inquisition. Hawkins lost forty-five more men on the way home, with the survivors having nothing but an ox hide to eat for the last seven days. Drake made it home separately. Two of the hundred left behind made it back to England in the aftermath of the battle. A few more got home years later, crippled and broken.

Between 1569 and 1571 Drake nevertheless sailed twice to the Caribbean to make preparations for an attack on a Spanish mule train bringing Peruvian treasure across the Isthmus of Panama to Nombre de Dios, for transshipment to Spain. Drake assaulted the Nombre de Dios mule train twice in 1572–1573. He failed the first time but eventually realized profits of 47 pounds for every 1 pound invested in the trip. Queen Elizabeth I was again an important investor. For these attacks Drake forged an alliance with African Maroons (escapees from Spanish captivity who lived in independent communities). They provided invaluable tactical, manpower and intelligence support. Drake returned to his hometown of Plymouth on August 9, 1573. He had lost forty of the seventy-three young men and boys who sailed with him fifteen months earlier. These included his two brothers. He himself had been wounded.

While preparing for his attacks Drake met some French Huguenot privateers, who joined with him and split the profits. He had also become, with the help of the African Maroons, the first Englishman to see the Pacific Ocean.

In 1586 Drake was back in the Caribbean, after taking time off to sail around the world. This time he headed a fleet of over thirty vessels, two of them seconded from the English Royal Navy by Queen Elizabeth, and containing 5,000–6,000 men.

England had joined the Reformation against the Roman Catholic Church in 1534 and Drake's father had been an anti-Catholic Protestant preacher. In Santo Domingo, Drake unleashed all the fury of a religious war. The English soldiers desecrated Spanish churches. They smashed religious statues. They opened sepulchers and filled them with the offal of cattle they slaughtered in the churches. They burned churches, nunneries, hospitals and monasteries and turned two of the cathedral's chapels into a jail. They made the cathedral their headquarters.

Once again Drake forged an alliance with the African Maroons, who were only too happy to join with anyone fighting their hated Spanish enslavers. Drake remained more than a month in Santo Domingo. He burned two-thirds of the city (though the stone buildings were not easily burned) and spared one-third for ransom.

From Santo Domingo, Spanish capital city of the islands, Drake sailed to Cartagena, capital of the Spanish Main. There he again burnt, looted and held for ransom. He lost about 500 men to fighting and illness.

Drake and Hawkins sailed together for their last voyage in 1595. This time there were 27 ships and 2,500 men. Hawkins died at sea between Virgin Gorda and Puerto Rico. Drake's subsequent attack on Puerto Rico was repulsed. He then returned to the Spanish Main where he burned Rio de la Hacha and Santa Marta. He tried another attack on the treasure shipments near Nombre de Dios but was defeated.

Drake died on board ship near Portobello on January 28, 1596. His men commemorated his passing by burning down Portobello.

Together with Dudley, Hawkins and Drake, Sir Walter Raleigh completed what might be called the "big four" of English sixteenth-century privateers attacking Spanish interests in the Caribbean. He was at pains to distinguish himself from ordinary low-level pirates. He could have spent his time sailing out of Cape Cod (Massachusetts) and elsewhere, he said, in search of ordinary prizes. He considered himself above that. He was bringing glory to his queen and country. Yet that distinction may not always have been apparent to the Spaniards he killed, the indigenous canoes he chased and the local pilots he kidnapped into service.

His main self-appointed tasks were to locate the Guianese El Dorado and to weaken the Spanish presence in the area. He was convinced that Spain's power derived from the vast treasures extracted from her New World territories. He was sure that the gold of El Dorado would surpass the treasure of Peru and Mexico and thereby enable England to greatly exceed Spain's power. "Guiana," he said (rendered here in modern spelling), "is a country that hath yet her maidenhead, never sacked, turned, nor wrought, the face of the earth hath not been torn . . . the graves have not been opened for gold, the mines not broken with sledges, nor their images pulled down out of their temples. It hath never been entered by any Christian prince."

And as if the gold were not enough, Raleigh thought that Guiana could also support a lucrative trade in timber, dyewood, cotton, gums, "Indian pepper," and other goods. Guiana was also exceedingly healthy. Of the 100 men he took there for over a month, not one became ill or contracted any disease. This despite the fact that they daily rowed and marched in the hot sun, were drenched in "great showers," slept in the open and ate all manner of "corrupt fruits," unseasoned fish and unfamiliar animals.

He professed never to have seen a more beautiful country. There were hills and villages, rivers winding into tributaries, plains of green grass without bush or stubble, hard sandy ground, easy to march on, with deer crisscrossing the way. And all crowned by "birds towards the evening singing on every tree with a thousand several tunes, cranes and herons of white, crimson, and carnation perching on the riverside, the air fresh with a gentle easterly wind, and every stone that we stooped to take up, promised either gold or silver by his complexion [modern spelling]."

Raleigh arrived in Trinidad, the staging post for his El Dorado mission, on March 22, 1595, only ten days after Dudley's departure. Like Dudley, he wandered about the southern part of the island at will, making no contact with Spaniards. He brought with him as interpreter an indigene who had been taken to England on a previous trip. Like the Frenchman Jean Retud in 1587 and Robert Dudley in 1595, Raleigh's earnest entreaties for gold led him to a mine of marcasite, a gold-like substance of little value.

Raleigh made his way north to Puerto de los Hispanioles via the Pitch Lake, where he caulked his ships. The Spaniards at Puerto de los Hispanioles seemed friendly, apparently because they were awaiting reinforcements from Margarita and Cumaná in Venezuela before confronting him.

Spanish governor Antonio de Berrio forbade the indigenes from trading with the English but they defied the ban. De Berrio executed two of them. Yet the Spaniards themselves willingly engaged in contraband trade with Raleigh. The poor Spanish soldiers, Raleigh said, had not had wine for years and a few drinks "made them merry."

Raleigh was bent on revenge, however, for de Berrio's killing of a party of Englishmen a year or two earlier. Raleigh therefore killed the Puerto de los Hispanioles garrison in a surprise attack. He then marched by night to the inland capital of San José de Oruña (St. Joseph). He burned down the town, supposedly at the instigation of the indigenes. He presented himself as their champion and the avenger of the suffering and torture inflicted on them by the Spaniards. Raleigh imprisoned de Berrio on board his ship, where he kept him as an informant for his trip to Guiana's El Dorado.

Raleigh did not renew Dudley's claim to Trinidad for the English crown, but he came close. After burning St. Joseph, he gathered the local caciques and "made them understand," through his interpreter,

that I was the servant of a queen, who was the great cacique of the north, and a virgin, and had more caciques under her than there were trees in their island: that she was an enemy to the Castellani in respect of their tyranny and oppression.

Raleigh explained that Queen Elizabeth had sent him to free them. He showed the assembled caciques a picture of his queen, "which they so admired and honored," as to be almost idolaters. Raleigh said he made similar speeches in Guiana and environs, so that the queen was now well known in the region as Ezrabeth Cassipuna Aquerewana, which translated as "Elizabeth, the great princess or great commander."

Raleigh left some of his party in Trinidad and took 100 men in small boats to Guiana. Among them were a nephew and two cousins, one bearing the engaging name of Butshead Gorges. There they lacked the time or resources to extract much gold, but were convinced that they were on the right track for the elusive El Dorado.

In the tradition of Drake and Hawkins, Raleigh attacked the Spaniards at Cumaná on his way home from Trinidad in 1595, but with disastrous results. He lost forty or more men in the initial assault and others died of their wounds on board ship. Some of his men were taken prisoner and had to be exchanged for de Berrio and another Spanish official still held by Raleigh.

Neither Raleigh nor anyone else ever found the elusive golden city of Manoa, though the general area remained an important source of gold for centuries thereafter. Raleigh made a last trip to Guiana in 1617–1618 and was executed on his return to England.

NORTHERN EUROPEAN COLONIES ESTABLISHED

After a hundred years of contraband trade, piracy and attacks on Spanish settlements and shipping, the Northern Europeans were by the early seventeenth century ready to plant colonies of their own. The Spaniards had fought back valiantly while simultaneously consolidating and expanding their empire in the

Europe Supported by Africa and America; J. G. Stedman's allegorical drawing done in Suriname in the 1770s.

Greater Caribbean and South, Central and North America. They could on occasion inflict devastating defeats on the likes of Drake, Hawkins and Raleigh.

A cursory look at a map of the Americas today reveals the extent and relative success of Spanish penetration. Spanish is today the almost universal language of South and Central America, and also a significant portion of the Caribbean. Such North American state names as Florida, Arizona,

California, New Mexico and Colorado attest to Spanish penetration.

From the mid-sixteenth century Spain also put in place elaborate and costly measures to combat the pirate menace. Commercial voyages to the Caribbean were consolidated into two fleets of twenty to sixty ships per year, escorted by warships. In Santo Domingo the fleets split in two, with one section going to the Isthmus of Panama and the other to Veracruz in Mexico. A few ships sailed along the Central American coast to supply that area. Squadrons of warships based in Santo Domingo and Cartagena added further support. Any corsairs found lurking in the path of these fleets were ruthlessly dealt with. The fleets reassembled in Havana for the return voyage. Menéndez de Avilés, captain general of Cuba and *adelentado* of Florida, was one of the principal architects of this system. His scheme included fortifying Spain's Caribbean harbors, a fortified base in Florida opposite Havana and a permanent naval patrol on the other side of the Atlantic, between the Azores and the Andalusian coast of Spain. He even proposed a Spanish naval base in the Scilly Islands, off the southwestern coast of England. Menéndez captured fifty corsair ships during his career.

In the late 1580s Philip II of Spain hired the Italian architect Juan Bautista Antoneli to strengthen Caribbean defenses. His efforts are credited with the Spanish defeats of Drake at Puerto Rico and Raleigh at Cumaná, both in 1595.

The Spaniards even took the battle to Northern Europe itself. In 1588 their famous *Armada* of 130 ships (40 of them warships, the rest troop transports and auxiliary vessels) attempted to invade England and neutralize the Netherlands. The invasion force carried about 8,000 sailors and perhaps as many as 19,000 soldiers. A further 30,000 Spanish soldiers waited in Flanders (now Belgium) to join the invasion. The Spanish intention was to defeat both England and the Netherlands, make them Spanish colonies and thus end the piracy menace in the Caribbean once and for all. The English and Dutch naval forces were able to save the day. There were heavy losses on all sides. Sir Francis Drake was second in command of the English fleet.

In 1595, even as Drake and Hawkins were preparing their last ill-fated foray into the Caribbean, four Spanish galleons landed in Cornwall on England's south coast, not far from Drake's and Hawkins' Plymouth base. They burned three towns, celebrated Roman Catholic mass on a convenient hill and got away unharmed and unchallenged.

Clearly there was no love lost between the Spaniards and their Northern European tormentors. Governor Antonio de Berrio of Trinidad expressed

this sentiment well in 1593 (two years before Raleigh captured him) when he referred to "these Englishmen whom I loathe and always injure" when they used Trinidad as a rest stop and place for contraband trade with the indigenes. An English ship landing at Tortuga in 1656 found a document written in Spanish with an English translation, warning French, Flemish and whatever other intruders to keep off. This was Spanish territory, it said, and any interlopers would be severely dealt with.

For all their valiant efforts, however, it was simply not humanly possible for Spain, or any country for that matter, to hold on indefinitely to the whole vast American continent in the face of such unrelenting and widespread opposition. Within a decade of Robert Dudley's unsustainable 1595 claim to Trinidad as a British colony, other tentative efforts were underway to colonize other islands. Some of these early attempts were associated with failed Northern European attempts to colonize the Wild Coast of Guiana. English settlers heading for the Wild Coast settled for St. Lucia instead in 1605. An Anglo-Dutch company sent over 200 settlers to Grenada in 1609. Both of these settlements were expelled by the Caribs, whose land they were presuming to encroach upon.

An Englishman, Captain Henry Powell, saw Barbados in 1622 on his way home from Bahia in Brazil. There were neither Caribs nor Spaniards living there and he returned to settle in 1627. The French occupied Martinique and Guadeloupe in 1635. The Guadeloupe settlers spread to Les Saintes, Désirade and Marie-Galante. The Martinique settlers investigated St. Lucia and Grenada, but did not immediately plant any lasting settlements in either place.

The first permanently settled island by Northern Europeans was, however, St. Kitts (St. Christopher). Thomas Warner, member of an English expedition to Guiana in 1620, landed at St. Kitts in 1622 and returned with English settlers in 1624. Some French people were already there growing cotton and tobacco and coexisting with the Caribs. In 1627 more French settlers came out. From St. Kitts the English spread out to Anguilla, Barbuda, Tortola and Nevis.

French and English governors on St. Kitts worked out arrangements of peaceful coexistence.

If any Caribs landed on the island, whichever community saw them first would alert the other. They would cooperate to repel any Spanish incursion. If war broke out between England and France whoever found out first should inform the other. But they should not automatically come to blows, unless they had a "special order" to fight, from their respective monarchs. Neither should enter the other's territory without permission. A 1655 visitor said that a dry ditch separated the two communities.

The Dutch, as already seen, initially emphasized trade over colonization. They nevertheless also established colonies in the early 1600s. They had won their independence from Spain in 1580 and continued to display a special animus toward Spain in the Caribbean.

From the late 1500s the Dutch were already exporting salt and rare woods from nominally Spanish Cumaná in eastern Venezuela. By 1621 Dutch fleets of privateers were using St. Vincent, Tobago, St. Martin, Bonaire and Curaçao as rest stops on their way to operations in Brazil and elsewhere.

The Dutch held Bahia, the Brazilian capital, from 1624 to 1625. They held north-east Brazil from 1630 to 1654. Some Jewish refugees expelled from Brazil after its recapture by the Portuguese, settled in the Caribbean. In 1628, the same year in which Piet Heyn captured the Spanish treasure fleet off Matanzas, Cuba, Dutch merchants from Flushing started a short-lived colony in Tobago.

In 1632 the Dutch built a fort on St. Martin and garrisoned it with 100 men. St. Martin became an important source of salt. The Spanish took the island in 1633 but the Dutch regained it in 1644. By 1634 the Dutch were also in Berbice, Corentine and Essequibo on Guiana's Wild Coast. In 1634 the Dutch also took Curaçao from the Spaniards. From Curaçao they wrested Aruba and Bonaire from the Spaniards as well, to form the Dutch Windward Islands.

In 1634 the Dutch founded New Zealand on St. Eustatius. From there they expanded to Saba. Saba, St. Eustatius and St. Martin became the Dutch Leeward Islands. In 1667 the Dutch exchanged New Amsterdam (New York) with the English for Suriname.

The Spaniards, meanwhile, did what they could to stem the burgeoning encroachment. In 1629 they destroyed the French and English settlements on St. Kitts. They maintained their own fort on St. Martin from 1635 to 1646. They destroyed the Dutch colony on Tobago in 1636.

By mid-seventeenth century the Dutch appeared to be leaders in the challenge to Spain (and to Portugal in Brazil). The Englishman Thomas Gage in 1648 urged his compatriots to learn from "our neighbours, the Hollanders." While the English were still trading port to port, he said, the Dutch had captured so much territory, both in the East and West Indies, "that it may be said of them, as of the Spaniards, *That the sun never sets upon their dominions.*" (This very expression later became the proud boast of the British Empire.)

Other colonies would later be established and as Spanish preeminence declined in the eighteenth century the northern Europeans would increasingly fight among themselves for various territories, some of which would change hands many times.

By the mid-seventeenth century, however, the Caribbean had already begun to assume linguistic and political outlines that would be recognizable three centuries later. The Spanish, Dutch, English and French (joined by the United States in the late nineteenth century) would remain the main colonizers. Germans, Danes, Swedes and others would also try their hands in the area.

German merchant bankers from The House of Welser actually ran part of Venezuela from 1528 to 1556. Charles V of Spain owed them money, was unable to pay and in effect gave them a mortgage on Venezuela. Beginning 1651 the Knights of Malta, the Roman Catholic religious military order and sometime owners of sovereign states, purchased St. Kitts, St. Martin and St. Bartolomé from the French *Compagnie des Iles d'Amérique*. They later added St. Croix, but sold them all to the French West India Company in 1665. The Danish West India and Guinea Company occupied St. Thomas in 1672 and St. John in 1683. They bought St. Croix from the French West Indies Company in 1733. The king of Denmark bought the islands in 1754, thereby making them royal Danish colonies. Norway was politically united with Denmark from 1536 to 1814 as the kingdom of Denmark-Norway, which made them part of the Danish involvement in the Virgin

Islands. Many of the seamen on Danish slave ships were in fact from Norway.

The German state of Brandenburg-Prussia, which includes Berlin, occupied St. Peter in the Virgin Islands in 1689. They were later expelled by the British. They tried unsuccessfully to buy Crab Island, St. Vincent, St. Croix and Tobago. The Baltic Duchy of Courland established a settlement in Tobago in the seventeenth century and continued to claim the island into the eighteenth. Sweden bought St. Bartolomé from France in 1784. The French repurchased it in 1878. Sweden also held Guadeloupe from 1813 to 1814.

Perhaps the most ambitious challenge to Spain by the mid-seventeenth century was the "Western Design" of Oliver Cromwell, "Lord Protector" of England from 1653 to 1658. Cromwell was a leader of the parliamentary coup which executed English King Charles I.

The Dutch had previously successfully attacked the Spaniards in the Dutch Windward Islands. Cromwell, however, aimed no less than to capture Hispaniola, capital of the Spanish Caribbean. Henry Whistler, who traveled with the expedition, has left an unusually lively and detailed account of the enterprise.

The force was under the joint command of Admiral William Penn, who commanded the fleet; General Robert Venables, who commanded the land forces; and three commissioners. Venables took along his new wife for a sort of working honeymoon, which became a cause of great resentment among his soldiers.

The 2,000–2,500 soldiers who embarked in England were a mixture of regular army conscripts and volunteer riffraff—"knights of the blade . . . common cheats, thieves, cutpurses, and such like lewd persons," not to mention some "sloathful and thievish servants. . . ."

When the gun was fired on December 26, 1654, as a sign for all to be on board, "many made it to be a warning for them to hide until we were gone [modern spelling]."

Some soldiers had to be forced on board. Whistler managed to capture the human side of soldiers leaving their loved ones as they headed to probable death, in a way that one does not often come by in such accounts. "This was a sad day with our married men," Whistler observed,

> they hanging down their heads with a demure countenance, acting loath to depart, and some of them professing more love the one to the other in one half hour than they had performed in all the time of their being together. And many of our young men that had entangled themselves in love with some young virgin: who think it very hard and a great cruelty to leave a young virgin to whom he hath engaged and wholly devoted his heart: others were weeping, and leaving and bequeathing unto them some pledge of their wanton love; receiving from them some cordial against sea sickness. . . .

The invasion force stopped in Barbados, where they raised another 3,000–4,000 men, already acclimated to the Caribbean. They raised about 1,200 more in Nevis, St. Kitts, Montserrat and Antigua. They were now up to about 8,000 men, plus a sea regiment of an estimated 1,080–1,200 sailors.

On the way to Hispaniola the invasion force sent one English ship, temporarily under Spanish colors, into the harbor at San Juan, Puerto Rico. They hoped by this ruse to capture a Puerto Rican pilot and force him to help them negotiate the local waters. The ruse did not work.

In Hispaniola the English landed troops several miles from Santo Domingo after a preliminary bombardment, and set out to assault the town by land. Residents of outlying areas had fled to the city. The invaders encountered a monastery, "but all the ballpated friars were gone." They had, however, left behind their "images," which the English soldiers, like Drake's decades earlier, had a fine time with. A soldier put a richly adorned Madonna and child on his head and brought her to the English ranks, where the soldiers pelted her with oranges and deformed her.

These soldiers of Oliver Cromwell, who had been particularly brutal in his campaigns in Ireland, now happened upon an Irish resident of Santo

Domingo. He promised to lead them to water (for they were very thirsty). Instead he led them into an ambush. General Venables, according to Whistler, "seeing the enemy fall in so desperately with their lances, he very nobly run behind a tree . . . being so much possessed with terror that he could hardly speak."

The English were routed in their initial encounters by a combination of "cow killers" and enslaved Africans. The cow killers actually killed cows for a living, to supply the hides and tallow exported from Hispaniola. They were, according to Whistler, "a sort of vagabond that are saved from the gallows in Spain and the king doth send them here."

Whistler did not think much of the other Spaniards who, he said, were so riddled by the pox (syphilis), "that they cannot go 2 mile but they are ready to die." In 1586 African Maroons had helped Francis Drake's assault on Santo Domingo. This time the Spaniards wisely promised their Africans freedom in exchange for fighting. Both Africans and cow killers wore talismans around their necks. The latter guaranteed papal forgiveness for sins past and present and promised immediate entry into Paradise should they be martyred in battle.

The English retreated to the beach where they had landed. While General Venables retired on board to the comfort of his new wife, his soldiers spent days on the beach, trying to regroup for another attack, and suffering greatly from the dreaded "bloody flux." "Nothing but shitting," Whistler picturesquely reported, "for they were in a very bad condition, 50 or 60 stools in a day. . . ."

On their second attempt on Santo Domingo the English were again ambushed and mauled by a much smaller local force. Admiral Penn was so disgusted with the English soldiers that he threatened to sail away and leave them. The surviving soldiers camped on the shore while the ships were readied for departure.

The country around them was full of wild cattle but the English were so traumatized by the cow killers and Africans that they preferred to starve rather than venture a mile from camp in search of food. The sound of crabs clattering at night caused soldiers to jump into the sea. They mistook fireflies for cow killers with matches and fired at them. Robert Dudley's men had similarly fired at fireflies in Trinidad in 1595. "For there is a certain fly," Capt Wyatt, a chronicler of Dudley's trip had observed, "which in the night time appeareth like unto a fire. . . ."

The defeated English remained in Hispaniola for three weeks. They were reduced to eating their dogs and horses. If a trooper tied his horse while he eased himself, Whistler noted, he might find his horse half-roasted by the time he was finished, "if he were not nimble." The English lost about 1,000 men in Hispaniola. A chastened General Venables begged Admiral Penn to take them to Spanish Jamaica, where the English might salvage some pride.

The whole Spanish population of Jamaica was only about 1,500. They decided to offer only token resistance to the 7,000 soldiers plus the sea regiment that the English still had at their disposal. The Spanish governor of Jamaica was in no condition to mount a defense. He was so incapacitated by the pox that he had to be carried on a hammock by two Africans to meet the English commanders.

Had the Jamaicans known how traumatized the English still were from their rout in Hispaniola perhaps they might have mounted a real defense. Those English soldiers who did not wish to fight were even given the option of staying on board, and many did just that.

Jamaica quickly turned into a sort of pyrrhic victory for the English. Of the 7,000 soldiers plus the sea regiment who arrived in May 1655, only 3,720 were still alive in November. The Spaniards had initially provided the English with food, but when that stopped, the English proved unequal to the task of feeding themselves. As in Hispaniola, they were once more reduced to eating dogs and horses. An Englishman in Jamaica painted a pitiful scene. "Never," he wrote home in November 1655, "did my eyes see such a sickly time, nor so many funerals, and graves all the town over that it is a very Golgotha."

Some graves in a nearby savannah were so shallow, he reported, that the Spanish dogs dug up the remains and ate them. "As for the English dogs," he said, "they are most eaten by our soldiery; not one walks the street that is not shot at unless well befriended or respected." The English in six months had eaten practically all the cattle, asses, horses and mules within 12 miles. The bloody flux and other diseases were rampant. Half of the survivors were "sick and helpless."

The Spaniards had called Jamaica the "Garden of the Indies" and Cromwell agreed. He thanked the "good providence of God," for the conquest of this "certain island called Jamaica, spacious in its extent, commodious in its harbours and rivers within itself, healthful by its rivers by its situation, fertile in the nature of the soil, well stored with horses and other cattle, and generally fit to be planted and improved, to the advantage, honour, and interest, of this nation." He urged English settlers in New England to abandon their "desert and barren wilderness" for Jamaica, the "land of plenty." He announced import and export duty concessions for any "planter or adventurer" who would come to Jamaica.

Cromwell's direct government-organized Western Design against Hispaniola and Jamaica represented a change from earlier practice, where Northern European colonies usually depended on private enterprise for initial incursion into new areas. Individual corsairs or merchants or groups of individuals organized into joint stock (i.e., limited liability) companies, usually took the initiative. They would often count among their stockholders members of their respective nobilities and governments. In time they would be granted "patents" by their home governments acknowledging their rights and responsibilities. Governors might be appointed by, or with the consent of, the home governments.

In 1627, for example, Charles I of England granted all the isles of "The Caribbees" (whether effectively occupied or not, it seems) to the Earl of Carlisle. His fiefdom included St. Kitts, Grenada, St. Vincent, St. Lucia, Barbados, Dominica, Marie Galante, Guadeloupe, Antigua, Montserrat and others. He was to pay a yearly rent of 100 pounds to the crown and had to keep a white horse always on the ready for whenever the king or his heirs or successors should visit the islands. In 1629 his proprietorship was reduced to Barbados only, while the Earl of Pembroke was made lord proprietor of the others.

Similarly in 1626 Cardinal de Richelieu, head of the French government, granted a commission to Belin d'Esnambuc and du Roissey giving them exclusive rights to settle St.Kitts, Barbados and "surrounding islands." The commission took into consideration the fact "that the inhabitants of the islands are not friendly people," and therefore enjoined the commissioners to Catholicize them and bring them under French jurisdiction.

Early commissioners and lord proprietors could be individuals. In time, though, they were frequently chartered companies with official "charters" for a stated number of years, granted by their home governments. Among these were the Courteen Company, which received a charter for Barbados in 1627; the *Compagnie des Iles d'Amérique*, 1635, a revised version of the *Compagnie de Saint-Christophe,* organized in 1626; and the *Compagnie des Indes*, which appointed its first governor of Saint Domingue (later Haiti) in 1665, before Spain had even recognized its encroachment onto the western section of Hispaniola.

The most illustrious of the early chartered companies and one which served as a model for the others was the Dutch West India Company. This was a powerful globalized multinational company with its headquarters in Amsterdam and territory in West Africa, South America (including Brazil), the Caribbean and North America. It had its own ships and army and was a vast agency for colonization by private enterprise.

The company received its charter from "Their High Mightinesses the Lords the States-General of Holland" in 1621. Governors had to be approved by and to take an oath of allegiance to the state.

SUGAR, POOR WHITES

The early North European settlers looked to agriculture for their economic prosperity. Sir Walter Raleigh, despite his Spanish-like determination to find El Dorado, had nevertheless eloquently assessed the agricultural potential of Trinidad in 1595. "This island of Trinedado," he wrote, was blessed with very fertile soil and would support "sugar, ginger, or any other commodity that the Indies yield."

The early North European colonies first tried cotton and tobacco. Tobacco was soon overproduced and they turned to sugar. Hispaniola had earlier allowed its sugar industry to decline in favor of ginger, so this marked a second beginning for sugar.

Barbados emerged in the 1640s as the Caribbean's major sugar producer. They (and Guadeloupe, Martinique and elsewhere) were aided in this enterprise by Jewish refugees expelled from Brazil, who brought sugar technology with them. The sugar-induced need for labor helped stimulate the importation of poor whites and, numerically more important, Africans. A typical British Caribbean sugar plantation at the end of the seventeenth century comprised about 100 acres, with 40 acres in cane, 40 fallow and 20 for such miscellaneous purposes as pasture, growing provisions and providing a nursery for new canes.

A sugar plantation also included a significant manufacturing element. This included, among other things, a boiling house, still house, curing house and drying house. A windmill would provide power. The typical plantation would utilize fifty enslaved Africans and seven poor white servants. There would be an overseer, doctor, farrier and carter. There would be six horses and eight oxen. The plantation would produce 80,000 pounds of sugar annually and 20 hogsheads of molasses, each weighing 700 pounds. All of this would generate a profit of almost 10 percent. On the Caribbean plantation you had a large socialized workforce operating sophisticated machinery and producing for an export market. Historian C. L. R James considered this to be a first in world history. This type of proto-industrial workforce did not become widespread in Europe for another hundred years or more.

The increasing productivity of the Northern European colonies led to the imposition of monopolistic trade practices variously known as mercantilism in the English territories and the exclusive in the French. These policies were little different from those long practiced by Spain. Since trade with the colonies was an extremely lucrative business, only the colonizing powers should benefit from trade with their respective colonies. The English codified these principles in the Navigation Laws of the 1650s. For the English colonies, goods would have to be imported from England on English ships captained by Englishmen. Crews would have to be at least three-quarters English. Sugar grown in British colonies must be refined in England and would have preferential entry into the English market.

The French exclusive was similar. Jean Baptiste Colbert (1619–1683), important architect of the exclusive, insisted that colonies existed for the economic benefit of the mother country. They were to be markets for French produce and stimulants to French industry.

The Dutch were the main initial targets of these exclusivist policies. With their massive merchant marine and effective distribution (including entrepôts and warehouses in the Caribbean), they had become principal suppliers to the entire area. The Spaniards alternated between hanging Dutch captains and trading with them.

With the advent of mercantilism, however, the Dutch now also had to confront British and French hostility. Charles I of England prohibited trade in 1637 with Dutch and other "strangers." Cromwell's Western Design force captured sixteen Dutch vessels in Barbados while on their way to Hispaniola and Jamaica. These ships were trading by mutual consent with the Barbadians, mercantilism or no mercantilism. In both English and French colonies the ban on Dutch shipping became a cause for grievance. The ban on trade with the Dutch (and later with the North American colonies, Bermuda and even Antigua) pushed Barbadians in 1651 to something close to a declaration of independence. Like the Americans who, a hundred years later, raised the cry of "no taxation without representation," the Barbadians asked, "Should we be bound to . . . a Parliament in which we have no Representatives . . . ?" They also anticipated the American Revolution's cry of "Give me liberty or give me death," the Haitian Revolution's "Liberty or death" and the twentieth-century Cuban Revolution's *"Patria o muerte, venceremos* [Fatherland or death, we will win!]". We would rather "choose a noble death," the Barbadians declared, "than forsake [our] old liberties and privileges."

The Barbadians had good reason to chafe at imperial control, for Barbados was by the mid-seventeenth century a wealthy place. Henry Whistler gave his trademark entertaining and detailed assessment of the island in 1655. "This island is one of the richest spots of ground in the world," he wrote, "and fully inhabited. But were the people suitable to the island it were not to be compared. . . ." Sugar was the main crop, but there was cotton, indigo and a variety of fruits. Bread was made from cassava flour.

"The gentry here doth live far better than ours do in England," Whistler noted. "[T]hey have most of them 100 or 2 or 3 of slaves, apes who they command as they please. . . ." They also had ample liberty, though, in his opinion, they abused it. The island already presented a polyglot and motley appearance. It was "inhabited with all sorts: with English, French, Dutch, Scots, Irish, Spaniards they being Jews: with Indians and miserable Negroes born to perpetual slavery, they and their seed. . . ."

The rapid growth of Barbados and other colonies led to the importation of poor whites to help populate them. As Columbus and the Spaniards had long done, and as many European nations would continue to do for hundreds of years to come, they looked to the dregs of European society to populate the new colonies. Richard Hakluyt, great advocate of English colonial expansion, had as early as 1584 suggested "multitudes of loiterers and idle vagabonds" as ideal candidates for the colonies which he envisaged. Better to put them to productive use in the colonies than leave them in jail where "at length [they] are miserably hanged, even 20 at a clap. . . ."

The poor whites were procured in various ways. Many were indentured servants, bound by a contract (indenture) to work three to seven years in exchange for a free passage out. At the end of their contracts they were given 3–5 acres of land. When the land in Barbados ran out in the 1640s they were given sugar or offered land in other islands instead. Most of the English indentured servants were young men. Many of the men who Cromwell's Western Design recruited in Barbados, St. Kitts and elsewhere for the attacks on Hispaniola and Jamaica would have come to the islands as indentured servants.

Some of the poor whites were kidnapped and transported by enterprising merchants who could sell them in the Caribbean. Children were kidnapped too, despite regulations against this practice.

Some were religious nonconformists or political dissidents who were banished to the Caribbean (or North America). Scottish and Irish prisoners sometimes shared a similar fate at the hands of the English.

After a campaign in Ireland in 1649, Oliver Cromwell reported to parliament that the Irish "officers were knocked on the head and every tenth man of the soldiers killed, and the rest shipped for the Barbadoes." The verb "to barbadoes" entered the English language at this time, connoting forced shipment to the island.

The Danish islands also sent out their convicts and what one Danish governor called their louts and vagabonds. French practice was similar to the others. French indentured servants were first called *alloués,* after a medieval French practice of placing oneself in voluntary bondage for a specified number of years. They were later called *engagés.*

The classic (and much quoted) description of the low-life European came once more from the engaging pen of Henry Whistler:

> This island is the dunghill whereon England doth cast forth its rubbish: rogues and whores and such like people are those which are generally brought here. A rogue in England will hardly make a cheater here: a baud brought over puts on a demure comportment, a whore if handsome makes a wife for some rich planter.

Whistler's commentary on Barbadian low life was corroborated by other sources. The historian Richard Ligon sailed to Barbados in 1647 and was scandalized by the behavior of women from London's seamier neighborhoods who sailed with him. When the ship stopped in the Cape Verde Islands the women immediately engaged in sexual escapades with "Portugals and Negroes," to Ligon's great horror. In 1656 the Venetian ambassador to London reported soldiers rounding up over 400 "women of loose life," for forced shipment to Barbados. The Venetian ambassador to France reported, while on a trip to London the same year, seeing soldiers looking for prostitutes with a view to deporting 1,200 to the Caribbean. This practice of deporting England's whores was still very much alive in 1789 when a few hundred of them were forced on board ship with London's "Blackpoor" (some from the Caribbean), to become the founding mothers of a new Sierra Leone settlement (and later colony).

JEWS

The establishment of the Northern European colonies brought to the Caribbean a substantial Jewish presence. Jews were simultaneously part of the white community and religiously and culturally distinct. Richard S. Dunn, examining the Barbados census of 1679, found the Jews concentrated in the town of Bridgetown, where 54 of the 405 households were Jewish. In 1724 a quarter of the whites in Charlestown, Nevis, were Jews. By the mid-eighteenth century Jews were more than half the whites in Suriname. In 1750 over half of the free people of St. Eustatius were Jews. Over half of Curaçao's white population were Jews at the end of the eighteenth century. In 1850 over half of St. Thomas' whites were Jews. The nineteenth century Pan-African intellectual Edward Wilmot Blyden, who grew up in St. Thomas and later made his home in West Africa, professed to being impressed as a youth by the Jewish religious services he witnessed. By 1881, nearly 20 percent of Jamaica's 13,800 whites were Jews.

These first Caribbean Jews were Sephardics, that is, those (as opposed to the Ashkenazi of Central and Eastern Europe) who originated in the Iberian Peninsula and North Africa. They had Spanish and Portuguese surnames. The Jewish presence in the Caribbean actually went back to Columbus. There is a lively but inconclusive literature suggesting that Columbus himself may have been a Jew. Whether he was or not, he certainly appeared to be a devout Roman Catholic. He left money in his will for the financing of a new Christian crusade to the Holy Land of Jerusalem. Luís Santángel, Gabriel Sanchez and Isaac Abrabanel—the three financiers who lent money to Ferdinand and Isabella to finance Columbus' first voyage—were Marranos (also known as New Christians, Crypto-Jews and Conversos). Marranos were Jews who converted to Roman Catholicism under duress but often continued to practice their Jewish faith in secret. When circumstances became favorable, even several generations later, they would re-emerge as openly practicing Jews. At least one member of Columbus' first crew, the interpreter Luis de Torres, was a Marrano.

Columbus' departure in 1492 coincided with the expulsion of 300,000 Jews from Spain. Columbus shared the harbor with these refugees as he prepared to sail. It has been suggested that Columbus sailed in 1492 from Palos, instead of the larger Cadiz, because the latter was too jammed with refugee ships.

The Spanish monarchs initially banned Jews and Muslims from the New World. Muslims, like Jews, were forced by the Spanish Inquisition to convert or face deportation or death. Those forced to convert were known as Moriscoes. Similar to the Jews, they were also called *Conversos* and Crypto-Muslims.

The ban on New World access did not prevent a large influx of Jews, principally New Christians, into the Spanish territories. Most of these came from Portugal, with some from Spain as well. So numerous were they in the Spanish New World colonies that in 1571 Philip II of Spain set up a tribunal of the Spanish Inquisition in Mexico, to "free the land which has become contaminated by Jews and heretics, especially of the Portuguese nation." Many more Portuguese Marranos moved to Brazil shortly after the Portuguese claimed it in 1500. It must be remembered that Brazil in this period was very much a part of the Caribbean–New World nexus.

These Portuguese Jews in the Caribbean constituted themselves into one tightly knit unit, the "Caribbean Jewish Nation" (sometimes simply "The Nation"), which transcended political borders. For much of the sixteenth and seventeenth centuries in the Spanish Caribbean, "Portuguese" and "Jew" were synonymous.

Small numbers of Jews also began arriving in the North European colonies practically from their inception. They began to arrive in Barbados in 1628, one year after the colony's inception in 1627. It was events in Brazil, however, which precipitated a sharp increase in Jewish arrivals to the new colonies. The Dutch captured north-east Brazil from the Portuguese in 1630, precipitating a wholesale "coming out" of Brazil's Marranos, who abandoned the clandestine Judaism of New Christians for a full-scale reversion to the open display of their faith.

When the Portuguese recaptured their territory in 1654, the Jews, having revealed the shallowness of their Christian commitment, had to leave. Some of these refugees became the first Jews in New Amsterdam (New York). Many shiploads of the refugees and their enslaved Africans roamed the Caribbean looking for safe haven. They brought with them from Brazil sugar-producing technology. They stimulated the emergence of sugar as the dominant cash crop in the new colonies. According to the *Encyclopedia Judaica*, "The first official warrant of residence given to a Jew [in Barbados]" was in 1654 to a refugee from Brazil and "his son, the sugar production specialist David Raphael de Mercado." The former Marrano, now openly Jewish refugee Benjamin d'Acosta, is said to have introduced sugar production into Martinique the same year. He was also a pioneer of commercial cocoa processing, using procedures borrowed from the indigenous people. Altogether over a thousand Brazilian Jews and a comparable number of their enslaved Africans arrived in Martinique and Guadeloupe in 1654. Some European Jews had actually been in Martinique managing Dutch businesses before the French colonized it in 1635.

English ruler Oliver Cromwell's 1655 Western Design into Jamaica happened just in time for the Brazilian Jewish refugees. Several Marranos of the Spanish-Portuguese Jewish nation had lived in Jamaica throughout its Spanish period. With the advent of the English they became openly practicing Jews. General Venables encouraged them to stay. It was in 1655 also that England removed its ban on Jews entering England itself, thereby further facilitating Jewish entry into Jamaica. Jamaica's Jewish community became a thriving one, with trading in buccaneer loot being one of its principal businesses.

Curaçao became a major center of Jewish population after the Dutch conquest. Samuel Coheno, a Jew, became first governor in 1634, under the Dutch West India Company. The English colonized Suriname from 1652 to 1667, when the Dutch took it. The English sent their evacuees, probably including Jews, to Jamaica. The Dutch West India Company occupied Cayenne in 1659 and encouraged Jews to settle. This group left in the face of English and French invasions in the 1660s.

In 1652 Latvian Courlanders settled one side of Tobago, with their capital at Jekabspills. In 1654 the Dutch settled the other side. Jews entered the Dutch area in 1659 and 1660 but remained impoverished and left to try their luck elsewhere. By the late seventeenth century, therefore, Jews could be found all over the greater Caribbean. This included St. Croix, Panama and Nevis, where Barbadian Jews relocated in 1671.

Whereas the South American Jews of Brazil and Suriname were plantation owners as well as traders, those in the islands concentrated primarily on trade. This included the trade in enslaved persons, where they were very prominent in the transportation (from Africa), warehousing, auctioning and reselling of Africans. They also owned ample numbers of "house slaves" for their domestic convenience. Bridgetown Jews owned "almost as many" enslaved Africans as their Christian counterparts. One of the most thriving Jewish communities was in eighteenth-century Dutch St. Eustatius. This became a trading entrepôt for the Caribbean and the world and an important shipper of arms to the Americans during the American Revolutionary War of the 1770s and 1780s.

Throughout the area the Jews were often able to receive various concessions. These included permission to work on Sundays, the privilege of having their own cemeteries, exemption from militia duty and the non-payment of certain taxes.

The Jews were for the most part very wealthy and various similar complaints followed them from place to place. Barbadians and Jamaicans accused them of bribing new governors to facilitate exemptions from duties and the like. Both places accused them of clipping coins and debasing gold and silver. The French colonies expelled Jews in 1683. This order was apparently not implemented immediately for the French *Code Noir* ("Black Code," directed primarily at the enslaved population) in 1685 again ordered authorities "to chase from our islands all the Jews who have established residence there." The code commanded them "to be gone within three months of the day of issuance of the present [order], at the risk of confiscation of their persons and their goods."

In 1691 and 1692 the English in the Jamaican legislative council accused the Jews of not doing productive work like planting. Instead, according to the charge, they manipulated money and took bread out of the mouths of English children. In 1739 Barbadians burned down the Jewish synagogue in Speightstown and drove the community out of town. In Coro, Venezuela, there were anti-Jewish riots in 1848 and 1854.

In most places the high proportions of Jews in the seventeenth and eighteenth centuries declined, as local hostility or new opportunities elsewhere siphoned off the Jewish populations.

PRESSURE ON THE CARIBS

Despite their sanctimoniousness and shedding of crocodile tears over the Spanish extermination of indigenous peoples, the Northern Europeans themselves sounded the death knell for the Caribs who inhibited the islands they claimed. It took two or three centuries to kill most of the Caribs in the Lesser Antilles, as opposed to half a century or less for the Arawaks of the Greater Antilles and the Bahamas. The Caribs had a few factors in their favor. They were somewhat on the periphery of Spain's initial genocidal blitz. They were not unwilling to put up a spirited defense (which is not to say that the Arawaks did not also defend themselves). Perhaps more than the Arawaks, the Caribs were sometimes prepared to take the offensive against the Europeans. The Caribs, possibly more than the Arawaks, also used mainland areas such as Venezuela and Guiana as areas for strategic retreat.

Yet, after all was said and done, history was against the Caribs, as it was against the Arawaks. They lived on islands vulnerable because of their small size to large-scale encroachment by technologically advanced, better armed and ruthless Europeans. They themselves had at best only limited access to any technological and industrial infrastructure capable of sustaining a successful protracted struggle against constantly innovating Europeans.

When the Spaniards early defined them (and anybody who offered effective resistance) as cannibals, they in effect declared open season on them. To be a Carib was to be a cannibal and therefore to exist, with royal sanction, in a perpetual fire zone of Spanish attack. Some, as already seen, were enslaved by Columbus himself and taken to Europe. Forty thousand enslaved indigenes were imported into Hispaniola between 1508 and 1513 from the Lesser Antilles, the Bahamas, Jamaica and Cuba.

Yet the Caribs did not respond aggressively to every instance of European encroachment. The Northern Europeans who made occasional rest stops from the early sixteenth century often found Caribs willing to trade, once they were satisfied that the Europeans were not planning to overstay their welcome. They even allowed small groups of stranded Europeans to stay a while. These early itinerant Europeans found Caribs in St. Kitts, Nevis, Montserrat, Guadeloupe and St. Vincent, among other places.

Spain's sixteenth-century invasion of Trinidad, the largest of the Lesser Antilles, signaled the first permanent European occupation of Carib territory. Both Caribs and Arawaks lived in Trinidad, which the indigenes called Cairi. Walter Raleigh in 1595 identified several "nations" in Trinidad, among them the Jaio, Arwacas, Salvaios, Nepoios and Carinepagotos.

Governor de Berrio seemed surprised that Trinidad's indigenes resented the Spanish presence in their land. He complained to the Spanish king in 1593 that the Caribs had tried to destroy the island, had killed eleven Spaniards sent against them, and had "eaten" 100 mercenary "Indians" in the Spanish forces. "I have only 70 men," he pleaded, "yet in this island are more than 6,000 war Indians, the major part of them by no means peaceable. . . ."

Walter Raleigh and Robert Dudley were not above ingratiating themselves with Caribs and other indigenes by presenting themselves as allies against Spanish tyranny. This tactic bore some unexpected fruit in 1590s Trinidad and Orinoco, when a Carib prophet appeared and foretold liberation from Spanish oppression with the help of the English and Dutch. Similar prophetic responses to European colonization could be seen among indigenous peoples at other places and times. Simon Kimbangu in the Belgian Congo in the 1920s envisaged African American help against the Belgian colonizers. Rumors were reportedly rampant in South Africa around the same time concerning African American soldiers who would land to help liberate the Africans from European oppression.

Walter Raleigh was warned in Guiana by the indigenous guide he pressed into service on pain of death, to give a wide berth to the Guanipa people who lived around the Guanipa and Berbice rivers. They had relocated there to escape the Spaniards in the islands and would surely kill Raleigh and his party if they encountered them.

Guiana, Trinidad and other islands had long been one vast area of trade, emigration and other interaction. Raleigh in 1595 noted extensive trade via canoe between the Caribs and Arawaks of Guiana and their compatriots in Margarita and Trinidad. They traded cassava, bread, gold, tobacco and girls.

Where the early North Europeans respected the rights to prior occupation this was limited to "Christian" occupation. When Captain Thomas Warner applied for a patent for St. Kitts and other islands in 1625 he assured London that the islands were inhabited only by "savage people," and not by Christians. The only problem presented by savage people was how best to enslave, kill or expel them. International law as understood in Europe apparently did not recognize the rights of indigenous people to their own lands. Louis XIV of France urged his people in 1661 to "exterminate or expel" the Caribs.

By the 1630s the Northern Europeans had already driven surviving Caribs from one island after another. The Caribs did not go willingly. They repeatedly chased Europeans off of Tobago, St. Lucia and Grenada. Henry Whistler noted in 1655 that St. Lucia had once been inhabited by the English, but the Caribs and French had driven them off. It was now uninhabited.

By the late seventeenth century, after the French had dramatically killed the remaining Caribs in Grenada, the Caribs were confined primarily to St. Vincent and Dominica. The French governor of Martinique signed a treaty with the Dominicans in 1660, acknowledging the Carib right to Dominica. The Dominicans guarded this right very jealously. When Henry Whistler's ships were becalmed off Dominica for three hours in 1655, a Carib pirogue appeared carrying fourteen indigenes. They fired a volley of arrows at the English, wounding five. They got away unscathed since their pirogue was too fast for any English vessel. Their action was reminiscent of the first Carib response to Columbus off Trinidad in 1498 and Columbus' first hostile encounter in the Caribbean, off the coast of St. Croix.

By the end of the seventeenth century, then, the Northern Europeans had, in a century or less, changed the Lesser Antilles for ever. They had exterminated the indigenes from many of the islands and had replaced them with rich and poor whites and Jews. They had also unwittingly laid the foundation for the Africanization of the Caribbean, which will be explored in Chapters 4 and 5.

Further Readings

Berenbaum, Michael, and Fred Skolnik, Eds. *Encyclopaedia Judaica*. Detroit, MI: Macmillan Reference USA, 2007.

Code Noir. http://chnm.gmu.edu/revolution/d/335/ [accessed June 5, 2010].

Dunn, Richard S. "The Barbados Census of 1680: Profile of the Richest Colony in English America." *The William and Mary Quarterly, Third Series,* 26, 1, January 1969, 4–30.

Mason, A. E. W. *The Life of Francis Drake*. London: Hodder and Stoughton, 1950.

Oviedo, Gonzalo Fernandez de. *Natural History of the West Indies*. Translated and Edited by Sterling A. Stoudmire. Chapel Hill: University of North Carolina Press, 1959.

Parry, John Horace. *The Spanish Seaborne Empire*. Berkeley: University of California Press, 1990.

Raleigh, Sir Walter. *The Discoverie of the Large, Rich, and Bewtiful Empyre of Guiana, With a Relation of the Great and Golden Citie of Manoa (which the Spanyards call El Dorado)*. . . . Imprinted at London by Robert Robinson, 1596.

Warner, George F., Ed. *The Voyage of Robert Dudley, Afterwards Styled Earl of Warwick and Leicester and Duke of Northumberland, to the West Indies, 1594–1595*. London: Printed for the Hakluyt Society, 1899. Reprinted by Kraus Reprint Ltd, Nendeln, Liechtenstein, 1967.

Whistler, Henry. Appendix E. "Extracts from Henry Whistler's Journal of the West India Expedition," in C. H. Firth, Ed., *The Narrative of General Venables: With an Appendix of Papers Relating to the Expedition to the West Indies and the Conquest of Jamaica, 1654–1655*. London: Longmans, Green and Co., 1900.

Williams, Eric. *Documents of West Indian History*. Port of Spain: PNM Publishing Company, 1963.

4

The Africans
Long Night of Enslavement

*Slavery in the West Indies is the forced servitude of every black man
found in those islands, who cannot by legal documents prove his liberty; this violent
constraint is exercised during his life without wages, while the master only is the judge
of the kind, degree and time of labour, and of the subsistence which the slave shall
receive. The master may, moreover, imprison, beat, scourge, wound,
and otherwise injure the body of the slave at his own discretion,
and may depute the same power to whom he
pleases, even to a fellow slave.*

*Slaves possess no legal right in any kind of property; for however
obtained, whatever they have belongs in point of law to their master, who may dispose
of that which they have acquired, as well as of themselves or of their children, in the
same manner as cattle or land may be sold; while the creditor or tax gatherer may
seize the slave and sell him to a distant proprietor, and so tear him
from his parents, his wife, his children, and his home, for the debts
of his master; or he may be devised by will to a cruel tyrant or
severe task master without the power of remonstrance
or even the right of redemption on any terms.*

—Speaker at an English antislavery rally, 1832

For 384 of the first 394 years after Columbus, from 1502 in Hispaniola to 1886 in Cuba, Africans could always be found enslaved somewhere or other in the Caribbean. Slavery in the British islands lasted for about 200 years, somewhat less than for its major rivals, France and Holland, and considerably less than the Spanish territories, which were both the first and the last to enslave Africans in the Caribbean. Brazil, closely associated with the Caribbean in the earliest period of slavery, ended the practice in 1888. Enslavement of Africans is an overriding reality of the Caribbean experience and its memory continues to hover over the regional consciousness. It is no accident that some of the most iconic emblems of Caribbean culture, such as Bob Marley's "Redemption Song" and the Mighty Sparrow's "The Slave," speak directly to that memory.

Yet it must be said that enslavement and Africans were not necessarily synonymous in the era of Columbus. Nor were the first enslaved Caribbean people Africans. A free African, one Diego, sailed on Columbus' third voyage. Historian Oviedo listed another African, Nuflo De Olano, among the "Noblemen and Gentlemen of quality" accompanying Spanish Explorer Balboa to the Pacific in 1513. There were African soldiers with Hernando Cortes on his conquest of Mexico, which was launched from Cuba in 1519.

The immediate origins of what became the transatlantic trade in enslaved Africans, the largest forced migration in history, are to be found in the activities of Portuguese sailors on the West African coast. In 1441 the Portuguese sailor Antam Gonçalvez landed an armed party somewhere on the North West African coast, probably in Rio De Oro. His men surprised, wounded and captured a lightly armed African man. An unsuspecting lone woman happened along soon afterward and they kidnapped her, too.

Gonçalvez then rendezvoused with the captain of another Portuguese vessel, one Nuño Tristão. Together they launched another attack on unsuspecting Africans, killing three and kidnapping ten, including men, women and boys. The Portuguese took these first victims of the transatlantic slave trade back to Lisbon. The Portuguese monarch, known to history as Prince Henry the Navigator, saw the potential for a new lucrative enterprise in human trafficking. He sought the approval of the pope, who obligingly extended forgiveness for their sins to all who would participate in this proposed crusade against the West African people.

The Portuguese kidnapping of Africans grew rapidly. Within a dozen years large military expeditions were yielding hundreds of captives. The beginnings of a settled trade nevertheless quickly replaced random raids as the preferred modus operandi. Middlemen on the coast could be found who were willing to supply the Europeans with gold, ivory, enslaved compatriots and other items. Englishman John Hawkins discovered

(as noted earlier) African rulers who were willing to provide prisoners of war to the Europeans in exchange for modern weapons and military assistance against their enemies.

In 1482 the Portuguese began construction of Elmina Castle (São Jorge da Mina) in modern-day Ghana, the first of many European forts along the West African coast. These forts provided heavily fortified enclaves from which the Europeans could sally forth to do business with, or wage war upon, neighboring Africans. They served also as holding stations for captured Africans awaiting forcible expulsion through the "doors of no return" to enslavement, first in Europe and later in the Americas. In due course the French, Dutch, English, Swedish and Danish-Norwegian people all built forts. The Dutch captured Elmina from the Portuguese in 1637.

For African chiefly collaborators with the European enslavers there were short-term rewards. Wars against neighboring rivals were won, geopolitical power was consolidated, weapons and European luxury goods (and junk items too) were procured. West Africa, however, paid a heavy price for these gains. Depopulation was massive and there was considerable destruction of the social fabric. Whole communities uprooted themselves and sought relocation in inaccessible places to avoid slave raiders. By the time the eleven-year-old Ibo Olaudah Equiano was kidnapped by fellow Africans in 1756, his community had in place a system of permanent, though in his case ineffective, lookouts for people snatchers.

Laws were changed to provide enslavement as penalties for petty crimes that were previously susceptible only to minor punishment. And whereas the Europeans, primary instigators of the enterprise, were ultimately rewarded with an industrial revolution, as will be seen, their African collaborators derived little developmental benefit. In fact, by helping ravage their countries they actually helped hasten their region's descent into nineteenth-century European conquest and African underdevelopment.

A special class of African collaborators must be mentioned. These were the so-called "mulatto chiefs" and "mulatto traders," children and descendants of European fathers and African mothers. They could be the offspring of Portuguese lançados; English, Danish or American slave traders; or any number of other Europeans who made their way to West Africa. In time many became less phenotypically "mulatto" and racially indistinguishable from the rest of the African population. They nevertheless maintained linguistic and cultural attachments to the European side of their ancestry. This they mingled with an intimate knowledge of their African milieu, an indispensable benefit for the prosecution of their specialty in slave trading. Like some of the Spanish conquerors in the Columbian and early post-Columbian period in the Caribbean, who strategically formed liaisons with the daughters of local nobles, some Europeans and their racially mixed descendants were able to marry into local nobility, thereby increasing their influence on the prosecution of the slave trade. This was typically the case of European unions with the "signare" or wealthy local women of Saint-Louis and Goree Island in Senegal.

These mulatto traders sometimes became very powerful players in local politics, complete with private armies. They could on occasion expel Europeans they had problems with or attack African kingdoms with which they were in dispute. In 1684 they attempted to set up an autonomous "republic" opposed to Portuguese rule on the Upper Guinea Coast. Though the institution of mulatto chiefs started very early in the slave trade, it was still alive and well in the nineteenth century. In 1836 Henrich Richter of the Gold Coast was described as one of the richest men around, with 400 enslaved persons, a private army and a stately home filled with enormous quantities of gold and silver. He was born in 1785, son of Johan Emanuel Richter, a Danish governor of the area and an African woman. He himself married an Ashanti princess.

Not all African leaders collaborated with the slave-trading Europeans, of course. Queen Nzinga (ca. 1581–1663) of the state of Matamba in Angola resisted Portuguese encroachment for decades by a combination of diplomacy and military strategy.

Around 1720 King Tomba of Baga, in present-day Guinea, put up a fierce resistance before being defeated by a combination of Europeans, mulatto chiefs and collaborationist Africans.

FIRST ENSLAVED AFRICANS IN THE CARIBBEAN

The Spanish king granted his subjects in Hispaniola permission to import enslaved Africans in 1501. By this time, the extermination of the indigenous population was well under way. The enslavement of neighboring indigenes appeared insufficient to satisfy the Spaniards' depleted labor supply. Requests were therefore made for the importation of African labor. The first enslaved Africans were accordingly introduced in 1502, a mere ten years after Columbus' initial encounter with the islands. These first Africans were drawn from the already enslaved population living in the Iberian Peninsula. Only Christianized Africans were allowed in.

The initial trickle of importations experienced its first "significant" increase in 1510 when 250 Africans were brought in from Seville in Spain. In 1517, as a result of continued requests from Hispaniola, Charles I of Spain initiated the "asiento," a licence which granted a monopoly to a large supplier to bring in a stated number of Africans over a stipulated period, directly from Africa. By order of August 18, 1518, Charles granted Lorenzo de Gorrevod, governor of Bresa and a member of the king's council, authority to import 4,000 enslaved Africans, "provided they be Christians," to the "Indies, the islands and the mainland of the ocean sea." This was the real beginning of the process which would in time kill millions of Africans, bring untold power and wealth to Europe and, as an unintended consequence, introduce an African population which would one day inherit much of the Caribbean.

The size and value of the asiento grew by leaps and bounds, eventually becoming the richest contract in international trade. Nations would one day go to war over the right to secure this lucrative monopoly.

MIDDLE PASSAGE

For the vast majority of Africans enslaved in the Caribbean their immediate journey began with embarkation on slave ships on the West African coast. The trip across the Atlantic Ocean, the horrendous Middle Passage, could take anywhere from three weeks to over three months, depending on port of embarkation, weather and other factors. By the time of their forcible embarkation, however, many of the Africans had already been captives for considerable periods. As the trade matured, slave hunters moved deeper into the continent in search of their prey. Captives could be caught hundreds of miles inland. Some might never have seen the sea before arriving at the coast on the way to the Caribbean. Many died before they reached the coast.

Olaudah Equiano reckons that he travell for six to seven months by land and river before arriving at the coast. He was sold and resold to various middlemen along the way. He was careful to say, however, that his African captors did not normally mistreat their prey. There was little here that could have prepared him for the cruelties of enslavement in the Caribbean.

Those Africans who were not captured directly by the Europeans underwent inspection and haggling

Door of no return, Goree Island, Senegal, photographed in 2003. The enslaved were led from their dungeons through this doorway to the small boats waiting on the beach a few feet away. They were then transferred to the larger vessels waiting off shore. They would never set foot on their native land again. This and similar forts along the West African coast have become places of pilgrimage for Africa's descendants in the Diaspora.

before purchase. A Danish observer in 1760 considered the Portuguese the most disgustingly fastidious buyers. They would spend four hours inspecting a single African. They would feel him or her everywhere, would make them jump up and down, laugh and sing. They would smell their throats. They would check to see if they had lost any teeth. They would lick the males to see if they had beards. English purchasers, according to this Dane, were almost as fastidious. Frenchmen, on the other hand, would buy anything black that moved.

Loading the Africans on board the slave ships began days before departure. The newly enslaved were rowed in canoes or ships' boats to the slave ships lying some distance from the shore. The first shock on board for some might be what Equiano described as "those white men with horrible looks, red faces and loose hair." Surely, thought Equiano and many others, these white men were about to devour them. The initial shock might be enhanced by sight of "a multitude of black people of every description chained together, every one of their countenances expressing dejection and sorrow.

The newly enslaved were accommodated in the ships' holds. A typical hold might be five or six feet high and subdivided into two or three tiers, respectively, like shelves on a bookcase. Africans were chained together, typically with one person's foot to his or her neighbor's ankle. Turning was difficult and sitting up was impossible. The Africans were let up on deck for brief periods of exercise, under very heavy guard. Prior to the ship's sailing, however, they were all locked up, for the Europeans feared that they might observe the workings of the vessel.

Conditions in the hold were intolerable. The enslaved defecated, were sick and died on one another. Disease was rampant. Especially deadly were smallpox and the bloody flux, whose victims defecated blood. Children often fell into tubs provided for excrement. Equiano reported a stench beyond description and an "absolutely pestilential atmosphere." The "galling of the chains," he said, the filth, the "shrieks of the women, and the groans of the dying, rendered the whole a scene of horror almost inconceivable." He might have added that sharks followed slave ships to devour the bodies thrown or otherwise deposited overboard.

Some of the slave ship operators were "loose packers," who preferred to take in less Africans in the hope that more would survive in a less crowded atmosphere. Others were "tight packers," who gambled that a severely overcrowded ship and consequently greater deaths among the enslaved would still net a large number of live deliveries in the Caribbean. The tight packers were in the ascendancy.

Either way, suffering was immense. Many Africans died of the dreaded "fixed melancholy," where they seemed to abandon the will to live under their new conditions. Some Africans refused to eat. They were flogged severely or worse. Placing burning coals at their mouths was among the means reported to induce the Africans to eat. An instrument known as a speculum oris (mouth opener) was universally used in the trade to force-feed those who would not eat. Mannix and Cowley in *Black Cargoes* describe it thus, "It looked like a pair of dividers with notched legs and with a thumbscrew at the blunt end. The legs were closed and the notches were hammered between the slave's teeth. When the thumbscrew was tightened, the legs of the instrument separated, forcing open the slave's mouth; then food was poured into it through a funnel."

Equiano, a mere child at the time of his capture, wished he could die and refused to eat. Two white men tied him up and flogged him severely. His desire to jump overboard was frustrated by the netting erected precisely for this purpose. Yet even the netting could not stop some of the newly enslaved. When the *Prince of Orange* docked in St. Kitts in 1737, over 100 enslaved men jumped overboard, of whom 33 were lost.

When the African coast was still in sight, they might attempt to swim back to land. The Africans at the time were in fact much better swimmers than the Europeans. It was they who during the period of slavery introduced to Europeans what later became known as freestyle swimming. Stedman in Suriname marveled at the aquatic feats performed by the enslaved of both sexes. Sometimes a slave ship might launch its boats to pursue an African who jumped overboard. If recaptured he or she would be flogged mercilessly.

Many of the enslaved believed, in keeping with African religions, that if they died, whether by suicide, revolt or otherwise, they would return home

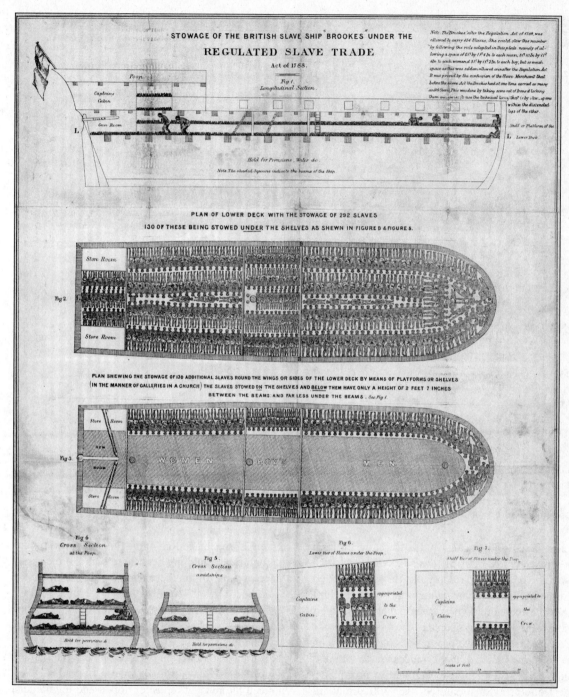

Cross section of the Liverpool slave ship *Brookes*, built in 1780–1781. This illustration was much used by antislavery campaigners and was featured in a British parliamentary investigation of 1788 into the slave trade. It has over the years achieved iconic status.

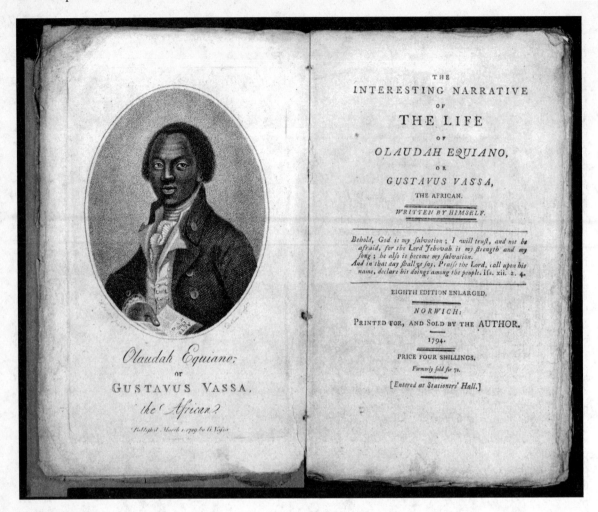

Olaudah Equiano.

to the land of their ancestors. Captain William Snelgrave in 1727 cut off the head of an African involved in a shipboard revolt. He had received information that Africans thought they would return home after being thrown overboard, but only if their bodies were not dismembered.

Despite extensive precautions against African maritime revolts and draconian measures to suppress them, revolts nevertheless frequently took place. Eric Robert Taylor identified over 400 shipboard insurrections for the eighteenth century alone. He thinks that the actual figure may have been much larger. Whether the Africans won or lost, the results were sure to be bloody. Despite the endemic warfare

among European nations at the time, the ships of one nation often would not hesitate to come to the assistance of those of another nationality in the throes of a shipboard revolt.

In 1704 four hundred Africans on the ship *Eagle*, off the coast of Ghana, killed their enslavers and liberated themselves. On the ship *Thomas* in 1797 the African women were released on deck for "fattening up," a few days prior to sale in Barbados. They noticed the musket repository open and unguarded. They seized weapons, overpowered their enslavers and freed their male counterparts. Unable to navigate home, the Africans drifted for forty-two days before being retaken by the English Royal Navy.

The case of the *Amistad* in Cuban waters in 1839 was similar. There the fifty-three Africans under Cinque killed some of the white crew. They spared the life of the pilot and ordered him to take them home. The ship was however captured by the U.S. Coast Guard off the coast of the state of Connecticut. U.S. abolitionists intervened to frustrate the attempts of the Spanish shipowners to recover their enslaved property. The U.S. Supreme Court eventually declared the Africans free in 1841. The court ruled that while slavery was legal in Cuba at the time, the importation of new Africans was not, and so the *Amistad* Africans were victims of a kidnapping and therefore entitled to recover their freedom by any means necessary. Thirty-five surviving Africans were repatriated to Sierra Leone in 1842.

In the seventeenth century, Africans in a slave ship from the Bight of Benin bound for Barbados were shipwrecked off the island of Bequia. They made their way first to Bequia and later to nearby St. Vincent, where they were absorbed into the Carib community. For a hundred years these "Black Caribs" (also called Garifuna) militarily defeated French and British forces. They were eventually defeated by the British in 1796 and deported to the island of Roatan, near Honduras.

An attempted shipboard rebellion is suspected to be the cause of one of the most horrendous disasters of the Middle Passage. In 1705 the Danish slave ship *Cron Prindzen* blew up at Principe Island in the Gulf of Guinea, with 826 enslaved persons aboard. Only five persons survived. Maritime accidents also exacted a terrible toll on Africans during the Middle Passage. Eric Robert Taylor has documented several—700 Africans aboard the Dutch vessel *Leusden* drowned off the coast of Suriname in 1738, when their vessel foundered on the rocks; the Liverpool ship *Pallas* blew up off the African coast in 1761 killing 600 enslaved Africans; in 1787 the *Sisters* capsized in the Caribbean on the way to Cuba. Nearly 500 Africans drowned. Taylor thinks that 1.5 million Africans died from ill-treatment and disaster in the Middle Passage alone.

Where the African efforts at revolt were unsuccessful the Europeans responded with beheadings, dismemberment, floggings and other forms of savagery. Such savagery could also be motivated by economic rather than military considerations. The most notorious of these cases involved the British

ship *Zong*, sailing out of Liverpool in 1781. There the enslavers threw 132 Africans overboard, after sighting land in the Caribbean. Over 60 of their 460 Africans had died on the way over. The ship's captain reasoned that if the remaining sick Africans were thrown overboard the insurers would have to pay, since they would be "jettisoned" cargo. Otherwise the owners would have to bear the financial loss caused by sick or deceased Africans. The crew therefore threw the unfortunate Africans overboard before putting into Kingston, Jamaica, on December 22, 1781. They sold the survivors in Jamaica. The insurers refused to pay, however, and the matter ended up in the courts, thereby establishing the notoriety of this case. A jury held for the owners in the lower courts, since "the case of slaves was the same as if horses had been thrown overboard." Lord Mansfield, who had earlier ruled slavery in England (but not in British colonies) unlawful, reversed the lower court on appeal. He set a precedent by rejecting the notion that Africans were no different from horses. Such was what Equiano called the "improvident avarice" of the slave traders.

Conditions similar to the *Zong* could also arise in the area of calms known as the Doldrums. If a sailing ship was unfortunate enough to be becalmed there for weeks with food and especially water running low, it sometimes happened that the Africans were jettisoned to save the lives of the Europeans.

Many Africans died during the Middle Passage, even in the absence of disaster, rebellion or insurance fraud. When the Danish slave ship *Fredensborg* sailed from Copenhagen to St. Croix via Ghana in 1767–1768, 30 of its 265 enslaved Africans, about 11 percent, died. Its successor vessel, *Fredensborg II,* in 1778 lost 145 of the 421 Africans embarked in Ghana or over 34 percent. The *Fredensborg* had made its maiden voyage, under the name *Cron Prindz Christian*, from Copenhagen to St. Thomas via the Gold Coast in 1753–1755, for the Royal Chartered Danish West India and Guinea Company. On that voyage 400 of the 600 enslaved Africans on board perished, for a mortality rate of 66 2/3 percent. Mortality rates among the Africans of over 50 percent were not uncommon. And these figures do not include deaths among those awaiting embarkation in Africa and the newly arrived in the Caribbean. The English

Privy Council in 1789 estimated an average mortality of 12½ percent during the voyage, 4½ percent among those awaiting sale after arrival in the Caribbean and 33 percent deaths during "seasoning" in the Caribbean, for a total of 50 percent, excluding deaths prior to embarkation in Africa.

Mortality could also be high among the European crews, who died from African fevers, shipboard accidents, drowning, diseases such as the bloody flux emanating from the slaveholds and battle with Africans making a desperate bid for freedom. This may be why Danish-Norwegian slave ship captains were mandated to "see to it that the fear of God is upheld on board the ship, and that prayers are said and hymns are sung every day. . . ."

Sanctimoniousness was indeed a standard part of the slaving business. Sir John Hawkins' *Jesus of Lubeck* and *Grace of God* have already been mentioned. One of Christendom's most enduring hymns, "Amazing Grace," was written in 1779 by John Newton, who spent several years as a slave factor on the West African coast and as a slave ship captain. He eventually found religion, not as a result of his slaving activities, but because of a near-death experience during a storm. "At midnight we weighed anchor in the name of Jesus," Danish captain Ferentz told his journal on Saturday April 23, 1768, as he set sail for the Caribbean with a ship full of enslaved Africans. His colleagues at the Danish fort had sent him a farewell message—"May God grant you a safe arrival in St. Croix, and we pray the Lord that you have a successful journey, and may God protect you." Among the estates in St. Croix where the *Fredensborg's* Africans may have ended up were "Jerusalem," "Sion Farm," "Bethlehem," and "Blessing." Early African arrivals in Virginia in 1619 had been captured by pirates from the Portuguese slaver *St. John the Baptist* (*São João Bautista*).

Newton kept a journal of his slaving activities between 1750 and 1754. The following extracts document a Middle Passage trip to Antigua. It was a typical trip, with attempted revolt, sickness, torture, suicide and death, culminating in a profitable sale in Antigua.

26th MAY. . . . In the evening, by the favour of Providence, discovered a conspiracy among the men slaves to rise upon us. . . . I've found near 20 of them had broke their irons. Are at work securing them.

27th MAY. . . . A hard tornado came on so quick that had hardly time to take in a small sail; blew extream hard for 3 hours with heavy rain . . . At noon little wind. . . . In the afternoon secured all the men's irons again and punished 6 of the ringleaders of the insurrection.

28th MAY. . . . Their plot was exceedingly well laid, and had they been let alone an hour longer, must have occasioned us a good deal of trouble and damage. . . . They still look very gloomy and sullen and have doubtless mischief in their heads if they could find . . . opportunity to vent it. . . .

29th MAY. . . . Buried a boy slave (No.86) of a flux. Had 3 girls taken with fevers this morning. . . .

12th JUNE. . . . Buried a man slave (No.84) of a flux, which he has been struggling with near 7 weeks. . . .

13th JUNE. . . . This morning buried a woman slave (No. 47). Know not what to say she died of for she has not been properly alive since she first came on board.

22nd JUNE. . . . I am much afraid of another ravage from the flux, for we have had 8 taken within these few days.

24th JUNE. . . . Buried a girl slave (No. 92).

27th JUNE. . . . When we were putting the slaves down in the evening, one that was sick jumped overboard. Got him in again but he dyed immediately between his weakness and the salt water he had swallowed. . . .

28th JUNE. . . . Put the boys in irons and slightly in the thumbscrews to urge them to a full confession.

29th JUNE. . . . In the morning examined the men slaves and punished 6 of the principal, put 4 of them in collars.

8th JULY. . . . Landed the slaves. Sold all to about 20.

A Danish slave ship captain began his journal in 1767 in the following manner—"IN THE NAME OF JESUS, I, Johan Frantzen Ferentz, Captain of the Royal Chartered Danish Guinea Company's Frigate called the *Fredensborg*, on 22 Dec. 1767, began to record in this journal . . . for the benefit and advantage of the Worthy Royal Chartered Company, and my eternal Welfare and Salvation." Before the ship left Copenhagen its owners had sent on board a supply of extra prayer books "for the purpose of spiritual healing."

Once arrived in the Caribbean the surviving Africans were spruced up for prospective buyers. Merchants and planters came on board for a preliminary view. Africans were made to jump up and down. They were poked and prodded and fondled without regard for normal tenets of decency. An English military visitor to Barbados in 1816 was horrified to see a female purchaser publicly fondling the private parts of a male African prior to possible purchase. When Equiano's ship arrived in Bridgetown he reported that the Africans were taken ashore to a merchant's yard, "where we were pent up all together like so many sheep in a fold; without regard to sex or age." Some of the female slaves by this time would be pregnant as a result of rape by the ships' crews, who sometimes organized makeshift harems on board. Pregnant women fetched higher prices.

J. G. Stedman gave a similar account of the procedures on arrival in Suriname. The Africans, he said, were led on deck and "refreshed with pure air, plantains, bananas, oranges, etc." They were cleaned up and then, with broken bottles and without the benefit of soap, they shaved one another's heads into figures of stars, half moons and the like, as was their custom at home. They were then sent ashore "with pieces of cotton to serve as fig leaves."

"Amongst these," the ever-observant Stedman noted, "should a woman chance to be pregnant, her price is augmented accordingly; for which reason I have known the captain of a Dutch Guinea vessel, who acknowledged himself to be the father, take advantage, with a brutality scarcely credited in the story of Inkle and Yarico, of doubling the value, by selling his own offspring to the best bidder; for which however he was highly censured by his companions."

And despite the last-minute sprucing up, the results of a long trip under horrible conditions were not easily concealed. Stedman described a group of newly arrived Africans in Suriname in the 1770s. He had to invoke scripture to adequately describe what he saw—

> The whole party was such a set of scarcely animated automatons, such a resurrection of skin and bones, as forcibly reminded me of the last trumpet. These objects appeared that moment to be risen from the grave, or escaped from Surgeons' Hall; and I confess I can give no better description of them, than by comparing them to walking skeletons covered with a piece of tanned leather.
>
> 'And the Lord caused me to pass by them round about, and behold there were many in the open valley, and lo they were very dry.
>
> 'And he said unto me, Son of Man, can these bones live? And I answered, O Lord God thou knowest.'—*Ezekiel*, XXXVII, ver. 2, 3.
>
> Before these wretches, which might be in all about sixty in number, walked a sailor, and another followed behind with a bamboo-rattan; the one serving as a shepherd to lead them along, and the other as his dog to worry them occasionally, should any one lag behind, or wander away from the flock.

Stedman was careful to add, however, to fulfill the demands of "equity," that none of the enslaved arrivals appeared dejected "and that the punishment of the bamboo was inflicted with the utmost moderation by the sailor who brought up the rear."

Equiano described a popular method of purchasing the enslaved—the Africans were sorted into "parcels" in the merchant's yard. At the sound of a drum, buyers rushed into the yard to select their parcels. This procedure, he reported, terrified the already confused Africans whose fears of being eaten by the whites were now rekindled. Once the Africans were disposed of, one or two might be kept back for removal to Europe, there to fulfill special orders from European-based purchasers.

SUGAR AND AFRICANIZATION

The African population grew rapidly and sugar provided the single most important reason. Led successfully by Hispaniola in the sixteenth century, Barbados and Martinique in the seventeenth, Jamaica and then Haiti in the eighteenth and Cuba from the nineteenth to the twenty-first centuries, sugar became a major factor in agricultural and economic life.

An immensely labor-intensive enterprise, sugar plantations had developed in Madeira after Portuguese settlement there in 1420. Diego Columbus, son of the admiral, already owned a sugar mill on the outskirts of Santo Domingo in 1522. About forty Africans worked it. By 1526 Hispaniola was importing about 400 Africans a year for its nineteen sugar mills.

Sugar was built on the labor of enslaved persons and enslavement quickly became synonymous with Africa. The result was what white policy makers feared but could not prevent, namely what they alarmingly called the "Africanization" of the Caribbean. They fervently desired a white majority population, but they also craved sugar and the economic prosperity it brought. Sugar meant Africanization. They could not have it both ways, a white majority and sugar.

By 1546 there were already about 12,000 Africans to less than 5,000 whites in Hispaniola. In 1586 smallpox killed over half of a now-increased African population, but nearly 10,000 survived. In Barbados in 1645 there were 5,680 enslaved Africans to 18,300 white men capable of bearing arms. Eric Williams cited a figure of 82,023 Africans in Barbados in 1667.

When Barbadian planter George Downing purchased 1,000 Africans in 1645, he gave thanks. In a year and a half, he exulted, they would have earned as much as he paid for them. By 1650 Africans were already the majority of nonindigenous people in the New World.

Racially conscious Europeans bitterly lamented these developments that they could not control. Oviedo could already ruefully describe Hispaniola as "New Guinea" in the mid-sixteenth century. The Portuguese Ambrósio Fernandes Brandão similarly described North East Brazil in 1618. Governor Lando of Puerto Rico observed in 1544 that the island was depopulated of Spaniards. One saw only Africans.

The same pattern of Africanization replicated itself in other colonies as they fell in with the sugar revolution. In Antigua in 1707 the ratio of whites to blacks was 1:4. In 1774 it was 1:15. After the restoration of the English monarchy in 1660, land grants to English settlers in Jamaica were made on condition that recipients would cultivate it using enslaved Africans.

In Cuba, the last of the islands to rise to sugar dominance, Africans, enslaved and free, went from 57 percent of the population in 1817 to 61 percent in 1855. Trinidad in 1783 was somewhat atypical. Still Spanish, still predominantly indigenous and not yet a sugar colony, it nevertheless already showed a preponderance of Africans over Europeans. The numbers were small, however. There were 126 whites, 295 free coloreds, 310 enslaved Africans and 2,032 indigenes.

Various European voices were raised in anguish at the Africanization which their own policies made it impossible to stop. They feared the preponderance of presumed mentally inferior beings in their midst. They feared the security risks inherent in being outnumbered by the people they chose to enslave. Despite their notions of white intellectual superiority, they contradictorily tacitly endowed the Africans with enough intelligence to revolt if opportunity presented itself.

Edward Long, the English Jamaican planter, condemned the "barbarous stupidity" of Africans in his *History of Jamaica* (1774). In a schema that was commonplace among European intellectuals of the period, he posited "gradations of the intellectual faculty" moving up from monkeys, through apes, next to Africans and eventually to white people, the apex of the intellectual chain. The "Divine Fabricator" had ordained all of this, he explained. And to prove his point, he insisted that race mixture in Spanish America had inevitably produced a "vicious, brutal, and degenerate breed of mongrels."

Long's contemporary Thomas Jefferson had similar views. He was a drafter of the U.S. Declaration of Independence, sometime president of the United States and sometime governor of Virginia, a state closely associated with the British West Indies. In his *Notes on the State of Virginia* (ca. 1782), he proclaimed Africans lacking in the ability to reason and devoid of humankind's more refined faculties, such as love, higher forms of music and the ability to experience real grief.

These attempts to dehumanize the Africans were reflected in the practice of giving the enslaved the fanciful names that some people give to pet animals. This practice existed all over the Americas, including the United States, where an enslaved person might sometimes officially have no name at all, and be simply "So-and-So's Nigger." In the Caribbean and elsewhere, where the enslaved did have a name it was often a single name only, which presented them with the problem of finding a surname if freedom should come their way. Mary Prince was actually derisively called Mary, Princess of Wales, by her enslavers. Thomas Pringle, English secretary of the Anti-Slavery Society, who edited and published her narrative, commented on this practice: "It is a common practice for the colonists to give ridiculous names of this description to their slaves," he wrote, "being, in fact, one of the numberless modes of expressing the habitual contempt with which they regard the Negro race." Olaudah Equiano was derisively renamed Gustavus Vassa by his English purchaser, Michael Pascal, an officer in the Royal Navy, after a Swedish national hero. Stedman noted in Suriname that European classical names like Caesar, Plato, Brutus, Cato, Nero, Pluto, Charon, Cerberus, Proserpine and Medusa were favorites among the names Europeans inflicted upon enslaved Africans. These were exchanged, he said, for the likes of Quacoo, Quacy, Quamy, Quamina, Quasiba, Adjuba and others. One of the leaders of the black mercenary rangers, his comrade in arms, was called Hannibal. Two African soldiers who remained loyal to the whites during the Daaga mutiny in the West India Regiment in Trinidad in 1837 were named Sergeant Mercy and Corporal Plague.

A listing of names on Thomas Thistlewood's Jamaican plantation in 1751 yielded the same pattern. There were European classical names like Achilles, Nero, Hector, Plato, Cyrus, Titus, Hannibal, Dido and Sibyl. There were biblical names like Abraham, Sampson and Hagar. (Hagar was popular in the United States as well, possibly in a more benign way. "Aunt Hagar" in abolitionist literature came to symbolize the enslaved, sexually exploited woman, reminiscent of the biblical Hagar, object of Abraham's extramarital adventure and mother of an outcast son who found sympathy from a compassionate God.) Several place names—Dover, London, Plymouth, Glasgow, Port Royal—seemed to suggest great mirth among the European providers of names for these Africans. On Thistlewood's plantation, as apparently all over the Caribbean, Africans from modern-day Ghana seemed most likely to maintain their African names. Amidst the Achilles and the Platos there remained a strong showing of Quacoos, Cudjoes, Quashes, Quashebas and Accubahs.

Various stratagems were attempted to stem Africanization. Laws were passed establishing maximum legal ratios of white to African, but to no avail. In North America Jefferson's fellow founding father, Benjamin Franklin, proposed restricted imports of Africans and other swarthy peoples. "Why," he asked, in his 1751 essay on *Observations Concerning the Increase of Mankind, Peopling of Countries, etc.,* "increase the sons of Africa, by planting them in America, where we have so fair an opportunity, by excluding all blacks and tawneys, of increasing the lovely white and red?"

More promising for a time, though ultimately unsuccessful in stemming the African demographic tide, was the seventeenth-century effort to bring in poor white indentured servants, already described in Chapter 3. The Africans, shackled, brutalized and enslaved, continued to grow in number, in a process that they did not control, but which would one day enable them to inherit much of the Caribbean.

ENSLAVEMENT

A large number of European countries participated in, and benefited from, the Caribbean portion of the slave trade. Even though Portugal owned no Caribbean colonies (due to the Papal Donation of 1496 which restricted it to Brazil in the Western Hemisphere), they were the major suppliers of Africans to the area up to the 1730s. Thereafter the British took over. Many of the Africans brought in by the British were smuggled into Santo Domingo and elsewhere. Dutch Curaçao, not itself a major plantation colony, became a major entrepôt for warehousing the enslaved for transshipment to such destinations as Venezuela and Colombia.

American ships brought many Africans to the Caribbean. Aaron Lopez, one of America's major slave traders in the colonial period, sent slave ships from his Newport, Rhode Island, base, to Africa and such Caribbean islands as Barbados, St. Kitts and Jamaica. He owned a sugar plantation in Antigua. Cuba in the nineteenth century emerged as an important transporter of Africans. Cuban ships brought Africans not only from West Africa, but also from as far away as Mozambique. This continued up to the 1870s, and possibly later. Between 1670 and 1807 vessels based in the Danish West Indies made eighty trips back and forth to West Africa. France, Denmark, Holland, Spain and Sweden all transported Africans to the Caribbean at one time or another.

Of the major regions involved in the slave trade to the Caribbean, namely Europe, North America, Africa and the Greater Caribbean, Africa was the only one absent from the more lucrative aspects of the business. They did not transport the trade's victims internationally, they built no modern ships, they developed no modern maritime industry and they made no super profits. Africa experienced no industrial revolution, like Europe and the United States did. Africans remained stuck in the debilitating role of suppliers of the human base of the trade.

LIFE FOR THE ENSLAVED

Despite the many nations involved in enslaving Africans, slave life was remarkably similar (though not necessarily identical) across the region, and indeed across the Americas. Caribbean island and mainland territories are physically close together. One can often see neighboring territories with the naked eye. Colonies changed hands frequently. They might be English today and French tomorrow. They traded with one another. Ships of many nations visited the region's ports. Plantation owners and managers from, say, Cuba, might travel to Jamaica or elsewhere to observe regional methods of cultivation or the adaptation of new plantation technology. European nations warred among themselves, ranging militarily all over the Caribbean. In times of peril, a slave uprising for example, one nation's troops might travel to a neighboring island to help avert a common danger. Africans might be sold or exiled from one nation's islands to another's. They often escaped from one jurisdiction, such as the Danish West Indies, to another, such as

Spanish Puerto Rico. This might prompt, for example, a Danish owner to sue for the return of his enslaved property in the courts of Puerto Rico. When the Anglican Church installed a vicar apostolic in Trinidad in 1820, his jurisdiction included the British, Dutch and Danish islands. Despite differences, the Caribbean was therefore an area of continuous interaction and mutual influence. The result was a relative unity of culture and experience which has endured. Similarities have greatly outnumbered differences.

Though not all Africans worked on sugar plantations, the typical African did. In Cuba in the 1860s close to 50 percent of the enslaved worked on sugar plantations. At the end of slavery in the British West Indies, 85 percent of the enslaved worked in agriculture or related work, with the figure for Tobago and British Guiana over 90 percent. Of nineteen British West Indian colonies at official Emancipation in 1834, only five were insignificant producers of sugar. These five—British Honduras, the Cayman Islands, the Bahamas, Anguilla and Barbuda— together accounted for only 16,000 of the 666,737 enslaved Africans in the British West Indies in 1834.

Sugar plantation work ranked with diving for pearls (notably in Margarita Island and Panama) as the most horrifyingly hazardous of slave work in the Americas. Here mortality was at its highest and fertility at its lowest. C. L. R. James reported in *The Black Jacobins* that the life expectancy of an African newly arrived in eighteenth-century Saint Domingue was six years. It was cheaper for the planter to work the African to death in six years and buy a new one, rather than nurture him or her into a ripe old age, at which point the African would, in strictly economic terms, become a nonproductive burden on the plantation. From statistics available to him, Olaudah Equiano calculated in the 1780s that the life expectancy for an enslaved person arriving in Barbados was sixteen years. And this despite his agreement that Barbados was one of the better places for an enslaved person to find himself. Richard S. Dunn corroborated Equiano's findings two centuries later. He found that the enslaved Barbados population stabilized itself at around 45,000 from the 1680s to the mid-eighteenth century. The planters imported 3,000 Africans a year but the new imports were offset by the high mortality rate. Planter Edward Littleton, Dunn reported, owned 120 enslaved

Africans in 1680. Littleton complained that a planter owning 100 Africans would have to import six a year just to maintain his numbers. This meant, said Dunn, that the original 100 could all expect to be dead in seventeen years. This was almost the exact result of Equiano's calculations.

Newly arrived Africans were "seasoned" into the brutal regime that would consign them to a life of wretchedness. A planter in the Windward Islands described the process in the 1790s. He had just bought twenty African boys and girls ranging from ten to thirteen years old. He distributed them among the Creole (Caribbean born) Africans who fed them, introduced them to the routine of plantation work and helped them learn their new language.

Creole seasoners were rewarded with knives, calabashes and iron pots. They were apparently happy to receive new arrivals, since these helped them in the gardens which Africans tended in their little spare time.

Female arrivals also underwent another "seasoning," namely their forcible induction into the world of sexual exploitation by white owners, overseers and others. The most notorious example of something akin to this in New World enslavement was the case of the enslaved girl Celia in Missouri, USA. Slave owner Robert Newsom bought the fourteen-year-old Celia for use as a concubine and immediately raped her on the way home from her purchase. She subsequently bore two of his children. When she started a relationship with a fellow enslaved person she asked Newsom to leave her alone. He refused and she beat him to death with a big stick. She burned his body in her fireplace, buried the surviving bones and got Newsom's own grandson to unsuspectingly help her take out his grandfather's ashes. A Missouri court executed her by hanging at the tender age of nineteen. Like the case of Solitude in Guadeloupe, which we will encounter later, Celia's executioners delayed killing her until after the birth of the baby with whom she was pregnant. The child was stillborn in jail, thus relieving her executioners of any concern over the Missouri law that prohibited execution of a pregnant woman.

In eighteenth-century Suriname a slave owner's wife forestalled sexual seasoning of a beautiful new arrival by horribly mutilating her before her husband could induct her into the world of plantation sexual exploitation.

Thomas Thistlewood in eighteenth-century Jamaica distinguished himself from other slave-owning rapists by openly admitting that he practiced rape as punishment. In 1762 he bought the nine to ten-year-old Congo Sally. By the time she was fifteen or sixteen, if not before, he was forcing his sexual desires on her, as he did on every enslaved woman on his pen (livestock farm). On July 2, 1770, he flogged her for stealing and eating a chicken. The next day he raped her on the ground, as he carefully noted in his diary. On August 7 Thistlewood's black concubine had Sally stripped naked and secured outdoors with her hands tied behind her back "for the mosquitoes to bite her," as Thistlewood explained. Sally broke loose and ran away. She was caught and brought back, whereupon Thistlewood secured her in the bilboes and immediately raped her again, on the ground once more.

On August 22, 1768, Thistlewood recorded that he "put a collar and chain about Sally's neck; also branded her TT on her right cheek." His enslaved woman Coobah ran away four times between 1770 and 1774. He flogged her, branded her in the face, chained and collared her and had excrement rubbed in her face. Yet Thistlewood himself lived with a succession of enslaved concubines, notable among them Phibbah, who was able to accumulate enough money to extend loans to Thistlewood on a couple occasions.

Plantation workers were typically organized into "gangs." Despite minor variations, this practice obtained throughout the Caribbean. Renny in his *History of Jamaica* (1807) described the gang system. There were three gangs. The first consisted of the "most healthy and robust" men and women. Before crop time (harvest) they cleared the land and planted the new canes. During crop time they cut canes, fed the mills which extracted sugar juice from the new canes and worked generally in the grueling and hazardous manufacturing aspects of sugarcane processing. About one-third of the plantation workforce was in the first gang, exclusive of artisans and domestic (house) slaves, who were outside of the gang system. First gangs often had a female majority.

The second gang consisted of young boys and girls, pregnant women and convalescents. They weeded the cane fields and did other relatively light work.

The third gang was made up of very young children working under an old African woman. They collected "green meat" for livestock animals and did some weeding and other light work. The main purpose of the third gang's tasks was not so much economic as to indoctrinate the children into the routine of plantation work—"merely to preserve them from the habits of idleness," as Renny put it.

The first gang was summoned to the field a little before sunrise by the blowing of a conch shell (abeng). They brought with them provisions for their breakfast. The white overseer and black drivers (foremen) accompanied them to the field. Overseers and drivers were the ones who administered corporal punishment.

The first gang broke for a half-hour breakfast around 8:00 or 9:00 AM. Breakfast was prepared by specialist women cooks, who did nothing else. The typical breakfast described by Renny would be familiar to many Jamaicans today—yams, eddoes, ocra, callaloo and plantains, all seasoned with salt and cayenne pepper—"a very agreeable and wholesome breakfast," as Renny observed. While all of this was going on, stragglers were being whipped for their tardiness.

After breakfast, work resumed until noon, which brought two hours of rest and refreshment. "Dinner" was served at this time. The menu was similar to breakfast, with the addition of some salt meat or pickled fish. At 2:00 PM. it was back to work "where," Renny assured us, "having been refreshed, both by rest and food, they now manifest some signs of rigorous and animated application. . . ." The Africans returned to their quarters at or shortly after sunset. If the day was wet or the work unusually burdensome, they received some rum to revive their spirits. Renny put the normal workday at about ten hours.

A description of plantation work in Martinique reveals little deviation from the Jamaican pattern. There the first gang (*grand atelier*) was also put at about one-third of the plantation workforce. Here, too, women outnumbered men in the first gang, since some men were siphoned off for jobs as drivers and skilled artisans. Here again the first gang handled the hardest work—digging cane holes, planting cane and provisions, clearing the forest, carrying green bagasse from the mills to the drying sheds, constructing roads, building stone walls and the like. Youngsters graduated to the first gang around the ages of fourteen to sixteen.

The second gang (*petit atelier*) in Martinique comprised the aged, weaker adults, convalescents, nursing mothers and ten-to-sixteen-year-olds. The third gang, known here also as the grass or weeding gang, included children from five years old.

The typical workday in the field was almost identical to that described for Jamaica. The Africans were awakened before dawn and started work around 5:00 or 6:00 AM. Breakfast came around 8:00 or 9:00 AM and lasted for thirty to forty-five minutes. Work resumed until midday. After a two-hour rest the Africans worked until sunset. Each African at some point during the day had to pick a bundle of guinea grass for animal fodder. In the evenings they prepared their own meals and were "relatively free."

Esteban Montejo of Cuba, who escaped slavery in the late nineteenth century, described a similar workday. A wake-up bell, the "Ave Maria," was rung in the barracoons (barracks or slave quarters) at 4:30 AM, he reported. A "line-up bell" rang at 6:00 AM. The Africans lined up outside the barracoons and were marched to the cane fields, where they worked until 11:00 AM. Breakfast of jerked beef, vegetables and bread followed. (Montejo gave no details of the second meal.) A "prayer bell" signaled the end of the workday. At 8:30 PM a "silence bell" signaled time to sleep in the barracoons.

Work was most grueling during the harvest season when the canes were cut and the manufacturing aspect of the sugar plantation swung into full gear. During this period the plantation changed from a primarily agricultural entity to a largely industrial operation with the enslaved Africans a sort of proto-industrial workforce operating sophisticated machinery.

The industrial process got underway with cartloads of cane being delivered into the plantation sugar mills. A worker fed cane into the mill's rollers while another extracted the bagasse (the refuse of the crushed cane stalks left behind after the cane juice was extracted) at the other end. The bagasse was taken to a drying shed from whence it went to the boiling house to be used as fuel. "So very dangerous is the work of those Negroes who attend the rollers," Stedman explained in Suriname, "that should one of their fingers be caught between them, which frequently happens through inadvertency, the whole arm is instantly shattered to pieces, if not part of the body. A hatchet is generally kept ready to chop off the limb, before the working of the mill can be stopped."

French Dominican priest Père Labat, who lived in Martinique and Guadeloupe from 1694 to 1705, documented the same practice of an ever-ready cutlass to sever the arm of any worker caught in the machinery. He related the horrendous death of an enslaved woman owned by Jesuits. Her shirt sleeves got caught in the cogs. Before anyone could rescue her, her whole body was drawn into the rollers and crushed. Her head, too big to pass, was severed at the neck and fell to one side. From Guadeloupe in 1845 came a report of the similar crushing of a twelve-year-old girl pressed into what was really theoretically first gang work. The girl's head fell on the mill table.

There was yet another danger. For, said Stedman, "should a poor slave dare to taste that sugar which he produces by the sweat of his brow, he runs the risk of receiving some hundred lashes, or having all his teeth knocked out by the overseer."

The liquid extracted by the rollers was conveyed to the boiling house. Work in the boiling house was dangerous, physically very demanding and uncomfortable. It involved prolonged exposure to high temperatures and the pungent smell of boiling cane juice. It also required highly skilled individuals at some points in the production chain. The head refiner or "boiler" has been described as the most important person on the plantation, enslaved or free.

Cuban enslaved were worked almost twenty hours a day during harvest time and kept awake by constant whipping. Victor Schoelcher, the French abolitionist, reported on a fact-finding visit to Puerto Rico in 1841 that the Africans were worked at harvest time from 3:00 AM to 8:00 or 9:00 PM with a further two to four hours on normally work free Sundays and public holidays. In nineteenth century Jamaica Africans worked in shifts all night in the sugar mills at harvest time. Harvest time was followed by the less frenetic dead season, devoted to planting, clearing new land, building and maintaining roads and the like.

Africans lived generally in very poor conditions, whether huts or barracks. Olaudah Equiano described the huts of the field slaves in Montserrat as damp "often open sheds" where the residents contracted diseases that contributed to the high mortality among the enslaved. Esteban Montejo described the Cuban barracoons as two long buildings facing each other. There was a door in the middle with a massive padlock which locked the Africans in at night. The floors were of mud and the buildings "as dirty as hell." Small holes in the wall or windows with bars provided the only ventilation. They were however kept cleanly whitewashed on the outside. The rooms were very small. Women washed clothes in tubs. In one corner of the barracoon there was one toilet for use by all its residents. Toiletry conveniences were rudimentary—"And to wipe your arse afterwards you had to pick leaves and maize husks." There was a slave cemetery on the plantation.

The enslaved living in or around their owners' houses in towns fared a little better, but still lived in poor conditions. Stedman reported that most houses in Paramaribo had wells "which afford but a brackish kind of beverage, only used for the Negroes, cattle, etc." The Europeans collected rainwater, sometimes filtered, in cisterns for their own consumption. Most people in Paramaribo slept in hammocks, "the Negro slaves excepted, who mostly lie on the ground. . . ."

The Africans were given a periodic very basic ration of clothes, called the *esquifación* in Cuba. In Suriname, Stedman said, they were "kept nearly naked." Their daily rations here consisted of "little more than a few yams and plantains." Twice a year or so this ration was augmented by a "scanty allowance" of salt fish and "a few leaves of tobacco." Everywhere the enslaved typically worked in decrepit, often tattered clothing, even naked. In warmer areas barefoot was the norm. Esteban Montejo described the typical Cuban slave attire for men as "Russian cloth," a sturdy linen and rawhide shoes. The old men, he said, wore African sandals. "This has always been an African fashion," he reminisced in the twentieth century, "though white women wear them now and call them mules or slippers." The basic ration for Cuban women was blouses, skirts and petticoats.

PUNISHMENT OF THE ENSLAVED

The slave plantation could be an incredibly brutal place. Several factors contributed to the reign of terror that prevailed. First of all the European enslavers were not particularly gentle people, even to one another. There were over 200 capital offences in England in the eighteenth century. They could hang you for stealing a handkerchief. Children were often executed for theft. Large crowds attended the public executions, with prominent citizens paying handsomely for good seats from which to observe the ghoulish spectacle. Prisoners, male and female, schoolchildren, soldiers and sailors were all flogged. Even on a slave ship one could see a European sailor being flogged for some misdemeanor or other.

Olaudah Equiano said, of his experience on the slave ship, "I had never seen among any people such instances of brutal cruelty; and this not only shown towards us blacks, but also to some of the whites themselves." He saw the white crew flog a fellow shipmate to death. "They tossed him over the side as they would have done a brute."

This tendency to brutality, however, took on a whole new dimension in a slave society where masters and slaves were mostly easily distinguishable from each other by race. In addition, in the Caribbean and elsewhere in the Americas enslaved Africans mostly had no rights. U.S. Chief Justice Taney's famous judgment in the *Dred Scott* case in 1857 that "black people have no rights that white people are bound to respect," was writ large in the Caribbean. An enslaved African in the Caribbean could not testify in court. Despite occasional laws to the contrary, a white person could generally kill, maim or flog a black person with impunity. There was no legal recourse for an African woman raped.

The reality of the inexorable Africanization of the Caribbean also hardened European dispositions toward brutality. In the European view whites were vastly outnumbered by their enslaved Africans. They very matter-of-factly determined that such a situation could not be maintained without a reign of terror. Pseudo-scientific notions of African inferiority and white supremacy also contributed to the brutality of the slave regime. Sometime U.S. president, Thomas Jefferson, asserted that Africans did not feel pain like other human beings, that their griefs were "transient." A Danish botanist, zoologist and doctor in Denmark's colonial medical service in 1848 considered Africans incapable of learning.

The Barbadian-English planter, slaveholder and historian Bryan Edwards unambiguously asserted the necessity of a reign of terror in his *History of the British Colonies in the West Indies* (1801). He wrote,

> In countries where slavery is established, the leading principle on which the government is supported is fear: or a sense of that absolute coercive necessity which, leaving no choice of action, supersedes all questions of right. It is vain to deny that such actually is, and necessarily must be, the case in all countries where slavery is allowed.

Frenchman Hilliard d'Auberteuil said essentially the same thing in eighteenth-century Saint Domingue—"Policy and safety require that we crush the race of blacks by a contempt so great that whoever descends from it even to the sixth generation shall be covered with an indelible stain."

The preamble to an 1807 law in Jamaica began, "And whereas it is absolutely necessary, that the slaves in this island should be kept in due obedience to their owners, and in due subordination to the white people in general. . . ." J. G. Stedman in Suriname, about as liberal as any European in the era of slavery, did not disagree with the need to keep the enslaved under "heavy manners." He argued, however, for stringent control to be tempered with some humanity. Was it possible, he asked, "to keep the African Negroes in habits of obedience and industry without the strictest and often the severest discipline?" "No," he answered, "But I ask again, Why is it necessary to inflict such inhuman tortures, according to the humor and caprice of an unfeeling master, or still more unprincipled overseer? Why should their reasonable complaints be never heard by a magistrate who has it in his power to redress them?"

Stedman, quite remarkably for his context, based his abhorrence of cruel and unusual punishments on the humanity of the enslaved. He disagreed with his European contemporaries on the alleged innate inferiority of Africans. "That these people are neither divested of a good

An enslaved woman with a weight chained to her ankle, drawn by J. G. Stedman in Suriname in the 1770s. As a full African or one of only limited European mixture, she was obliged in Suriname to keep her upper body uncovered.

ear, nor poetical genius," he observed, "has been frequently proved, when they have had the advantages of a good education." He quoted a poem by the enslaved pioneer African American poet Phillis Wheatley, whose *Poems on Various Subjects,* *Religious and Moral* appeared in London in September 1773. This was mere months after Stedman's arrival in Suriname, and he may well have read Wheatley there. Thomas Thistlewood similarly read Adam Smith's *The Wealth of Nations* (1776) in

Jamaica immediately after its publication in London, suggesting a literary-minded element in the white Caribbean population, more significant than hitherto acknowledged.

"What can be more beautiful and sublime?" asked Stedman of Wheatley's poem. Thomas Jefferson, on the other hand, found her poetry so awful that, as far as he was concerned, it did nothing to disprove his notions of the mental inferiority of Africans.

The most obvious emblem of white privilege and brutality was the whip. The whip, often a cat o' nine tails with a single handle and nine thongs, was ubiquitous and applied unceasingly. Victor Schoelcher called it "the bell of the plantations." In some French Colonies, he explained, the crack of a whip was the "bell" that signaled wake-up time in the morning, lunchtime in the fields and so on. In Paramaribo, said J. G. Stedman in the 1770s, "my ears were deafened with the clang of the whip, and the shrieks of the Negroes."

Overseers accompanied the enslaved to the fields whip in hand. Latecomers were whipped. Those who fell behind in their tasks were whipped. Women who resisted the sexual advances of white men were whipped. Africans who refused to eat on the slave ships were whipped. Recaptured runaways were whipped. Pregnant women were stripped naked and placed face down on the ground with a hole dug to accommodate their bellies, and whipped. House servants whose owners did not feel like applying the whip themselves were sent for public whippings to the "public executioner," who plied his whipping trade near the gallows. "As to the numbers who are excoriated from their neck to their heel, by constant whipping," said Stedman, "they may cure themselves, or do their work without a skin, if they think proper."

Various slave laws prescribed maximum lashes for various offences, but these were honored mostly in the breach. The supposedly liberal French *Code Noir* of 1688 allowed for whippings of the enslaved. Laws in eighteenth-century Martinique allowed first fifty and later twenty-nine lashes maximum. In the Danish West Indies, Governor Philip Gardelin in 1773 included breaking on the wheel, pinching with glowing tongs, cutting off of ears, amputation of limbs and hanging among his legally authorized modes of slave torture.

The notorious Thomas Thistlewood, who lived in Jamaica from 1750 to his death in 1786, had excrement rubbed into the faces of Africans and had others defecate into their mouths as punishment. C. L. R. James also reported the enslaved in Saint Domingue being forced to eat their own excrement and drink their urine. Thistlewood also detailed in his diaries the administering of 50–300 lashes to various enslaved men and women. A mixed-race boy on his plantation received 300 lashes for various "crimes and naughtiness." Thistlewood said the boy could not work for nine days afterward. Yet some contemporaries thought that fifteen severe lashes were enough to disable a strong man.

Stedman in Suriname came upon a girl being flogged at the command of a white overseer for refusing his sexual advances. She "was a beautiful Samboe girl of about eighteen, tied up by both arms to a tree, as naked as she came into the world, and lacerated in such a shocking manner by the whips of two negro-drivers, that she was from her neck to her ancles [sic] literally dyed with blood." Stedman remonstrated with the overseer, who responded by increasing the 200 lashes already administered to 400, for Stedman's benefit. On another occasion Stedman was more successful when he saved a black girl from 100 lashes by replacing some china she had inadvertently broken.

Esteban Montejo in Cuba described the whip as the most common form of punishment. It was made of rawhide or the "fibres of some jungle plant which stung like the devil and flayed the skin off in strips." He saw pregnant women flogged.

Few accounts of the application of the whip can be more heartrending than those of Mary Prince, author of the slave narrative, *The History of Mary Prince: A West Indian Slave, Narrated by Herself.* Prince's narrative, the first by a woman in the Americas, was published in London in 1831. This was thirty years before Harriet Jacobs' *Incidents in the Life of a Slave Girl* (1861), thought to be the first slave narrative by an African American woman.

Prince was enslaved in Bermuda, Turks Island and Antigua. She recounted years of brutal whippings suffered by herself and others she worked with. Sold away from her family in Bermuda at the age of twelve, she found herself the property of a sadistic female owner, who "caused me to know the exact difference between the smart of the rope, the cart whip and the cow-skin, when applied to my naked body by her own cruel hand." This woman beat two young enslaved boys continuously. "I have seen their flesh ragged and raw with licks," Prince lamented. Soon Prince was suffering the same fate as the two boys— "to strip me naked—to hang me up by the wrists and lay my flesh open with the cow-skin, was an ordinary punishment for even a slight offence."

Prince witnessed the horrific beating of a pregnant "French" African named Hetty. A cow that Hetty had tied to a stake dragged its rope away. This became the cause for a fatal beating for the unfortunate Hetty. Mary Prince recalled,

> My master flew into a terrible passion, and ordered the poor creature to be stripped quite naked, notwithstanding her pregnancy, and to be tied up to a tree in the yard. He then flogged her as hard as he could lick, both with the whip and cow-skin till she was all over streaming with blood. He rested and then beat her again and again. Her shrieks were terrible. The consequence was that poor Hetty was brought to bed before her time, and was delivered after severe labor of a dead child. She appeared to recover after her confinement so far that she was repeatedly flogged by both master and mistress afterwards but her former strength never returned to her. Before long her body and limbs swelled to a great size; and she lay on a mat in the kitchen, till the water burst out of her body and she died. All the slaves said that death was a good thing for poor Hetty; but I cried very much for her death.

On another occasion an already cracked earthenware jar finally came apart as Mary Prince tried to empty it. The result was a ferocious flogging from her mistress followed by 100 more lashes from the slave master. The mistress "stripped and flogged me long and severely with the cow-skin; as long as

she had strength to use the lash, for she did not give over till she was quite tired." This was but prelude to the master's 100—"He tied me upon a ladder and gave me a hundred lashes with his own hand, and Master Benjy stood by to count them for him. When he had licked me for some time he sat down to take a breath; then after resting, he beat me again and again, until he was quite wearied, and so hot (for the weather was very sultry), that he sank back in his chair, almost like to faint." This beating was terminated by what might have seemed like an act of God, namely an earthquake. In the confusion, Mary Prince crawled away and spent the rest of the night under the front steps, scarcely able to move. The next morning her owners forced her back into her normal strenuous work routine, despite her bloody, bruised and stiff condition.

While it is possible to find in the record exceptional cases of a slave owner or overseer being legally reprimanded for injuring or killing an enslaved person, and despite the presence of a few slave laws setting limits to punishments, cases such as these enumerated here were routine and did not attract any judicial concern. Mary Prince herself noted this most poignantly when describing her regular beatings from a Mr. D. in Turks Island. He often stripped her naked and flogged her until her "body was raw with gashes." "Yet," she noted sadly, "there was nothing very remarkable in this; for it might serve as a sample of the common usage of the slaves on that horrible island."

The punishments here described were, as seen, always prescribed and often carried out by white owners and overseers. Often, however, the punishment, though ordered by a white person, would be carried out by a driver, a sort of black foreman figure who existed all over the Caribbean, or by a black public executioner, who was somewhat akin to a driver. Drivers (also called "bombas" by the Dutch and Danes) were appointed even before Africans arrived in the Caribbean. A few physically very strong captives might be singled out during the Middle Passage for this purpose. They must not speak the language of the majority. They were given some authority over the other captives and were taught a smattering of the European language. They were expected to help with general chores around the ship. The Danes at the Gold Coast expressly did not recruit them from the local Asante or Crepe people. Despite their relative freedom they were closely watched and had to sleep in the hold at night.

At their worst, drivers could beat their own family at the white man's behest. "The driver was a Black man like myself," Esteban Montejo told the Jamaican writer Andrew Salkey in 1968. He "was on the make, with his master, and he had to show how cruel he was, all the time. He used to have a good time. He had women, as he liked, and extra food from the master's kitchen, and he would have certain little privileges. He used a leather whip. He would prepare the whip in salt and water. He would cure it like meat. He pickled it like pork, you see. I got twenty-five lashes, once, because I slept with a slave girl I liked very much. . . . We lived so close together, in the dirt, in the shit, in the heat, always together. . . ."

Sometimes, however, drivers were cast in positive roles. In Suriname they emerged as leaders of the enslaved community in their efforts to resist the cultural encroachments of Christian religion. Drivers and "headmen" emerged as leaders in the revolutionary struggle in Haiti. Quashe, a driver under the infamous Thomas Thistlewood in Jamaica, once made some "threatening remarks" about Thistlewood's pursuing of an enslaved woman. There were cases of drivers joining the runaways who fled the plantations.

Mary Prince related the story of a former driver in Antigua who begged forgiveness for his excesses when he was converted to Christianity. "He confessed that he had treated the slaves very cruelly," she related, "but said that he was compelled to obey the orders of his master. He prayed them all to forgive him, and he prayed that God would forgive him. He said it was a horrid thing for a ranger ['head Negro of an estate,' according to Pringle, her editor] to have sometimes to beat his own wife or sister; but he must do so if ordered by his master." Like the free colored and free black holders of enslaved persons, the drivers were a complex lot.

The whip may have been the most ubiquitous emblem of enslavement, but it was far from the sole instrument of brutality. These could be as many and

varied as the imaginations of the enslavers could concoct. Some, such as the stocks, were imported from Europe. Others, such as stuffing gunpowder into the anus of an African and blowing him or her to bits, appear to have been the inventions of a tropical European depravity. C. L. R. James described this technique, euphemistically called "to burn a little powder in the arse of a nigger," in his study of the Haitian Revolution.

The reputedly liberal French slave code, the *Code Noir* of 1688, banned *private* torture and mutilation, albeit ineffectively. It nevertheless allowed judicial authorities to inflict upon the Africans such punishments as burning alive, dismemberment and branding with hot irons. It prescribed crippling by hamstringing for runaways and authorized breaking alive upon the rack. Stedman described a breaking upon the rack, "without the benefit of the *coup de grace* or mercy-stroke" which he witnessed in Suriname. The victim was stretched out on a wooden frame, legs and arms spread wide. The executioner, a black man acting on the orders of white officials, first chopped off his left hand with a hatchet. He then "took up a heavy iron bar, with which, by repeated blows, he broke his bones to shivers, til [sic] the marrow, blood, and splinters flew about the field. . . ." The victim underwent excruciating pain. When he appeared to be clinging to life against all odds Stedman and some American sailors among the spectators had to restrain members of the crowd from kicking and spitting on the man as he lay close to death. Later that day Stedman saw the victim's head on a stake, being eaten by vultures.

Esteban Montejo considered stocks the most cruel of the devices used to brutalize the Africans. These stocks were thick wooden planks with holes in them to accommodate the head, feet and hands. He reported Africans left in the stocks for two to three months "for some trivial offence." Some were kept in a standing position, some lying down. They might be left in the open to be bitten by insects.

Slaves were often chained to a heavy iron weight attached to a large log. The victim would have to lift the encumbrance whenever he or she attempted to walk. The heavy iron shackles often chafed the skin and induced sores. In seventeenth century Barbados male

Africans were castrated for running away. Thomas Thistlewood, as seen, inflicted rape as punishment.

In the notorious LeJeune case of 1788 in Saint Domingue, a slave owner killed four Africans and severely burned two others while torturing them. Local authorities refused to reprimand him. In 1814 Lieutenant-Governor Bentinck of Berbice suggested that the colony's Court of Policy ban a form of torture euphemistically called "Little Ease," practiced on several plantations. Here the victims were placed inside an old iron boiler. Others were forced to beat on the outside with hammers. The victims sometimes lost their sense of hearing as a result.

The Englishman Hans Sloane, in *A Voyage to the Islands Madera, Barbados, Nieves, S. Christophers and Jamaica*(London, 2 vols, 1707–1725), matter-of-factly enumerated some forms of punishment. Rebellious Africans, he said, were burned to death. They were first nailed to the ground with crooked sticks applied to each limb. Fire was then applied to the victims' feet and hands. The whole body was burned gradually, upward toward the head "whereby," Sloane commented laconically, "their pains are extravagant." For less serious crimes the torturers could choose between castration and chopping off half of one foot with an axe. "These punishments," Sloane observed, "are suffered by them with great constancy." Other observers also noted the frequent stoicism of the Africans under torture.

For running away Sloane described "iron rings of great weight" affixed to the ankles of the Africans. Alternatively they might be fitted with "pothooks about their necks." These pothooks were iron collars with protruding spikes which made it impossible for the wearers to lie down in a comfortable position. They might have to endure this discomfiture for months. For "negligence," Sloane said, the usual punishment was being tied up by their hands in the mill house, followed by a whipping with "laice-wood switches till they be bloody and several of the switches broken."

In his Suriname narrative Stedman repeatedly apologized to his readers for the recurring descriptions of cruelty meted out to the enslaved. By confronting these harsh realities, he said, he hoped that some alleviation might come to the sufferings of the poor victims. In 1730 in Suriname the colonists executed eleven rebel Africans in the following manner, as

described by Stedman: "One man was hanged alive upon a gibbet, by an iron hook stuck through his ribs; two others were chained to stakes, and burnt to death by a slow fire. Six women were broken alive upon the rack, and two girls were decapitated. Such was their resolution under these tortures, that they endured them without even uttering a sigh." Stedman on another occasion described a number of Africans "roasted alive by half dozens in a shocking manner, being chained to stakes in the midst of surrounding flames. . . ." He witnessed an old African chained to a furnace that distilled "kill-devil," a fatal (so thought Stedman) rum made from the "scum and dregs of sugar cauldrons," and the only alcohol the slaves were allowed to consume. This poor man lived "in the intense heat of a perpetual fire night and day, being blistered all over, till he should expire by infirmity or old age. . . ." Stedman thought the chances of the latter very slim.

Stedman was aware of nine Africans having their legs amputated for running away during his stay in Paramaribo. "This punishment," he said, "is a part of the Surinam administration of justice" and was per-formed by a surgeon. Four of the victims died immediately after the operation. A fifth committed suicide by tearing away his bandages, as a result of which he died during the night. "These amputated negroes are common in this colony," Stedman noted, "and are employed in rowing the boats and barges of their masters. Others are seen deprived of an arm; and this is the forfeit for daring to raise it against an European."

On one occasion Stedman, ever willing to intervene when he could, cut down a boy and girl who an overseer had hung "by a rope fastened to their thumbs, which were tied behind their backs; this almost dislocated their shoulders. . . ." An Italian planter, he reported, had caused an eight months' pregnant African woman to be flogged until her intestines spilled out. "[T]here was not a slave belonging to his estate but was cut by the lash of his whip from the neck to the heel." Stedman's dreary catalog of horrors included an owner wantonly shooting a slave he was tired of, leaving victims naked in the forest to be stung to death by insects, drowning them by throwing them overboard with a weight attached to their legs, breaking out their teeth for tasting sugarcane, slitting their ears and cutting

off their noses. Stedman also documented in a drawing from life the killing of the previously mentioned
enslaved man who was hung up from a gibbet to die
a slow, painful, public death. His hands were pin-
ioned behind him and an iron hook attached to a
chain pierced his rib cage. He was suspended from
the gibbet by this hook, which bore the full weight of
his body. There he remained for several days, dying
a gruesome death while passers-by stopped to stare
and even to converse with him.

The "peculiarly tyrannical" Mr. Ebber, an
overseer on the Hope plantation, Stedman reported,
tyrannized a fourteen-year-old boy named Cadetty
for a whole year, by subjecting him each month to
cruel and unusual punishments. He flogged him
every day for one month; tied him down flat on his
back with his feet in the stocks for another; placed a
pot-hook around his neck for a third month—the protruding hooks made it impossible to escape into the
forest or even sleep, except in an upright position;
"chain[ed] him to the landing-place, night and day, to
a dog's kennel, with orders to bark at every boat or
canoe that passed for a fourth month"; and so on. The
boy eventually went mad. "The wretch Ebber" was
succeeded by the "*humane*" Mr. Blenderman,
Stedman noted ironically. Blenderman began his
tenure as overseer by flogging every enslaved person
on the plantation for oversleeping by fifteen minutes.

Whereas saving the life of a white person could
sometimes be the occasion for manumission, such
was not necessarily the case. Stedman related one
episode where an enslaved boy saved his overseer's
life during an attack by Maroons. He told the overseer
to lie flat on his belly in a canoe while, swimming
with one hand, the boy guided the canoe to safety with
the other, through a hail of Maroon bullets. However,
Stedman drily noted, "for this material piece of
service, [the boy] was recompensed the week after
with three hundred lashes by the same master, only for
having forgotten the sluices or floodgates."

One noteworthy element in this catalog of horrors was the significant involvement of white women
in administering these cruelties. Mention has already
been made of Mary Prince's female torturer and we
will soon encounter Alice Mills, the Barbadian castration specialist. White women slave owners in
Barbados, it will be seen, were more likely than their

male counterparts to hire out their female slaves as
prostitutes. It was a well-known fact, Stedman
recalled, "that by the orders of a *woman,* Negro slaves
have been privately burned to death, miserably
chained in a surrounding pile of flaming faggots."
Stedman thought that female slave owners in
Paramaribo were more oppressive than male owners.
Although a few urban enslaved lived comfortably, he
noted, "the greatest number are wretched, particularly
those governed by a *lady,* who have many wales to
show, but not the smallest indulgence to boast of."

The excesses of Ebber and Blenderman might
seem unparalleled, Stedman wrote, "but this is not
the case, they were even exceeded, and by a female
too." He recounted the action of one Mrs. S—lk—r
who held her slave woman's baby underwater until
the infant drowned, because she was offended by the
infant's cries on a river barge. The enslaved mother
tried to drown herself in her grief but was prevented
by Africans rowing the vessel. Mrs. S—lk—r then
had the woman receive 3 or 400 lashes "for her
daring temerity," as Stedman put it.

This incident, gruesome as it was, did not
exhaust the reputed crimes of Mrs. S—lk—r, "that
infernal fiend," and "monster of a woman," as
Stedman called her. "[S]he was accused of still
greater barbarity," Stedman said, "were greater barbarity possible." Stedman was on hand at the waterfront in front of Mrs. S—lk—r's house to witness
"the dreadful spectacle of a beautiful young mulatto
girl, floating on her back, with her hands tied behind,
her throat most shockingly cut, and stabbed in the
breast with a knife in more than eight or ten different
places." The apparent motive for this horror was Mrs.
S—lk—r's apprehension that her husband might be
attracted to this young woman.

On another occasion, Stedman reported, Mrs.
S—lk—r, on a visit to her plantation, noticed a
"fine negro girl about fifteen years of age," newly
arrived in Suriname. "Observing her to be a remarkably fine figure," Stedman reported, "with a
sweet engaging countenance, her diabolical jealousy instantly prompted her to burn the girl's
cheeks, mouth, and forehead with a red-hot iron;
she also cut the tendon Achilles of one of her legs,
thus rendering her a monster of deformity. . . ."
Some of the enslaved Africans remonstrated with

Mrs. S—lk—r, whereupon she "knocked out the brains" of a quadroon child. Two of the child's relations tried to stop her and she had their heads chopped off. When she ended her estate visit, Stedman reported, some of the surviving relatives of the victims took the two heads in silk handkerchiefs to the governor, who branded them all liars and ordered a vigorous whipping for them. "Such is the consequence of the law of the colony," Stedman commented, "that the testimony of a Negro is never to be taken. Had any one white person been present at the above carnage, the evidence would have been good, but even then this fury would have escaped by paying a fine of fifty pounds for each murder."

"A Jewess, impelled by a groundless jealousy," someone told him, had similarly "put an end to the life of a young and beautiful Quadroon girl, by the infernal means of plunging into her body a red-hot poker." Incredibly, Stedman observed, the perpetrator's only punishment was banishment to the settlement of Jew's Savannah.

Stedman looked out of his window on one occasion in time to see one Miss Sp—n "give orders that a young black woman should be flogged principally across the breasts, at which she seemed to enjoy peculiar satisfaction." He was once the guest of a Mr. and Mrs. Goetzee at their beautiful plantation. Mrs. Goetzee ordered a whipping for a boy who did not rinse the glasses to her satisfaction. The boy preempted her by blowing his brains out in Mr. Goetzee's bedroom. The couple then ordered his body thrown out the window to the dogs. This couple were later poisoned by their enslaved workers, but not before Stedman witnessed another extreme example of what he called Mrs. Goetzee's "barbarity." Mrs. Goetzee had a female "mulatto" woman "stripped stark naked, and in a very indecent as well as inhuman manner flogged by two stout Negroes before the dwelling house door (while both her feet were locked to a heavy iron bolt) until hardly any skin was left on her thighs or sides." This was two weeks into Stedman's stay as a guest on the Goetzee plantation. Five days after this punishment he was able to prevail upon the torturers to remove the poor woman's iron bolt, which was locked against her shins. The cause of her punishment was some remark made in jest about Mrs. Goetzee.

No sooner did Stedman obtain relief for the poor woman from her iron bolt, however, than "a Mrs. Van Eys, alledging [sic] she had affronted her also by her *saucy* looks, prevailed on Mrs. Goetzee to renew the punishment the same week; when she was actually so cruelly beaten, that I expected she could not have survived it."

Stedman knew of two cooks who, like Mrs. Goetzee's kitchen servant, had committed suicide rather than face a whipping for spoiling dinner. Another boy who attempted suicide after a flogging was not so fortunate. He jumped out of a window but was revived, tortured and then sent by the lady of the house to the public executioner for a *"spanso-bocko."* Stedman described this punishment: "The prisoner's hands being lashed together, he is laid down on the ground on one side, with his knees thrust between his arms, and these confined by a strong stake, which separates them from his wrists, and is driven perpendicularly into the ground, insomuch that he can no more stir than if he was dead. In this locked position, trussed like a fowl, he is beaten on one side of his breech by a strong Negro, with a handful of knotty tamarind branches, till the very flesh is cut away; he is then turned over on the other side, where the same dreadful flagellation is inflicted, till not a bit of skin is left, and the place of execution is dyed with blood: after which the raw lacerated wound is immediately washed with lemon-juice and gun-powder to prevent mortification, and then he is sent home to recover as well as he can." This form of "cruel and indecent punishment," Stedman said, "is sometimes repeated at every street in the town of Paramaribo, to men and women indiscriminately, which is a severity absolutely beyond conception. . . ." The *spanso-bocko* (also rendered "Spaanse bok") was known in other New World slavery societies. The name itself, translated as "Spanish whip," bore testimony to this. It was called the "buck" in the southern United States.

These, then, were some of the results of a tendency to violence in Europe, wedded to unrestrained authority over the enslaved of another race in the Americas. The resulting horrors knew no bounds. Mary Prince related the plight of one Old Daniel at the salt works of Turks Island. He had the misfortune of living to a ripe old age in slavery and being "lame in the hips." He was unable to keep up with the rest of the gang and the slave master therefore beat him regularly "with a rod of rough brier till his skin was quite red and raw." This slave owner would then throw a bucket of salt over the wounds while the old man, naked and tied to the ground, "writhed on the ground like a worm, and screamed aloud with agony." As a result of this constant torture the old man's wounds never had time to heal. "I have often seen them full of maggots," Mary Prince reported.

Olaudah Equiano, such a valuable witness on account of his own enslavement and his extensive travel as a seaman throughout the Caribbean, reported that "It was very common in several of the islands, particularly in St. Kitts, for the slaves to be branded with the initial letters of their master's name; and a load of heavy iron hooks hung about their necks. Indeed on the most trifling occasions they were loaded with chains; and often instruments of torture were added. The iron muzzle, thumb screws, etc., are so well known as not to need a description, and were sometimes applied for the slightest faults. I have seen a Negro beaten till some of his bones were broken, for only letting a pot boil over." Equiano witnessed attempted suicides induced by these forms of torture. This entire situation, he noted, spoke to the "small account in which the life of a Negro is held in the West Indies. . . ." He quoted an act of the Barbados Assembly, but typical of the Caribbean, excusing from any penalty whatsoever any master whose slave inadvertently died or suffered loss of limb while undergoing punishment. Where, however, the death of any slave was caused by "wantonness, or . . . bloody-mindedness, or cruel intention" the perpetrator would be fined fifteen pounds.

Up until the late eighteenth century at least, castration was a brutal punishment inflicted on enslaved males. It was practiced by individual planters on their own whim and was also sometimes officially recognized under the law. This was true both in British islands such as Antigua and Bermuda and in their British North American counterparts of Virginia, Pennsylvania, the Carolinas and New Jersey. Striking a white person and running away

were among the offences punishable by castration. In 1693 after an uprising of the enslaved in Barbados, one Alice Mills was paid ten guineas for castrating forty-two Africans, "an episode which," commented Winthrop Jordan, "says a good deal about Barbados and something about Alice Mills."

SEXUAL EXPLOITATION OF ENSLAVED WOMEN

White planter society turned the enslaved environment into an orgy of sexual abuse. Sexual liaisons with African women actually began in Africa. White men stationed in the coastal forts gave themselves access to whichever of their newly enslaved women caught their fancy. Sometimes they established familial relations with free African women from neighboring communities. These latter were more likely to be stable, socially acceptable relationships than concubinage in the Caribbean. West African society, unlike its Caribbean counterpart, did not make interracial marriage the object of social ostracism.

During the Middle Passage crew members were able to help themselves to harems from among their naked female captives. The Englishman T. S. St. Clair in *A Residence in the West Indies* (1834) described his visit to a newly arrived slave ship in Demerara. The emaciated condition of most of the new African arrivals contrasted sharply with the healthy-looking occupants of the harem that the captain and mate had put together in their cabins. These consisted of "five or six young girls, as naked as they were born, who formed the seraglios of these two sultans and were kept fat and in good condition."

Plantation society was not above sanitizing and romanticizing this exploitation of African women. Bryan Edwards, no lover of African people, reproduced in the frontispiece to Volume II of the third edition of his *History of the British Colonies in the West Indies* (1801) the famous painting, "The Voyage of the Sable Venus from Angola to the West Indies." This was by Thomas Stothard, Esq. of the English Royal Academy, and was apparently inspired by the Italian Sandro Botticelli's celebrated "Birth of Venus" (ca. 1485). The painting represented a beauteous idyllic African woman borne over the Atlantic with an escort of winged cherubs and other adornments from classical European mythology, while Cupid shot an arrow at Neptune, god of the sea. An accompanying poem explained that black women were no different from white in the midnight hour. Daniel P. Mannix and Malcolm Cowley observed that "Meanwhile the Sable Venus, if she was a living woman borne from Angola to the West Indies, was roaming the deck of a ship that stank of excrement, so that, as with any slaver, 'You could smell it five miles down wind.' She had been torn from her husband and her children, she had been branded on the left buttock, and she had been carried to the ship bound hand and foot, lying in the bilge at the bottom of a dugout canoe. Now she was the prey of the ship's officers, in danger of being flogged to death if she resisted them. Her reward if she yielded was a handful of beads or a sailor's kerchief to tie around her waist."

In the Caribbean, white slave masters literally owned their enslaved women, who could be raped at will, even if in a stable relationship with an enslaved man. Stedman reported that in Suriname "if a Negro and his wife have ever so great an attachment for each other, the woman, if handsome, must yield to the loathsome embrace of an adulterous and licentious manager, or see her husband cut to pieces for endeavoring to prevent it. This," he said, "in frequent instances, has driven them to distraction, and been the cause of many murders."

On the other hand, white male access to enslaved women might have had the strange consequence of reducing the otherwise-all-powerful white man to in effect sharing women with his male African subjects. Thomas Thistlewood in Jamaica might rub feces in the faces of his male and female Africans, administer 300 lashes at a time and hang one man and stick his head on a pole for running away, but he still found himself in the presumably unseemly (for him) position of having to take back presents he had given to one of his enslaved concubines, because she continued to see a fellow enslaved lover. Thistlewood confided to his diary all the gory details of the sexually transmitted disease he brought with him from England. These, too, doubtless represented a shared affliction with the African men and women over whom he held the power of life and death. Thistlewood forced himself sexually (he acknowledged that some of his

victims actually tried to avoid his charms) on practically every enslaved woman under his control. Assuming that most of them did not remain celibate after encountering him sexually, he must have directly or indirectly infected pretty much all his enslaved charges, both male and female, with venereal disease.

Stedman also related the story of an African woman captured by his fellow anti-Maroon troops. She escaped, but "considerably increased in size from her connection with the troops, and likely to present a new recruit to her dusky monarch." Mary Prince, who married in Antigua, recounted the pathetic inability of her husband to protect her from the brutality and indignities visited upon enslaved women.

Women and their partners could strike back or run away, but the stakes were high, with floggings, dismemberment, castration for males and other horrific punishments awaiting the unsuccessful. J. A. Thorne, in *Emancipation in the West Indies* (1839), noted of Barbados, "The managers and overseers, commonly unmarried, left no female virtue unattempted. Those who yielded were sometimes rewarded, but those who did not were flogged or imprisoned."

On the few occasions when African men were able to retaliate against this degradation of their women, their wrath could be terrible. The ferocity of their response indicated their deep resentment at this state of affairs. In Suriname the revolutionary eighteenth-century Maroon leader Jolly Coeur had a rare opportunity to strike back. On a Maroon raid on the New Rosenback plantation in Jew's Savannah, he captured the manager, one Schults. Schults recognized Jolly Coeur as his former property. He pleaded that he had always been good to Jolly Coeur and that his life should be spared. While still a child, Jolly Coeur had witnessed Schults rape his mother. Now with the former rapist in his power he reminded Schults of this incident. The African recounting this story to Stedman vividly recalled Jolly Coeur's reply to Schults—"But you, O tyrant, recollect how you ravished my poor mother, and flogged my father for coming to her assistance. Recollect, that the shameful act was perpetrated in my infant presence—Recollect this—then die by my hands, and next be damn'd." Jolly Coeur cut Schults' head off with a single blow of a hatchet and played bowls with it on the beach.

He flayed Schults and used his skin to keep the priming on one of his cannons dry.

Planters and overseers raped enslaved girls from the age of prepubescence and up. Hilary Beckles has shown that on the Newton Plantation in Barbados in 1796 all four of the female field-workers listed as having "mulatto" children had been impregnated between the ages of thirteen and sixteen. In Cuba in 1834 a fourteen-year-old light-skinned enslaved girl, Florencia Rodriguez (or Hernandez), lodged a complaint with the Mayor of Havana against her owner, one Don Ramón Saíz. Ramón had promised to free her if she would have sex with him. Once he got his wishes he reneged on the deal and instead punished her frequently. He even, she deposed, "tried to place silver rings in the most secret parts" of her body. She testified that though Ramón failed to insert the rings in her, he had succeeded with her friend, Inés. Florencia begged not to be sent back to Ramón, in which case, she said, she would surely die. Her plea fell on deaf ears.

The enslaved Puerto Rican woman Maria Balbina testified in 1859 to a tribunal set up to ameliorate the lot of enslaved in the dying years of the institution. She said, "On the promise of freeing me, when I was barely a teenager my master made me the mother of his three children, born one after another. But now, unmindful of his given word and the lamentation of his conscience, he intends to sell me." After two years of fruitless litigation, Maria ran away.

This kind of child rape of the enslaved was common throughout the Americas and had in fact started in the time of Columbus, as indicated earlier. In 1880s Brazil (where emancipation came only in 1888), one Honorata, a prepubescent girl, was raped by her owner, a known child molester. Four doctors testified that she was in fact prepubescent, but her owner was nevertheless acquitted by the court. In the United States, founding father Thomas Jefferson is thought to have fathered six children by his enslaved charge Sally Hemings. A possible seventh is said to have died shortly after birth circa1789, when Sally would have been around sixteen. Long after emancipation, in 1919, the Trinidadian civil rights worker in London, F. E. M. Hercules, was still complaining that British officials in the colonies were raping little girls.

In the Caribbean, as elsewhere in the Americas, slave masters sometimes lived in open polygamy with a white wife and an enslaved concubine, with separate sets of white and black children coexisting under the same roof. The black offspring would be the house slaves of their white siblings. "On first arriving here [Jamaica]," wrote planter historian Edward Long in the 1770s, "a civilized European" would be thoroughly "shocked at seeing a group of white legitimate and mulatto illegitimate children, all claimed by the same married father and all bred up, under the same roof. Habit, however, and the prevailing fashion reconcile such scenes and lessen the abhorrence cited by their first impression."

The plantation environment itself was a place of frequent licentiousness. Enslaved children, boys and girls, often went naked to puberty. Adults were sometimes worked in nudity or near nudity in the fields. Domestic servants were sometimes forced to wait at table in a similar condition. In the late eighteenth-century Suriname of Stedman's observations, black women were forced to go naked from the waist up. "Mulatto" women could cover one breast. Quadroons were allowed to cover their entire upper bodies. "In Surinam the slaves are kept nearly naked," he observed, and his book was peppered with references to and drawings of naked enslaved male porters carrying equipment for the soldiers, naked girls chasing gnats out of rooms at night so that the Europeans might sleep comfortably, a naked girl accidentally falling out of a window onto a heap of broken glass, slaves stripped naked and publicly flogged and the like.

All of this scandalized some European visitors newly arrived in the Caribbean, and they were the ones who mainly documented these practices. Adriaan van Berkel in late seventeenth-century Berbice described Africans worked in the nude because their owners refused to provide clothes. George Pinckard, physician to the British expedition against Dutch Demerara in the late 1790s, saw six naked African men transporting two Dutch women in a chaise. T. S. St. Clair, newly arrived in Demerara around 1803 after the English conquest, wrote incredulously of four young enslaved women, forced to wait table "as naked as they came into the world," during his visit to one of Demerara's

An enslaved quadroon woman, drawn by J. G. Stedman in Suriname in the 1770s. Note that quadroon women were allowed in Suriname to cover their upper bodies.

most prominent white families. His host lived in one of the country's most imposing mansions. His companions at dinner consisted of the host and his wife, their two daughters and a white widow. "I was astonished," wrote St. Clair, "at such an exhibition before persons of their own sex." Stedman had been similarly shocked in Suriname a few years earlier during dinner at a plantation owner's home. "Here we saw a great novelty indeed," he observed, "the young women waiting at table all stark naked, as they came into the world." The ever curious Stedman enquired of his hosts the reason why, and received an unusual answer. The lady of the house claimed that this was the way the girls' "mothers and matrons" kept them under sexual surveillance as a deterrent to too early intercourse, which would ruin their figures and stunt their growth. Stedman conceded that he had never beheld finer figures than those on both the male and female enslaved on this plantation.

Male house guests were routinely provided with an enslaved sexual partner for the night. These enslaved women and girls, observed the Rev. Thomas Cooper in his *Negro Slavery as it Exists In . . . Jamaica* (1817), had been made into "the mere instruments of licentious gratification." "[W]hen visitors stay all night on an estate," he noted, "they are accustomed on going to bed to desire the domestic who attends them to bring them a girl with almost as little ceremony as they would ask for a candle. . . ."

When visiting naval vessels were in port, enslaved women were rounded up and placed at the sailors' disposal. Prostituting their female slaves was a source of income for many a slave owner. As far as formal prostitution was concerned, female slave owners were often the principal perpetrators. This may be because formal prostitution tended to be an urban phenomenon, and women owners often predominated in the towns. In 1817, according to Hilary Beckles, 58 percent of Bridgetown's owners of enslaved persons were women. They owned 54 percent of the enslaved. These white women owned more females than males. They also owned more females than their male counterparts did. These facts led Beckles to surmise that "many black women suffered their greatest degree of social exploitation at the hands of white women. . . ."

Incest was not uncommon in the panoply of sexual abuse visited upon the enslaved women.

B. McMahon, in *Jamaica Planters* (1839), recounted the case of one Richard P. Martin, a white magistrate who had a "mulatto" daughter. He incestuously abused his daughter and the result was some quadroon (one-quarter black) children. He then fathered octoroon (one-eighth black) children with his quadroon daughters.

The African American historian W. E. B. DuBois, himself of part Haitian and part Bahamian heritage, addressed the following accusatory lament in his *Souls of Black Folk* to the perpetrators of these sexual evils: "The rapes which you gentlemen have done against helpless black women in defiance of your own laws is written on the foreheads of two millions of mulattoes, and written in ineffaceable blood."

The mixed-race progeny of this carnival of sexual abuse was highly prized by European men. The Brazilian saying, documented by Abdias do Nascimento, was equally applicable to the Caribbean: "White woman to marry; mulatto woman for sex; black woman to work." Not that the use of the racially mixed women exempted black women from further sexual abuse.

In time, as the mixed-race population increasingly gained their freedom and developed into an oftendistinct buffer group between black and white, colored and black women (both free and enslaved) themselves exploited their position of sexual desirability. In a society which provided them few other options for upward mobility they now often actively sought the attention of white men, their tickets to economic improvement, and, for those notyetfree, their ticket to freedom. "We see in the country," wrote a Frenchman in Saint Domingue in 1713, "only Negro women and mulatto women who have bargained off their virginity for their freedom. . . ."

Women would offer their daughters to newly arrived European males. Stedman, newly arrived in Suriname, was visited by "an elderly Negro-woman, with a black girl about fourteen" who the old lady offered him as "what she was pleased to call my wife." "The girls here who voluntarily enter into these connections are sometimes mulattoes, sometimes Indians, and often Negroes," Stedman explained. "They all exult in the circumstance of living with an European. . . . Young women of this description cannot indeed be married or connected in any other way, as most of them are born or trained up in a state of slavery. . . ." The clergy availed themselves of this practice as did secular white men. Enslaved concubines, and black and colored women generally, often had to endure the wrath of jealous white wives who took out their frustrations on these unfortunate objects of their husbands' lust.

The famous quadroon balls of New Orleans and elsewhere in the United States had their counterparts in the Caribbean. In the United States, as in the Caribbean, these balls brought together light-skinned women and white men looking for relationships approximating marriage, in societies where formal marriage between white and colored was not normally acceptable. Barbados had "dignity balls" in taverns owned by colored women who had usually amassed money through their own concubinage. As in New Orleans, only white men could attend.

Stedman attended what he called a "mulatto ball" in Paramaribo in January 1776. This was for free coloreds only and it is not clear whether non-white men were welcome. "Here the music, the lights, the country dances, the supper, and, above all, the dresses were so superb, and their behaviour so decent and genteel, that the whole might serve as a model for decorum and etiquette to some of the fairer and more polished inhabitants."

When Stedman did fall for an enslaved girl, he found himself the pursuer of a reluctant object of his infatuation, rather than the more usual recipient of easily accessible proffered or commandeered sexual favors. His infatuation with the teenaged Joanna has become probably the most celebrated episode in the literature of the colored Caribbean people. Joanna was the oldest daughter of a Dutch "respectable gentleman," one Kruythoff, and an African mother whose father, a member of his native ruling class, had been taken captive in war and enslaved in Suriname. Kruythoff had tried in vain to purchase the freedom of Joanna and her four siblings from their slave owner and died brokenhearted, leaving his five children still in bondage. Their owner was known for his cruelty, with the result that a large number of his enslaved people ran away and joined the rebel Maroons. One of these became the special protector of Joanna's mother, Cery, and her children.

He was none other than the feared Jolly Coeur, who had flayed his former tormentor Shults and played bowls with his head. Joanna's uncle, Cojo, decorated by the Europeans for fighting *against* the Maroons, took care of Jolly Coeur's little daughter Tamera, after her father's defection to the Maroons.

The elegance of Stedman's prose, his gift for storytelling, the depth of feeling he expressed, his poetic waxings, his famous drawing of Joanna and the inherent qualities of the story which made of it a veritable Greek tragedy, all combined to capture the imaginations of many who read it. The story became the basis for several works of fiction by European writers. It also illustrated many of the features of colored life in Caribbean society. It illustrated the prevalence of concubinage, the hapless position of those colored persons who were brought up in a genteel way but were not formally manumitted and the legal difficulties in the way of manumission, even in the face of the best intentions. It also illustrated the cruelties of Caribbean enslavement and its inevitable consequence of rebellion.

Stedman met "the beautiful mulatto maid Joanna" shortly after arriving in Suriname. She was an enslaved girl of only fifteen in the household of a high Dutch official at whose house he breakfasted daily. "Rather taller than the middle size," he wrote,

> she was possessed of the most elegant shape that nature can exhibit, moving her well-formed limbs with more than common gracefulness. Her face was full of native modesty, and the most distinguished sweetness; her eyes, as black as ebony, were large and full of expression, bespeaking the goodness of her heart; with cheeks through which glowed, in spite of the darkness of her complexion, a beautiful tinge of vermillion, when gazed upon. Her nose was perfectly well formed, rather small; her lips a little prominent, which, when she spoke, discovered two regular rows of teeth, as white as mountain snow; her hair was a dark brown inclining to black, forming a beautiful globe of small ringlets, ornamented with flowers

Joanna, teenage concubine of J. G. Stedman, engraved from a drawing by Stedman in Suriname in the 1770s. Note that Joanna, as a half-white, half-black female, was allowed to cover only one breast.

and gold spangles. Round her neck, her arms, and her ancles, [sic] she wore gold chains, rings and medals: while a shawl of India muslin, the end of which was negligently thrown over her pol-ished shoulders, gracefully covered part of her lovely bosom: a petticoat of rich chintz alone completed her apparel. Bare-headed and bare-footed, she shone with double lustre, as she carried in her delicate hand a beaver hat, the crown trimmed round with silver. The figure and appearance of this charming creature could not but attract my particular attention, as they did indeed that of all who beheld her: and induced me to enquire from Mrs. Demelly, with much surprise, who she was, that appeared to be so much distinguished above all others of her species in the colony.

Joanna saved Stedman's life several times when he was perilously ill. He was able to get her a temporary reprieve when she was about to be sold into uncertain plantation slavery by the administrator of her deceased owner's estate. She declined his first proposals for a liaison on the remarkable grounds, given the near-universal concubinage of the colored female population, that, as Stedman reported it, "should I soon return to Europe, she must either be parted from me for ever, or accompany me to a part of the world where the inferiority of her condition must prove greatly to the disadvantage of both herself and her benefactor, and thus in either case be miserable."

Stedman eventually induced Joanna to move in with him and she bore him a son, Johnny, who he was eventually able to manumit, thanks to the help of his friend the governor. He had witnessed the suffering of well-bred colored children whose parents had died without being able to manumit them, and this had made him "tremble for my little boy." His efforts to manumit Joanna, on the other hand, met with failure. Even after a benefactor came forward to help him financially, Joanna insisted that she be mortgaged to the good lady until her purchase price be paid off. Stedman valiantly began to liquidate the debt in installments. With his return to Holland approaching and despite his benefactor's willingness to let her go, Joanna nevertheless still refused to accompany him to Europe. Joanna once again demonstrated a sense of pride and self-respect quite amazing for one so young (she was now nineteen) and in her unfortunate circumstances. Stedman once again sadly reported her refusal "first, from a consciousness that, with propriety, she had not the disposal of herself; and secondly, from pride, wishing in her

present condition rather to be one of the first among her own class in America, than a reflection or burthen on me in Europe, as she was convinced must be the case, unless our circumstances became one day more independent."

Five years after his departure from Suriname, Stedman received news that his Joanna had died, apparently poisoned by persons jealous of her rise in Suriname society. "But she is no more!" Stedman exclaimed to his readers. "Reader!—the virtuous Joanna, who so often saved my life, is no more!!!" Joanna had in the intervening years accumulated enough wealth to leave little Johnny a substantial legacy. The boy was sent to Stedman, who educated him well in England. Johnny then joined the navy, where he saw successful combat against the Spanish fleet. But he, too, died a tragic and untimely death. "But, Oh!" lamented Stedman, "he also is no more, having since *perished* at sea off the island of *Jamaica*." As he had often done when overcome with emotion for Joanna, Stedman sought the solace of poetry to memorialize his son:

> Oh! agonizing pain—pain never felt before—
> My manly boy—my John—my Sailor is no
>   more . . .
> Fly, gentle shade—fly to that blest abode,
> There view thy *mother*—and adore thy God. . . .

Esteban Montejo in Cuba related an interesting piece of folklore on the question of white male access to black women. White Cuban males, he said, contracted a strange illness "of the veins and male organs." This illness could only be cured, they thought, by sleeping with a black woman. This remedy was sure to effect an instant cure.

J. M. Phillipo in *Jamaica, Its Past and Present* (1843) suggested that "concubinage was almost universal, embracing nine-tenths of the [white] male population." A 1774 census in Saint Domingue enumerated approximately 7,000 free women of color, of whom 5,000 were mistresses of white men.

Concubinage did not ordinarily lead to marriage, despite its open practice. As the French historian P. Vaissière put it in a 1909 study of Saint Domingue, "Numbers of masters, instead of concealing their turpitude glory in it, having in their house their black concubines and the children they have had by them, and showing them off with as much assurance as if they were the offspring of marriage. Neither the color, nor the odor, nor any other natural disgust, nor the idea of having a slave as offspring and to see him ill-treated or worked at the vilest of labor, or sold, keep them from these monstrous unions. . . ." While the institution was near universal and openly practiced, formal marriage was a different matter. A white man marrying any nonwhite woman would be subject to ostracism from white society. The exceptions were European adventurers who married rich colored women and used their wives' money to establish or reestablish themselves in European society. The French *Code Noir* had allowed marriage with black people. A 1724 amendment annulled the earlier provision. Such laws were however mostly irrelevant to actual practice.

One consequence of this widespread white-initiated miscegenation was further impetus to the much-feared Africanization of the population. To make matters worse, from the white perspective, many rich white fathers were sending their colored offspring to Europe for superior educations. They were also endowing their concubines and colored children with considerable wealth, including even enslaved persons, via their wills. This prompted the Jamaican assembly in 1762 to pass a law "to prevent the inconvenience arising from exorbitant grants and devises made by white persons to Negroes and the issue of Negroes." A 2,000 pound sterling cap was put on all bequests of real or personal property to nonwhites. Some efforts were made, not always successful, to circumvent this law by the setting up of trusts for offspring.

Some of the issue of concubines did well in Europe. General Alexander Dumas of Saint Domingue served in Napoleon's army. His son, Alexander Dumas *fils* (son), and grandson of the same name were both distinguished French writers. The second Alexander Dumas authored the novel *The Three Musketeers.* Joseph de Bologne, better known to history as Le Chevalier St. Georges (1745–1799) was the son of a French aristocrat and a teenaged enslaved girl in Guadeloupe. His extraordinary career included a stint as a young Gentleman of the King's Chamber (personal assistant to the French king), virtuoso violinist, champion swordsman, conductor, composer and all-round athlete. He was a founder of

the *Société des Amis des Noirs,*(Society of Friends of the Blacks) the premier French abolitionist society.

Some of these beautiful and wealthy West Indians in England married into aristocratic circles. The English novelist William Thackeray in *Vanity Fair* featured the character Rhoda Swartz, a beautiful and fabulously rich Caribbean colored daughter of a German Jew. She was presented at the English court and eventually married the future Lord Castletoddy.

Interracial sex during slavery was a one-way affair, with white males having access to black and colored women. Hilary Beckles has however been able to identify at least four marriages between Africans and poor white indentured women in Barbados in the late seventeenth century. Similar exceptional marriages were recorded in the English North American colony of Virginia in the same period. Winthrop Jordan has shown that in New England, by contrast, early legal marriages between black men and white women of "the meaner sort" were "far more common than is generally supposed." He thinks that here the very small African population and absence of plantation society may have initially induced a relatively more relaxed atmosphere.

Once slavery became an established institution, black male–white female liaisons were extremely rare. Olaudah Equiano related the fate of a fellow enslaved in Montserrat, who succumbed to the enticements of a white prostitute, "the most abandoned woman of her species." The man was "staked to the ground, and cut most shockingly, and then his ears cut off bit by bit. . . ." Equiano contrasted this with the white men he knew to "gratify" with impunity "their brutal passion with [black] females not ten years old. . . ." Stedman drew a similar contrast in Suriname. "All these fine [quadroon] women have European husbands [that is, partners in concubinage]," he observed, "to the no small mortification of the fair Creolians; yet should it be known that an European female had an intercourse with a slave of any denomination, she is forever detested, and the slave loses his life without mercy.—Such are the despotic laws of men in Dutch Guiana over the weaker sex."

White indentured women probably initially had no principled objections to liaisons with black men. Their short-term affairs with Africans while in transit in Cape Verde have already been noted. In the Caribbean environment, however, they and their

Chevalier de Saint George, 1787.

impoverished descendants (such as the "Redlegs" of Barbados) developed the practice of racial exclusiveness and endogamy.

There was often a sexual imbalance in the enslaved population, with men outnumbering women. This, plus the large-scale resort of white men to black women could mean a shortage of women for enslaved men. Cuban Esteban Montejo said that as a result enslaved males often had either to resign themselves to a life without women, or turn to homosexuality. "I don't think [that homosexuality] can have come from Africa," he opined, "because the old [African] men hated it." Montejo (1860–1973) escaped slavery some time during the Ten Years War (1868–1878) and lived the life of a solitary runaway in the jungle for many years. He narrated his remarkable life in 1963 at the age of 103.

Slave breeding was yet another way in which the enslaved were sexually degraded. This practice became especially prevalent after the slave trade from Africa (but not slavery itself) was outlawed at various points in the nineteenth century. With the supply from Africa reduced, slave owners turned to "breeding" their own locally.

Esteban Montejo explained that the owners selected tall healthy men and women, shut them up in the barracoons, and commanded them to mate. Their children fetched premium prices. Women were expected to produce a child a year. If any woman failed to have children she was returned to the fields. "I tell you," Montejo commented, "it was like breeding animals."

Further Readings

Code Noir. http://chnm.gmu.edu/revolution/d/335/ [accessed December 16, 2009].

Dunn, Richard S. "The Barbados Census of 1680: Profile of the Richest Colony in English America." *William and Mary Quarterly, Third Series*, 26, 1, January 1969, pp. 4–30.

Equiano, Olaudah. *The Interesting Narrative of the Life of Olaudah Equiano, or Gustavus Vassa, the African. Written by Himself. Vols. I and II.* London: Author, 1789.

Hall, Douglas, Ed. *In Miserable Slavery: Thomas Thistlewood in Jamaica, 1750–86.* Kingston: University of the West Indies Press, 1999.

Jordan, Winthrop D. *White Over Black: American Attitudes Toward the Negro, 1550–1812.* Chapel Hill: University of North Carolina Press, 1968.

Mannix, Daniel P., with Malcolm Cowley. *Black Cargoes: A History of the Atlantic Slave Trade, 1518–1865.* New York: Viking Press, 1962.

Moitt, Bernard. *Women and Slavery in the French Antilles, 1635–1848.* Bloomington: Indiana University Press, 2001.

Montejo, Esteban. *Autobiography of a Runaway Slave.* Ed. by Miguel Barnet. Willimantic, CT: Curbstone Press, 1994.

Prince, Mary. *The History of Mary Prince, a West Indian Slave. Related by Herself.* London: Published by F. Westley and A. H. Davis, Stationers' Hall Court, 1831.

Rodney, Walter. *A History of the Upper Guinea Coast, 1545–1800.* Oxford: The Clarendon Press, 1970.

Rogers, Joel Augustus. *Sex and Race, Vol. II.* St. Petersburg, FL: Helga M. Rogers, 1942.

Shepherd, Verene, and Hilary McD. Beckles, Eds. *Caribbean Slavery in the Atlantic World.* Kingston: Ian Randle Publishers, 2000.

Sloane, Hans. *A Voyage to the Islands Madera, Barbados, Nieves, S. Christophers and Jamaica, with the Natural History. . . .* London: Printed for the Author, 2 vols, 1707–1725.

Stedman, John Gabriel. *Narrative of a Five Years' Expedition Against the Revolted Negroes of Surinam In Guiana on the Wild Coast of South America From the Years 1772 to 1777.* Amherst: University of Massachusetts Press, 1972. First pub. 1796.

Svalesen, Leif. *The Slave Ship Fredensborg.* Kingston: Ian Randle Publishers, 2000.

Taylor, Eric Robert. *If We Must Die: Shipboard Insurrections in the Era of the Atlantic Slave Trade.* Baton Rouge: LSU Press, 2006.

Tomich, Dale. "Slavery in Martinique in the French Caribbean," in Verene Shepherd and Hilary McD. Beckles, Eds., *Caribbean Slavery in the Atlantic World.* Kingston: Ian Randle Publishers, 2000, pp. 413–436.

5

The Enslaved and the Manumitted
Human Beings in Savage Surroundings

Enslaved or not, the Africans were still human beings. Most of them lived their entire lives within the institution of slavery. Somehow, they still had to find ways to do what human beings do. They loved, they hated, they attempted as far as the reality of their condition allowed, to seek material comfort, to provide for their children, to find a mate, to practice a religion, to dance and sing and fight and play, to achieve some upward mobility where they could.

HIERARCHY OF THE ENSLAVED

While the majority of the enslaved performed manual labor on plantations, not all did. Even within slavery there was a division of labor and a social hierarchy of sorts. Artisans were at the top of the enslavement hierarchy. The supreme example of this was the head refiner or boiler, arguably the most important person on the plantation, enslaved or free, black or white. Upon his skill and experience depended the success or failure of the entire sugar crop. As Dale Tomich has said of the head boiler in Martinique:

> The fate of the entire crop, thus profit or loss for the estate was in his hands. The entire operation of manufacturing the sugar took place under his guidance and demanded his constant attention around the clock during the harvest season. . . . The job required intimate knowledge of the process of sugar making and the particularities of the cane juice, furnace, and kettles. The head refiner had to judge the quality of the cane juice and, therefore, had to be familiar with "the way the cane has been raised and treated; the kind of soil it grows upon; if that soil has been high or low manured; the age of the cane; the species it is of; whether it has been topped short or long in the cutting; if it has been arrowed, bored or rat-eaten. . . ." He had to prepare and apply the temper according to the quality of the cane juice. He determined how long the juice boiled in each of the kettles, supervised its transfer from one to another, and, most importantly, decided when the sugar was ready to strike. He also had to see to the proper crystallization, packing, and draining of the sugar. In the absence of scientific instruments and methods of sugar refining, control over these procedures depended upon individual skill, judgment, and a wide range of empirical knowledge. . . . If [the refiner] failed to demonstrate the requisite skill or trustworthiness the consequences for

the estate could be severe. . . . Despite growing scientific interest and enquiry, for all practical purposes knowledge of the techniques of sugar refining remained a craft secret and could be acquired only by long practice and experience. This knowledge was the property of the slaves whose permanence on the estate was assumed, and, in a society organized by the most extreme social and racial hierarchy, the exercise of the refiner's art came to be seen as their special province. Wrote one observer, "The Negro boilers must be more perfect in their business than any white can pretend to be." Although the white sugar master nominally oversaw the boiling house, the slave refiner was in practical control of its activities.

Other skilled workers performed various other boiling house tasks. Artisans might be coopers, carpenters, ships' carpenters or versed in one or another of the other building trades. Sometimes artisans were hired out to work on their own in the towns and remitted their wages, or some portion thereof, to their owners.

House slaves followed in the pecking order of the enslaved. Light-skinned girls would normally be house slaves (domestics) although, again, not all house slaves would be light-skinned and not all light-skinned girls would be house slaves. Domestics performed the full range of household chores, which might include wet-nursing the white people's children, cooking, cleaning, sewing, washing, tending livestock kept near the house, waiting at the table and babysitting. Male house slaves might be coachmen, butlers and handymen, among other things.

Mary Prince was a house slave for much of her life of enslavement. Her career, as it were, began with her purchase as a pet for little Miss Betsy, a white girl her own age, much the way that others might purchase a puppy for a young child. "I was made quite a pet of by Miss Betsy," Mary Prince recalled, "and loved her very much. She used to lead me about by the hand, and call me her little nigger. This was the

happiest period of my life; for I was too young to understand rightly my condition as a slave. . . ."

House slaves generally lived better than the field slaves, the plantation workers who came below them in the hierarchy of the enslaved. House slaves were often the children of the slave masters and had access to the castoffs of a more affluent lifestyle than generally was available to the field slaves.

Their closeness to the master both literally and metaphorically placed them in an ambivalent position in the plantation world. They not infrequently betrayed slave conspiracies. In the folklore of slavery they have become the objects of much opprobrium. Malcolm X, African America's revolutionary son of a Grenadian mother, fixed the house slave as a figure of loathing for all time. When Ole Massa was sick, said Malcolm, the Uncle Tom house slave would enquire, "Massa, *we* sick?" If Massa's house was on fire, on the other hand, said Malcolm, the field slave would pray for a strong wind.

While these generalizations were somewhat true, they were not writ in black and white. Mary Prince's experience showed that the life of a house slave could be absolutely wretched. And house slaves and artisans could often be revolutionary leaders in the struggle against slavery. The maximum leader of the Haitian Revolution, Toussaint L'Ouverture, had been a house slave, a coachman. Denmark Vesey of St. Thomas and Haiti was a ship's carpenter. As a freedman in Charleston, South Carolina, in 1822, he led one of the greatest attempted uprisings of the enslaved in North American history.

Esteban Montejo of Cuba, however, tended to corroborate Malcolm X's view of house slaves. Montejo never saw a house slave badly punished. He said they acted as proselytizing agents for Roman Catholic priests, who themselves would never dare enter the barracoons. They sometimes visited the barracoons to see relatives among the field hands. They caused friction by trying to woo barracoon women. On the whole, Montejo said, the barracoon dwellers did not like them.

House slaves were just as likely to be used as symbols of conspicuous wealth by their owners as for any real productive purpose. In eighteenth-century Jamaica there might be as many as twenty to thirty servants in a single household. On a large Martiniquan plantation each member of the family would typically have his or her personal servant. Additionally there might be a cook, two or three washerwomen, two or three seamstresses and two or three "women to run errands." Racially mixed girls here, as elsewhere, were the domestics of choice and the domestics were typically Creole (that is, Caribbean born) and born on the plantation which employed them.

Rev. Ohm, a Lutheran Priest in St. Croix in 1792, maintained five domestics— a cook, a washer and her two daughters and a seamstress. Carl Holten, adjutant to the St. Croix governor from 1799, recorded in his memoirs, as cited by N. A. T. Hall, an entourage of fourteen servants—"A mulatto servant; 2 black boys; a cook; an assistant cook; a washer; two chamber maids and an old biddy who supervised the women and looked after the [five] children." Stedman corroborated this general situation for Suriname.

It was Stedman who penned the classic description of white planters ("these West-India nabobs," he called them), luxuriating in a life of gross indolence and indulgence at the expense of their house servants:

A planter in Surinam, when he lives on his estate, (which is but seldom, as they mostly prefer the society of Paramaribo) gets out of his hammock with the rising sun, *viz.* about six o'clock in the morning, when he makes his appearance under the piazza of his house; where his coffee is ready waiting for him, which he generally takes with his pipe, instead of toast and butter; and there he is attended by half a dozen of the finest young slaves, both male and female, of the plantation, to serve him; at this *sanctum-sanctorum* he is next accosted by his overseer, who regularly every morning attends at his levee, and having made his bows at several yards distance, with the most profound respect informs his Greatness what work was done the day before; what Negroes deserted, died, fell sick, recovered, were bought or born; and, above all things, which of them neglected their work, affected sickness, or had been drunk or absent, etc.; the prisoners are generally present, being secured by the Negro-drivers, and instantly tied up to the beams of the piazza, or a tree, without so much as being heard in their own defence; when the flogging begins, with men, women, or children, without exception. The instruments of torture on these occasions are long hempen whips, that cut round at every lash, and crack like pistol-shot; during which they alternately repeat, *'Dankee, massera,'* (Thank you, master). In the mean time he stalks up and down with his overseer, affecting not so much as to hear their cries, till they are sufficiently mangled, when they are untied, and ordered to return to their work, without so much as a dressing.

This ceremony being over, the dressy Negro (a black surgeon) comes to make his report; who being dismissed with a hearty curse, for *allowing* any slaves to be sick, next makes her appearance a superannuated matron, with all the young Negro children of the estate, over whom she is governess; these, being clean washed in the river, clap their hands, and cheer in chorus, when they are sent away to breakfast on a large platter of rice and plantains; and the levee ends with a low bow from the overseer, at it begun [sic].

His worship now saunters out in his morning dress, which consists of a pair of the finest Holland trowsers [sic], white silk stockings, and red or yellow Morocco slippers; the neck of his shirt open, and nothing over it, a loose flowing night-gown of the finest India chintz excepted. On his head is a cotton night-cap, as thin as a cobweb, and over that an enormous beaver hat, that protects his meagre visage from the sun, which is already the colour of mahogany, while his whole carcass seldom weighs above

A Suriname overseer, drawn by J. G. Stedman in the 1770s, to illustrate his famous description of the "West-India nabob" steeped in a life of indolence, intolerance and excess. Note again that the enslaved African woman has to leave her upper body uncovered.

eight or ten stone, being generally exhausted by the climate and dissipation. To give a more complete idea of this fine gentleman, I in the annexed plate present him to the reader with a pipe in his mouth, which almost everywhere accompanies him, and receiving a glass of Madeira wine and water, from a female quaderoon [sic] slave, to refresh during his walk.

Having loitered about his estate, or sometimes ridden on horseback to his fields, to view his increasing stores, he returns about eight o'clock, when, if he goes abroad, he dresses, but if not, remains just as he is. Should the first take place, having only exchanged his trowsers for a pair of thin linen or silk breeches, he sits down, and holding out one foot after the other, like a horse going to be shod, a Negro boy puts on his stockings and shoes, which he also buckles, while another dresses his hair, his wig, or shaves his chin, and a third is fanning him to keep off the musquitoes [sic]. Having now shifted, he puts on a thin coat and waistcoat, all white; when under an umbrella, carried by a black boy, he is conducted to his barge, which is in waiting for him with six or eight oars, well provided with fruit, wine, water and tobacco, by his overseer, who no sooner has seen him depart, than he resumes the command with all the usual insolence of office. But should this prince not mean to stir from his estate, he goes to breakfast about ten o'clock, for which a table is spread in the large hall, provided with a bacon ham, hung-beef, fowls, or pigeons broiled; plantains and sweet cassavas roasted; bread, butter, cheese, etc. with which he drinks strong beer, and a glass of Madeira, Rhenish or Mozell wine, while the cringing overseer sits at the farther end, keeping

his proper distance, both being served by the most beautiful slaves that can be selected;—and this is called breaking the poor gentleman's fast.

After this he takes a book, plays at chess or billiards, entertains himself with music, etc. till the heat of the day forces him to return into his cotton hammock to enjoy his meridian nap, which he could no more dispense with than a Spaniard his *siesta*, and in which he rocks to and fro, like a performer on the slack-rope, till he falls asleep, without either bed or covering; and during which time he is fanned by a couple of his black attendants, to keep him cool, etc.

About three o'clock he awakes by natural instinct, when having washed and perfumed himself, he sits down to dinner, attended as at breakfast by his deputy governor and sable pages, where nothing is wanting that the world can afford in a western climate, of meat, fowls, venison, fish, vegetables, fruits, etc., and the most exquisite wines are often squandered in profusion; after this a cup of strong coffee and a liqueur finish the repast. At six o'clock he is again waited on by his overseer, attended as in the morning by Negro-drivers and prisoners, when the flogging once more having continued for some time, and the necessary orders having been given for the next day's work, the assembly is dismissed and the evening spent with weak punch, sangaree, cards and tobacco.—His worship generally begins to yawn about ten or eleven o'clock, when he withdraws, and is undressed by his sooty pages. He then retires to rest, where he passes the night in the arms of one or other of his sable sultanas (for he always keeps a seraglio) till about six in the morning, when he again repairs to his piazza walk, where his pipe and coffee are waiting for him; and where, with the rising sun, he begins his round of dissipation, like a petty monarch, as capricious as he is despotic and despicable.

Such absolute power indeed cannot fail to be peculiarly delightful to a man, who, in all probability, was in his own country, Europe, a ——nothing.

"As for the ladies," Stedman continued, "they indulge themselves just as much, by giving way to their unbounded passions, and especially to the most relentless barbarity." He readily admitted that there were outstanding exceptions to these generalizations, both for men and women. As for the majority of white women, however, he preferred on this occasion to "draw a veil over all the imperfections, too common to their sex in this climate." Elsewhere in his narrative, though, he did provide graphic descriptions of the savagery of white women against their enslaved Africans of both sexes. He also elsewhere described his shock at being openly sexually solicited by a married white woman. On the positive side, Stedman corroborated the evidence of other visiting Europeans throughout the Caribbean regarding the astonishing hospitality of planter society to visiting Europeans. A table and bed were always available to any stranger who happened along.

British government statistics for its enslaved population at Emancipation in 1834 suggest a field slave population of 74.6 percent of the workforce. (The workforce excluded children under six, the aged and infirm). Domestics made up 12.9 percent. Tradesmen (artisans) accounted for 6.2 percent. Those who worked on the wharves or on shipping comprised 1.3 percent. Agriculturally based "head people" were 5.0 percent.

GARDENS, PROVISION GROUNDS AND ENTREPRENEURSHIP

Despite the horrors of slavery, which endured until the very end of its days, a combination of factors continually tested the viability of slave society. The Africanization of the Caribbean, already noted, was one such factor. The sheer size of the enslaved population put the institution's viability under constant pressure. Various forms of rebelliousness among the enslaved, as will be seen, were another constant strain on the institution. In the phenomenon of gardens and provision grounds slavery encountered another reality that tugged at the edges of its viability. For here enslaved persons, legally without rights, considered subhuman by white society and subjected to the severest of physical abuse, nevertheless managed to carve for themselves an important niche in the market economies of their respective territories.

As time went on, the practice evolved of letting the enslaved cultivate "gardens" near their quarters and eventually larger provision grounds further away. Gardens were small plots of land in the immediate vicinity of the enslaved's quarters where the Africans grew food and raised livestock. Provision grounds (also called "pollinks" in Jamaica) were much larger allotments, on otherwise-noncultivated land outside the plantation's official use area. They could be considerable distances away, as much as 5 to 7 miles in Jamaica.

In both gardens and provision grounds the enslaved were allowed to produce for their own subsistence. This considerably lessened the financial and administrative burden on plantation management. The enslaved by these devices would in effect be to some extent feeding themselves. The industry of the enslaved was such, however, that they produced surpluses, established markets and injected themselves into the cash economies of their territories. They even impacted the export industry and all in all became important players in the economic life of their societies.

Provision grounds in Martinique were introduced by the Brazilian Jewish refugees who pioneered sugar and plantation slavery in the seventeenth century. The idea is said to have copied practice in São Tome, off the coast of West Africa, dating back to the sixteenth century. There were provision grounds in Curaçao in 1692. By the time slavery matured in the Caribbean, provision grounds were an important part of the landscape of slavery. In smaller, intensively cultivated islands like Barbados and St. Kitts, where spare land for provision grounds simply did not exist, Africans had to be content with the smaller gardens.

But even here the Africans were able to impact the local economies through their thrift, industry and initiative.

The Africans cultivated their gardens and provision grounds in their free time. In St. Vincent and probably elsewhere, this included their two-hour lunchtime break. In Jamaica in 1707 they utilized Saturday afternoons, Sundays, Christmas day, Easter (also called Little or Pickaninny Christmas) and whatever holidays came their way. European observers often wondered where they got the strength from, but enslavement's rare opportunity to do something for self was a great motivator. So too was the opportunity to provide a healthier and more varied diet than the food provided by the slave owners, which relied heavily on salted, smoked and pickled fish and meats.

In the initial gardens and provision grounds, the Africans adapted and continued the Arawak *conucos*. They grew such indigenous crops as cassavas, sweet potatoes and corn. They also grew eddoes, Guinea yams, dasheen, ackee, plantains and cocoyams, among others. In the gardens, as opposed to the provision grounds, they grew herbs, fruit trees and plants requiring frequent attention.

Out of this activity came the surpluses that gave rise to a network of markets, reminiscent of markets in Africa. The Africans themselves developed these markets. It was usual for owners to provide market passes to enable Africans to leave the plantations on market day.

Provision grounds were cultivated not only by sugar workers but also by the enslaved on other types of estates, including livestock farms (called "pens" in Jamaica). Jamaica's pens in 1832 employed 13 percent of the island's enslaved. In 1810 the figure was 5 percent each in Antigua, Barbuda and Berbice; 0.5 percent in Demerara-Essequibo; and 0.2 percent in St. Lucia. Verene Shepherd has shown that the pen enslaved also generated surpluses from their provision grounds. They also had additional ways of making money, such as attending to their owners at horse races and driving livestock to and from the market.

European observers were astonished at the variety of goods exchanged at these markets. Many goods were bartered but the money economy inevitably intruded. As the markets grew, they attracted nonenslaved persons, drawn by the opportunities for large-scale commerce. The Rev. R. Bickell in *The West Indies as They Are* (1835), as quoted by Sydney Mintz and Douglas Hall, recalled his visit to a Sunday market in Kingston, Jamaica. There were thousands of Africans present, with a large number of others as well, cashing in on the opportunities for business. "Here were Jews," he said, "with shops and standings as at a fair, selling old and new clothes, trinkets and small wares at cent. per cent. [usurious rates] to adorn the Negro person; there were some low French men and Spaniards and people of colour, in petty shops and with stalls; some selling their bad rum, gin, tobacco, etc; others, salt provisions and small articles of dress; and many of them bartering with the slave or purchasing his surplus provisions to retail again; poor free people and servants also, from all parts of the city to purchase vegetables, etc., for the following week."

Several years earlier, in 1774, English Jamaican planter-historian Edward Long aired the complaint of a contemporary, alarmed by the fact that observant Christian businessmen were losing out to Jews on the Sunday African generated business. This person suggested a Thursday market day instead, which would "prove of great advantage to all Christian shop keepers and retailers; the Jews now grossing the whole business of trafficking with the Negroes every Sunday, at which time there is a prodigious resort of them to the towns, and a vast sum expanded for drams, necessaries, and manufactures. This alteration would therefore place the Christian dealers upon an equal footing which they do not at present enjoy."

According to Mintz and Hall, enslaved Africans had a "virtual monopoly" of internal marketing in Jamaica by the 1770s. Tomich reports that almost all the cassava consumed on most large and medium-sized plantations in Martinique was bought from the enslaved. Martinique depended on them for a "substantial portion" of its food. Edward Long estimated that of 50,000 pounds in currency circulating in Jamaica, at least 10,000 pounds were held by enslaved Africans, mostly in small coins. By the end of the eighteenth century some goods originating with the enslaved were being exported via middlemen in the towns.

In Cuba the liquidity Africans accumulated from their provision grounds provided a market for immigrant Chinese, Turkish and white peasant (*guajiro*) peddlers, who came around the barracoons selling various items.

Not all enslaved Africans opted for provision grounds. Less enterprising ones opted for the plantation's food handouts, which were sometimes made an alternative to provision ground rights. At the other extreme, some of the enslaved in Martinique were so successful that they actually hired fellow enslaved to work for them.

In Barbados, which had gardens but no provision grounds, Hilary Beckles reports that the enslaved still managed to dominate provision sales in Bridgetown market. They also developed a vibrant huckstering tradition.

Provision grounds developed to the point where the enslaved actually developed a well-organized system of passing on their grounds to relatives at their deaths. Since the enslaved could not legally own the land, they were in fact passing on the right to cultivate it as long as the owners allowed them to. The fact that owners respected these arrangements, however, spoke to the importance of the provision ground phenomenon.

Provision grounds provided benefits of improved diet, self-esteem and some further space to preserve African culture. They also provided the wherewithal for the enslaved to discard the rags and tatters of their legally imposed servile status. Montejo reported that in Cuba those who had provision grounds bought their own clothes, and even gold rings and earrings from visiting Turk and "Moor" peddlers. While some might still work on the plantation in rags, on Sundays and holidays they came out in finery that belied their enslaved condition. Frock coats, satin vests, ruffled shirts and boots and shoes (both banned for the enslaved during an earlier period in Martinique) were all in evidence. Women wore necklaces and earrings of gold and semiprecious materials.

An observer in the Danish Virgin Islands around 1787 could not believe the "chintz and finery" worn by the enslaved on their way to church on Sunday. Since provision grounds and their benefits represented a potential threat to the preservation of servile status, the law tried repeatedly to keep these developments in check. A 1786 ordinance in St. Croix forbade house and field slaves from wearing silk, gold, silver, etc., to their parties. House slaves were allowed to wear a simple silver clasp.

Esteban Montejo described the atmosphere in a Cuban barracoon on Sunday, the "liveliest" day he called it, when the earnings from provision grounds could be put to good use. Drumming began early and was a signal for the residents to go down to the nearby stream to bathe. Some women bathed in the big tub or two that each barracoon had. Women who chose to utilize the stream might rendezvous with a lover and slip away for a private moment.

Men had haircuts. Women had their hair done up in various styles. Teeth were cleaned with "strips of soap-tree bark." "The overseer and deputy overseer came into the barracoon and started chatting up the black women." The Chinese indentured workers remained aloof. There were lots of drumming and dancing. The *marimbula*, an African instrument, could be heard. (He says the white peasant *guajiros* did not like it). Peddlers came around.

Folks put on their Sunday best. This might include rawhide boots, red and green scarves, gold rings on fingers and ears and silver bracelets. These may have been bought from the general stores situated near the barracoons. These stores sold everything, including rum. They were often run by old Spanish army veterans and were constructed of wood and palm bark. Jute sacks served as seats. The owners, said Montejo, often cheated the Africans. Though some slave owners prohibited their enslaved from visiting these stores, others allowed their Africans to visit them during the daylight hours. Some might exceptionally allow their enslaved to visit the shops (which also doubled as taverns) in the evening.

In St. Croix, recreation could include stick fighting, which the government unsuccessfully legislated against. New Year's Day was an especially big occasion in St. Croix (and in several other islands too). Carnival-type processions paraded through the streets. The enslaved serenaded their owners in exchange for gifts. Songs of social commentary and protest were sung, some alleging that the Danish king had granted a freedom which the local authorities were withholding. The Africans elected kings, queens, princes and princesses to preside over their dances.

A 1711 Jamaican law forbade the enslaved from "hawking and selling" goods except for provisions, fruits and other stipulated items. The penalty for transgression was up to thirty-one lashes. A 1735 law permitted enumerated items only with a written ticket from the owner. Still, as the eighteenth century wore on, the growing importance of provision markets to national economies tempered efforts to suppress them.

The ultimate official fear of provision grounds was doubtless that the self-actualization, self-confidence, sense of self-worth, access to money, access to news of the wider world and the huge gatherings they generated would eventually prove a ripe environment for dissatisfaction with the institution of slavery. People who cleared their "own" land, cultivated their crops without supervision, established markets that attracted large numbers of free people of all description, and did business with free people, even their own owners, as quasi-equals, probably would chafe at the bit of continued enslavement.

Large gatherings especially had often provided a cloak for conspiracy. This is partly why slave mobility was severely prescribed. A Havana slave ordinance from as early as 1574 typically prescribed thirty lashes for any enslaved person found outside without a pass after the curfew bell rang each night. In eighteenth-century Paramaribo no African could appear on the street or the river at night without a pass signed by his or her owner. Any caught without the proper documentation, Stedman noted, were "taken up, and infallibly flogged the next morning." When missionaries began converting the enslaved to Christianity in the early eighteenth century, unsupervised prayer meetings among the enslaved were vigorously suppressed.

These provision ground fears may perhaps have been realized with the Haitian Revolution (1791–1804). The revolution's planners came from a wide area and met regularly. Some, such as Jean-François and Boukman, appear to have been Maroons (enslaved who successfully escaped permanently from plantations). It is speculated that their meetings may have been facilitated by Sunday market passes, whether real or forged. (Forged passes were common in Saint Domingue). If this is so then the provision grounds would have given rise to the markets which would have provided the enslaved mobility and opportunity to gather unnoticed in fairly large numbers to plan the greatest revolution of the enslaved in history.

As important and impressive as provision grounds were, they did not exhaust the entrepreneurial spirit of the Africans. Some of the enslaved actually expanded into petty trading as avenues of capital mobilization with which to purchase their freedom. The urban enslaved, as will be seen shortly, had the best opportunities for doing this, though others also found ways to trade on their own behalf. One such was Olaudah Equiano, who worked as an enslaved seaman out of Montserrat for many years. Beginning with almost nothing, he used his tips to do a little trading on his own account. A tumbler in St. Eustatius, some turkeys in Savannah, Georgia, barrels of pork in Charleston, South Carolina, gin in St. Eustatius—these were some of the motley items that Equiano traded. He was predictably robbed on occasion since, as he put it, "being a Negro man, I could not oblige [a white man] to pay me." He nevertheless accumulated enough this way to eventually purchase his freedom.

While enslaved in Antigua, Mary Prince had a similar opportunity to demonstrate entrepreneurial initiative. "The way in which I made my money," she said, "was this."

> When my master and mistress went from
> home, as they sometimes did, and left me
> to take care of the house and premises,
> I had a good deal of time to myself, and
> made the most of it. I took in washing, and
> sold coffee and yams and other provisions
> to the captains of ships. I did not sit still
> idling during the absence of my owners;
> for I wanted, by all honest means, to earn
> money to buy my freedom. Sometimes
> I bought a hog cheap on board ship, and
> sold it for double the money on shore; and
> I also earned a good deal by selling coffee.
> By this means I by degrees acquired

a little cash. A gentleman also lent me some to help to buy my freedom—but when I could not get free he got it back again. His name was Captain Abbot.

FAMILY LIFE

The institution of family life came under severe stress during enslavement. Pseudoscientific notions of Africans as subhuman beasts incapable of feeling human love, grief and pain naturally helped harden white society to the distress caused by disregard for African families. The assault on enslaved families began in Africa itself, continued during the Middle Passage, was intensified during initial sale in the Caribbean and continued as long as slavery existed. Its effects lingered into the postslavery era.

Olaudah Equiano described in heart-wrenching language his forcible separation from his sister, his brief reuniting with her and a final separation, after which he never saw her again. All of this happened in Africa, before he ever saw a white man or a slave ship. The initial separation came as he and his sister, still young children, lay clinging to each other. "[S]he was torn from me," he reported, "and immediately carried away, while I was left in a state of distraction not to be described. I cried and grieved continually; and for several days I did not eat anything but what they forced into my mouth."

The siblings were later unexpectedly reunited: "As soon as she saw me she gave a loud shriek, and ran into my arms—I was quite overpowered: neither of us could speak; but, for a considerable time, clung to each other in mutual embraces, unable to do anything but weep. Our meeting affected all who saw us. . . ."

The joy of this reunion was short lived. The siblings were again wrenched apart, this time forever. The pain of these experiences haunted Equiano for the rest of his life. "Though you were early forced from my arms," he wrote to his long lost sister, "your image has been always riveted in my heart, from which neither *time nor fortune* have been able to remove it. . . ." He commended her to the protection of heaven, "if your youth and delicacy have not long fallen victims to the violence of the African trader, the pestilential stench of a Guinea ship, the lash and lust of a brutal and unrelenting overseer."

Families who traversed the Middle Passage together, and persons who became close quasi-families along the way, might suffer another traumatic separation on initial sale in the Caribbean. Several brothers were among Equiano's shipmates sold apart from one another in Bridgetown. "It was very moving," he recalled, "on this occasion to see and hear their cries at parting."

Though formal marriage was usually not permitted among the enslaved, nuclear families did exist wherever the enslaved could wrench this basic concession to decency from the system. Substantial numbers of nuclear families were found for the enslaved in Trinidad, Jamaica and the Bahamas.

Still, very often every obstacle was placed in the way of family formation. Esteban Montejo described the Cuba of his experience, where children were reared collectively in the infirmary. Wet nurses and cooks looked after them. Some never knew their parents, who may have been sold away to other plantations. At age six or seven they were moved from the infirmary to plantation gangs.

For those lucky enough to maintain some semblance of a nuclear family, life was not easy. The father might be on a different plantation with only limited access. The siblings might have different fathers, due to the realities of enslaved life. The sexual debauchery of mothers and daughters, the flogging of pregnant women, forcible slave breeding—all of these realities would have exacerbated already difficult enslaved life.

For those who were able to hold together a family through all of these vicissitudes, there was the ultimate dread of forcible separation. Siblings could be sold away from one another. Parents could be sold away from children. Families could be split apart and scattered for any number of reasons. Death of an owner might result in family members being bequeathed to different persons. An owner might sell to raise money to pay off a debt or avoid bankruptcy. The desire to be rid of an enslaved person deemed troublesome might result in sale away from his or her family.

Mary Prince's owner in Bermuda sold Mary (about twelve years old) and two younger sisters away from their mother and two brothers, in order to raise money for his wedding. Mary was placed in the

An enslaved family from Angola, drawn by J. G. Stedman in Suriname in the 1770s.

middle of a street, the better to be exposed to the scrutiny of would-be bidders at the auction. "I was soon surrounded by strange men," she recalled, "who examined and handled me in the same manner that a butcher would a calf or a lamb he was about to purchase, and who talked about my shape and size in like words—as if I could no more understand their meaning than the dumb beasts. I was then put up for sale." After she was sold to the highest bidder her anguish continued for, she said, "I then saw my sisters led forth, and sold to different owners; so that we had not the sad satisfaction of being partners in bondage. . . . It was a sad parting; one went one way, one another, and our poor mother went home with nothing."

Mary Prince was enslaved in the relatively small colony of Bermuda. She therefore knew where to find her mother. When the frequent and horrendous floggings inflicted by her new owners became too much to bear, she ran away to her mother. The powerlessness of first her mother, and later her father, to help her was as sad a reflection on enslavement as the breakup of her family and the brutality she had to endure. All her mother could do was hide her "up in a hole in the rocks" and bring her food late at night.

Her father, who lived some distance away, eventually heard of his daughter's plight. He felt unable to do anything but take her back to her owner and make the following pathetic plea: "Sir, I am sorry that my child should be forced to run away from her owner; but the treatment she has received is enough to break her heart. The sight of her wounds has nearly broke mine. I entreat you, for the love of God, to forgive her for running away, and that you will be a kind Master to her in future." As Mary Prince commented in her narrative, "I had run away to my mother; but mothers could only weep and mourn over their children, they could not save them from cruel masters—from the whip, the rope, and the cow-skin."

The only benefit of this sad return to Mary was no floggings for the rest of that day. She endured five more years of almost daily brutality until her owner shipped her off to the saltworks of Turks Island, there to endure further brutality and sleep "in a long shed, divided into narrow slips, like the stalls used for cattle."

Years later Mary's mother unexpectedly turned up in Turks Island with a party of enslaved persons brought there to work in the salt industry. It was a sad meeting. Her mother had gone mad on the way over. She brought with her a four-year-old, Mary's sister, who she was seeing for the first time.

Olaudah Equiano often witnessed the forcible breakup of families, not merely to different owners in the same island, but to other islands altogether, or even to North America. "Oftentimes my heart has bled at these partings," he said, "when the friends of the departed have been at the waterside, and with sighs and tears, have kept their eyes fixed on the vessel, till it went out of sight."

The strains on family life again intruded into Mary's reality when she married a free man in Antigua some years later. "We could not be married in the English [Anglican] Church," she explained. "English marriage is not allowed to slaves; and no free man can marry a slave woman." The Moravian Church married her, but her owner, spurred on by his wife, whipped her for getting married. "It made my husband sad to see me so ill-treated," Mary commented, but he could no more figure a way to protect her than her father had been able to.

Free people of color, as seen, were not exempt from the stresses imposed by slave society on family life. Some who could have been freed with a little luck or the active help of their white fathers, were instead abandoned to slavery. Stedman in Suriname almost intervened physically to try and rescue "a lovely mulatto girl, aged fourteen, who had been christened in 1775, and educated as a young lady," when he beheld her "dragged to court in chains, with her mother and a few more of her relations, the whole surrounded by a military guard." Her white father had died without securing her manumission. "Such were the fatal consequences of not having been timely emancipated;" Stedman observed, "and such were they that they made me tremble for my little boy." His friend the governor happily freed Stedman's little Johnny soon afterward, waiving the customary burdensome fees, as a special favor to Stedman.

While some white fathers manumitted their colored offspring and provided well for them, others added to the woes of family life by recklessly fathering and abandoning children. Stedman was aware of "near forty beautiful boys and girls . . . left to perpetual slavery by their parents of my acquaintance, and many of them without being so much as once enquired after at all." The most shocking aspect of this for Stedman was that "while the well-thinking few highly applauded my sensibility, many not only blamed, but publicly derided me for my paternal affection, which was called a weakness, a whim."

In addition to bemoaning the "harlotization" of colored women, J. B. Philippe pointed out that Governor Ralph Woodford of Trinidad imposed such excessive fees for marriage licenses on coloreds that poor members of their community were thereby encouraged into concubinage. Free coloreds were also susceptible to kidnap and sale into slavery, never to see their families again. "Why are parents to lose their children, brothers their sisters, or husbands their wives?" asked Olaudah Equiano of slave society. "Surely this is a new refinement in cruelty. . . ."

Where the enslaved had the opportunity to maintain family relationships, no matter how tenuous, there can be no question of their commitment to family. In the United States in the years after Emancipation in 1865, formerly enslaved African Americans could be seen wandering the country for years trying to relocate family members torn away during slavery. In the Caribbean those able to manumit themselves before Emancipation usually had as their first priority the effort to free their still-enslaved relatives. Like Mary Prince's parents, the enslaved tried to protect their abused relatives in whatever little way they could. The *Barbados Globe* ran an advertisement in 1829 for one Amelia, a light-skinned runaway. She had run away from a new purchaser and had returned to her mother and father. She was apprehended but promptly ran away again. Her owner suspected her father and associates were hiding her.

Englishman Hans Sloane in his *Natural History of Jamaica* (1707) testified to the power of family love among the enslaved. He wrote:

> The parents here, although their children are slaves for ever, yet have so great a love for them, that no master dare sell or give away one of their little ones, unless they care not whether their parents hang themselves or no. . . .

The efforts of some enslaved to bequeath their provision grounds to relatives has already been noted. An observer in early nineteenth-century Jamaica noted the practice among the enslaved of burying family members in specially landscaped gardens adjoining their huts.

AFRICAN CULTURAL SURVIVALS

While it is true that concerted efforts were made to eradicate, demonize and trivialize African culture, much of it managed to withstand and survive slavery. The naked Africans loaded on to slave ships clearly brought no tangible cultural objects with them. Even the amulets they wore were torn off and thrown overboard, though religious leaders among the enslaved in the Caribbean widely dispensed obias or amulets—"as some hypocrites sell absolution in Europe," Stedman noted. Some aspects of African culture, such as Cuban Santería and other religions, became synthesized with Western cultural forms over the years. Others emerged from legal proscription in new guises. The Trinidad steelband is the outstanding example of this, emerging, as it were, from many attempts to ban the African drum.

The impact of African culture on the Caribbean was felt from the very beginning. In 1503, just one year after the introduction of the first enslaved Africans, their importation was briefly halted. The Spaniards had become fearful of the influence of African "idolatry" on the indigenous people. This situation was rendered doubly significant by the fact that only Africans born in the Iberian Peninsula, and therefore theoretically Christians, were allowed in at that time. As the slave trade expanded and millions of people were brought direct from Africa, it can be presumed that the African cultural presence became more widespread.

Though a child of only eleven when transported to the Caribbean, Olaudah Equiano testified to the power of cultural memory: "[The] manners and customs of my country . . . had been implanted in me with great care," he recalled, "and made an impression on my mind, which time could not erase, and which all the adversity and variety of fortune I have since experienced served only to rivet and record. . . ."

Esteban Montejo in Cuba noted that the African-born old men on his plantation were treated with special respect by their fellow enslaved "because they knew all [African] religious matters."

The proportion of African-born persons in the enslaved populations varied over place and time. While the Creole element would have trended generally upward, this trend could on occasion be reversed. In 1804–1805, 54.4 percent of enslaved people in the Danish Virgin Islands were African born. There had in fact been an upsurge in importations in the decade leading up to the abolition of the slave trade in 1802, as owners scrambled to stock up before the ban went into effect. Most of the liberation soldiers in the Haitian Revolution were born in Africa.

African cultural survivals could be found in a large number of areas. Recreational activities were rife with evidence of such survivals. African dances such as the bongo and limbo survived slavery. These were often considered lewd and lascivious by Europeans, whose sense of morality could seemingly be turned on and off at will. "As for the dancing," wrote one observer of nineteenth-century Trinidad carnival, quoted by John Cowley, "it is nothing, but the most disgusting obscenity pure and simple, being an imitation more or less vigorous and lustful by the male and female performers of the motions of the respective sexes whilst in the act of coition."

In Suriname at least, Stedman found the local white women quite fond of these dances. "However indelicate" they might be, he said, the European and Creole white women enjoyed watching these dances as much as their men did, even though "such scenes would change an English woman's face from white to scarlet." He was referring here particularly to a dance he witnessed performed exclusively by Angolans, male and female. The dance consisted "from first to last in such a scene of wanton and lascivious gestures, as nothing but a heated imagination and a constant practice could enable them to perform." The dancers were accompanied by drums and clapping hands and the dancing went on for hours. Both white men and women crowded around the dancers in their zeal to witness the spectacle.

All over the Americas the culture of the despised Africans exercised this kind of fascination over Europeans and resulted in time in the domination of popular culture by such African-derived and often-banned art forms as calypso, samba, reggae, salsa, blues, jazz, meringue, tango (from Argentina), steel-band and others. The sexually suggestive "wining" that continues to be a fixture of Caribbean dance was doubtless an element in the "lascivious" performance that Stedman saw.

Calypso music was found to retain some of the stylistic features of West African Yoruba songs, such as the repetition of the first two lines in traditional calypsoes. Stick fighting (cudgeling), documented during slavery in Suriname, Trinidad, Dominica, St. Croix and elsewhere, has occasionally remained a vibrant martial art, notably in Trinidad. African musical instruments such as the banjo found their way to the Caribbean.

Various *lingua francas* and vernaculars, such as the French-influenced *patois* of Haiti, St. Lucia, Martinique, Guadeloupe, Grenada, Trinidad and elsewhere, and the Patwa of Jamaica, *Creolesk* in the Danish Virgin Islands, *Sranan Tongo* in Suriname and Papiamentu in Curaçao, retained West African grammatical and linguistic influences. Sometimes the same words might appear in more than one of these vernaculars. Stedman, who pronounced himself a master of the Surinamese vernacular, mentioned at least two such words. His "ananassy tory" was obviously the "nancy story" of Trinidad and the Anansi stories of other territories and their original Ghana. His "peekeeneenee," which he defined as "very small," was obviously the pickney (young child) of Jamaica and picaninny (used derisively by Europeans) of elsewhere in the Caribbean and West Africa.

Berbice Dutch Creole, an amalgam of the Zeeland dialect of Dutch, the Ijo language of the Ijaw people in modern Nigeria, Arawakan and Guyana Creolese (the dominant Guyana vernacular), was officially declared extinct in 2005. The last speaker of this language, which survived in Berbice, Guyana, was one Bertha Bell who died in 2005 at approximately 104 years old. Skepi Creole Dutch, spoken in Essequibo, now part of Guyana, officially became extinct in 1998. It was an entirely different language from Berbice Dutch. Rupununi Creole, said to be mutually unintelligible with the Berbice Dutch and Skepi Creole, was also spoken in Guyana.

By 1770 two ABC books had been produced in *Creolesk* (also known as *Negerhollands* or Negro Dutch) in the Danish Virgin Islands, together with a grammar, hymnal and catechism. A *Creolesk* translation of the New Testament followed in 1779 and an unpublished translation of the Old Testament in 1781. *Creolesk* readers were published in 1798 and 1827, more hymnals in 1799 and 1823, a children's Bible in 1822 and a catechism in 1827. The last native speaker of this language died in 1987. J. J. Thomas in Trinidad published a *Creole Grammar* in 1869.

The prenuptial *kwe-kwe* ceremony in Guyana has also survived slavery. The Anansi folktales of Ghana are likewise part of the cultural patrimony of the Caribbean, from Suriname to Jamaica and beyond. West African agricultural practices led to the introduction of rice farming into Guyana. West African–derived modes of women's dress have become the traditional folk dress of many territories.

The Caribbean *susu* (*esusu* of West Africa) has survived as an ingenious method of capital mobilization among poor communities. The carnivals, jonkonnus and masquerades which flourish all over the Caribbean all have large elements of African cultural survival. The wood carvings of Haiti, Suriname and elsewhere bear obvious testimony to their African origin. The same is true for calabash decorations. Stedman noted in Suriname that the Africans "generally adorn them by carving on the outer skin many fantastical figures, and filling up the vacancies with chalk-dust, which sometimes has a very pretty effect." African military strategies among the mostly African-born soldiers of the successful Haitian Revolution contributed to the triumph of that epochal event. Sometimes the survivals have been so seemingly insignificant as to be easily overlooked—the institution of "Saturday soup" in West Africa and the Caribbean, for instance, or the practice by fruit vendors of peeling their oranges and piling them into little pyramids as they vend them from wooden trays on the roadside.

Esteban Montejo documented many of these everyday cultural retentions in barracoon life in Cuba. He recalled the *margombe*, a large pot containing supernatural powers. People made offerings to the pot and asked for health and other favors. The Africans also made *enkangues*, charms of cemetery earth.

"When a master punished a slave," Montejo remembered, "the others would collect a little earth and put it in the pot. With the help of this earth they could make the master fall sick or bring some harm upon his family. . . . This was how the Congolese revenged themselves upon their master."

Montejo described the *marimbula*, a "very small" musical instrument "made of wickerwork." It carried a large sound despite its size, and was used to accompany Congo drums. He mentioned a dance done by "French" enslaved persons to the accompaniment of two big drums and songs sung in patois. Stedman documented eighteen African instruments in Suriname—flutes, "trumpets of war," a guitar-like instrument, the conch shell, and various drums and other percussion instruments.

Montejo also described some aspects of religious practices in the barracoons. The two main religious traditions there were the Congo and the Lucumí (the Yorubas of present day Nigeria). He considered the Congoes the more important. Montejo mentioned several Congolese words as he described the activities of the Congo-born *chicherekú* (priest) who could cast spells and even induce death. "The Congolese," he said, "were more involved with witchcraft than the Lucumí who had more to do with the saints and with God." The Lucumí spoke "in their own tongue" and foretold the future with the aid of *diloggunes*, round white shells from Africa. They also used *obi*, sacred coconut shells. Obatalá was their chief "saint" and he recalled their greeting of "Alafia" ("all is well"). The Lucumí wore white. They kept images of their gods in the barracoons. Changó (Shango), god of thunder and Yemaya, the water goddess, were carved in wood. (The water goddess, Watra Mama in Suriname and Maman Dlo in Trinidad, was present all over the Caribbean.) Elegguá, god of the crossroads, was made of cement. The Lucumí also made saints' marks on walls with charcoal or chalk. Montejo's observations on the Lucumí religion (also known as Orisa and Shango) would also be recognizable to adherents elsewhere in the Caribbean.

Some of the everyday uses of African religions in Cuba, such as the preparation of love potions, have survived in the popular Caribbean imagination. An aspirant to a woman's charms, Montejo said, might grind up a hummingbird's heart to powder and slip it into the woman's tobacco. Similar stratagems have been immortalized in several twentieth-century Trinidad calypsoes.

One of the most widely noted African religious beliefs in the Caribbean was the ability of some persons to escape enslavement by flying back to Africa. Slave ship crews went to great lengths, as has been seen, to prevent Africans from committing suicide to hasten their flight home. Montejo said he heard, but did not believe, stories of frequent African suicides in Cuba. Cuban Africans preferred to fly back, he said, without suicide. The Masundi Congoes, he said, flew the most.

The first incursions of Protestant missionaries into the slave quarters in the eighteenth century met protracted cultural resistance. Even after ostensibly accepting Christianity, many Africans continued to venerate their traditional gods. In Jamaica supposedly Christianized Africans continued to display African religious paraphernalia in their houses and to venerate the silk cotton tree, as they did in Suriname and elsewhere.

Humphrey Lamur has documented the persistence of African religious practice on the large (240 enslaved persons) Vossenburg sugar plantation in Suriname before Emancipation in 1863. Large wooden religious carvings for group worship and smaller icons for individual devotion proliferated in the slave quarters. These included the *kwa kwa banji*, small wooden benches which doubled as drums. The priest/obeahman/lukuman divined causes of sickness and death and prescribed medicines. A *wissiman* could cause illness or death. The enslaved worshipped Andranga ("The Most Secret"). Andranga's shrine was an hour's walk into the forest. Africans from neighboring plantations also attended his ceremonies.

The enslaved also performed *pakasaka,* a religious ritual, in their huts. They worshipped *Mamasneki,* a snake deity. They continued to do all this while attending Moravian Christian missionary meetings.

Although Islam is not indigenous to West Africa, it can be considered an African religion for this discussion. It had been practiced in some parts of the area for

near 600 years when the European trade in enslaved persons began. The Muslim Almoravid empire which ruled Spain in the eleventh and twelfth centuries stretched from historical Ghana (modern-day Senegal and Mali) to North Africa and eventually to Spain. The Almoravid conquest inevitably brought West Africans as conquerors into Spain.

Some Muslim Africans found themselves, via the transatlantic trade, transported to North and South America and the Caribbean. Their numbers and the extent to which they were able to preserve their religion in the Caribbean have not been definitively established. There were, however, several communities of free Muslims in Trinidad in the waning years of slavery, principally composed of disbanded veterans of the West India Regiment, who were settled there between 1817 and 1825. These practiced their religion. Some were literate in Arabic.

The Europeans expended much energy banning expressions of African cultural survival, both during and long after the end of slavery. Obeahmen and obeahwomen were outlawed in St. Vincent when it was discovered that they were dispensers of poisons used to kill slave owners and their families and associates. Stedman described the female African oracles or "prophetesses" whose work was banned, often without success by the Dutch authorities. They had the power to command devotees to kill their owners. Both before and after Emancipation the Dutch jailed Africans in Suriname for participation in "pagan festivals." Obeah was still banned in Trinidad and elsewhere in the twentieth century, though this did not prevent members of officially Christianized society from resorting to its practitioners. In Scott's Hall, Jamaica, in 1935, one Samuel Pink was fined 6 pounds for practicing obeah.

African horns and drums were already banned in Jamaica by 1707. Sometimes, as in the case of the "big drum" in Trinidad, the banned instrument or practice never recovered. Very often the power of African cultural retention survived the legal bannings, even where survival drove the African practices underground. Sometimes, as in Cuban Santería, African cultural and religious manifestations even attracted sizeable European followings. Haitian Voodoo, derived from West Africa, was actually imported back into Togo in its Caribbeanized form.

Even after independence in the late twentieth century, independent governments did not always move quickly to eradicate these legal vestiges of a repressive past. President Forbes Burnham of independent Guyana removed the colonial ban on obeah in the 1970s. In Trinidad the 1917 ban on the African-influenced Shouter Baptists was removed in 1951, before independence. In Trinidad, nevertheless, a 1980 compilation of laws still included a Summary Offences Act which banned the playing of African instruments (but not those of other ethnicities) at night. The law defined African instruments as "any drum, gong, tambour, bangée [banjo], chac-chac, or other similar instruments." The law also banned nighttime performances of the "bungo" (bongo) dance, traditionally performed by Africans at wakes. The police were authorized to enter any house or yard where the bongo was being danced and to seize the offending instruments. African culprits offending against European cultural preferences were liable to a fine of $400.00. Police were still incongruously trying to enforce this law against African drumming in Port of Spain during Emancipation celebrations near the end of the twentieth century.

URBAN ENSLAVED

Urban areas could also have substantial numbers of enslaved, many of them women. This practice was already well enough established to be recognized in the Havana slave ordinance of 1574. "Many citizens hire Negroes to work for wages," said this law. "Such Negroes are employed in different occupations, and go about like free men, working at what they please, and at the end of the week or month they hand over their wages to their masters. Others run lodging houses to board travelers, and have in such houses their own Negro women. . . ." Although tavern keepers were generally prohibited from selling wine to enslaved persons, the law made an exception for this class of the Havana enslaved. "[S]ince many slaves . . . work for wages which they bring to their masters whom they support thereby," the law explained, "and those Negroes travel far to work, and sometimes need to drink wine, the tavern-keepers may allow them to drink not more than half a pint in their taverns. . . ."

According to Monk Lewis, a Jamaican planter, male mixed-race enslaved tended to be artisans. Some were domestics in white households. Some owners who owned no plantations bought slaves for the express purpose of hiring them out. Some of the urban enslaved were runaways, often protected by the urban free black community, into which they could easily blend. Some plantation enslaved came into town periodically for market. Many were hucksters/higglers, petty traders who sold a variety of goods, including grass for horse fodder, firewood, sweetmeats and fruits. Urban enslaved typically needed passes to legally move around the towns. By dint of hard work and thrift, they might sometimes save enough to eventually buy their freedom. Since they were enslaved persons, however, in societies where they had no rights, their thrift could often be frustrated by dishonest whites. These might not pay them for their work, take their fodder without paying, flog them if they complained and so on.

Olaudah Equiano, enslaved for ten years, mostly in Montserrat, and sailing regularly between the islands and North America as an enslaved seaman, observed many of these injustices. He visited fifteen of the Caribbean territories altogether. Speaking of the enslaved women who brought fodder for sale in town, he remarked,

> Nothing is more common than for the white people on this occasion to take the grass from them without paying for it; and not only so, but too often also, to my knowledge, our clerks, and many others, at the same have committed acts of violence on the poor, wretched, and helpless females; whom I have seen for hours stand crying to no purpose, and get no redress or pay of any kind.

"Is not this," Equiano commented, "one common and crying sin enough to bring down God's judgment on the islands? He tells us the oppressor and the oppressed are both in his hands; and if these are not the poor, the broken-hearted, the blind, the captive, the bruised, which our saviour speaks of, who are they?"

In Charlotte Amalie, St. Thomas, two-thirds of the town's inhabitants in 1797 were enslaved, though the number declined thereafter. In eighteenth-century St. Thomas, as elsewhere, the authorities sought continuously to control the activities of the urban enslaved. Free and enslaved urban blacks formed a sort of underworld which white European elements sometimes participated in. A 1741 St. Croix ordinance accordingly prohibited whites from drinking and gambling with the enslaved. A 1774 ordinance prohibited whites from attending dances where enslaved persons were present. The penalty for transgression was fourteen days' imprisonment on bread and water.

The purely human qualities displayed by the enslaved in general, in spite of their condition, received a characteristically sympathetic appraisal from Stedman. The Africans, he said, were prone to great gratitude when circumstances warranted. But they could be ferociously vengeful if done wrong. They were modest. He never saw an African man so much as offer to kiss a woman in public. They showed a touching "maternal tenderness." Women breast-fed their babies for two years and abstained from sex in that period. "The cleanliness of the Negro nation is peculiarly remarkable," he observed, as the early Spaniards had noted for the indigenous people, "as they bathe above three times a day. The Congo tribe in particular are so fond of the water, that they may, not improperly, be called amphibious animals."

The Africans, he said, were "spirited and brave, patient in adversity, meeting death or torture with the most undaunted fortitude. . . . [N]o Negro sighs, groans, or complains, though expiring in the midst of surrounding flames." He had never seen an African shed a tear, he said, though they would beg for mercy if about to be flogged without just cause.

FREE PEOPLE OF COLOR

Widespread white-initiated miscegenation inevitably resulted in sizeable mixed-race populations. "Colored" and "mulatto" became generic terms for this group. "Mulatto" supposedly derived from mule, the unnatural barren offspring of two dissimilar species, the horse and ass. It more narrowly defined the result of a black and white parent. Vincent Ogé,

leader of a colored revolt against the whites of Saint Domingue in 1790, considered "mulatto" an "injurious epithet."

In societies based unabashedly on race, the intermediate status of free coloreds, between whites and enslaved blacks, was assured. And since phenotypical closeness to whites generally ensured higher status, an amazing welter of names developed, to demarcate various gradations of racial mixture. The precise number and meaning of terms and the terms themselves varied from place to place. A quadroon would normally be the offspring of a "mulatto" and a white person. An octoroon would be the result of a quadroon and a white. A "mulatto" and a black would produce a sambo. But even this relatively simplified scheme was susceptible of variations.

Trinidad's official slave registry of 1813 listed the following racial categories in descending order of privilege: white, quadroon, mestee, costee, mulatto, cabre, mongrel, sambo and black. The Martinique-born French historian, Moreau de Saint-Méry (1750–1819) listed 128 legally recognized color categories for the French colonies. John G. Stedman, the indefatigable and irrepressible observer of 1770s Suriname society, drew a diagram of Suriname's color gradations.

Some of the coloreds became very rich, more so than many of the white colonists. Their white fathers, forefathers and benefactors had often provided them, as seen, with a formidable head start—plantations, money, European educations, even enslaved Africans. Some have suggested that the *affranchis* (free people of color, including free blacks) may have owned one-third of the land-based wealth and a quarter of the enslaved persons in Saint Domingue by 1789. They comprised 45 percent of the population of France's flagship colony, the richest of any nation in the world.

The material conditions of coloreds varied widely. Olaudah Equiano cited Nevis resident James Tobin, who witnessed half-white Martiniquans being worked "in the fields like beasts of burden" by a French father who deliberately bred them for this purpose. Olaudah's own experience corroborated Tobin's account. As in North America, free coloreds and blacks were always vulnerable to kidnapping and sale into slavery.

Though people of mixed race largely defined the category of free people of color in the popular imagination, the category also included varying numbers of free blacks. Many of these were the manumitted concubines of white men. They might be the mothers of free coloreds. Other freed blacks would often have achieved their status through some meritorious acts benefiting white society. They may have helped retrieve runaways, or fought valiantly against foreign invaders, or informed on enslaved conspirators, or perhaps saved the life of a white person. Artisans or others might save enough from their earnings to purchase freedom for themselves and family. Sometimes an unscrupulous owner might "free" an old and infirm worker rather than provide medical benefits. And of course there were the runaways, who took their own freedom, but who are not included in the free colored communities discussed here.

Free blacks were usually lumped together with coloreds in population statistics and it is therefore not always easy to determine their precise numbers. In Barbados between 1825 and 1829 free coloreds and blacks were 53 percent and 47 percent, respectively of the free people of color. Separate free black (pardo) and free colored (moreno) militias existed throughout Spanish Colonial America by the eighteenth century. The same was true for Martinique, Suriname and Curaçao.

On the eve of British West Indian Emancipation, in the 1820s and 1830s, Trinidad had one of the highest percentages of free coloreds and blacks. According to figures compiled by Carl Campbell, 81.9 percent of Trinidad's free population were free people of color in 1825. They constituted 39.2 percent of the nonwhite population. By comparison Grenada in 1826 had 82.4 percent free colored and blacks in its free population, with 13.7 percent of the nonwhites free. Figures for Dominica, St. Vincent and the Grenadines in 1823 were 75.4 and 16.0 percent respectively; ; for St. Lucia (1824), 75.4 and 21.2 percent; Guyana (1829), 67.7 and 8.4 percent; Suriname (free coloreds only—free blacks not included), 66.0 and 9.3 percent in 1830; St. Kitts (1826), 57.3 percent and 11.3 percent; Martinique (1826), 52.0 and 11.7 percent; Jamaica (1820), 48.5 and 8.8 percent; Curaçao (1817, free coloreds only),

44.6 and 24.8 percent; Puerto Rico (1827), 38.2 and 74.5 percent; Cuba (1817), 30.1 and 33.2 percent.Barbados (1825) had the lowest numbers of free persons of color, both as percentages of the free population (23.6 percent) and of the nonwhite population (6.0 percent).

Trinidad, an underpopulated frontier colony in 1783, underwent a rapid advance in its nonwhite population thereafter. By its Cedula of Population in 1783 Spanish Trinidad began the process by inviting in Roman Catholic "French Creoles" from other islands to populate the largely empty colony. The principal inducement offered was the grant of free land. While most of the beneficiaries were white, about 5 percent of the free land distributed between 1783 and 1812 went to the free colored and black French Creoles. Each free person of color received 5 *quarrés* of land (1 *quarré* equal 3.20 acres). Each white person received 10 *quarrés*. This was nevertheless enough to constitute Trinidad's French Creole free persons of color into an important landowning class. They concentrated in the Naparimas in Southern Trinidad where, by 1813, they owned 35 percent of the estates and 30.1 percent (862) of the field slaves. Two of the three sugar estates with more that 100 field slaves were owned by colored proprietors. There were at least thirty-eight free colored proprietors in the area, collectively accounting for seventeen sugar estates, three coffee estates, one in coffee and provisions and ten in provisions. Others owned land in other parts of the country. Of these free coloreds, 65.2 percent lived in rural areas.

Trinidad's high percentage of free people of color was fed also from other nontraditional sources. African American veterans of the British-American War of 1812 were relocated to Trinidad. They had abandoned their enslavement to join the British forces attacking their hated American slave masters. After the war the British shipped them out to save them from re-enslavement by the Americans. They settled in the "Company Villages" of Southern Trinidad and were given some land, some of which had to be in provisions. Free demobilized veterans of the mercenary West India Regiment were also settled, with land, in Manzanilla, in the east of the island.

The white ruling race simultaneously welcomed the coloreds as a buffer against the blacks and tried their best to keep them in a subordinate position. In Saint Domingue they were forcibly impressed into the *maréchaussée*, a police force that hunted fugitive slaves, among other things. After three years in the *maréchaussée* they were forced to serve in the local militia. There they had to provide their own weapons, ammunition and uniforms, and to serve at the pleasure of their white commanders. They could not serve in the navy and regular army, could not practice law or medicine or hold public office. They were segregated in public places. They could be enslaved for certain offences. They were unjustly treated in the courts. A free man of color who struck a white man could have his right arm judicially severed.

The disabilities faced by the free coloreds and blacks in Trinidad were cataloged in exhaustive detail by Jean-Baptiste Philippe, a leader of the community. In 1823 he travelled to London to present a petition to the secretary of state for the colonies, Earl Bathurst, seeking relief from the discriminations suffered by his community.

Philippe, the largest estate owner among Trinidad's free persons of color, also owned more enslaved Africans than any of his class. He had qualified as a medical doctor at the University of Edinburgh around 1815, at the age of about nineteen. He died in July 1829, aged thirty-three, just before the final emancipation of the free people of color of Trinidad.

Apart from being one of the largest free colored populations in the Caribbean, the Trinidad coloreds also thought themselves the most liberally treated, prior to the English conquest of 1797. The Spanish had allowed old anticolored laws to become obsolete and had enacted others extending equal treatment. Free blacks and coloreds had been granted commissions in the Spanish colonial militia. The local Spanish administration had rejected the advice of the initiator of the Cedula project, Grenadian Roume de St. Laurent, that post-Cedula black and colored immigrants should receive only half as much land as whites. The authorities in Spain overruled Trinidad on this point. The treaty of capitulation in 1797 had likewise sought to preserve the relative equality enjoyed by free people of color under the Spaniards.

With the coming of the British, however, the coloreds found themselves "degraded by the illiberal prejudices of the whites," as Philippe complained.

A new law modeled on the French *Code Noir* was introduced. Free coloreds now needed permission to have parties at night. They were not to invite enslaved persons to such parties. They were to be conscripted into the marshalsey (m*aréchausée*) under degrading conditions. Formerly commissioned militia officers were relegated to the ranks under a white sergeant. Those who objected to these developments were subjected to hanging, jail or banishment.

In 1804 free people of color were required to present proof of manumission or be enslaved. By an 1810 proclamation free coloreds had to carry a lighted lantern if they ventured out at night. At one point the English seemed ready to revive an obsolete law allowing amputation at the wrists of any free person of color striking a white person. Private persons were allowed to extra-judicially flog free coloreds with impunity. An old colored man of almost eighty was flogged in this way. In 1819 all enslaved persons and free persons of color were to be off the streets after 10 PM. Neither group could sell goods without obtaining onerous permissions. Unqualified and undocumented white persons were allowed to practice medicine, while qualified free coloreds were prevented from doing so. One Dr. Francis Williams, who qualified in London at the Royal College of Surgeons, was rejected by Trinidad's Medical Board, on the ground that his enslaved birth would compromise the dignity of the profession. He later appealed successfully to the secretary of state in London. Under Governor Ralph Woodford, the most virulent perpetrator of these indignities, no free person of color was to be addressed as "Mr." or "Mrs." at government gatherings. Coloreds could not assemble together. A young people's literary society was prevented from gathering and the owner of the house fined. In 1820, John Lynch, a twelve-year-old freed colored boy, was sentenced to fifty lashes and two months' hard labor for petty theft.

Trinidad's coloreds were jim-crowed in Protestant churches and in burial grounds, including Port of Spain's Lapeyrouse Cemetery. When a coastal steamer, appropriately named the *Woodford*, was introduced on December 20, 1818, free coloreds and blacks were segregated into an area near the chimney. (This was the first steam vessel in the "West Indies," according to contemporary Trinidad historian E. L. Joseph.) As in the more famous North American case of Martin Luther King's Birmingham Bus Boycott in 1955, the Trinidadians successfully boycotted the ships. The "partition which prejudice had erected," said Philippe, was removed.

Philippe was also upset at the continued sexual exploitation of colored women. "The colored females, for the most part over the West Indies," he lamented, "have been nurtured on [concubinage]. . . . they are destined to be harlots of white men or others. . . ." Their families had little or no redress against the debauchery of their women. Practically as he was writing, the itinerant Englishman, H. N. Coleridge, seemed to mock Philippe's concern for the virtue of colored women, with a paean of praise for the nonwhite beauties he saw in Trinidad. "I think for gait, gestures, shape and air, the finest women in the world may be seen on a Sunday in Port-of-Spain. The rich and gay costumes of these nations sets off the dark countenances of their mulattoes infinitely better than the plain dress of the English." This was in his *Six Months in the West Indies*, published in 1826.

Those few white men who wished to do the right thing by marrying colored women were frustrated in their efforts. An old Frenchman in Trinidad who wished to marry his concubine of many years on her deathbed was refused this privilege by a priest. A young Frenchman "desirous of espousing a virtuous woman," was likewise refused permission. He had to go to Grenada to get married. Philippe nevertheless held out hope that the increasing prosperity of the free people had brought some diminution in the vulnerability of their women.

Philippe also advocated for Trinidad's nontraditional free people, the African Americans, ex–West India Regiment soldiers, Venezuelan peasant "peons," and the indigenous peoples. He considered the treatment of his own Naparima planters "trifling," compared with the suffering borne by the indigenous and peons. The indigenous at the Roman Catholic mission at Savanna Grande were "infinitely more to be pitied than . . . African slaves." They were whipped

almost daily. The Roman Catholic priest in charge, one Fr. Francisco Carrillo, debauched the indigenous girls under his care. Mothers who protested were stripped naked and "castigated." Protesting fathers were placed in the stocks and whipped.

Despite his own slave ownership, Philippe demonstrated great sympathy for the enslaved. He defended them against pseudoscientific allegations of inmate inferiority. He particularly rejected the Hamitic Myth, which tried to use the biblical story of Ham, the supposed progenitor of the African race, to support enslavement of Africans. Philippe denounced the slave trade, "by which so many myriads of victims were annually sacrificed at the shrine of avarice. . . ."

The picture of Trinidad's free coloreds suggested by these remarks may possibly contrast with Toussaint L'Ouverture's view of Saint Domingue's free coloreds. "As . . . anticipated," he wrote in 1799, "the men of color, many of whom were slaveholders, had only been using the blacks to gain their own political demands."

The Trinidad petition of 1823 was far from unique. Petitions had long been a principal means of protest by free populations of color, as they chafed under the weight of their myriad disabilities. The year 1823 was an important one for such petitions, as a commission of inquiry into the administration of justice in the British West Indies toured the area in 1823 and 1824.

In Montserrat in 1813, sixty free coloreds petitioned against the invalidation of their electoral votes. In 1815 free people of color in the British Virgin Islands petitioned against a law limiting them to the ownership of eight acres of land and fifteen enslaved persons. In 1811 their Barbadian counterparts petitioned for the right to testify in judicial proceedings. In Martinique in 1789 authorities hanged a white man for assisting free coloreds with a petition. In St. Pierre, Martinique, in 1790 a petition for the right of free coloreds to participate in the Corpus Christi parade led to riots. The French authorities hanged thirty-four free colored militiamen for participating in these protests.

Despite inevitable variations from place to place, the discriminations described for Trinidad were more or less replicated everywhere. In the non-Spanish islands discriminatory legislation targeting free people of color began appearing in the early eighteenth century, as the community's numbers began to approach critical mass. Discriminatory legislation was widespread by the late eighteenth century.

Freed people were banned from a variety of professions. Medicine was prominent among these. Cuba either banned outright or made difficult the practice of medicine, surgery and pharmacy. Freed Cubans had to apply for permits to engage in any trades save farming. They could not trade in gold or silver. They could not be priests, lawyers or holders of various prestige positions. St. Kitts and Grenada also kept freed people out of medicine.

Exclusion from the professions and priesthood in the Spanish colonial possessions went back to the sixteenth century. In the Anglican Church in Barbados and elsewhere nonwhites sat in segregated seating, could not be ministers and had a segregated communion ceremony. Like early black police in the southern United States, who could not arrest white people, nonwhite Barbadian teachers could not teach white children. Nor could nonwhite militias in Curaçao intervene in white people's business.

Freed persons generally could not vote in islands such as Barbados, St. Kitts and Grenada, which had elected assemblies. Nor could they testify against whites, serve on juries, hold public office or be magistrates or justices of the peace. As in the United States, freed people in Curaçao, St. Kitts, Grenada, Cuba and elsewhere had to carry lighted lanterns at night, as they had to in Trinidad. They were widely banned from carrying sticks or other actual or potential weapons. In Cuba a freed person needed one white man to accompany him for every eight head of cattle he drove through the streets. As in Trinidad and the American South, Barbadian whites generally did not dignify freed people with titles such as "Mr.," "Mrs." and "Miss." .

Freed people generally could not hold meetings, dances, weddings or funerals without special permission. In Curaçao they could not play music or buy liquor after 9 PM. Cuban self-help groups ("cabildos") were severely restricted. Free people of color were segregated everywhere, in the militias, in libraries and after death in cemeteries. In Barbados they could not join white literary associations.

As previously noted, enslaved people were often given the kinds of fanciful and outlandish names sometimes given to pets. In Martinique, Guadeloupe and Saint Domingue they were forbidden, upon manumission, from assuming the family names of white people. Martiniquans therefore evolved the practice, upon manumission, of converting their mothers' first names into surnames.

As the numbers of freed people increased in the latter eighteenth century, manumission fees became widespread. A Grenada law of 1767, as quoted by Edward Cox, was designed to prevent "the Further Sudden Encrease [sic] of Freed Negroes and Mulattoes." In Martinique persons were often sent overseas for manumission to jurisdictions with less onerous manumission taxes. On their return they were not treated as fully freed and formed a *Soi-disant Libres* (nominally free) class, between the fully enslaved and the locally manumitted. A 1764 law sought to end the practice of seeking freedom overseas.

Inheritance taxes eliminated or circumscribed receipt of property via will from white fathers. Various eighteenth- and nineteenth-century laws in Guadeloupe and Martinique prevented the few white men so inclined from marrying colored women. Similar laws or unwritten understandings existed elsewhere. In 1781, authorities in Suriname wrote to Holland for advice on whether to allow a white man to marry a black woman. They pointed out in their covering note that the woman was wealthy and her money would more than likely revert to the white race. Holland found no legal basis for withholding permission. This was a mere three years after Stedman returned to Europe without his beloved Joanna. Her fear of the social repercussions of returning to Europe with him were clearly not unfounded.

Several other attempts were made to prevent the acquisition of wealth by freed persons. A proposed Barbados law of 1803 to limit property holding (including enslaved persons) among coloreds did not pass. Edward Cox reports two colored women being denied permission to purchase land in St. George's, Grenada, in 1773. The British Virgin Islands restricted land and ownership of enslaved persons, as already noted. Nonwhites there could not be legal freeholders, but needed a white freeholder to represent them. Laws were introduced (e.g., in St. Kitts in 1763) attempting to prevent free people from accumulating capital through huckstering.

These discriminations all came out of the similar circumstances that would eventually evolve into the segregated American South and apartheid in South Africa. In the Caribbean, as elsewhere, blacks and coloreds unable to participate in white society, often formed their own clubs, sporting groups, literary associations and the like. Barbadian freed people had a "company to act plays" in 1805 and their own theatre, the Lyceum, in Bridgetown by 1828.

The question of ownership of enslaved persons among free people of color is widely noted in the literature, but mostly in passing without analysis. N. A. T. Hall says that freed people owned about 30 percent of the enslaved in Charlotte Amalie around 1802. Léo Elisabeth says that free people of color owned 12,348 of the 76,117 enslaved persons in Martinique in 1844. Jerome Handler and Arnold Sio suggest that freed people owned probably only a small proportion of the enslaved persons in Barbados in 1803. In Trinidad, as noted earlier, freed persons were significant owners of enslaved persons in the years leading up to Emancipation. Edward Cox noted 24 colored landowners in Grenada owning 385 enslaved persons in 1772, for an average of 16 enslaved per holding. Whites owned seventy-eight enslaved persons per holding. In 1833 in St. Kitts, Cox reports eleven "identifiable free coloreds" owning seventy-two enslaved persons.

When the Danish ship *Fredensborg* arrived in St. Croix in 1768 from the Gold Coast, one Captain Peter Tongerloe, a free black and Maria Elizabeth, a free colored, purchased one enslaved African each. Tongerloe owned a small plantation with nine enslaved Africans. He had a fine house in town.

Stedman noted in Suriname that an exceptional few urban enslaved artisans were able to buy their own freedom and even purchase enslaved people. One blacksmith named Joseph accumulated money but refused to buy his freedom, because of the taxes and other expenses involved. He preferred to stay with an indulgent owner and use his money to buy some enslaved of his own.

Inheritance of enslaved persons from white fathers and lovers seems to have been the major initial reason for black and colored slaveholding. Those who inherited sometimes subsequently augmented their holdings via purchase. Many freed persons acquired their own families as enslaved persons as a means of rescuing them from white owners. Once they acquired family members they were often unable to officially free them due to the prohibitive manumission taxes. Léo Elisabeth was able to document this reality in Martinique from a perusal of notarial records and parish registers.

There may be some tenuous similarity between inheritance of enslaved persons by freed persons in the Caribbean and the mulatto slaving chiefs of West Africa. There appears to be no evidence however of freed Caribbean people developing into a specialist slave-owning and -trafficking class, as happened in West Africa.

N. A. T. Hall has tentatively suggested that freed-person slaveholders could be very cruel and that there is evidence of marronage from them. Haitian revolutionary leader Toussaint L'Ouverture, though allied with the free coloreds on occasion, considered them unreliable opportunists. His successor, Jean-Jacques Dessalines, who led Haiti to freedom in 1804, initially belonged to a white Frenchman before being bought by a black owner, from whom he took (and kept) his surname, Dessalines. After the revolution Dessalines loved his former black owner sufficiently to take him into his house and give him a job. Jean-Baptiste Philippe of Trinidad, as seen, attacked the institution of slavery. Edward Cox has shown that Ralph Cleghorn, the most prominent colored person in St. Kitts, freed his enslaved people, around 1829–1830. He then tried unsuccessfully to become "Protector of Slaves," a position established in the ameliorative buildup to Emancipation.

A Jamaican law of 1733, unique in the British West Indies, recognized as legally white anyone three generations removed from African ancestry. As late as the First World War (1914–1918), the British were still attempting to legally define whiteness. Only whites could be officers in the newly formed British West Indies Regiment. Whites were defined as persons with 1/16 or 1/32 African blood or less. In Puerto Rico, coloreds could buy certificates of whiteness. The distinctions between blacks and coloreds could also be made fluid by considerations of money. A popular Caribbean saying asserted that a rich black was a "mulatto" and a poor "mulatto" was black.

Free persons of color began to get some legislative relief in the years leading up to Emancipation of the enslaved, as their agitation, the increasing threat of rebellion from the enslaved and the growing humanitarian sentiment in Europe all combined in their favor.

In the British territories, full emancipation for free people of color came in 1829 to Trinidad. Jamaica followed in 1830 with the Disabilities Act, which conferred on the free people of color the same rights as "born Englishmen." Freedom came to Barbados in 1831, to Grenada in 1832 and to St. Kitts in 1833. Freedom came mostly after pressure from the Colonial Office in London on colonial legislatures. In the newer "crown colonies" of St. Lucia, Trinidad, Demerara, Essequibo and Berbice the British ruled directly without local white assemblies, thereby making it easier to enforce the dictates of the Colonial Office.

CONCLUSION

Why did slavery last so long? Extreme forms of oppression have often lasted for a very long time. Serfdom in Europe, the exploitation of the working class in early European capitalism, apartheid in Southern Africa, caste in India—all of these oppressive systems lasted for long periods, sometimes much longer than slavery in the Caribbean and the Americas. The reasons everywhere are similar, though not always identical. In the Caribbean, as elsewhere, you had the full weight of state power unabashedly mobilized to maintain injustice. Most enslaved persons (and often free people of color as well) lived practically their whole lives under some form of curfew. They were typically locked down at night, needed special passes to be away from the plantation, could not carry weapons and so on. Education was generally denied to the enslaved. The law usually did not protect them from extreme abuse, including wanton loss of life. They could not testify in courts. They could not prevent the sexual debauching of their women and girls. The Europeans who made the laws frequently went on the record, as has been seen, to deem the Africans subhuman creatures worthy of being kept in a perpetual state of terror.

Of course here, as in other forms of bondage, the human spirit chafed under oppression. Resistance was endemic to Caribbean slavery from the very beginning and contributed mightily to its eventual demise. This will be the subject of Chapters 6, 7 and 8.

Further Readings

Campbell, Carl C. *Cedulants and Capitulants: The Politics of the Coloured Opposition in the Slave Society of Trinidad, 1783–1838*. Port of Spain: Paria Publishing Co., 1992.

Cox, Edward L. *Free Coloreds in the Slave Societies of St. Kitts and Grenada, 1763–1833*. Knoxville, TN: University of Tennessee Press, 1984.

Cox, Edward L. "Ralph Brush Cleghorn of St. Kitts, 1804–42," *Slavery and Abolition: A Journal of Slavery and Post-Slave Studies*, 28, April 2007, pp. 41–60.

Equiano, Olaudah. *The Interesting Narrative of the Life of Olaudah Equiano, or Gustavus Vassa, the African. Written by Himself. Vols. I and II*. London: Author, 1789.

Hall, Neville A. T. *Slave Society in the Danish West Indies: St. Thomas, St. John, and St. Croix*. Ed. by B. W. Higman. Mona: University of the West Indies Press, 1992.

Montejo, Esteban. *Autobiography of a Runaway Slave*. Ed. by Miguel Barnet. Willimantic, CT: Curbstone Press, 1994.

Philippe, Jean Baptiste. *Free Mulatto: An Address to the Right Hon. Earl Bathurst by a Free Mulatto*. Port of Spain: Paria Publishing, 1987. First pub. 1824.

Prince, Mary. *The History of Mary Prince, a West Indian Slave. Related by Herself*. London: Published by F. Westley and A. H. Davis, Stationers' Hall Court, 1831.

Shepherd, Verene, and Hilary McD. Beckles, Eds. *Caribbean Slavery in the Atlantic World*. Kingston: Ian Randle Publishers, 2000.

Stedman, John Gabriel. *Narrative of a Five Years' Expedition Against the Revolted Negroes of Surinam in Guiana on the Wild Coast of South America from the Years 1772 to 1777*. Amherst, MA: University of Massachusetts Press, 1972. First pub. 1796.

Tomich, Dale. "Slavery in Martinique in the French Caribbean," in Shepherd and Beckles, Eds., *Caribbean Slavery in the Atlantic World*, op. cit., pp. 413–436.

6

The Big Fight Back
Resistance, Marronage, Proto-States

Some Afric chief will rise, who scorning chains,
Racks, tortures, flames, excruciating pains,
Will lead his injur'd friends to bloody fight,
And in the flooded carnage take delight;
Then dear repay us in some vengeful war,
And give us blood for blood, and scar for scar.

—JOHN G. STEDMAN, *Narrative of an Expedition*
Against the Revolted Negroes of Surinam

Their next attack was soon after on a sugar plantation at Rosalie,
belonging to the Lieutenant-governor [of Dominica] and other persons in England.
There they came also in the night-time, murdered Mr. Gamble, the manager, Mr. Armstrong,
carpenter, Mr. Hatton, and Mr. Lile, the overseers, together with the chief Negro driver
belonging to the estate. Having glutted themselves with murdering these persons, after
stripping them of their cloaths [sic], they set fire round the bodies; doing the same to the
sugar works, principal buildings, and canes; and committing other considerable damages,
to the amount of several thousand pounds.

Elated with their success, and having satiated themselves for that time
with murder, plunder, and devastation, they retired to the dwelling-house on the estate,
where they regaled on the stock, provisions, and liquors they found in plenty, their chiefs
being served in the silver vessels of the Lieutenant-governor, which, together with other
valuable articles, to a great amount, they afterwards carried away with them. On this
plantation they continued two days, riotting [sic] and revelling, blowing conk [sic] shells
and huzzaing, as for a great victory, having taken the precaution to stop up the roads to
the estate by felling large trees, and placing centinels [sic] to give them notice, in case of
the approach of the legions.

—THOMAS ATWOOD, *The History of the Island of Dominica (1791),*
on a late eighteenth-century Maroon raid, led by Chief Balla.

117

The [Black] Charaibs have been regarded by some persons in Great Britain as an independent
nation, the original and rightful possessors of the island of St. Vincent's. . . .

—Sir William Young, *An Account of the Black Charaibs in the Island of St. Vincent's (1795)*

The first shipload of enslaved Africans to the Americas landed in Hispaniola in 1502. Some of the Africans immediately escaped into the hills and became Maroons. They were never caught. The English term Maroon and the French *marron* are said to have been derived from the Spanish *"cimarrón,"* denoting formerly domesticated cattle after escape into the wild. The term was applied in Hispaniola to the indigenous Maroons who preceded the Africans. With the rapid extermination of the indigenes the term quickly became associated exclusively with Africans. The term *marronage* (used in both French and English, but occasionally rendered "marooonage" in English) denoted the state of being a Maroon.

These first African Maroons hit the ground running. They set in motion a protracted struggle against enslavement that was to continue, unabated, for almost 400 years.

Despite the formidable odds against them, facing state power of the most powerful nations and empires in the world, the Africans were able to meet the European reign of terror that was slavery, with something at least approximating perpetual war. They forced the European colonizers into a state of constant mobilization against African attack. Sometimes the formerly enslaved were able to wring concessions in the form of treaties from the colonizing powers. Sometimes they were able to achieve state power for limited (and sometimes substantial) periods. In the case of the Haitian Revolution (1791–1804) the majority African-born insurgents were able to do what no other enslaved people anywhere in the world have ever done. They permanently wrested state power from an enslaving nation, in the process defeating armies from France, Britain and Spain, three of the world's most powerful countries.

By the time that formal Emancipation came to the British West Indies (1834), a critical mass of European abolitionists had emerged to pressure the home government as a relentless wave of continuing marronage and large-scale uprisings threatened to render the slave regime unsustainable. Objective economic forces also joined the many-pronged final assault on British West Indian slavery. Similar combinations of factors were also at work in the French, Danish, Dutch and Spanish Caribbean empires.

"It is said that of all human possessions none is more valuable or more beautiful than freedom," said the Spanish liberal Fray Alonso de Sandoval in 1627. As "the divine Plato said," he continued, "captivity and slavery constitute one continuous death." The enslaved lived in death, he said, but in opposing slavery they had a chance to die like men. For slavery was real death, subjecting its victims as it did "not only [to] exile but also subjugation, and hunger, gloom, nakedness, outrage, imprisonment [and] perpetual persecution," making it "finally, a combination of all evils."

The enslaved of course did not need Fray Sandoval to explain this to them. The immediacy with which they transformed Spanish colonial society into a state of permanent apprehension of African attack spoke eloquently to this fact.

Over the entire period of Caribbean slavery the principal forms of active resistance were running away individually or in small groups (*petit marronage*), running away and joining large groupings, some of them permanent communities, which engaged in ongoing warfare with the colonial states (*grand marronage*) and full-scale rebellions, which may or may not have involved the Maroons of *petit* and *grand marronage*.

Malingering was perhaps a less important form of resistance, though it is impossible to know how successful this tactic could have been. Even suspected malingering was liable to result in savage punishments. Thomas Thistlewood regularly flogged his Africans for suspected malingering. On one occasion he subsequently confided to his diary that the suspected female malingerer he had beaten was in fact very ill, but he offered no indication of remorse.

Petty sabotage and destruction of property may also have presented some opportunities for retaliation. Thistlewood's diary contains several references to crops damaged, a horse with its belly ripped open and its guts hanging out, and similar incidents, which he attributed to sabotage. Retaliation could come, too, via what the Europeans described as larceny. "Shew [sic] me a Negro," wrote Thomas Atwood in Dominica in 1791, echoing what he described as a "proverb current in all the islands," "and I will shew you a thief." The contemporary literature of slavery is full of material to corroborate the widespread nature of this European belief. Urban enslaved were accused of hawking stolen goods. Maroons plundered plantations. Field slaves had their mouths fastened to prevent them imbibing cane juice. In Suriname the enslaved might have their teeth knocked out if caught drinking the juice they toiled to produce.

In the wretched conditions of life imposed on them by slavery, the enslaved clearly considered it to be no crime to liberate whatever they could from those who had stolen their very liberty. Atwood admitted this, though without understanding the significance of his own observations. "Thieving from their owners they look upon as no crime," he observed. Stedman was nearer the mark when he said, "nor can we wonder that slaves, who in their own persons suffer the most flagrant violation of every right, should be disposed to retaliate," by theft or otherwise.

A possibly surprising corroboration of Stedman's attitude came from African American educator Booker T. Washington, considered by many to have been a conservative figure. "The early years of my life," wrote Washington in his autobiography, *Up From Slavery,* "which were spent in [a] little cabin, were not very different from those of thousands of other slaves. My mother, of course," he continued,

had little time in which to give attention to the training of her children during the day. She snatched a few moments for our care in the early morning before her work began, and at night after the day's work was done. One of my earliest recollections is that of my mother cooking a chicken late at night, and awakening her children

for the purpose of feeding them. How or where she got it I do not know. I presume, however, it was procured from our owner's farm. Some people may call this theft. If such a thing were to happen now, I should condemn it as theft myself. But taking place at the time it did, and for the reason that it did, no one could ever make me believe that my mother was guilty of thieving. She was simply a victim of the system of slavery."

There was undoubtedly some poisoning of owners as well, a reality which filled the white ruling class with dread. "Fear of poisoning used to be common among cruel masters and managers," noted visiting British abolitionists Joseph Sturge and Thomas Harvey, of pre-Emancipation Antigua. "Such would lock up the filtering apparatus which supplied them with water, and commit the key to a favorite slave. Others would employ none but hired servants in their houses, not daring to trust their slaves." A case of poisoning excessively cruel owners in Suriname has already been noted. "In the art of poisoning," Stedman further noted, "not even the Accaww Indians are more expert; [the Africans] can carry it under their nails, and by only dipping their thumb into a tumbler of water, which they offer as a beverage to the object of their revenge, they infuse a slow but certain death."

On Plantation Egypt in early nineteenth-century Berbice the enslaved used poison to send several of their tormentors to untimely graves. In informally changing the plantation's name to Egypt the Africans, newly exposed to Christianity, associated themselves with the sufferings inflicted on God's people in Biblical Egypt. "Near to the buildings," reported a European chronicler, "was a long row of tombs of managers and overseers who had died there. One result of the cruelty practiced on the slaves was that they bound themselves together by what they deemed an oath of the most solemn and terrible character, that no manager or overseer should live more than six months on the estate." A female house slave was appointed the grim task of introducing a slow acting poison into the water jars of those the enslaved wished to kill.

The appearance of a young unusually kindly overseer in Egypt at one point presented the Africans with a serious moral dilemma. They did not wish to kill him but some insisted that he must die in order to preserve the sanctity of their sacred oath. (Oaths among the Africans were treated with great solemnity and not easily broken, a fact noted by Stedman in Suriname, among others.) The Africans finally figured out a way to save the young overseer's life while still preserving their oath. The female poisoner was directed to bring to his attention as many horror stories as she could concoct concerning the fate of his predecessors. The young man got the message and returned to his country before his allotted six months, thus sparing the Africans the necessity of reluctantly killing him for the sins of his predecessors. Many years later, as an old woman on her death bed, the poisoner unburdened her soul in a confession to a European missionary.

C. L. R. James noted that poison was also widely utilized in Saint Domingue. In Guadeloupe in 1802 enslaved women posing as nurses poisoned hospitalized French soldiers. This was during Napoleon's campaign to reestablish slavery in Guadeloupe, after a brief period of Emancipation during the upheaval triggered by the French Revolution. This time the women were caught and shot by the French.

Thomas Atwood, sometime chief judge in both the Bahamas and Dominica, dismissed Dominica's obeahmen and obeah-women as charlatans in 1791, as he did most manifestations of surviving African culture. He nevertheless identified them as important purveyors of poison directed at white people. "These people are very dangerous on any plantations," he wrote, "for although there is no credit to be given to the power of their pretended charms, yet, they are in general well acquainted with the quality of many poisonous herbs that grow in the West Indies, and which they often give to others who apply to them for charms to be administered to the persons upon whom they are to operate. By this means many white people have been killed by poison under the persuasion of these Obeah men, that it was to make them love their slaves by whom it was obtained."

The Africans also poisoned their enslavers' animals. Reports out of the French Antilles in the late 1830s, cited by Alexis de Tocqueville, lamented the growing inability of the slaveocracy to control the Africans, who now clearly had freedom on their minds. The Africans left their huts at night, the report said, robbing, smuggling and holding meetings. They were too tired to work in the day, but the masters dared not do anything about it. If they attempted to, the Africans replied by idleness and poisoning cattle. The governor of Martinique said in 1839 that fear of poison made owners reluctant to raise cattle.

A similar revolutionary use of African religion was described by Stedman, who described the female African oracles or "prophetesses" whose work was banned, often without success, by the Dutch authorities. He described "these sage matrons dancing and whirling round in the middle of an assembly, with amazing rapidity, until they foam at the mouth, and drop down as convulsed. Whatever the prophetess orders to be done during this paroxysm," he said, "is most sacredly performed by the surrounding multitude; which renders these meetings extremely dangerous, as she frequently enjoins them to murder their masters, or desert to the woods. . . ."

Suicide could also be a form of retaliation, since it meant a financial loss for the owner. Stedman described a technique, especially among those they called Coromantyns in Suriname, of throwing back their heads in the midst of very severe whippings and swallowing their tongues, thereby inducing death. The Dutch devised an antidote to tongue-swallowing. They held a firebrand to the victim's face, which burnt his face and distracted him from his suicidal mission. Eating earth, a widespread practice throughout the Americas, could result in prolonged debilitation and eventual death. According to Stedman, "some even have leaped into the cauldrons of boiling sugar, thus at once depriving the tyrant of his crop and of his servant."

Despite the draconian punishments for striking a white person or running away, it was inevitable that some of the enslaved would have retaliated on the spur of the moment under the pain of severe punishment. The nineteenth-century African American statesman Frederick Douglass famously recounted the beating he inflicted on an oppressive overseer before eventually running away to freedom. Alvin Thompson has documented a similar story concerning the disappearance of William McWatt, an oppressive "massa" in Berbice in 1826. McWatt and his horse disappeared without trace. Search parties utilizing enslaved persons and indigenous Amerindians were unable to locate him. When what appeared to be the remains of man and horse turned up at the bottom of a trench many years later, some surviving Africans were induced, on condition of no reprisals, to tell what happened.

The survivors were now advanced in age and the plantation was under new management. The unsolved mystery of McWatt's disappearance was now merely of academic interest. McWatt, it was now revealed, had come on horseback among some Africans hoeing a field, his customary whip in hand. Without warning he dealt a severe lash across the back of a "tall and powerful slave." The enraged victim immediately swung around and hit McWatt on the back of the head with his hoe, killing him instantly. After some consultation the Africans decided to bury McWatt in a nearby trench. They killed the horse and carefully stanched the flow of water into the trench while they buried horse and rider. By the time the remains were accidentally found years later the African who slew "ole massa" and many of the others present were dead. None of them, including presumably any drivers present, had ever revealed the secret of that dreadful day.

Individual acts of revenge were also inevitable. While some like Mary Prince may have endured punishment over long periods, others committed suicide rather than suffer any more. Some women practiced abortion to prevent bringing more enslaved into the world. Stedman mentioned a "vegetable or flower" called seven-boom and green pineapples as substances "too frequently used by the young Negro girls to promote abortion. . . ." Individual acts of revenge could be absolutely devastating. Africans could be the most grateful people if well served, Stedman thought, but most unforgiving when done wrong. He related the case of a house slave who locked up his owners' house in their absence with himself and their three young children inside. When the owners returned home and enquired why he had locked them out he replied by throwing their infant child to its death at their feet, from high up in the building. "[T]hey threatened—he tossed down the

brother: they intreated [sic] but to no purpose, the third sharing the same fate, who all lay dead at their parents' feet." He then told the parents he was adequately revenged and jumped to his own death. Enslaved persons seeking revenge, Stedman said, could kill whole families and even scores of their fellow enslaved to destroy their masters' property.

THE EARLY SPANISH PERIOD: 1502 TO THE EARLY 1600s

As early as 1514, a mere twelve years after the first enslaved arrived in Hispaniola, King Ferdinand I of Spain was moved to advance proposals to lessen the incidence of marronage and revolts. He suggested bringing in more African women, since men involved in relationships might be less inclined to run away. He cautioned against the importation of young African males for a church under construction. These would cause the Spaniards too much trouble. This was still three years before the asiento ushered in the first really big leap forward in African importations.

In 1515, on the eve of the asiento, the Spaniards decided to bring in Africans direct from Africa, thus ending the insistence on Christianized Africans from the Iberian Peninsula. The Spaniards now argued that Africans from Spain spoke Spanish, which would facilitate communication among them and increase chances of rebellion.

What is usually described as the first African rebellion in Hispaniola (though others had clearly preceded it), took place in Santo Domingo in 1522. The Africans killed six Spaniards and wounded several.

In the 1540s the Hispaniola Maroons were described as living in organized societies. They had reconstituted their African religions and even had a fiscal system in place. They regularly raided Spanish settlements and plantations. They were able to procure some lances and other Spanish weapons, as well as horses. In 1543 the Spaniards were venturing out of their plantations only under escort of fifteen to twenty armed men.

Spanish officials put the number of Maroons around Santo Domingo at this time at 2,000–3,000. The audiencia of Santo Domingo put the figure in

1546 at more than 7,000. These Maroons engaged in extensive trade, utilizing in part goods liberated from plantations. Urban enslaved persons working on their own and remitting their wages to their owners (already an established phenomenon in the 1540s), were said to be in league with the Maroons.

The principal Maroon leader at this time was Diego de Campo. He regularly burned sugar estates and other Spanish property, freeing enslaved Africans in the process. The Spaniards actually negotiated a treaty with Campo but he disregarded it and resumed his burning, looting and killing. In what was to become a familiar pattern in years to come, Campo eventually defected to the Spaniards, who then utilized him to track down other Maroons.

Spanish society responded to the Maroon reality in various ways. Signing a treaty with Campo and eventually encouraging his defection reflected two approaches to the Maroon problem. Laws were passed prohibiting the harboring or aiding of runaways. The already-savage punishments of slave society were obviously applied to captured Maroons. By 1540 castration of runaways was so common that a Spanish royal decree sought to end the practice.

The sense of Spanish panic mixed with awe at the achievements of the Maroons was summed up by Alvaro de Castro, archdeacon of Hispaniola, in a 1542 dispatch to the Council of the Indies in Spain. "[I]f the Negroes wish to rebel outright," he thought, "one hundred of them are sufficient to conquer the island, and twenty thousand Spaniards would not suffice to bring them to subjection. The island is large and well wooded, and they are warlike and expert at hiding out in the forests." The Audiencia of Hispaniola seemed to throw up its hands in despair in a dispatch to Emperor Charles V in 1546. The Africans were so prone to rebel, it said, that "the settlers dare not give their slaves an order except in the gentlest manner." By this time, the dispatch stated, special excise taxes and duties were already long in place to "sustain the war with the Negroes and the siege of their strongholds." The clergy, who had paid these taxes along with everyone else, were now seeking exemptions.

Bartolomé de Las Casas, the pioneer abolitionist whose desire to save the indigenes had led him to agree to the introduction of Africans in their place, was by 1559 very regretful of his decision. He now realized that Africans died as frequently as the indigenes when subjected to similar harsh conditions. They also, he wrote in his *History of the Indies*, "whenever they can . . . run away in bands; they rise in rebellion, kill the Spaniards and wreak cruelties on them. As a result the small towns of Hispaniola are never very safe. . . ."

Maroons also appeared very early in the other Spanish islands, such as Cuba, Puerto Rico, Margarita and Jamaica. A Havana slave law of 1574 blamed excessive cruelty on the part of owners for the prevalence of runaways, admitted the difficulty the Spaniards faced in trying to dislodge the Africans from their fortified positions and prescribed severe penalties for those aiding runaways. It also offered rewards for those apprehending runaways.

"Many people treat their slaves with great cruelty," the law stated, "whipping them brutally, larding them with different kinds of resin, burning them, and inflicting other cruelties from which they die. The slaves [as a result] kill themselves, or throw themselves into the sea or run away, or rise up in rebellion, and one has merely to say that the master killed his slave, and no proceedings are instituted against him."

African rebellion in the Spanish islands was duplicated in Spain's Greater Caribbean colonies. In fact many of the early enslaved Africans in such places as Mexico, Honduras, Guatemala, Nueva Granada and Venezuela had been brought there from Santo Domingo. In 1548 Africans in San Pedro, Honduras, rebelled. They were put down with reinforcements from neighboring Spanish settlements.

Miguel, a Maroon leader, escaped from the Buría mines in Honduras. He gathered a force of Africans and indigenes and attacked the Spanish settlement of Barquisimeto. He was eventually defeated by reinforcements brought in from El Tocuyo. Africans rose up in Coro, Venezuela, in 1532. Other Maroon and insurgent activity in this period took place in such places as Darien (Panama), Mexico and Lima (Peru).

The most successful African revolutionary enterprise of this early period was the Palmares Republic (1605?–1694) in Northeast Brazil. A case can be made for considering Brazil almost a part of the Greater Caribbean in this period. Portuguese and other ships travelled regularly between Brazil and the islands. When the Dutch briefly wrested Brazil from Portugal (1630–1654) it was under the auspices of the Dutch West India Company. It will be remembered also that it was refugees (and their enslaved Africans) from Portugal's reconquest of Brazil from the Dutch who introduced sugarcane cultivation into the French and British islands in the seventeenth century. These refugees also came from Northeast Brazil. It is not inconceivable that the odd former resident of Palmares might have ended up in Martinique or Barbados.

The first enslaved Africans are thought to have arrived in Brazil in 1552. They, too, hit the ground running. Maroons were terrorizing Pernambuco before the century ended. Palmares may have been in existence even before the suggested 1605 date. Maroons continued living in the area after their centralized state was finally defeated by the Portuguese in 1694. Palmares brought together approximately ten Maroon settlements, (known as *quilombos* or *mocambos),* most of whose residents originated in Angola. The state was ruled by a Ganga Zumba or "Great Lord." Palmares lasted as an independent state for close to 100 years. It withstood and repulsed numerous attacks from both Portuguese and Dutch. Many consider it the first country in the Americas to win independence from Europe. Zumbi was its most renowned military leader. The population of Palmares in the 1690s is estimated by some at 20,000.

Within a few short years of the introduction of enslaved Africans by the Spaniards the Maroons had become such a formidable independent force that the European enemies of Spain began seeking their assistance in anti-Spanish operations. These were limited alliances of convenience. Spain's enemies, whether pirates or regular state forces, were slave traders and representatives of slave-trading nations. The Maroons could not have been unaware of this. But the enemy of my enemy is my friend and both sides were willing to cooperate for limited periods for clearly defined objectives of mutual benefit. On these occasions the European allies treated the Maroons like the equal allies that they were. Their slave-trading backgrounds were put out of the equation for as long

as joint operations lasted. At the end of a successful operation both parties got what they wanted—infliction of damage on the Spaniards—and went their respective ways.

In 1538 Cuban Maroons helped French pirates sack Havana. Sir Walter Raleigh, in recounting the history of Spanish attempts to locate the fabled El Dorado, related the exploits of the Spaniard Aguirre (or Agiri) who sailed in the 1560s in search of the golden city, in an expedition led by Pedro de Osua. Osua sailed across South America from Peru, by way of the Amazon River. Aguirre mutinied and killed Osua and attempted to return to Peru via Margarita Island, Caracas, Santa Marta and points further west. In Margarita, Aguirre slew the Spanish governor and others. There he "tooke with him certaine Cemerones [Maroons], and other desperate companions" to Cumana, where they again slew a Spanish governor.

While on the South American coast Aguirre met Francis Drake, England's slave-trade pioneer and state-supported pirate extraordinaire. Drake would himself depend heavily on assistance from Maroons on his two most successful Caribbean missions. These were his two attacks on the Spanish mule train bringing Peruvian treasures across the Isthmus of Panama to Nombre de Dios in 1572–1573 and his sack of Santo Domingo in 1586.

Drake's three earlier assaults on Spanish targets in the area had all failed. Maroon support, it turned out, made the difference between success and failure. The Maroons were invaluable to Drake because first, they knew their terrain intimately. They could act as guides and help Drake set up ambushes and supervise attacks. Second, they were excellent fighters. Third, they were a priceless source of intelligence. They knew the movements and disposition of the mule train and the strength of Spanish forts. They could mingle with Africans still in captivity and obtain further intelligence. Fourth, they were implacable foes of the Spaniards. After the successful mule train assault Drake actually had to take extraordinary measures to protect Spanish prisoners from the wrath of the Maroons.

Drake's introduction to the Maroons of Nombre de Dios came via some enslaved Africans he met on some islands off the Central American coast while he was preparing an attack on the town. They were loading timber and told Drake that the material was to build a fort to protect Nombre de Dios from Maroons. The Maroons in the area, Drake learned, were very numerous. They married indigenous women and formed two nations, each under a king. Drake established a strategic alliance with the Africans. He later transported them to the mainland and facilitated their escape into marronage.

The Spanish preoccupation with a possible Maroon attack helped Drake in many ways. He found, for example, that the town's seaward defenses were negligible, since the Spaniards had organized their defenses on land, facing the forests from which they expected the Maroons to emerge.

Drake was able to enter Nombre de Dios but failed in his bid to sack the town's treasury. He nevertheless met one Diego, a Maroon, who approached him with important intelligence and an offer of cooperation against the Spaniards. Diego explained that 150 fresh Spanish troops had just arrived to guard against the Maroons. Drake retreated to an offshore island to recuperate from injuries sustained in the failed attack. He used his time there to develop his friendship with Diego and other Maroons.

The Maroons agreed to help Drake on his next exploit, namely an attack on the Spanish mule train. This train regularly brought a half year's supply of gold, silver and other Peruvian treasure across the Isthmus of Panama from Panama City on the Pacific coast to Nombre de Dios on the Atlantic. Ships then took the treasure from Nombre de Dios to Spain.

Pedro, the Maroon king, and Drake cemented their deal by an exchange of hostages. Pedro said that the Maroons sometimes attacked the mule trains just for fun. Indeed, for several years the numerous Maroons in the area had been helping pirates of various nations attack the Spanish treasure convoys.

Drake's encounter with these Maroons provides important glimpses into their modus operandi. Drake's men and the Maroons marched for several days through the jungle. Each night the Maroons quickly set up camp by building six houses from posts, thatched plantain leaves and other materials.

After three days' march the assault party reached a Maroon town built on a hillside. It contained fifty to sixty houses. The area was clean and the people dressed in the Spanish style. A 10-foot-high wall and a dyke protected the town. The town contained one broad street.

After several days' march, Pedro showed Drake the Pacific Ocean. Drake's biographer describes the occasion:

> The next morning they climbed the ridge, and upon a word from Pedro halted. Pedro took Drake by the hand. In the trunk of the highest tree steps had been cut, and at the top of it an arbour had been built in which twelve men might sit. To this arbour Drake now mounted. A fair breeze kept the day clear, and as he gazed out upon the Pacific Ocean, the first Englishman to see it since the dawn of time, he besought Almighty God of His Goodness to give him life and leave to sail once in an English ship upon that sea.

The new allies eventually arrived at Venta Cruz, an intermediate stop for the Spanish treasure-laden mule train. In Venta Cruz, Pedro sent one of his Maroons into the town to gather intelligence. This man learned from friends still in bondage that a large 350-ton ship had arrived at Nombre de Dios to transport the treasure back to Spain. The governor of Lima, Peru, was also planning to sail home on that ship. The governor would be starting that very night from Panama with fourteen mules. Eight would be laden with gold, one with jewels and the rest with luggage. He would be followed by two mule trains of fifty mules each. One would be carrying food and a little silver. The others would be carrying gold and jewels.

Drake and the Maroons sprang an ambush, but one of the Englishmen botched the job by striking too quickly at the van, instead of waiting patiently for the body of the mule train. A Maroon pulled him down, but it was too late. He had already been seen by the Spaniards, who promptly turned back. All the attackers got was luggage and a little silver.

Drake returned to sea for a while after his failure. A chance encounter with a French Huguenot pirate ship brought him some French allies for his attack on the next Spanish mule train. Drake and the French captain exchanged gifts, with Drake receiving in the exchange "a fine gilt scimitar," once owned by King Henry II of France.

The Maroons again helped Drake's party. This time the attackers captured three trains, one of fifty mules and two of seventy mules each. A grateful Drake offered Diego anything he wanted as a token of his gratitude. Diego chose the gilt scimitar, and thus did the sword of a king of France end up in the possession of Diego, leader of the Maroons in the vicinity of Nombre de Dios. Thus also did the Maroons help Drake to his first real victory in five attempts in the Greater Caribbean.

When Drake, now Admiral Sir Francis Drake, attacked Santo Domingo on New Year's Day, 1586, it was only after forming another careful alliance with the area's Maroons. These lived in the hills and jungles around the town. Drake first sent his vice admiral, Martin Frobisher (better known as an explorer of Canada's east coast), on a secret mission to establish contact with the Maroons. These undertook to help out by wiping out the Spanish garrisons in the city's castle and watch house, which they duly did. Drake eventually sacked the city with great savagery, as noted earlier. During negotiations for a truce Drake sent an African boy with a letter for the Spaniards, under a flag of truce. The Spaniards killed the boy and Drake retaliated by hanging two Spanish friars he had captured.

MARRONAGE CONTINUES UNDER THE NORTHERN EUROPEANS

As the Northern Europeans filled the Caribbean area from the seventeenth century onward, marronage became an instant part of their reality, as it had been and continued to be for the Spaniards. The African desire to be free did not differentiate between Spain and Northern Europe. The general patterns of petit and grand marronage were the same as in the early Spanish period. Africans ran away singly or in groups large and small. On one extreme some may have simply been absenting themselves for a limited period to see a loved one or for some other private purpose. There were even rare strikes, where the

enslaved would abscond into the bush and refuse to return until a brutal overseer was removed or some other demand was met.

On the other extreme Africans, either singly or in groups, might escape and join or found Maroon settlements. These might periodically raid nearby plantations or, if they were in a remote enough area, might even exist undiscovered by the Europeans for many years. The most successful, as will be seen, became virtual independent states and defied European attacks, sometimes permanently.

Marronage, petit or grand, existed everywhere in the Caribbean. The French West Indian experience was typical. As early as 1639 a Maroon band in St. Kitts, thought to be 60 strong, was firing arrows on white settlers from their mountain fastnesses. In 1641 the French king pardoned an African condemned to death for marronage in Guadeloupe.

In 1657 in Martinique enslaved Africans killed one La Planche and his wife and took to the forests. Even women with seven- to eight-day-old infants joined the exodus. Contemporary historian Père Du Tertre was moved to lament, in words almost identical to those quoted previously from the Audiencia of Santo Domingo a hundred years earlier, that "In Martinique colonists were reduced to the point where they did not dare utter an unpleasant word to a Negro, nor try to correct him, for fear that he would run off to the forest."

By 1665 the Martiniquan Maroon leader Francisque Fabulé was heading a band estimated at 400–500. The Europeans could not defeat him and negotiated a treaty of peace. In 1668 the governor of Guadeloupe estimated over thirty Maroons in Grande Terre, then otherwise uninhabited. In 1671 the Supreme Council of Martinique reported that Maroons had cleared land and planted crops. They were terrorizing their neighborhood.

By the 1690s one of the most important of Caribbean Maroon communities, Le Maniel, was already in existence on the border between French Saint Domingue and Spanish Santo Domingo. Le Maniel was to survive a hundred years of attacks, before negotiating a treaty with the French in 1776. Moreau de Saint-Méry reported sixty-year-old Maroons who had lived their entire lives in the forest at the time of signing. Here, as elsewhere, the

"Le Negre Marron," Monument to the Unknown Maroon, facing the presidential palace, Port au Prince, Haiti, was created by Haitian sculptor and architect Albert Mangones. The palace was destroyed in the earthquake of 2010 but the statue remained intact. The Maroon is blowing an *abeng* (conch shell). On his left ankle is a broken chain. In his right hand he holds a cutlass.

Maroons agreed to apprehend other Maroons for a fee. From Cayenne in 1707 came news of Maroon leader Gabriel, also known as "The Governor," whose band included indigenous people.

In 1726 officials in Guadeloupe were estimating a Maroon population of 600, "divided into four bands." Guadeloupe in 1737 tried forty-eight Maroons, eighteen of them in absentia. The French in 1730 killed Plymouth, a Maroon leader originally from an English island, in Saint Domingue. Guadeloupe in 1744 tried sixty-six Maroons after some of them abducted and killed a plantation bookkeeper. This was in retaliation for the bookkeeper's murder of a pregnant Maroon woman. The French king pardoned these Maroons. Serious Maroon disturbances were reported in Grenada in 1725, Antigua in 1729 and St. John in 1734.

Where the topography was helpful, as was mostly the case, Maroon communities retreated into dense jungle and inaccessible mountains. Where the topography provided little cover, as in Barbados and St. Thomas, Maroons ran away to towns and blended into the urban enslaved and free populations. The enslaved everywhere fled by ship or boat to neighboring islands, and sometimes to such distant destinations as England and Denmark.

Advertisements for their return were a permanent feature of regional newspapers. One such ad in the Jamaica *Royal Gazette* in 1782 bemoaned the loss of Maria, a washerwoman, who was probably "harbored among the shipping. . . ." One William had escaped to sea by passing himself off as a free person. He was apprehended on board but managed to escape again on being brought ashore. Ships' masters were warned not to harbor him, on pain of "righteous" prosecution.

The *Royal Gazette* likewise sought the whereabouts of "MARY, a stout, young House Wench, about 16 years old," last seen selling plantains in Kingston. She had been seen twice in Liguanea near her owner's pen, but had escaped apprehension.

Runaways from Curaçao turned Coro, Venezuela, into a Maroon haven. Escapees from the

Danish Virgin Islands were particularly adept at maritime marronage. Charlotte Amalie was an *entrepôt* port serving the ships of many nations. Nearby Puerto Rico and Vieques Island were favorite destinations. They could be reached easily on improvised or commandeered craft and the Spanish authorities were often (though not always) loath to return foreign enslaved persons escaping to their shores. In 1748 forty-two enslaved in St. Croix seized a sloop and sailed to freedom in Puerto Rico.

Africans escaping to Denmark were less fortunate since the Danish supreme court decreed in 1802 that escape of enslaved persons to Denmark did not confer freedom. The English supreme court, on the other hand, had ruled just the opposite in the celebrated Somerset's case of 1772. The common law of England, it held, did not recognize slavery, whatever might have been the practice in England's colonies.

The fact that some free people of color in the Danish islands were ships' captains was helpful to maritime Maroons. Many Africans, including the enslaved, also worked on ships sailing out of the Danish and other islands. Olaudah Equiano, as seen, sailed out of Montserrat as an enslaved person for many years. Denmark Vesey, leader of the massive planned slave uprising in Charleston, South Carolina, in 1822, is thought to have been a ship's carpenter from St. Thomas before settling in Haiti and eventually making his way to the United States.

Formal Emancipation in the British islands in 1834 made them an attractive destination for Maroons from still-enslaved areas. In 1845, thirty-seven Maroons escaped from Danish St. John to British Tortola in two boats sent from Tortola expressly for that purpose. From the 1840s the Danes responded by increasing naval patrols with orders to shoot to kill maritime Maroons. One such incident in 1840 elicited a British protest when a Danish naval vessel killed an escaping woman and apprehended a mother and child in British waters off Tortola.

Maritime marronage *to* the Danish islands was also frequent, because so many ships visited the Danish ports. N. A. T. Hall reported runaways in Charlotte Amalie in the early nineteenth century from St. Bartolomé, Nevis, Antigua, Curaçao, Barbados, Tortola and St. Croix. He characterized Charlotte

Amalie as a kind of sea-borne underground railroad terminus. In 1819 seven women and one man commandeered a St. Thomas sloop when it arrived in St. Vincent. The extent of maritime marronage can be gauged from the fact that ads for the recapture of Barbadian Maroons could be found in the newspapers of Demerara, St. Vincent and St. Lucia. Michael Toussaint has shown that substantial numbers of enslaved Trinidadians escaped to Venezuela.

In Tobago there were Maroon communities in the Central Range. In Trinidad Maroon communities existed in Diego Martin, Brigand Hill near Manzanilla and the environs of Savana Grande. Trinidad's militia launched two expeditions from Savana Grande against Maroon settlements in 1819. The first campaign reportedly killed three and captured about twenty-five. A month later they captured twenty-seven east of Mt. Tamana. In 1825 the militia raided a village of twenty-eight Maroons at Terre Bouillant. They captured fifteen and killed two, Ralph Short and Carlo. They burned down the village, according to their standard practice. The militia captured nine more Maroons in 1827.

When Puerto Rico heavily defeated Sir Ralph Abercromby's attempted British invasion in 1797, Africans, including Los Morenos (Moors), a force of former Maroons, bore the brunt of the fighting. The numerically superior British force (over 14,000) actually landed units at Loiza, an African area and home of many former Maroons. Abercromby withdrew under cover of night, leaving behind large quantities of arms, horses, rations and cooking utensils. His defeat came after successful campaigns in St. Lucia, Demerara, Essequibo, St. Vincent, Grenada and Trinidad. He also utilized black and colored troops, including units from Martinique, then under British occupation.

THE MAROON PROTO-STATES

The Republic of Palmares in Brazil is sometimes acknowledged to be the first New World state independent of Europe, achieving this distinction maybe a century and a half before the United States of America. Several Caribbean Maroon states can arguably make similar claims, Le Maniel among them. Some lasted a century or more. Some were never defeated and maintain some vestiges of quasi-autonomy into the twenty-first century. Several negotiated treaties with European powers as de facto sovereign states.

Their lack of full recognition as at least the New World's first post-Columbian proto-states emanates from several factors. First, circumstances forced them into varying degrees of physical and diplomatic isolation. They were societies perennially under attack. Second, they did not generally leave behind any substantial body of documentation of their own reality written by themselves. Perhaps the circumstances of their existence made this impossible. What glimpses we have of their kings, their social structure, their defenses, the layout of their towns, the furnishings of their dwellings, their lands under cultivation, their military tactics and their diplomacy come mostly from those who fought against them. In this section we will briefly consider two of these outstanding Caribbean possible proto-states, if not independent nations. These are Dominica and the so-called Black Caribs (Garifuna) of St. Vincent. Two more, Jamaica and Suriname, will be examined in Chapter 7.

Dominica

For decades up to 1814 the Maroons of Dominica were among the most formidable in the Caribbean. English contemporaries considered them second only to Jamaica's Maroons as a major threat to the British West Indies. The island was long "neutral" by common agreement among Britain, France and Spain. The French nevertheless encroached on the island before the English officially possessed it in 1763. France captured it in 1778 but Britain regained it via treaty in 1783.

In Dominica, as elsewhere, the Africans took advantage of war and political instability to greatly augment the number of Maroons. Thomas Atwood reported in 1791 that their numbers escalated greatly after the island's acquisition by the British in 1763. French Jesuit slaveholders sold their Africans to the English. Large numbers absconded in the confusion, followed by others, including women and children, from other estates.

Atwood says the Maroons formed four companies, each under a chief. They built good houses,

planted the land and raised poultry, hogs and other livestock. They also fished in the rivers and seas and traded with their colleagues still enslaved on the plantations. Altogether, he said, "they lived very comfortably and were seldom disturbed in their haunts."

When the French retook Dominica in 1778 the Maroons were a sufficiently formidable presence for the French to enter into alliance with them. According to Atwood the French administrator, Marquis Duchilleau, utilized the Maroons as an official military force to aid in the defense of the island. He supplied them with muskets, bayonets, powder and balls confiscated from the English.

The Maroons quickly moved from raiding English plantations for food crops and small livestock to taking away cattle and plundering and burning down whole estates. Their first English victim was one Mr. Grahame. "Him they shot on his knees," Atwood wrote, "as he was begging for mercy, using him in the most shocking, barbarous manner while he was dying; and after stripping the house of every thing of value, they set it on fire."

The Maroon attacks on the English grew even bolder. They sometimes attacked in broad daylight, "with conk [sic] shells blowing and French colors flying," even venturing close to the capital, Roseau. The English, "Driven to the greatest distress, and in dread of being destroyed by those cruel wretches," Atwood explained, abandoned their estates and took their families to Roseau, "leaving their property to the mercy of the runaways." The English eventually secured weapons through the help of the French governor of Martinique "to endeavor to put a stop to the sanguinary and shocking ravages committed against them." This helped, but did not stop the Maroon attacks.

On resuming control in 1783 the English formed a Maroon-chasing militia composed entirely of free people of color. These showed little enthusiasm for the job and did not apprehend a single Maroon.

The English legislature now issued several proclamations offering amnesty to such as would surrender. The Maroons responded with derision and threats of escalated attacks. In 1785 the English were forced to levy special taxes for three years to fund a new anti-Maroon drive. A 10 percent tax was levied on the assessed value of all houses. Doctors, lawyers, merchants, tavern keepers, overseers and what the law described as "every other white man" had to pay. So did free people of color. Slave owners paid per "house Negro" (the terminology of the act), for other enslaved persons, and for the sugar, rum and coffee they produced.

This was a considerable strain on the colony's finances. Anti-Maroon activities in 1785–1786 cost Dominica 50,000 pounds, "a sum so considerable," Atwood thought, "that it appears hardly credible how, or in what manner it was raised or applied." The first year's special taxes raised only 17,014 pounds.

The new taxes paid for a special anti-Maroon force of 500 men, officered by regular English army officers stationed on the island. Whites and free people of color were mobilized, as well as "able Negro men belonging to the different plantations." English regular soldiers who volunteered for this special force were rewarded with extra pay.

Things nevertheless got worse for the English before they got better. The Africans in nearby Martinique and Guadeloupe were fired up by the hope of wresting liberty from the confusion caused by the French Revolution. This revolutionary spirit spread to the enslaved on French-owned plantations in Dominica. Many of these now united under the Maroon leader Farcelle (also rendered Farcel, Farcell and Pharcelle) to wreak more havoc.

The English negotiated a treaty with Farcelle in 1794 whereby he, his two wives and selected followers were offered freedom. Crown lands would be provided for Farcelle and his people. In exchange the ex-Maroons would help capture future runaways. Farcelle apparently cooperated for a while and then reneged on the deal.

Two decades later the Maroons were still unconquered. In 1813 the English governor issued yet another proclamation of amnesty to Maroons who wished to surrender. He enlisted a former Maroon to courier it to Quashee, now the most prominent Maroon chief. Quashee's reply was to have the messenger shot. The governor then offered a reward for Quashee's head. Quashee reciprocated with a $2,000 reward for the governor's head.

The Maroons were finally defeated in 1815.

St. Vincent

The people who came to be known to history as the Black Caribs of St. Vincent ruled much of their island for over a hundred years. Their sovereignty over the island was both tacitly and explicitly acknowledged by the French and English who tried repeatedly and unsuccessfully to dispossess them. Sir William Young, the Afrophobic English apologist for his country's assault on the Black Caribs, acknowledged the existence of a body of opinion, even within England, which saw St. Vincent as "an independent nation," and the Black Caribs "the original and rightful possessors of the island. . . ."

Both the French and British nevertheless schemed over ways to annex the island. In the early seventeenth century England had claimed St. Vincent as an "appendage" to Barbados, but had been unable to effectively occupy it. In 1748, by the Treaty of Aix La Chapelle, France and England declared St. Vincent neutral territory, as they had done with Dominica. In 1763 by the Treaty of Paris, France "acknowledged" British sovereignty in St. Vincent.

All of this blissfully ignored the reality on the ground, where the Black Caribs were sovereign in their area. The British in 1763 preferred to argue, as the Spanish had earlier done as a pretext for annihilating the indigenous people, that the existing owners of the land did not live up to the norms of civilized ownership. Civilized nations had, especially, to recognize private property and aggressively pursue endless capital accumulation beyond their subsistence needs. Anything short of the English conception of these matters made other people savages and worthy of forced removal.

The Black Caribs were long thought to have originated, following Sir William Young's opinion, with the 1675 shipwreck of the Dutch slave ship *Palmira* on its way from the Bight of Benin to Barbados. The Africans escaped to the island of Bequia in the Grenadines, just a few miles from St. Vincent. The indigenous "Red" Caribs brought the Africans to St. Vincent, where water and other subsistence requirements were more plentiful.

An alternative view acknowledges the arrival of the shipwrecked Africans in 1675 but sees the

Black Caribs as the result of an ongoing process of racial and cultural amalgamation that began with Maroons escaping from Barbados, St. Lucia and elsewhere, and augmented by other shipwrecks.

A Spaniard, Fray Vasquez Espinosa, reported 500 Africans shipwrecked in the Grenadines in the 1620s when the Portuguese slave ship they were on ran aground. The Africans killed their Portuguese enslavers and were thought to have joined the Caribs of St. Vincent. In 1635 two Spanish slave ships were also lost near St. Vincent, with their surviving Africans possibly joining the Caribs. The Caribs were also said to have augmented their numbers from Africans captured on raids against European settlements.

The Black Caribs adopted the language and some of the culture of their indigenous hosts and in time may have become the larger of the two communities, Red and Black, though this numerical ascendancy is not universally acknowledged. After some friction between the two groups of Caribs the island was partitioned between them in 1700. The French governor of Martinique acted as arbitrator. He drew the "Barre de L'isle" line which became the border between the Reds on the western or Leeward side and the Blacks on the eastern or Windward side.

The Blacks thereafter became the dominant community, though they continued to intermarry and cooperate with the Reds. The communities held periodic joint councils and cooperated in time of war.

The Black Caribs from 1700 always considered "Le Barre de L'isle" to be the legal border of their territory which, as far as Sir William Young was concerned, was an indication of savagery. The 1700 boundary, he said, "grew shortly into prescription in the short memorials [sic] of a savage people. . . ."

The 1675 Africans were, according to Sir William Young's colorful account, from the "warlike Moco tribe from Africa." The Caribs, according to Young, "incommoded by the refractory spirit of these Africans, decided to kill all their male children." The Blacks instead rose up and withdrew to the high mountains of Northeast St. Vincent. "In these almost inaccessible fortresses they found many other Negroes from the neighboring islands, who, murderers or runaways, had fled from justice, revenge, or slavery."

According to Young the Red Caribs invited some French people to live among them for protection. When in 1719 the French governor of Martinique sent an invasion force of 400 volunteers to establish a more substantial French presence, the Black Caribs attacked them with arrows and muskets. The leader and many of the French rank and file were killed. The survivors had to flee "in dismay," Young said, back to Martinique. The French thereafter abandoned hostile attacks in favor of encroaching via settlements on the leeward side of the island.

None deterred by the French defeat of 1719, English King George I granted St. Vincent to his Duke of Montague. One Captain Braithwaite duly landed in St. Vincent in 1723 to inform the island's rulers of their new king. He met with both the "General of the [Red] Indians" and the "Chief" of the Black Caribs. The former was attended by about 100 armed men. The latter had an armed bodyguard of 400 men, equipped with muskets and cutlasses. Both seemed to prefer the French to the English, Young reported, "and both parties declared their resolution to oppose the English settlement, and pretensions of English sovereignty." The English, lacking the force to impose their will, withdrew. In 1762 they resumed their aggression by occupying some of the non-Black section of St. Vincent. Other European nations confirmed their "sovereignty" by the Treaty of Paris in 1763.

The Caribs, both Red and Black, appointed a Frenchman, the Abbé Valladares, to represent them in negotiations with the British. Valladares, now and later, seemed quite comfortable in selling out the Caribs whenever he could. He went along with the British desire to grab Carib land. For Sir William Young, himself a British planter on the island, the case for naked British aggression was clear. The Black Carib area coveted by Britain comprised, he argued, "the most fertile part of the island [and] was occupied mostly in common, as by an erratic nation of savages, warriors and hunters. . . ." European international law, he said, spoke expressly to such a situation: "A general appropriation of country for so partial use and benefit, was not deemed consistent with the common law of nations, with the general interest of the colony, or with the rights of the British crown." Carib rejection of

British aggression only confirmed their savagery, as far as Young was concerned. The British pretext for aggression, he acknowledged, comprised "considerations difficult to impress on the minds of the Charaibs. . . ."

The Carib rejection of these specious arguments, both before and after 1762, was clear enough. Yet the historian again wishes that their own views, expressed by themselves, could have entered the documentary record. Young nevertheless seems to have represented them accurately, despite his hostile spin, when he reported that the Caribs "as a people . . . obstinately persevered in declaring against all interference within *the country they called their own* [my emphasis], and in disclaiming allegiance to the British crown."

The British, buoyed by the Treaty of Paris, were now set on a course of relentless aggression, though it would be thirty-five years, many skirmishes and two wars against the Black Caribs before they would realize their goal. In 1764 they appointed a board of commissioners to effect British conquest of Black Carib territory. Sir William Young, governor of Dominica and father and namesake of the English chronicler of these events, headed the commission. The senior Young produced a pamphlet encouraging British "adventurers" to occupy St. Vincent, "That when the Black Charaibs of St. Vincent's [sic] are duly apprized of the humanity and generosity of our gracious Sovereign, and assured of the enjoyment of their lands, freedom, favor, and protection, they may be gained over to our cause, and even rendered useful."

By 1765 the British commissioners had had enough of the Caribs' refusal to meekly capitulate to their aggression. They claimed, not for the first time, "That the charaibs are altogether uncivilized, and the *Blacks* [their emphasis] particularly of an idle untractable [sic] disposition." Cleared Carib land was seen as in the way of proposed British plantations. Their slash-and-burn agriculture the British interpreted as nonuse of land that the British wanted. They now therefore proposed forcibly removing the Caribs to Bequia. In 1766 they suggested some place else, since Bequia lacked rivers.

In 1768 the British published revised "sundry propositions" concerning their intentions. They would seize the best Carib land and relocate the Caribs to reservations (like the bantustans of apartheid South Africa). If the Red Caribs wished at that point to separate from the Blacks, "it shall be done."

Later in 1768 the British sent Abbé Valladares (now looking more and more like a double agent) to explain their position to the Caribs. Valladares met Chief Chatoyer at Grand Sable, the Black Carib capital. "What King of England is this?" Chatoyer enquired, "who is presuming to take Carib territory?" The Caribs realized that they would have to prepare for war, so they sought time by pretending to go along with the British plan, while obtaining military supplies from neighboring islands and generally preparing for the conflict to come. These sophisticated tactics, which would have done credit to any nation, Young (the younger) once again interpreted as the mark of a savage people. The Carib, he explains, "attains, what is the glory of each savage race, the accomplishing his purpose by cunning, and destroying his enemy by surprise."

Meanwhile Carib canoes moved busily back and forth between St. Vincent, Martinique and St. Lucia, procuring arms and other supplies for the impending conflict. It was not long before the first skirmishes began, in what would eventually become the first Carib-British War of 1772–1773. In 1769 the British decided to construct a road, the first of several they hoped to build through Carib territory. The Caribs knew very well that roads would facilitate the introduction of enemy troops and heavy weaponry into their midst. They let the British begin the road, but stopped it when it reached their border on the Calonery River.

Forty British troops guarding the road had commandeered a house for use as a barracks. Three hundred armed Black Caribs appeared and removed the roof. The British commander agreed to halt work on the road while he awaited further instructions. The Caribs therefore allowed the soldiers to repair the house and stay.

The Black Caribs then decided to surround the barracks, cutting the British off from everything, including their water supply. The 100 remaining British regular troops on the island, augmented by all available British men capable of bearing arms, marched to the rescue. The Carib chiefs led by

Chatoyer offered to release the hostages if the British would cease and desist from building roads and otherwise interfering with their country. The British agreed, the hostages were released, and they all marched back to their settlement on the leeward side of the island.

The Abbé Valladares had apparently tried to warn the British of the Carib intention to stop the British road at the Calonery River. The Caribs got wind of this and decided to punish the apparent double agent. Once the British party abandoned their road, the Black Caribs raided Valladares' house. They chopped up his nephew, but he later recovered from his wounds. They killed his black servant. Valladares himself had left home earlier that morning, thereby escaping the Caribs' wrath.

Things continued to get worse. Caribs were now regularly raiding British settlements. An armed British sloop patrolling the waters between St. Vincent and St. Lucia sank four large Carib canoes, carrying twenty armed men each and transporting ammunition for the war effort. The British captain then retreated as the Caribs, cutlasses in their mouths, swam toward his ship in an attempt to board it. The British suffered two killed and one wounded of their nine-man crew. Carib losses were not known.

On January 22, 1770, British settlers in St. Vincent petitioned their home government to move decisively against the Black Caribs who, despite British benevolence, were "nevertheless, from groundless fears and jealousies assembled in arms" and terrorizing His Majesty's subjects. The British commissioners on the island proposed the assembling of a large military force to "awe and control" the Blacks, much as the United States, in the early twenty-first century, launched its military offensive to "shock and awe" Iraq.

By December 1770, however, the commissioners, seemingly daunted by the task of militarily subjugating the Black Caribs, now proposed a compromise. They suggested a royal proclamation "declaring that the king has taken compassion on their ignorance, distrusts, and jealousies, and rather than be the author of their destruction, is generously pleased, that they shall *continue to hold the lands they now possess* [emphasis here and later in the original] under his royal favor, on condition *only*,

that they become his good and faithful subjects" and never alienate their lands without the king's permission.

The commissioners met in June 1771 with Chief Chatoyer and about forty other Carib leaders. The Caribs rejected any proffered British benevolence. Their prime minister, Jean Baptiste, insisted, as reported by Sir William Young, whose account benefited from access to the British commissioners' records held by Sir William Young the elder, "that they were independent of the kings either of France or England," despite their attachment to the French.

"The Charaibs declared repeatedly and in the most unqualified terms," Young wrote, "that they were resolved that at no time whatever, any European should settle within the country they claimed: and they absolutely denied any right in the crown of Great Britain to their allegiance. They said they knew of no king and would acknowledge no king. . . ."

The independent-mindedness of the Black Caribs was now more than the British commissioners could take. They declared in July 1771 that the question was no longer one of land, but of the very "honor of the crown . . . against a race of lawless people. . . ." They now suggested resuming their road building program through Carib territory by force. They would then, they proposed, "keep them in order, by mixing white inhabitants amongst them."

At the end of 1771 four St. Vincent settlers proposed resettlement of the Black Caribs to West Africa "or some desert island adjacent thereto." (In 1789 the British founded their Sierra Leone colony by deporting London's "Blackpoor" there. In 1796 they deported Jamaican Trelawney Maroons to Nova Scotia, Canada and later, in 1801, to Sierra Leone, at the Jamaicans' request.)

The British government in 1771, however, preferred the commissioners' idea of forced road building protected by "a sufficient military force." The nakedness of British aggression was not lost on antiimperialist dissidents within England itself. One such, quoted by Bernard Marshall, urged the British government "to put a stop to the murderous commission sent out . . . to extirpate" the Black Caribs. He accused his government of "reviving the Spanish cruelties at the conquest of Mexico, to gratify avaricious merchants, land holders and venal commissioners."

Such a radical voice was no less able to stem the aggressive intent of the British government in the eighteenth century than similar radicals would have been able to do in the nineteenth or twentieth. The British now began to consider recruiting troops in Grenada, Dominica and North America (itself soon to throw off the yoke of British hegemony).

Here again eighteenth-century "awe and control" presaged the international supporting force assembled by "shock and awe" in Iraq in the twentieth and twenty-first centuries. As in the Iraq counterpart, the British in St. Vincent first launched a diplomatic offensive as part of their preparations for war. Sir William Young the elder, governor of Dominica and chief commissioner, visited the Count de Nosière, governor of Martinique, to brief him on British preparations. The French, obvious potential Carib allies in the impending conflict, heartily supported the British plans, according to Sir William Young the younger. If this account is accurate, then the French government, like the Abbé Valladares earlier, proved to be unreliable allies of the Caribs, and not for the last time.

By 1772 the Caribs, meanwhile, were in a state of high alert for the inexorably unfolding conflict. In August the British sent a seaborne "expedition" to sail around the island, gathering intelligence, attempting landings in Carib territory and generally probing Carib preparedness. At each attempted landing they were greeted by hostile fire from Carib forces. They were unable to effect a single landing. "During this interval of mutual preparation," Sir William Young the younger noted sardonically, "the colony remained in gloomy tranquility." The Black Caribs reiterated meanwhile that they had received their land from their ancestors and were prepared to die in its defense.

Reflecting on the eve of the first Carib-British War of 1772–1773, Young the younger assessed the Carib preparations for a defensive war. He considered this their best option. "The rugged face of the country," he suggested, "the almost impenetrable woods, and above all the approaching rainy season, would serve them best in a protracted campaign." Delay "would probably be fatal to British troops, forced to extraordinary fatigue, under the strong vicissitude of sultry suns, and torrents of rain, and exposed to pestilential vapours in an uncleared country so fatal to the European constitution." Delay, he noted, also fostered Carib hopes for renewed British-French hostilities which would turn the French into more reliable Carib allies.

The British commenced the war on September 24, 1772. Their immediate objective was to establish military posts at strategic locations in Carib territory. These would physically split up Carib land, impede communication among the Caribs, and generally hem them in. Young the younger was uncharacteristically silent on the details of the fighting. He defended the British forces against changes of serious losses spread by opposition politicians in England. A treaty was signed between the warring parties on Wednesday, February 17, 1773, five months after hostilities began.

The Caribs' defensive war had proved, as anticipated by Young, a difficult hurdle for the British in St. Vincent to negotiate. "The conduct of the Charibbs [sic] is more serious and formidable . . . than I expected," Young confessed. They were very good, he said, at exploiting their knowledge of their country.

Bernard Marshall gave officially admitted British casualties as 72 killed, 80 wounded, 110 felled by disease, 428 sick and 4 deserted, out of a total British force elsewhere reported to be 2,273 strong. Official statistics are notoriously unreliable in time of war and the temptation to underreport casualties is often irresistible. Even if these figures are accurate, though, almost one-third of the British force had been put out of commission after only five months. This and their acknowledgement of the formidable defensive campaign of the Caribs doubtless hastened their willingness to negotiate a settlement. With similar statistics from the Black Carib side now unknowable, one has to suppose that the privations of a war fought on their home territory also made them willing to negotiate.

The treaty of "peace and friendship" was concluded on February 17, 1773. The terms appeared on the surface to favor the British, but later events were to suggest otherwise. Young the younger had often excoriated the Black Caribs for feigning submission to buy time. This treaty seemed no different. Their apparent acquiescence in British sovereignty was nullified by subsequent events.

The treaty contained twenty-four clauses and was signed for the Caribs by twenty-eight of their leaders, including Chatoyer. These represented the Carib settlements of Grand Sable, Massiraca, Rabacca, Macaricau, Byera, Coubamarou, Jambou, Colonrie, Camacarabou, Ouarawarou and Point Espagniol.

The terms stipulated that hostilities must cease. The Caribs were to lay down their arms and acknowledge the British king as sovereign. English law was to prevail in all but intra-Carib matters. There was to be no "undue intercourse" with the French islands. The Caribs were to give up runaways they were currently harboring from European plantations and must not harbor any more in the future. It would be a capital offence for Caribs to take runaways off the island. They were to help Britain in times of external attack. The British would help any Caribs who wished to emigrate. The British would have unfettered access to Carib land in pursuit of runaways. British deserters and French "runaway slaves" were "to be delivered up. . . ." Carib chiefs were to provide population statistics for their areas. They were "to attend the Governor" when required. The British would help them trade with other islands. "No strangers, or white persons" could settle among the Caribs, without written permission of the British governor. Caribs would receive amnesty for "past offences." Caribs would have to swear the following oath: "We . . . do swear, in the name of the immortal God, and Christ Jesus, that we will bear true allegiance to his majesty George the Third, of Great Britain, France, and Ireland, King, defender of the faith. . . ."

Events would soon cast doubt on the Caribs' intent to observe the stipulations of this British wish list. Young the younger said that they continued to menace road building after the treaty. These roads, he said, were completed, but only on a scale less ambitious than initially envisaged. The Caribs had by 1775 reoccupied the 2,000 acres given up after the war.

When the French invaded St. Vincent in 1779 the Caribs were on hand to help. When the British tried to recapture the island in 1780 the French repulsed them with Carib assistance. Carib hatred for the British was such that their French allies on occasion tried to restrain them from wreaking too exuberant revenge on the British. Englishman Francis Drakes, it will be remembered, had similarly tried 200 years earlier to restrain his Maroon allies at Nombre de Dios from tearing Spanish prisoners to pieces. In 1783 France returned St. Vincent to the British, again treating the Caribs like the allies of convenience that they were.

The Carib-British war of 1795–1797 came at a time of great upheaval in the Caribbean, much of it influenced by repercussions from the French Revolution of 1789. The Haitian Revolution had begun in 1791. Martinique and Guadeloupe were in upheaval, with the British occupying Martinique and French revolutionaries taking Guadeloupe. Fedon's Rebellion, one of the major conflicts in the region, erupted in Grenada in 1795. Revolutionary French held sway in St. Lucia, before being expelled by the British in 1795.

These revolutionary happenings inspired the British in St. Vincent to make feverish plans for their defense. They also inspired the Caribs, who were very much in touch with events, through their long association with Martinique and through contact with emissaries of Victor Hugues, the revolutionary French leader of Guadeloupe. Hugues undertook to help arm the Caribs as they prepared for war in 1795.

On March 7, 1795, the St. Vincent governor invoked Article 17 of the British-Carib treaty of 1773 to summon Chiefs Chatoyer and Duvallé to a meeting. These chiefs declined to attend but the governor assured himself that rumors of an imminent Carib attack were groundless. On March 8 several English residents attended a Carib-sponsored "Maroon dinner," an apparent gesture of goodwill. The organizers of the dinner shortly afterward appeared at the head of Caribs attacking British plantations.

These were apparently the opening skirmishes of the Second Carib-British War. On March 10 a British force sent to engage Caribs burning a plantation was ambushed. "As soon as the perfidious villains perceived [the British] were completely exposed to their fire," English chronicler Charles Shephard lamented, "they opened upon them a most tremendous volley of musketry, which they maintained with unabating ardour. . . ." The British were routed and retreated to Kingston in disorder.

The British suffered greatly in this encounter. According to Shephard, writing around 1830 and with the benefit of interviews with veterans of the war, diaries kept by combatants and other primary sources,

> In this unsuccessful expedition, thirty-one British persons lost their lives, the greatest part of them the most promising young men in the colony; those who were wounded or made prisoners, received no quarter, but were murdered with every circumstance of savage barbarity; some had their arms and legs cut off while the living trunks were left writhing in the agonies of pain; others were mangled and cut up in a manner too shocking to relate. This fatal event produced a scene too tragical [sic] and melancholy for description. The defeated and disheartened troop, in their precipitate and disorderly flight to Kingston, communicated terror and dismay as they passed. . . .

The Caribs set fire to all sugar works, cane fields and British houses in their path. They killed British cattle. They continued their onslaught to Calliaqua only 3 miles from the British capital at Kingstown. Two days after the outbreak of violence they reached Dorsetshire Hill, a strategic point near Kingstown, where they trampled the British flag and hoisted the tricolor of revolutionary France.

This destruction on the windward side of the island was under the command of Chief Duvallé. On the leeward side, commander in chief and Paramount Chief Chatoyer was similarly engaged, though he spared some British property in the expectation of occupying it when the war was over. Chatoyer arrived at the town of Chateau Belair on March 10, 1795. There all the local French residents joined him in this effort to expel the British.

The Caribs captured three young Englishmen at Chateau Belair and took them to Dorsetshire Hill, where the two Carib columns linked up. Here, said Shephard, "the Caribs killed them in a most shocking manner," though he could not bring himself to provide details. Chatoyer himself hacked the Englishmen to pieces. The Carib chief "reviled these unhappy victims, and the English nation at each blow of the sabre. . . ." To add insult to English injury, Chatoyer used a "silver-mounted broad sword" given him by an Englishman after the First Carib-British War of 1772–1773. The sword was engraved with the Englishman's family's arms. It was once owned by a family member who fell with it at the Battle of Saratoga in 1777, during the American Revolution.

About 200–300 Caribs and 150 French allies (white and persons of color) were now on Dorsetshire Hill. They fortified their positions, laid up provisions and, Shephard said, "with infinite labor and difficulty" they dragged two pieces of heavy artillery up the hill. The beleaguered British governor in Kingstown moved his headquarters and burned cane fields on the town's outskirts to slow the expected Carib assault. They even armed some of their enslaved Africans for use as scouts.

With an attack from Dorsetshire Hill imminent and defeat staring them in the face, the British had one of the lucky breaks that were to recur at crucial times during the conflict. In short succession British troops landed from Martinique (now under British occupation), and a sloop of war and a British warship arrived. There reinforcements decided to attack Dorsetshire Hill on the very night that all of them were safely on land. Time was of the essence, said Shephard, "as the apparent superiority of the enemy began to shake the fidelity of the Negroes, and to tempt them to abandon the weak and defenseless standard of the colonists. . . ." The British counterattacking force consisted of regular soldiers, sailors, merchant seamen, militia "and some armed Negroes, in whom [the British] could confide." The attackers caught the Caribs by surprise and regained the hill.

Among the dead the counterattackers found on the field of battle was Chief Chatoyer, now fairly advanced in years. He fell with his heirloom English sword in hand. On his person was a "silver gorget" (an ornament on a chain worn around the neck by military officers as a mark of rank). This gorget had been given him by none other than the then king of England, George III, when, as Prince William Henry, he had visited St. Vincent. The exact manner of Chief Joseph Chatoyer's death is uncertain, but the

British cultivated a legend of his demise by the bayonet of one Major Leith of the local militia.

In Chatoyer's pocket the British also found a proclamation to the French on the island. It was dated Chateau-bellair [sic], March 12, 1795, "the first year of our Liberty." "Where is the Frenchman," the proclamation asked, "who will not join his brothers, at a moment when the voice of liberty is heard by them?" For those Frenchmen too timorous to join the Caribs against the British Chatoyer's proclamation had this to say: "We do swear that both fire and sword shall be employed against them, that we are going to burn their estates, and that we will murder their wives and children, in order to annihilate their race." The local French around Chateau Belair apparently all fell in with the Caribs, rather than face the consequences. After the setback on Dorsetshire Hill the French deserted the Caribs and tried to return to their estates. Several who were caught were hanged by the British.

Though the death of Chatoyer was a great blow to the Caribs, the war continued. For the next year it would ebb and flow as the Caribs demonstrated a great capacity to retreat into their inaccessible areas, resupply themselves from St. Lucia and Guadeloupe, and mount large-scale attacks.

The British, lacking the manpower to press home the advantage after retaking Dorsetshire Hill, tried to pursue the Caribs with the help of ranger units, made up of conscripted enslaved Africans. They initially discontinued the practice due to difficulties in controlling the armed Africans. As the war progressed, though, Rangers became a regular fixture. Some of the enslaved also defected to the Caribs.

In the immediate aftermath of Dorsetshire Hill, small bands of newly escaped Maroons, Caribs and French raided plantations on the leeward side of the island. They partially destroyed the town of Chateau Belair. On one estate, said Shephard, they killed an overseer "by inhumanly passing his body between the cylinders of the sugar-mill."

The Caribs next set up three encampments very near a British base at Sion Hill. Their raiding parties came to the very base of the hill to fire some estates and kill uncooperative enslaved Africans. They also burnt down most of Calliaqua.

On April 5, 1795, two British transports arrived with troops straight from a three-year tour of duty at Gibraltar. These were considered ideal for the St. Vincent theatre, because of Gibraltar's rocky topography and warm climate. A Liverpool ship at this time also put nine sailors ashore, unaware of the state of war on the island. The Caribs promptly took them prisoner. A rescue party from Sion Hill failed to secure them.

The British next decided to attack the Caribs in the vicinity of Calliaqua, but they were thoroughly routed. The British "van fell back upon the rear with such impetuosity," Shephard reported, "that many were thrown down and trampled upon. . . ." A second British attempt was more successful. Shephard reported twenty Caribs found dead on the field of battle and several British killed. The nine Liverpool sailors were left behind unharmed by the Caribs.

With the British unable to win any decisive victories they once more resorted to arming those enslaved Africans they thought they could trust. Some of these, as seen, had run away to the Caribs. Some had taken advantage of the turmoil to do some burning and destruction of their own. Others, spurning Carib overtures had become fair game for Carib wrath. Many, as previously noted, appeared on the brink of mass escape during the early days of the war. There had been earlier limited efforts to arm some enslaved people.

Now the exigencies of war moved the British to arm their Africans once more. This was not a unique experiment. Two decades earlier the British had effectively armed large numbers of African Americans in their struggle against American Independence. In Suriname and elsewhere in the Caribbean, ranger units, as they were known, were frequently utilized against Maroons. The lure of freedom was usually sufficient to induce these enslaved soldiers to fight.

A force of 500 Rangers was accordingly raised in St. Vincent. Each African was appraised on enlistment. If he was lost in battle his owner would be remunerated his appraised value. White officers from the militia and regular army commanded the Rangers. "They very soon became a most useful and active body of men," Shephard reported.

Rangers were in an attacking party that sailed from Kingston on April 25 to attack Duvallé's camp.

They burnt twenty-five Carib houses, destroyed "vast quantities of provisions," sixteen canoes and four swivel guns.

Meanwhile the Caribs and "those English and French Negroes who joined them" built fortifications on the Vigie, a hilly area about 6 miles north-east of Kingstown. The Vigie was within sight of the British in the Kingstown area. The Caribs had been reinforced by 110 French revolutionaries from Guadeloupe, about 40 of them white. They had also been resupplied with "remarkable long pikes," which the British had not seen them with before.

On May 7, in full view of the British, an estimated 800 of the Caribs and their allies descended the Vigie in eight columns. A "young French officer" approached the British with a flag of truce. He invited them to surrender, in which case they would be assured safe passage to any British island "where the flag of liberty was not yet unfurled." The British declined the invitation.

A British warship once more arrived in the nick of time and landed sailors. At about 1 AM the newly arrived French troops and what Shephard called the "disaffected Negroes and Mulattoes of the Island" defeated them. A British counterattack proved successful, with forty-eight of the enemy killed, nineteen of them white.

In May and June the British augmented their troops with more Rangers and fresh arrivals from Martinique. During a renewed attack on the Caribs the latter ran out of ammunition and retreated even deeper into their windward area, with the British in pursuit.

The tide of war now seemed to be turning against the Caribs. The British were able to destroy vast stockpiles of Carib food and material. They destroyed about 200 Carib canoes, some "so large," wrote Shephard, "as to be stiled [sic] 'their men of war.'"

The British were also able to make some strategic seaborne landings, cutting off Carib access to many of the bays where they would receive supplies. The British lost several men in effecting these landings and in the ensuing skirmishes. In the midst of all this almost all the British militia broke rank and fled back to Kingstown in what Shephard considered most "unmilitary-like behavior."

The Caribs now had a stroke of good luck as the British evacuated St. Lucia, abandoning it to the French. The Caribs immediately dispatched soldiers to St. Lucia for reinforcements of men and supplies, which managed to get through to them.

In July the British again attacked Chateau Belair but were repulsed with "a more than ordinary loss" of twenty-three killed and forty-five wounded. In September the Caribs were again reinforced by about 500 men plus provisions from St. Lucia. They now surrounded the British position on the Vigie. A British relief force refused orders to advance further on the enemy. Instead they turned tail and fled with the Caribs in hot pursuit. The Caribs retook the Vigie and killed or captured about sixty British soldiers.

On September 29 the British again received reinforcements. Several hundred fresh troops landed and assaulted the Vigie. They retook it, but at a cost, as reported by John William Fortescue in his *History of the British Army*, of 150 killed and wounded. Then the tide of war once more turned in favor of the Caribs. Two British deserters provided information to the Caribs which allowed them to mount another devastating attack. This time they killed or wounded 135 British privates, in addition to killing, wounding or taking prisoner several officers. Bryan Edwards put British losses in this engagement at 400.

"In this anxious and desponding hour," as Shephard put it, Major General Hunter arrived from Martinique, once again bringing in fresh reinforcements for the beleaguered British. Hunter left a garrison on the Vigie and pulled all British forces back to defend Kingstown. The Caribs now massed to assault the Vigie and Hunter decided to evacuate it rather than risk further severe losses in its defense. The Caribs immediately took the Vigie once more. Several skirmishes continued, in one of which the British lost about fifty killed and wounded. Three hundred more British reinforcements arrived.

Carib fortunes turned downward on March 27, 1796, when British General Ralph Abercromby retook St. Lucia from the French. This cut off the main source of Carib resupply. On June 3 Abercromby arrived in St. Vincent with almost 4,000 troops. They included 260 of the mercenary black, white-officered West India Regiment, Rangers and German mercenaries.

Abercromby assaulted the Vigie once again. Three officers and fifty-one men, mostly from the West India Regiment, lost their lives in the early stages of this encounter. The British nevertheless retook the Vigie with a further loss of about 40 killed and 141 wounded. Shephard estimated that the Caribs and their allies may have lost half that amount. Four hundred and sixty of the French defenders at Vigie now unilaterally surrendered, leaving their Carib allies in the lurch.

The Caribs seemed poised to renew attacks, but their position had now become dire and they offered a truce. They were badly in need of provisions and ammunition. The British destruction of their food stockpiles and material and the loss of St. Lucia as a source of resupply left them without the means to prosecute the war effectively. The war now ended, not with any decisive battle, but rather by petering out, though with disastrous consequences for the Caribs.

The Caribs proposed a peace which would have allowed them to retain their lands. The British demanded unconditional surrender. The Caribs requested until June 18 to confer with their chiefs. The deadline passed and the Caribs simply went back to their peacetime pursuits. There were no more hostilities. The British seized the Caribs' canoes. On June 24, 1796, the British governor declared an end to martial law, terminating over a year of all-out war between the Black Caribs of St. Vincent and the British empire.

The British Council and Assembly of St. Vincent had demanded in 1795 *"that the British planters, or the Black Charaibs, must be removed from off the island of St. Vincent's* [emphasis in original].*"* The administration now moved to do just that. The Caribs, no longer mobilized for war, were rounded up piecemeal, with some heeding British demands that they surrender themselves. A few escaped the British net.

The deportation order against the Caribs was signed by Sir William Young the younger, planter, council member, author of *An account of the Black Charaibs in the Island of St. Vincent's* and the man after whom Sir William Young's Hill and Sir William Young Bay were named.

About 5,000 Caribs were interned in a concentration camp on the tiny Balliceaux Island off the coast of St. Vincent. Charles Shephard's account of the war, so rich in detail, suddenly fell silent on the internment in Balliceaux. It appears that Balliceaux became the scene of one of the more horrific genocidal episodes in the whole blood-spattered history of the post-1492 Caribbean. More than half (ca. 2,500 of nearly 5,000) of the Carib men, women and children incarcerated on Balliceaux Island died in the four months between October 1796 and February 1797. The British had consistently described the Black Caribs as savages for vigorously defending their territorial integrity. In 1795 the British governor of St. Vincent had announced that he would not apply the rules of war to such an enemy. The extermination of the interned Caribs on Balliceaux Island was a logical outcome of this mind-set.

In St. Vincent the British could finally possess themselves of the fertile lands they had coveted for so long. In 1801 Governor Henry Bentinck gave away 5,260 acres to British settlers. In 1804 a law officially converted Carib lands into crown (state) lands. In 1807 the government promised 6,000 acres of Carib lands to a loyalist veteran of the American War of Independence. There was a settler outcry at the size of the grant and it was reduced in 1809 to 1,700 acres. The government also sold Carib lands. They piously contributed 5,000 pounds from this money in 1820 toward the rebuilding of a Kingstown church destroyed in the hurricane of 1780.

On March 11, 1797, ten British ships, under escort of the *HMS Experiment,* deported 722 men, 806 women and 720 children, for a total of 2,348 Caribs. The trip took thirty-one days, including a ten-day stopover in Jamaica. The destination was Roatán, a Spanish island near Honduras. The Spaniards naturally resisted having 2,000 British deportees deposited in their midst. The British had to assault the Spanish garrison. In the process the Spaniards captured and sank one British ship, with 289 Caribs aboard. In 1805 the assembly granted pardons to remaining Caribs who had escaped deportation. They were "granted" 250 acres of their own land.

In 2002 the independent nation of St. Vincent and the Grenadines made Chief Joseph Chatoyer its first national hero and erected a monument in his honor. The descendents of the Roatán deportees now constitute the Garifuna community widely dispersed through Central and North America. In 2007 and

2008 they were trying to have a street in the Garifuna community in Bronx, New York, renamed for Chief Joseph Chatoyer.

The Second Carib-British War of 1795–1796 was an epic conflict of ongoing warfare that the Caribs could conceivably have won with a little luck. Even through the jaundiced lens of Englishman Charles Shephard, the main chronicler of the war, the Caribs were revealed as fearless, highly disciplined, excellent guerrilla fighters and sound military strategists. They initially had ample provisions in store for a protracted campaign. They were able for a while to benefit from an alliance with revolutionary republican French elements. Martinique was occupied by the British, which turned it into a source of resupply and general assistance for the British in St. Vincent. But Guadeloupe remained under the control of Republican France and provided some assistance for the Caribs. St Lucia, nearer to St. Vincent than Guadeloupe, was even more crucial. Carib canoes plied the waters between St. Vincent and St. Lucia bringing supplies of arms and ammunition. In fact it was the fall of French St. Lucia to the British General Ralph Abercromby, together with the unilateral surrender of the Caribs' French allies in St. Vincent, which provided the fatal blow against the Caribs. In one fell swoop almost, the Caribs were cut off from supplies and allies. Additionally, once Abercromby secured St. Lucia he was able to inject into the St. Vincent conflict a huge force (nearly 4,000 fighting men) which put great strain on the Caribs, now themselves about to lose several hundred French allies.

Prior to these final setbacks the tide of war had raged back and forth. More than once the British were saved from imminent defeat by the fortuitous arrival of reinforcements—transports from Martinique, British veterans from Gibraltar, fresh troops from England, etc. These military resources of a vast empire were a decided advantage to the British. The relatively small size of St. Vincent, contrasted with, say, Suriname or Jamaica, also worked against the Caribs. The British were sometimes able to bombard Carib positions from the sea and otherwise launch seaborne attacks.

Further Readings

Atwood, Thomas. *The History of the Island of Dominica.* London: Frank Cass, 1971.

Bilby, Kenneth M. *True-Born Maroons.* Gainesville, FL: University Press of Florida, 2005.

Marshall, Bernard A. "The Black Caribs: Native Resistance to British Penetration into the Windward Side of St. Vincent, 1763–1773." *Caribbean Quarterly,* 19, 4, 1973, pp. 4–19. Also in *Pan-African Journal,* 8, 2, 1975.

Marshall, Bernard A. "Marronage in Slave Plantation Societies: A Case Study of Dominica, 1785–1815." *Caribbean Quarterly,* XXII, 2/3, June/September 1976, pp. 26–32.

Price, Richard, Ed. *Maroon Societies: Rebel Slave Communities in the Americas.* Garden City, NY: Anchor Press, 1973.

Price, Richard. *First-Time: The Historical Vision of an Afro-American People.* Baltimore, MD: Johns Hopkins University Press, 1983.

Shephard, Charles. *An Historical Account of the Island of Saint Vincent.* London: Frank Cass. 1997. First pub. 1831.

Sweeney, James L. "Caribs, Maroons, Jacobins, Brigands, and Sugar Barons: The Last Stand of the Black Caribs on St. Vincent," http://www.diaspora.uiuc.edu/news0307/news0307.html#7 [African Diaspora Archaeology Network], accessed May 2009.

Thompson, Alvin O. *A Documentary History of Slavery in Berbice, 1796–1834.* Georgetown, Guyana: Free Press, 2002.

Young, Sir William. *An Account of the Black Charaibs in the Island of St. Vincent's.* London: Frank Cass and Co., 1971.

7

The Big Fight Back
Suriname and Jamaica

The Negro's revolutionary history is rich, inspiring, and unknown. . . .
The docile Negro is a myth. . . . The only place where Negroes did not revolt is
in the pages of capitalist historians. . . . It is not strange that the Negroes
revolted. It would have been strange if they had not.

—C. L. R. JAMES, *1939. ["The Revolution and the Negro,"* New International,
Volume V, December 1939, pp. 339–343. Published under the name
J. R Johnson; Transcribed by Ted Crawford. http://www.marxists.org
/archive/james-clr/works/1939/12/negro-revolution.htm]

If you think black people are nonviolent, why don't you hit one?

—ELOMBE BRATH, *Harlem lecture, New York, circa the 1980s*

SURINAME

Marronage and Maroon wars continued unabated in Suriname for 200 years, from "earliest remembrance," as Stedman described it. Africans began deserting the plantations and fighting back during the initial English occupation (1651–1667) and continued under Dutch colonization. The last Dutch military expedition against the Maroons was in 1862, one year before Emancipation. In the intervening years various bands of Maroons coalesced into independent nations which still retain a distinctive quasi-national status in independent Suriname.

Maroon struggles against the Suriname plantocracy ranged from the endemic raids on plantations to full-scale wars lasting as many as seven years. Plantation society never ceased trying to militarily defeat the Maroons. They never succeeded. What they did do was negotiate treaties with some Maroon nations, acknowledging their independence and paying them tribute. Suriname's Maroon population was put at about 60,000 circa 1990, divided into the following communities:

Saramaka	25,000
Ndjuka	25,000
Matawai	2,500
Paramaka	2,500
Aluku	2,500
Kwinti	500

Another 3,000–5,000 were in Cayenne and about 5,000 had emigrated to the Netherlands.

By 1717 Maroon communities were sufficiently established for the Dutch to be able to identify several by name. In the late 1720s the Saramakas, Ndjukas and Aluku began to coalesce into national entities. They were able to plunder firelocks and lances from European plantations and terrorized the Europeans, who were unable to contain them. In 1730 the Dutch staged what Stedman called "a most shocking and barbarous execution" of eleven captured Saramakas. They hanged one man on a gibbet suspended by an iron meat hook through his ribs. They chained two of the Africans to stakes and burned them to death over a slow fire; they broke six Maroon women alive upon the rack; they decapitated two Maroon girls. As was often the case, none of these victims uttered even a sigh under torture.

The Dutch hoped to scare the Maroons with this show of barbarity but it had the opposite effect. In 1731 Governor De Cheusses offered the Maroons an amnesty but they showed no interest. David C. Nassy, a leader of the Suriname Jewish community, claimed to have alone led over thirty expeditions against the Maroons between 1731 and 1749. In 1738 the Jewish community, a significant proportion of the plantation ownership class, mounted a campaign against the Maroons after a Maroon attack on the plantation of one of their number, Manuel Pereyra. Pereyra was killed during the campaign.

By the 1750s only two of the last twenty-eight European expeditions against the Maroons could boast of anything resembling success. Six hundred fresh troops from Holland in 1751 made no appreciable difference. Government reprisal excursions had, of necessity, to include large numbers of enslaved porters, bush whackers and other menial laborers. To add to the European discomfiture many of these enslaved, once in the forest, deserted the European patrols to join the Maroons. About

30 of nearly 300 escaped on one occasion in 1755. On another occasion in 1756 about 200 of 345 Africans similarly engaged ran away to the Maroons.

By 1749 the Dutch governor had had enough and he opened negotiations with the Saramakas. He used as a precedent a British Maroon treaty of 1739 in Jamaica. He had the approval of the Dutch authorities in Holland, but the local legislators remained opposed to negotiations with their former enslaved property. The governor presented Captain Adoe, a Creole and chief of the Saramakas, with a "fine large cane" with Suriname's coat of arms engraved on it, as a present. Captain Adoe gave him "a handsome bow" and arrows, which he had made himself.

As part of the negotiations the Dutch undertook to provide the Maroons with tribute consisting of arms, ammunition, cloth, tools, salt beef and pork and other items. The promised presents were intercepted by another Maroon leader, Zam Zam, on their way to Adoe. Adoe thought that the Dutch had reneged on the deal and were only buying time pending the arrival of their fresh troops in 1751. The negotiations therefore broke down.

In February 1757, amidst continuing fighting with the Saramaka and others, a new revolt broke out in the Tempaty Creek area. The enslaved Africans cut off the hand of an overseer, one Bruyere, and chopped the commander of a military post, Van Hertzbergen, on his head.

They then attacked the soldiers, who surrendered the next day. The Africans let them go with their arms and some refreshments. They had pity on the poor mercenary soldiers, said the Africans—for they were practically enslaved themselves. The revolt spread to all seven plantations and about 250 enslaved Africans in the Tempaty area. The European military failed to quell the revolt. The rebels were still in control of the area in July 1757, when they went into the jungle to join the Ndjukas. Nearly twenty years later, when European troops moved through the area, the Tempaty plantations were still in ruins.

The Europeans, explained Stedman, now "saw themselves once more reduced to sue for peace with their own slaves. . . ." In their anguish the Europeans sentenced one of their own, a Captain Mayer, to be shot through the head for cowardice. The governor later pardoned him.

In a preliminary meeting between the parties Captain Boston (also known as Adjaka) of the Ndjukas turned up with a bodyguard of 1,000 armed men. He, like the Dutch governor, was aware of the Jamaican precedent. There is even some speculation that he may have been originally from Jamaica himself. He spoke English and was literate.

The Maroons demanded a yearly tribute of firearms, ammunition and other items which they normally procured on their raids into European settlements. Peace would dry up this supply and the tribute would be a substitute source of supply. The list of tribute items was signed by Paramount Chief (Gaanman) Araby and his six chiefs—Mafunge, Titus, Kwauw, Kwaku, Kofi Semprendre and Boston.

Late in 1759 an official Dutch embassy journeyed into the bush to negotiate the treaty. They met with Paramount Chief Araby, "a very handsome negro," as Stedman described him. Araby had been born in the jungle. He was very gracious and assured the two Dutch emissaries of safe conduct.

When it was ascertained, however, that the Dutch came bearing only trinkets—knives, scissors, combs, small mirrors and the like—Captain Baron became agitated. None of the promised gunpowder, arms and ammunition were forthcoming. Boston "demanded, in a thundering voice, whether the Europeans imagined that the Negroes could live on combs and looking glasses. . . ." He proposed detaining the embassy until the promised negotiated items were forthcoming.

Captain Quaco now intervened, suggesting that these were only emissaries and should not be held responsible. Chief Araby then said that the emissaries should write down a new list dictated by himself. He would give the Dutch a year to comply and deliberate whether they wanted war or peace.

Another Maroon captain then addressed the emissaries in a remarkable speech, reproduced by Stedman:

We desire you to tell your government and your court, that in case they want to raise no new gangs of rebels, they ought to take care that the planters keep a more watchful eye over their own property,

and not to trust them so frequently in the hands of drunken managers and overseers, who by wrongfully and severely chastising the Negroes, debauching their wives and children, neglecting the sick, etc. are the ruin of the colony, and willfully drive to the woods such numbers of stout and active people, who by their sweat earn your subsistence, without whose hands your colony must drop to nothing; and to whom at last, in this disgraceful manner, you are glad to come and sue for friendship.

Treaties were eventually signed with the Ndjukas in 1760, Saramakas in 1762 and Matawai in 1767. The Africans would be recognized as free. They would receive their annual tribute and would deliver up runaways, for which they would be paid. No more than five would appear armed in Paramaribo at any one time. They would keep their settlements at a "proper distance" from European towns and plantations. Both sides would exchange resident envoys.

Not all the Maroons desired peace, but the majority prevailed. The agreement was solemnized, at the Maroons' insistence, by an African blood oath. Chief Araby said he did not trust European oaths, which he had seen them break too many times. Each of the negotiators had to cut himself and let the blood flow into a calabash of clean springwater. A few particles of dry earth were mixed in. Some was poured on the ground as a libation and then everybody had to drink some. The gadoman (priest) then "with a most audible voice and in a most awful manner" invoked the curse of God on anyone who would break this sacred treaty. The Maroon multitude answered "Da so! [Amen]." The Africans, Stedman explained, "are uncommonly tenacious of these solemn engagements. . . ."

In 1762 the Dutch governor received the Ndjuka and Saramaka envoys in state in Paramaribo. There was a parade through the town, with the Africans riding in the governor's private carriage. They were treated to a banquet, where the Maroons sat at the governor's table.

The Saramaka treaty had almost become undone when the renegade Zam Zam repeated his earlier feat of intercepting the Dutch tribute on its way to the Saramaka. Captain Muzinga of the Saramakas, thinking that the Dutch had reneged on their promise, attacked a force of over 150 of Suriname's best troops, killing a large number and carrying off all their baggage and ammunition. Zam Zam's action was later realized, and the Dutch replaced the lost tribute.

The treaties held thereafter, though the Maroons were uncomfortable with the stipulation requiring the return of runaways. During the negotiations the Ndjukas had this requirement modified to exclude runaways who had been off the plantation for a long time and those deserting due to very bad treatment. After signing they continued to resist complying and new Maroons continued to escape from the plantations. It was the activity of some of these, the Cottica Maroons, which led to the seven-year Boni Maroon War (1769–1776). Stedman considered this the "most sanguinary" episode in the history of Maroon–European conflict in Suriname. During that conflict the Europeans actually asked the Ndjukas and Saramakas for assistance against their new Maroon adversaries, but they both refused.

It was this war that brought Stedman to Suriname. He has been cited so many times in this work, on so many aspects of Suriname's plantation society, that it is easy to forget that his primary purpose in the colony was to fight the Maroons. He was an officer in the Scots Brigade, a mercenary outfit in the service of the Dutch crown. Despite his officer status he had an unusual rapport with the European common soldiers, the mercenary black Rangers (his favorite government troops) and even the enslaved African "beasts of burden" (his expression) who carried the soldiers' baggage, cleared paths for them through the jungle, built temporary shelters and transported the sick, dead and wounded.

Little escaped Stedman's attention—the military tactics of his commander, the Swiss Col. Fourgeoud, the extraordinary privations suffered by the European soldiers, the Maroon settlements, and the flora and fauna that he meticulously drew and described. The result was a description of a European–Maroon encounter probably unmatched in the literature of the Caribbean. This was not only a macro view of grand strategies and battles, but also a unique micro view of

the day-to-day drudgery of his campaigns in the sometimes nearly impenetrable jungles of Suriname.

Stedman and his regiment were in Suriname from 1773 to 1778. They came at the behest of the local white population, who felt they were on the brink of destruction by the Cottica rebels (also known as Aluka). Stedman estimated that the Cotticas grew from around 3,000 people in the 1760s to 15,000–20,000 a decade later, as new runaways swelled their numbers. They had become "overbearing and even insolent," he thought.

The Cotticas were so called after the Cottica River, in whose vicinity they lived. By 1772, Stedman said, they had nearly delivered the death blow to Suriname. Plantations everywhere were in flames and ashes, "while the reeking and mangled bodies of their inhabitants were scattered along the banks of the river Cottica, with their throats cut, and their effects pillaged by their own Negroes, who all fled to the woods, men, women and children, without exception."

The whites fled their estates and crowded into Paramaribo. Unable to cope, they turned in desperation "to the dangerous resolution of forming a regiment of manumitted slaves to fight against their own countrymen." Stedman could not believe that "this hazardous resolution had providentially the desired effect." The colonists still felt uneasy, however, with their reliance on Rangers, as these black troops were known in Suriname and around the Caribbean. Hence the request for troops from Holland.

The Cottica rebels were led by Baron, formerly enslaved by one Dahlbergh, a Swede. Baron was literate and a skilled mason. Dahlbergh had taken him to Holland and had promised Baron his freedom. "But Mr. Dahlbergh breaking his word. . . . and selling him to a Jew, Baron obstinately refused to work. . . ." He was therefore publicly flogged under the gallows. He escaped to the woods and swore vengeance on all Europeans.

As in the pre-Stedman era, the enslaved Africans pressed into infrastructural support for the war effort were not reluctant to run away. Sometimes plantation Africans in the vicinity took advantage of the turmoil to make a dash for freedom. On one occasion "twelve fine Negro slaves" defected to the Maroons from the Gold Mine estate. On another occasion seven Africans actually deserted the troops and returned to their estates. Their living conditions among the troops were abominable and they were now emaciated and unwilling to continue. They lived on half rations and were in a state of endemic semi-starvation. They foraged for cabbage trees, seeds, roots, berries and whatever they could find. Stedman described them descending on the stinking carcass of a manatee and tearing it to pieces to supplement their meager rations. They did the same with dead fish they found floating in the water. They offered Stedman, who got along well with them, the limb of a monkey they were eating, but he declined. (Stedman himself was not averse to eating monkeys on his own.) The result of all this, added to the privations of the soldiers, was an outbreak of the bloody flux (also, as previously noted, the scourge of slave ships). Almost everybody, soldiers and enslaved, was affected. Colonel Fourgeoud was not excepted.

The privations of the soldiers were also intense. On one occasion Col. Fourgeoud simply sent his very sick soldiers to die on the riverbanks. Two soldiers perished from eating bitter cassava in a rebel field they were destroying. A marine was taken in a river by a large alligator and never seen again.

With no water for days, the "Negro slaves found means to procure us some, which, though stagnant and stinking like a kennel, we drank, straining it through our shirt-sleeves." On another occasion of no water for days some soldiers, Stedman said, "crept on all fours and licked scanty drops of dew from the fallen leaves" on the ground.

The soldiers waded through swamps in chest-high water, were "terribly mangled" by thorns and were stung by "Patat lice, ants, and *wassy-wassy*, or wild bees. . . ." Worse than all of this "was the fatigue of marching in a burning sun, and the last two hours in total darkness, holding each other by the hand; and having left ten men behind, some with agues, some stung blind, and some with their feet full of chigoes."

Mosquitoes were a major problem. Camping at night in the forest with the Maroons nearby, the soldiers dared not light any fires to reveal their positions. This meant that there was no smoke to help drive away the mosquitoes. The soldiers were reduced to digging holes in the ground with their bayonets. They put their heads in the holes, stopped

up the space with their hammocks and slept on their bellies, all in the effort to escape the mosquitoes. Stedman took the advice of an African and slung his hammock high up in a tree while the swarm of buzzing insects devoured his colleagues below. He had to dig bush worms out of his arms.

In the rainy season the soldiers marched through heavy rains. The mornings were so cold and damp, Stedman said, that it was like sleeping in a frost, especially when they had spent the night in wet clothes. Stedman later imitated the Rangers and marched half naked, thereby partially eliminating the wet clothes problem, and being altogether "more comfortable than any of my trembling, ghastly looking companions."

When a sentry reported a Maroon with a lighted pipe nearby, soldiers scrambled out of their hammocks, only to be informed by an African that it was a firefly. Robert Dudley in Trinidad in 1595 and the English in Santo Domingo in 1655 had been similarly fooled by fireflies.

By the end of 1775 even the indomitable Stedman had had enough (even though it was to be three more years before his tour of duty ended). December 31, 1775, found him in an "encampment . . . intolerable beyond every description being constantly overflowed, so that the ammunition and provisions were stowed for preservation on wooden rafts; nor could we step out of our hammocks without being up to the knees in mud and water, where it was most shallow, while the gnat and other insects devoured us alive." The result was "*another* barge full of dying wretches," a "floating *charnel-house*," sent down river to the hospital. "My heart now began to sink with accumulated disasters," Stedman confessed. He could see no end to the misery, and he "became weary of life." He fell on his "naked knees" and begged heaven to hurt him if he didn't find a way out of his awful situation.

Stedman participated in seven campaigns against the Cotticas during his five years in Suriname. For most of that period his unit bore the brunt of the fighting. The pattern of engagement that developed was classic guerilla warfare, similar to that fought throughout the Caribbean. The broad outlines of these campaigns would also have been familiar to twentieth-century conflicts in such places as Viet Nam.

The Cotticas knew their environment very well and were much more mobile than the European forces.

The Cotticas won most of the direct military encounters with the Dutch. Like all guerillas they tried to choose the place and time of firefights. They relied on ambushes, booby traps (sharpened stakes concealed under bush, for example) and their knowledge of the jungle. They would fire on the enemy from the tops of trees, sometimes descending and making their escape with an agility that the Europeans found astonishing.

They regularly attacked Dutch jungle patrols, Stedman said, sometimes killing everybody and capturing guns and ammunition. While Col. Fourgeoud's troops were tramping through the jungle in search of an elusive foe, the Maroons would often double back and attack plantations.

While patrolling a river on the lookout for the Cotticas, Stedman received a report that they had just burnt three estates and "cut the throats of all the white inhabitants that fell in their way." On this occasion several of Stedman's sick soldiers crawled on their hands and knees to arms and "several . . . dropped dead on the spot." In a similar strike the Cotticas burnt an estate and killed all the white people except one man who miraculously escaped by hiding in mangrove. When Col. Fourgeoud left Jew's Savannah, where he had been operating for some time, the Maroons, whose intelligence was usually very good, moved in to pillage and burn.

The typical Maroon plan for attacking estates was to "lurk" in the surrounding bushes all night. They would attack just before daybreak. They would kill all the Europeans and abduct the black women, "whom they had with the spoil," Stedman commented, "and treat with the utmost insolence should they make opposition." The Maroons could be exceedingly patient while laying an ambush or preparing an attack. "[N]or can I help remarking the generalship of the rebel Negroes," said Stedman, "who had kept lying quiet till the removal of the Society troops from Devil's Harwar, and seized the very first day of their departure," to launch their attack.

African cemetery, Jew's Savannah, Suriname, photographed in 2008.

Stedman, who wrote his diary entries, drew his sketches and read books even in his hammock in the jungle, has provided a new famous drawing and literary sketch of a "Rebel Negro Armed and on his Guard."

This rebel Negro is armed with a firelock and a hatchet; his hair, though woolly, may be observed to be plaited close to his head, by way of distinction from the rangers, or any other straggling Negroes, who are not as yet captured amongst them; his beard is grown to a point, like that of all the Africans, when they have no opportunity of shaving. The principal dress of this man consists of a cotton sheet negligently tied across his shoulders, which protects him from the weather, and serves him also to rest on: while he always sleeps under cover in the most obscure places he can find, when detached from his companions. The rest of his dress is a camisa, tied around his loins like a handkerchief; his pouch, which is made of some animal's skin; a few cotton strings for ornament around his ancles [sic] and wrists; and a superstitious *obia* or amulet tied about his neck, in which he places all his confidence. The skull and ribs are supposed to be the bones of his enemies, scattered upon the sandy savannah.

A Surinamese Maroon, armed and on his guard. This now iconic portrait, drawn by J. G. Stedman in the 1770s, has been reproduced many times, often without attribution and creating the impression that it originated in some other part of the Caribbean.

The Maroon Cottica guerillas won most of their direct clashes with the Dutch forces, usually in spectacular fashion. They were now in a position to return the savagery practiced on the enslaved population by the Dutch and they did so with little quarter asked or given. Stedman's description of one such encounter also illustrates the superior intelligence capabilities and general guerilla tactics of the Maroon fighters. It involved a detachment of European soldiers led by one Lt. Lepper, whose attacking party of around thirty men was completely wiped out.

> But the rebels being apprized [sic] of his intentions by their spies, which they constantly employ, immediately marched out to receive him; in his way they laid themselves in ambush, near the borders of a deep marsh, through which the soldiers were to pass to the rebel settlement. No sooner had the unfortunate men got into the swamp and up to their armpits, than their black enemies rushed out from under cover, and shot them dead at their leisure in the water, while they were unable to return the fire more than once, their situation preventing them from reloading their muskets. Their gallant commander, being imprudently distinguished by a gold-laced hat, was shot through the head in the first onset. The few that scrambled out in the marsh upon the banks were immediately put to death in the most barbarous manner, except five or six, who were taken prisoners and carried alive to the settlement of the rebels.

A survivor reported that the Maroon chief cut off the heads of the fallen enemy and took them home as trophies.

While marching against the Maroons during one campaign in 1775, Stedman's men came upon two or three heaps of bones of colleagues previously annihilated by the Maroons. One, "a spectacle sufficient to shock the most intrepid," consisted of "the ground strewed with skulls, bones, and ribs still covered with human flesh, and besmeared with the blood of those unfortunate men who were killed with Captain Meyland." The Dutch had actually buried the remains, but the Maroons dug them up for their clothes and then proceeded "to mangle the bodies, which, like ferocious animals, they had torn limb from limb."

The spectacle gave Stedman one of his rare episodes of misgivings on the wisdom of "engag[ing] with Negroes." It nevertheless filled the common soldiers with a desire for revenge. A sergeant broke down at the spectacle. Stedman poetically called him a "pale coward," despite his own misgivings—"With chattering teeth he stands, and stiff'ning hair, / And looks a bloodless image of despair."

The Europeans, for their part, continued their savagery against the enslaved in peacetime into their treatment of Maroons who fell into their hands. A young Maroon, about twenty years old or less, was captured with his thigh "shot to shivers." The troops tied him like a hog on a pole and brought him 6 miles through the jungle, "bearing all the weight of his body upon his shattered limbs," without bandages. He expired.

Stedman and his troops fought a war of attrition against the Cotticas. They suffered great losses to fighting and illness. They were greatly aided by the Rangers, who Stedman considered much better fighters than the Europeans in the jungle warfare that engulfed them. Joining Stedman's force as privates were two African veterans of a recent Berbice uprising, Okera and Gowsary. They had perpetrated "most inhuman" murders against whites in Berbice but were pardoned by the Berbice governor when they delivered up their chief, Atta, to the Dutch.

Despite his loss of most firefights with the Maroons, Col. Fourgeoud doggedly pursued his overall plan, which would be equally consistent with antiguerilla warfare in the twentieth century. His plan was to locate and destroy Maroon settlements and crops, thereby depriving them of the means of sustaining themselves. The Maroons were well aware of Fourgeoud's plans. They fortified and concealed their settlements and prepared elaborate contingency plans to evacuate women, children and fighters in the event of European attack on their towns.

All of these features were illustrated in the battle for Gado Saby ("I shall molder before I shall be

The Sculls of Lieut. Leppar; & Six of his Men.

European soldiers in Suriname overcome by the discovery of the mutilated remains of thirty of their colleagues who were completely wiped out by Maroons; drawn by J. G. Stedman in the 1770s.

taken"), major town of the Cottica Maroons. Gado Saby was the home of Bonny, "a relentless mulatto." He was born in the jungle. His mother escaped to the Maroons while pregnant with him, after being raped by her white owner. Other contemporary rebel chiefs were Baron, who was thought to have linked up with Bonny, Quammy, Coromantyn, Cojo, Arico and Joli-Coeur, "the last two being celebrated captains, whose revenge was insatiable against the whites, particularly Joli-Coeur. . . ."

Baron's town of Boucou ("I shall perish before I shall be taken") provides a classic example of a Maroon settlement's defense. It was built on a quasi-island completely surrounded by a swamp and approachable only by underwater paths, known only to the Maroons. Baron placed loaded swivel guns (captured from plantations) before these paths. The entire area was fenced in by several thousand palisades.

Stedman's troops tried to bridge the swamp around Baron's town but lost several men in the process. With ammunition running short and many of their men killed, they were about to give up when the Rangers discovered the secret paths. This enabled the troops to ford the swamp on one side. They drew Baron's troops by a feint while the Rangers attacked from the other side.

They captured Boucou, but Baron and most of his people were able to escape, thanks to their care-fully laid contingency plans. Before leaving, Baron's people cut the throats of ten to twelve Rangers who had lost their way in the swamp. They cut off the ears, nose and lips of one unfortunate Ranger and sent him to his friends. The poor man expired shortly afterward.

Stedman's major battle was the taking of Gado Saby, Bonny's town. He provided a graphic account of the field of battle:

the continued noise of the firing, shouting, swearing, and hollering of black and white men mixed together; the groans of the wounded and the dying, all weltering in blood and in dust; the shrill sound of the Negro horns from every quarter, and the crackling of the burning village . . . the clouds of smoke that every where

surrounded us, the ascending flames, etc. etc. formed on the whole, such an uncommon scene as I cannot describe. . . .

At Gady Sabo, Col. Fourgeoud was able to destroy several flourishing fields of rice and provisions. They found the skulls of three white soldiers and the fresh skulls of two young Maroons who had been executed on the eve of battle for speaking favorably of the Europeans. (After taking some other Maroon towns the Europeans had discovered the skulls of seven of their colleagues stuck on stakes, while their bodies lay moldering on the ground underneath their heads. A captured rebel woman explained that the seven had been captured alive, taken to the town, stripped naked and flogged to death for the amusement of Maroon women and children.)

At Gabo Saby the Maroons were able to safely evacuate their women and children. They then very calmly and deliberately burnt the town. Fourgeoud had to be content with destroying more of the Maroons' food supply. While this weakened the Maroons' ability to continue fighting in that area, it robbed Fourgeoud of military victory, prisoners and booty. This greatly upset Fourgeoud, who, as Stedman explained, "on finding himself thus foiled by a naked Negro, was unable any longer to restrain his resentment, and swore aloud that he would pursue Bonny" to the end of the world.

Fourgeoud immediately sent his Captain Bolts with European soldiers and Rangers to pursue Bonny. The remainder were left on half rations to beat their own rice using the rebels' mortars, made from purple heart wood. Bonny's men attacked Bolt's party and inflicted a heavy defeat. They spared the Europeans but wrought dreadful havoc among the Rangers, who they especially hated, considering then traitors to the race. The Maroons also returned to the evacuated and scuttled town that very night, to harass the soldiers. Their fighting capacity was not impaired by their evacuation of Gado Saby. In the ensuing days they continued to mount attacks on European targets.

Fourgeoud's men meanwhile were sick, wounded, starving or dying. Ammunition was running low. The enslaved porters were occupied carrying the sick and wounded in hammocks while they themselves could hardly find subsistence. The bloody flux broke out once more. They were now living on rice, yams, peas and corn. Although "that kind of nourishment will keep the Indians and Negroes strong as horses," Stedman explained, "the Europeans cannot long subsist without animal food, which was at this time so very scarce, that even the Jew soldiers of the Society troops devoured salt pork as fast as they could catch it."

The enslaved were so starved that they killed a monkey and "boiled it with skin, hair, intestines and all." They tore it to bits before it was even properly cooked. They offered Stedman a limb but he was unable to accept, though he was not averse to eating properly prepared monkey. These laborers, now thoroughly emaciated, were sent back to their owners and replaced by a fresh draft. But these "*beasts* [Stedman's emphasis] of burden" were "not only overloaded and starved, but beat like mules or asses by every ill-tempered individual."

Yet Stedman could claim a victory at Gado Saby. The troops had "neither captured any rebels, nor gained booty," but this was, he thought, nevertheless an "almost decisive victory." The Maroons had been forced to withdraw deeper into the jungle, where they would less easily raid plantations and attract new runaway recruits. This was very much better, he thought, than the "Dutch making a shameful peace with them," as they probably would have done without the military help.

Fourgeoud now returned to the remains of Gado Saby, where he was able to destroy four more fields of cassava, yams, plantain, pistachio nuts, corn and pigeon (or Angola) peas. On one of these raids Fourgeoud's soldiers captured a pregnant Maroon woman and her eight-year-old son. A Maroon girl of about fifteen escaped. Because of "her great agility, and being stark naked," she was able to slip out of the hands of her would-be capturer. The eight-year-old had not seen white people before and would not let them touch him. He called whites "Yorica," signifying devil.

Weeks after the scuttling of Gado Saby, in December 1775, the Maroons were still mounting attacks. They burned a house on the Killestyn Nora estate with the overseer in it, "ransacked the whole

plantation," and "chopped off the limbs" of a colored boy child to avenge themselves on his white father. In August 1776, long after Fourgeoud claimed eliminating them as a threat, news reached Paramaribo that the Maroons had attacked the Bergendal estate and taken away "all the black women," despite the presence of a European military post in the vicinity.

Earlier in 1776 the Dutch had in desperation actually sent an embassy to the Owcas (Ndjukas) and Saramakas requesting their cooperation against the Cotticas. This is after Fourgeoud had plied them with presents. The Ndjukas and Saramakas absolutely refused.

Word came in November 1776, over a year after the battle of Gado Saby, that the Maroons had crossed the Cottica River into Cayenne where the French were willing to accommodate them.

The Dutch now began a road around Suriname, to be equipped with military posts at intervals. And Fourgeoud claimed victory, based on his assertion of 21 Maroon villages or towns destroyed, and 200 fields demolished. The Bonny Maroons nevertheless later resumed war against the Dutch. Marronage continued until independence in 1863.

JAMAICA

The Jamaican Maroons, together with the Surinamese probably the best known in the Caribbean, had a history similar in broad outline to the others. While the Spaniards were trying to cope with the British invasion of 1655 many Africans were able to resort to marronage. They grouped in the Clarendon mountains under the leadership of Juan Lubolo, later known as Juan de Bolas.

These Maroons were induced to help the Spanish resistance by promises of official freedom. In one encounter in 1656 they killed forty British soldiers. Somewhere around 1659–1660 de Bolas went over to the British who made similar promises of freedom. The Maroons helped the British find and defeat Arnaldo de Yassi, leader of the Spanish resistance. De Bolas and his followers were granted their freedom and de Bolas was appointed colonel of the black militia. Some Maroons nevertheless spurned the British offers of pardons, freedom and 20 acres each.

The British utilized de Bolas in the attack on these Maroons and he was killed in this endeavor.

Maroons continued to be a permanent fixture of the Jamaican landscape but their numbers increased significantly after an enslaved revolt of 1690. Many of these Maroons now coalesced, again in the Clarendon hills, under the leadership of Cudjoe. By the 1730s repeated efforts to wipe them out had failed. Other communities existed in the east of the island (the Windward Maroons) and elsewhere.

In 1730 the government offered a bounty of 10 pounds for each Maroon captured. Three major expeditions were sent against them that year. Indigenous people from the Mosquito coast of Honduras were introduced to help hunt the Maroons. Military outposts were set up to destroy Maroon provision grounds. Ranger units and "Confidential Black Shot" were also thrown into the fight. Cudjoe decided to relocate to the more inaccessible cockpit country of Trelawney.

In 1734 the British finally destroyed Nanny Town of the Windward Maroons, after several attempts. Nanny Town was named after Nanny, a Maroon leader of Ashanti background, and currently a national hero of Jamaica. The few documented details of her life are supplemented by oral tradition. Considerable legend also attaches to her history.

By the late 1730s the British regime in Jamaica felt itself under so much stress from the Maroons that they decided to sue for peace. A British delegation went to Cudjoe's headquarters at Petty River Bottom. After taking elaborate precautions against surprise attacks, Cudjoe spoke with the delegation.

The British historian R. C. Dallas, in his *History of the Maroons* (1803), presented an unlikely story of Cudjoe prostrating himself and kissing the feet of Colonel John Guthrie, chief British negotiator. This story is not corroborated anywhere. The treaty was signed on March 1, 1739. It gave 1,500 acres to Cudjoe's people. They could hunt anywhere except within 3 miles of any settlement. Two European ambassadors would live among them. Cudjoe could administer justice in his own community, short of imposing the death penalty. The Maroons promised to capture and hand over rebels and runaways, for a price. Like the Surinamese Maroons later, Cudjoe insisted on a blood oath.

The British signed a similar treaty with Quao's Windward Maroons on June 23, 1739. This was after a force of 200 seamen, plus militia, supported by 70 enslaved porters, had been routed by Quao at the "Spanish River Fight." Here too it was the British who initiated negotiations.

After the treaties the British tried to whittle away Maroon independence by restrictions on the time Maroons could spend outside their towns and other petty regulations. The Maroons captured runaways but simultaneously maintained close relationships with the enslaved and even continued to harbor some. They may have made it more difficult for new runaways to establish themselves in the forest, though several new small communities of Maroons appeared between the treaties and Emancipation. In 1760 the Maroons killed Tackey, leader of the important rebellion that bore his name.

The "treaty Maroons" were now consolidated into five towns. Trelawney Town, the biggest, was Cudjoe's town. Accompong Town and Scotts Hall were also associated with Cudjoe. Charles Town and Moore Town (new home of Nanny's followers) constituted the Windward Maroons.

After decades of relative peace the Trelawney War of 1795–1796 provided one of the most serious clashes between Maroons and the British in Jamaican history. As in so many Maroon-European wars, the Maroons, though greatly outnumbered, were able to win practically all the military skirmishes. Their ambushes, mobility and general guerilla tactics again enabled them to inflict substantial casualties on their enemy. They suffered practically no known casualties, but as in the case of the Black Caribs, they eventually agreed to negotiate as a result of the destruction of their provision grounds by the British. Like the Black Caribs they were deported (in 1796, one year before the Caribs). Their deportation, to Nova Scotia in Canada, was a deliberate act of treachery on the part of the British, who reneged on an express undertaking not to deport them if they laid down their arms.

Hostilities broke out in July 1795 after two Trelawney Maroons were flogged in the Montego Bay workhouse, accused by two white men of killing some hogs. The sentence violated the terms of the Maroon treaty. This incident was joined to other

Jamaican Maroon Capt. Leonard Parkinson, 1796.

festering grievances, including upset at the now inadequate size of their land allocation.

The British preemptively declared martial law on August 2, 1795. They recalled 1,500 troops on their way to intervene in the Haitian Revolution. They also mobilized several thousand militia and conscripted an enslaved contingent of Confidential Black Shot. All of this against 500 Trelawney men, women and children, only 167 of whom were actual fighters.

On August 8, Lt. Governor Lord Balcarres issued a proclamation calling on all Trelawneys to surrender by August 12. A bounty would be paid for all captured thereafter. About thirty older Trelawneys surrendered, including Montague James, the venerable old chief. Six more were arrested on their way to surrender. The remainder burned their Old and New Towns, as part of a scorched earth policy.

The British policy, already a classic antiguerilla strategy, was to destroy the Trelawney provision grounds, denude the forests which gave them cover, encircle them with military posts, and isolate them politically. The British were able to mobilize not only white troops, but colored militia, enslaved conscripted Black Shots, Accompong Maroons and a few Windward Maroons (though most of these refused to cooperate). Some enslaved persons joined the Trelawneys and many others took the opportunity to become independent Maroons and harass the British on their own. The Trelawneys meanwhile retreated, in the words of Lord Balcarres, as cited by Mavis Campbell, "into a Country of Rocks beyond description—wild and barren into which no white person has ever entered."

From August to December 1795 the virtual handful of Trelawneys wrought havoc among British forces. "As it is impossible to get up with the Savages, without first receiving the fire of their Ambush," wrote General George Walpole, commander of British forces, again as cited by Mavis Campbell, "our loss in every affair is constantly from 8 to 12 men killed and wounded."

In mid-August the Trelawneys ambushed a force of British dragoons, militia and volunteers, killing thirty-seven and wounding many more, and without a single Trelawney casualty. Among the British dead were Colonel Sandford, overall commander of the British war effort and Colonel Gallimore, commander of the militia.

In December 1795 the British in desperation deployed 40 Cuban *chasseurs* (professional Maroon hunters) and their 104 ferocious dogs. (Dogs, as already seen, had been a part of the Spanish arsenal since the early depredations against the indigenous people.) Shortly after the dogs were introduced, however, General Walpole for the British and Chief Montague James for the Trelawneys, signed a peace treaty on December 28, 1795. James had earlier been released from British custody to communicate British peace proposals to the Trelawneys. He had instead remained among his people and joined their struggle against the British.

At the time of the treaty the Trelawneys had not been defeated militarily though their access to provisions and water was more difficult than before. According to the peace agreement the Trelawneys were to beg pardon (shades of the first Carib-British War), they were to return to their Old Town or wherever the British determined and they were to give up runaways. General Walpole swore on oath that the Trelawneys' demand for no deportation as a condition for laying down their arms would be respected. Once the Trelawneys gathered up their old, women and children and laid down their arms, however, the British reneged on the no-deportation promise. General Walpole was chagrined and voiced his upset at this betrayal, but to no effect. Walpole's words, in a letter to Lord Balcarres, cited by Mavis Campbell, speak eloquently to his own integrity and to the foul play of the British authorities:

My Lord, to be plain with you it was thro [sic] my means alone that the Maroons were induced to Surrender from a Reliance which they had in my word; from a Conviction impressed upon them by me that the white people would never break their faith. All these things strongly call upon me as the Instrumental Agent in this business to see a due observance of the Terms or in case of Violation to resign my Command and if that should not be accepted to declare the facts to the world and to leave them to judge how far I ought or ought not to be Implicated in the Guilt or Infamy of such a proceeding.

Five hundred and sixty-eight Trelawneys were deported from Jamaica on June 6, 1796. Only 167 were fighting men. The rest were women, children and the elderly. About fifty who were not caught up in the net of the deportation left voluntarily rather than be separated from their families. Their destination was cold, inhospitable Nova Scotia in Canada, a British colony since 1749. For any of them to return to Jamaica would be a capital offence. The guilty would be executed "without benefit of clergy." After four years in Nova Scotia they asked to be sent back to Africa. They arrived in Sierra Leone in October 1800.

The remaining treaty Maroons continued to fulfill their treaty obligations, including the capture of runaways. They were last used in the Jamaica Rebellion of 1865, when they captured Paul Bogle, the rebellion's leader and now, like Nanny and Cudjoe, a national hero of Jamaica.

THE MAROONS: REASONS FOR SUCCESS

The Maroons were generally pretty successful. Whether we consider an Esteban Montejo who lived alone in the Cuban bush for ten years, or those from places like Suriname who were able to match and often defeat European armies and their vassals, the picture is an impressive one. Yet the obstacles to Maroon success were formidable. The Europeans pursued them relentlessly and the Maroons often had no reliable easily accessible source of arms and supplies. Yet they persisted, survived and on occasion achieved spectacular success.

The first reason for Maroon success was that Maroons had only limited options. Once the Rubicon into marronage was crossed, it mostly became a de facto declaration of liberty or death, or at best liberty or very severe punishment, possibly involving loss of limbs, castration, brutal whipping and the like.

The case of the Maroon woman Zabeth in Saint Domingue in 1768 is illustrative. She was placed permanently in chains for running away, but her owner was prevailed upon to unchain her, since she was near death. She promptly ran away again but was apprehended and chained in a mill house. There she put her hands between the mills and suffered three broken fingers before they could extricate her. They next chained her in a hospital. Her owner was again prevailed upon to release her chains since she seemed very near death. He did so and had her grave dug in her presence. She absconded again. This time, the owner told his diary, he chained her in the mill, there to await death in chains.

The "Mulatto Nancy" in 1700s Christiansted repeatedly ran away, once with her eleven-month-old child, despite bearing the marks of previous escapes— "sundry scars" from beatings on her face, shackles still attached to one foot, sores from shackles on another foot.

This is why Maroon communities were usually ruled by strong persons (often elected kings and queens) who maintained harsh, even military-like, discipline. New runaways might have to undergo lengthy periods of probation before being accepted as trusted members of the community. Two Cottica Maroons who spoke favorably of the Europeans were executed on the spot and their heads put on poles.

Maroons also practiced a vigorous lifestyle that produced intrepid fighters, and outstanding physical specimens. Their British adversaries in Jamaica praised the Maroons for their fine physiques, even surpassing those of their enslaved counterparts. Their agility in the jungle was often a cause of comment by Europeans.

The Maroons also developed a whole range of survival strategies for the harsh life in the jungle. They learnt the medicinal properties of herbs and plants. They improvised substitutes for unavailable comforts of plantation or urban living. Montejo made a tobacco substitute from the leaves of the macaw tree. He distilled a coffee substitute from roasted *guanina* leaves. He found bees' honey in the hollows of trees and concocted a delicious drink by mixing it with stream water.

Stedman said that the Suriname Maroons made salt from "palm-tree ashes." They made butter by "clarifying the fat of palm-tree worms". They also made butter from pistachio and other nuts, which sounded similar to today's peanut butter. They made palm wine. They used calabashes for cups and allied purposes. They wove hammocks from the leaves and fronds of the silk grass plant and maurecee tree. They made brooms, candles, wax, corks and other necessities from the materials at hand. Some of this know-how was doubtless brought from Africa. Palm wine and the use of nut butter in cooking doubtless came within this category.

They caught fish and game, either by hunting or appropriating from accessible plantation provision grounds. They preserved meat by barbecuing it. Montejo said that if he was able to procure a small pig he was assured of food for a couple weeks.

When Maroons formed settled communities they cultivated extensive fields of food crops. These then became the target of anti-Maroon forces. Whether singly or in communities, Maroons often chose the most inaccessible places imaginable. In eighteenth-century St. Thomas, Maroons lived in virtually unapproachable caves on cliffs, too steep to be scaled from the sea and too obstructed by vegetation to be easily approached by land. The whites organized three Maroon-hunting parties a year but could not dislodge them.

Large Maroon villages and towns might be located on islands surrounded by swamps, or perched high in inaccessible rugged country approachable only by secret (even underwater) paths or only via a narrow single-file-only track where defenders could easily mount an ambush. There was usually some equally secret or obscure way of evacuating women and children, and later the fighters themselves, in the event of attack. In Suriname, Maroons might cross a waterway by sitting on a tree trunk, and then being "ferried" over by the best swimmers.

An anti-Maroon fighter in Cuba in 1830 marveled at the ditches full of pointed sticks; the steep, winding paths leading apparently nowhere; the ambushes; the Maroons' ability to negotiate seemingly unclimbable cliffs; the secret escape paths; and the dwellings so spread out that an intruder could not surprise more than two or three at a time, so low that they could not be seen over the bush or detected until one was right up on them. If those people had firearms, he said, they would be absolutely invincible. Many of the Cuban *palenques* survived to the end of slavery and became the nuclei of small towns.

When expecting an attack, Maroon communities might even go so far as to erect temporary settlements to wait out the invaders or serve as muster points for an orderly evacuation. Religion and political ideas also contributed to success. African religions were adapted to fit new environments. Sometimes a fierce hatred of white society played a role in doctrinal cohesion. The case of the eight-year-old Surinamese boy who thought that white people were devils, comes to mind. The very names of Maroon towns sometimes reflected their spirit of hatred toward and defiance of white society. In Suriname there were Boucoo ("I shall molder before I shall be taken"), Gado Saby ("God only knows me, and none else"), Cofaay ("Come try me, if you be man") and others. A Maroon village in Trelawney, Jamaica, was named Me-no-sen-you-no-come.

The Maroons also mastered the art of guerilla warfare. At a time when European soldiers might still be encumbered by layers of gaudy clothing, Maroons were sparsely clothed in a manner calculated to make them less conspicuous targets. The Africans, both Maroons and European-led Rangers, fought in an intricate set-piece maneuver. A captain with a horn led a small detachment of eight to ten men. They spread out and lay on the ground, firing from behind cover. Each warrior was supported by two unarmed colleagues. One took his place if he was killed while the other removed the body.

Stedman described in text and drawing their set-piece action. One man fired and then moved away to a predetermined spot to reload, while another then fired from a predetermined spot and moved away and so on. They fired from a prostrate or kneeling position. When the bush was thick, "each Negro skulks behind a thick tree," firing from relative safety and "usually resting his piece against the trunk or the forked branches, like the *Shawanese* and *Delaware* Indians." All of this was obviously novel to most of the European soldiers.

Maroon fighters ran quickly in a zigzag fashion or tumbled along the ground, making it difficult for opposing forces to shoot them. All of this was based on exhaustively practiced drills. During a period of peace in Jamaica, Maroon fighters actually staged a military display for a British governor, where they showcased these skills. European troops, unaccustomed to these maneuvers, would sometimes try to imitate them in an ad hoc way in the thick of battle.

During battle, Maroons communicated via horns (e.g., the abeng or cow's horn of Jamaica, or conch shells in Suriname). Commanders could communicate orders to advance, retreat or whatever by the use of these horns, which were the field telephones of Maroon forces. The horns could also provide several hours advanced warning in the event of approaching enemy forces.

Maroon communities were protected by a network of spies and lookouts which made it difficult to take them by surprise. In extreme circumstances, if even their commanders deemed it wise to avoid a pitched battle, their lookouts would normally provide enough time for the community to burn their own town if necessary, and take their women and children to safety in an orderly manner. In such cases one or two fighters might stay behind to coolly fire their town with all deliberate speed, within full view of the advancing European troops. Once the Europeans occupied the smoldering ruins some fighters might circle back and attack them.

These towns, it must be said, could be quite pleasant and comfortable places. Furniture, silver plate and other conveniences of plantation society were often brought back after raids. Gado Saby in Suriname contained about 100 houses, some of 2 stories. "[W]e arrived in the most beautiful field of ripe rice," Stedman wrote, of his approach to Gado Saby, "in the form of an oblong square [sic], from which the *rebel town* appeared at a distance, in the form of an amphitheatre, sheltered from the sun by the foliage of a few lofty trees, the whole presenting a *coup d'oeil* romantic and enchanting beyond conception [Emphasis in original]."

When Chief Bonny evacuated his temporary settlement after scuttling Gady Sabo, Col. Fourgeoud actually stayed in his house of "four pretty little rooms, and a shed or piazza inclosed [sic] with neat manicole palisades."

Some guerilla tactics adapted to the scarcity of guns and bullets. If guns were in short supply Maroons might carve wooden guns that looked from a distance like the real thing, in order to fool the opposing forces. Nails, stones and even buttons were sometimes made to do for nonexistent bullets. Sharpened bamboo and other sticks camouflaged in the bush were designed to impale unsuspecting enemy troops. Sometimes, mounting an ambush from high ground overlooking a narrow single-file-only path, Maroons could conserve ammunition by rolling large boulders down on the Europeans trapped below. What firearms and ammunition the Maroons did have were obtained largely from raids on plantations and capture of enemy supplies in battle. The firearms so procured could be formidable, including heavy-duty swivel guns.

The Maroons knew that they were in a state of perpetual war against a ruthless enemy bent on re-enslaving them and capable of extreme brutality. The Maroons dealt with this reality by asking no quarter and giving none. Planter society, which had no qualms about beheading, dismembering, drawing and quartering, castrating and raping its enslaved, delighted in describing Maroons as savages. The Maroons responded with, yes, a savagery that could strike fear into the heart of even so well-seasoned a professional soldier as Stedman. Whether in Dominica, St. Vincent, Suriname, Haiti or elsewhere, they could quite literally tear their enemies limb from limb, stick their heads on poles, strew their mangled bodies over the ground, and generally match planter society, outrage for outrage.

The Maroons also developed a good sense of realpolitik. They did not mind joining the English at Nombre de Dios against their more immediate enemies, the Spanish. The Black Caribs similarly did not mind allying themselves with the French against the English. When negotiations seemed feasible, they did not mind going that route. In Jamaica especially some argue that they were outsmarted by duplicitous English negotiators. This was clearly the case in the betrayal and deportation of the Trelawney Maroons after they laid down their arms. It may be the case in the Jamaican Maroons' acceptance of treaty provisions mandating capture of runaways. The Surinamese Maroons seem to have more successfully extricated themselves from the full impact of similar treaty clauses. Here, perhaps more than anywhere else, the absence of the Maroons' own documentary historical record is a severe impediment to understanding what really happened.

If the guerilla tactics of the Maroons would have been at home in the twentieth century, so too would have the antiguerilla campaigns of their more enlightened persecutors. The general tactic was to reduce the Maroons' area of operations by destroying provision grounds, denuding forest cover, encircling them by land (or sea if available) and generally cutting them off from food, material, reinforcements and even water. These tactics offered more hope of success than direct military confrontation. For established Maroon communities in places such as St. Vincent, Jamaica and Suriname, the Europeans never really won any decisive military battles, even where, as in St. Vincent and Jamaica, they were able to deport large numbers.

One factor which cannot be overlooked in Maroon success was the quality of leadership that arose among them. Leaders tended to be accomplished warriors, strong administrators and able military strategists. They were strong leaders, as they had to be, existing in a state of war, and usually commanded the fierce loyalty of their followers. Stedman characteristically gave the Maroon leadership its due. "This was certainly such a masterly trait of generalship in a savage people," he said on one occasion, "whom we affected to despise, as would have done honor to any European commander and has perhaps been seldom equaled by more civilized nations."

A widespread European tactic against Maroons was the use of "loyal" African troops to fight their freedom-seeking compatriots. "Ranger" units existed in several Caribbean territories. They were made up of enslaved persons specially freed or promised freedom in exchange for service. They became professional soldiers, occupying a niche in plantation society different from that of normal enslaved persons. There were also the "Confidential Black Shot," raised from among the enslaved. Sometimes, when the situation was dire enough, whites might arm their enslaved on an ad hoc basis. With his soldiers all dead, dying, sick or wounded, Stedman was once "obliged to convert the slaves into soldiers: these I armed with a hatchet, not daring to trust them with a fire lock."

There were also mercenary units, most notably for the British colonies, the West India Regiment (WIR). This unit, which eventually grew into several battalions and served until the 1920s, was begun in 1795 with a nucleus of African American veterans of British forces during the American War of Independence. It was augmented over the years by "liberated Africans" captured from foreign slave ships after the British ended their own slave trade. Ranger and other units of the enslaved, in addition to free colored and black militias, were also on occasion drafted into the WIR.

The WIR served in the Caribbean, Mobile (Alabama), New Orleans, West Africa and, during the First World War, in East Africa. They fought against the Black Caribs in St. Vincent, helped put down the Jamaica Rebellion of 1865 and helped win Ashanti for the British. Elements of the WIR mutinied in Dominica in 1802 and in the Daaga Rebellion in Trinidad in 1837.

The list of black forces arrayed against the Maroons includes free colored and black militias everywhere from Saint Domingue to Suriname. And of course treaty Maroons were officially obliged to fight against nontreaty Maroons. The colored and black militias were everywhere forced to undertake anti-Maroon activities as a kind of specialty. In Suriname at least, however, some volunteered for anti-Maroon service.

This widespread use of black troops was based in part on a realization that they performed better than whites in jungle warfare conditions. The Rangers were Stedman's favorite troops. The use of black troops, through force or the promise of freedom, was also a cynical effort to divide and rule.

Stedman, not surprisingly, provides the most detailed account of Ranger operations. They were just as African as the Maroons, often coming from the same "Coromantee" (Akan cultural) group. They knew the jungle very well, were more inured to its hardships than the white soldiers and were quite comfortable in their mercenary role. (They did pack up and go home at least once though, due to a dispute with the Dutch authorities.) Stedman marveled at how seemingly easy it was to enlist enslaved Africans to risk their lives against their freedom-seeking compatriots. He concluded that the promise of freedom from the Dutch was like money in the bank for the Rangers, and more certain than the precarious freedom of Maroon life.

Between the Rangers and the Maroons of Suriname there developed a bitter animosity, with the Maroons unable to forgive the Rangers for their treachery to the African race. On one occasion a Maroon unit promised to leave the European troops alone and get the Rangers. They fulfilled their promise with great ferocity. The Rangers also mutilated the bodies of Maroons who fell into their hands.

Stedman recorded a fascinating exchange of insults which went on one night between the two groups of Africans, "each party cursing & menacing the other at a very terrible rate." The Maroons called the Rangers "poltroons and traitors to their countrymen." They challenged the Rangers to single combat next day, expressing a wish to wash their hands in the blood of these scoundrels who were primarily responsible for destroying their settlement.

The Rangers called the Maroons "a parcel of pitiful skulking rascals, whom they would fight one to two in the open field, if they but dared to shew their *ugly* faces [Emphasis in original]." They had only deserted the plantation, said the Rangers, because they were too lazy to work. Both sides indulged in a "war-whoop," sang "victorious songs" and blew their horns.

Further Readings

Campbell, Mavis C. *The Maroons of Jamaica, 1655–1796: A History of Resistance, Collaboration and Betrayal.* Granby, MA: Bergin and Garvey, 1988.

Hoogbergen, William. "The History of the Suriname Maroons," in Gary Brana-Shute, Ed., *Resistance in Suriname: Old and New. Studies in Third World Societies*, Vol. 43, November 1990.

Mair, Lucille Mathurin. "The Rebel Woman in the British West Indies During Slavery," in Verene Shepherd and Hilary McD. Beckles, Eds., *Caribbean Slavery in the Atlantic World.* Kingston: Ian Randle Publishers, 2000.

Robinson, Carey. *The Fighting Maroons of Jamaica.* Kingston: Collins and Sangster, 1969.

Stedman, John Gabriel. *Narrative of a Five Years' Expedition Against the Revolted Negroes of Surinam in Guiana on the Wild Coast of South America from the Years 1772 to 1777.* Amherst, MA: University of Massachusetts Press, 1972. First pub. 1796.

Terborg-Penn, Rosalyn. "African Diaspora Women Resist Oppression: An Historical View," in Leonard L. Bethel, Ed., *Africana: An Introduction and Study.* Dubuque, IA: Kendal/Hunt Publishing Company, 1999.

8

The Big Fight Back
From Rebellion to Haitian Revolution

The Commander in Chief to the People of Haiti
Citizens:

It is not enough to have expelled the barbarians who have bloodied our land for two centuries; it is not enough to have restrained those ever-evolving factions that one after another mocked the specter of liberty that France dangled before you. We must, with one last act of national authority, forever assure the empire of liberty in the country of our birth; we must take any hope of re-enslaving us away from the inhuman government that for so long kept us in the most humiliating torpor. In the end we must live independent or die.

Independence or death . . . let these sacred words unite us and be the signal of battle and of our reunion. . . .
We have dared to be free. . . .

—Declaration of Independence of Haiti, 1804

Ladies and gentlemen: I have been requested to offer you a sketch, . . . of one of the most remarkable men of the last generation, — the great St. Domingo chief, Toussaint L'Ouverture, an unmixed Negro, with no drop of white blood in his veins. . . . I am engaged tonight in what you will think the absurd effort to convince you that the Negro race, instead of being that object of pity or contempt which we usually consider it, is entitled, judged by the facts of history, to a place close by the side of the Saxon. . . .

Some doubt the courage of the Negro. Go to Hayti, and stand on those fifty thousand graves of the best soldiers France ever had, and ask them what they think. And if that does not satisfy you, go to France, to the splendid mausoleum of the Counts of Rochambeau, and to the eight thousand graves of Frenchmen who skulked home under the English flag, and ask them. And if that does not satisfy you, come home, and if it had been October, 1859, you might have come by way of quaking Virginia, and asked her what she thought of Negro courage.

You may also remember this,—that we Saxons were slaves about
four hundred years, sold with the land, and our fathers never raised a finger to end
our slavery. They waited till Christianity and civilization, till commerce and the discovery of
America, melted away their chains. Spartacus in Italy led the slaves of Rome against the
Empress of the world. She murdered him, and crucified them. There never was a
slave rebellion successful but once, and that was in St. Domingo. Every race has
been, some time or other, in chains. But there never was a race that,
weakened and degraded by such chattel slavery, unaided, tore off its own
fetters, forged them into swords, and won its liberty on the battlefield,
but one, and that was the black race of St. Domingo. . . .

So much for the courage of the Negro. Now look at his endurance.
In 1805 [sic] he said to the white men, 'This island is ours; not a white foot shall
touch it.'. . . . Hayti, from the ruins of her colonial dependence, is become a civilized
state, the seventh nation in the catalogue of commerce with this country [the United States],
inferior in morals and education to none of the West Indian isles. Foreign merchants trust her
courts as willingly as they do our own. Thus far, she has foiled the ambition of Spain, the greed
of England, and the malicious statesmanship of Calhoun. Toussaint made her what
she is. In this work there was grouped around him a score of men, mostly
of pure Negro blood, who ably seconded his efforts. . . .

I would call him Napoleon, but Napoleon made his way to empire
over broken oaths and through a sea of blood. This man never broke his word. . . .
I would call him Cromwell, but Cromwell was only a soldier, and the state he founded went
down with him into his grave. I would call him Washington, but the great Virginian
held slaves. This man risked his empire rather than permit the slave-trade
in the humblest village of his dominions.

You think me a fanatic tonight, for you read history, not with your eyes,
but with your prejudices. . . . But fifty years hence, when Truth gets a hearing, the Muse
of History will put Phocion for the Greek, and Brutus for the Roman, Hampden for England,
Fayette for France, choose Washington as the bright, consummate flower of our earlier
civilization, and John Brown the ripe fruit of our noonday [thunders of applause],
then, dipping her pen in the sunlight, will write in the clear blue, above them all,
the name of the soldier, the statesman, the martyr, TOUSSAINT
L'OUVERTURE. [Long-continued applause.]

—WENDELL PHILLIPS, *speech delivered in New*
York and Boston, December 1861

REBELLIONS

Rebellions among the enslaved were <u>endemic</u> to slave society. They were closely allied to marronage. Sometimes <u>Maroons</u> instigated revolts. Often, in the immediate aftermath of a revolt the rebels, whether successful or not, would depart into marronage.

Revolts were large and small, and occurred all over the Caribbean. The most successful, the Haitian Revolution (1781–1803), became the most successful revolution of the enslaved in history.

Full-scale rebellions were merely the ultimate manifestation of the manifold types of resistance already described. The possibility of revolt was therefore never far from the surface. There were even cases where the enslaved downed tools and walked off the job, like workers in the age of capitalism. Stedman, visiting the Hope plantation in Suriname, "found the whole of the slaves on the estate in a mutiny on account of the cruel usage inflicted by the managers. . . ." Happily for all concerned, Stedman observed, the military intervened and quelled the unrest. "These frequent disturbances," he noted, "plainly indicate the inclination of the Negroes to break out in open rebellion; and this would certainly have been more often attempted, had they not been awed by the troops."

What is considered the first big uprising (that is, a revolt not by Maroons but by persons still on the plantation) took place on December 26, 1522, on the Santo Domingo plantation of Admiral Diego Colon, brother of Columbus and governor of the colony.

On July 29, 1690, all 500 plus Africans on Mr. Salter's Jamaican estate revolted. They killed the caretaker of the main house and captured weapons and ammunition. They marched to a neighboring plantation, again killed an overseer and burnt down a plantation house. They had an inadequate supply of weapons and were eventually defeated. So many escaped, however, that the governor predicted that they would never be caught and would harass the island as Maroons.

In 1731 more than 250 rose up on a plantation in Santiago de Cuba. St. John in the Virgin Islands, colonized by Denmark in 1718, experienced a major revolt in 1733. The revolutionaries, Twi-speaking Akan people from modern Ghana, included persons with military experience from their homeland. They abolished slavery from November 23, 1733 to May 27, 1734, when they were finally defeated.

Two of the three major leaders, Kanta and Bolombo, were an assistant driver and driver, respectively. The third was Quashi. The revolt began with an attack by a few Africans on a Danish fort. Armed only with cutlasses, the Africans killed all but one of the seven Danish soldiers in the fort. They then fired a cannon to signal to the other Africans that the revolt was on.

Ninety-two plantations were involved in the uprising. Sixty British troops from Tortola and fifty from St. Kitts arrived to help put down the rebellion.

Both detachments withdrew after suffering several men killed. Forces from Danish St. Thomas were equally unsuccessful. Two hundred and twenty-eight French soldiers eventually ended the revolt which was thought to have been staged by 146 African men and women. The Danish also mobilized, as common in these situations, a "free Negro corps."

In August 1734 Quashi and fourteen fighters, still at large, were induced to lay down their arms in exchange for a pardon. As happened later with the Trelawney Maroons of Jamaica, the Europeans double-crossed them. They beheaded Quashi and tortured and executed most of the others. Thirty-eight Africans committed suicide rather than submit.

The Akan-dominated Tackey's Rebellion of 1760 in Jamaica lasted six months. Tackey himself was killed by treaty Maroons who answered the British call to duty. Many of Tackey's followers opted for mass suicide over capture.

The Berbice Rebellion of 1763 was the largest (as distinct from Maroon wars) in the Dutch Caribbean. It was the fifth Berbice uprising in thirty years, in addition to fourteen recent foiled plots. It lasted over a year and at times seemed close to total victory. Akan Africans Cuffy (Kofi), Atta and Akara (Accara) were again in the initial leadership, though "Congoes" (from Congo and Angola) were also well represented. The Africans captured most of the Colony's plantations within the first month and set up their headquarters in the Dutch Fort Nassau. The Dutch were gradually able to recover from their initial setbacks with the help of multinational military assistance from Holland, Suriname, St. Eustatius, Demerara, Britain and indigenous people.

For much of the rebellion the Africans controlled the southern section of the colony, where Cuffy was recognized as king. The whites held on to the northern coastal section. There is some indication that in the early stages Cuffy and his followers may have intended to join the Maroons of neighboring Suriname. Efforts to march into Demerara and initiate revolt there were foiled by paths made impassable during bad weather. Cuffy twice formally proposed partitioning the colony to Governor Van Hoogenheim.

The rebellion was weakened by internal dissention which led to intra-African fighting, culminating in Cuffy's suicide. Internal problems became disastrous when some rebels delivered up Atta to the Dutch. The two traitors were enlisted as privates in Colonel Fourgeoud's Suriname forces.

The Europeans also had their internal problems. Forty-two of their reinforcements from Suriname deserted and sought asylum among the rebels. The suspicious Africans executed twenty-eight of them, enslaved others and retained three as instructors in the proper care of firearms.

Stedman accused the Berbice revolutionaries of "abominable cruelties" against the whites. He said they chopped up "their mistresses with child, even in their master's presence. . . ." The Dutch put down the uprising with characteristic ferocity. They executed 124–128. They gouged out pieces of Atta's flesh with hot pincers every fifteen minutes for some hours before burning him to death at the stake. As was also characteristic of these situations, he bore his torture with stoicism.

A Tobago revolt of 1770, led by Sandy, killed twenty white people. Sandy escaped from British Tobago to Spanish Trinidad and was not extradited. Further Tobago revolts followed in 1771 and 1774.

Some of the bloodiest struggles against slavery took place in Guadeloupe from the 1790s to 1802. A major catalyst was Victor Hugues, a French-born revolutionary who was sent out as commissioner to Guadeloupe from the French Revolution in 1794. Sir John Fortescue, in *A History of the British Army*, described Hugues as of mixed race, though this has not been universally accepted. The French government, under pressure from its own revolution and the Haitian Revolution, then in full swing, abolished slavery in 1794. Hugues arrived in the Caribbean in June 1794 to discover that Britain had just invaded the French islands of Martinique and Guadeloupe, frustrating the abolition of slavery in the process.

The British were able to remain in Martinique until it was restored to Napoleon in 1802. Slavery was never abolished in Martinique in this period. Hugues however used the 1,500 troops at his disposal to enforce Emancipation in Guadeloupe. He mobilized many of the now-free ex-enslaved into his army. They defeated the British and expelled them early in 1795. Some outstanding black military men rose to prominence in Hugues' forces.

Even before Hugues' arrival the enslaved in Martinique and Guadeloupe had been striking blows against slavery. There were revolts of the enslaved in St. Pierre, capital of Martinique, in 1789 and 1791. Revolts occurred in 1790, and twice in 1793 in Guadeloupe.

After expelling the British, Hugues' forces massacred several hundred French Royalist planters who had supported the British pro-slavery occupation. Hugues also spread his agents and troops into St. Vincent, St. Lucia and Martinique, in each of which the French and British were in a contest for power. He communicated with Fedon, leader of the Grenada uprising and is said to have sought an alliance with the Spanish in Trinidad against the expected British invasion, which eventually materialized in 1797. He exhumed the body of General Thomas Dundas, short-lived British governor of Guadeloupe, and had it flung into a sewer. On the spot he erected a monument deploring British crimes against humanity. Hugues became the de facto dictator of Guadeloupe, but was recalled to France in 1798.

When Napoleon Bonaparte gained power in France he moved to reimpose slavery. His troops were heavily defeated in Haiti but succeeded in reimposing slavery in French Guiana in 1801. The British had maintained slavery during their occupation, so their return of Martinique to France in 1802 did not affect the status of black Martiniquans.

The attempt to reintroduce slavery into Guadeloupe resulted in a bitter war led by some of the black commanders who had risen to prominence under Hugues. Most important of these was Louis Delgrès, a colored Martiniquan and former enslaved.

The antislavery forces fought desperately under the slogan "*Vivre libre ou mourir* (liberty or death)." In the final battle at Matouba in 1802 Delgrès performed a mass suicide bombing calculated to take as many French soldiers along with him as possible. Bernard Moitt calculates that about 500 Guadeloupian men, women and children died, including Delgrès himself. They managed to take along about 400 French troops.

Many African survivors moved into marronage and continued the resistance. The figure of a young African woman, Solitude, emerged from this conflict as a heroine of now-legendary proportions. In the inevitable tortures and executions that followed the defeat of the freedom fighters, she was sentenced to death. She was pregnant, so the French awaited the birth of her child, not wanting to bear the economic loss of two enslaved persons. They executed Solitude shortly after she gave birth. Moitt says that 7,000 Africans were killed in combat or executed afterward. Three thousand more were deported to French Guiana and Senegal or imprisoned at Brest in France.

Hundreds of enslaved rebelled in Tortola in 1790. Farcelle's rebellion (limited to Maroon activity described earlier), started in Dominica in 1791. There was an uprising in St. Lucia in January 1791. An April 1793 uprising at Trois-Rivières, Guadeloupe, killed twenty whites. In August that year one Auguste, a free colored, led 1,000–1,200 Africans in revolt in Guadeloupe. From 1794 to 1798 the largely colored and black French forces of Victor Hugues in Guadeloupe operated in St. Vincent (allied with the Black Caribs), St. Lucia, Dominica and Grenada. They fought the British and tried to spread the freedom that had come to Guadeloupe in 1794. The British called this The Brigands' War. In Grenada Fedon's Rebellion lasted from March 2, 1795 to June 1796. Julien Fedon was a free colored owner of large cocoa and coffee estates. With an army of free coloreds, Africans and Frenchmen, he launched his attack on British Grenada. Within twelve hours he had killed several British whites and captured the British Lt. Governor Ninian Home. Fedon emancipated his Africans. He controlled the whole island save for the capital, St. Georges, and its immediate environs. A British attack in April 1795 on his Belvidere estate headquarters failed. Fedon thereupon executed twenty-eight of his fifty-one British prisoners, Governor Home among them, as he had promised to do in the event of a counterattack.

British General Ralph Abercomby arrived in June 1796 and saved the day for the British, as he had done, or was soon to do, in St. Lucia, St. Vincent and elsewhere. A 500-pound reward on Fedon's head

failed to secure his capture. He was never found. Some thought he escaped to Trinidad.

In 1795 also a rebellion erupted in Curaçao, led by Tula Rigaud and Bastiaan Carpata. Tula and forty to fifty Africans refused to work on August 17. They freed some enslaved persons imprisoned in a cage on their own estate. They then marched from estate to estate freeing the enslaved, who fell in with them. They were offered a pardon by the Dutch but Tula would accept nothing but freedom. The uprising was put down after about two months of fighting. The Dutch cut open Tula's body, burned his face and beheaded him. Carpata was made to watch the torture of Tula before suffering the same fate. Their heads were placed on stakes. A monument to Tula and the revolutionaries now stands at the place where Tula was executed. August 17 is celebrated as a key date in Curaçao's struggle for freedom.

Rebellions were recorded in Cuba in 1805, 1809, 1812, 1820, 1823, 1825, 1826, 1830, 1833 and 1843, and in Tobago in 1807. In Jamaica the 2nd West India Regiment mutinied in 1808. They were recruited from enslaved Africans and were upset that their freedom was not forthcoming fast enough. They killed two of their officers. Twenty-one mutineers were killed and seven more executed. Units of this black but white-officered mercenary regiment also mutinied in Dominica in 1802 and Trinidad in 1837. The regiment also fought against Maroons and others in addition to fighting Britain's colonial and imperialistic wars in the Caribbean, North America, West and East Africa and Palestine.

Further enslaved revolts took place in 1815 and 1822 in Jamaica and in 1822 in Martinique. In 1823 hundreds of enslaved revolted on Pickering's estates in Tortola, as they had done in 1790. The Demerara Revolt began on August 18, 1823 and involved an estimated 11,000–12,000 enslaved persons in about fifty-five plantations in East Coast Demerara. Here, as in some other rebellions, there was a widespread belief that the English king had decreed freedom but that the recalcitrant local whites were fraudulently withholding the information. This fused with other grievances endemic to plantation society, such as increasingly onerous tasks, severe punishments and obstacles placed in the way of the Africans attending church services. Christian evangelization had recently come to the area and the English missionary Rev. John Smith was believed by the authorities to have instigated the uprising. The Africans had in fact planned their own uprising, though Smith's Christian teachings no doubt inadvertently provided more grist for the freedom mill. Christian assertions that all men were created of one blood and that God's people were delivered from pharaoh resonated among the enslaved. Rev. Smith was arrested shortly after the outbreak of hostilities and died in a Demerara prison before news of his reprieve reached the colony from England. Here too, as in many other revolts of the enslaved, those higher up the enslaved hierarchy tended to be leaders. Jack Gladstone, principal leader, was head cooper on Plantation Success, where the revolt started. Unlike earlier revolts, however, higher echelon positions in enslaved society now included high-ranking positions such as deacons in Bethel Chapel, Rev. Smith's church. Gladstone's father, Quamina, also a leader of the revolt, was head carpenter on the estate as well as chief deacon at Bethel Chapel. The final preparatory meeting took place on Sunday August 17 after church. The leaders of this revolt seem to have been less well prepared, more poorly armed and less ruthless than was the norm. They contented themselves with putting their first white captives in the stocks. They suffered about 200 killed during a pitched battle on August 20 against a well-armed military. The revolt was put down in about a week, with the whites in no way inclined to reciprocate the gentleness of the rebels. They hanged 47, reprieved 25 more, stuck heads on poles and delivered floggings of up to 1,000 lashes to the African survivors.

Pompey led a revolt in Exuma, the Bahamas, in 1803. Once again rumor spread among the Africans that they had been freed in London but the local whites were refusing to give them the news. There was another revolt in Tortola in 1830 as well. In 1816 Bussa's Rebellion gave Barbados its first major revolt since 1692. It broke out on Easter Sunday night, April 14, after months of planning. Preparations began soon after the white local assembly rejected the ameliorating Registry Bill drafted in London. This seemed to signal local white rejection of Emancipation. Here again, headmen, drivers and other upper-level enslaved were the leaders. Washington Franklin and Nanny Grigg, a

house servant, were Bussa's lieutenants. The rebels destroyed about 25 percent of Barbados' anticipated sugar crop. About 400 rebels were defeated on April 16 by the militia and the mercenary West India Regiment. About 3,900–5,000 Africans are thought to have participated in the revolt. One white man and two West India Regiment soldiers died. Almost 1,000 Africans are said to have died, with 144 executed. One hundred and twenty-three were deported to Honduras for two years and then to Sierra Leone. An Emancipation statue unveiled in Barbados in 1985 quickly became associated with Bussa. He was named first national hero of Barbados in 1999.

By now the countdown to the 1833 Emancipation Act for the British colonies was well underway and African America, always close to Caribbean affairs, now provided at least two developments of some relevance to the fast-approaching Caribbean denouement. In 1829 David Walker's *Appeal* appeared in Boston, arguably the most militant and erudite of antislavery works. Walker relied on biblical and other history of antiquity to demonstrate that no prior slavery had ever been as vicious as that visited upon Africans in the Americas. He said that white people were the natural enemies of black folk and called for the violent overthrow of slavery.

Walker's was one of the first books authored by an African American. It came two years after the appearance of African America's first newspaper, *Freedom's Journal*, copublished by Rev. Samuel Cornish and Jamaican John B. Russwurm. Walker was a contributor to, and distributor for *Freedom's Journal*, which contained extensive coverage of slavery and freedom in the Caribbean. Walker directed his book especially at African America, but also to the "Colored Citizens of the World."

Walker's *Appeal* evinced an impressive knowledge of both the historical and contemporary Caribbean. He lambasted the "wretch" Las Casas for encouraging the importation of enslaved Africans. He deplored the large percentage of murderers and convicts with whom Europe had populated the Americas, including the Caribbean. He praised the English in the Caribbean for their recent amelioration program: "Though they have oppressed us a little and have colonies now in the West Indies, which oppress us *sorely*." He embraced Haiti, "the glory of the blacks and terror of tyrants. . . ." He couldn't understand why Afro-Jamaicans, outnumbering whites 22:1, did not rise up and end their oppression.

Walker also had important Caribbean connections in his private life. He was a member of Prince Hall's African Lodge. Hall, major civil rights campaigner and African America's pioneer of Freemasonry, is thought by some to have been born in Barbados. He earlier campaigned successfully for the release of three free Boston men kidnapped into slavery in the Caribbean.

Walker operated a second-hand clothing store for sailors where many of his clientele would have been African American seamen who sailed to the Caribbean and the Caribbean sailors (like the enslaved Olaudah Equiano) who sailed to North America. Sailors were an important part of his distribution network and copies of his book were seized in port cities as far south as New Orleans. It is plausible to speculate that some of his books might easily have reached the Caribbean. Walker was found dead in 1830, possibly murdered, three months after the appearance of the third edition of his book.

A year after Walker's death, in August 1831, Nat Turner's rebellion erupted in Virginia. It was the most successful insurrection of the enslaved in African American history. Turner was a literate preacher who was convinced that he had a God-given mission to strike a blow against slavery. He escaped from the plantation once but returned voluntarily, to the dismay of his fellow enslaved, so that he could fulfill his mission. He was ably assisted by his lieutenant "Will, the executioner . . . with his fatal axe." These were Nat's own words as reported in the *Confessions* which he narrated from jail. When Will showed up, apparently uninvited, at the final preparatory session in the woods, Nat asked him what he was doing there. Will explained that "his life was worth no more than others, and his liberty [was] as dear to him." He was ready, he affirmed, to obtain his liberty "or lose his life." Similar sentiments have resonated through the pages of Caribbean history. Nat and his colleagues killed over fifty white people, mostly on the first night, as they methodically moved from house to house. Many commentators have suggested that Walker may have influenced Turner, thereby providing a tenuous link to the unfolding events in the Caribbean. It might be mentioned in passing also that the Male revolt, one of Brazil's most important, took place in Bahia in 1835.

There was a revolt in Antigua also in 1831. In St. Pierre, Martinique, Africans fired eight plantations and eleven houses to launch an uprising. It was eventually put down by superior arms. And four months after Nat Turner, Jamaica erupted on December 25, 1831 in the Jamaica Christmas Rebellion, also known as the Baptist War. It was one of the largest of the Caribbean enslaved revolts and is credited with hastening Emancipation in the British Caribbean. Sam Sharpe (1801–1832) was the principal leader. He was literate and a deacon at the First Baptist Church in Montego Bay. The leaders were again representative of the upper echelon of enslaved society. As in Demerara, church officials provided leadership. Sharpe planned a strike for the Christmas period, with contingency plans for armed struggle if these pacific means failed to achieve freedom. There was once again a widespread belief that Emancipation had already been decreed in London, but the locals were not implementing it.

The struggle involved up to 60,000 enslaved and a few free supporters. The leaders swore on the Bible to fight against the white people as long as there was one left on the island. The rebels inflicted severe property damage, largely via burnt-out plantations. St. James parish was at the center of the struggle but it spread to over half of Jamaica's parishes. Six hundred and nineteen rebels were killed, including 312 executed. The usual savage whippings, wanton killings and torture accompanied official reprisals. Some rebels were deported to Nova Scotia and England.

From 1832 to 1834 there were uprisings in Exuma, Eleuthera and Cat Island in the Bahamas and in 1833 in Cuba and Martinique. The year 1837 witnessed Daaga's rebellion in Trinidad, where enslaved Africans impressed into the West India Regiment mutinied. Daaga, a Popo, and his chief fellow leader, Maurice Ogston, a Yoruba, seized arms and ammunition but were apparently not yet skilled in their use. About forty persons, mostly mutineers, died. Daaga, Ogston and one other were executed. In 1839 the Amistad Mutiny took place in Cuban waters. Enslaved men and women being transported by ship rose up and killed some of the ship's white occupants—others escaped overboard. They spared the life of the pilot and ordered him to take them back to Africa. They were apprehended by the U.S. Coast Guard when they stopped in the United States to take in water. In the United States white abolitionists took up their cause and after trials all the way to the U.S. Supreme Court they were repatriated to Sierra Leone. In St. Croix in 1848 occurred perhaps the most unique of enslaved uprisings. As will be seen later, 8,000 Africans marched to Fort Frederik and demanded immediate freedom. Governor-General Peter von Scholten capitulated to the crowd and issued an immediate order for emancipation. In 1866 in Matanzas, Cuba, some enslaved struck for work with pay. Here again they thought that the *Cortes* in Spain had freed them. The many revolts enumerated here do not include countless conspiracies which failed for one reason or another to come to fruition. Nor do they include rumored planned revolts, which the authorities were unable to verify. Two such were reported from Trinidad, in 1819 and 1823. Some plots, though abortive, still resulted in executions of enslaved conspirators.

These revolts and conspiracies, together with the Maroon conflicts which were going on at the same time, placed a severe strain on Europe's ability to maintain the regime of enslavement. The governor of Guadeloupe in 1838 reported a general panic in the island due to fear that the Africans "were disposed to reclaim their liberty forcibly, if it were not granted by the first of January." The feared uprising did not materialize but he was sure that the danger was not averted. Here, as elsewhere, a series of economic and humanitarian realities combined with expediency and sheer necessity to help forward the struggle for freedom in the Caribbean.

HAITIAN REVOLUTION

The Haitian Revolution (1791–1803) represented the crowning achievement of all the Maroon struggles and rebellious activity of the slavery period in general and the latter eighteenth century in particular. It incorporated the elements of earlier struggles into one glorious revolt on a scale never before or since matched in human history. The Haitian Revolution remains the only one in which enslaved people permanently wrested state power from their enslavers. And the Haitians did so in the richest colony in the world and one which the enslaving power, France, absolutely did not want to lose. The Africans struck in August 1791, two years after the outbreak of the French Revolution in 1789. Haiti, known as Saint Domingue under the French, was rent by factional struggle in the wake of events in France. The ruling 35,000-strong white population was divided between royalists and (revolutionary) republicans. The upper class, *grands blancs* (French officials, clergy, businessmen, estate owners and the like), chafed under the French exclusive. By French decrees of 1789 and 1790 they received local white autonomy, comparable to that existing in British colonies. The lower-level whites, *petits blancs* (overseers, artisans, soldiers, etc.), were more likely to be republican and therefore politically opposed to the *grands blancs*. They won a "civil war" against the *grands blancs* in 1791. The 30,000-strong colored caste suffered from the same increased eighteenth-century discrimination as their group did in the rest of the Caribbean. Many here, as elsewhere, had built significant wealth on the education and inheritances bestowed by their white fathers. It is suggested that they may have owned a quarter of the enslaved Africans and a third of the agricultural-based wealth of the island. Yet, like coloreds elsewhere in the Caribbean, they labored under severe social discrimination. They were excluded from public office, were given double the punishments meted out to whites for crimes committed, were segregated in schools, could not enter white churches and were buried in segregated cemeteries. In towns coloreds had to dismount and lead their horses on foot.

After revolution broke out in France in 1789, the coloreds lobbied in Paris for relief. The French National Convention seemed to accord them some relief but the new Colonial Assembly of local whites refused to ameliorate their condition. Then in October 1790 the free people of color rose up unsuccessfully under Vincent Ogé, recently back from lobbying in Paris. The assembly broke him on the wheel before drawing and quartering him. They displayed a quarter of his body in each of the principal cities of Saint Domingue. They confiscated his property. In 1791 the coloreds were more successful under André Rigaud.

Various factions of whites and coloreds had enlisted support among the Africans. In 1791, however, the Africans rose up in their own interest. They planned long and carefully, possibly taking advantage of market days and forged passes to congregate for their meetings. The Africans already had a long history of struggle. Maroon communities were endemic and some were of very long duration. Abortive conspiracies had been reported in 1679, 1691, 1703, 1704, 1758, 1775 and 1778. The best known, that of 1758, was led by Mackandal, a Maroon and Voodoo priest. He was said to have planned a massive poisoning of the white population. Survivors were to be run off the island. Mackandal was betrayed and executed.

The revolution began in the North Plain in August 1791. The Africans planned to set fire to houses, kill the whites and take the northern city of Le Cap during the night. The rebel flag proclaimed death to the whites. Some overzealous rebels struck early, thus giving the whites in Le Cap time to strengthen their defenses and evade destruction for the time being.

Within eight days, according to Caroline Fick, the rebels "devastated" seven parishes and "completely destroyed" 184 sugar plantations in the northern province. By September, they had destroyed all the plantations within 50 miles of either side of Le Cap. By late November perhaps 80,000 rebels were in arms of an enslaved population of about 170,000 in the North Province. Several free blacks and coloreds joined the rebels.

The rebel modus operandi was similar to that developed over the years by Maroons, whether operating independently of each other or in concert. They set up bases in inaccessible places. They were experts at guerrilla warfare. They designed camouflaged booby traps, blocked roads to impede French forces, disguised tree trunks to look like cannon and even improvised workable bulletproof vests, stuffed with cotton. They subjected white prisoners to the same barbaric tortures inflicted upon enslaved Africans.

The revolutionaries were also helped by the presence, within their ranks, of veterans of North American, Caribbean and African wars. Henri Christophe, a future emperor of Haiti and André Rigaud, early leader of the free coloreds, had both fought with a French expedition that aided the Americans at the Siege of Savannah (Georgia) during the American War of Independence. Rigaud had also fought in Guadeloupe. Many of the majority African-born fighters had been enslaved after becoming prisoners of war in African conflicts. Some of the African armies they served in were as large as 30,000 men and used muskets. Some had defeated European forces, as happened in Angolan struggles against the Portuguese between 1788 and 1791.

The most important early rebel leader was Zamba Boukman, a Voodoo priest and former plantation headman. Under Boukman, "a man of Herculean strength, who knew not what danger was," as John R. Beard described him, "the Negroes on the night of August 21st, 1791, arose in the terrific power of brute force." Within a week, "Conflagration raged everywhere. The mountains, covered with smoke and burning fragments, borne upwards by the wind, looked like volcanoes. The atmosphere, as if on fire, resembled a furnace. Everywhere were seen signs of devastation . . . the soil running with blood, dead bodies heaped the one on the other, mangled and mutilated, a prey to voracious birds and beasts."

Three days after the Africans rose, on August 24, the newly established white Colonial Assembly appealed to the British in Jamaica for help. "[F]ire lays waste our possessions," they wrote; "the hands of our Negroes in arms are already dyed with the blood of our brethren. Very prompt assistance is necessary to save the wreck of our fortunes—already half-destroyed; and confined within the towns, we look for your aid."

Boukman was killed in action in November 1791. The French cut his head off and placed it on a stake in a square in Le Cap. The Africans similarly adorned their stockades with the heads of Frenchmen.

The other major early African leaders were Jean François and Biassou. The latter had been the enslaved property of a religious order, the Fathers of Charity. When the French governor called on them to end their uprising they told him that it was too late.

They had watered the colony with their blood and toil. They would cease hostilities if every single white person left the country. In the meantime, they assured the governor, their motto would be "Liberty or Death."

Toussaint L'Ouverture, who more than anyone else came to symbolize the Haitian Revolution, joined the conflict a month after it started. A Creole, he was, like Boukman, a member of the upper echelon of enslaved society, a coachman. He was married, literate, forty-five years old and a man of some influence over his fellow enslaved. He may in fact have been freed some years before the revolution, though continuing to work on the plantation. "The following books were conspicuous in the library of Toussaint," reported Marcus Rainsford, who met him in 1797, "a list of which was handed to the author in consequence of his inquiries respecting the progress of his mind." The list suggests a Toussaint in a guise not generally recognized, as a student of the great classical texts on military history. These were

Scriptores de re Militari.
Caesar's Commentaries, French translation, by De Crisse.
DesClaison's History of Alexander and Caesar.
D'Orleans' History of Revolutions in England and Spain.
Marshal Saxe's Military Reveries.
Guischard's Military Memoirs of the Greeks and Romans.
Herodotus, History of the Wars of the Persians against the Greeks.
Le Beau's Memoirs of the Academy of Inscriptions and Belle's Lettres.
Lloyd's Military and Political Memoirs; the Works of the English Socrates [sic], Plutarch, Cornelius Nepos, &c. &c. &c.

Toussaint had also read the Abbé Raynal, who saw the treaties signed with Maroons in Suriname and Jamaica as the "lightnings [which] announce the thunder. A courageous chief only is wanted," Raynal predicted. "Where is he? that great man whom Nature owes to her vexed, oppressed, and tormented children. Where is he? He will appear, doubt it not; he will come forth, and raise the sacred standard of liberty. This venerable signal will gather around him the companions of his misfortune. More impetuous than the torrents, they will everywhere leave the indelible traces of their just resentment."

John R. Beard, from whose 1853 work this quotation comes, softened in his translation those of Raynal's words that he thought too "vengeful." John G. Stedman in Suriname, Raynal's contemporary, made essentially the same prediction as Raynal, vengefulness included. The African liberator, he said, would

Then dear repay us in some vengeful war,
And give us blood for blood, and scar for scar.

Both Stedman and Raynal wrote a little over a decade before the revolution began.

Once the revolution erupted, C. L. R. James reported, Toussaint was overcome by a premonition of impending greatness. He could not say precisely how the feeling would manifest, but as sometimes happens with persons destined for greatness, his life's experiences may have been quietly preparing him for his grand entry onto the historical stage. French General Laveaux is said to have called Toussaint "the Spartacus, foretold by Raynal, whose destiny it *was* to avenge the wrongs committed on his race." Toussaint sent the owner of his plantation to safety in Le Cap, and from thence to Baltimore. He removed his own wife and children to a safe place, and joined the rebels as secretary to Biassou and an army physician.

Haiti quickly slid into a state of confusion as each group, royalists, republicans, coloreds and Africans fought for advantage. Various alliances of convenience were formed and broken—coloreds with republicans, Africans with coloreds, and so on. The republican government in France sent commissioners to try and straighten things out in 1791, 1792 and 1796.

In late 1791 Jean François and Biassou, with the cooperation of Toussaint, offered the French commissioners and local assembly a peace deal in exchange for guaranteed freedom for 400 rebels. Toussaint later reduced the number to 60. The local white assembly refused and Toussaint resolved to fight on. He trained an elite force. When war broke out between the French and neighboring Spanish Santo Domingo in 1792, Biassou, Jean François and Toussaint all went over to the Spaniards. From this point on, Toussaint's shifting alliances were motivated by an effort to best end slavery for good. When French Commissioner Sonthonax abolished slavery on his own authority on August 29, 1793, Toussaint remained with the Spanish. He did not think that Sonthonax had the power to bind his French superiors in so important a decision. He was still nominally subordinate to Jean François and Biassou but was now leader of the strongest armed force in the conflict. It was only when the French Assembly in Paris officially abolished slavery on February 4, 1794, that Toussaint left the Spanish and rejoined the French. He defeated Jean François and Biassou, still allied to the Spanish. He drove the Spanish back into Santo Domingo in 1795 and in 1796 rescued French military commander General Laveaux from captivity during a colored uprising. He routed the coloreds. A grateful Laveaux proclaimed Toussaint, still avowedly loyal to France, as lieutenant governor in May 1796. In May 1797 Toussaint was made commander in chief of French forces by Sonthonax, who was again in Saint Domingue, heading a third French board of civil commissioners. By 1797 Toussaint felt strong enough to expel Sonthonax.

Englishman Captain Marcus Rainsford of the Third West India Regiment, who spent some time shipwrecked (and masquerading as an American) in Haiti in 1797, described a country where Toussaint and his officers mixed easily with the populace in civilian life, but where the army was highly disciplined and efficient. Martial law prevailed across the land. All men capable of bearing arms could be mobilized at a moment's notice. Like Stedman in Suriname and the British who fought the Maroons of Jamaica, Rainsford spoke in awe of the military ability of Toussaint's soldiers. In his book, *An Historical Account of the Black Empire of Hayti* (1805), he described, here rendered in modern spelling, some military exercises he witnessed in Le Cap. He said that 60,000 troops took part.

Two thousand officers were in the field, carrying arms, from the general to the ensign, yet with the utmost attention to rank, without the smallest symptom of the insubordination that existed in the leisure of the hotel. Each general officer had a demi-brigade, which went through the manual exercise with a degree of expertness seldom witnessed, and performed equally well several manœuvres applicable to their method of fighting. At a whistle a whole brigade ran three or four hundred yards; then, separating, threw themselves flat on the ground, changing to their backs or sides, keeping up a strong fire the whole of the time, till they were recalled; they then formed again, in an instant, into their wonted regularity. This single manœuvre was executed with such facility and precision, as totally to prevent cavalry from charging them in bushy and hilly countries. Such complete subordination, such promptitude and dexterity, prevailed the whole time, as would have astonished any European soldier who had the smallest idea of their previous situation [of enslavement.]

With Sonthonax expelled, Toussaint and Rigaud then teamed up to expel the British from their last stronghold in Western Saint Domingue. The British had been there since 1793. The white colonists had welcomed them. They signed a secret deal with Britain whereby Saint Domingue would become a British colony and slavery would be reinstated. Free people of color would be deprived of citizenship.

Toussaint defeated Sir Thomas Maitland, the British commander in chief, in October 1798. Maitland, a colonel in the 10th West India Regiment, withdrew to Jamaica, whence he had come. Toussaint helped him on his way with a secret promise not to invade Jamaica, as he had earlier threatened to. Fortescue, historian of the British army, determined that the Saint Domingue campaign cost Britain almost 100,000 dead and disabled.

Along the way Toussaint had declined a British offer of support for a Toussaint declaration of independence from France, guaranteed by British support. Toussaint had no desire to have an independence underwritten by the slaveholding British. Toussaint later considered sending a force to West Africa to end the slave trade at its source. Later still, U.S. governments would live in fear of a Haitian invasion aimed at liberating enslaved African Americans. Meanwhile General Hédouville, French replacement for the expelled Sonthonax, arrived in Saint Domingue in April 1798. By October, Toussaint felt strong enough to expel him too, for intriguing with the local whites against Toussaint. Toussaint now methodically moved to destroy whatever obstacles remained to his complete control of the island. He defeated Rigaud, colored strongman in the West, in 1800, after a year's civil war which French officials were happy to encourage. Against the wishes of new French strongman Napoleon Bonaparte, he invaded Santo Domingo, motivated largely by a desire to end a slave trade which had reappeared there. Santo Domingo fell in January 1801.

Toussaint was now the ruler of all Hispaniola, namely French Saint Domingue and Spanish Santo Domingo. He could presumably have claimed independence if he had so desired. His reluctance to do so in the past was now however strengthened by a new development, namely the rise of Napoleon Bonaparte. Bonaparte, soldier extraordinaire, had assumed power in France in a coup of 1799. He had been preoccupied with campaigns in Europe, Egypt and the Middle East. Now, in 1801, he had acquired some breathing space and could fix his gaze on Toussaint, Saint Domingue and France's vast Western empire. Napoleon wished to be the world's most powerful leader. He hated Africans. He was determined to restore French power to Saint Domingue and to reinstate slavery in the Caribbean. Having to deal with the formerly enslaved Toussaint with anything approximating equality was a source of great mortification for him. He called Toussaint the "gilded African" and "revolted slave."

Toussaint, well aware of Napoleon's intentions, stood between him and his Western ambitions. There ensued a life and death chess game between the two men, which was in short order to result in Napoleon's horrible murder of Toussaint, the most devastating military defeat for Napoleon to date, the

loss of Saint Domingue to France, and the Louisiana Purchase of 1803, where Napoleon sold Louisiana territory (in fact part or all of fourteen present-day U.S. states and two Canadian provinces) to the United States for a pittance. For Napoleon was now bereft of Saint Domingue, and therefore unable to fulfill his dream of a Western empire anchored by Saint Domingue and Louisiana. Furthermore, the army he had intended sending on to Louisiana from Saint Domingue was now destroyed. The 828,800 square miles (2,147,000 square kilometers) of the Louisiana Purchase doubled the size of the United States. The loss of Saint Domingue and Louisiana also ended France's challenge to Britain for supremacy in the Caribbean.

Toussaint, the consummate diplomat, attempted, as was his wont, to get what he wanted by dissimulation and without directly confronting Napoleon any more than he needed to. What he wanted was an irrevocable end to slavery, independence (whether de facto or de jure seemed not to matter), and his own power constitutionally enshrined for ever as a hedge against Napoleon's ambitions, which threatened to destroy everything that he had struggled for. He appeared to get all three via his constitution of 1801.

In Napoleon, however, Toussaint encountered an adversary who was arguably the most powerful figure in Europe, ruthless, and a master of deceit and treachery. He was consumed by the quest for personal aggrandizement and the glory of France. Where Toussaint was willing to dissimulate for the noble purpose of consolidating freedom, Napoleon was prepared to practice every deceit, utilize any atrocity, in the attempt to effect the ignoble purpose of reimposing slavery.

Toussaint and Napoleon had skirmished immediately on the latter's assumption of power in 1799. Napoleon's December 25, 1799, proclamation to Saint Domingue promised, with a straight face, that "the SACRED principles of the freedom and equality of blacks will NEVER SUFFER among you the least attack or modification." Napoleon simultaneously issued a decree ordering the following inscription to be emblazoned in gold letters on the flags of the Saint Domingue army: "Remember, brave blacks, that the French people alone recognize your freedom and the equality of your rights." This hypocrisy was too much for Toussaint and he departed from his usual tact and circumspection to offer a sharp, principled rebuke to Napoleon: "It is not a circumstantial freedom conceded to ourselves alone that we want. It is the absolute adoption of the principle that any man born red, black or white cannot be the property of his like. We are free today because we are the stronger party. The Consul maintains slavery in Martinique and Bourbon; we will thus be slaves when he will be the stronger."

Toussaint's 1801 constitution was promulgated on July 8, 1801. It was debated and approved by a Central Assembly of eight white men and one colored, which Toussaint brought into being and which would have a continuing role as a legislative body subject to regular elections. Power nevertheless resided unequivocally with Toussaint and his military.

In Article 28 a grateful Central Assembly expressed profound indebtedness to "Citizen" Toussaint, General Chief of the Army, for his extraordinary service to the country. In an outpouring of love they nominated him governor "for the remainder of his glorious life."

The outpouring of love continued into Article 30, which gave Toussaint the right to nominate his successor.

> In order to strengthen the tranquility that the colony owes to [the] steadfastness, activity, indefatigable zeal and rare virtues of the General Toussaint-Louverture, and in sign of the unlimited trust of the inhabitants of Saint Domingue, the Constitution attribute[s] exclusively to this general the right to designate the citizen who, in the unfortunate event of the general's death, shall immediately replace him.

The constitution abolished slavery in all of Hispaniola. There would henceforth be no difference in treatment of citizens, except on the basis of virtue and merit. Toussaint's Roman Catholic faith became the only officially sanctioned religion. Marriage was to be encouraged. Divorce was outlawed. It proclaimed freedom from arbitrary arrest. Private property was declared inviolate and

the rehabilitation of agriculture, the country's lifeblood, was encouraged. To this end, absentee owners were allowed to preserve title to their property. A ban was placed on imports of goods already manufactured locally and free trade was proclaimed. This was a major challenge to France, whose exclusive had long tried to reserve a monopoly of manufacturing to metropolitan French concerns, and at the expense of local entrepreneurs of all colors. It also signaled Toussaint's favorable disposition toward the United States, a much more liberal trading partner. Both Britain and the United States were now treating Toussaint as a virtual leader of an independent country, as they jockeyed for favorable trade arrangements with the emerging nation. The constitution also established a system of municipal government.

The 1801 constitution was a virtual declaration of independence. It ushered in what historian John R. Beard called "a constitutional dictatorship of indispensable necessity." It was a culmination of the game that Toussaint had been playing for a long time. He could rescue a French commissioner from his enemies one day while expelling him the next. His power was paramount before the constitution, but strategically and carefully exercised in the name of France. This time, as previously, Toussaint threw a few sops to France. The constitution described Saint Domingue as a colony of the French empire but one requiring unique legal arrangements. Though there was absolutely no provision for French oversight or input, Toussaint inserted a first-person promise to forward it to France for approval. He added that the urgent need to rehabilitate Saint Domingue, the absence of existing laws and the unanimous wish of the entire country made immediate implementation, without prior French approval, a necessity. Toussaint repeated these explanations in a letter of July 16, 1801 to Bonaparte.

Bonaparte was not amused. His response was to send against Toussaint the largest military expedition ever to set sail from France. He also wrote a letter of reply on November 18, 1801. He dispatched this letter with the invasion force, but it was only delivered to Toussaint after fighting was well underway, so that for Toussaint the appearance of Napoleon's hordes off the coast constituted the first definitive intimation of a Napoleonic response to his constitution. As part of a grand deception to camouflage the real purpose of his invasion force, Napoleon entertained Toussaint's two sons, Isaac and Placide, who were being educated in France. He assured them that his expedition's intentions were simply to strengthen Saint Domingue's defenses. He praised their father and promised to send the boys home in advance of the armada, to apprise Toussaint of the pending arrival of his pacific force. He did not keep this promise. Instead, he sent the boys back with the expedition.

In seemingly agreeable language, Napoleon immediately sought, in his letter, to impress upon Toussaint his enormous power and Toussaint's subservience to it. "Citizen General," he began,

> The peace with England and all the European powers, which has established the Republic in the highest degree of power and grandeur, now allows the government to occupy itself with the colony of Saint-Domingue. We are sending there Citizen Leclerc, our brother-in-law, in his quality as General to serve as first magistrate of the colony. He is accompanied by a considerable force in order to ensure the respect of the sovereignty of the French people.

Napoleon was willing to give Toussaint some kudos for preserving Saint Domingue for France, but was he really sincere in his protestations of fealty to France? Napoleon called on him to demonstrate the sincerity of his pro-French sentiments: "It is in these circumstances that we hope that you will prove to us, and to all of France, the sincerity of the sentiments that you have regularly expressed in the letters that you wrote." Napoleon now called on Toussaint to withdraw from his seeming insubordination and acknowledge French sovereignty, or have the ground swallow him up.

> The constitution you made, while including many good things, contains some that are contrary to the dignity and sovereignty of the French people, of which Saint-Domingue forms only a portion.

> The circumstances in which you found yourself, surrounded on all sides by enemies without the metropole being able to either assist or revictual you, rendered articles of that constitution legitimate that otherwise would not be. But today, when the circumstances have changed for the better, you should be the first to render homage to the sovereignty of the nation that counts you among its most illustrious citizens thanks to the services you have rendered it and by the talents and the force of character with which nature has graced you. A contrary conduct would be irreconcilable with the idea we have conceived of you. It would have you lose the many rights to recognition and the benefits of the republic, and would dig beneath your feet a precipice which, in swallowing you up, could contribute to the misfortune of those brave blacks whose courage we love, and whose rebellion we would, with difficulty, be obliged to be punished.

Napoleon again promised freedom for the black people of Saint Domingue and honors and material rewards for a compliant Toussaint.

Toussaint, meanwhile, faced the classic dilemma of many postrevolutionary and post-Emancipation regimes. His country was ravaged by war and short on the managerial skills needed to quickly rehabilitate agriculture, the overwhelming basis of the country's economy. White former slave owners had the needed skills. Should he reach out to such of them as seemed to be now reformed and reconstructed? He answered in the affirmative. Should he allow the black laborers the freedom to desert the plantations, if even for good reason, and thereby risk further economic deterioration, at least in the short term? He answered "No." He needed a quick economic recovery to purchase arms and strengthen the country generally against the assault which would inevitably come from one or another of the big powers at the first sign of weakness.

After the Russian Revolution Lenin allowed members of the defeated middle class to assume managerial positions. When in the nineteenth century Emancipation came to the rest of the Caribbean the white rulers mostly imposed periods of forced labor or "apprenticeship" on the newly freed. In the United States after 1865 the former enslaved were enmeshed in a welter of "vagrancy" laws and "Black codes," which sometimes virtually re-enslaved them. After the Cuban Revolution of 1959, the revolutionary government had to maintain and expand sugar production, as Toussaint tried to do, since the reality was that this was the area of the country's comparative economic advantage.

Toussaint imposed a military discipline on the black laborers, restricting their ability to freely desert the estates. He considered bringing in new Africans, to be used as free laborers. Unlike the white Caribbean planters of the apprenticeship period and the white Southern whites of postslavery United States, Toussaint's purpose was clearly not to further debase a long-suffering race. Plantation profits would be shared between workers, owners and the state.

Production and trade began to recover, public works were undertaken and schools were built. He allowed some French to return to their estates. Abolitionist Wendell Phillips, Toussaint's great American eulogizer, considered Toussaint's policies evidence of near-saintly magnanimity. For some within the black population they became the reason for an uprising, led by his nephew, Moise, who killed 600–700 whites in the process. Toussaint put down this rebellion in September 1801 and had Moise executed. Toussaint's attitude of reconciliation toward whites, coupled with an apparent taking of his black base for granted, were soon to prove a fatal mistake, when Napoleon forced his day of reckoning on Toussaint and Saint Domingue.

On February 2, 1802, Napoleon's invading army arrived, led by his brother-in-law, General Leclerc. This was part of the same wider design that reinstated slavery in Guadeloupe that same year. Leclerc commanded 60 ships and over 30,000 men, including 20,000 veteran troops. "The Alps, the Nile, the Rhine, and all Italy," wrote African American William Wells Brown in his 1863 book, *The Black Man, His Antecedents, His Genius, and His Achievements*, "had resounded with the exploits of the men who were now leaving their country for the

purpose of placing the chains again on the limbs of the heroic people of St. Domingo." Among Leclerc's entourage were Rigaud, Pétion and Boyer, the three most important colored leaders of the period. Isaac and Placide L'Ouverture realized in due course that they had been deceived. They remonstrated in writing with Leclerc, but to no avail. Beard reckoned Toussaint's forces to be 16,000 at the most, and they were scattered around the whole island.

Napoleon had entrusted Leclerc with four secret instructions, namely first, to entice away Toussaint's supporters; second, to apprehend and deport Toussaint; third, to disarm the black population; and fourth, to reintroduce slavery.

These were bad times for Toussaint. His troops in Santo Domingo were tricked into surrendering to Leclerc. The colored-led forces in the South went over to the French. Whites generally welcomed and joined Leclerc. Toussaint's black base remained lukewarm to him, as a result of his efforts at reconstruction. At Toussaint's urging, General Henri Christophe burned down Le Cap before Leclerc landed. Toussaint wrote to his general, Jean-Jacques Dessalines, on February 8, 1802: "the soil bathed with our sweat must not furnish our enemies with the smallest aliment. Tear up the roads with shot; throw corpses and horses into all the fountains; burn and annihilate everything, in order that those who have come to reduce us to slavery may have before their eyes the image of that hell which they deserve."

Half of Toussaint's disaffected troops deserted to the French, lured in part by false assurances that slavery would not be reinstituted. Leclerc was greatly helped by the fact that he came clothed in the authority of "Captain-General and First Magistrate," that is, Toussaint's superior in the colonial hierarchy that Toussaint's 1801 constitution had ostensibly recognized. Several days into the fighting Leclerc sent Isaac and Placide L'Ouverture to Toussaint with Napoleon's letter of November 18, 1801, which Toussaint now saw for the first time. The sons pleaded Leclerc's case for Toussaint to submit to Leclerc's authority. Toussaint refused. He said he placed his duty to his race above his paternal affection and sent his sons back to Leclerc with his negative answer. Leclerc sent them back with a renewed request for Toussaint's submission. Toussaint told his sons that they could stay with him or go with Leclerc. Either way he would love them just the same. Placide, actually Toussaint's adopted son, decided to stay with his father. He was the son of Toussaint's wife by a former marriage. She was a widow when she married Toussaint. Toussaint immediately placed Placide in charge of a battalion and he saw service a few days later. Isaac, the son of Toussaint and his wife, preferred to go with France. His mother prevailed upon him to stay.

On February 17, 1802, after the failure of Leclerc's attempt to use Toussaint's sons, Leclerc issued a proclamation in the name of the French government declaring Toussaint and Christophe outlaws and rebels. Any citizen could legitimately arrest them. Rebel soldiers coming over to Leclerc would be incorporated into the French army. Toussaint explained the situation to the soldiers of his guard. "General," they shouted, "we will all die with you."

Toussaint and his generals were able to inflict considerable damage on Leclerc's forces, by a combination of their scorched earth policy and guerilla warfare waged from the mountains. At the battle of Ravine-à-Couleuvres (Snake Gully) on February 23, 1802, Toussaint was able to avoid encirclement and deprive Leclerc of a quick victory. Here he addressed his troops in one of the most moving perorations of this epic struggle, so marked by moving speeches. "You are going to fight," he told his troops, as they prepared to lay in ambush for Leclerc's forces,

against enemies who have neither faith, law, nor religion. They promise you liberty, they intend your servitude. Why have so many ships traversed the ocean, if not to throw you again into chains? They disdain to recognize in you submissive children, and if you are not their slaves, you are rebels. The mother country, misled by the Consul [Napoleon], is no longer anything for you but a stepmother. Was there ever a defense more just than yours? Uncover your breasts, you will see them branded by the iron of slavery. During ten years, what did you not undertake for liberty? Your masters slain or put to flight; the English humili-

ated by defeat; discord extinguished; a land of slavery purified by fire, and reviving more beautiful than ever under liberty; these are your labors, and these the fruits of your labors; and the foe wishes to snatch both out of your hands. Already have you left traces of your despair; but for a traitor, Port-au-Prince would be only a heap of ruins; but Léogane, Fort-Dauphin, the Cape, that opulent capital of the Antilles, exist no longer; you have carried everywhere consuming fires, the flambeaux of our liberty. The steps of our enemies have trodden only on ashes, their eyes have encountered nothing but smoking ruins, which you have watered with their blood. This is the road by which they have come to us.

What do they hope for? Have we not all the presages of victory? Not for their country, not for liberty do they fight, but to serve the hatred and the ambition of the Consul, my enemy, mine because he is yours; their bodies are not mutilated by the punishments of servitude, their wives and their children are not near their camps, and the graves of their fathers are beyond the ocean. This sky, these mountains, these lands, all are strange to them. What do I say? As soon as they breathe the same air as we, their bravery sinks, their courage departs. Fortune seems to have delivered them as victims into our hands. Those whom the sword spares, will be struck dead by an avenging climate. Their bones will be scattered among these mountains and rocks, and tossed about by the waves of our sea. Never more will they behold their native land; never more will they receive the tender embraces of their wives, their sisters, and their mothers; and liberty will reign over their tomb.

After this successful battle Toussaint was able to rendezvous with his family, who had been nearby.

Greatly outnumbered by Leclerc's newly rein-forced troops, Toussaint now withdrew to the Artibonite mountain range. This was classic Maroon country of deep gorges and narrow paths, similar to the Cockpit country strongholds of Jamaican Maroons. Toussaint appointed Dessalines to guard this area, and particularly the fort of Crête-à-Pierrot which commanded its main entrance. Dessalines slaughtered whites on his way and imprisoned many others. He killed 400 in one village and 700 in another. His mixed-race troops slaughtered their white fathers to avenge their abuse of their black mothers and neglect of their children. Some blacks, moved by compassion, helped whites to escape. Whites committed similar massacres. The "scenes were horrible," wrote John R. Beard. Some people went mad or committed suicide under the strain of such carnage. After several days' fighting Leclerc was able to capture Crête-à-Pierrot, but at the price of much larger casualties than suffered by Toussaint.

Leclerc was now greatly weakened but still able to expect fresh reinforcements from time to time. He opened negotiations, now in conciliatory mode, first with Christophe and then Dessalines and succeeded in winning them to the French side. Others of Toussaint's generals followed, including two brothers and a nephew. Toussaint, astonished and weakened by the turn of events, eventually agreed to meet with Leclerc. Attended by a guard of 400 mounted soldiers with swords drawn, Toussaint met Leclerc to discuss peace. Leclerc offered to retain Toussaint as governor, but subordinate to himself as French representative on the island. (Napoleon's memoirs referred to this as a vice-governorship.) He agreed to allow Toussaint's officers to retain command of their troops. All Toussaint's officers would maintain their ranks. These two provisions would prove crucial when Toussaint's generals later abandoned Leclerc to push the revolution to final victory. Their reconciliation, Leclerc promised, would assure the renewed progress of Saint Domingue. Leclerc swore not to reinstitute slavery. He returned one of Toussaint's sons, captured in the fighting, as a token of goodwill. In what may have been a fatal error, Toussaint accepted all Leclerc's proposals, except for his own governorship. He opted to retire to private life. His

troops came down from the mountains and he bade them an emotional farewell.

Key elements in these agreements, relating to slavery and respecting Toussaint's freedom as a private citizen, proved once more to be illusory. Toussaint retired to his farm, too dangerous a person, from the French perspective, to be left alone. Scarcely a month had elapsed since his solemn accords with Leclerc when the Napoleonic regime perpetrated one of the greatest acts of treachery in all of Caribbean history. In 1503 the Spaniards on Hispaniola had invited the welcoming Cacica Anacaona and her entourage of eighty nobles into a large building. The Spaniards massacred them all. After the St. John rebellion of 1734 the Danes nego-tiated a pardon with Quashi, the revolt's leader, only to execute him and his followers as soon as they laid down their arms. The British had induced the Trelawney Maroons of Jamaica to lay down their arms in 1796 and had then treacherously broken their word on no deportation. Now it was the turn of Toussaint.

Invincible on the battlefield, even when out-numbered by the full weight of Napoleon's hordes, Toussaint now fell to a supreme act of treachery. On June 7, 1802, almost sixty years old and ill, Leclerc's General Brunet lured him to a meeting where, with only two aides to defend him, he was arrested and placed on board a waiting ship, the *Creole*.

The French first prepared the ground by fabri-cating a dispute concerning the tardiness with which Toussaint was disarming his bodyguard. This allowed them the pretense of introducing a large body of white soldiers into his neighborhood to effect, with some difficulty, the expedited disarming. General Brunet's letter of June 7 invited Toussaint to visit him to discuss some outstanding issues. Brunet assured him of his honorable intentions. He offered to send some horses for Mme Toussaint, whose acquaintance he wished to make. Toussaint went without his wife. After some pleasantries Brunet withdrew. Eighteen to twenty soldiers then entered with swords and pistols drawn. Toussaint drew his saber and prepared to take as many as he could with him to his death. The officer in charge lowered his sword and assured Toussaint that it was not an assas-sination, but merely an arrest. Like Fidel Castro, who asserted as a prisoner of the Batista regime that "History will absolve me," Toussaint promised that "The justice of Heaven will avenge my cause."

Next day a detachment of Leclerc's soldiers kidnapped Toussaint's family, stole his savings and destroyed his property. Toussaint and his family were placed on the warship *Héros* and dispatched to France. His youngest son, St. Jean, who Leclerc had earlier restored to him, was already on the *Creole* when Toussaint got there. Leclerc rounded up over a hundred of Toussaint's close associates and placed them on board vessels in the harbor, from where they were presumed executed by drowning. Toussaint was not allowed to see his family on the *Héros* until a brief encounter on deck when the ship reached Brest. There Marcus Rainsford described a scene as heart-wrenching as any in the history of enslavement's forced separation of families. "Their agonizing separation," he wrote, "will be long remembered by the seamen who witnessed it, notwithstanding the means taken to impress an unfavorable opinion of the blacks, and render them insensible to the emotions of humanity. . . ."

Toussaint was, Rainsford wrote, "treated as the worst of criminals.—He who had been the benefactor of white people in a country where their enormities had provoked hatred, whose power was never stained by malevolence, and who was greater in his fall, than his enemies in their assumed power. . . ."

Napoleon had Toussaint locked up in a stone dungeon in the Castle of Joux on the Swiss border. It measured 12×12.8 feet . The floor was ice-covered in winter and waterlogged in summer. Napoleon gave orders that Toussaint was to be treated with a minimum of comfort and respect. "In this living tomb," said Wendell Phillips, "the child of the sunny tropic was left to die." When Toussaint seemed not to be dying fast enough Napoleon had his food rations reduced. "This prison may be considered the sepulture [sic] of Toussaint," added Rainsford. "France forgot awhile the habits of a civilized nation, to entomb one she should have graced with a public triumph. . . ."

Toussaint had written a letter to Napoleon from aboard ship pleading for the safety of his family. From

LE MINISTRE D'HAÏTI ET MADAME NEMOURS DANS LE CACHOT DE TOUSSAINT-LOUVERTURE

Dungeon at Fort de Joux, France, where Toussaint L'Ouverture died at the hands of Napoleon Bonaparte. In this photo Alfred Nemours, Minister of Haiti to France, 1926–1929 and Mrs. Nemours make a pilgrimage to the spot. They are standing next to a flag of Haiti and a wreath.

his freezing dungeon, denied newspapers and even a clock to tell the time of day, he wrote a memoir proclaiming his innocence of any wrongdoing, reiterating his loyalty to France, recalling the bullet still lodged in his hip, his teeth almost all knocked out by a cannon ball and the fifteen other wounds he had sustained fighting for France.

He asked for a judicial hearing. "If they no longer needed my services and wished to replace me," he wrote, "should they not have treated me as white French generals are always treated. . . . Doubtless, I owe this treatment to my color; but my color,—my color,—has it hindered me from serving my country with zeal and fidelity? Does the color of my skin impair my honor and my bravery?"

He was once rich, Toussaint said, worth 648,000 francs, but he had spent it all in service to his country. Now, he said, "I am made the most unhappy of men; my liberty is taken from me; I am separated from all that I hold dearest in the world,—from a venerable father, a hundred and five years old, who needs my assistance, from a dearly-loved wife, who, I fear, separated from me, cannot endure the afflictions which overwhelm her, and from a cherished family, who made the happiness of my life."

Far from home, denied access to friends and family and facing certain agonizing death in freezing solitary confinement, this sad appeal to fair play was the best that Toussaint could muster. It was lost on Napoleon.

Toussaint died on April 3, 1803. French newspapers barely mentioned his passing. Rainsford paraphrased *The London Times'* report: "The fate of this man has been singularly unfortunate, and his treatment most cruel. He died, we believe, without a friend to close his eyes. We have never heard that his wife and children, though they were brought over from St. Domingo with him, have ever been permitted to see him during his imprisonment."

In exile in September 1817 in St. Helena, whither he had been banished by the British, Napoleon implausibly denied that he had killed Toussaint. (He may perhaps have been alluding to rumors that he had him poisoned, rather than to the slow and agonizing death that he subjected Toussaint to.) He also sought to extricate himself from blame for the invasion of Saint Domingue. "One of the greatest follies I ever was guilty of," he told his interviewer,

> was sending that army out to St. Domingo. . . . I committed a great oversight and fault in not having declared St. Domingo free, acknowledged the black government, and before the peace of Amiens [with the British], sent some French officers to assist them. Had I done this . . . [y]ou would have lost Jamaica, and your other colonies would have followed.

Napoleon now claimed that he had been pressured into the Leclerc expedition by the planters and merchants' lobby. This sounded more like an effort after the fact to exonerate himself from blame. It did not accord with his enthusiasm before the project. Neither did it accord with his own expressions in other conversations. In one of these he explained that "I am for the whites because I am white; I have no other reason, yet that is reason enough." He said he could not possibly sanction Emancipation for "Africans . . . without any kind of civilization. . . ." Emancipation, he said, would be tantamount to enslaving whites.

News of Toussaint's capture had sent some of his old generals and others into an immediate state of renewed revolt. Christophe and Dessalines initially operated against them. Then news of the reimposition of slavery in Guadeloupe reached Haiti. In October 1802 Dessalines, the Grenadian-born Christophe and the colored Pétion now left the French and returned to the bosom of their people, with Dessalines in overall command of the liberation forces.

Leclerc, meanwhile, died in November 1802 and was succeeded by General Rochambeau, a former Saint Domingue slave owner. Rochambeau, like Leclerc before him, tortured, drowned and massacred large numbers of blacks and coloreds. Leclerc had drowned 1,000 blacks in Le Cap harbor on one occasion. Rochambeau converted the holds of ships into gas chambers. Blacks were crammed

Jean-Jacques Dessalines, General, Governor-General and Emperor of Haiti.

into the holds and gassed by the burning of brimstone (sulphur dioxide, plentifully available locally). On one occasion his troops surrounded and massacred 600 Africans. The air became putrid with the stench of decaying bodies. Black residents combed the beaches trying to identify loved ones from among the corpses washed up after being dumped overboard. Some boat captains saved the lives of those delivered to them for execution. Others saved them only to sell them into slavery in neighboring islands.

Sixteen of Toussaint's generals were chained by their necks to rocks in an uninhabited island and left to die over seventeen days. These atrocities were very much in the tradition of Napoleon, who in 1799 in Jaffa in the Middle East had spent three days bayoneting men, women and children to save bullets. Toussaint's brother, Paul L'Ouverture, driven to distraction at news of the drowning of his wife, burned to death thirty shipwrecked French travellers near a main entrance to Le Cap. He erected a plaque proclaiming the reason for his actions.

The French-based Guadeloupean scholar Claude Ribbe, in *Le Crime de Napoléon* (*Napoleon's Crimes*), attributed Rochambeau's crimes to Napoleon's instructions for a final solution against the Africans of Haiti. Ribbe reported possibly 100,000 Africans gassed to death in the holds of French ships. In a letter to Napoleon written on October 7, 1802, shortly before his death on November 1, and quoted by Carolyn Fick, Leclerc very expressly advocated a final solution. He blamed his now-desperate military position, exacerbated by the redefection of Dessalines, Christophe and others,

Dessalines' soldiers hanging 500 French prisoners within sight of the French lines, in retaliation for the French massacre of 500 Haitians.

not only on the yellow fever which had afflicted his soldiers, but also on what he considered the premature reimposition of slavery in Guadeloupe, which had been accompanied by French atrocities similar to those perpetrated in Saint Domingue. This ultimate expression of Napoleonic perfidy, once it became known in Saint Domingue, had reinvigorated the popular resistance to Leclerc and cost him his black generals. For Leclerc a final solution now provided the only hope of French victory. "We must destroy all the blacks in the mountains—men and women—and spare only the children under 12 years of age," he counseled. "We must destroy half of those in the plains and must not leave a single colored person in the colony who has worn an épaulette."

As early as 1797 Toussaint had vainly complained to the French Directory of Rochambeau's insistence on blaming the African victims and accusing them of reverse racism. There was liberty in Saint Domingue, Toussaint quoted Rochambeau as saying, "only for the commanders of Africans and men of color. . . . The whites are everywhere vexed and humiliated." Now Rochambeau imported 1,500 bloodhounds from Cuba, as the British had recently done in their war against the Maroons of Jamaica. Historian John R. Beard reported white girls kissing the dogs in anticipation of a public spectacle in the amphitheatre at Le Cap where the dogs tore blacks to shreds. In a subsequent siege of the city, said Wendell Phillips, "these same girls, in their misery, ate the very hounds they had welcomed."

Dessalines reciprocated. While Dessalines was governor of the South, Toussaint once had to restrain him from killing too many white people. Now he killed any whites he encountered, leaving their unburied corpses rotting to slow down French troops pursuing him. When Rochambeau killed 500 Africans at Le Cap, Dessalines famously hanged 500 French prisoners within view of the whites. Dessalines designed a new flag. He is said to have ripped the white out of the French red, white and blue. He replaced the French flag's "R.F.," signifying Republic of France (*République Française*), with "Liberty or Death." The conciliatory approach of Toussaint had taken the struggle as far as it could go. Now only a Dessalines, it seemed, prepared

to answer terror with terror, could assure for the struggle its ultimate victory.

Rochambeau issued a challenge to Dessalines: "When I take you, I will not shoot you like a soldier, or hang you like a white man; I will whip you to death like a slave." Dessalines, said Wendell Phillips, "chased him from battle-field to battle-field, from fort to fort, and finally shut him up in Samana. Heating cannon-balls to destroy his fleet, Dessalines learned that Rochambeau had begged of the British admiral to cover his troops with the English flag, and the generous Negro suffered the boaster to embark undisturbed."

Rochambeau fled the country on November 29, 1803. Of 60,000 French soldiers and sailors (including subsequent reinforcements) who had left France for Saint Domingue, C. L. R. James reported, almost all had perished. Army chiefs Dessalines, Christophe and Clerveaux presented a preliminary Declaration of Independence on the same day of Rochambeau's departure. "THE Independence of St. Domingo is proclaimed," it began. "Restored to our primitive dignity, we have asserted our rights; we swear never to yield them to any power on earth; the frightful veil of prejudice is torn to pieces, be it so for ever. Woe be to them who would dare, to put together its bloody tatters."

The declaration invited back white landowners, as Toussaint had earlier done, who had renounced their former errors and were now sympathetic to the new realities. It regretted the killing of some by soldiers who, remembering in the heat of war the suffering they had endured at the hands of whites, were unable to distinguish the good whites from the bad ones. The most ringing denunciation was reserved to any who might in the future presume to revisit Haiti with the threat of slavery. "Nothing is too dear, and all means are lawful," the declaration said, "to men from whom it is wished to tear the first of all blessings. Were they to cause rivers and torrents of blood to run; were they, in order to maintain their liberty, to conflagrate seven eighths of the globe, they are innocent before the tribunal of Providence, that never created men, to see them groaning under so harsh and shameful a servitude." This was essentially the whole of this short and relatively moderate preliminary declaration.

Dessalines, acknowledged by his fellow military chiefs as supreme leader, declared Haiti officially independent at Gonaïves on January 1, 1804. The victorious revolutionaries changed their new country's name to Haiti, the indigenous Arawak name, in a remarkable act of solidarity with the pre-European owners of the land.

The final Declaration of Independence was a more elaborate and more forceful document, worthy of the Caribbean and the world's most successful revolution of the enslaved. It proclaimed liberty or death. It vowed to expunge forever all trace of "this barbarous people," the French oppressors. When, it asked rhetorically, "will we tire of breathing the air that they breathe? What do we have in common with this nation of executioners? The difference between its cruelty and our patient moderation, its color and ours, the great seas that separate us, our avenging climate, all tell us plainly that they are not our brothers, that they never will be, and that if they find refuge among us, they will plot again to trouble and divide us."

Dessalines, through the declaration, promised to give the world "a terrible, but just example of the vengeance that must be wrought by a people proud to have recovered its liberty and jealous to maintain it. Let us frighten all those who would dare try to take it from us again," the declaration continued. "Let us begin with the French. Let them tremble when they approach our coast, if not from the memory of those cruelties they perpetrated here, then from the terrible resolution that we will have made to put to death anyone born French whose profane foot soils the land of liberty."

The declaration promised, as Toussaint had earlier done, that Haiti would not become exporters of revolution to the rest of the Caribbean. "Peace to our neighbors," it proclaimed, "but let this be our cry: 'Anathema to the French name! Eternal hatred of France!' " Dessalines ended the declaration on a poignant personal note : "Remember that I sacrificed everything to rally to your defense; family, children, fortune, and now I am rich only with your liberty; my name has become a horror to all those who want slavery. Despots and tyrants curse the day that I was born."

Dessalines changed his title from governor-general to emperor later in 1804. In 1805 he massacred large numbers of the French whites who still remained. On May 20, 1805, as Emperor I of Haiti he issued a new constitution. It began,

> We, H. Christophe, Clerveaux, Vernet, Gabart, Petion, Geffard, Toussaint, Brave, Raphael, Roamin, Lalondridie, Capoix, Magny, Daut, Conge, Magloire, Ambrose, Yayou, Jean Louis Franchois, Gerin, Mereau, Fervu, Bavelais, Martial Besse . . .
>
> As well in our name as in that of the people of Hayti, who have legally constituted us faithfully organs and interpreters of their will, in presence of the Supreme Being, before whom all mankind are equal, and who has scattered so many species of creatures on the surface of the earth for the purpose of manifesting his glory and his power by the diversity of his works, in the presence of all nature by whom we have been so unjustly and for so long a time considered as outcast children.
>
> Do declare that the tenor of the present constitution is the free spontaneous and invariable expression of our hearts, and the general will of our constituents, and we submit it to the sanction of H.M. the Emperor Jacques Dessalines our deliverer, to receive its speedy and entire execution.

The new constitution confirmed that the country would be called Haiti. It again abolished slavery forever. It further decreed that "No whiteman of whatever nation he may be, shall put his foot on this territory with the title of master or proprietor, neither shall he in future acquire any property therein." Exceptions were made for white women and "Germans and Polanders" who had been naturalized. (The Polanders were Polish troops in Napoleon's army who had deserted to the Haitians. A small community of German settlers had lived in Haiti since the late eighteenth century.) The constitution sought to end the excessive preoccupation with gradations of color bequeathed by slavery when it decreed that all Haitians would henceforth be known "only by the generic appellation of Blacks." There would be no official religion. "All property which formerly belonged to any white Frenchmen" was "incontestably and of right confiscated to the use of the state." A system of public schools was set up. The national colors were to be black and red. (The blue and red were reinstated after the assassination of Dessalines in 1806.) "No person is worthy of being a Haitian," the constitution proclaimed, "who is not a good father, good son, a good husband, and especially a good soldier."

The Haitian victory inspired the struggle against slavery everywhere. The African American–attempted uprisings of Gabriel Prosser in Richmond, Virginia (1800) and Denmark Vesey in Charleston, South Carolina (1822), were inspired by it. Enslaved people from Haiti were not welcome in American slave states, for fear that they would foment insurrection. John Brown Russwurm, coeditor of African America's first

newspaper, *Freedom's Journal* (1827), chose the revolution as the subject of term papers and his valedictory commencement address at Bowdoin College. "You think me a fanatic tonight," said Wendell Phillips in 1861, "for you read history, not with your eyes but with your prejudices." History, he said, would proclaim Toussaint a greater hero than George Washington of the United States and other Europeans and white Americans of similar stature.

English poet William Wordsworth wrote of Toussaint,

Though fallen thyself, never to rise again,
Live and take comfort. Thou hast left behind
Powers that work for thee: air, earth and skies.
There's not a breathing of the common wind
That will forget thee: thou hast great allies:
Thy friends are exultations, agonies,
And love, and man's unconquerable mind.

Further Readings

Beard, John R. *The Life of Toussaint L'Ouverture: The Negro Patriot of Hayti; Comprising an Account of the Struggle for Liberty in the Island, and a Sketch of its History to the Present Period.* London: Ingram, Cooke and Co., 1853.

Boromé, Joseph A. "Dominica During French Occupation, 1778–1784." *English Historical Review*, 84, 330, January 1969, 36–58.

Dubois, Laurent. *A Colony of Citizens: Revolution and Slave Emancipation in the French Caribbean, 1787–1804.* Kingston: Ian Randle Publishers, 2004.

Fick, Carolyn. *The Making of Haiti: The Saint Domingue Revolution from Below.* Knoxville: The University of Tennessee Press, 1990.

Gaspar, David Barry. *Bondmen and Rebels: A Study of Master-Slave Relations in Antigua.* Durham, NC: Duke University Press, 1993.

Gaspar, David Barry, and David Patrick Geggus, Eds. *A Turbulent Time: The French Revolution and the Greater Caribbean.* Bloomington: Indiana University Press, 1997.

Haitian Declaration of Independence, 1804, as translated *by* Laurent Dubois and John Garrigus in *Slave Revolution*

in the Caribbean 1789–1804: A Brief History with Documents.* http://news.duke.edu/haitideclaration/declarationstext.html [accessed April 12, 2010].

Hall, N. A. T. *Slave Society in the Danish West Indies: St. Thomas, St. John, and St. Croix.* Ed. by B. W. Higman. Mona: University of the West Indies Press, 1992.

James, C. L. R. *The Black Jacobins.* New York: Vintage Books, 1963. First pub. 1938.

Marshall, Bernard. "Slave Resistance and White Reaction in the British Windward Islands, 1763–1833." *Caribbean Quarterly*, 28, 3, September 1982.

Ribbe, Claude. *Napoleon's Crimes: A Blueprint for Hitler.* Oneworld Publications, 2007.

The Louverture Project. http://thelouvertureproject.org/index.php?title=Main_Page [accessed January 31, 2011].

Thornton, John K. "African Soldiers in the Haitian Revolution." *Journal of Caribbean History*, XXV, 1 & 2, 1992, 58–86.

Tyson, George F. *Toussaint L'Ouverture.* Englewood Cliffs, NJ: Prentice-Hall, 1973.

9

Emancipation
Help from Europe, Final Push from the Enslaved

Humanity and Morality have often claimed, and sometimes perhaps with imprudence, the abolition of slavery. It is now a measure of political necessity.

—ALEXIS DE TOCQUEVILLE, *Report Made to the Chamber of Deputies on the Abolition of Slavery in the French Colonies, 1839*

For the latter half of the eighteenth century the Caribbean was consumed by an unending revolutionary conflagration. There were Maroon wars in Suriname; the First and Second Black Carib-British wars in St. Vincent; the Trelawney War and other Maroon conflicts in Jamaica; the 1790 revolt in Tortola; the so-called Brigands War in Guadeloupe, St Lucia, Grenada, Dominica and St Vincent; the revolts in Martinique and Cuba; the Berbice Rebellion; Fedon's Rebellion in Grenada; the revolts in Tobago, the Bahamas and Curaçao; Maroons everywhere; and more. And all culminating in the Haitian Revolution, where the three biggest enslaving powers—France, Spain and Britain—were all crushed at the hands of an insurgent army of the formerly enslaved.

Something had to give. By the end of the eighteenth century it was obvious that Africans in the Caribbean could not, would not, be enslaved for ever. Slavery did not end overnight and Napoleon actually reimposed it in French Guiana in 1801 and Guadeloupe in 1802, though he failed comprehensively to reimpose it in Haiti.

It was in this atmosphere of a Caribbean on fire that help arrived, as it were, from Europe. European abolitionists constituted a de facto antislavery lobby in the belly of the beast, providing the kind of international support that most liberation struggles in the twentieth century would find indispensable. But they were a superstructure, and the infrastructure of antislavery struggle came from the enslaved themselves. The African American abolitionist Frederick Douglass recognized this clearly in his famous "West India Emancipation" speech of 1857. A "share of the credit" for the abolition of slavery, he said, "falls justly to the slaves themselves."

"Though slaves, they were rebellious slaves." . . . What [abolitionist William] Wilberforce was endeavoring to win from the British senate by his magic eloquence the slaves themselves were endeavoring to gain by outbreaks of violence. The combined action of one and the other wrought out the final result. While one showed that slavery was wrong, the other showed that it was dangerous as well as wrong. Mr. Wilberforce. . . . warned the British government of the danger of continuing slavery in the West Indies. There is no doubt that the fear of the consequences, acting with a sense of the moral evil of slavery, led to its abolition. The spirit of freedom was abroad in the Islands. Insurrection for freedom kept the planters in a constant state of alarm and trepidation. A standing army was necessary to keep the slaves in their chains. . . .

Those white people who joined the struggle against slavery in the non-Spanish Caribbean were primarily from Europe. There was little homegrown white antislavery movement to talk of. European help came in the form of Christian missionary activity, the abolitionist movement, abolition of the slave trade, amelioration and the interplay between capitalism and slavery.

MISSIONARIES

The Roman Catholic slave states of Spain and France (and Portugal in Brazil) had sought to Christianize their Africans from the beginning. The Portuguese baptized Africans en masse in West Africa. The newly enslaved were often marched past a cleric who doused them with a bucket of holy water. The Spaniards originally insisted that only Christianized Africans could be introduced into the Caribbean. The French Code Noir of 1685 made provision for the Christianization of the enslaved. The possibility of any incompatibilities between Christianity and enslavement did not unduly bother the Roman Catholics, at least not in theory. Things may have been less clear in practice. Alexis de

Tocqueville, reporting in 1839 for the commission appointed by the French Chamber of Deputies into the abolition of slavery, noted that "In many countries where the Europeans have introduced servitude, the masters have always opposed, openly or in secret, the preaching of the Gospel to the Negroes. Christianity is a religion of free men; and they fear, lest in exciting it in the soul of the slave, they may also awaken there some of the instincts of liberty."

For the Protestant slave trading nations—Britain, Holland, Denmark and the rest, the situation was different. They early decided that it was not right to enslave one's brothers and sisters in Christ. The easiest way out of any resultant moral dilemma was simply not to Christianize the enslaved. This made it easy to rationalize slavery on the following grounds (some shared with the Roman Catholics):

(a) Africans were heathen savages and hence eminently enslaveable.
(b) Africans were not quite human so that the question of enslaving fellow human beings did not really arise.
(c) They appropriated the Curse of Ham idea from a Jewish tradition going back 1,000 years, in the process making it their own. According to this tradition God, through Noah in the biblical book of Genesis, cursed his son Ham, supposedly the progenitor of the African race and his Canaanite descendants. These would, as a result, forever be the enslaved hewers of wood and drawers of water for the European and Asiatic races.

In the British colonies the "established" state church, the Anglicans, mostly kept the enslaved beyond the pale of Christianity for over a hundred years. A Jamaican law of 1696 allowing for baptism of the enslaved became an instant dead letter. It was early established that baptism in any event would not alter the status of the enslaved. A Barbados law of 1667 expressly outlawed proselytization since it led to "notions of equality." The Scottish Presbyterian church shared the views of their Anglican compatriots.

Clerics of all denominations were generally indistinguishable from the lay population in their interaction with the enslaved. They were slave owners. They lived in concubinage. Jesuits in Santo Domingo were said to engage in slave breeding.

Bartolomé de Las Casas in the sixteenth century bore witness to the excesses of his fellow clerics against the indigenous people. Roman Catholic Fr. Francisco Carillo debauched the indigenous girls at his Savana Grande mission in early nineteenth-century Trinidad. He had twelve iron stocks made in honor of the twelve apostles. He assembled the indigenous people, gave them benediction, sprinkled holy water on them and put an indigene in one of the stocks to act a godfather.

In St. Kitts, Edward Cox reports, Anglican Rev. William Davis beat an enslaved person to death in 1813. The British governor ruled that such conduct was "unbecoming the sacred character of a clergyman." No further sanctions were applied. In 1818 the Rev. Henry Rawlins of St. Kitts flogged a runaway to death. A white coroner's jury, seemingly made up of comedians, found that the African died from a "visitation of God."

Things began to change in the Protestant islands with the rise of "dissenting" and "nonconformist" denominations in the eighteenth century. The pioneers were the Moravians (the United Brethren of Germany), the English Methodists and the Baptists, originally from African America but later from England. The Moravians were first in the field in St. Thomas in 1732. They entered the Jamaican missionary field in 1754, where they baptized all of 1,000 persons in fifty years. Between 1765 and 1795 they amassed forty African converts in Barbados. Antigua (where Mary Prince joined them), became their great success story. In 1812 they had 8,994 members in Antigua.

The Methodists or Wesleyans had 6,570 members, mostly enslaved persons, in Antigua in 1793. There the governor, a Methodist convert, facilitated their activities. The pioneer Baptist missionary was George Lisle, an African American from Savannah, Georgia. Lisle, a freedman, was evacuated to Jamaica in 1782 after fighting for the British in the United States War of Independence. He pioneered black Baptist churches both in Savannah and in Jamaica.

All of these nonconformists made Africans the main focus of their activity. They were severely persecuted by the establishment. Laws were passed or reinterpreted to retard their work. George Lisle was imprisoned in chains. There were riots against them. In St. Vincent, missionaries were subject to

corporal punishment. A Jamaican Assembly resolution of 1815 deplored "the dark and dangerous fanaticism" of Methodists. In 1823 rioters in Bridgetown destroyed the Methodist chapel. In 1827 a clergyman in St. Lucy, Barbados, was fined a shilling and convicted of a misdemeanor for teaching "equality" to the enslaved. An 1828 committee of the Jamaican Assembly likewise deplored the teaching of "equality."

In early 1832, in the aftermath of Jamaica's Christmas Rebellion (the "Baptist War"), an Anglican clergyman, Rev. Bridges, formed a terrorist "Colonial Church Union" with tactics like the later Ku Klux Klan in the postslavery United States. They burnt down twelve Baptist chapels.

The new missionaries were however not necessarily revolutionaries. They were willing on occasion to preach a gospel of obedience to white people. As in the United States, where St. Paul's admonition, "Slaves, obey thy masters," was a standard text, Moravians (who owned enslaved people themselves) promised Surinamese authorities in 1734 to "admonish [the enslaved] to be loyal and industrious and therefore not to long for freedom." Even the Rev. John Smith was willing to toe the line. He was sentenced to death for his alleged role in the Demerara rebellion of 1823. In 1822, however, he stopped using hymns with "freedom lyrics" at the behest of the slave owners.

Yet, by bringing the gospel to the enslaved these missionaries were being revolutionary in spite of themselves. The church did indeed provide notions of equality for those who could read the whole Bible for themselves. It also provided another avenue for the practice of leadership skills that could be transferred into revolutionary activity. The Demerara rebellion and Jamaican Christmas rebellion proved this. Toussaint L'Ouverture said that the Bible consoled him.

The large Jewish populations in Suriname, Curaçao, Jamaica, Barbados and elsewhere require mention here. The Jews did not engage in Christian-style missionary activity. They are said to have joined the antinonconformist terrorist activity of the Colonial Church Union in Jamaica in 1832.There were no Jewish abolition societies, as there were among the Christians.

In Suriname and Curaçao especially, a distinct group of "Jewish mulattoes" existed, separate from the rest of the free colored population. In eighteenth-century Suriname they were the object of special Jewish community bylaws, promulgated by both Sephardic and Ashkenazi governing bodies which formally defined their inferior status. Both mixed-race Jews and white ones who married mixed race females were defined as "second rate members." They were segregated in the synagogues, and could not receive a blessing. Those officially accepted as second-rate members were buried in a segregated part of the Jewish cemetery. Colored and black Jews not so formally recognized could not be buried in the Jewish cemetery at all. "[C]onsidering the Respect of the Holy Place," said the Sephardic regulations, as reported by Robert Cohen, no colored, black or indigenous female was allowed into the synagogue, even if employed as a nanny for Jewish children.

Second-rate members were, despite their disabilities, subjected to the same taxes and other obligations as first-class members. In 1793 the "mulatto" Jews complained to the Surinamese governor for relief from their discriminations. The governor upheld the position of the Jewish community leaders and enjoined the mixed-race Jews to accept their subordinate status or face being charged with disturbing the peace.

ABOLITIONISTS, AMELIORATION

The sixteenth century produced Bartolomé de Las Casas, one of the great abolitionists of Caribbean history. Those who followed in his footsteps were few and far between. It was only in the late eighteenth century that a critical mass of white persons opposed to British slavery came together. This happened in England. Whites in the Caribbean itself were mostly intransigently opposed to anything resembling a movement against slavery. Two resolutions of the Jamaican Assembly in 1823 called British ameliorative slavery "fanaticism."

Organized abolitionism coincided with the enslaved's own violent push for freedom and was inextricably bound to it. The abolitionists also had links to the missionary movement. William Wilberforce, the doyen of the English abolitionists, was a prominent Anglican evangelical Christian.

Among Wilberforce's collaborators were Granville Sharp, whose advocacy had helped secure Lord Mansfield's supreme court decision of 1772 outlawing slavery in England. The 1772 decision (Somersett's Case, involving an enslaved Jamaican who came to England) resulted in the freeing of about 15,000 enslaved Londoners, who quickly became the city's destitute "Black Poor." Sharp was instrumental in shipping them off to Sierra Leone in 1787. A number of English prostitutes were tricked on board, plied with liquor and involuntarily sent to Sierra Leone as well. These odd couples became the founding mothers and fathers of British-controlled Sierra Leone, of which John Clarkson, brother of abolitionist Thomas Clarkson, became governor. An 1814 publication described Sierra Leone's white founding mothers as "chiefly of the lowest order, in ill health, and of but moderate character."

The pioneer 1787 Society for Effecting the Abolition of the Slave Trade contained nine Quakers and three Anglicans. Sharp and Thomas Clarkson were among the latter. Wilberforce became the main parliamentary voice for the group. Clarkson became their great pamphleteer and historian.

These abolitionists initially confined their advocacy to ending the slave *trade*, but not slavery itself. Like their counterparts in the United States, who often ran segregated abolition societies, they did not necessarily consider Africans equal to whites. Even so avowed a liberal as J. G. Stedman vociferously disagreed with anything but a very gradual abolition from slavery for the enslaved "savages." The liberal founding father Thomas Jefferson in the United States favored Emancipation with deportation out of the United States. President Abraham Lincoln took the same position in the 1860s.

The abolitionists were nevertheless very passionate in their propaganda war against slavery. They held public meetings, wrote books and pamphlets and introduced motions in Parliament. By the 1830s Britain was also engulfed in a popular movement which culminated in the Reform Act of 1832, liberalizing the electoral system. It was a good time for radical causes such as abolition.

The abolitionists lobbied successfully for the end of the British slave trade in 1807 and later for the Emancipation Act of 1833. The later phase was spearheaded by the Antislavery Society, formed in 1823 by Wilberforce, Thomas Fowell Buxton, Zachary Macaulay, Thomas Clarkson, Thomas Babington Macaulay and others. Thomas Pringle, who helped Mary Prince write her narrative in 1831, was secretary. Whatever their limitations, these abolitionists brought a genuine missionary zeal to their campaign. In *An Appeal on Behalf of the Negro Slaves of the West Indies* in 1823, for example, Wilberforce scoffed at those who contended that the enslaved were better off than British workers. Was there any husband or parent in Britain, he asked rhetorically, who would allow "his wife or daughter to be subjected to the brutal outrage of the cart-whip—to the savage lust of the driver—to the indecent, and degrading, and merciless punishment of a West-Indian whipping?"

Caught between the hammer blows of the Caribbean uprisings and the lobbying efforts of the abolitionists, the European governments instituted a series of ameliorating measures. These were designed to restrain the harshest excesses of slavery, thereby hopefully removing some of these reasons for the rage exhibited by the enslaved. Similar measures were introduced in all the Caribbean jurisdictions, though at varying times.

The abolition of the slave trade was presented in this context. It would hopefully encourage domestic slave breeding and natural increase in population, since fresh importations would be prohibited. (There was, in fact, considerable illegal smuggling of Africans after abolition of the trade). At this point abolition did not mean Emancipation of the enslaved. Wilberforce was clear on this. The abolitionists' desire, he emphasized in 1814, was merely "to produce by abolition a disposition to breed instead of buying." He opposed a parliamentary suggestion that all Africans imported illegally into the Caribbean should be immediately set free.

The Foreign Slave Act of 1806 banned sending enslaved persons to foreign countries and newly acquired colonies, such as Trinidad. Imports into other British colonies were outlawed in 1807. Intercolonial importations remained legal until 1811. The British next introduced "slave registers" as a means of keeping track of the legally enslaved and discouraging illegal importations. The first register was set up in Trinidad in 1813. Any person not enrolled would be deemed free.

The institution of "crown colonies" was another British ameliorative measure. This related to the new territories conquered from France and Holland in the late eighteenth century—Trinidad, St. Lucia and British Guiana (formerly the separate colonies of Berbice, Essequibo and Demerara). The older colonies had internally self-governing planter-dominated legislative assemblies. The Colonial Office in London ruled the crown colonies directly through "orders-in-council" transmitted to handpicked British governors. London saw this as less oppressive than rule by planter-dominated assemblies hostile to African rights. While Britain had ultimate authority over the island assemblies, implementing legislation could sometimes involve tricky maneuvering around reactionary local representatives hostile to ameliorative legislation.

In 1823 the Colonial Office sent a comprehensive list of ameliorative suggestions to governors of islands with assemblies. (These measures were directly imposed on the crown colonies). Governors were asked to:

- remove unnecessary obstacles (such as taxes) to manumission.
- stop selling Africans "in satisfaction of the debts of their owners."
- schedule punishments for the day after the alleged offence. One free person must be present, in addition to whoever was inflicting the punishment.
- allow the enslaved to enjoy whatever property they were able to acquire.
- move "with all possible dispatch. . . ."
- end flogging of enslaved women.
- ban the whip in the field.
- maintain a registry of punishments.
- allow compulsory manumission for those enslaved who could afford to purchase their freedom.
- admit testimony of the enslaved in courts of law.

In addition, "protectors of slaves" were to be appointed. Savings banks were to be established for the enslaved. (The U. S. Freedmen's Bureau did a similar thing in 1860s postslavery United States.) Sunday markets were to be abolished with an alternative day for markets, thus making Sunday a real day of rest. Marriage was to be officially recognized.

Families were not to be separated. There was to be a six-day week and a nine-hour working day. Provisions were to be made for religious and moral instruction.

Planters, ever intolerant, loudly proclaimed their customary rights to flog enslaved women. During the transitional "apprenticeship" period (1834–1838) that followed Emancipation, visiting English abolitionists could still document the unregulated whipping of women in Barbados until the skin was entirely beaten off their legs and they could scarcely crawl away from the scene of their torture. Free colored spokesman J. B. Philippe complained in Trinidad that the protector of slaves appointed as part of these ameliorative measures was himself an owner of enslaved persons.

The French abolished the slave trade in 1815. In 1833 an ordinance abolished mutilation and branding. In 1840 the enslaved were placed under the protection of the *procureurs généraux* (attornies general). The Macau law of 1845 limited the workday from 6 AM to 6 PM with two and a half hours siesta in between. During harvest time, however, the enslaved could be worked night and day, Sundays included, though a small stipend was payable. Men and women were given equal pay. The maximum legally allowed number of lashes was reduced from twenty-nine to fifteen.

Denmark-Norway abolished the slave trade in 1792, to take effect from 1802, but to the Danish Islands only. They continued their flourishing re-export trade. The ban precipitated a frenzy of imports to beat the prohibition. The history of amelioration and Emancipation in the Danish West Indies has come to be largely connected to the name of Peter Carl Frederik von Scholten, governor-general from 1827 to 1848. His 1834 proposal for gradual Emancipation, inspired by events in the British colonies, was not implemented. In 1843 he made Saturday a free day of rest for the enslaved, together with Lutheran Church feast days and royal birthdays.

He shortened the workday, reduced owners' power to punish, improved housing for the enslaved, banned the public auctioning of Africans and, in 1841, introduced public education for enslaved children.

Dutch ameliorative measures included improved medical care, food rations and housing, and a right of the enslaved to take grievances direct to government officials.

There was some initial ameliorative activity in the Spanish colonies from the 1760s to the 1820s. A Magistracy for Slave Defense allowed the enslaved to file grievances. Spain abolished the slave trade in 1817 under pressure from the British. Africans were nevertheless imported in large numbers up to the 1860s. Spain (but not its colonies) abolished slavery in 1836.

CAPITALISM AND SLAVERY

The rebellious enslaved found a de facto lobby in the abolitionist movement. The objective economic relations of the time were also on their side. Eric Williams, in his seminal *Capitalism and Slavery,* documented this relationship for the British empire. The connection can succinctly be described in three points:

First, the slave trade and its associated economic spin-offs—sugar production, rum distilling, manufactured goods to supply the trade, the monopolist (mercantilist) laws that reserved colonial trade for British ships, and so on.—catapulted England into the world's first industrial revolution. The triangular trade (Europe to Africa to the Americas and back to Europe) provided the monumental super profits and capital accumulation that made this possible. A ship would leave England laden with goods for trade in West Africa—iron bars for currency, firearms for African accomplices, fine cloth, alcohol and other luxury items, iron handcuffs, leg restraints and other instruments of torture, gaudy junk items ("pacotille"), etc. These items would be exchanged in West Africa for enslaved persons, realizing a great profit.

The ship would next head for the Americas, where it would exchange its enslaved Africans for sugar, molasses (raw material for rum distillers), other agricultural products, hides, etc. Another large profit would be realized. These products would be sold in Europe for another large profit.

These profits also stimulated the English shipbuilding industry and encouraged the development of a merchant marine and navy. English seaport towns like Bristol and Liverpool were practically built upon the slave trade.

Second, Williams demonstrated that many of the industrial and commercial pillars of England's pioneer industrial revolution were financed directly in part from slave trade profits. James Watts' steam engine, the defining technological breakthrough of the age, received Caribbean-derived venture capital.

The Quaker David Barclay of Barclay's Bank was a slave trader and Jamaican plantation owner. "The earliest extant advertisement referring to Lloyd's [of London Insurance Company], dated 1692," Williams reported, concerned the auction of three ships "cleared for Barbados and Virginia."

Third, having been fueled by the triangular trade, the industrial revolution then caused England to outgrow the very trade that had helped give it birth. Britain no longer needed the monopoly it had on the British Caribbean market. The massive low-cost productive capacity of the industrial revolution made it possible for Britain to undersell its rivals, monopoly or no monopoly.

Nor was it now economically sensible to maintain the preferential tariffs provided to British Caribbean sugar in the British market. New, rising sugar suppliers in India, Brazil and elsewhere could now provide Britain's needs more effectively and cheaper, once the preferential tariffs were removed. Britain eventually equalized the sugar duties between British Caribbean and other sugar in 1846.

The significance of all this was that the British abolitionists could now lobby Parliament while the country's economic need to end slavery coincided with the humanitarian thrust to do so. Without this coincidence, Williams argued, humanitarianism alone would not have worked.

Williams' *Capitalism and Slavery* has been ferociously attacked by a small but vocal group of European (and some American) scholars, who see his diminution of the central role of the European "saints" in Emancipation as heresy. They have however been singularly unable to refute Williams' demonstration of the contribution of slavery to the industrial revolution in England, and the other points enumerated above. Instead they have concentrated on the argument, by no means generally accepted, that the British Caribbean was in economic advance leading up to Emancipation, rather than in decline. Therefore, they argue, there was no

economic incentive for the British abolition of slavery. Their arguments here do not address Williams' demonstration that the British economy no longer needed Caribbean slave-grown and subsidized sugar to undersell the world.

So the Africans rebelling on the ground, the humanitarians agitating in Britain and the objective economic forces all came together in this final push against British slavery.

EMANCIPATION

The culminating step in the amelioration process was Emancipation. Africans, of course, had been emancipating themselves since the first Maroons took to the hills in Hispaniola in 1502. As already noted, some of the stronger Maroon communities were de facto independent nations, recognized as such by the Europeans. On occasion, as in the 1733 revolt in St. John, the Africans officially abolished slavery, in this case from November 23, 1733 to the defeat of their insurgency on May 27, 1734. In Haiti, as seen, Emancipation occurred in 1793, 1794 and finally and definitively in 1804. The Haitians abolished slavery in the Dominican Republic in 1801 and again in 1822, at the beginning of their twenty-two-year occupation. As the movement toward Emancipation appeared irresistible in the British islands, some slaveholders sold their enslaved to Spanish islands or relocated there with their enslaved.

"An Act for the Abolition of Slavery throughout the British Colonies; for promoting the Industry of the manumitted Slaves; and for compensating the Persons hitherto entitled to the Services of such Slaves," passed the British Parliament on August 28, 1833, to take effect on August 1, 1834. Its provisions extended to the British West Indies, Mauritius and South Africa. Britain was now the major slaveholding power in the Caribbean, thanks to the French loss of Haiti. According to parliamentary resolutions of June 12, 1833, repeated in the act, all children under six at the time of the act or born thereafter were declared free but subject to whatever restrictions on their freedom might be "deemed necessary." Any such "free" child under twelve becoming destitute could be indentured to the mother's owner up to the age of twenty-one years.

Emancipation monument, New Kingston, Jamaica.

Persons enslaved in 1834 were pronounced both free and unfree in an amazing piece of double-speak. They were to become "apprenticed laborers and to acquire thereby all rights and privileges of free men; subject to the restriction of laboring under conditions and for a time for their present owners." Agricultural ("praedial") enslaved were apprenticed for six years. Nonpraedials would be apprenticed for four years. Apprenticeship was in actuality a device for forcing the enslaved to fund some of the compensation paid to owners, via free labor. Government-subsidized indentured immigration, mostly of Indians, further compensated the planters, by providing a new source of cheap labor, for which the newly freed had to bear some of the tax burden. In both the British West Indies and Suriname, the first Indian indentureds arrived shortly before the end of apprenticeship. Continuing protective tariffs favoring British Caribbean produce further compensated the planters.

Upset among the supposedly freed eventually caused the British to end apprenticeship prematurely in 1838. August 1, 1838, rather than August 1, 1834, thus became the preferred date for the celebration of British Emancipation. Trinidad was very nearly the exception to the early ending of apprenticeship. With the other affected British colonies already on board for change, Trinidad's planters strenuously opposed ending apprenticeship early. With his council deadlocked Governor George Fitzgerald Hill had to use his casting vote to pass the measure. This was on July 25, 1838, less than a week before apprenticeship ended. Trinidad's crown colony council comprised the governor, plus six "official" (British) and six "unofficial" (local) members, all appointed by himself. The necessity for the governor's casting vote seemed to vindicate the views of Under-Secretary of State at the Colonial Office, James Stephen, that "popular franchises in the hands of a great body of owners of slaves were the worst instruments of tyranny which were ever yet forged for the oppression of mankind."

Special justices were appointed to administer the provisions of the act. Whipping and other punishments could be administered only with their concurrence. Women must not be flogged or beaten. (This provision was not always observed). Apprentices who could afford it must not be prevented from manumitting themselves.

Local legislatures were permitted to pass similar acts with enhanced benefits, thus Antigua and Bermuda dispensed with apprenticeship altogether. The largest portion of the act actually dealt with the 20 million pounds compensation paid to slave owners. The preamble to the act did not express any profound regret for the institution of enslavement, except to say that "it is just and expedient that all such Persons should be manumitted and set free. . . ." The British emancipatory template of amelioration, Emancipation, compensation and apprenticeship was faithfully followed, with here and there an exception, by the entire Caribbean.

British Emancipation also generated immense further pressure on neighboring slave states, already in the throes of African upset. Danish Governor-General von Scholten's unsuccessful 1834 effort at gradual Emancipation has already been noted. British colonies became even more attractive destinations for would-be Maroons from other jurisdictions. Guadeloupe's privy council stated in December 1838 that the proximity of now-free British islands made Emancipation in Guadeloupe an urgent necessity. The French Chamber of Deputies established a commission, led by Alexis de Tocqueville, to enquire into the question of Emancipation. The commission's report acknowledged the impact of events in the British colonies. It studied the British emancipatory process in great detail. Its 1839 report concluded that the Africans were now practically ungovernable. "It is no longer a state of regular and established order"; de Tocqueville noted, "it is a transitory and stormy condition; the dreaded revolution is already begun." It suggested quick and decisive Emancipation, without apprenticeship as that term was understood in the British colonies. It recommended compensation for slave owners, to be paid in part from the wages of the newly freed.

The Danish, Spanish and Dutch Emancipations all imposed the gradualism of the British precedent. The French were the big exceptions. De Tocqueville's commission concluded that gradual Emancipation was unworkable. The premature termination of British apprenticeship in 1838 was fresh in their minds and seemed a harbinger of what would happen if gradualism were tried in French colonies. Victor Schoelcher, like de Tocqueville a major French abolitionist, was won over from gradualism to immediate Emancipation in 1842. This was after a trip to slave states in the French West Indies, Puerto Rico and elsewhere.

The Provisional Government of France that followed the revolution of 1848 set up an Emancipation Commission in March 1848. Schoelcher, under-secretary of state of the Navy and Colonies in the new government, presided. As a result of the commission's efforts, the government announced Emancipation in the French colonies on April 27, 1848. The decree was however to take effect two months after the document reached each colony. The Africans of Martinique heard the news before the decree arrived and mounted militant protests. The government killed sixty-seven to seventy-five of the protesters on May 22. The Africans retaliated by burning down twenty-one houses in St. Pierre, killing thirty-five white people in one house alone. They murdered other whites and set fire to plantations. On May 23 the authorities capitulated and announced immediate abolition, which was officially ratified on June 4. Guadeloupe decreed Emancipation on May 28, in an effort to avoid similar bloodshed. French Guiana, where things were quieter, got its freedom on August 10. As in the case of the British colonies, French Emancipation incorporated not only the Caribbean, but also Africa (Senegal and the Isle of Bourbon, renamed Reunion in 1848) as well as French possessions in India.

French slave owners received 126 million francs in compensation. In August 1848 Schoelcher was elected deputy in the French parliament for both Martinique and Guadeloupe. He chose Guadeloupe.

Dutch St. Maarten, sharing a tiny island with French St. Martin, had little choice but to emancipate in 1848, the year of French Emancipation. For the rest of the Dutch Caribbean, Emancipation was formally agreed in 1844 but the law was not enacted until 1862, with effect from July 1, 1863. Almost 10 million guilders were paid to slave owners in compensation for 26,825 freed field-workers and 6,086 domestics. A ten-year apprenticeship was instituted, from 1863 to 1873, but for Suriname only. There was no apprenticeship in Curaçao, Aruba, Bonaire, St. Eustatius, Saba, or earlier for St.Maarten. Apprenticed field and boiling house workers had to sign contracts of at least one year, other freedpersons for three months to a year. They could change plantations after expiry of their initial contracts.

District commissioners were appointed to monitor and adjudicate issues pertaining to apprenticeship. The formerly enslaved could now buy shoes, the wearing of which had been legally permitted for free people only.

A Danish royal decree of July 28, 1847 freed all children born thereafter. The rest of the enslaved would be free in 1859. Here as elsewhere the enslaved short-circuited the process. On July 2–3, 1848, the Africans of St. Croix assembled to the call of bells and conch shells. They destroyed some houses of white authority figures. About 8,000 gathered at Fort Frederik and demanded freedom by 4 PM. News of French Emancipation had come to the Virgin Islands and they had heard rumors that Denmark had abolished slavery. Governor-General von Scholten eventually arrived at the fort and acceded to their demands in a statement written in Danish and English. Von Scholten's proclamation stated that (1) everybody was free immediately, (2) estate workers could remain in their homes for three months, (3) allowances to the enslaved were ended but they would be paid for their labor and (4) the old and infirm would be maintained until further notice.

This did not end the disturbances. Danish troops were reinforced on July 8 by 580 Spanish troops from Puerto Rico. Several Africans were killed and eight were summarily executed by court-martial in the week after Emancipation. Von Scholten complained that the women were more aggressive and violent than the men. Von Scholten had cohabited in St. Croix for twenty years with Anna Heegaard, a free colored woman, his earlier marriage to a Danish woman notwithstanding. Heegaard is sometimes credited with having put in a good word for her suffering kinfolk.

Population of French Colonies, 1825–1832

Colonies	Census of	Whites	Free Col.	Enslaved	Total
Martinique	1832	9,410	18,832	80,753	107,995
Guadeloupe	1831	10,596	10,772	90,743	112,111
Marie-Galante, Etc.	1823	2,570	279	11,600	14,440
French Guiana	1832	1,291	2,220	19,173	22,684
Isle of Bourbon (Réunion)	1830	20,000	11,500	66,000	97,500
Senegal, Etc.	1825	240	3,573	12,297	16,110
French Factories in India	1825	1,021	107,986	1,194	110,501

Source: Tocqueville, Alexis de. *Report Made to the Chamber of Deputies on the Abolition of Slavery in the French Colonies, 1839*. Boston: James Munroe and Company, 1840. Reprinted by Negro Universities Press, Westport, CT, 1970.

Danish reprisals against the Emancipation victory of the Africans continued for decades, culminating in the brutally suppressed 1878 "Great Fireburn" uprising in St. Croix, to be discussed in Chapter 10. Emancipation in 1848 had been followed in 1849 by an apprenticeship program much more severe than in the British islands. It forced the ex-enslaved to become indentured workers with renewable contracts of one to three years. The period from 1848 to 1878 became arguably the longest and most repressive apprenticeship period in the Caribbean.

Von Scholten was recalled to Denmark in July 1848. Even though a royal proclamation of September 22, 1848, accepted the *fait accompli* of Emancipation, von Scholten was nevertheless found guilty, on February 5, 1851, of dereliction of duty. The Supreme Court acquitted him on April 29, 1852. One of the leaders of the Africans, "General" Buddhoe, also known as John Gottliff, was deported to Trinidad. He had helped the authorities appeal for calm after the initial disturbances. He made his way to Curaçao and eventually to New York, where he met the abolitionist Lewis Tappan in 1850.

The Spanish National Assembly ended slavery in Puerto Rico on March 22, 1873. A local abolition movement had developed here, led by Ramón Emeterio Betances, founder of the Secret Abolitionist Society, Segundo Ruiz Belvis and others. Betances and other abolitionists also doubled as pro-independence activists and helped lead the short-lived *Grito de Lares* (Declaration of Lares) uprising on September 23, 1868. Enslaved Africans participated in this revolt. As often the case in such situations they were promised freedom. The ameliorative Moret Law of 1870, discussed below, applied to Puerto Rico as well as to Cuba. The Spanish government set aside 35 million pesetas to compensate owners whose enslaved were emancipated as a result of this law. The Africans were required to work as apprentices for three more years.

By the time slavery officially ended in Cuba in 1886 it had largely withered away. The Ten Years War of 1868–1878 was launched by Carlos Manuel de Céspedes, a plantation owner of enslaved persons, in his famous *Grito de Yara* ("Declaration of Yara") on October 10, 1868, two and a half weeks after Puerto Rico's *Grito de Lares*. Céspedes and his associates wanted independence from Spain. Some of the insurgents freed their enslaved at the start of the conflict and mobilized them as fighters. Yet the official rebel platform envisaged Emancipation only after the war, and with compensation to the slave owners. The rebels also decreed the death penalty for anyone inciting the enslaved to revolt. Political and military expediency quickly forced the insurgents to switch their position to immediate Emancipation. In July 1869, as Rebecca J. Scott has shown, the

Puerto Rican freedpersons, ca. 1873.

rebels imposed forced labor on their formerly enslaved. Genuine Emancipation only came from the rebels late in 1870.

The emancipatory actions of the rebels, however circumscribed or opportunistic, and the general confusion of war, nevertheless provided the cover for many enslaved to escape to de facto freedom. This situation also put pressure on Spain to make some gesture toward Emancipation.

Spain responded to events in Puerto Rico and Cuba with the ameliorative Moret Law of 1870, officially conceived as a preliminary measure for eventual gradual Emancipation. Children born to enslaved mothers after November 17, 1868, were declared free, though they still had to provide unpaid labor for their mothers' owners up to the age of eighteen. Those sixty years old and above and those belonging to the state were also freed. The law abolished the whip and promised freedom for any enslaved subjected to excessive cruelty. As earlier in the Caribbean and the United States, special tribunals were set up to monitor the process. The law met with much planter opposition, but some enslaved managed to benefit from it.

The 1878 Cuban peace treaty formally recognized the freedom of combatants on both sides (*los convenidos*). The remaining enslaved thereupon demanded similar privileges. The eastern planters gave in, promising freedom in four years and wages in the interim. The Spanish government agreed on a gradual Emancipation, beginning in 1879. A transitional period of apprenticeship (*patronato*) would continue to 1888. These arrangements broke down with many more Africans than anticipated managing to secure their freedom. An approximately 200,000 enslaved Africans in Cuba in 1877 had dwindled to 100,000 apprentices by 1883 and 53,000 by 1885. By 1886 only 25,000 were still apprenticed. Spain therefore ended apprenticeship early in 1886.

Emancipation in the Caribbean was part of a larger movement that ended enslavement in many countries around the world. In the Americas freedom, usually gradual rather than immediate, came between 1777 and 1804 to the northern U.S. states of Vermont, Massachusetts, Pennsylvania, New Hampshire, Connecticut, Rhode Island, New York and New Jersey. The rest of the U.S. slave states were emancipated with the thirteenth amendment to the U.S. Constitution in 1865, after the War of the Slaveholders' Rebellion (Civil War). Between 1813 and 1888 the South American countries of Argentina, Colombia, Chile, Bolivia, Uruguay, Ecuador, Peru, Venezuela and Brazil proclaimed Emancipation, usually also on a gradual basis. The Central American Federation (Costa Rica, El Salvador, Guatemala, Honduras and Nicaragua) emancipated its few Africans in 1824. Mexico followed in 1829.

Further Readings

"An Act for the Abolition of Slavery throughout the British Colonies; for promoting the Industry of the manumitted Slaves; and for compensating the Persons hitherto entitled to the Services of such Slaves," August 28, 1833. http://www.pdavis.nl/Legis_07.htm [accessed November 24, 2010].

Caldecott, Alfred. *The Church in the West Indies*. London: Frank Cass, 1970. First pub. 1898.

Cohen, Robert. *Jews in Another Environment: Suriname in the Second Half of the Eighteenth Century*. New York: E.J. Brill, 1991.

De Tocqueville, Alexis. *Report Made to the Chamber of Deputies on the Abolition of Slavery in the French Colonies, 1839*. Boston: James Munroe and Company, 1840. Reprinted by Negro Universities Press, Westport, CT, 1970.

Dookhan, Isaac. *A History of the Virgin Islands of the United States*. Mona: Canoe Press. 1994. First pub. 1974.

Hall, N. A. T. *Slave Society in the Danish West Indies: St. Thomas, St. John, and St. Croix*. Ed. by B. W. Higman. Mona: University of the West Indies Press, 1992.

Jennings, Lawrence C. "Slavery Emancipation." *Encyclopedia of Revolutions of 1848*. http://www.ohio.edu/chastain/rz/slavery.htm [accessed November 28, 2010].

Moitt, Bernard. *Women and Slavery in the French Antilles, 1635–1848*. Bloomington: Indiana University Press, 2001.

Scott, Rebecca J. *Slave Emancipation in Cuba: The Transition to Free Labor*. Pittsburgh: University of Pittsburgh Press, 2000.

Williams, Eric. *Capitalism and Slavery*. Chapel Hill: University of North Carolina Press, 1944.

10

After Emancipation
Obstacles and Progress

*England is to pay twenty million of pounds sterling for your gradual freedom.
You can only deserve or understand this blessing by a course of good conduct, by obeying
the laws, and being dutiful to all those entitled to your services, and to whom you will
have to look for the rewards of your labor when you become perfectly free.*

—GOVERNOR OF BARBADOS, *Proclamation explaining
forthcoming Emancipation Act, January 22, 1834*

*The returns for 1857 show that no less than 8,209 persons were then living
in their own houses built by themselves since emancipation—illustrating in the most
satisfactory manner the material progress made by the Creole laborers of St. Vincent during
the last twenty years. More remarkable still is the fact that, within the last twelve years, from
ten to twelve thousand acres have been brought under cultivation by small proprietors,
owning from one to five acres, and growing arrow-root, provisions, and minor
articles for export. The statistical returns from which I gather these figures
further state that there are no paupers in the island—quite sufficient,
in my opinion to disprove the erroneous idea that, unless compelled
to work, the Negro will lie all day in the sun and live on a piece of
sugar-cane. I have seen nothing in the British West Indies that
lends any countenance to such a supposition.*

—WILLIAM G. SEWELL, *The Ordeal of Free
Labor in the British West Indies, 1861*

APPRENTICESHIP: SAVAGE INTERLUDE

Some anti-Emancipation British campaigners predicted, as one suggested in 1833, that the enslaved
who "we design to civilize and to make happy, may be driven back to the barbarianism, the vices and
the sufferings of savage life." In a sense apprenticeship was an attempt to make this a self-fulfilling

prophecy. All over the British West Indies the newly freed Africans expressed dismay at the continuing six years of unfreedom. In Trinidad a delegation of the newly emancipated marched to the governor's residence. "*Point de six ans*," they told him in the French-influenced patois, "No six years." The king had given them freedom, they said, and, like the Africans in Martinique and St. Croix in 1848, they wanted it now. The police dispersed this group of mostly very old men and women, together with children. Some were sentenced to floggings with the cat o' nine tails.

The British authorities mobilized troops, including warships throughout the colonies. Many of the newly emancipated began their freedom by being flogged, jailed or hanged for demanding real rather than illusory freedom. The governor of the Windward Islands surveyed the situation on August 26, 1834. In the immediate aftermath of Emancipation Grenada was "partially disturbed by refractory Negroes on two estates," he reported. Civil and military authorities had "immediately restored order." In St. Vincent, one estate had struck work, but "order was soon restored." In Tobago and Barbados everything was calm. Demerara, Trinidad, St. Kitts and Dominica were all "considerably agitated."

He had refused a request from Trinidad for troop reinforcements. He thought that things were "fast subsiding" there. Martial law had been imposed on St. Kitts and "some severe examples made." The Windward naval squadron "afforded as usual the most cheerful and important services in aid of the troops. . . ." He was about to send a warship each to Grenada and Trinidad "to aid in maintaining the public tranquility." Less than a month after freedom supposedly came, it looked a lot as if the more things changed, the more they remained the same.

The governor of Antigua in his proclamation of June 1834 warned that the new magistrates would have the power to bring "deserved punishment" to "all such as shall wander about in idleness" or be dishonest. This was a lot like the "Black Codes" of postslavery United States, which deemed unemployed freedmen "vagrants" and locked them up, often into a situation of neo-slavery. The former slavemasters, the governor advised, had to allow "orderly and reputable" former enslaved persons

to remain in their homes for twelve months. But, he warned, the "insubordinate, quarrelsome," and otherwise "disorderly" would risk expulsion. The governor of Barbados was more to the point: "The law is strong, and the law will punish you if you do not work [for your former slaveowners]."

In Essequibo, British Guiana, Africans declined to work on August 2, 1834, supposing that Emancipation gave them that right. Led by Damon, they staged a peaceful vigil in Trinity Parish churchyard on August 4. Damon unfurled a flag in the process. Governor Carmichael Smith had Damon publicly hanged as a result. His unfurling of a flag was defined as an act of rebellion. The total passivity of Damon and his followers was not reciprocated. Four of Damon's associates were sentenced to jail and "severe floggings." Two were transported. Thirty were sentenced to the treadmill, but "pardoned" by the governor.

The savage repression of the almost semi-pacific Demerara rebellion had come in 1823, year of the Amelioration Act. Damon was hanged for a series of pacific actions beginning the day after the Emancipation Act came into force. With ameliorative measures like these, the Africans of Guyana probably wondered, who needed repressive legislation?

The planters reinforced their immediate post-slavery repression by making it as difficult as possible for the newly emancipated to avoid continued work on plantations. The Barbados assembly recommended the destruction of provision grounds to starve the Africans into working on plantations in order to buy food. In Guyana the planters destroyed fruit trees for a similar purpose. A European missionary in Berbice considered apprenticeship by 1836 a complete failure. Apprentices were defrauded of their time and the planter-merchant assembly was oppressive.

Drivers were now unable to carry the whip in the field. They carried a staff instead. Whippings, as savage as during slavery, nevertheless continued. Two visiting English abolitionists, Joseph Sturge and Thomas Harvey, described the situation in Barbados in 1836. At the Bridgetown jail, male prisoners had to break thirty baskets of stones a day. Female prisoners had to break twenty-five. A woman far advanced in pregnancy was observed thus employed. Men and women were flogged for failure to meet their tasks. Stronger men would voluntarily exceed their tasks and hand over their excess baskets to the weak, to save them from a flogging.

A treadmill was in operation with fifteen males "from boys to men" on it when observed. The treadmill, a recent English invention (1818), was one of the more barbaric forms of torture imported into the Caribbean from Europe. It was introduced into Trinidad in 1824 and into Jamaica in 1828. It became the defining penal innovation of the apprenticeship period. The treadmill was a hollow cylindrical frame constructed of iron. Around it were built wooden platforms serving as steps. Prisoners stood on the steps holding on to a bar above head level. As the mill was put into motion prisoners had to keep walking upward in order to remain in one place. If they missed their step or could not keep up they could fall off the machine. If, as often the case, they were strapped by the wrists to the bar, then, if they could not keep up their body would dangle from the bar. In that case the moving steps would inflict serious damage (broken bones, clipped toes, skin scraped off of shins, mangled bodies) as they bumped against the dangling bodies. The cat o' nine tails (whip), the abolitionists noted, was applied constantly to the "sides, shoulders and legs" of the prisoners on the treadmill. Those victims too weak to hold on to the treadmill were held up at the wrist of one arm, by others employed for that purpose.

The abolitionists described a room of 30 × 35 feet in which 110 persons were "herded" from 4 PM until the following morning. They could not imagine how anyone could survive in those conditions. Some spent twelve months there before being released without trial. Cases were often adjourned for six months because the prosecutor found it inconvenient to show up in court. "How iniquitous a system is this!" commented the abolitionists.

Women on the treadmill fared as badly as the men, with the "brutal driver" flogging them with the cat as savagely as he had done to the males. Their hair had been shaved off and handkerchiefs tied around their heads. (As late as 1920, Marcus Garvey's First International Convention of the Negro Peoples of the World was still calling for an end to the shaving of women's heads in jails.) The driver beat the women as he pleased, with his whim being the only guidepost as to how much torture they had to endure. "We were dreadfully shocked," reported the abolitionists, "but determined to witness the whole proceeding."

A colored woman of about thirty was on the treadmill "dreadfully exhausted." The driver flogged her relentlessly. "She was literally suspended by the bend of the elbow of one arm, a Negro holding down the wrist at the top of the mill for some minutes; and her poor legs knocking against the revolving steps of the mill until her blood marked them. There she hung groaning, and anon receiving a cut from the driver. To which she appeared almost indifferent." When her stint on the mill was up "she fell on the floor utterly unable to support herself. . . ."

The abolitionists observed an eighteen-year-old black girl suffering similarly on the treadmill. She too was suspended, totally exhausted, by one arm, which the machine had broken. The abolitionists engaged the driver in conversation to run out the clock and save the girl a few minutes' punishment.

The colored woman had had a dollar sized piece of skin on her leg entirely torn away by the cat. "The poor black girl had lost the skin of the bend of her arm. . . ." "Thus then," the abolitionists commented, "it appears, that in Barbados women committed to the tread-mill are catted *ad-libitum*— the driver's feelings alone being the rule which governs him in the use of his scourge." The Barbados assembly was in session 30 yards from the scene of these tortures.

Sexual exploitation of black women and girls also continued into the apprenticeship period. Sturge and Harvey reported from a Moravian day school in Antigua in 1836 that "Dreadful evils" befell some of the new scholars "from the lax morals" of some white Antiguan men. Within the preceding three months the school had lost three students to "improper connections with white men." The only student for whom an age was given was sixteen years old. The abolitionists praised the work of an Antiguan orphanage for girls which "rescue[d] them from a life of almost inevitable degradation and profligacy."

Apprenticeship also gave rise to the "Demerara slave trade." Sturge and Harvey traveled on board ship in 1836 with a Demerara labor recruiter who went up the islands buying out apprentices' remaining time. In exchange the apprentices (and free recruits from Antigua, which dispensed with apprenticeship) would be indentured for periods usually of one to four years. He had already secured thirty from Montserrat, thirty-two from Antigua and varying numbers from St. Kitts, Nevis and Barbados. He was on his way to collect eighty from Tortola. Sturge and Harvey worried that there was no guarantee that the recruits might not be sold to New Orleans, the Spanish Main or some other slaveholding place.

EFFORTS TO THWART AFRICAN PROGRESS

The efforts to marginalize the formerly enslaved continued unabated after 1838, however. In Trinidad the recently freed first collectively bargained to bid up the price of labor to a fair level. This worked for a while but the planters were able to reduce their wages, thus precipitating an exodus of the newly freed from plantation labor. The exodus was however not precipitous, as William Sewell explained in an 1859 dispatch to the *New York Times*. The Africans waited until they had saved enough to buy some land, before quitting.

And quitting involved the freed persons in losses that they would not have sustained in a just environment. For Trinidad's "tenancy at will" laws allowed planters to force laborers residing on their estates to work for them only, and at a reduced pay (in exchange for housing and medical attention). When workers left the plantations the planters took their houses and destroyed their provision grounds, thus robbing the workers of crops already planted but not yet harvested.

Brian L. Moore has detailed similar processes as they operated in British Guiana. There the newly freed had bought plantations, pooling their money to get around restrictions on purchase of small plots, designed to frustrate African land acquisition. By 1850 Afro-Guianese had acquired 16,850 acres, enabling 80 percent of the newly freed to relocate off the estates and on to their own land. After 1850, however, they faced increasing prices for crown lands, renewed reluctance of planters to sell to them and regressive taxation from the planter and merchant dominated court of policy (assembly). The mule and donkey carts of the peasants were taxed, for example, while the implements and supplies required by planters were not. Most of the African land was badly drained. Subdivision and other factors reduced the average size of plots to uneconomic units, less than one acre each. The government imposed taxes for dubious village "improvements." And in 1852 the planter-merchant legislature put a cap of twenty persons on the number that could pool their resources to buy land.

After August 1, 1838, there was a standoff in St. Vincent of several weeks between the finally freed, acting in concert, and the planters. The latter eventually felt forced to sell to the Africans in small lots. In some cases the Africans collectively bought larger estates and subdivided among themselves.

Similar conditions applied to the ex-enslaved's efforts to get into trade and commerce. The phenomenal success of provision grounds during slavery made an attempted move into commerce a natural development. Sewell was so impressed by the entry of African Trinidadians into business by 1859 that he thought they had won the battle for commercial success, despite planter society's stringent efforts to thwart their entry into this area. Sewell referred to "the large and utterly disproportionate numbers of colored people engaged in trade—from keeping a store down [sic] to selling a sixpence worth of mangoes on the street." This rush into commerce was fed by both the free persons of color who obtained a pre-Emancipation head start and the newly freed who joined them. The latter, Sewell noted, "made every exertion to bring up their children as traders or mechanics, and the consequence is, that today these professions in Trinidad are almost entirely supplied by the colored population." He estimated that four-fifths of the "Creoles of African descent" in Port of Spain were engaged in trade. Their condition, he said, was "one of prosperity and independence."

The negative stereotype of indolence among African Caribbeans has been matched over the years by one of African inability to do business. Yet what Sewell saw in 1859 made him think that the "Creoles of African descent" had already won the race for commercial viability. "I have personal knowledge," he said, "of many instances where great wealth has been accumulated by men who were slaves themselves a quarter of a century ago. Trade seems to be the destiny of the Trinidadian Creoles, for the position they once occupied as tillers of the soil is already filled by another race."

Sewell's enthusiasm for the new black merchants was, however, ominously tempered by his noting the hostility of the ruling white planter class to these developments. They "adopted most stringent measures to prevent the increase of small proprietors and keep up, by such unnatural means, a sufficient laboring force for the estates. They imposed heavy taxes on all lands and buildings except those devoted to sugar manufacture." Yet Sewell thought that these efforts up to 1859 had not succeeded in stemming the forward march of black business in Trinidad, which had a larger wealthy black merchant class than other colonies.

Khalleel Mohamed has documented the process of forcing the formerly enslaved out of business in the case of Guyana. There the unending search for a buffer group against the Africans bore early fruit with the Portuguese immigrants, who began arriving in 1835, during apprenticeship. The Portuguese had much going for them as a potential buffer. They were mostly white, though initially poor. They were mostly religiously different (Roman Catholic). They spoke a different language and they seemed to embrace enthusiastically their role as buffers. They were also a numerically significant community.

The Portuguese met a huckstering trade dominated by free people of color. Many had accumulated some money from their provision grounds and Sunday markets. In June 1838, two months before the end of apprenticeship seemed poised to release a flood of new black and colored hucksters, the legislature revived huckster licenses, which had fallen into disuse. Licenses became a major device for squeezing the formerly enslaved business people. They were differentially applied and enforced, with the Portuguese routinely paying lesser fees or no fees at all. Once the new licenses were in effect the Portuguese and others colluded with police to arrest, imprison and confiscate the goods of any of the formerly enslaved found without the licenses on their persons. Police received half of the confiscated goods.

Portuguese entry into the rum retail (which they monopolized by 1855) and other businesses was accompanied by similar assistance. They received easy credit from white merchants while business-people of color received credit on harsh terms or not at all. By 1845 the Portuguese were bringing trading goods and new immigrants from their Madeira homeland in their own ships. Portuguese merchants accordingly dominated peddling and the retail trades by the 1850s. Their sharp practices (short changing, weight fraud, currency manipulation, etc.) precipitated anti-Portuguese riots in the 1840s and 1850s, culminating in the serious riots of February 1856, usually blamed on John Sayers Orr, the "Angel Gabriel."

Orr was a colored Guianese of possibly some means and certainly some educational accomplishment. His wide international travel, his history of radical activity overseas and his return home to agitate against perceived injustice, all invite comparison with such later nineteenth- and twentieth-century Caribbean radicals as Henry Sylvester Williams, Marcus Garvey and Walter Rodney. Several contemporary and subsequent commentators wrote him off as a lunatic, but he was probably no more demented than a Marcus Garvey, a Fidel Castro or a John Brown of U.S. antislavery fame. He deserves more serious study. Like similar Caribbean historical figures, he developed a clear ideological orientation early in life and did not materially deviate from it thereafter. Like some other Caribbean radicals, returning home proved his undoing. Orr's ideology and political practice included hostility to Roman Catholic "popery," insistence on the right of free speech and opposition to slavery. He delivered his message everywhere through itinerant open-air preaching.

Orr described his father as a paymaster in Georgetown. His mother was a "respectable" colored woman. He once said he was born in England. He certainly spent many years there. The several newspapers in the United Kingdom, the United States and even Australia which mentioned him, tended to be silent on his racial appearance. One source mentioned that he wore his hair down to his shoulders, as part of his biblical makeup which included a white robe and a flag.

Orr returned home in December 1855 after decades of religious/political activism in the United Kingdom and North America, where he involved himself extensively in the social agitations of the day. Irish immigrants bore the brunt of his anti-Catholic wrath. For approximately a year and a half prior to his return home he had engaged in an intense campaign of street preaching which placed him at the epicenter of serious riots between Irish immigrants and native populations. He moved like a hurricane through Manchester, New Hampshire; Bath, Maine; Manhattan and Brooklyn, New York; East Boston and Chelsea, Massachusetts; and Greenock and Paisley, Greater Glasgow.

Orr typically blew his trumpet to announce his open-air sermons. Crowds quickly assembled. He had a remarkable ability to move into a new community and almost instantly mobilize huge throngs of people. He brought out 10,000 white Yankees to the steps of City Hall in Manhattan. Two thousand followed him in procession into Brooklyn, where the Irish met them in pitched battle on Fulton Street. Orr's forces emerged victorious from an engagement described at the time as one of the most intense in the history of Brooklyn. He could just as easily raise a crowd of Protestants in Scotland as he could Africans around the Stabroek Market in Georgetown.

In the United States many of his riots were actually precipitated by the Irish, who were ever ready to offer armed preemptive aggression to anyone preaching against their faith. In Guiana too the proximate cause of the riots would be Portuguese violence against Orr's followers, despite the fact that Orr, not on the scene when the violence began, has traditionally been blamed for what transpired. Serious injury to life and limb, the destruction of Catholic churches and mobilization of police and armed forces were all routine appendages of Orr's appearances. Orr was arrested many times but seemed to escape personal injury at the hands of hostile mobs.

Orr saw himself as a champion of the masses. He informed Governor Wodehouse of British Guiana on January 1, 1856, that he desired "in every way possible to get at the masses of the Poor, the ignorant and despised. . . ." His agitation against the

Catholic Irish in the United States was linked to the popular feeling of antislavery campaigners who blamed the Southern-based Democratic Party for passage of the 1854 Kansas-Nebraska Act, which they interpreted as opening the door for the expansion of slavery into the new territories of Kansas and Nebraska. The Irish Catholics, overwhelmingly pro-slavery and virulently anti–African American, supported the pro-slavery Democrats.

The Kansas-Nebraska Act became law on May 30, 1854. Between May and July Orr swept through the Eastern United States, with pitched battles, loss of life, serious personal injury and sometimes the destruction of Catholic churches in his wake. The violence swirling around Orr was but part of a wider turmoil which engulfed much of the United States around the Kansas-Nebraska question. In 1856 John Brown, the great white martyr of the antislavery cause, led Kansas antislavery elements in a successful little "war" which killed some pro-slavery militants.

Orr returned home, fresh from these encounters, to find Afro-Guianese locked in a struggle for economic survival with the Portuguese. The position of the Catholic Portuguese vis-à-vis the Afro-Guianese would have seemed very similar to that of the Catholic Irish in relation to African Americans.

On January 1, 1856, Orr took the precaution of writing Governor Philip Wodehouse. He advised the governor that he planned to work with the poor, but expected to have his right to free speech respected, since he intended to break no law. Orr began holding street corner meetings to protest Roman Catholicism and Portuguese business practices. Tobago-born Guyanese politician A. R. F. Webber summarized Orr's charges against the Portuguese: "that they had taken the bread out of the mouths of the creoles; that they had driven the colored hucksters and peddlers out of the business—which was largely true—and that they with ready cash cornered every supply of vegetables, as soon as it was offered at the market by the farmers—no doubt equally true!" Orr's return coincided with efforts on the part of the Creole (African and colored) shopkeepers to form a Mutual Aid Society to recover a fair share of the retail trade.

As he had done for decades elsewhere, Orr summoned the crowds to his meetings by blowing his trumpet. He was known here, too, as the Angel Gabriel. Like the Irish the Portuguese, probably emboldened by the government partiality they enjoyed, prepared to violently confront Orr. A body of Portuguese men, armed with sticks and whips, lay in wait for him at his accustomed meeting place. His followers interpreted this as an indication of Portuguese intent to murder Orr. Orr did not show up. His supporters ran through the town shouting anti-Portuguese slogans. The police next banned Orr's gatherings at the instigation of the Portuguese consul and clashed with Orr's followers a few days later. Orr, who was not present at any of these events, was then arrested. In the midst of all this the Portuguese stabbed a black man. The perpetrator was badly beaten by Orr's followers before being rescued by the police. Three Portuguese were arrested and tried. They received relatively light sentences while by contrast Orr, who was not even present at these altercations, was arrested, detained and committed to trial before the Supreme Criminal Court (which tried more serious cases). This was the final straw for Orr's followers and the riots ensued.

Governor Philip Wodehouse blamed the riots on "the gross and brutal character of the female population." (Similar references to female militancy had been heard concerning protesting women apprentices in Trinidad in August 1834 and from Governor-General Peter von Scholten on the St. Croix Emancipation Riots in 1848. The theme would be repeated in relation to the Water Riots of Trinidad in 1903, the Butler Riots of Trinidad in 1937 and elsewhere.) Shops were looted and Portuguese people were assaulted.

Governor Wodehouse led a group of volunteer special constables to the Charlestown section of Georgetown where, he reported, there were six or seven Portuguese shops in each street. The Africans beat one policeman to death in Charlestown. The police shot two blacks and arrested hundreds of people, including a few Portuguese. The riots spread to the rural villages and estates, where Portuguese shops were also looted, as were houses of some Portuguese farmers.

Reminiscent of the days of enslaved rebellions, French and Dutch gunboats that happened to be visiting, were both enlisted in anti-African activities. Also reminiscent of the slavery period, the government mobilized Arawaks and Caribs against the black rioters. Governor Wodehouse expressed satisfaction at the behavior of indentured Indian immigrants, who helped protect Portuguese property and some of whom were badly beaten for their trouble. The locally based units of the West India Regiment (WIR) were also called out, with further WIR reinforcements brought in from Barbados. There were unconfirmed reports of black troops being reluctant to fire on their fellow Africans in Essequibo.

The new Afro-Guianese *Creole* newspaper supported Orr's people. Protestant missionaries backed Orr against the Catholic Portuguese and helped pay for his legal defense against a charge of holding an unlawful assembly. He received the inordinately harsh sentence of three years at hard labor. His imprisonment became a de facto capital sentence, for he died in jail in November 1856, supposedly of dysentery. Three Portuguese who were apprehended trying to assault Orr with sticks and horsewhips were fined and sentenced to a relatively light six months in jail, without hard labor. Hundreds of Africans were arrested and sentenced, with twelve in Essequibo condemned to deportation from the colony for ten years. When the prisons overflowed detainees were placed in penal settlements.

Governor Wodehouse had at the start of the riots piloted special new laws imposing heavy fines, imprisonment and flogging on persons looting or assaulting persons of another race. He later imposed a poll tax "to compel the lower classes, who had perpetrated the damage," to compensate the Portuguese, who had presented 615 claims for alleged losses. The largest Portuguese claims came from West Coast Demerara, followed by Leguan Island, Essequibo and Georgetown. The special tax was in effect a collective punishment against the entire African population. It was withdrawn in 1858 after protests by the Anti-Slavery Society and others.

The Angel Gabriel affair, with its wholesale imprisonments, floggings and deportations of Africans, its death to Orr and the collective reparations exacted from the African population, represented a sort of final savage crushing of British Guiana's black and colored effort to stave off Portuguese economic competition and the government's insistence on reinforcing the Portuguese buffer at all costs. It was part of the Caribbean-wide package of repressive measures which included the excesses of apprenticeship, immigration to depress African wages, the taxation of Africans to fund indentured immigration and the various measures to stymie African commerce and land purchases.

Together with the death in jail of the English missionary Rev. John Smith in 1824 and the judicial murder of the inoffensive Damon in 1834, the Gabriel affair represented the completion of a trilogy of repression from which Guiana's African population probably did not soon recover. When Governor Wodehouse left at the end of his tour of duty, it was at the dead of night to avoid a barrage of dead cats and dogs which the Africans had laid up to salute his exit.

MORE POST-EMANCIPATION RIOTS AND UPRISINGS

Orr and Rev. John Smith paid with their lives for championing the cause of the African oppressed. Such was the case also of George William Gordon during the Jamaica (Morant Bay) Rebellion of 1865. The Jamaica Rebellion, like the Angel Gabriel riots, was symptomatic of the continued frustrations of the mass of Afro-Caribbean people in the existing climate of extreme repression. Unlike pre-Emancipation days, these riots were not the full-scale wars of some Maroon campaigns or the carefully planned revolts of enslaved rebellions. They were more typically the spontaneous or near-spontaneous eruptions of people nursing unresolved grievances and provoked beyond endurance.

In 1865 peasants in St. Ann parish, facing hard times, petitioned Queen Victoria for some crown land to cultivate as a cooperative. The queen's reply, written by Colonial Office officials, based itself on the old Thomas Carlyle premise of black people as indolent and working only intermittently and just enough to satisfy their basic pumpkin (the Caribbean equivalent of the American watermelon stereotype) needs. The reply, and the revolt that it helped stimulate, were an ultimate and logical consequence of all the measures put in place since 1838 to hinder the advance of the African Caribbean masses. The efforts to keep the newly freed on sugar plantations, the laws frustrating

purchase of land, the racist commentary of Thomas Carlyle, all seemed to come together and explode in the Jamaica Rebellion of 1865. The queen said:

> THAT THE PROSPERITY of the laboring classes, as well as of all other classes, depends, in Jamaica, and in other countries, upon their working for wages, not uncertainly, or capriciously, but steadily and continually, at the times when their labor is wanted, and for so long as it is wanted: AND THAT if they would thus use this industry, and thereby render the plantations productive, they would enable the planters to pay them higher wages for the same hours of work than are received by the best field laborers in this country [Britain]. . . .

Petitions sent to the queen had to pass through the governor for his approval and commentary. The petitioners therefore assumed that the queen's insensitive and insulting response must have been influenced by comments of the governor, Edward Eyre.

It was in this atmosphere that authorities imprisoned a black man for allegedly trespassing on an abandoned estate. Villagers from Stony Gut protested and one was arrested. The protesters rescued the arrested man from prison. Paul Bogle subsequently discovered that a warrant had been issued for his arrest and that of twenty-seven other protesters.

On October 11, 1865, Bogle marched with a group of protesters to the town of Morant Bay. The militia fired on them, killing seven. The protesters retaliated by burning down the courthouse while the parish council was in session. They killed the chief magistrate and eighteen other white people, including some militia.

Governor Edward Eyre mobilized troops, including Maroon fighters. There was no organized resistance at this point and the soldiers were allowed to wantonly massacre whoever they felt like, whether involved in the protests or not. They killed 439 black people, according to official figures. Three hundred and fifty-four more were executed afterward. Soldiers burned down over 1,000 homes of the black population. Many were sentenced to long prison terms.

Over 600 people, including pregnant women, were flogged, receiving up to 100 lashes from the cat o' nine tails. H. Pringle, a former stipendiary magistrate in Jamaica, was horrified enough at the flogging of women to write several London newspapers. The indecent exposure and public flogging of African women, he noted, had been one of the most potent factors mobilizing English public opinion against slavery in the Caribbean. Yet over 300 of those flogged now were women and young girls. Men were flogged on their backs and shoulders. In Jamaica, however, women and girls were flogged "in shameful nakedness."

"I am altogether at a loss," Pringle stated, "to conceive that, under any possible circumstances of insurrection or warfare, it could be necessary to resort to this abominable and ferocious punishment of women. It is absolutely necessary for the ends of justice, and a due regard for outraged humanity, that these things should be known to the women of England."

Governor Eyre also took advantage of the situation to judicially murder George William Gordon, a wealthy, outspoken colored member of the Jamaica assembly. Gordon was also a journalist and businessman and a persistent critic of the governor. He also had an independent Native Baptist Church, in which Paul Bogle was a deacon.

Governor Eyre had Gordon arrested in Kingston. He had him transported to Morant Bay, which was under martial law and where, therefore, constitutional guarantees were suspended. Gordon was immediately tried by court-martial and hurriedly hanged. Gordon had no connection to Paul Bogle's protest.

English intellectuals and public figures ranged themselves for and against Eyre. Philosopher John Stuart Mill organized a Jamaica Committee which tried unsuccessfully to have him prosecuted for murdering Gordon. Charles Darwin was a member of Mill's committee. Thomas Carlyle, author of *An Occasional Discourse on the Nigger Question,* organized a committee in Eyre's defense. Charles Dickens and poet Alfred Lord Tennyson were in Carlyle's committee. James Hooker, a friend of Darwin, supported Eyre because "the Negro in Jamaica . . . is pestilential . . . a dangerous savage at best."

Eyre and the British government used the opportunity of the uproar to dismantle the Jamaica Assembly of over 200 years. Colored politicians, as exemplified by Gordon, were poised to become the dominant party, which was anathema to both local whites and British imperial administrators. Jamaica became a crown colony.

Bogle and Gordon are national heroes of independent Jamaica. Marcus Garvey, Jamaica's great Pan-African leader of the twentieth century, was a native of St. Ann and an admirer of Gordon. Garvey's early newspaper, *Garvey's Watchman,* was apparently named after Gordon's paper, *The Watchman.*

While the British colonies were grappling with the challenges of post-Emancipation realities, other jurisdictions were only slowly emerging out of slavery. In 1853 Denmark agreed to pay former owners $50 compensation per enslaved person.

On October 1, 1878, "Contract Day," workers in St. Croix rose up in "The Great Fireburn" against the neo-slavery conditions still existing. Emancipation in 1848 had been followed in 1849 by an apprenticeship program much more severe than in the British islands. It forced the ex-enslaved to become indentured workers with contracts of one to three years and severe restrictions on breaking the contracts.

The workers had staged several strikes and protest actions since 1849. On October 1, 1878, an annual public holiday on the eve of contract signing, several events precipitated the outbreak of violence. Passports (even for travel to the sister Danish island of St. Thomas) appeared to be unobtainable. Workers were reported detained on their way to Vieques Island, Puerto Rico. A worker was reported to have died in police custody. These factors appeared to have precipitated an outbreak of violent protest, though some suggest that there may have been some prior planning.

Workers burned fifty plantations and buildings. They demanded abolition of the 1849 Labor Act under which they suffered. The Danish authorities killed eighty-four workers. Some ameliorative measures were put in place and labor unions were formed in the aftermath. Some Barbadian and Jamaican immigrant workers were said to be implicated in the leadership of the revolt. The most celebrated leader, however, was an estate worker known as Queen Mary Thomas. Other leaders included Queen Agnes and Queen Matilda.

Less spontaneous and more similar to the pre-Emancipation rebellions was the 1876 workers' rebellion in Barbados. Workers, led by a laborer, "General Green," destroyed plantations and other property over much of the country. Several were shot by the authorities.

In 1779 Vincentians tried to revive their previously banned carnival. Many policemen were injured in the resulting clashes. A warship was summoned from Barbados.

In 1881 in Port of Spain and in 1884 in San Fernando and Princes Town, Trinidad police and auxiliary forces under English Police Chief Arthur Baker precipitated clashes with bands of carnival masqueraders. Canboulay (*"cannes brulées"* or lighted torches) processions had traditionally marked the start of Emancipation Day (August 1) commemorations. The practice was also incorporated into carnival, possibly as early as 1838. Canboulay and carnival processions were also accompanied by drumming, chanting and singing, masquerading and fighting between rival bands. Carnival represented a period when the black masses took over the streets, celebrated their African culture in their own way, parodied white society and were very difficult for authorities to control.

Soon after the canboulay parade started at midnight on February 27–28, 1881, police laying in wait and canboulay "stick men" engaged in a bloody battle lasting three hours. The police were unable to obtain a clear-cut victory. In 1884 in Princes Town the stickmen took the battle to the waiting police massed in the station yard. The police opened fire killing a boy and seriously wounding two persons.

It was on October 30, 1884, that the Hosay riots/Muhurram massacre took place in San Fernando, Trinidad. There the police fired into a crowd of people celebrating the Shia Muslim Hosay festival. The police had fought with canboulay celebrants in the same town earlier in the year but had allowed Hosay participants to carry torches in 1881 while engaging in a pitched battle

to prevent canboulay participants from carrying them.

Hosay was primarily a festival of Indian Muslims although by 1884 it had already been significantly infiltrated by Afro-Trinidadians. Indian Hindus also joined in. Casualties for the Hosay massacre are variously put at 16 to 22 killed and over 100 wounded.

POST-APPRENTICESHIP STRUGGLE FOR AFRICAN PROGRESS

The end of apprenticeship accelerated efforts at progress. African flight from estates continued. Peasant villages sprang up, with the newly freed often pioneering the commercial production of such new crops as arrowroot in St. Vincent, nutmegs in Grenada and bananas in Jamaica.

William G. Sewell, on his investigative journalism trip in 1859–1860, was impressed by the energy, thrift and initiative he saw. In Barbados he was "surprised that these proverbially indolent people should exhibit so much energy in the prosecution of their business." Poor neighborhoods were much cleaner than their New York counterparts. Of about 28,500 blacks and coloreds in St. Vincent 8,209, according to the 1857 census, were living in their own homes, built by themselves. In twelve years up to 1859 the former enslaved had brought 10,000–12,000 acres into peasant cultivation, growing arrowroot, provisions and other crops instead of sugar.

In Trinidad, Sewell noted, many former enslaved had left the "virtual slavery" of sugar estates for peasant proprietorship. Of about 11,000 field-workers in 1838 only about 4,000 remained on the estates in 1839, and most of those had migrated from sugar to cocoa. Five-sixths of the 7,000 deserting the estates were now proprietors of 1–10 acres each. They had set up about twenty new villages in the process. A few squatted on Trinidad's abundant state (crown) lands. About 4,000–5,000 of the newly independent former estate workers still performed casual labor on sugar estates, especially at crop time. Now, however, they did it based on their availability and needs, and not under compulsion.

EDUCATION

Education provided an important means of upward mobility for the post-Emancipation population. Formal education did not normally exist for the enslaved during slavery. There were a few private schools for whites and free coloreds. Some children of both of these groups were sent to Europe (England, France, Holland, Denmark, etc.) for schooling. There was the exceptional black Francis Williams of Jamaica, who was sent to Cambridge University in the mid-eighteenth century. He was supposed to be an experiment to see if Africans were educable or whether they were really, as alleged, subhuman beings. Williams did alright. He returned to Jamaica, an anomaly in plantation society, wrote Latin verses and opened a school.

In the years leading up to British Caribbean Emancipation, the missionary churches opened a few schools, mostly religious. In early 1834 in Jamaica, 800 students were attending such Moravian schools. Half of the students were enslaved. Four hundred attended their regular day schools, of necessity limited to whites and freed coloreds. In the crown colonies of Trinidad and British Guiana, some "urban slave schools" were set up by the government as part of the ameliorative arrangements of 1823. In St. Vincent the government made its first grant to parochial schools in 1834. In 1849 it assumed wider responsibility for education with grants to twenty-seven schools, including the new coeducational St. Vincent Grammar School.

The British Emancipation Act of 1833 promised education for the newly freed. This was administered via the Negro Education Grant of 1835–1845. The British government granted funds to private concerns such as the Mico Charitable Trust and to religious bodies to implement programs in infant and primary schools and also noon and night schools for adults. The government felt that basic literacy and inculcation of Christian values would prevent the newly freed from slipping into "savagery," to the detriment of colonial rule.

The new education program generated many debates concerning the advisability of industrial versus classical education, the need for agricultural studies, the fear of overeducating the children of the poor and unfitting them for lowly occupations, the role of education in making British a polyglot island like Trinidad (where two-thirds of the population spoke only French or Spanish in 1841), secular versus religious education, and the resistance of Indian immigrants to having their children in the same schools as Africans.

The question of the educability of blacks persisted for some time as a topic of debate among white administrators. Dr. Richard Rawle, principal of Codrington College in Barbados, was astonished to discover in 1848 that his "blackies" were "above the average of Staffordshire [England] children in intelligence." A Moravian in Jamaica in 1854 noted cautiously that "it has been affirmed that [black people] are every way inferior to the white people; that their intellect is capable of cultivation only to a certain extent and that then it becomes stationary. We cannot altogether agree to this."

Primary school curriculum suggestions circulated by the British Colonial Office in 1847 seemed to embody notions of limited capacity for their African-descended subjects. The guidelines suggested religious education, English language ("the most important agent of civilization for the colored people of the colonies"), sufficient writing and arithmetic to enable a small farmer to "enter into calculations and agreements," and a section called "Relationships with authority." This section would teach the "rational basis" of the British–colonial relationship and the "domestic and social duties of the colored races."

In similar vein Governor Robert Keate of Trinidad in 1857 hoped that the new Tacarigua Orphanage for Indian children would provide a wonderful opportunity for Westernizing a future leadership cadre of Trinidad Indians, whose education would make them Indian "in descent and natural characteristics but English in education and feeling, and having no home associations beyond the limits of the colony." They would be a captive cadre, far "from the debasing influence of caste and heathenism."

Similar practices were implemented with Native American children in the United States. This type of policy reached its horrific zenith with the "stolen generations" of British Australia. Here mixed-race Aborigine children were kidnapped wholesale from their indigenous mothers, usually never to see them again. The children were taken to orphanages far away to be force-fed European culture. In the twenty-first century, Australian governments belatedly acknowledged with regret the country's guilt for this amazing episode.

Secondary education came late to the British Caribbean and was initially closed to the black population. The exceptional Lodge Grammar School of Codrington College opened in 1749 in Barbados. This was the result of a private bequest. Queens College, originally a state-aided Anglican school, opened in Guyana in 1842. Queen's Collegiate School (later Queen's Royal College) opened as a fully state-owned school in Trinidad in 1859. St. Joseph's Convent (Roman Catholic) opened for girls in Trinidad in 1836. Roman Catholic St. George's College (later St. Mary's) opened in Trinidad in 1837.

Tertiary education was, with some minor exceptions, virtually nonexistent in the British territories until the University College of the West Indies opened in Jamaica in 1947. The University of Havana, by contrast, was founded in 1728. The Dominican Republic (Hispaniola) had a university in the sixteenth century.

Whatever the shortcomings of the new education system, a critical mass of the former enslaved was able to seize the opportunities education afforded. By 1881, 45.7 percent of Jamaicans were literate (at least able to read). By the nineteenth century, some of them were already beginning to distinguish themselves academically and professionally.

Despite the absence of universities in the British Caribbean, some professions could be accessed locally. Teaching and preaching were among these. The solicitors' (as opposed to barristers') branch of the legal profession could be pursued at home. Exam papers were sent to England for marking. Pharmacists could also study at home. A few persons studied overseas and returned home.

While most of the non-British Caribbean still languished under slavery after 1834, Haiti provided the major exception. A few private schools had existed there for whites and coloreds, but these did not survive the revolution. Toussaint was literate but his immediate successors Jean-Jacques Dessalines and Henri Christophe were not.

They nevertheless initiated free primary schools and allowed private ones from 1805, shortly after independence. In 1848 President Faustin Soulouque created a system of rural schools. Under Elie Dubois, minister of public instruction, the number of schools in Haiti increased from 118 to 229. These included two *lycées* or high schools. Colleges of Law and Medicine, already in existence, were reorganized. The College of Medicine included Schools of Pharmacy and Midwifery.

The first professional school, a School of Health, was started as early as 1806. The first secondary school, the *Lycée* Alexandre Pétion, opened in 1816. The first vocational school, *La Maison Centrale*, began in 1846.

The official curriculum for state and private primary schools in 1848 consisted of reading, writing, linear drawing, arithmetic, grammar, Bible stories and the history and geography of Haiti. For secondary schools the 1848 curriculum comprised writing, linear, drawing, academic drawing, French, Latin, Spanish, Greek, mythology, history and geography (with an emphasis on Haiti), cosmography, mathematics, zoology, botany, rhetoric, philosophy, chemistry and experimental physics. Haiti, not surprisingly, eventually produced a significant cadre of outstanding intellectuals.

In the Danish islands, as seen, Governor-General von Scholten introduced schools for enslaved children in 1841. The Dutch in Suriname allowed Moravian and Roman Catholic missionaries to educate a small number of enslaved children prior to Emancipation in 1863. They provided education subsidies to these groups after Emancipation. Education was made compulsory in 1876.

AFRICAN INTELLECTUALS, NEWSPAPER PUBLISHING

A region-wide cohort of African Caribbean intellectuals began to take shape. Though slavery-derived distinctions between black and colored persisted, especially in such personal contexts as marriage and club membership, these distinctions gradually diminished. This was especially the case among the politically and intellectually activist. Edward Wilmot Blyden left St. Thomas in 1850 for Liberia via the United States. He became one of the most distinguished Pan-African intellectuals of his day. John Jacob Thomas of Trinidad wrote a *Creole Grammar* in 1869. In 1887 he published the famous polemic *Froudacity; West Indian Fables by James Anthony Froude; Explained by J. J. Thomas,* a response to the racist polemicizing of the Regius Professor of Modern History at Oxford University. Froude had expressed horror at the prospect of a future black Caribbean dominion (quasi-independent territory within the British Empire) with a figurehead white governor-general. "No English gentleman would consent to occupy so absurd a situation," he opined. Black people were inferior, he wrote. If Britain wanted to keep its Caribbean colonies it would have to maintain undemocratic rule. Haitian Anténor Firmin in 1885 published *On the Equality of Human Races*, a response to the French Count de Gobineau's pseudoscientific work on *The Inequality of Human Races*. All of these men, it will be noted, used their learning to confront racist ideas among European intellectuals.

In 1888 poet Egbert "Leo" Martin of Guyana won a British empire–wide competition run by a London newspaper, to compose two additional verses for the British national anthem.

This growing class of nineteenth-century intellectuals explored whatever means they found available to move themselves and their group forward. Some obtained admission into influential Masonic and similar secret societies. Sir Conrad Reeves broke new ground as attorney general of Barbados. Lawyer Maxwell Phillip was mayor of Port of Spain. Several prominent Afro-Trinidadians were on the Port of Spain City Council when the British abolished it late in the century.

This new black and colored middle and professional class was conscious of its historical mission of racial uplift. When the British administration in Trinidad tried in 1888 to play down the golden jubilee commemoration of Emancipation, Edgar Maresse-Smith, a solicitor and others insisted on a proper identification with their enslaved ancestors and a renewed commitment to racial unity and progress.

Much of the energy of this class also went into newspaper publishing. In 1830 there were twenty-five white-owned and four free colored newspapers in the British Caribbean. Henry Loving, who held a variety of high-ranking government posts in Antigua, Montserrat and Barbados, coedited with colored William Hill Antigua's first newspaper of any race, the *Weekly Register,* from 1814. Edward Jordan and Robert Osborn started the antislavery *Watchman and Jamaica Free Press* in 1829. Generations of the Cable family (Samuel, Richard, Thomas, et al.) ran the *St. Christopher's Advertiser* from 1782. William Baker ran the pro-slavery *Grenada Chronicle.*

By the time these colored newspapers appeared, Roderick Cave has shown, enslaved Africans had already entered the ranks of skilled printing workers. There was at least one African pressman in Jamaica in 1783. By 1794 Africans were handling most of the skilled printing work in Jamaica. A white Antiguan in 1819 bequeathed his printing business to his six enslaved sons by an African woman. He had been training all of them to be compositors.

Caribbean people of this period also pioneered newspaper publishing in African America and Africa. African America's first newspaper, *Freedom's Journal,* began publication in 1827 in New York City, under Jamaican-born John B. Russwurm and African American Rev. Samuel E. Cornish. In 1830 Russwurm published the *Liberia Herald. Freedom Journal's* ringing declaration in its first editorial could just as easily have been issued to a Caribbean audience: "We wish to plead our own cause. Too long have others spoken for us." When Marcus Garvey began learning the printing trade around the beginning of the twentieth century he was therefore heir to a tradition of over 100 years.

In the post-Emancipation period, Bahamian-born, U.S.-educated and former Haitian resident Dr. J. Robert Love published the influential *Jamaican Advocate.* Tobagonian Samuel Carter published Trinidad's *New Era* from 1869 to 1891. Carriacou-born Alexander Murray published Trinidad's *San Fernando Gazette* from 1850.

The Freeman's Sentinel appeared in British Guiana in 1842. It was owned by De Vries (a Surinamese), Oudkirk and Belgrave, all colored and

Mc Farlane (black). These men were also founders in the same year of the British Guiana African Association. The association encouraged its constituency to build and unite the African community. They struggled against unfair employment practices in the civil service.

When Peter Rose, Richard Hayes and other blacks and coloreds formed the Reform Association in 1845, the *Freeman's Sentinel* provided a base of support. They advocated electoral reform. Several other short-lived black and colored papers followed in the 1850s. Then came one of the most enduring, *The Creole* (1856–1907). Its first publisher was William S. Stephens. George William Braithwaite was its first editor. The *Creole's* appearance coincided with the "Angel Gabriel riots" against Portuguese shopkeepers in 1856. Later nineteenth-century black and colored Guyanese newspapers included *The Working Man* (1872), the *Villager, Echo (1884), Reflector (1889)* and *Liberal.*

EMIGRATION

Emigration of mostly Afro-Caribbean people continued throughout the period of post-Emancipation Asian and other immigration. Trinidad and Guyana early solicited Caribbean immigrants. Densely populated Barbados sent many people to both places in the 1840s and thereafter.

Some Caribbean emigrants found themselves in Panama during railway construction there in the 1850s. When the French attempted to build a Panama Canal in the 1880s thousands more Caribbean workers went over. George Roberts reported 1,000 a month leaving Jamaica for Panama, Mexico and Yucatan in 1882. The French discontinued their project in 1888. Caribbean emigration to Panama reached a crescendo between the U.S. resumption of work in 1904 and its completion of the canal in 1914. The United States, reports Bonham Richardson, established its main recruiting station in Barbados in 1905. Barbados supplied 20,000 of the 45,000 workers contracted for the Canal for the next ten years, more than any other place. Richardson estimates that another 25,000 Barbadians went over on their own, without official contracts, for a total of 45,000 of a total island population of about 200,000.

More Caribbean workers entered Panama for the aborted Third Locks Project (1940–1942) to increase the capacity of the Canal. Between 1850 and 1950, 200,000 Caribbean workers entered Panama.

Railway construction in the 1880s and banana plantations attracted Caribbean workers to Costa Rica. The emigrants fanned out across Latin America. They went to Honduras, Guatemala, Colombia. Trinidadians went to the gold-producing area of El Callao in Venezuela.

Barbadians went to Liberia. Afro-Caribbean professionals, after studying in England, went to such places as Ghana and South Africa, rather than return home. Some of their Chinese-Caribbean counterparts went on to China. The British government recruited Caribbean civil servants, policemen and railway workers for Nigeria and Ghana. A Caribbean community grew up in the late nineteenth century and early twentieth century in Cape Town, South Africa. Jamaicans ended up in nineteenth-century gold rush Australia.

Peter Jackson, "The Black Prince," born in St. Croix in 1861, moved to Australia with his fisherman father and family at the age of six. He became heavyweight boxing champion of Australia and the British empire. He campaigned in the United States seeking a match with the white world champion John L. Sullivan. Sullivan absolutely refused.

Some emigrants went to Europe, initially as students or sometimes as seamen or laborers. Some went to Cuba to work on the railways. By the early twentieth century, with the Panama Canal completed, the United States supplanted Panama as the major destination.

A few Barbadians even settled in Brazil. By the early twentieth century large numbers of British Caribbeans and Haitians were going to Cuba to cut cane. Some were going to the Dominican Republic for similar work (see Chapter 11). Between 1881 and 1891 there was a net emigration from Jamaica of 69,000 people. Between 1911 and 1921 the figure was 77,000.

The sacrifice and thrift of these emigrants made "Panama money," their remittances back home, major sources of national revenues in Barbados and Jamaica (which together furnished the bulk of emigrants), and elsewhere.

Peter Jackson of St. Croix, nineteenth-century heavyweight boxing champion of Australia and the British empire.

HAITI

In Haiti, meanwhile, the victorious revolution embarked on an obstacle course of seeming unending duration. A free, black, revolutionary country that had just defeated Europe's finest was not welcome in the comity of powerful nations. Europe ostracized it. Haiti initially tried to continue a coercive plantation agriculture to maximize production and maintain a strong military in the face of threats of renewed aggression, especially from France. Less commercially oriented peasant agriculture eventually prevailed, however.

Jean-Jacques Dessalines, who proclaimed independence on January 1, 1804, was assassinated in 1806. He was succeeded by Henri Christophe, a fellow commander in the liberation wars. After civil strife Haiti was divided in 1807 into the Republic of Haiti, ruled by the colored Alexander Petion in the South, and the State (later Kingdom) of Haiti, ruled by Christophe in the North. Christophe enforced his authority with the help of several thousand Royal Dahomets, a military force recruited in Dahomey (now Benin). When Christophe committed suicide after a stroke in 1820, Boyer seized the opportunity to reunite the country, which he ruled from 1818 to 1843.

In 1825 President Boyer agreed under some duress to French demands for an indemnity of 150 million francs. In exchange France would recognize Haiti, thus easing its international isolation. British and U.S. recognition followed in 1833 and 1862, respectively. The indemnity was supposed to be reparations to France for the loss of its thousands of plantations and human property during the revolution. In a sense Haiti, after triumphing on the field of battle over the horribly repressive French slave regime, was now being asked to do what the British and others did for their slave owners, namely pay them compensation.

The French insisted that Haiti raise a commercial loan in France at usurious terms, to pay the first installment. Haiti did not pay off this debt until 1947. It made very difficult the availability of adequate funds for development. President Jean-Bertrand Aristide in 2004 demanded $21.7 billion from France as reparations for the indemnity.

President for Life Boyer fled to Jamaica and then to France in the face of an insurrectionary army in 1843. It was under his watch that Haiti occupied the Dominican Republic (1822–1844). There were twenty-two heads of state between 1843 and 1915, with only one of them serving out his whole term. Fourteen were deposed by armed uprisings after periods varying between three months and twelve years in office. One was blown up, one was presumed poisoned and one was hacked to death by the populace. The rest died in office.

Historians have debated the weight of the various factors bearing on Haiti's inability to fully realize the promise of its glorious beginnings. These include the unstable political system, corrupt politicians and an endemic destabilizing conflict between coloreds and blacks. Most important was the effect of the indemnity. Both Thomas Carlyle and the U.S. administration which invaded Haiti in 1915 put the blame on black people's (including coloreds') alleged inability to govern themselves.

The post–British Emancipation decades were therefore a time of significant progress for the former enslaved, despite serious obstacles put in the way of that advancement.

Further Readings

Cave, Roderick. "The Use of Slave Labour in West Indian Printing Houses." *Library*, s5-XXX, 1975, pp. 241–243.

Clément, Job B. "History of Emancipation in Haiti: 1804–1915 (First Part)." *Revista de Historia de América*, No. 87, January–June, 1979, pp. 141–181.

Cowley, John. *Carnival, Canboulay and Calypso: Traditions in the Making*. New York: Cambridge University Press, 1996.

Cox, Edward L. "William Galwey Donovan and the Struggle for Political Change in Grenada, 1883–1920." *Small Axe*, No. 22 (Volume 11, Number 1), February 2007, pp. 17–38.

Gordon, Shirley. *A Century of West Indian Education*. London: Longmans, 1963.

Marsh, Clifton E. "A Socio-Historical Analysis of the Labor Revolt of 1878 in the Danish West Indies." *Phylon*, 41, 4, 1981, pp. 335–345.

Mohamed, Khalleel. "The Establishment of the Portuguese Business Community in British Guiana." *History Gazette* (Guyana), No. 60, September 1993.

Moore, Brian L. "The Social and Economic Subordination of the Guyanese Creoles after Emancipation," in Winston McGowan, James G. Rose, and David A. Granger, Eds., *Themes in African-Guyanese History*. Georgetown: Free Press, 1998.

Roberts, George. *The Population of Jamaica*. London: Oxford University Press, 1957.

Saunders, Gail. *Bahamian Society After Emancipation*. Kingston: Ian Randle Publishers, 1994.

Sewell, William G. *The Ordeal of Free Labor in the British West Indies*. New York: Augustus M. Kelley, Bookseller, 1968. First pub. 1861.

Sturge, Joseph, and Thomas Harvey. *The West Indies in 1837*. London: Frank Cass, 1968. First pub. 1838.

11

Immigration in the Nineteenth and Twentieth Centuries

IMMIGRATION

The history of the Caribbean after 1492 is overwhelmingly one of successive immigrations of motley peoples. Some came voluntarily as conquerors. Some came involuntarily in chains. The rest came in every conceivable circumstance between these two extremes—as refugees from persecution, indentured laborers, escapees from economic deprivation, seekers of fortunes in a new environment and more.

For the planters in the British, French and Dutch territories immigration was a response to the impending, and then actual Emancipation of the formerly enslaved. G. W. Roberts and J. Byrne calculated 536,310 immigrant arrivals into the British Caribbean "mainly under indenture" between 1834 and 1918. Over 80 percent of these (429,623) were from India. Over 56 percent of the immigrants (300,967) went to British Guiana, followed by Trinidad (157,668), Jamaica (53,940), Grenada (6,207), St. Vincent (5,610), St. Lucia (5,198), St. Kitts (2,877), Antigua (2,627), British Honduras (652) and Dominica (564). The overall breakdown of these immigrants' origins was as follows:

India (1838–1918)	429,623 immigrants
Madeira (1835–1881)	40,971
Africa (1834–1867)	39,332
China (1852–1884)	17,904
Europe (1834–1845)	4,582
Other (1835–1867)	3,898

The planters sought to justify this flood of new cheap labor in various ways. They claimed that Africans were lazy, thriftless and would work only enough to satisfy their immediate daily needs. This was manifestly untrue, as the significant progress the Africans made in spite of obstacles amply demonstrates.

William Sewell addressed this point convincingly in the 1850s. "I am sick of the statement so constantly and so thoroughly repeated that the African won't work," he wrote. "It is the instinct of human nature to aspire to independence," he continued, and the Africans could not be faulted for seeking a life as independent farmers off the sugar plantations. "In spite of the extraordinary price of land and the lower rate of wages," he showed, "the small proprietors of Barbados have increased from 1100 to 3537. . . . This is certainly an evidence of industrious habits, and a remarkable contradiction to the prevailing idea that the Negro will only work under compulsion."

Sewell could envisage no other people anywhere in the world capable of matching the progress Afro-Caribbeans had made in twenty years up from slavery. "Won't work?" he sneered. "Why should they work for the planter, and bind themselves to a new tyranny?"

Yet this notion of African "indolence" causing the "ruin" of the British Caribbean sugar industry dies hard, due to constant repetition. The quintessential expression of these ideas came from the eminent Scottish historian Thomas Carlyle in his essay, "Occasional Discourse on the Nigger Question" (1849). Carlyle presented Quashee, his stereotypical freedman personified, who labored half an hour a day to satisfy his subsistence needs, consisting of pumpkins. Carlyle warned that a terrible fate awaited Quashee if he did not soon rouse himself and start producing for white people:

> If Quashee will not honestly aid in bringing out those . . . products of the West India islands, for the benefit of all mankind, then, I say, neither will the powers permit Quashee to continue growing pumpkins for his own lazy benefit. . . . Quashee, if he will not help . . . will get himself made a slave again (which state will be a little less ugly than his present one), and with beneficent whip, since other methods avail not, will be compelled to work. . . . He that will not work shall perish from the earth—and the patience of the gods has limits.

In the 1930s, Barbadians from the Forum cultural group had to complain to a British commission of enquiry into education. They cited British textbooks (some published in Carlyle's Scotland) which were still asserting that the islands were "ruined" because the Africans, their wants easily supplied, refused to work after Emancipation.

CHINESE

Chinese immigrants were brought to Trinidad as early as 1806, the year of the abolition of the slave trade to Trinidad and one year before its abolition to most of the rest of the British Caribbean. They came from Penang (Prince of Wales Island, Malaya), Macao (the Portuguese enclave on the coast of China) and Calcutta in India. In the intensely globalized world ushered in by Columbus, Chinese from Spanish Manila in the Philippines and elsewhere had actually long preceded the 1806 arrivals to the New World. Spanish shipping regularly plied the route between Manila, Spanish hub in Asia, and Acapulco in Mexico. As a result Chinese sailors and workers found themselves from the late sixteenth century in such places as Mexico, Peru and Minas Gerais in Brazil. Some were reported in Cuba in the late eighteenth century. Walton Look Lai mentions an unconfirmed report of five Chinese in Spanish Trinidad in 1796, one of whom may have stayed on in the island.

In 1806 the British were already anticipating inevitable Emancipation and, from their perspective, a resultant shortage of cheap labor. The Chinese were to be an experiment in alternative labor. One strand of British opinion saw Chinese immigration with the active assistance of the East India Company as a means of making Trinidad an entrepôt for the lucrative Asian-South American trade. One hundred and ninety-two Chinese men accordingly arrived in Trinidad on October 12, 1806 on the *SS Fortitude* of the East India Company. This was 314 years to the day after Columbus' landfall in the Bahamas. Eight of the original 200 had died along the way. They had sailed for five months from Bengal in India to St. Helena off the African coast. A further thirty days brought them from St. Helena to Trinidad.

An important part of the motivation in bringing the 1806 immigrants was the ongoing European effort to find buffer groups to interpose between the African majorities and themselves. During slavery the Europeans had tried, mostly unsuccessfully, to limit the black over white racial demographic imbalance. The introduction of white indentured workers and the effort to induce free people of color into a buffer role had met with varying degrees of success, as already noted. The Chinese represented a new round (but not the last) in the enduring effort to find an effective buffer group. As with all buffer groups, it would be necessary for the intermediate group to receive preferential treatment. Conflict between Africans and the buffer would, ideally, deflect hostility away from the European ruling minority.

This apprehension of a fast-approaching majority free (though politically disfranchised) black population gave urgency to the quest for a buffer group. As one British official said when later advocating Indian immigration to Dominica, these colonies were too important to be left for Africans to inherit. A secret memorandum from the British Colonial Office, written in 1803 on the eve of final Haitian independence, saw the introduction of a Chinese buffer as admirably suited to thwart any attempt at a free African state in Trinidad. "It is conceived that no measure would so effectually tend to provide a security against this danger [of a Haitian style revolution in Trinidad]," it said, "as that of introducing a free race of cultivators into our islands, who, from habits and feelings would be kept distinct from the Negroes, and who from interest would be inseparably attached to the European proprietors."

A few months after the arrival of these first Chinese the Trinidad attorney general considered their further importation "one of the best schemes possible." For, he wrote to the Colonial Office, "It will be a barrier to us and the Negroes, with whom they do not associate; and consequently to whom they will always offer a formidable opposition."

The 1806 pioneers received free passages to Trinidad, free return passages home and subsistence payments for one year. Shortly after arrival they were given the option of doing work similar to that done by the enslaved, or receiving free land grants in Cocorite where they might form themselves into a Chinese community, grow food crops for the local market, receive a salary and have the services of a doctor and a free colored nurse. They were in effect being paid to become self-sufficient and hence a better buffer group. The government also bought them a fishing boat, which became a major source of their economic advance. Enslaved African labor constructed their Cocorite dwellings.

Seven more Chinese had died by March 1807. Of the remaining 185, only 24 were still employed as agricultural labor by planters. The community's headmen Affat, Awar, Ayo and Ayong and 139 of their men were living in Cocorite. Sixty-one returned with the *Fortitude* to Bengal or China in July 1807.

Contemporary Trinidad historian E. L. Joseph reported about thirty still in the island in 1809 and only two or three still alive in 1838. Those that stayed inevitably formed liaisons with African women and were, according to Joseph, devoted family men. Like many manumitted Africans before them, they bought their enslaved wives to free them and their offspring from slavery. Headman Awar used his government-subsidized fish business to build some economic success. When he won the right to run the government fish house on tender, the Cabildo (town council) helped him by banning (but apparently ineffectively) African would-be competitors from huckstering fish. Awar and his son owned five enslaved Africans between them at Emancipation in 1834.

These first Chinese nevertheless proved a disappointment to the Trinidad planters. A British official described them as "obtained from the diseased and profligate refuse of the indolent and degraded population of a Portuguese town, unaccustomed to the habits of their industrious countrymen, and total strangers to the qualifications requisite for their future employments in the West Indies."

Chinese indentured immigration nevertheless resumed later. Most of those coming to the British West Indies arrived in the 1850s and 1860s. Roberts and Byrne reported 17,904 Chinese to the British Caribbean between 1852 and 1884—13,533 went to British Guiana, 2,645 to Trinidad, 1,152 to Jamaica, 474 to British Honduras and 100 to Antigua.

The first immigrant ship, the *Lord Elgin*, arrived in British Guiana in 1853. Sixty-nine of the original 154 died on the way over, giving a mortality rate of 44.8 percent. The *Lord Elgin* had actually departed British Guiana in 1851 for India, where it deposited 146 returning Indian indentured workers before continuing on to China. As in 1806, there was a close connection between Chinese immigration and India. India and China were part of the same British Asia–New World nexus fueled by the East India Company. British Indian troops, sepoys and lascars, protected British territory in China and on occasion sailed as security on Chinese emigrant ships. Cecil Clementi reported an Indian "Parsee gentleman" resident in England in 1858 being interested in privately bringing Chinese immigrants to British Guiana.

Cuba was the most important destination for Chinese immigrants to the Caribbean. Here Chinese immigration began in 1857, with workers coming in on eight-year contracts. According to the British consul in Cuba, 76,829 Chinese had embarked for Cuba up to 1865—66,447 landed alive, with 10,382 deaths at sea. By 1877 there were 53,811 Chinese in Cuba, amounting to 3 percent of the population. Some worked alongside the enslaved Africans, some separately. Their numbers were augmented in the late nineteenth century by about 5,000 arrivals fleeing racism in California, USA. As elsewhere in the Caribbean, some free Chinese immigrated to Cuba in the early twentieth century, fleeing political upheaval and in search of economic opportunity. Cuba at one time hosted the largest Chinatown in Latin America. The Castro revolution of 1959 led to an exodus of Chinese, as the revolution nationalized their grocery shops and other businesses. Most went to Florida. Cuban-Chinese restaurants became an important part of the landscape in some areas of Manhattan, New York. Those Chinese remaining in Cuba are mostly miscegenated into the other ethnic sectors of the Cuban population.

About 2,780 Chinese workers came to Suriname between 1853 and 1873. They came from Dutch Java, Macao and Hong Kong. Here too there was heavy remigration and assimilation into the host society. About 1,000 Chinese workers came to Martinique in 1859, with a further free migration in the twentieth century. A few hundred reached Guadeloupe after 1855.

Chinese immigration to the Caribbean was part of a vast network of Chinese emigration in the nineteenth century. Chinese were simultaneously leaving for such destinations as Australia, the Pacific, South-East Asia, South Africa, the United States, Peru and elsewhere in Latin America. Poverty and political conflict were important push factors expelling Chinese. One British official in 1802 even thought that emigration to Trinidad might alleviate financial distress sufficiently to moderate the Chinese practice of infanticide induced by poverty.

Mass emigration to the Caribbean in the 1850s also coincided with an increasingly intrusive European military presence in China. Britain and China fought Opium Wars from 1839 to 1842 and again from 1856 to 1860, as Britain insisted on illegally trading opium to China, thereby profiting from China's massive drug addiction problem. Large sums were exacted from the defeated Chinese in the form of reparations and the British forced the cession of Hong Kong to themselves after the first war, initially in perpetuity. This helped stimulate frequent outbreaks of popular Chinese violence against Westerners, including labor recruiters. In the Tientsin riot of 1870 a crowd beat the French consul to death and killed over twenty Europeans. France exacted heavy monetary reparations and forced the Chinese government to send a delegation to Paris to apologize. The murder of a British consular official in 1874 was likewise followed by reparations imposed by the British and a Chinese embassy on an apologetic mission to London.

Western governments established recruitment agencies on Chinese territory and worked to varying degrees with Chinese middlemen known as crimps. Money, free rations and other inducements were given to would-be emigrants. In an environment where crimps sometimes resorted to kidnapping and false promises, the British fancied themselves the most decorous and honest of recruiters. This seems to be borne out by statistics for shipborne revolts among Caribbean and South America–bound Chinese.

Walton Look Lai reports sixty-eight such revolts between 1847 and 1874. A British official in 1874 compiled a list of thirty-four Chinese "Coolie Ships on board of which mutinies have occurred, or in which the vessels or passengers have met with disaster" from 1845 to 1872. Fifteen of the vessels were en route to Peru (principally to the port of Callao near Lima). Thirteen of the ships were headed for Havana. Only two were headed for British West Indian destinations (Demerara).

On several occasions the Chinese killed the ships' captains and crews. Sometimes they set fire to the ships. Sometimes they commandeered the ships and brought them to a nearby shore. Often they suffered horrendous losses at the hands of the well-armed crews. On at least one occasion Indian soldiers (lascars) aboard ship helped put down the revolts. On the *Delores Ugarte* bound for Peru in 1870 the Chinese allegedly set fire to the ship. Six hundred of them perished while the European captain and crew escaped to safety in the ship's boats. On the *Jeddo* bound for Demerara in 1866 about 300 Chinese either perished in the flames or drowned after reportedly setting fire to the ship. The *Flora Temple* bound for Havana in 1859 encountered a hurricane. The captain and crew rowed the ship's boats to the safety of nearby Vietnam leaving behind 850 Chinese, presumed drowned.

Mutinous activity and shipboard natural disasters were compounded by intra-Chinese violence. The emigrants were a heterogeneous group, sometimes speaking mutually unintelligible languages and drawn from mutually hostile communities. What was one supposed to do, asked a British official charged with brutalizing Chinese on board the *Persia* bound for British Guiana in 1862, "when 500 Chinese were fighting all over her. . . ; yells and noises sufficient to stun you; billets of fire-wood, choppers, chopping-blocks, holy stones, boards, iron bars, knives, etc. flying about, and glass bottles breaking in all directions?"

If official British reports were accurate, the Chinese immigrants were a mixed bag and difficult to generalize accurately about. The nineteenth-century European penchant for stereotyping the "other" nevertheless found abundant rein when it encountered the Chinese immigrants. Many of the stereotypes were mutually exclusive, some at least must have been accurate, and all were unintentionally entertaining. The Chinese were said, in 1802, to show "indefatigable industry and habits of frugality." Europeans were drawn to comparisons with the Indians, their contemporary immigrants. "From all the inconvenient prejudices of Hindoostan," wrote a British official, "they are wholly free. They like to

make money, but they have not the faculty of hoarding it that distinguishes the penurious Hindoo, for they live more comfortably. . . ." For another British official, "any comparison with the Indian coolies who have been sent to the West Indies would be a gross injustice to the Chinese." To the ship's surgeon on a mutinous emigrant ship, the Chinese were savages. A Guyanese estate manager in 1853 found them equal in strength to the Africans. Another found them "more muscular and athletic than the East Indians." A Guyanese official report of 1871 found them more intelligent than Africans or Indians. Trinidad's *Annual Immigration Report* for 1865 found, probably accurately, that their turbulence was more likely during the early years of their indenture, "when crimes of violence, including both murder and suicide, not infrequently occur. . . ." Thereafter they mellowed, as knowledge of the fundamental fairness of the host society's laws became apparent. "It is different with the Indian," however, this official report continued. For "although gentle externally, no length of residence weans him from the love of blood, no year passes over without one or more murders, characterized by the most determined recklessness and ferocity. . . ."

Possibly the most entertaining stereotypes came from British writer Henry Kirk remembering his twenty-five years in British Guiana, from 1872 to 1897. "The Chinese are so much alike in features," he allowed, "that it is very difficult to distinguish one man from another," thereby making difficult the apprehension of deserters from the estates. "The Negro population," he opined, "who make a butt of the patient Hindoo and bully his life out of him, are afraid of the Chinaman, and leave him alone."

"All generalizations are dangerous," Kirk conceded, before proceeding to generalize about the distinguishing criminal propensities of Guiana's many races:

> but still I think we may concede that murder and felonious assaults in the colony were mainly committed by East Indians and Chinese; larcenies by black and coloured people; wounding with knives and razors by coloured Barbadians; forgeries and embezzlements by partly

educated coloured creoles; breaches of the revenue laws and cheating by the Portuguese; whereas perjury, bearing false witness, profane swearing and indecent language seem pretty evenly distributed among all nationalities.

The non-Portuguese Europeans appeared to be without crime.

The Chinese experience on the British West Indian estates was as varied as the British stereotypes seemed to suggest. Early arrivals in Trinidad were by 1854 striking and generally refusing to work. Their contracts protected them from pay cuts unless they were sick for more than fourteen days continuously. "As the Chinese are not proverbially deficient in cunning," explained an official British report, they reported sick for fourteen days, worked on the 15th, and became "sick" once more from the 16th until the end of the month, after which they collected a full month's wages. Planters responded by sentencing some to stints on the treadmill.

Their shipboard violence could sometimes be transported ashore. Governor Henry Barkly of British Guiana reported a huge confrontation in 1853 between Chinese on Plantation Blankenburg and neighboring Africans in Den Amstel Village. He marveled at the Chinese willingness to attack 600 Africans arrayed in defense of their community. He judged the Chinese to be the aggressors and sentenced six ringleaders to imprisonment. Some 1865 arrivals in Trinidad were considered so fractious and prone to theft that planters were asking to be rid of them, even if it meant having to continue paying their indenture fees.

Some Chinese, like their African predecessors on the estates, were subjected to harsh and unfair treatment by drivers and overseers. They were brutalized and had their wages unfairly reduced. According to Joseph Beaumont's antiimmigration treatise, *The New Slavery* (1871), Indian and Chinese drivers in British Guiana extorted money from the immigrants. (Black drivers never did this, he said.) Like the Africans before them, Chinese workers in British Guiana and Antigua killed overseers and managers who provoked them beyond endurance.

Not all the immigrants had been agriculturists in China and some left the plantations at the earliest opportunity. An 1861 report in Trinidad showed that of 460 Chinese on the island almost all had become traders. Some were now affluent. Chinese in British Guiana deserted the estates, even while under indenture, more frequently than did the Indians. By 1879 half the British Guiana Chinese had left the plantations.

The aspects of immigrant Chinese culture which attracted most attention from the host society were their use of opium and love of gambling. The 1806 Trinidad arrivals taught locals gambling. The signature Chinese game of Whe Whe was quickly absorbed into the culture of Trinidad. Chinese on the plantations put aside a section of their barracks for gambling operations. "There," said an 1871 British Guiana report, "the opium smokers and gamblers among them assemble, with occasionally a good-for-nothing Hindoo or Negro. They play cards or dominoes . . . ." Planters complained frequently of opium smoking and its deleterious effects on health and productivity. The "good-for-nothing" Indians also brought their own drug tradition in ganja (marijuana), later their great gift to Rastafarianism, which was used as openly and legally in the Indian community as opium was among the Chinese.

One of the most intractable problems confronting Chinese contract immigration was the shortage of Chinese women. Various cultural and legal factors militated against the emigration of women. Women made up only about 1 percent of all the Chinese immigration to Latin America and the Caribbean. Of 66,447 Chinese landed alive in Cuba up to 1865 only fifty-two were women. The first Chinese women to British Guiana arrived in 1860, seven years after the first men. Where women became available as emigrants they tended to be displaced rural women trapped into enslavement or prostitution. And a large percentage of the few women available were "small footed" and consequently unfitted for agriculture. (The widespread Chinese practice of binding up the feet of young girls restricted normal development thereby consigning the girls to abnormally small and delicate feet for life.)

In 1853 the British West Indian agent in China proposed obtaining "respectable" girls of ten to fifteen years old for $40 a piece. The Colonial Office in London vetoed the idea, fearing its degeneration into a new slave trade. In the early 1860s, British agents in China began providing gifts of $20 each to Chinese men bringing their wives or daughters. This scheme quickly degenerated into abuse. Men procured "wives" to obtain the bounty and abandoned them on the way over or after arrival in the Caribbean. The ship's surgeon on the *Whirlwind* bound from Hong Kong to Demerara in 1861 described the result of the wife bounty—he had on board, he said, "two notorious prostitutes, four idiots, one helpless cripple—one hunchback—one deaf and dumb, and several much disfigured by scars." A large number of the women were small footed and unable to do agricultural work. They were forced to eke out an existence, sometimes in morally questionable ways. There was also a belief that the bounty encouraged the kidnapping of women.

The immigrants made up for the shortage of Chinese women by a willingness to cohabit with local women. They had already demonstrated this willingness in South-East Asia and other emigrant destinations. This willingness had been evident among the 1806 immigrants to Trinidad, as already seen, and continued into the free migration of the twentieth century. The "half-Chinese," most often an African–Chinese mixture, became a permanent fixture of some Caribbean racial landscapes.

Even though Indian-African miscegenation was by no means unknown, European observers were struck by the much greater openness of the Chinese to cohabitation and social contact with the Africans, in addition to a greater willingness to adopt Christianity and Western modes of dress. The Chinese "have not the same objection to living with females of a different race than themselves that the Indians have," commented an official report on British Guiana in 1871. "This may be owing in some degree to the small proportion of women who have emigrated from China, but the principal reason for it is that the Chinese have not the difficulty of *caste* to get over that the Indian has, and are more cosmopolitan in their habits."

In the British West Indies at least, the local demographics actually favored Chinese procurement of local partners. The Trinidad *Annual Immigration Report* of 1863 perceptively noted that "In the last Census the males of Trinidad outnumber the females, but when the Indian element, which does not inter-marry with the others, is eliminated, the females preponderate as in nearly all the other British West Indian colonies."

By the 1890s in the British West Indies the exodus of Chinese from plantations was complete. Many became shopkeepers and other businessmen. Like other upwardly mobile and restless Caribbean people they moved around the Caribbean and further afield. Some 3,000 Chinese left British Guiana for Trinidad, Suriname, Cayenne, Panama and points more remote, between 1872 and 1887. Some also returned to China, sometimes taking with them sizeable amounts of money accumulated in the Caribbean. In 1874, according to Clementi, 135 British Guianese Chinese left for Suriname, 44 for St. Lucia (the result of a special recruitment effort by a Guianese Chinese), 10 each to Trinidad and Jamaica and 2 to China. Emigrants to Suriname and Trinidad mailed back their passports for others to use them.

The sexual imbalance of Chinese contract workers and consequent miscegenation made difficult the maintenance of an undiluted racial presence in their host countries. This was offset by a new immigration of free Chinese beginning in the 1890s and accelerating after 1910. Between 1918 and 1950, 5,000–6,000 free Chinese voluntarily immigrated, mostly to Jamaica and Trinidad but also to British Guiana in the British territories. A thousand entered Suriname. Others went to Martinique and Cuba.

Most of the established Chinese families in the former British West Indies actually are derived from this new free immigration, rather than from the earlier indentured immigrants. The new arrivals came to dominate such areas as small retail shops, laundries and restaurants. As they accumulated money they branched out into a wide array of businesses. The successful among them followed similar paths to those of the upwardly mobile African and other ethnic groups. They educated their children well, sending them to the United Kingdom, North America and occasionally Ireland for higher education and sometimes for secondary education as well. At least one successful Guianese Chinese in the early twentieth century sent his son to Harrison College in Barbados for secondary school. Some sent their children back to China for primary or secondary schooling. Edinburgh University was popular with the Chinese community, as it was with the children of upwardly mobile Afro-Caribbeans.

Some of the Chinese children returned to their Caribbean homes to enter such professions as law and medicine. Some remained abroad. Like Afro-Caribbean students overseas, who often ended up in Africa through contacts or marriages made in the metropolis, Chinese-Caribbean students might sometimes end up in some such place as Singapore or China instead of returning home to the Caribbean.

Successful businessmen sent home to China for family members to join them. Some resorted to arranged marriages, whereby they accepted, sight unseen, brides selected for them by relatives back home. Some maintained contact with the wives and children they had left behind, while not neglecting the new families they raised with Caribbean women. The most successful tended to have very large Caribbean families, with seven to twelve children the norm for very successful Chinese-Guianese families studied by Clementi. This Chinese "procreative recklessness," said Clementi, was just what British Guiana needed.

The Chinese formed a plethora of social, ethnic and political organizations. These often mirrored political, regional and ethnic loyalties derived from their China experience. They formed sporting clubs, often seeking sports such as hockey, tennis and netball, outside the big two (in the British West Indies) of cricket and football. Like the Indians, Chinese sports clubs exchanged visits with their compatriots in other territories. British Guiana–Trinidad exchanges were especially frequent.

Like other ethnic groups, the Chinese used the church and Masonic lodges as facilitators of upward mobility. Some Baptist churches in British Guiana offered Chinese language services. The St. Saviour's Chinese Anglican Church, opened in 1875, became a venerable institution in British Guiana. (The word "Chinese" was later dropped from its name.) When upwardly mobile Guyanese Chinese were refused membership in the white Union Masonic lodge they joined the "colored" Mt. Olive lodge in 1900. In

1907 they formed their own Silent Temple Lodge. Jamaica developed a Chinese Freemason Society.

In the three-tiered white–brown–black social pyramid of the Caribbean the Chinese, like other immigrant groups, tried to maneuver themselves into the interstices of the pyramid, as high up as they could. The 1806 immigrants to Trinidad were treated socially as quasi-coloreds. As free immigration replaced indentured labor, the ratio between the sexes made a more normal intra-Chinese mating pattern possible, making interracial mating no longer an absolute necessity. Interracial marriage and relationships continued nevertheless. Upwardly mobile Chinese who mated across racial lines were more likely to choose equally affluent colored mates, rather than the darker working-class mates of their indentured forebears. Eugene Chen, Trinidadian four-time foreign minister of China, married into the colored section of the affluent Gantaume family. He also had a Chinese-African half sister, for good measure. Affluent Chinese, like affluent members of other groups, eventually settled near the top of the pyramid. When in 1969 the Trinidad government held an inquiry into allegedly racist practices at the traditionally whites-only Trinidad Country Club, it was triggered by allegations of visiting African Americans who claimed to have been denied entry by a Chinese functionary of the club.

Cuba and British Guiana had Chinatowns, the former the largest in Latin America and the latter destroyed by fire in 1913. Trinidad had a small China Town in Belmont, Port of Spain and a Chinese Village in La Brea. British Guiana had Chinese settlements established with government assistance in the 1870s and 1880s. These included the flourishing rice-growing village of Hong Kong (or Chinaland) in the Upper Corentyne.

From 1865 to 1914 British Guiana was home to Hopetown, a Chinese settlement at Kamuni Creek, 30 miles outside Georgetown, set up with government assistance. The settlement was the brainchild of Wu Tai-Kam, a Malay Straits–born Chinese Church Missionary Society evangelist. He had become aware of the Chinese presence in British Guiana while visiting the Strangers' Home for Asiatics and other institutions in England. Wu was appointed official missionary to the Chinese with a

Eugene Chen of Trinidad, four-time foreign minister of China, seated second from the right, as a Chinese delegate to the League of Nations, Geneva, 1920.

salary of 300 pounds a year. The government agreed to financially support his proposal for a new Chinese immigration scheme that would bring arrivals straight to Hopetown.

Then Wu got a "colored" Georgetown woman pregnant. Unable to live with his now-sullied reputation he absconded with three accomplices in 1867. They stole a Hopetown boat, apparently raised funds via robbery and made a hurried exit. They were presumed headed for Trinidad. One report located Wu back in China organizing an illegal emigration scheme, after spending some time in the United States. "So much prosperity seems to have had a deteriorating effect on the man's character," commented Governor Cecil Clementi, chronicler of the Chinese presence in Guyana.

Hopetown had 567 residents in 1871. Charcoal burning, growing food crops and pig rearing were their main activities. In 1903 Governor Sir J. A. Swettenham converted 915 acres of the Hopetown land into free grants to the Chinese settlers. The residents continued to leave, however, largely for work in retail establishments. By 1914 Hopetown's population had dwindled to seventy-five, of whom nearly a third were a motley assortment of Chinese–African, Chinese–colored and Chinese–Portuguese mixtures. There were also, according to Clementi, seven Africans, four East Indians and three coloreds among the residents. By this time the settlement had largely reverted to bush.

Despite mostly harmonious relations with the host societies, the new immigrants did experience periods of tension. Anti-Chinese riots in Jamaica in 1918 resulted in 452 local people arrested and 300 convicted. The West India Regiment was mobilized in defense of the Chinese. Underlying tensions between Jamaicans and Chinese shopkeepers exploded when an off-duty Jamaican policeman was assaulted by some Chinese. A Chinese immigrant to Jamaica in this period described his Chinese employer selling to the local folk with a sharpened cutlass always on the ready under the counter.

The Caribbean Chinese community produced several personalities of international reputation. Most prominent was undoubtedly Eugene Chen (1878–1944), Trinidad lawyer (solicitor) and four-time foreign minister of China. Chen was for years a prominent figure in the administrations of Sun Yat-sen,

Chiang Kai-shek and other Chinese nationalist leaders. Chen's son Percy followed his father into Chinese politics. His daughter, Sylvia Chen, was a well-known dancer in Trinidad before joining her father in China in the late 1920s. There, and later in Russia and the United States, she continued her distinguished career.

Trinidad contributed another outstanding dancer to China in Dai Ailian (previously Aileen Isaac Tai). After the emergence of the Peoples Republic of China (1948) Dai became vice chairman of the Dancer's Association of China and director of the Central Ballet Group.

Several Chinese participated prominently in politics in twentieth-century Trinidad. Alfred Richards, son of a Chinese immigrant and a black Barbadian woman, was variously head of the Trinidad Workingmen's Association and mayor of Port of Spain. In 1936 he was deputy mayor of Port of Spain and vice president of the Chinese Commercial Association. Sir Solomon Hochoy served as governor of Trinidad and Tobago from 1960 to 1962 and then as first postindependence governor-general (ceremonial head of state) from 1962 to 1972. Arthur Chung served as president of Guyana from 1970 to 1980 upon Guyana's adoption of a republican constitution. Hendrick Chin A Sen was appointed prime minister and then president of Suriname by the leaders of military coups in 1980. He served until 1982.

CARIBBEAN IMMIGRANTS

Intra-Caribbean immigration, as already seen, had been a feature of Caribbean life since time immemorial. The Arawaks, Caribs, early Europeans and enslaved and free Africans had always been in a state of constant motion. The nineteenth century began with an influx of over 30,000 Haitian refugees from the Haitian Revolution to Cuba. Many more went to Jamaica, Trinidad and elsewhere, not to mention New Orleans and Philadelphia in the United States. In the early nineteenth century the British relocated demobilized African American soldiers to Trinidad. They also demobilized mostly African-born veterans of the West India Regiment to Manzanilla and environs in Trinidad. Jorge Chinea has documented 1,407 Caribbean immigrants, mostly free coloreds, to Puerto Rico from 1800 to 1850.

In the immediate aftermath of British Emancipation planters from Guyana and Trinidad, with their large unused land area and small populations, went up the islands in search of labor, giving rise to the "Demerara slave trade" (see Chapter 10). Planter-generated stereotypes of indolent Africans notwithstanding, Trinidad planters paid ships' captains a reward for bringing in Caribbean workers. The system led to some fraud, with enterprising captains bringing in the same workers more than once. These workers were furthermore not bound by any contract and could come and go as they pleased, not an ideal arrangement for planters. Some were migrant workers and returned home after the peak harvest period. Some of them followed their Trinidad counterparts into peasant proprietorship and trade. Trinidad's agent general for immigration documented 3,832 Trinidadians and 4,041 other islanders on sugar estates circa 1859. Workers on cocoa plantations brought the numbers up to about 5,000 Afro-Trinidadians and the same number of other islanders on Trinidad's estates in 1859.

Sewell put the number of Caribbean, African and African American workers brought into Trinidad after Emancipation at 20,000, with only 13,000 remaining on the estates in 1859. The rest had bought land, gone into commerce or domestic work or returned to their homes. Between 1835 and 1893, 40,656 Caribbean immigrants reached British Guiana. Suriname received 1,495 Barbadians up to 1870.

Most of this intra-British Caribbean immigration eventually became voluntary, without benefit of bounties to ships' captains or other inducements. It never really stopped, and continued, especially into Trinidad, into the twenty-first century. The oil industry in Trinidad in the post–World War I years and the establishment of oil refineries in Aruba from the late 1920s were among the further stimulants to this immigration.

With the abolition of slavery in Cuba in 1886, the U.S. occupation of the island in 1898 and the massive centralization of Cuban sugar plantations by U.S. capital, Cuba arrived late at the Caribbean tendency to massive influxes of new post-Emancipation labor. Cuba was by this time into its frenzied attempt to de-Africanize the country and African immigration had been rendered illegal. Chinese immigration had officially ended. As so often previously in Caribbean history, economic need trumped racial paranoia. U.S. corporations (especially in the sugar industry) were able to get around the ban on African immigration by importing Jamaicans and Haitians as contract laborers. (Many thousands were deported in the most deplorable conditions in the 1930s.) There was also a sprinkling of workers brought in from throughout the Anglophone and Francophone Caribbean and Bermuda, but they tend, in historical accounts, to be subsumed under the designation "Jamaican." According to Juan Pérez de la Riva 102,972 Jamaicans entered Cuba between 1907 and 1929. Between 1912 and 1929, 183,983 Haitians entered, for a total influx of 304,955. This was more than the entire official "black" Cuban population of 1907 and about half of the combined "black" and "mulatto" populations, to use the census terminology of Cuba's notoriously inaccurate racial statistics.

The immigrants were concentrated in the eastern provinces of Oriente and Camaguey, where the bulk of the Afro-Cuban population also resided. While the Haitians were overwhelmingly illiterate, the Jamaicans enjoyed a much higher literacy rate than the Afro-Cubans, and access, however limited, to the diplomatic support of a powerful nation, Great Britain.

The Cuban press kept up a hysterical tirade against the newcomers, and especially the Jamaicans. They accused them of corrupting their "docile" Afro-Cuban kinsmen. They also accused the newcomers of sacrificing white Cuban children for their obeah rites. At least one Jamaican was lynched in 1919 on a false charge of obeah. Despite the expulsions of the 1930s, the descendants of these immigrants still constitute a significant portion of Afro-Cuba. They are often bilingual and recognizable by their English or French surnames.

Caribbean immigrants also entered the Dominican Republic (DR) as cane cutters from 1884. They came mostly from St. Kitts, Nevis, Anguilla, Antigua, Montserrat and St. Martin. From 1900 to 1930 they came annually as seasonal migrant workers, but some inevitably remained. A 1920 census recorded 5,763 permanently resident. A further 9,272 entered in 1935. Most lived in San Pedro de Macoris. The great Barbadian man

of letters, H. A. Vaughan, lived in the Dominican Republic as part of this immigration. A much larger cross-border immigration of Haitian laborers into the Dominican Republic resulted in the massacre of perhaps 35,000 Haitians on the orders of Dominican President Rafael Trujillo in 1937.

By the early 1950s 3 percent of Suriname's workforce were employed in the oil refineries of Aruba and Curaçao. Workers from elsewhere in the Caribbean were also there in significant numbers.

The massive movement of Caribbean workers to such greater Caribbean destinations as Panama, Costa Rica, Mexico, Guatemala, Honduras, Colombia and Venezuela has been treated as emigration in Chapter 10. This movement can equally qualify as immigration. When one adds the 200,000 Caribbean workers (per Michael L. Conniff) moving to Panama alone between 1850 and 1950 to the over 300,000 going to Cuba early in the twentieth century, it becomes apparent that primarily African voluntary intra-Caribbean migration generated a greater migratory flow than Indian immigration. White immigration to Cuba (discussed below) was the biggest migratory movement of all.

AFRICANS

Immigration was further augmented by "liberated Africans" seized from foreign slave ships by the British navy. In 1859, 2,885 "native Africans" were working on Trinidad's estates.

Between 1834 and 1867, according to Roberts and Byrne, 14,060 "liberated slaves and other Africans . . . mainly under indenture" entered British Guiana, 11,391 went to Jamaica, 8,854 to Trinidad, 2,406 to Grenada, 1,036 to St. Vincent, 730 to St. Lucia, 455 to St. Kitts and 400 to Dominica, for a grand total of 39,332. These Africans were actually the third largest group of new immigrants into the British Caribbean, after the Indians and Portuguese Madeirans. Most came via St. Helena, Sierra Leone, Rio de Janeiro and Havana. These were the ports where the British navy brought enslaved people seized from foreign ships.

A few hundred voluntary Kroo workers also came in from Liberia. After 1842 indentured Africans in the British territories were subjected to one-year contracts, with the figure rising later to three years. They generally merged into the general populations, though often establishing separate villages based on their African ethnicities. About 9,000 indentured Africans were taken to Martinique to 1861, with 5,800 to Guadeloupe and about 1,500 to French Guiana. Thousands more went to the Dutch colonies.

AFRICAN AMERICANS

African American veterans of the British-U.S. War of 1812 were already a numerically important component of Trinidad's free African population before Emancipation. Trinidad's New York–born planter William Burnley went to his birthplace and other eastern U.S. cities in 1839 to recruit African Americans. Two hundred and sixteen arrived in Trinidad in November, their passages paid by the government. Other Trinidad recruiters followed Burnley to the Eastern United States. By 1847, 1,301 African Americans, primarily from New York, Pennsylvania, Delaware, Maryland and New Jersey, were in Trinidad. British Guiana also recruited African Americans. These were mostly mechanics and artisans, though, and not the laborers the planters wanted. Most eventually returned to the United States. In 1851 Trinidad passed an ordinance

attempting to capitalize on the draconian Fugitive Slave Law passed in the United States, which placed free African Americans under the peril of re-enslavement and which precipitated a scramble of relocations to Canada, Haiti, West Africa and elsewhere. (African American immigration to Haiti in this period is discussed in Chapter 13.)

INDIANS

Over half a million indentured Indian laborers were introduced into the Caribbean between 1838 and 1917, a major part of the great effort of the European rulers to deprive the newly emancipated Africans of the bargaining benefits of free labor. It is no accident that both in the British West Indies and Suriname the first Indians arrived just before the end of apprenticeship. Trinidad planter William Burnley, later instrumental in bringing in African Americans, suggested Indian immigrants as early as 1814, shortly after the Chinese pilot program of 1806. The first indentured Indians arrived in British Guiana in May 1838 on the ships *Whitby* and *Hesperus*, about three months before final Emancipation. The 1806 Chinese had similarly arrived in the year of the abolition of the slave trade to Trinidad. Trinidad received its first Indian immigrants on the *Fatel Rozack* in 1845.

A Trinidad indentured
Indian family, ca. 1890.

As in the case of the Chinese before them, the nineteenth-century immigrants were not the first Indians to set foot in the Caribbean. English adventurer Sir Robert Dudley actually had two apparently enslaved East Indians with him on his trip to Trinidad in 1594–1595. He had procured them from his cousin Thomas Cavendish who sailed around the world from 1586 to 1588. On February 17, 1595, one of these men jumped ship to become the first East Indian immigrant in the Caribbean, 243 years before the 1838 arrivals in British Guiana. He escaped, either to the Spaniards or the indigenes, while Dudley's men were preoccupied with their work. (A free African had sailed with Columbus on his third voyage in 1498, during which he encountered Trinidad.) Another Indian showed up as a *lançado* (mostly Portuguese slave traders settled among the Africans) in Sierra Leone in the same period.

According to George Roberts and Joycelyn Byrne, from 1838 to 1918, 238,909 Indians came to British Guiana, 143,939 to Trinidad, 36,412 to Jamaica, 4,354 to St. Lucia, 3,200 to Grenada, 2,472 to St. Vincent and 337 to St. Kitts, for a grand total of 429,623 to the British West Indies. Up to 1916, 111,303 had returned to India. Between 1853 and 1885 French Guadeloupe received around 45,000 Indians, with 25,509 going to Martinique and 9,200 to French Guiana. Dutch Suriname received 34,000 Indians between 1873 and 1916, of whom 70 percent remained in Suriname. French and Dutch Indians were brought from British India, with the British government overseeing their welfare. By 1911 Indians were already officially the largest ethnic group in British Guiana (helped by the separation of "Coloreds/Mixed" from "Blacks" in the census). By 1940 they were 30 percent of the Suriname population, excluding Maroons and Amerindians. By 1901 they were 33 percent of Trinidad.

As in the case of the failed 1806 attempt to settle Chinese in Trinidad, Indians were consciously developed into a buffer by the European rulers in an effort to deflect African agitation away from themselves. The search for a buffer group was never ending. The Portuguese filled the need very well and even Caribbean immigrants were on occasion presented as hoped-for buffers. "One thing more," wrote a committee of white leaders in Trinidad in 1919,

when the Indian buffer arrangement seemed in danger of disintegration,

> in the years gone by the large East Indian indentured population, numbering many thousands and largely under the control of their respective plantation owners, managers and overseers, was looked upon as a substantial safeguard against trouble with the Negroes and *vice versa*. With the abolition of immigration such a counterpoise has ceased to exist and the 'creole coolie' will either remain an interested spectator or join the mob.

In 1897 an assistant under-secretary at the British Colonial Office urged increased Indian immigration and its spread to new areas such as Dominica "not as a means of procuring labor, but with the distinct object of not leaving any of these Islands entirely to the Negro race." Joseph Chamberlain, secretary of state for the Colonies, was sympathetic to the idea of immigration "to maintain and strengthen the leaven of East Indians in the population." Influential French opinion in Martinique in 1855 saw the buffer value of Indians as the strongest argument for preferring them to other immigrants. Indians, it was argued, would stand aloof from African-fomented strikes and disturbances. Such a thing did indeed happen in British Guiana in 1848, when Indian and Portuguese workers refused to support an African-called general strike, and in 1856, when Indians helped protect Portuguese interests during the Angel Gabriel Riots.

Buffer policies were facilitated by residential separation and differences in race, religion, language and legal status between indentured Indians and Africans. Furthermore, though most Indians remained in the Caribbean, the fact that as many as 25 percent of those in the British West Indies exercised their option to return to India may long have contributed to a psychology of transience. Two decades after the end of indenture in 1917, specially chartered ships still encountered more Guyanese and Trinidadian Indians wishing to return home than there was space for.

The Indians were indentured workers, under contract. They were bound to their plantations during the period of indenture and required a pass to venture outside. They came primarily to cut cane, though some worked on cocoa plantations in Trinidad and Grenada and on banana plantations in Jamaica. Accommodation varied from colony to colony. In Trinidad they lived in barracks, one small room to a family, with no privacy. In Suriname they inherited the quarters of the enslaved. In Grenada, where Sewell reported 300–400 already imported by 1859, estates were required to have clean and "good-sized" lodgings for the Indians, with separate apartments for each family. Each estate had to have a doctor and medical attention was free. Wages had to be paid in cash with no deductions unless by mutual consent. The flip side of all this solicitude was that the Indians, like other indentured workers, labored under a measure of unfreedom while still under indenture. Contractual infringements, such as absence without authorization, were treated as criminal offences.

There was a general consensus among European commentators that the Indians were not as physically strong as the Africans or the Chinese, who seemed to be considered second on the ladder of physical strength. A tradition eventually developed of giving Africans the most physically demanding jobs, such as clearing forests. Sewell thought that arriving Indians seemed almost too delicate for plantation labor. Yet their sheer numbers, their restriction to the plantations during indenture and their perseverance eventually made them excellent plantation workers. Sewell added his two cents to the sometimes wildly conflicting white stereotypes of the working populations. He saw the Indians as "mild in disposition, almost to effeminacy, docile and obedient, contrasting very favorably, in this respect, with the Negro and the Chinaman."

British arrivals were closely overseen by the Colonial Office in London, the British government in India and the local legislatures. Britain also maintained a protective oversight over Indians in the French and Dutch colonies, who also originated mostly in British India. Indian immigrants typically signed five-year contracts from 1862, with some variation of terms before that date. They were given free passage and medical attention. They were guaranteed a specified number of hours work per week at an agreed wage. They sailed under the supervision of sirdars (headmen).

Protectors of immigrants involved themselves intimately in the welfare of the Indians, even to the point of ensuring that families were not separated, and persons from the same home districts stayed together. A special orphanage for Indian children was established in Trinidad. This attention gave rise to a stereotype of Indians as a "pampered" class. "It is impossible to imagine the rights of any people more securely guaranteed than are those of the Indian coolies who emigrate to Trinidad," Sewell thought in 1859. Those arriving before 1898 were entitled to a free return passage home, initially after five years' service but, after 1854, only after ten years' service. After 1898 returnees received half of the fare if male and two-thirds if female. Up to 1924 one in four of those in Guyana and one in six in Trinidad returned home, sometimes considerably wealthier than when they arrived. Sewell thought it "a hardship, if not a positive injustice," that after Indian immigration was financed by taxes levied on the rest of Trinidad's population, and Indians were cocooned in a web of special protections, that they should then be returned home at the further expense of the very populace already burdened by the cost of their importation and upkeep.

In order to induce the Indians to stay at the end of their initial contracts, Trinidad, Guyana, Jamaica and Suriname provided free land to those opting to remain. In Trinidad the land-for-return-passage commutation program, as it was called, lasted for twenty years, from 1869 to 1889. From 1869 to 1873 Indians received 10 acres in lieu of a free passage home. From 1873 to 1879 they received 5 acres plus 5 pounds cash. From 1879 to 1889 they received 5 pounds cash, enabling them, in theory at least, to purchase land wherever they wished, instead of depending on whatever land grant was selected for them. Walton Look Lai calculates that about "3,979 grants . . . involving about 11,933 people" were made between 1869 and 1889 in Trinidad. The Indians received 19,055 acres, presumably excluding whatever they bought with their 5 pound cash grants.

It was this free land program, Look Lai demonstrates, that established the Indians as a distinct landowning peasantry in Trinidad, despite the fact that many of their settlements failed. Following the Presbyterian missionary to the Indians, Rev. John Morton, Look Lai attributed the failure of many of the Indian settlements to, among other things, the "inexperience and improvidence" of the Indians, their lack of experience dealing with woodland, and "the absence of a sense of real community" among them, resulting in intra-community praedial larceny.

Between 1880 and 1882 British Guianese Indians in Essequibo received 49 free "residential lots" of a quarter of an acre each and 69 "cultivation lots" of 2 acres each in commutation of return passages. Between 1897 and 1902, 2,711 received free land in East Coast Demerara.

For Jamaica, Look Lai reported an intermittent free land program between 1869 and 1910. There were 10 acre land grants for some and 10–12 pound cash payments for "a large number of Indians" in lieu of passage home. With this money they purchased "an unquantifiable amount" of land.

State-aided procurement of land for time-expired Indian immigrants also found its way to Fiji, where Indian immigrants were introduced in 1879 under an array of Caribbean influences. When Sir Arthur Gordon arrived in Fiji as first British governor in 1875, it was after serving as governor of Trinidad from 1866 to 1870. His successor, Sir William Des Voeux, considered himself something of an expert on immigration questions, due to his eighteen-year experience in, as he put it, "four coolie-importing colonies, British Guiana, St. Lucia, Trinidad, and Fiji."

When Gordon introduced Indians to Fiji in 1879, the first shipload contained some former Trinidad indentured workers who were about to reindenture themselves to Trinidad but were persuaded to try Fiji instead. Observers in the Caribbean had often noted the improved physical and material conditions of Indians returning home, contrasted with those arriving for the first time. William Sewell, an advocate of Indian immigration, contrasted the arrivals, "naked, half-starved, gibbering savages, ready to eat any dead, putrid animal, fish, flesh, or fowl that lay in their path," with the returnees, "clothed, sleek and well fed, strong and able-bodied, speaking English with tolerable accuracy, and looking the intelligent people they really

are." Many returnees to India actually found that they could not readjust to the relatively depressed conditions back home and returned voluntarily to the Caribbean. Some came as reindentures, others as free persons paying their own way.

Perhaps the presence of these "improved" Trinidadians among Fiji's first Indian immigrants helps explain a future British Fiji governor's observation that "The men are a very fine set of fellows. . . . The women seem a good full-bodied lot of wenches, and the children are a jolly lot of little things."

Traditional landholding in Fiji made it mostly impossible for immigrants to purchase (as opposed to leasing) land, but the British nevertheless did the next best thing. They set up an Indian Settlements Fund in 1898 to procure and prepare land for the time-expired immigrants. As in the Caribbean, the Indians could use the bounties paid after the expiry of their indentures, to procure land.

Eric Williams demonstrated that the success of Indian immigration in its avowed objective of rehabilitating sugar was a mixed bag. Trinidad and British Guiana, the largest recipients of Indians, saw dramatic increases in sugar exports (13,285 tons in 1828 and 54,622 tons in 1895 for Trinidad). Corresponding figures for British Guiana were 40,115 and 101,160 tons, respectively. On the other hand sugar exports from Jamaica in the same years fell from 72,198 to 19,546. In Grenada exports went from 13,493 tons to nothing. In 1866 planters actually relocated some Indians from Grenada to British Guiana. From Trinidad in 1859 Sewell saw Indian immigration as the "salvation" of the island. He nevertheless acknowledged that the Africans had rightly exercised their prerogative for independence by leaving the plantations and were emphatically not the indolent and thriftless "Quashees" of Thomas Carlyle and other detractors.

Indenture was expensive. It was funded in St. Vincent by a special duty on sugar, rum, molasses, arrowroot, cotton and cocoa. A further amount was charged to general revenue. In Guyana and Trinidad in 1896 about 30 percent of the cost was borne by general revenue. This meant that the former enslaved whose wages were being depressed by the artificial surplus labor created by immigration were doubly penalized by having to subsidize those who, in effect, were destroying their ability to bargain for a fair wage. In Jamaica, to add insult to injury, African emigrants leaving home in search of properly remunerated work elsewhere were forced to pay a special departure tax.

Eric Williams pointed out that for every Indian coming in, three Africans left the Caribbean in search of work with dignity. For every pound remitted home to India, Williams calculated, 4 pounds were being sent back to the Caribbean by Barbadian emigrants alone, in a striking example of the thrift and desire for economic advance that drove the African Caribbeans from their homes. When Sewell considered the significant wealth taken back to India by returnees he concluded that the heavy taxes imposed on the populace to provide free return passages were "a hardship if not a positive injustice."

If the impact of immigration on sugar production was a mixed bag, its impact on slowing down the progress of the newly freed was probably more in keeping with the expectations of the planter and official elites. The efforts to frustrate the African move to viable independent villages in places such as Guyana clearly had some effect. The mass emigration of the African population in the wake of the new arrivals speaks eloquently to one effect of immigration. The extra taxes levied on the general population to support immigration siphoned off some resources that might have gone into peasant agriculture or other areas. This was mitigated by the remittances of African emigrants, but families were disrupted and most emigrants did not return.

The European desire to develop new immigrants into a buffer class also met with some success, as future developments were to show. Policies such as taxing the general population to fund free passages for Indians or providing Indians with free land after extraordinary efforts had been taken to frustrate African landownership all contributed to interracial tensions later on. The perception of encouragement to the sharp practices of Portuguese shopkeepers led to tensions such as those manifested in Guyana's "Angel Gabriel" riots of 1856.

By the turn of the twentieth century the gradual Indian acceptance of the Caribbean as a place of permanent residence was underway. Some affluent Indians had begun to make an appearance.

Occupations listed in the Trinidad censuses of 1891 and 1921 indicated some upward mobility. In 1891 there were 334 mechanics and handicraftsmen. In 1921 there were 997. There were three lawyer's clerks in 1891 and no lawyers listed. In 1921 there were five "members of legal profession." In 1891 there were two Christian ministers and forty-one Hindu and Muslim "priests." In 1921 there were ninety "ministers of religion." There were thirty Indian and one "Anglo-Indian" commercial "merchants, agents and dealers" in 1891 and 70 in 1921. Peasant proprietors rose from 720 in 1891 to 4,254 in 1921. There was one Indian policeman in 1891 and eight in 1921.

Indian indentured immigration to the British colonies officially ended in 1917. Over 400 more Indians nevertheless came to British Guiana under contract in 1921–1922. Others came in as voluntary noncontracted immigrants. Planter response to the termination of Indian immigration into British Guiana provided a rerun of the 1830s post-Emancipation period. They feared ruin due to the diminution of their labor supply. Guianese Africans, already reduced to a minority due to Indian immigration, were apprehensive about a further imbalancing of the colony's racial composition. The government accordingly set up a Colonization and Labor Committee. A Colonization Scheme of 1919 followed. A seven-member delegation was sent to London to meet with the Colonial Office on the matter. It comprised Attorney General Sir Joseph Nunan, three Indo-Guianese and three Afro-Guianese. The understanding was that the Indians would proceed to India after London, to explore further immigration from India. The Africans would proceed to West Africa on a similar mission. In London the West India Committee, representing the planters, vetoed the idea of African immigration. The Afro-Guianese delegation therefore had to return home. The Indo-Guianese went on to India and Ceylon.

In India the delegation met with Mahatma Gandhi, leader of the Indian nationalist struggle, on three occasions. They were able to obtain from him agreement on a resumption of emigration for a trial period of six months. They were however unable to extract an agreement from the Indian government.

A three-member Indian government delegation (two Indians and one Britisher) therefore visited British Guiana in 1922 to evaluate conditions. They voted 2–1 against a resumption of immigration. Guianese planters kept up the pressure and in 1924 Nunan returned to India to lobby. He was accompanied by Joseph A. Luckhoo, prominent Indo-Guianese lawyer and politician and a veteran of the 1919 delegation, and two members of the British Guiana East Indian Association. The Negro Progress Convention (NPC) sought assurances that African immigration would also be facilitated, as a quid pro quo. The NPC was founded in 1921 by E. F. Fredericks, recently returned from England, a veteran Pan-Africanist and lawyer, and a native of Buxton, one of the pioneer African villages established after Emancipation.

As a follow-up to the 1925 delegation, the Indian government in 1925 sent Kunwar Maharaj Singh on yet another mission into conditions in Guiana. He reported favorably that the standard of living for Indian immigrants was higher in Guiana than in rural India. Guianese Indians did not face discrimination as their compatriots did in South Africa. They were generally prosperous, though not as much as in Mauritius, where Indians owned 40 percent of sugar lands, or as in Trinidad, where Indians now owned 100,000 acres. Singh was nevertheless against the resumption of old-style immigration. He advocated instead a trial scheme of 500 families comprising approximately 1,500 free immigrants. In 1926 India nevertheless approved a new indentured scheme. About fifty families comprising 173 people came over. The supplementary immigration officially ended in 1928.

The African Guianese population meanwhile continued to seek equal facilities for African and Caribbean immigration. A. R. F. Webber raised this question in 1924 in his reply to the governor's speech, read on behalf of the elected members in the colonial legislature. The electives wanted a more vigorous government pursuit of Caribbean immigration, instead of "pursuing feverishly our activities in India." Webber warned of "a large body of public opinion [which] feels that it is essentially necessary to preserve the balance of the races in the colony, and not allow any one race to become too predominant." In 1925 members of Marcus Garvey's Universal

Negro Improvement Association (UNIA) were among those appointed to a government committee looking into the possible importation of "agricultural families of African race and origin" under the Colonization Scheme of 1919. A year earlier the Negro Progress Convention petitioned the governor to appoint a committee to visit the Caribbean and Africa in search of immigrants who would come in "on the same terms and conditions as are being offered to the Indians." In 1919 a large delegation had asked Lord Milner, secretary of state for the colonies, to facilitate African immigration. The banning of African American race uplift publications (including Marcus Garvey's *Negro World)* compounded the apprehensions of the Afro-Guianese.

Once free of indenture the Indians, too, adopted to some extent the wanderlust endemic to Caribbean history. Communities of free Guianese Indians arose in Suriname. Trinidad Indians followed their Afro-Trinidadian counterparts into Venezuela.

The Indian adjustment to a sense of permanence in the new environment was accompanied, uniquely for immigrant groups, by an underlying tension with the Africans. This was due to more than one factor. First, there was the sheer size of the Indian population. By 1911 as noted, they were the majority ethnic element in British Guiana and new immigrants were still being brought in. They were leaving their Caribbean home territories less than the Africans and having larger families. The preponderance of males in the Indian population was not sufficient to stem their demographic advance. It was already clear that the Indians and Africans would eventually have to compete for political prominence in British Guiana, Trinidad and Suriname.

Europeans often commented on the Indian reluctance to interact with the rest of the polyglot Caribbean society in general, and with the Africans in particular. These factors made of the Indians the group most likely to eventually fulfill the buffer role that the Europeans desired.

Demerara Indians, according to an 1852 report, referred to Africans "with the greatest disgust, saying that they are a coarse woolly-headed race, more like monkeys than human beings." They said they shunned the company of Africans. Such Indian antipathy toward Africans was rooted in the color-caste system of Hinduism, which held light skin in high regard.

While intra-Indian caste distinction tended to diminish in the Caribbean, the majority-Hindu Indian community as a whole incorporated Africans into their scheme of things as the blackest and lowest of outcasts. K. O. Laurence, Dale Bisnauth and others have noted the Indian immigrants' association of Africans with Rakshasa, a demon of the Mahabharata and Ravan, the enemy of the God Rama of the Ramayana. The Mahabharata and the Ramayana are India's most important sacred texts.

Indo-Trinidadian nationalist H. P. Singh similarly pointed out in the 1965 work, *The Indian Struggle for Justice and Equality Against Black Racism in Trinidad and Tobago (1956–1962),* that Hinduism recognized four main castes. "Outside the pale," he said, "was a fifth class, the Panchamas, . . . the 'untouchables, the unapproachables and the unlookables. . . .'" Below these outcasts came the rest of humankind [but, in this context, Africans specifically]."

Such sentiments, together with resistance to Christian proselytization, help explain the widespread early Indian refusal to send their children to school with Africans. The 1869 Keenan Report into Trinidad education noted that the Indian

is able fully to appreciate the importance and value of education. But he is proud of his ancient lineage, is influenced by the prejudices of caste, and declines to associate intimately, or to bring up his children in the same school, with creoles of the African race. If, therefore, it be deemed desirable to educate the Coolies, exceptional provisions and arrangements are indispensable.

The Trinidad census of 1921 corroborated these observations. Many more Indian children were attending government-assisted schools (6,457), including the Presbyterian Canadian Mission schools catering near-exclusively to Indians, than government (and therefore racially mixed) schools (1,967). Private schools, presumably exclusively or primarily for Indians, contained the smallest number of school-attending students (381), doubtless because of cost. But they significantly had the highest percentage of Indian girls enrolled. The fear of Indian girls intermingling with African boys at school was deeply rooted, and the census figures bore this out. Twenty-seven percent of the Indian children at government schools were girls. The figure for government-assisted schools was 29 percent of a much larger total. An impressive 45 percent of Indian students at private schools were girls. The vast majority (31,110) of Indian children were nevertheless not attending school at all. The figures are shown in the table at the bottom of this page.

As late as 1939 Indians in Jamaica and Trinidad were preferring to keep their daughters at home and uneducated rather than letting them attend racially integrated schools. Jamaica's East Indian Association requested a return to the racially exclusive schools of the indenture period, but that island's director of education preferred a policy of "no race discrimination." In Trinidad an Indian government representative, like Keenan in 1869, endorsed local Indian requests, which included enhanced recognition for Hindu and Muslim schools, "non-Christian Indian teachers," and a technical institute exclusively for Indians, although the last-mentioned never materialized. In Suriname also most Indian children in general, and girls in particular, were initially kept out of school, causing

Indian Students Attending School, Trinidad, 1921

	Boys	Girls	Total
Government Schools	1456	531	1987
Government-Assisted Schools	4562	1895	6457
Private Schools	210	171	381
Not attending school	14,633	16,477	31,110

Source: Adapted from Trinidad Census of 1921, as reproduced in Walton Look Lai, *Indentured Labor, Caribbean Sugar: Chinese and Indian Migrants to the British West Indies, 1838–1918.* Baltimore: The Johns Hopkins University Press, 1993.

the authorities not to enforce laws requiring compulsory school attendance.

These attitudes naturally found expression in a widespread Indian abhorrence of Indian–African sexual connections. Severe sanctions were imposed by the religious and cultural leaders of the Indian community. These included forcing women in such relationships to leave their community. The practice of child brides (with girls as young as ten being given away in arranged marriages) was also, among other things, a hedge against miscegenation. According to H. P. Singh, any Indian–African miscegenation would be a violation of Indians' "sacred laws."

Some commentators have concluded from this type of sentiment that Indian men did not "like" African women. The reality, however, was less simplistic (if not mischievous). For one thing, Indian emigrant avoidance of Chinese-style liaisons with local women was observed in the Malay Straits and elsewhere as well. And despite the strong community disapproval of Indian–African miscegenation, the practice took place anyway, although initially not on a scale comparable with most other groups.

Several of the first 1838 Indian arrivals in British Guiana formed liaisons with African women. There was additionally a surprisingly high proportion of females among the Indian parents of mixed-race children. Jack Harewood's figures for estimated net Indian immigrants in Trinidad give 3,037 Indian men to every 1,000 Indian women for the period 1901–1911, for a ratio of approximately 3:1. Look Lai reports 1,514 mixed Indian–other Trinidadians according to the 1911 census, the last before the end of Indian immigration. Of these, 975 had an Indian father and 539 an Indian mother, for a ratio of under 2:1. The census did not indicate the ethnic composition of the non-Indian parents and the overall numbers are small. Yet these numbers show that Trinidad Indian women were proportionately more likely than their men to parent mixed-race children around 1911. These women were presumably quite happy to walk away from the 3:1 ratio of Indian males to females in which they could luxuriate if they wanted to.

If some, maybe even most of the males enumerated here were motivated by sexual necessity due to the shortage of Indian women, this cannot explain the number of Indian women involved in interracial arrangements. It is hardly likely that Indian immigrant men had access to European, Chinese or other non-African women in meaningful numbers. The large preponderance of Africans over non-Indian groups in the population makes it reasonable to assume that most of the partners of miscegenating Indian women were also Africans. Indian women nevertheless had a wider choice than their male counterparts. European male authority figures such as managers and overseers had long encroached into the short supply of Indian women. Mohammed Orfy, the activist champion of Trinidad's Indian destitutes, bemoaned the fact in 1917 that three-quarters of Indian women, as he saw it, were kept openly as concubines by Europeans, Africans, "Americans," Chinese and other unspecified ethnicities. To make matters worse, rich Indian men were further diminishing the pool by arrogating to themselves more than one concubine. For many Indian men chances of an Indian mate were slim, thereby arguably forcing them outside the race for sexual interaction. This was happily made easier for them by a surplus of females in the non-Indian Trinidad population of 1901–1911.

"Official" Indian disgust at race mixture nevertheless did not abate. The word "Dougla," which came to designate the offspring of Indians and Africans in the Caribbean, continues to bear eloquent testimony to Indian community pressure against African–Indian miscegenation. Dougla is derived from a Hindi word most often rendered in its Caribbean context as "bastard," and sometimes as "son of a whore" and "half-breed." This places it in the same category as "mulatto," described above. It also invites comparison with the once popular "black bastards" of less refined British citizenry and with the "Rhineland bastards" of Nazi Germany. These latter were the offspring of white German women and French colonial African troops occupying the Rhine after World War I. Hitler also categorized the women involved in these liaisons as whores.

Women scholars such as Shaheeda Hosein and Rhoda Reddock have emphasized the independent-mindedness of some female Indian immigrants, despite pervasive stereotypes to the contrary. When the going got tough some were quite capable of physically fighting with oppressive mothers-in-law or husbands. They walked away from arranged marriages and entered voluntary sexual relations of their own choosing. Some who arrived in the Caribbean as adults had already been forced by circumstances in India (e.g., widowhood or absconding from home) into lives of some independence.

Indian disdain for Africans was also influenced by Indian attitudes toward Europeans. Despite occasional fatal clashes between Indian workers and European plantation managers, there was often a deep Indian posture of admiration and respect for Europeans. Whites had brought the Indians to the Caribbean in conditions of semi-slavery, but they also occupied a special paternalistic and benevolent relationship with them. Whites were also the power elite in a multiracial society. Several benevolent Europeans founded and participated in Indian organizations. Suriname's first important Indian organization, the Surinam Immigrants' Association, was founded in 1910 by a Dutch immigration agent general. The Susamachar East Indian Young Men's Society, founded in British Guiana in 1919, was the brainchild of an English Methodist missionary. Other British missionaries followed the founder as leaders of the organization.

Indians respected the Canadian Mission to the Indians of Trinidad, said historian Brinsley Samaroo, in part "because they were white." The Canadians, he argued, in turn championed political causes seen as anti-African by the African community and helped institutionalize Indian exclusivism.

An important element in the panoply of European influences on Indo-Caribbean racial attitudes was the nineteenth and early twentieth-century flowering of Aryan racial superiority thought. Englishman Rudyard Kipling, "poet laureate of British imperialism," whose 1899 poem "White Man's Burden" defined this era of white triumphalism, was born in India. He won the Nobel Prize for Literature in 1907 and was buried in

Westminster Abbey in 1936 among monarchs of the British empire.

Aryanism postulated a racial kinship between white people and presumed Aryan-derived Indians, with the rest of humankind relegated to an inferior status. These ideas eventually found their logical culmination in Adolf Hitler. The supposed Aryan super race had thousands of years ago allegedly subjugated India and enshrined the idea of a master race via the caste system. All-conquering Europe of the modern age had become the latest manifestation of Aryan genius. For British official Sir William Hunter of the Indian Civil Service, the Aryan was the common glorious progenitor of the Brahman, the Rajput and the Englishman. This was in his *Imperial Gazeteer of India* (1881). For Samuel Laing, a British Finance Minister in the Government of India in 1862, Britain's sacred duty in India was to help up the weaker Indian Aryan brother, once preeminent among Aryans, but now fallen on hard times.

By judiciously offering a limited promise of Indian–European racial kinship, the European community could provide for Indo-Caribbeans the hope of exalted status, at least over the Africans. At the inaugural meeting of the Susamachar East Indian Young Men's Society in British Guiana in 1919, the acting governor, Cecil Clementi, delivered an address on "The Kinship between the Indian and British Races." These ideas found ready acceptance in some influential circles. They probably reinforced the notions of anti-African disdain already independently present in Indo-Caribbean thought. Surinamese historian Sandew Hira saw Suriname's "Indian compradors," even in the postindependence era, as still promoting "the colonial view according to which Indian culture was more close to the 'normal' white culture."

Some Indo-Caribbean intellectuals could be found who accepted with relish these offers of racial kinship. The outstanding example was F. E. M. Hosein, arguably the leading Caribbean Indian intellectual of his day and an important politician. He was a graduate of Canadian Mission schools, Queen's Royal College (where he won an Island Scholarship in 1901), Oxford University and Lincoln's Inn. Hosein, usually portrayed by historians as a liberal, and even a champion of African–Indian solidarity, in

1913 likened his African compatriots to "an inferior race." The occasion was a major address at an "inaugural" meeting of the East Indian National Congress which he headed. Before a multiracial (but predominantly Indian) audience which included the British Governor Sir George R. LeHunte and the visiting British administrator of St. Vincent, Hosein predicted the demise of the African population and the ultimate control of Trinidad by Indians. In language indistinguishable from the rhetoric of European pseudoscience, Hosein declared, as reported by the *Port of Spain Gazette*, that

> The Indian was full of his racial prejudice. The time was not when he was not civilized. He had heard of the great races of the earth. But among the great sons of the earth Africa was not mentioned, and when mentioned it was in a humble capacity. From him, the son of India had nothing to learn,—unless, perhaps, something to ridicule. . . .

He saw extinction as the ultimate fate of the inferior African race in Trinidad.

> If the East Indian showed that progressive increase in number which they had shown up to now, and taking into account their natural productivity, it was no mere hyperbolical statement that Indians would people the colony and drive out the rest of the inhabitants. The African was not as productive as the East Indian: and if circumstances did not compel him to leave the colony, he would naturally die out. Such a thing had taken place at Mauritius. And Trinidad would be maintained and owned by the Indian in the field, the office and the shop.

Hosein's remarks drew instant reprimands from the administrator of St. Vincent and Governor LeHunte. The African Trinidadian writer Algernon Burkett responded in the press and the Chinese-owned but Afro-Trinidadian-edited *Argos* editorially

blasted this "tirade of a half baked East Indian collegian against the Afro-Trinidadian and tacitly others. . . ."

The complex provenance of Hosein's ideas, involving possibly contemporary Aryan supremacy notions wedded to ideas independently rooted in Indian color and caste consciousness, had an intriguing parallel in Mahatma Gandhi, most revered of modern Indian leaders. Gandhi was a contemporary of Hosein and involved in a similar struggle in another major theatre of Indian indentured immigration, namely South Africa, where he lived from 1893 to 1914. Both men qualified as barristers-at-law at the Inns of Court in London. In South Africa, as in the Caribbean, Indian immigrants found themselves in a multiracial society in which whites, Africans, Indians and others were obliged to interact, however unequally. Gandhi cofounded the Natal Indian Congress in 1894 and was its first honorary secretary. Both Hosein and Gandhi therefore presided over "Indian Congresses." The similarity in nomenclature may not necessarily have been coincidental. The Natal Indian Congress' constitution in 1894 promised

> To promote concord and harmony among the Indians and the Europeans residing in the Colony. . . .

> To induce Hindustanis—particularly Colonial-born Indians—to study Indian history and literature relating to India. . . .

> To inquire into the conditions of the indentured Indians and to take proper steps to alleviate their sufferings. . . .

Like Hosein, Gandhi's liberal, even saintly, image has obscured several statements of his considered by many to be racist. He insisted on using the derogatory term "Kaffir" for Africans. He wrote that they were only minimally removed from animals. He thought it a grave insult to Indians for whites to lump the two groups together. He lambasted South Africa's whites in 1906 for imposing nuisance restrictions on Indians designed, in his opinion, to degrade them to the level of "raw" Africans. Expressing ideas reminiscent of Carlyle's *Occasional Discourse on the Nigger Question*,

Gandhi thought that the African's life ambitions were satisfied when he accumulated enough cows to buy himself a wife. Carlyle thought that once "Quashee" procured sufficient pumpkins to satisfy his immediate needs, his life's goals had been achieved. Carlyle considered Africans "lazy." Gandhi thought them "indolent." Carlyle, Hosein and Gandhi were all giving expression to prevailing British orthodoxy on this question.

Afro-Caribbean spokespersons struggled persistently against these negative stereotypes. In January 1932 a committee of the Forum Club of Barbados comprising Clennell W. Wickham, J. C. Hope and H. A. Vaughan, together with two members of the Barbados Elementary Teachers' Association, met with a Commission of Enquiry into the educational needs of the British West Indies. They protested passages identical with the sentiments of Carlyle, Hosein and Gandhi, which had made their way into British-authored school textbooks for Caribbean children. One of the texts, *Our Empire Overseas*, postulated that "With the abolition of slavery the prosperity of Jamaica declined. The present population consists largely of blacks most of them averse to work as their wants are few and easily satisfied." The other, J. M. D. Meiklejohn's *School History of England*, told Caribbean children where the blame lay for the "ruin" of Caribbean planters after Emancipation—"Negroes are lazy, and finding that they could make as much money as they wanted by working only two or three days a week they could not be persuaded to work more and most of the West Indian planters were in consequence ruined."

Trinidad's Colonial Indian Committee told the West Indian Royal Commission in 1939 that Trinidad Indians had saved the country from ruin. Rev. J. D. Ramkeesoon, Anglican minister, first regular nonwhite columnist in the *Trinidad Guardian* and member of the Colonial Indian Committee, had in 1936 blamed Africans for the "necessity" of importing Indian labor. He was taken to task by prominent African Trinidadian lawyer, Henry Hudson-Phillips.

In 1950 the Indo-Guyanese historian Dwarka Nath was still broadcasting the sentiments of Carlyle, Gandhi and the others —"But nothing could induce [the Africans] to work regularly," he lamented. "The greater number did nothing at all, but lived on such fruits and ground provisions as they could get."

The rise of Indian political and quasi-political organizations in the late nineteenth and twentieth centuries brought with it heightened expressions of racial tension. In 1897 Trinidad Indians memorialized a visiting West India Royal Commission for communal representation in the Legislative Council. Indian communalism in politics could on occasion be used as a weapon to frustrate or delay constitutional advance sought by Africans. The case of the Wood Commission of 1921–1922 is illustrative of this. The commission was sent to the Caribbean from London in response to demands for democratization of the political process. These demands figured prominently in the primarily African riots of the postwar period in Belize, Trinidad and elsewhere.

Several Trinidad Indians appearing before the commission opposed introduction of the elective principle into Trinidad politics. The East Indian National Congress (EINC) demanded proportional or communal representation "on the ground," as Wood explained, "that otherwise there was a danger of their being outvoted." C. B. Mathura, later editor of the *East Indian Weekly* and one of an Indian minority favoring an elective franchise, saw the position of the EINC and its chief spokesman, Rev. C. D. Lalla, as the introduction into Trinidad of "a miniature India with class legislation, perhaps caste representation—Brahmin for Brahmin, Hindu for Hindu and so on."

The East Indian National Association of Princes Town and several prominent Indians preferred to keep undemocratic crown colony rule, since they did not think that there were enough qualified Indians to compete successfully in an elective system. Several of the Indian leaders advanced as a further reason for opposing the African quest for democracy what F. E. M. Hosein described as "the veiled and some times open hostility of the coloured race."

The positions of the Indian leadership were finely nuanced, however. They were overwhelmingly separatists, and disagreed only on how best to secure this objective. F. E. M. Hosein felt that noncommunal elections need not be an obstacle "to preserve the purity and pride of race." The entire leadership, he said, was "at one in its aim; namely, the advancement and prestige of East Indians separate and distinct from the rest of a heterogeneous community. This," he said, "is a laudable desire with which the whole [Indian leadership] fully sympathizes. . . ."

Major Wood partly acceded to the Indian demands. He denied their request for communal representation while nevertheless retaining a strong nonelective element making it possible for the government to simply appoint Indians to the Legislative Council, if they should fail to secure adequate representation via elections. His arguments against communalism were nevertheless interesting:

> . . . it would accentuate and perpetuate the differences which, in order to produce a homogeneous community it should be the object of statesmanship to remove. The East Indians are an important element in the community, and it would be a great misfortune if they were encouraged to stand aside from the main current of political life instead of sharing in it and assisting to guide its course. Finally, if a concession of this kind were granted to the East Indians, there would be no logical reason for withholding it from persons of French, Spanish or Chinese descent, a situation which would became impossible.

A similar demand from the British Guiana East Indian Association in 1936 elicited a similar official response.

In objecting to Indian communal requests, Trinidad's Legislative Reform Committee, as recorded by the Wood Report, "deprecated differentiation between East Indian and Creole, since they formed one community and the difference between them was one of domestic life only. . . . In their view any system of communal representation involving preferential treatment to one race would create friction."

Among the key elements feeding communalism was an intense interaction with emissaries from India. Whether secular or religious, such emissaries encouraged attitudes of separatism and bolstered feelings of racial pride. Well after the end of indenture, members of the Indian Civil Service visited periodically. They lobbied on behalf of local Indians, encouraged feelings of closeness to Mother India and arbitrated disputes within the Indo-Caribbean community. (From the late 1940s diplomatic representatives of independent India played a similar role.)

When in 1938–1939 London sent out a West Indies Royal Commission (once more following rioting, primarily among the African population), the (British) Indian Government sent along a special "officer on deputation" to mobilize Caribbean Indians and help them put their grievances before the commissioners. While full publication of the commission's report was withheld until after World War II, the separate *Report on the Condition of Indians in Jamaica, British Guiana and Trinidad* was published right away in 1939. This represented merely the latest episode in a hundred years of special British solicitude for its Caribbean Indian population, which gave rise, as early as the nineteenth century in British Guiana, to the expression "pampered coolie."

Visits by India-based religious missionaries were even more frequent than those of the Indian Civil Service representatives and equally influential, if not more so. Both Hindu and Muslim missionaries traveled the circuit from Trinidad to Guyana to Suriname, with sometimes a stop in other Caribbean destinations or the United States. Missionaries commanded great respect among their overseas compatriots. They founded local religious organizations and local branches of Indian ones. They also explicitly preached racial pride and encouraged racial exclusiveness. Their missionary zeal was exemplary. Visiting Vedic missionary to Trinidad, Pundit Mehta Jaimini, visited thirty-eight towns and villages and delivered seventy-nine lectures in less than three months in 1928–1929.

The parting advice given by visiting Pandit Ayodha Prasad to the Arya Samaj Association of Trinidad in 1936 was instructive. He was on his way to Suriname, he explained, when he discovered the Indian community of Trinidad. He completed his work in Suriname and retraced his steps to Trinidad, where, despite some local opposition (possibly from rival religious groupings), he was welcomed by Indian Hindus, Muslims and Christians. "I am leaving Trinidad," he said on his departure, "but I want Indians to think that they are Indians first and everything else after." He continued, "They must maintain their national identity and their language."

His local followers were profuse in their gratitude. "[You have achieved] the redemption of sons of India who had been denationalised and alienated," they confessed. In an address presented to Prasad, Professor Satya Charan and B. T. Shastri showed the close relation between religious proselytization and racial consciousness. Arya Samaj, said the address, had "infused new life in Indian Society." It had made Indo-Trinidadians proud of Indian civilization. It had "engendered in our hearts a love for the ancient glory and culture of our Motherland." It had brought home the need to preserve Indian "mother tongues." The Arya Samaj Movement had in fact "saved the Indian community from the perilous plight of being hopelessly absorbed by alien religions and alien culture." It had taken a disillusioned community and transformed it into a model of hope for a glorious future.

While Hinduism and Islam may have seemed natural vehicles for Indian communalism and racial pride, the Christian denomination most closely associated with the Indians in Trinidad played a similar role. The Canadian Mission (Presbyterian Church of Canada) was unique among Christian churches in its single-minded concentration on the Indian community. Its missionaries often trained in India for Caribbean work. They studied Indian religions and spoke Indian languages. Their local catechists and clergy were Indian. The churches and schools (elementary, secondary and teacher-training) they established were overwhelmingly Indian, as were the local teachers they recruited. Classes were taught in Hindi, which was a compulsory subject in their teachers' colleges.

Communalism found further expression in the media. Some major newspapers and periodicals in Trinidad carried special Indian sections in the 1930s. (A Trinidad Garveyite leader noted in 1937 that the big dailies carried Indian, Portuguese, Spanish and Chinese sections, but no African sections.) Yet the Afro-Trinidadian-owned *East Indian Weekly* and the Afro-Guianese-owned radio station VP3BG, as seen,

played important roles in facilitating this nationalism. By the mid-1930s, movies imported from India had become important vehicles of cultural rejuvenation and racial awareness.

The 1930s activity represented a general upsurge in group consciousness which found parallels in the African and other communities. The "Indian News and Views" section of the *Trinidad Guardian* in 1936 welcomed the growing popularity of saris among Indian women as a manifestation of this consciousness and commented, "It is hoped that others will identify themselves in like manner and thus preserve their national characteristics as true and loyal daughters of Mother India." (Interestingly, the dhoti, the most characteristic form of Indo-Caribbean male attire, was mostly allowed to die a natural death.)

One of the most enduring aspects of Indo-Caribbean nationalism has been the demand for Hindi in schools. The Canadian Mission schools, as already seen, accommodated these demands. Schools run by Hindu organizations continued the practice later. By 1938 forty-nine Guyanese schools were receiving government grants for the teaching of Hindi. Public interest in this subject remained strong.

The teaching of Hindi and the broader question of Indo-Caribbean nationalism generally were ventilated in 1936, in what may be the definitive debate on these questions. 'Trinidadian' initiated the exchange with a letter to Trinidad's *Sunday Guardian*. He agreed with Indian missionary P. Kodanda Rao of the Servants of India Society, Poona, and a personal friend of Mahatma Gandhi, that there was no need for the compulsory teaching of Hindi to Indian children in Trinidad schools. (Rao, who also labored among the Indians of British Guiana, was not the last Indian to consider Indo-Caribbean nationalism excessive.) Trinidadian reviewed the pronouncements of "prominent" Indo-Trinidadians on the issue. One had said that if Hindi were not taught, Indians would lose their culture. Another said that Indians would become denationalized, and no longer true Indians.

It was all right for Indians to learn Hindi, Urdu, Arabic or any of the multitudinous languages of India, Trinidadian thought. But it was unreasonable to advocate the compulsory teaching of Hindi.

Suppose for the moment that the government did indeed grant the Indian request. This would, in Trinidadian's view, open a Pandora's Box of inter- and intra-ethnic strife. Trinidadian's views here were reminiscent of those expressed earlier in the Wood Report:

> What will be Government's position when the Negroes of Trinidad also demand that one of the languages of Africa must be compulsorily taught to Negro children in our schools. . . ? Is it to be expected that Government will begin to reorganize our schools to suit the whims of every national community of Trinidad which has representatives of almost every people under the sun. . . ? And if even the Negroes do not agitate because of a broader outlook, is it not a certainty that among the Indians who constitute about one hundred and fifty thousands, you will find one-third approaching Government [for the teaching of Tamil, since Tamils are one-third of the Indian population]?

A demand for Bengali would be next, Trinidadian thought, and the process could potentially be never-ending. The writer perceived a misapprehension among Trinidad Indians to the effect that India was a cohesive society with a single mother tongue.

The "Indian News and Views" section of the *Trinidad Guardian* provided the forum for the Indian response. It came from H. M. Khan of St. Joseph. In a minor concession to Trinidadian he urged the teaching of both Hindi and Urdu, the two most popular local Indian languages. "In advocating the claims of the East Indians," he wrote, "I am not unmindful of the claims of the African race. . . ." Yet "the fact that no similar demand is made by the African people" he ascribed not to "their broader outlook, but [to their] apparent, and to me, sad and deplorable loss of national consciousness. Sad it is indeed," he said, "for the majority of them have merged themselves in custom, culture and language foreign to their own. Their national spirit seems to be

almost dead." He thought that "East Indians have not as yet reached that phase of life, but if no cognisance is paid to their languages and culture, their story some day will be like their African neighbors."

In dismissing the African claim to "broader outlook," Khan in fact overlooked a great strength of African nationalism. For people like Henry Sylvester Williams, Garvey, F. E. M. Hercules and George Padmore had salvaged what they could from their much repressed African heritage and had built a new racial consciousness, less dependent on the mechanical transference of African cultural forms, but no less potent for that. This may explain why Africans from the Caribbean often played leadership roles in Pan-African struggle (not infrequently on the African continent itself), while Caribbean Indians were more likely to be *recipients* of cultural largesse from Mother India. Khan's ideas nevertheless were then, and long continued to be, orthodoxy among some influential segments of Trinidad Indian opinion. In 1988 the small Trinidad Hindu journal, *Sandesh,* editorialized in similar vein, though with a slightly new twist:

> The Europeans spared no moment in denuding the Africans of their culture and religion and left no stone unturned in trying to do the same to the Indians. But the Indians were made of stener [sic] stuff . . .

Khan said that the East Indian Educational Board had extracted a promise of part-time Hindi and Urdu teachers in schools where Indians predominated. He acknowledged that Trinidad was now home for its Indian community. But his was a Trinidad where Indians would aggressively "mould their character from Indian Culture, thereby retaining their national consciousness."

Trinidadian predictably took exception to Khan's disparaging remarks on African racial consciousness. He saw Trinidad Indians' fierce communalism as reflective of the worst of India itself, where communalism and intolerance were responsible for most of the country's problems. "The Indian mind is probably the most intolerant in the world," he declared,

And this communal and caste intolerance has defied even the vastnesses of the Atlantic and Indian Oceans. It scorns the distance of many thousand miles between India and Trinidad. . . . And the worst part of it is, they are called Cultures of India, and if you dare to go against them, you are termed denationalised!

Trinidadian finally contrasted the extreme communalism of Trinidad Indians with more progressive elements in India itself, as Eric Williams would later do in his conflict with Trinidad Hindus. He quoted J. M. Len Gupta of the Indian National Congress, addressing his own people, in terms reminiscent of Karl Marx's essay on "The British Rule in India":

If it is found that Hindu Culture means purdah, and Mohammedan Culture means the harem, both [cultures] must go. If Hindu Culture means caste system and marriage before puberty, and Mohammedan culture means polygamy, none of them should have a place in our social reforms.

The insistent advocacy of racial nationalism on the part of Indo-Caribbean leaders did not completely stem the tide of acculturation to the larger societies. The twentieth century witnessed a steady increase in Indian participation in such African-dominated cultural expressions as Trinidad carnival. Sometimes such acculturation took place in spite of the strident efforts of the Indian leadership.

Newspaper photographs of the 1930s, even on the pages set aside for Indian opinion, already showed the inexorable progress of acculturation. There were scenes of Western-style weddings. There was the exceptional photo of the marriage of a prominent Indian businessman to an Afro-Caribbean woman. There was the picture of Ms. Guyadeen's dance class in Trinidad, featuring girls, predominantly but not exclusively Indian, posing in the stylized gestures of European dance. Prominently featured in Ms. Guyadeen's class was Freida McBurnie, sister of Beryl McBurnie, the great doyenne of Trinidad's Afro-Caribbean dance.

Powerful elements within the Indian leadership cautioned against such signs of acculturation. Attacks on the "denationalization" of their people and programs of "re-Indianization" were the largely successful devices to whip the Indian masses back into line. "The process of denationalization of the Indian born in this colony is even now proceeding rapidly apace and unchecked," F. E. M. Hosein wrote in 1922; "and there is every indication that the younger generation of East Indians will be completely assimilated with and absorbed by the coloured race" if something were not done soon. He sought to forestall assimilation and "preserve the purity and pride of race."

Trinidad's *East Indian Weekly* in 1929 bemoaned the increasingly denationalized young generation which had done nothing to advance the race and was "day by day, becoming increasingly disrespectful to their women folk." Missionary Pundit Jaimini had reversed this trend, however, for "whereas previously there has been [a] sort of losing of ground, now a spirit of renaissance, or of race-determination, or race consciousness has gone forward throughout the whole Indian community."

The Indian government's emissary, J. D. Tyson, provided the formula for continued successful re-Indianization in 1939 when he astutely pointed out that while some acculturation was unavoidable, it was not necessarily inconsistent with the laudable goal of Indian nationalism. The correct strategy, he advised, was for "the Indian, while retaining his purity of race [to] become a Trinidadian in outlook. . . ."

Despite the competing nationalisms, there has often been a lingering perception on both sides that this did not amount to serious racial animosity. C. L. R. James ventured the opinion in 1938, perhaps unduly sanguine even for that period, that there was "no racial ill-feeling" between Indians and Africans in Trinidad. One Muslim and two Hindu organizations informed the visiting British Moyne Commission at about the same time that there was no racial prejudice in Trinidad. In 1966, after the worst racial riots in British Caribbean history, Marxist Cheddi Jagan still argued that "Race has never been a serious problem" in Guyana.

It is certainly true that Indian–African violence remained rare if it happened at all, until the 1960s events in Guyana. There appears to be no counterpart of the occasional anti-Portuguese and anti-Chinese outbreaks. Sandew Hira has shown that the ten major instances of Indian plantation violence between 1873 and 1902 in Suriname were all antiwhite. A possible explanation for this seeming paradox was the residential separation that limited everyday contact between the races. Even when residential separation began to break down in the twentieth century, however, there was no corresponding escalation of intercommunal violence.

Nor was the African population reluctant to encourage the more benign expressions of Indian nationalism. Such an opportunity was afforded by a celebratory banquet in 1936 for Leslie Grant Dookhie, Trinidad's fifth Indian Island Scholarship winner, and the first to capture the Jerningham Gold Medal in the process. Dookhie, a "son of India," had distinguished himself, thereby proving "not only a credit to himself, or his parents, but to the East Indians of the colony." C. Henry Pierre, a featured speaker for the occasion, considered it "a natural and laudable" thing for Indians to be proud of one of their own. "This race-consciousness is a difficult if not impossible thing to cast into the Stygian waters of oblivion," he said. "In spite of every effort, it proves irrepressible and asserts itself at every odd moment." But he did not favor the demand, coming from some quarters, for a specially Indian education for Indo-Trinidadian youth.

Progressive nationalist movements, whether Indian or African, and even where articulated in racial terms, could often be tolerant or even welcoming of each other. Thus the secretary of Marcus Garvey's UNIA in Montreal, Canada, was for many years an Indo-Caribbean. Hucheshwar G. Mudgal of India and Trinidad edited Garvey's *Negro World* newspaper in the 1930s and was a staunch defender of Garvey's African nationalism.

During the primarily Afro-Trinidadian stevedores' strikes and disturbances of 1919, Indo-Trinidadian plantation workers also initiated radical action against the white plantation structure. The Trinidad Workingmen's Association and its successor Trinidad Labor Party both attracted substantial Indian

participation in the interwar years. The very radical "Butler the Black" in Trinidad from the 1930s worked closely with Indian colleagues. The National Joint Action Committee (NJAC), which led Trinidad's Black Power movement in 1970, made several overtures to the Indian community. Indian religious-cultural leaders were the ones most likely to strongly oppose such initiatives.

The *East Indian Weekly* (1928–1932), Trinidad's most important Indian nationalist newspaper to that time, was owned by Leonard Fitzgerald Walcott, an African nationalist and Garveyite. The "Indian National Hour," begun in January 1936 on British Guiana's first "legal" radio station, VP3BG, pioneered the broadcast of Indian music. It had an enthusiastic short-wave listenership in Trinidad. The station was started on January 13, 1935, by Afro-Guianese James Leonard Rowe.

Indians outside of Trinidad, Guyana and Suriname, for their part, have often been less resistant than in the areas of major Indian population to an accommodation with African culture. In St. Lucia in the 1940s, three Indian members (ethnicity confirmed by both their names and photographs) of the Garveyite New York–headquartered Universal African Nationalist Movement answered "Yes" on their application forms to the question, "Are you of African blood and descent?"

Indo-Caribbean nationalism was over the years supported by a plethora of racially focused organizations extending into every sphere of life. The East Indian Institute was founded circa 1892 as British Guiana's first "organized attempt to bring Indians together" for social, economic, political and other reasons. This was followed in 1916 by the omnibus British Guiana East Indian Association (BGEIA, founded at Berbice by Joseph Ruhomon). The association's constitution was an articulate and representative statement of Indo-Caribbean nationalist aspirations. It promised in part:

1. To unite the members of the East Indian race in all parts of the colony for representative purposes. . . .
5. To secure representatives of East Indian nationality in the Legislature and in all corporations where the interests of

East Indians are concerned or stand to be affected, every candidate selected, to give a pledge, beforehand, to protect and further the interests of the race, as far as it lies in his power. . . .

7. To urge the establishment of special Government Schools under East Indian Masters for the teaching of both Hindi and English to children of East Indian parents. . . .

11. To advocate and promote, by all possible legitimate means, the intellectual, moral, social, economical, political and general public interest and welfare of the East Indian community at large. . . .

Trinidad's counterparts to the BGEIA were the East Indian National Association (1897) and the East Indian National Congress (1909). Jamaica in 1938 boasted an East Indian National Association and a "newly formed" East Indian National Union. The pioneering Surinam Immigrants' Association appeared in 1910. Throughout the twentieth century exclusively Indian organizations permeated every sphere of existence. An East Indian Literary and Debating Association was active in Trinidad in 1917. Clubs bearing similar names were still active decades later. There was an East Indian Cricket Club in Guyana in 1914 and both individual clubs and an East Indian Cricket Board of Control in Trinidad. International matches were arranged between Indian teams from both countries.

The Balak Sahaita Mandalee (Child Welfare Society) founded in Guyana in 1936 had as its motto, "Better mothers, better children, better house life and a better Indian community." Trinidad boasted a Trinidad Girls in Training described as specifically for Indian girls in the Canadian Mission church. In an apparent effort to parallel the work of Trinidad's premier social worker, Audrey Jeffers, Indian leaders in 1936 attempted to establish a "Breakfast Shed for Indian children." The moving force behind the effort was A. C. B. Singh, president of the Trinidad Indian League and chairman of the East Indian Social Workers of Port of Spain.

During the Second World War some Trinidad Indians wished to form a separate Indian contingent.

(There was also some talk of a Chinese contingent.) There was a short-lived Indian Teachers Union in Trinidad combining the Canadian Mission Teachers Association, the Sanatan Dharma Maha Sabha (Hindu) Teachers Association and the Muslim Teachers Association. A 1947 editorial in the Trinidad *Observer,* edited by H. P. Singh, referred to recently abortive efforts at an Indian motor insurance company, an Indian Chamber of Commerce and an Indian Welfare Committee.

The India Club (1942–1954), an ostensibly social organization in Port of Spain's exclusive Queens Park West, was started by Dr. D. P. Pandia, a visiting Indian Congress Party member. "Clearly," commented an Indo-Trinidadian historian of this development, "the Indian community [in Trinidad] viewed itself as a distinct and separate community, one nation living in a common space with other nations." Pandia also founded several other Indian political, cultural and welfare associations throughout Trinidad. Other social clubs of this period and later carried names such as the West India Club and Himalaya Club. By the 1980s and 1990s, with Indo-Trinidadian nationalism possibly at its most strident ever, the University of the West Indies (Trinidad campus) boasted a Society for the Propagation of Indian Culture (SPIC), which was inevitably followed by the Society for the Propagation of African Nationalism (SPAN).

Indian organization has been paralleled over the years by Indian publications. In Trinidad these have included *Koh-i-noor* (1898–1899), the *East Indian Herald* (1919), the *East Indian Patriot* (1921–1925), *East Indian Weekly* (1928–1932), *The Indian Magazine* (1937), *The Sentinel* (1946), *The West Indian Magnet* (1932), *The Statesman* (1940s), *The Observer* (1941) and *Sandesh* (1980s). Guyana in the 1930s published *The Indian Opinion* and *The Guiana Indian.*

In politics Indian nationalism has run the gamut from the early efforts at communal representation to open advocacy of Indian parties, to calls for secession and the building of an Indian "homeland" or empire in the West. There has also been a continuing effort at coalition building with parties of other ethnicities.

In 1944 the communal representation idea was still alive and well when Trinidad's Adrian Cola

Rienzi (born Krishna Deonarine) threatened unsuccessfully to demand "special representatives on all elective and representative bodies." Trinidad's Indian Association sought, also unsuccessfully, to have proportional representation enshrined in the country's 1962 independence constitution. A three-man delegation (H. P. Singh, Lennox Deyalsingh and Kenneth Lalla) was dispatched to London for this purpose. In the 1970s Vernon Jamadar, representing one faction of the Indian-dominated Democratic Labor Party, renewed the call for proportional representation. In Guyana, where ethnic animosity led to serious violence, all major political players, including the British government, had by 1964 come around to advocacy of proportional representation, though there was no agreement as to its precise implementation.

The plethora of separatist cultural and social organizations and the early and frequent calls for communal representation did not automatically translate into exclusively Indian political parties. From the limited representative government introduced into Trinidad by the Wood Report of the 1920s, to Universal Adult Suffrage in 1946 (and beyond), Indian politicians often participated in multiracial parties and groupings. This was true of both major early parties, the Trinidad Labor Party of A. A. Cipriani and the British Empire Workers and Citizens Home Rule Party of Tubal Uriah Buzz Butler. Timothy Roodal was leader of the southern section of the former in the 1920s; Adrian Cola Rienzi, a veteran of the Indian National Party of the 1920s, became a leading Butler collaborator in the 1930s. In Guyana, Joseph A. Luckhoo in 1916 became the first Indian to be elected to the legislature. He did so as a candidate for the multiracial People's Association.

To many, both observers and participants, it was universal adult suffrage (1946 in Trinidad and Tobago, 1948 in Suriname, 1953 in Guyana), with its new potential for appeals to the mass of citizens, that brought race to the forefront of electoral politics. Trinidadian Dr. Patrick Solomon, an electoral candidate in 1946 and later deputy prime minister under Eric Williams, blamed Indians for this development. H. P. Singh blamed Africans. From this point on the Hindi expression meaning "Vote for your own" passed into the political vocabularies of Trinidad

(*apan jhaat*), Suriname (*apanjaht*) and Guyana (*appan jaat* or *apanjaht*). In 1958 Chief Minister Eric Williams of Trinidad deplored a letter (possibly spurious) from "Yours Truly, Indian" to "My Dear Indian Brothers," said to have been circulated by partisans of the Indian-dominated Democratic Labor Party. The letter contained "nothing of taxation or Government policy," he noted. It was "sheer race. . . ." In 1961 Janet Jagan, American-born wife of Indo-Guyanese politician Cheddi Jagan, denied a newspaper allegation that she had openly advocated "appan jaat." Her husband blamed "Indian racist leaders" for "originat[ing]" the term.

Indian nationalism became entrenched in Trinidad politics with the appearance of the People's Democratic Party (PDP) to contest the 1956 elections. Bhadase Sagan Maraj doubled as leader of the major Hindu organization, the Sanatan Dharma Maha Sabha, and the new party. The result was a party that was perhaps closer to Hindu communal association than orthodox political party. It lacked the basic political structures (party groups, a constitution, etc.) and relied instead on pundits, prayer meetings and the like to spread a political message clothed in the authority of religious and racial sanctions.

The PDP's offspring, the Democratic Labor Party (DLP), inherited the mantle of an Indian party, though with an infusion of multiracial appointees imposed from the top of its still haphazard party structure. Some Indo-Trinidadian intellectuals were among the critics of the communalization of Trinidad Indian politics. "It was a great pity," they wrote of the DLP, "that the broader, national issues were not emphasized as against the narrow racial problems." On the PDP/DLP continuum of the 1950s and 1960s they observed:

> The link between the Maha Sabha and
> the politicians ensured a pre-occupation
> with the cultural concerns of one racial
> grouping and discouraged the mass of
> East Indians from looking critically at
> the society and their leaders. A leader
> was judged by his ability to erect
> temples or chant the rudiments of Hindi.
> His ability to discuss the problems of

an emergent country was hardly even considered.

The communalization of Indian politics in Trinidad was heightened with the rise of Eric Williams and his People's National Movement (PNM) in 1956. Williams was heir to a hundred years of African struggle at the center of Trinidad politics. Africans inevitably predominated in the PNM's hierarchy and membership. Williams' gifted leadership unleashed the pent-up African nationalist fervor of decades, as British colonialism seemed headed for certain demise. Yet the PNM was never a narrowly communal party, in the manner of the PDP and the DLP. It aspired to be a genuine national party reflective of its multiracial society.

For H. P. Singh in 1956, "A vote for a PNM candidate [would be] a vote against the Indian community. . . ." And PNM rule meant, in the words of a Singh disciple, "racist black fascist neo-colonial domination." Singh was an executive member of the DLP but chafed at the efforts of its leaders to impose a multiracial executive on its Hindu base. He insisted on a totally "Indian organization—call it a political party if you will. . . . We are conscious of the full implications of the advocacy of such a measure. . . ." It was to this end that he formed the small Indian Association of Trinidad and Tobago in 1962.

Criticism of this nature, compounded by a PNM defeat at the federal elections of 1958, caused Williams to call the Hindu-based DLP a " 'recalcitrant and hostile minority'. . . masquerading as the Indian Nation and prostituting the name of India 'for its selfish and reactionary political ends.'" In India itself, Williams showed, the Trinidad Maha Sabha's namesake had been denounced by Prime Minister Jawaharlal Nehru as representing "small upper class reactionary groups taking advantage of the religious passions of the masses. . . ."

The historic quest for Indian communalism has sometimes led to extremist demands for partition and/or secession. In the 1940s and 1950s there were calls for a Guyana–Trinidad unification, to constitute an "East Indian Empire." Trinidad's Indian Association in its 1962 preindependence memorandum to the British government demanded "parity" (defined as 50 percent of civil service, police, legislative and other appointments) or "partition," presumably as happened in India/Pakistan.

In the 1980s some Indo-Trinidadians sought entry into Canada as "refugees" from alleged political persecution in Trinidad. Others sought entry into the United States on similar grounds. Such "refugees" may have been among those who constituted themselves into the Indesh Freedom Party in 1990. From Canada they claimed a substantial portion of Trinidad for the establishment of an "Indian homeland."

A coalition of Trinidad-based Indian groups countered with the more grandiose proposal of a federated homeland of Bharatiyadesh/Industan, comprising Trinidad, Guyana and Suriname. Its 1991 "Declaration on the Question of the Creation in the Americas of an Indian Homeland" announced that

> it is only with the creation of
> Bharatiyadesh/Industan can the Indian
> spirit realize its full potential. This
> vision of Bharatiyadesh/Industan is
> latent in the very being of every Indian,
> it has been a persistent and strong desire,
> a longing, a dream—a vision awaiting
> realisation.

Secessionist tendencies in most countries have been accompanied by violence. Indo-Caribbean nationalism has also been characterized by persistent undertones of threatened violence. H. P. Singh saw violence as inevitable where two peoples coexisted in the same space—"one must as a rule become the HAMMER," he warned, "and the other the ANVIL." His disciples in 1993 saw violence as a viable option for attainment of an Indian homeland. If "peaceful constitutional means" proved ineffective, they wrote, "Indians should not hesitate to use militant means for ultimate freedom." In Suriname ethnic tensions peaked in the preindependence early 1970s as Hindustanis and others confronted the Creole-led independence movement with stonings and arson.

As early as 1913, F. E. M. Hosein resorted to ambiguously militaristic metaphors to "play the prophet" and suggest that the "invasion from India" would in time drive the Africans from Trinidad.

Governor G. R. LeHunte rose from the audience in an unusual gesture to object, *inter alia,* to Hosein's use of the terms "invasion" and "master."

During the election campaign of 1964 in Guyana, Afro-Guyanese People's Progressive Party candidate Brindley H. Benn is said to have urged Indians to "sharpen your cutlasses." In Trinidad, DLP leader Rudranath Capildeo in 1961 told an election campaign audience variously estimated at 17,000–35,000 people, "I am asking you to arm yourselves with a weapon in order to take over this country."

It was in Guyana, however, that the potential for violence inherent in the coexisting nationalisms became manifest. Universal adult suffrage in 1953 brought an electoral victory for the People's Progressive Party (PPP), led by the Indian Cheddi Jagan and the African Forbes Burnham. Some see this collaboration as a golden age of interracial cooperation, while others see it as an enlightened effort at the top which did not permeate down through the ranks of the PPP. The British ousted Jagan from government after 133 days for his Marxist rhetoric. Then followed a split in 1955 between Jagan and Burnham. Burnham's PPP faction eventually became the People's National Congress (PNC). The predominantly Indian PPP won elections of 1957 and 1961 with the predominantly African PNC forming the major opposition party. The period 1962–1964 saw interracial violence on a scale hitherto not known in the Anglophone Caribbean. The British government introduced proportional representation in 1964, resulting in a PPP defeat at the polls that year. Some voices could be heard in the period from 1953 to 1964 in favor of partition of the country. It is noteworthy, however, that even in the most perilous times both major parties sought to maintain at least an appearance of interracial cooperation in their respective ranks.

Indo-Caribbeans have at times seen themselves as the Jews of the Caribbean, invoking analogies with Nazi Germany and Palestine. "Hindus are like Jews," Indo-Trinidadian businessman Motilal Moonan told an interviewer, "they have an inner drive to do the best they can. Moreover, in Hinduism it is no sin to be wealthy." For H. P. Singh the analogy had violent implications—"[Trinidad] is Nazi Germany and

the Jews are the Indians." The British Moyne Commission in 1938–1939 had warned against the potentially disastrous consequences of this analogy: "We would avoid any system of sectional quotas which would lead to the deplorable system of 'government by arithmetic,' the adoption of which in Palestine . . . if anything exacerbates communal feelings instead of allaying it." President Janet Jagan, American Jewish leader of Guyana's People's Progressive Party, in 1997 saw the Jewish connection more benignly, as predisposing her to empathy with society's underdogs.

The efforts to reconcile political separatism with a racial modus vivendi have been at their most pragmatic in Suriname, where the three major political parties unabashedly based themselves on the three largest ethnic groups of Hindustanis (Indians), Creoles (primarily Africans, but not including the majority of African Maroons) and Indonesians. (Creole and Hindustani emigrants in Holland even vote for different Dutch parties.) Major efforts at coexistence were directed at building coalition governments rather than forcing integration within each party. At one time in the 1950s and 1960s the Creole and Hindustani parties remained in coalition for fifteen years. The military government's effort (1980–1987) at what one writer called "anti-apanjaht Utopianism" gave way eventually to a resumption of coalition politics.

The tendency to Indian-focused opposition parties in Trinidad and Tobago underwent a monumental shift when the National Alliance for Reconstruction (in power from 1986 to 1981) overwhelmingly ended the thirty-year incumbency of the Peoples National Movement. The traditional Indian-based party, United National Congress (UNC), provided the backbone of this very broad coalition, which was led electorally by an Afro-Trinidadian prime minister, A. N. R. Robinson. The coalition fell apart quickly. The UNC finally became the government in 1995, with the help of the mainly African Tobago-based remnants of the NAR, but the precedent of a broad coalition defeating the all-powerful PNM remained too strong a temptation to ignore. In 2010 a similar broad coalition, the People's Partnership, again dealt a crushing defeat to the PNM. The traditional Indian-based party, UNC, again provided the anchor, but with a more integrated leadership than before, and led by the country's first woman prime minister, Kamla Persad-Bissessar.

The triumph of the People's Partnership sparked hopes among opposition parties in Guyana that something similar might end the incumbency of the Indian based Peoples Progressive Party, in power since 1992. With a much larger ethnic base than similar parties in Trinidad and Tobago or Suriname, the PPP appears unassailable to some. The oft repeated, but until 2010 unanswered question was whether disgruntled Indian supporters of the PPP would cross over or at least abstain from voting, the way the Afro-Trinidadians were thought to have done, to facilitate the Partnership victory.

EUROPEANS

Europeans were among the earliest Emancipation-era immigrants introduced to the British territories. Roberts and Byrne recorded 4,582 European arrivals to the British Caribbean between 1834 and 1845, with 4,087 to Jamaica, 381 to British Guiana and 114 to St. Lucia. Jamaica created a special highland settlement, Seaford, in 1837, for Germans. The hope was that the German buffer would force the Africans down from the cooler areas into the hotter, sugar-growing areas. This would lessen the land available to Africans and force them into sugar labor. Initial high mortality rates among the Germans and desertion of their agricultural communities made Seaford a failed experiment.

White immigration was much more massive in Cuba which, together with other Latin American republics, embarked on large-scale whitening projects in the nineteenth and twentieth centuries. Here the intent was not simply to introduce buffer groups but to overwhelm the black (and where applicable, indigenous) populations with white majorities. A special White Immigration Bureau (*Junta de Inmigración Blanca*) in 1817 provided free land and tax concessions to white immigrants, not unlike the practice in the British colonies. Cuba imported Spaniards and Canary Islanders in the 1830s and 1870s, though liberal José Antonio Sacó preferred "superior" North Europeans. African immigration was banned after Emancipation. Official Cuban censuses of 1817, 1827 and 1846 gave combined black/free colored majorities. In 1862 whites regained their official majority. In 1900, during the American occupation, the state again began subsidizing white immigration. Nearly a million whites entered during the next three decades.

PORTUGUESE

Portuguese immigrants arrived in Trinidad from the Azores in 1834. Most of the later Portuguese immigrants were however not literally from Europe but from Madeira, famine-stricken in the 1840s, off the coast of Northwest Africa. A few came from the Cape Verde islands, off West Africa. As in the case of the Indians and Chinese, most went to British Guiana, making them numerically second only to the Indians. Between 1835 and 1881, according to Roberts and Byrne, British Guiana received 32,216 Portuguese, Antigua 2,527, St. Vincent 2,102, St. Kitts-Nevis 2,085, Trinidad 897, Grenada 601, Jamaica 397 and Dominica 164. A few went to Martinique and Guadeloupe as well. Suriname received 275 by 1855 and a further 205 in the 1860s.

Portuguese came initially as agricultural workers but quickly branched out into retail and other businesses and later into big business as well. Early arrivals to St. Vincent worked under contract for one year, after which they received free land, an allowance and supplies for a limited period. Portuguese indenture also ended early (1858 according to Roberts and Byrne) in British Guiana, with the emphasis on developing them into a free buffer business class (see Chapter 10). Portuguese were primarily Roman Catholics with a few Presbyterian religious refugees to Trinidad.

As with the Chinese, Portuguese immigration continued into the twentieth century. Almost a quarter of the approximately 4,000 who came to Trinidad up to 1975 arrived between 1900 and 1950.

The Portuguese, as primarily relatively poor whites, initially occupied a social position below the established white ruling class. Over time, however, and with white ruling class support and economic success (see Chapter 10) they were able to find a niche somewhere in the higher echelons of the social pyramid.

A large proportion of the community emigrated to North America and the United Kingdom, and in the case of Guyanese, to Trinidad, in the late twentieth century. Much of the population was also miscegenated out of identifiable existence, except for the Portuguese surnames which still proliferate. A few Portuguese personalities became important political figures. These included Albert Gomes, virtual chief minister of Trinidad and Tobago in the early 1950s, Peter D'Aguiar, leader of the United Force in Guyana and political ally of Forbes Burnham and Ralph Gonsalves, elected prime minister of St. Vincent and the Grenadines in 2001.

JEWS

For a brief moment in the late 1930s and early 1940s, Trinidad became an unlikely major refuge for Jews fleeing Nazi Europe. The Dominican Republic also became one of the most important welcoming destinations in the world, as Jews scrambled frantically from the Hitlerian onslaught. The Dominican Republic's safe haven was constructed on the deliberate welcoming policy of dictator Rafael Trujillo. Trinidad became a haven by accident, because its lax immigration policies provided a virtual open door and because colonial unrepresentative government made it impossible for local politicians to control their country's immigration policies.

The United States and Great Britain, traditional friends of world Jewry, both found it inexpedient to relax their immigration procedures to accommodate the large numbers of Jews looking for somewhere to escape to. The Caribbean for a brief and important moment filled the breach. By February 29, 1940, a year after Trinidad's laws were belatedly tightened, 585 Jewish refugees had entered. Thousands more were in various stages of preparing to join them. Some were caught on the high seas desperately trying to beat the ban when the new stringent procedures went into effect in January 1939. Once World War II started in September 1939, those arrivals considered "enemy aliens" were interned at Port of Spain's St. James Barracks.

The Jews happened into Trinidad around the time of the Butler Riots, the country's major labor disturbances to that time. Unemployment was rife and there was considerable agitation against Lebanese and Chinese immigrants, who were seen as unwelcome competition for the already suffering local workers.

As in the case of the Portuguese and some other earlier immigrants, the Jews, too, benefited from economic favors not easily available to local workers and entrepreneurs. Local wholesalers gave them instant credit on arrival. Many Jews joined the Syrians/Lebanese as peddlers selling cloth to housewives out of their suitcases. With the Syrians/Lebanese phenotypically similar to many Jews and engaged in the same peddling business, the terms "Arab" and "Jew" became incongruously synonymous for many Trinidadians. The fact that these Lebanese were mostly Christians rather than Muslims, facilitated Jewish–Lebanese interaction.

Financial assistance came also from the local Jewish Association and from overseas Jewish agencies. One U.S. agency provided the refugees with a revolving fund to set up in business. Trinidad's refugees were allowed to borrow start-up capital from the fund. When their businesses became profitable they repaid the initial seed money into the fund for the next in line to repeat the process. Some Jews defaulted on their loans but the fund on the whole had the desired effect of launching Trinidad's Jews into business at almost no cost, since when the fund became no longer necessary the seed money was returned to the United States. For most of Trinidad's Jews, Trinidad was a temporary stepping stone toward hoped-for-entry into the United States, Canada or elsewhere. Once the war was over, the community declined, eventually by the 1970s to almost nothing.

A sprinkling of other Jews managed to get to other Caribbean territories, including Barbados, Curaçao and Jamaica. In early 1939, 165 would-be refugees on the ship *Koenigstein* were not allowed to land in British Guiana, though 130 were accommodated in 1942. Here, as elsewhere, most left when they obtained alternative havens, primarily in North America.

On May 27, 1939, the Hamburg-Amerika Line ship *St.Louis* arrived in Havana with over 900 Jews who were initially promised but later denied entry. After six fruitless days in Havana the *St. Louis* left and loitered for a few days more between Havana and Miami, which also refused the Jews asylum. The

St. Louis eventually docked in Antwerp, Belgium, from where its passengers were distributed to Belgium, England, France and Holland.

British Guiana, which had earlier absorbed more Indians, post-Emancipation Africans and Portuguese than anywhere else in the British West Indies, came very close to becoming the Palestine of the West. Britain proposed its colony as a Jewish homeland in 1938. The governments of Britain and the United States, together with representatives of organized world Jewry, were in an advanced stage of implementing this proposal when the outbreak of World War II halted their plans. A joint British Guiana Refugee Commission toured the country early in 1939. They pronounced it suitable for 1,000,000 Jewish immigrants, more than triple the existing Guianese population of slightly over 300,000. The commission proposed an immediate pilot scheme of 5,000 carefully selected European Jews. British prime minister Neville Chamberlain promised the fullest possible financial and technical support to ensure the settlement's success. World Jewry would doubtless have significantly supplemented British contributions. The commission proposed splitting the country, with slightly more than half (42,000) of Guyana's 83,000 square miles to go to a new largely autonomous Jewish state. The commissioners noted the vast hydro-electric, agricultural, mineral and other economic possibilities of the proposed Jewish half of British Guiana. Commissioner Dr. Joseph A. Rosen of the American Jewish Joint Distribution Committee noted that Guiana's crown colony government (with no local representative element) made effecting the proposals politically simple.

The British government planned to begin settlement in the fall of 1939, but World War II intervened. If this scheme had gone into effect it would have dwarfed most other nineteenth- and twentieth-century immigrations into the British West Indies, including Indian immigration. It is unlikely that such a relatively wealthy, technologically advanced state, supported by massive economic inflows from the major powers, would not also have developed a military capability far in advance of anything known to the British Caribbean.

A new independent Jewish state or an overwhelmingly Jewish-majority state within British

Guiana's existing borders might well have been the ultimate outcome. British government officials referred to the British Guiana proposal as the new Balfour Declaration. This was in reference to the 1917 letter by British Foreign Secretary Arthur Balfour to Zionist leader Lord Rothschild, pledging British government support for Zionist aspirations for a Jewish homeland in Palestine.

British commitment to the Guiana project encouraged the Netherlands in December 1938 to pledge acceptance of 10,000 Jewish refugees to Suriname and the Dutch East Indies, provided Britain and the United States provided a financial underpinning. This did not materialize.

In 1934 and 1935 the League of Nations had similarly considered but rejected British Guiana as a home for 10,000 Assyrian refugees from Iraq. Like many Lebanese/Syrians of the Caribbean, these Assyrians were Christians. They had been a pro-British element and had served as British mercenaries during the British mandate in Iraq from 1920 to 1932.

While Jewish settlement schemes to British Guiana were not resuscitated after World War II, a new scheme was proposed for neighboring Suriname. The U.S.-based Freeland League for Jewish Territorial Colonization, with $35,000,000 at its disposal, persuaded the Suriname *Staten* (parliament) in 1947 to accept in principle the settlement of up to 30,000 Jews in the Saramacca region (earlier made famous as a theatre of Maroon struggle). The government in Holland preferred to characterize the agreement as a mere preliminary understanding. The *Staten* itself was unable to agree to Jewish requests for autonomy and import tax exemptions for the settlers. Afro-Surinamese Creoles also voiced concern and invoked memories of Jewish enslavers of an earlier time. Conflicts surrounding independence for Israel in 1948 caused Suriname to have further misgivings and helped shift the project to a back burner.

Just as Britain was offering the Jews British Guiana in 1938, President Rafael Trujillo was offering 100,000 Jews a place in the Dominican Republic. He was fresh from his massacre of 35,000 Haitians in 1937. Replacing the African Haitians with white European Jews may have served the dual purpose of taking attention away from the massacre while simultaneously whitening the population. Between 1940 and 1945 the Dominicans issued 5,000 visas to Jews but only 645 actually settled, in the seaside agricultural town of Sosua. Each Jewish settler was given 80 acres, 10 cows, 1 mule and a horse. As elsewhere, most of the Jews later moved on, mostly to the United States. Those who stayed received an enormous bonanza when the Sosua area became a tourist destination in the 1980s. Their real estate grants made some of them the wealthiest persons in the area.

OTHERS

Javanese from Dutch Indonesia were a very important part of the Surinamese immigration landscape, with 32,976 arriving between 1890 and 1931. Over 20 percent returned to Indonesia before World War II. A further 1,000 returned in 1954. Some 20,000 emigrated to the Netherlands before independence in 1975. As of the 2004 census the Javanese were officially the fourth largest ethnic group in Suriname, after the Hindustanis (Indians), Afro-Surinamese and Maroons.

About 210 Mayans were brought to Cuba in 1849. Another 2,000 were brought in between 1849 and 1861. Twelve Maldive Islanders arrived in British Guiana in 1862. The French brought 272 of their colonized Vietnamese to Guadeloupe in the late nineteenth century. Five hundred Japanese entered Guadeloupe in 1894. A few hundred black Portuguese from Cape Verde came to Trinidad in the mid-nineteenth century.

LEBANESE-SYRIANS

The Lebanese-Syrian community in the Caribbean also includes some Palestinians. They are sometimes designated Levantines or Arabs, though some Lebanese (the majority component) have argued that they are not Arabs, but descendants of Phoenicians. The Lebanese-Syrians have become, all over the Caribbean, a numerically small but economically powerful group. Political, economic and religious problems at home fueled successive waves of emigration, beginning in the late nineteenth century. The result was a large Diaspora spread all over the world.

Over 105,000 entered the United States, Latin America and the Caribbean between 1880 and 1914. In the Caribbean these and later arrivals went to Cuba, Haiti, the Dominican Republic, Jamaica, Trinidad, Dominica, St. Lucia, British Guiana and elsewhere. Most were Greek Orthodox, Maronite or Melkite Christians. The latter two faiths were in communion with the Roman Catholic Church, making it easy for immigrants to adopt Catholicism in their new environments. Some were Sunni Muslims. Ironically, some Palestinians came in the 1940s as refugees from the Jewish conquest of Palestine, a few short years after many Jews sought refuge in the Caribbean from Hitlerian Europe.

Between 500 and 15,000 Lebanese-Syrians had arrived in Haiti by 1914. About 2,000–3,000 were estimated there in 1980. About 100 families were in Trinidad before World War I, with many more coming in the 1920s and 1930s. Trinidad's 1960 census listed 1,591, with almost half in Port of Spain. About 10,000 were in Cuba by 1920. The 1920 census in the Dominican Republic reported 1,187 Levantines.

Most of the early immigrants were Turkish nationals and citizens of the Ottoman Empire, which troops of the British West Indies Regiment helped conquer for the Allies during World War I. They started everywhere as peddlers, selling fabric and other wares house to house to housewives. They penetrated rural areas where there was little competition. They were initially widely disliked and accused of usury. Several Caribbean territories tried to restrict their presence or deport them. (Australia, Canada, the United States and Ivory Coast made similar efforts. There were anti-Lebanese riots in Sierra Leone in 1919.)

Haiti tried several times from 1904 to restrict Lebanese influence. By this time the Lebanese-Syrians were controlling most of the trade with peasants and the urban poor. They had supplanted indigenous commercial elites and the European firms which were entrenched in Haiti. In 1903 there were anti-Syrian riots. *L'Anti-Syrien (The Anti-Syrien)* newspaper appeared. The French promised a gunboat to assist them and the U.S. embassy gave assurances of assistance. In 1904 Haiti tried to restrict their trading activities and access to Haitian citizenship. A Haitian law of 1905 sought, in response to a widespread Lebanese-Syrian scam, to expel all Lebanese-Syrians who had illegally falsified naturalization papers. Hundreds left though many returned later.

In Haiti the Levantines benefited from a high level of U.S. protection, which often blunted Haitian efforts to move against them. The United States found in the Levantines a useful tool to introduce American commercial interests and extend the reach of the Monroe Doctrine. The Lebanese-Syrians imported mostly American goods, making them valuable proxies for U.S. penetration. During the U.S. occupation of Haiti (1915–1934), the occupation regime gave the Levantines preferential treatment which ensured their increased prosperity. The Lebanese eventually found favor with President François Duvalier (1957–1971), Haiti's longest-serving president of the twentieth century. In 1920 there were unsuccessful governmental attempts to expel the Lebanese from the Dominican Republic. Like Haiti, the DR was by this time under U.S. occupation and therefore constricted in its ability to implement policies.

Local labor leaders and politicians, including Captain A. A. Cipriani, pressured the Trinidad government into passing an Immigration (Restriction) Ordinance, No. 4 of 1936 in an unsuccessful attempt to stem the influx of Chinese and Lebanese-Syrian immigrants. Local labor was in the throes of great distress brought on by the Great Depression and workers' leaders resented the activity of Lebanese peddlers targeting the poorest consumers with their easy credit and high interest rates.

The Lebanese-Syrians were also seen as among the major beneficiaries of the Shop Closing Ordinance, proposed in 1936 in the midst of this new immigration and passed into law in 1938. The Shop Closing Ordinance, in the tradition of the pro-Portuguese economic measures in nineteenth-century British Guiana and similar measures elsewhere, sought to eliminate the still substantial Afro-Trinidadian presence in the small retail sector in Trinidad's downtown areas. The large retail establishments, dominated (but not monopolized) by white merchants, closed at 4 PM. Smaller stores, as in many countries, stayed open later and were able to attract the custom of working-class people who shopped after work. The new ordinance compelled

the small merchants to close at the same time as the big establishments. There was a widespread, but in the end unsuccessful campaign against the new ordinance. Bukka Rennie has argued that this ordinance sounded the death knell for the black-dominated small retail sector in downtown Port of Spain. These businesses increasingly passed into the ownership of Lebanese, Chinese and Jews.

Like successful business elites of other ethnic groups, the Lebanese were able to use their initial profits to diversify into a wide array of businesses of varying size. They remained probably the most endogamous of Caribbean ethnic groups, though the degree of marital exclusivism varied. Wives were sometimes imported from ancestral home districts. In the Dominican Republic they were less ethnically reclusive than in Trinidad, Jamaica and other places. In Jamaica they were less socially exclusive than in Trinidad. When David Nicholls published his study of the Trinidad Lebanese in 1981 he found very few exogamous marriages, and those only to light-skinned spouses. Marriage between first and second cousins greatly exceeded marriage with community outsiders.

There was an early Syrian residential district in Haiti. In Trinidad the Levantines have tended to cluster together in what by at least the 1950s would have been middle- or upper-class neighborhoods. As time went on some entered the professions. They reached out to their host cultures only late in the twentieth century, with the appearance, for example, of a Lebanese calypsonian or two in Trinidad.

Lebanese have often been amalgamated with Jews in the popular Caribbean imagination. The fifty or so Jewish families in Haiti to the end of World War II were entwined into the Lebanese-Syrian group. The vice president of Haiti's Syrian Commercial Club in 1920 was a Jew. In Trinidad until at least the 1950s the terms "Arab" and "Jew" were used interchangeably. The British-American-Jewish proposal in 1939 to settle 1,000,000 Jews in British Guiana was preceded in 1935 by a League of Nations commission to study the country as a possible refuge for Assyrians from Iraq.

By the later twentieth century the Lebanese were ready to leverage their great economic power into forays into politics. In 1950 Trinidad's British governor appointed the half-Lebanese, Roy Joseph, former mayor of San Fernando, as minister of education. In the Dominican Republic Jacobo Majluta served as vice president under President Antonio Guzman from 1978 to 1982. He was president for 43 days in 1982 after the death of Guzman. In 1986 Majluta lost the presidential election to Joachin Balaguer, after defeating Jose Francisco Pena Gomez, the DR's first fully black major political figure, for his Dominican Revolutionary Party (PRD's) presidential nomination.

In Haiti in 1993 Robert Malval, a protégé of Jean-Bertrand Aristide, served as interim prime minister. Edward Seaga, grandson of a Lebanese store owner, was prime minister of Jamaica from 1980 to 1989. From the 1960s in Trinidad, a succession of Lebanese have participated actively in politics, holding ministerial posts and the mayoralty of Port of Spain.

COMPARATIVE IMMIGRATIONS

Nineteenth- and twentieth-century immigrants obviously came over in conditions less severe than the horrors of African enslavement. It is nevertheless possible to identify several similarities (and differences) both among the various new waves of immigration and between the new immigrations, the African slave trade and other earlier immigrations. Though the new immigration was mostly voluntary, the push factors driving emigrants to leave home sometimes approximated coercion. Famine and wars in China and India forced many to seek emigration as almost a necessity. A preponderance of the Indians who came from the 1830s to the mid-1850s were low-caste Hindus, non-Hindu aboriginal peoples ("Hill Coolies"), Madrasi vagrants and Untouchables (now called Dalits), many of them coming from conditions of near slavery. Many of the Untouchables came from a state of real slavery, as that term is understood in relation to the African slave trade. An Indian slave trade had long sold Untouchables to such places as Mauritius, Reunion and Malaya. When Indian immigration was initially terminated in 1839 after the first arrivals in Guyana, it was the British Anti-Slavery Society which spearheaded the campaign. The abuses revealed by the

Anti-Slavery Society were reminiscent of African slavery—brutal floggings followed by the rubbing of salt in the wounds of the Indians, for example. The abuse of African women during the Middle Passage was apparently also not unknown on the Indian immigrant ships. Verene Shepherd has documented the case of Maharani, a young Indian woman who died on board ship in 1885 on her way to British Guiana, apparently the victim of a brutal rape by two British sailors.

Near-slavery conditions in some parts of China were revealed in the use of the term "barracoon" (previously used on the west coast of Africa) for holding areas among the Macao emigrants. Indian immigrants sometimes inherited the plantation quarters left behind by the emancipated Africans. Chinese and Indian indentured laborers were subject to pass laws restricting their mobility away from the plantations. This was reminiscent of slavery, except that for the Africans the pass laws were a lifelong curfew, rather than a temporary inconvenience.

Africans developed feelings of quasi-family among those transported on the same ships. These relationships could be long-lasting, though even this new form of "family" was often torn asunder at the auction block on arrival in the Caribbean. Other immigrants undoubtedly developed similar bonds on the long sea voyages over. The Indians were fortunate enough to have these relationships actually encouraged by the British authorities, giving rise to the concept of *jahajibhai*, shipmates who were often encouraged to settle in the same areas on arrival.

The people-stealing crimps of China had their counterparts in India, as they did in the European kidnappers of poor white indentured servants before them. British body snatchers "barbadoed" their poor white brothers and sisters in the seventeenth century as their Chinese counterparts "shanghaied" their own compatriots in the nineteenth. Even in the African slave trade, which was a case of wholesale kidnapping, there were cases of free people, sometimes slave-sellers themselves, being kidnapped and shipped along with the captives they had come to deliver to double-crossing Europeans.

The Chinese came closest to the Africans in their shipboard rebelliousness. Their willingness to kill white captains and crews and the horrendous losses they sometimes suffered in the course of revolts and maritime calamities most nearly approximated the Middle Passage experience of the Africans.

For most of the emigrants the push factors of destitution and famine ensured a fair proportion of the worst off of the exporting societies. The Europeans, from the fifteenth century, had deliberately sent over a large proportion of their worst elements. Chinese governments tried, not always successfully, to prevent criminals avoiding punishment via emigration. The African slave trade distorted the definitions of "criminal" to provide fodder for the trade and then sentenced the newly defined criminals to enslavement overseas. The early Indians included a large proportion of the enslaved, Untouchables and vagrants. Look Lai quoted Dr. Bunyun of the Colonial Land and Emigration Commissioners using language similar to that of William Sewell in describing Madrasi immigrants in an 1848 report on British Guiana—they were "extremely filthy . . . eating every species of garbage, even to the extent of picking up the putrid bodies of animals from the nearest trenches, cooking them and eating them mixed with curry."

The chronic shortage of women also existed across immigrations. It was a feature of early immigration of the white Spanish conquerors. They and their European successors, unlike many later immigrants, were strong enough to simply commandeer the indigenous women and, later, the enslaved African women. Many of the enslaved Africans had to do without women, or, as Esteban Montejo suggested for Cuba, resort to homosexuality, however much the African elders frowned on the practice. The Chinese simply married or lived with the African (and sometimes other) women.

The woman-short Indians developed wife-killing and mutilation into their community's signature crime. Various authors have quantified this crime—all twenty-seven murders committed by Trinidad Indians between 1859 and 1863 were killings of wives or partners; in British Guiana between 1895 and 1900 thirty-three of the forty murders of Indian women were wife killings; sixty-five of the eighty-seven Indian women murdered

between 1872 and 1900 in Trinidad met death at the hands of their husbands. Wife killing was also rife in Suriname. John Edward Jenkins in *The Coolie: His Rights and Wrongs* (1871) reported seven Indians in British Guiana hanged in a single week for wife murder. " In one case," he reported, "I saw a Coolie come to [Magistrate] Des Voeux with his wife, a fine-looking girl, who stood meekly by his side while he expressed a resolution to 'chop her up'— the favourite method among these people of abolishing matrimonial inconveniences, the cutlass being a handy weapon."

Judith Ann Weller has noted that wife-killing figures may have been understated, since only cases of judicial convictions entered the statistics and convictions were difficult to obtain. All of the killings appear to have been perpetrated by Hindus.

European authorities were alarmed by wife-killing, not least because the practice might discourage further potential immigrants. They debated whether the practice was even a peculiarly immigrant problem, since some considered wife-killing to be a long-standing problem in India itself. In 1863 in British Guiana authorities sent out circulars promising the gallows for wife murderers. In 1865 the Colonial Office enjoined estate officials to preemptively notify authorities at signs of potential violence. Stipendiary magistrates were empowered to relocate one or both spouses at signs of impending mayhem. Various complexities arose, however, such as the reluctance of some magistrates to separate husband and wife except as a last resort. Also, when the wife-stealer was a free Indian, removing the object of his affection would not prevent him from himself relocating to wherever she was sent. There was also the case, reported by Jenkins, where one Nobeebuxus came to Guiana with his wife, Astoreah. She left him after a year for Maighoo. Seven years later she returned to Nobeebuxus, only to have Maighoo the outside man threaten to kill her for returning to her husband.

Laws were introduced imposing fines on immigrants seducing others' wives, though there were no penalties for errant wives or for husbands who deserted their wives. Some officials suggested an annual flogging, spread over several years, combined with life imprisonment, as an alternative to hanging for wife murder. These felt that flogging was more of a deterrent to Indians than the gallows. Shaving the heads of errant women was also proposed. Both ideas were voted down.

Magistrates also dealt with the occasional case of Chinese infidelity, such as where Chee Shee abandoned her husband, Woo-a-lee, in the 1860s in favor of Chin-a-foo. Chee Shee absolutely refused to return to her marital abode, Woo-a-lee's threats of suicide notwithstanding. So the magistrate favored transferring Chin-a-foo, preferring to maintain the marriage at all costs.

In trying to stamp out Indian wife-killing, British officials were perhaps inadvertently illustrating the paradox of British rule posed by Karl Marx in his contemporary (1853) essay on "The British Rule in India." Traditional Indian culture, Marx argued, included slavery and caste and "rendered murder itself a religious rite in Hindostan." It was true, he said, that England, "in causing a social revolution in Hindostan, was actuated only by the vilest interests, and was stupid in her manner of enforcing them." The central reality nevertheless remained for Marx the fact that "whatever may have been the crimes of England she was the unconscious tool of history" in rooting out unacceptable cultural practices.

Polyandry also became common in Indian immigrant communities, probably inevitable due to the great resistance to exogamy among male Indians. Women were known to have more than one husband and to be unfaithful to all. Women had serial relationships with several men, one after the other, after which they might return to the original partner. It was a sort of female equivalent of the male "visiting" relationships described by sociologists for Afro-Caribbean families.

The demographic sexual imbalance was responsible for marked declines in the populations of Africans and Chinese in various parts of the New World after the cessation of their respective immigrations. The African populations in the Caribbean eventually stabilized but suffered large losses due to emigration. New free postindenture Chinese immigration and absorption of half-Chinese into the Chinese community eventually normalized the sexual balance for Chinese. Despite the shortage of Indian women up to the end of indenture, Indians in

Trinidad, Guyana and Suriname nevertheless continued to outstrip other groups in their rate of demographic advance. One reason was the sheer magnitude of Indian immigration. Additionally, the shortage of Indian women was not as severe as for Chinese. Also, by the end of indenture more women were being brought in than hitherto.

One important demographic advantage enjoyed by the Indians was the near-universal practice of child marriages. Parentally arranged marriage of girls from as young as ten was the norm until well into the twentieth century. This practice was rooted in Indian custom. It was exacerbated in the Caribbean by the eagerness of parents to capitalize on the shortage of women, by exacting bride price from prospective husbands.

The Trinidad-based Presbyterian missionary Sarah Morton reported a case of a father selling his daughter into marriage nine times to pocket the multiple bride prices. In each case he refused to deliver up the child and sold her again. Basdeo Mangru reports one British Guiana immigrant selling his three daughters for a handsome profit, which allowed him to retire to India with over 1,000 pounds and jewelry. Fifty-year-old Guianese Seecharan received eleven-year-old Etwarea in marriage in exchange for a cow, a calf, $50 cash and a will naming his young wife and their expected progeny his sole heirs. When, at age sixteen, she showed some susceptibility to extramarital temptations, he chopped off her right hand with a cutlass. She died. He went to the gallows.

Child marriages also provided a hedge against miscegenation and secured culturally desirable virgin brides. Mangru quoted a Colonial Office official explaining in 1887 that Guianese parents "laboriously enlarge the private parts of the poor child by mechanical means until she is ready for the aged purchaser." Even where these prepuberty brides did not consummate their marriages immediately, by the time they did they would typically have been several years younger than first-time mothers of other communities, thus encouraging a high rate of Indian fecundity. In fact, Indian girls were routinely and legally mothers at ages which would have landed fathers from other communities in jail for statutory rape.

Indian traditional marriages were countenanced by various immigration ordinances but required further civil registration to come within the full purview of divorce, bigamy and other legal provisions. Until well into the twentieth century, most Indians refused to register their marriages. This gave them the freedom to terminate marriages, enter into new arrangements and receive more bride price without the encumbrance of divorce, bigamy and similar sanctions.

This began to change in the 1930s, with the introduction of Indian marriage laws. These brought ceremonies officiated by Muslim and Hindu marriage officers within the purview of the general civil laws, without the necessity for further registration. Trinidad's Muslim Marriage and Divorce Act of 1936 fixed the legal marriageable age for Muslims at sixteen for boys and twelve for girls. Trinidad's Hindu Marriage Act of 1946 set the ages at eighteen for males and fourteen for females. Jamaica's Hindu Marriage Act of 1957 set the ages at sixteen for both sexes. British Guiana set the ages at sixteen for males and fourteen for females. Suriname introduced an Asiatic Marriage Decree in 1940.

Very interestingly for the subject peoples, it was the Africans, who came over in the worst conditions and continued therein until at least Emancipation, who documented their own experiences on the way over and during enslavement. The Chinese and Indians produced nothing comparable to the slave narratives of the Africans. It was well into the twentieth century before any Indian or Chinese works appeared documenting for themselves their immigrant experiences. Firsthand accounts of the Indian and Chinese shipboard experience and their accommodation to the New World were all written by Europeans—ship's surgeons, missionaries and the like.

All immigrants maintained a soft spot for their respective homelands. They all brought with them the memory and continued practice of aspects of their home cultures. This might be culinary practices for all groups, or agricultural methods, or musical styles. Chinese and Lebanese sent home for brides. Indian repatriation was long facilitated by contractually guaranteed free return passages. Chinese, for the most part not similarly favored, nevertheless sometimes returned home, even on occasion sending their children to China for schooling.

Africans, in pioneering the Pan-African movement, carried the connection with home to a higher level than any other groups. They relocated to Africa in large numbers, especially after Emancipation. Many who went back had lived in the Caribbean for generations. Whether in Africa itself or from their homes in the Diaspora, they inserted themselves prominently into the African struggle against colonialism. Edward Wilmot Blyden of St. Thomas became Liberian ambassador to Great Britain. Arthur Barclay of Barbados became president of Liberia. A. S. Shackleford of Jamaica dominated the market for bread in Nigeria and Ghana. Frantz Fanon of Martinique became a leader of the Algerian revolution. George Padmore of Trinidad was adviser on African affairs to President Kwame Nkrumah of Ghana. Marcus Garvey of Jamaica had a profound impact on Africa, acknowledged universally on the continent, even without ever setting foot there.

By contrast the Indians brought over missionaries from India and sought to steep themselves as far as they could in the Indian culture they nostalgically remembered. They did not intervene in political affairs in India as the Pan-African movement did in Africa, though they celebrated the triumphs of Indian nationalism against European colonialism.

Here, as elsewhere, the Chinese experience more closely approximated that of the Africans. Eugene Chen, Trinidad's first Chinese solicitor (lawyer), husband of a colored Trinidadian woman and later four-time foreign minister of China, easily fit into the Pan-African mould. Chen studied law in Trinidad and was "articled" (apprenticed) for five years to Edgar Maresse-Smith, a veteran anticolonial radical, a Pan-Africanist and a leader of the Trinidad branch of Henry Sylvester Williams' Pan-African Association (see Chapter 12). Chen (under his earlier name of E. Bernard Acham) was very much a part of this radical milieu. In 1904 he delivered a paper on "Trinidad and Reform," critical of Acting Colonial Secretary Hugh Clifford. This was a year after Maresse-Smith played a leading role in instigating the Water Riots of 1903. Chen's younger brother, David Acham Chen, was also a solicitor. David served in the Port of Spain City Council in the 1920s, together with M'Zumbo Lazare, former head of the Trindad Pan-African Association. It is impossible to escape the speculation that Chen's exposure to Pan-Africanism and Trinidad's anticolonial politics must have influenced his own Chinese nationalism. Chen's children Percy and Sylvia followed their father to China. Percy Chen's autobiography was appropriately entitled *China Called Me*.

Further Readings

Brereton, Bridget. *Race Relations in Colonial Trinidad, 1870–1900*. New York: Cambridge University Press, 1979.

Chen, Percy. *China Called Me: My Life Inside the Chinese Revolution*. Boston: Little Brown Company, 1979.

Clementi, Cecil. *The Chinese in British Guiana*. Georgetown: The Argosy Company, 1915. Reprinted by Caribbean Press, Georgetown, 2010.

"Gandhi and the Immigration Proposals," http://www.guyana.org/features/guyanastory/chapter98.html [accessed December 4, 2010].

Higman, Barry W. "The Chinese in Trinidad, 1806–1838." *Caribbean Studies,* 12, 3, October 1972, 21–44.

Hira, Sandew. "The Evolution of the Social, Economic and Political Position of the East Indians in Suriname, 1873–1983," in David Dabydeen and Brinsley Samaroo, Eds., *India in the Caribbean*. Hertford: Hansib, 1987.

Hoefte, Rosemarijn. "The Javanese of Suriname." *Inside Indonesia,* 102, October–December 2010. http://www.insideindonesia.org/edition-92/the-javanese-of-suriname [accessed December 5, 2010].

Hosein, Shaheeda. "'Until Death Do Us Part?' Marriage, Divorce and the Indian Woman in Trinidad." *Oral History*, 30, 1, Spring 2002, pp. 63–72.

Jenkins, John Edward. *The Coolie: His Rights and Wrongs*. N.p.: The Caribbean Press, 2010. First pub. 1871.

Laurence, Keith O. *Immigration into the West Indies in the 19th Century*. Aylesbury, Bucks: Caribbean Universities Press, 1971.

Look Lai, Walton. *Indentured Labor, Caribbean Sugar: Chinese and Indian Migrants to the British West Indies, 1838–1918*. Baltimore: The Johns Hopkins University Press, 1993.

Look Lai, Walton. *The Chinese in the West Indies, 1806–1995: A Documentary History*. Kingston: The Press, University of the Wrest Indies, 1998.

Mangru, Basdeo. "The Sex Ratio Disparity and its Consequences under the Indenture in British Guiana," in David Dabydeen and Brinsley Samaroo, Eds., *India in the Caribbean*. Hertford: Hansib, 1987.

Martin, Tony. "Jews to Trinidad." *Journal of Caribbean History*, XXVIII, 2, 1994, pp. 244–257.

Martin, Tony. "African and Indian Consciousness in the 20th Century," in Bridget Brereton, Ed., *UNESCO General History of the Caribbean*, Vol. 5. London: Macmillan and Paris: UNESCO, 2003, pp. 224–281.

Morgenstern, Aryeh, and Mordecai Arbell. "Guiana," in Michael Berenbaum and Fred Skolnik, Eds., *Encyclopaedia Judaica*. Detroit, MI: Macmillan Reference USA, 2007.

Nicholls, David. "No Hawkers and Peddlers: Levantines in the Caribbean." *Ethnic & Racial Studies*, 4, 4, October 1981 pp. 415–431.

Plummer, Brenda Gayle. "Race, Nationality, and Trade in the Caribbean: The Syrians in Haiti, 1903–1934." *The International History Review*, 3, 4, October 1981, pp. 517–539.

Reddock, Rhoda E. "Freedom Denied: Indian Women and Indentureship in Trinidad and Tobago, 1845–1917." *Economic and Political Weekly*, 20, 43, October 1985, pp. 109–133.

Reddock, Rhoda E. *Women, Labour and Politics in Trinidad and Tobago: A History*. Kingston: Ian Randle Publishers, 1994.

Rennie, A. Bukka. *The History of the Working-Class in Trinidad & Tobago, in the 20th Century (1919–1956)*. 2nd ed. Port of Spain: The Majority Press, 2011.

Roberts, George W., and Joycelyn Byrne. "Summary Statistics on Indenture and Associated Migration Affecting the West Indies, 1834–1918." *Population Studies*, 20, 1, July 1966.

Sewell, William G. *The Ordeal of Free Labor in the British West Indies*. New York: Augustus M. Kelley, Bookseller, 1968. First pub. 1861.

Shepherd, Verene A. *Transients to Settlers: The Experience of Indians in Jamaica, 1845–1950*. Leeds: Peepal Tree/University of Warwick, 1994.

Speckmann, Johan D. "The Indian Group in the Segmented Society of Surinam." *Caribbean Studies*, 3, 1, April 1963.

12

The Caribbean and Africa Through the Early Twentieth Century

Mr. H.O. Beresford Wooding, President of the Union of Students of African Descent of Great Britain, was appointed an honorary member of the [West African Students' Union] . . . for though a West Indian by birth, he has shown such widespread interest in general Negro questions—African and other—that most of us have come to regard him as a man of exceptional value—an agboni agba—for the whole Negro race. . . .

—WASU magazine, 1927

During enslavement there were many manifestations of African consciousness in the Caribbean. Maroon communities, for example, recreated the African environment through language, religion, architecture, military practice, social organization and in other ways. But this is not surprising, for many of the Maroons were born in Africa.

As time went on and increasing numbers of Africans were born in the Caribbean, that desire to reunite with Africa did not disappear. Songs of the enslaved, sometimes with lyrics couched in religious language, expressed a desire to go back to Africa. Some Africans went so far as to commit suicide in the hope and expectation that having departed this life, their spirits would reunite with their ancestors in the African homeland.

Revolutionary Africans often had the idea of Africa not very far from their activities. No sooner had Toussaint L'Ouverture vanquished his European adversaries and imposed his will on revolutionary Haiti than he turned his thoughts to Africa. He made elaborate plans for leading a military expedition to West Africa to end the slave trade at its source.

In 1800 some 500 deported Jamaican Trelawney Maroons were shipped from Nova Scotia to Sierra Leone at their own request. The Amistad mutineers in Cuba in 1839 ultimately returned to Africa after their court trials in the United States. The Daaga mutineers of Trinidad in 1837 likewise tried to get back to Africa.

Once slavery ended, the thoughts of thousands of the formerly enslaved turned to the question of how they could reconnect to Africa. For some it was literally a desire to go back home. For others, including some who were already free before Emancipation, there was an urge to impart some of the knowledge which they had gained in the West. There was a sense of needing to help Africa, still ravaged by the slave trade and its aftereffects. Out of evil cometh good, they said, and the evil of enslavement had made possible learned, energetic pioneers from the West who were ready to make a contribution to their fatherland. The Rev. Alexander Crummell, prominent African American missionary to Liberia, writing in the *African Repository*, organ of the American Colonization Society in 1868, praised the arrival in Liberia in 1865 of 346 emigrants from Barbados. "Whose work is this?" he asked. "Who has prompted this movement of Christian black men from Barbados, back to the land of their ancestors; laden with gifts, and talents; sanctified, as numbers of them are, by the spirit of grace?" The answer was clear. "Who but God himself. . . ."

Some Caribbean Christian missionaries were among the early returnees to Africa after Emancipation. White missionaries in Africa often had a reputation for being accomplices to European colonialism and conquest. Black missionaries, from colonized societies themselves, were less likely to see themselves as part of the European colonizing mission. Sometimes they were active agents of resistance to European imperial penetration. Black missionaries, Caribbean and African American, sometimes found themselves drawn into conflict with their white counterparts. Black missionaries went to Africa both under the auspices of white missionary societies and independent of white sponsorship. White missionary bodies eventually saw black missionaries as a positive hindrance and tried to prevent or restrict their entry into Africa. An international missionary conference meeting in Le Zoute, Belgium, in 1926 actually passed resolutions attempting to prevent the entry into Africa of black missionaries, except for those traveling under white supervision. By this time the European "scramble for Africa" was virtually complete and white missionaries were in a position to encourage their home governments to implement their requests.

One of the earliest groups of Caribbean missionaries to Africa was the West Indian Church Association out of Codrington College in Barbados. Codrington College, the oldest Anglican theological college anywhere, occupies a unique place in the history of higher education in the Caribbean. It was funded by a bequest from Christopher Codrington, a Barbadian English plantation owner and sometime governor-general of the Leeward Islands who died in 1710. The college opened in 1745. Beginning in the 1850s these Codrington graduates, some from other Caribbean colonies as well, worked in the Rio Pongo, in modern Guinea.

One of the outstanding persons who joined the missionary trek to Africa was Edward Wilmot Blyden. Blyden left his home in St. Thomas in 1850 and went to the United States. There he tried to enroll in a theological seminary, but he was refused on account of his color. This ended his hoped-for missionary career, but he nevertheless left immediately, in 1850, for Liberia. He later became one of the most outstanding Pan-African intellectuals of the nineteenth and early twentieth centuries. He had a very great influence on two or three generations of African intellectuals and one of the most important persons who Blyden influenced was Marcus Garvey.

In Trinidad in the 1830s there was a group of Mandingoes who made strenuous efforts to get back to their home in the Gambia. One of them, Mohammedu Sisei, a Muslim, succeeded. In Cuba around the turn of the twentieth century several thousand Africans from the Congo organized in an effort to return home. A few succeeded.

During this period Caribbean people were already beginning to emigrate to the United States. Several of the African Americans who distinguished themselves in this Pan-African quest for an African connection were in fact people born in the Caribbean. One such was John B. Russwurm, the Jamaican who cofounded the first African American newspaper, *Freedom's Journal,* in New York in 1827. Russwurm emigrated from the United States to Liberia in 1829. There he published the first English-language newspaper in West Africa, the *Liberian Herald.* He later became governor of Maryland, later incorporated into Liberia.

In 1859 another Jamaican, Robert Campbell, a chemistry teacher at the prestigious Institute for Colored Youth in Philadelphia, joined the African American Martin R. Delany in a two-man Niger Valley Exploration Mission. Campbell was the son of a colored woman and a Scottish father. He and

Delany went to Abeokuta in modern Nigeria. Their idea was to settle there and encourage Africans from the Diaspora to come back home. This mission failed, partly due to opposition by the British who were then establishing themselves in Nigeria, and partly because of the onset of the U.S. Civil War. But Robert Campbell, his wife, and four children settled in Lagos, Nigeria, in 1862. There he became a well-known and distinguished member of the community. Like Russwurm, he published a newspaper, *The Anglo-African*, which appeared in Lagos from 1863 to 1865. One of the Barbadians who emigrated to Liberia in 1865, Arthur Barclay, became president of the republic from 1904 to 1912. His son, Edwin Barclay, was secretary of state and later president from 1930 to 1944.

In the late nineteenth century there emerged in the Caribbean, Europe and African America the first generation to self-consciously describe themselves as Pan-Africanists. The first post-Emancipation African-conscious activists were primarily interested in going back to live, to teach, to help, to contribute. In the case of the pioneer Pan-Africanists, however, even though some of them did go back to live, this was not their primary aim. Their primary aim was to develop a worldwide community of African peoples. They were imbued with the idea that Africans, no matter where they lived, were basically one people. Whether they were living in Africa or the Diaspora, Africans had a similar history, similar aspirations and a similar culture.

These early Pan-Africanists were also acutely aware of the fact that Africa was about to be gobbled up by the European "scramble" for the continent. Between 1870 and the First World War of 1914–1918, practically the whole of Africa was conquered by Europe. Even though Europeans had enslaved Africans for over 400 years from the 1440s, most of Africa still remained independent. The European slave traders rarely got much further than certain coastal enclaves. But beginning around 1870 that was to change.

Many of the people who distinguished themselves in this struggle to save Africa from European imperial conquest were from the Caribbean. They included Benito Sylvain, a Haitian who lived in France for many years. In the 1890s Sylvain journeyed to

Ethiopia, where at the Battle of Aduwa in 1896 the Emperor Menelik II had become the only African to inflict a definitive military defeat on the Europeans in the midst of their scramble for Africa. Emperor Menelik made Sylvain an honorary representative of Ethiopia. In 1898 Sylvain founded the Black Youth Association of Paris. In 1900 he was one of the people who participated in the famous first ever Pan-African Conference, organized by Trinidadian law student in London, Henry Sylvester Williams.

Williams, a former primary school teacher in Port of Spain, had travelled in the United States and studied in Canada, from where he proceeded to England to study law. In England in 1897 he founded the African Association. Williams was now living in London at the heart of the British empire and so he was in a very strategic position to lobby on behalf of Africa. He was very concerned about the scramble for Africa in general, but he was especially concerned about South Africa, which, long before the official inception of the white supremacist apartheid policy, was already responsible for some of the worst atrocities in European-controlled Africa.

In London in 1900 Williams convened the Pan-African Conference, in the process providing a name for the African-conscious movement that had gathered momentum since Emancipation. Over thirty prominent men and women got together from the Caribbean, African America, Canada, Europe and Africa. They shared information on the state of the African race in their respective countries. They discussed how they could try to unite the African world to lobby effectively for its interests. They formed a Pan-African Association (PAA) and prepared to begin publication of an organ, *The Pan-African*.

Williams moved rapidly to implant the Pan-African Association in the Caribbean. He toured Trinidad and Jamaica in 1901, lecturing and organizing branches. The quality and enthusiasm of the response in both places attested to the potency of racial consciousness as a mobilizing force in the Caribbean. The Trinidad branch of the PAA was formally established during Williams' visit in early July 1901. Attorney Emmanuel M'Zumbo Lazare was president of the central executive, with Mrs. Philip John as secretary. Lazare's rationale for joining the association may be inferred from his motion carried unanimously at Williams' first Port of Spain lecture, to a crowd of over 1,000 persons. "The meeting assembled here," he moved, "appreciates the successful efforts made by the Pan-African Association in London to ameliorate the condition of our oppressed brethren in Africa, and is of the opinion that the organization should be strongly supported by members of the race in this island." Lazare had actually collaborated with Williams in London in 1897 on the launch of the African Association.

For Lazare, as for his middle-class African-conscious contemporaries, the struggle at home (in this case, Trinidad) was largely indivisible from the struggle for African advancement around the world. Their strong commitment to Africa did not prevent them from playing leading roles in the struggles not only for racial justice, but also for broad political reform at home. Edgar Maresse-Smith, a foundation member of the Trinidad PAA, had led the famous campaign in 1888 for a strong Afrocentric observance of the fiftieth anniversary of Emancipation. So had Rev. Philip Henry Douglin, head of the Pan-African Association in San Fernando. A Barbadian by birth, Douglin had labored for seventeen years with the West Indian Church Association at the Rio Pongo.

Williams had stopped in Jamaica on his way to Trinidad. There he reported 500 members enrolled during his visit and a further 500 by the time he got to Trinidad. The rapid growth in Jamaican PAA membership was facilitated by the affiliation, en masse, of the People's Convention, led by Dr. J. Robert Love.

In 1903 Williams emigrated to Cape Town, South Africa, where there was already a small resident Caribbean community. He practiced law and was very active in community affairs for a couple of years. Back in London he was elected to the Marylebone Borough Council in 1906 and represented African political delegations visiting London. He visited Liberia at the invitation of President Arthur Barclay in 1908. He returned to Trinidad on August 29, 1908, and died there in 1911.

Caribbean people in England (as elsewhere in the metropolis) remained active in the Pan-African struggle after Williams. This is a tendency which has never really stopped. In 1927 H. O. B. Wooding, future chief justice of Trinidad and Tobago, was made an honorary member of the London-headquartered West African Students' Union. In 1928 he married a Ghanaian.

Trinidadian F. E. M. Hercules, born in 1888, provided a fine example of this tendency. While a student at Queen's Royal College in Port of Spain he founded a Young Men's Colored Association. In 1907 he was a founder of the Port-of-Spain Colored Association. Hercules went to England during the First World War and became a leader of the black community there. The community at this time comprised seamen, students and travelers, in addition to a small number of black people born in England.

All over Britain in 1919 there were very bloody race riots and quite a few Caribbean people were forcibly repatriated. The riots were caused by returning servicemen competing for jobs with black residents, white upset at black male liaisons with white women, and the racial provocations of British Commonwealth troops from such places as New Zealand.

During these riots there appeared in the *London Times* a letter from a retired British colonial administrator who had worked in Grenada and Africa. This old colonialist suggested the deportation of Britain's black population and blamed the riots on black men who were having affairs with white women. The average Englishman, he wrote, was revolted by the idea of sexual contact between white women and black men. Hercules wrote a reply to the *London Times* in which he pointed out that when the European colonizers left Africa and the Caribbean that would be enough time for English people to talk about black people leaving England. He pointed out that in the Caribbean and Africa the slave masters and their descendants had always forced their attentions on black women. Hercules recalled from his own Caribbean experience cases where girls as young as twelve had fallen victim to the white man's lust. He reminded the former colonial official that in South Africa there were millions of so-called coloreds. And where did they come from? They were the children of white South African men.

Hercules was also secretary of the London-based Society of Peoples of African Origin (SPAO). The SPAO's mostly West African and Caribbean leadership included Audrey Jeffers of Trinidad, who in 1921 founded her well-known Coterie of Social Workers. Hercules, like Henry Sylvester Williams before him, and like Marcus Garvey in 1937, made a lecture tour of the West Indies in 1919. In Jamaica the British authorities accused him of causing strikes and unrest. He came through Trinidad and spoke to packed audiences. Many people joined his SPAO. From Trinidad he went to British Guiana. A few weeks later he returned to Trinidad, but the authorities would not let him land, despite the presence there of his wife and children. Trinidad at the time was in the grip of strikes and unrest. Anticolonialist and antiwhite feeling were running high, and the authorities were alarmed at the enthusiastic local response to Hercules' call for race pride, freedom and self-reliance.

Caribbean people were also involved in a variety of African American–sponsored Pan-African initiatives. Edmund Fitzgerald Fredericks of British Guiana served on the executive committee of the 1919 Paris Pan-African Congress convened by African American W. E. B. DuBois.

Fredericks had taught school in British Guiana and Trinidad before going to the United States in 1903. There he became an attorney-at-law and director of colored schools in Mooresville, North Carolina. He attended the Universal Races Congress in London in 1911. He returned to England and enrolled as a law student at Gray's Inn, London, in 1914. He was called to the English bar in 1918. Fredericks attended the Paris congress as a delegate of the recently founded (1918) London-headquartered African Progress Union. He returned to British Guiana in 1919 and founded the Negro Progress Convention in 1921. He was elected to the legislature in 1930. He was subsequently appointed to the colony's Executive Council, the first African so honored.

T. A. Marryshow of Grenada attended the London leg of W. E. B. DuBois' 1921 Pan-African Congress. Further sessions were held in Paris, Brussels and Lisbon. The newly elected executive included Gratien Candace, a Guadeloupean member of the French Chamber of Deputies and Isaac Beton, a Guadeloupean high school teacher in Paris. Audrey Jeffers of Trinidad was mentioned about this time as a possible host for a DuBois congress.

Several of these early Caribbean Pan-African activists operated in both North America and Europe. Edmund Fitzgerald Fredericks was one. Pan-African

movement pioneer Henry Sylvester Williams lived in the United States and Canada in the late nineteenth century, before going to London. George Padmore, coconvener with Kwame Nkrumah of Ghana of the Manchester, England, Pan-African Congress of 1945, lived in the United States in the 1920s before relocating to the USSR, Germany and later London. Trotskyist Pan-Africanist C. L. R. James left Trinidad for England in 1932. He relocated to the United States in 1938 and remained there until the United States deported him back to England in 1953. After his World War I period activism in England, F. E. M. Hercules emigrated to the United States. Amy Ashwood Garvey, first wife of Marcus Garvey and important Pan-Africanist in her own right, lived for several periods in both the United States and England from the 1920s to the 1960s.

Amy Ashwood Garvey, Pan-Africanist, feminist and the first Mrs. Marcus Garvey

Among Caribbean people who experienced Africa in the nineteenth and early twentieth centuries were soldiers and civil servants. Some of these, such as the men of the West India Regiments, played a somewhat negative role. They took part in the ill-fated British expedition to New Orleans in 1814–1815 and the more successful British assault on Mobile, Alabama, in 1815. They were used to help put down the British Guianese Angel Gabriel riots in 1856 and the Jamaica Rebellion in 1865. They were used all over Africa. They participated in the conquest of large pieces of West Africa for Britain. A lot of the British soldiers in the Ashanti wars were actually men from the West India Regiments. C. D. B. King, president of Liberia in the 1920s, was the son of a Jamaican ex-soldier. During the First World War the West India Regiments (not to be confused with the British West Indies Regiment formed especially for the First World War) served in Sierra Leone, the Cameroons and East Africa.

The overwhelming majority of the WIR's members in the earlier decades of the nineteenth century were African born. These included over 12,000 "liberated" Africans (seized by the British navy from slave ships of other nations) by 1840. The fear of another Daaga rebellion, though, caused the British to ease up a little on this kind of recruitment after 1837. By the end of the century African-born soldiers were in the minority. There were some African American recruits too, in the eighteenth century. These regiments remained in service right up to after the First World War. The officers of course were white, as usual in this period.

Some, at least, of the WIR veterans lived long enough to regret their use as mercenary soldiers. When the Marcus Garvey movement came into being in 1914 some of the members were West India Regiment ex-soldiers who, because of Garvey's Pan-African sentiments, were able to turn their knowledge of Africa to a more positive purpose.

Several Caribbean civil servants also worked in Africa. In the nineteenth century the British actually recruited civil servants from the Caribbean to work in Sierra Leone. The high mortality among white officials led them to seek educated Caribbean people who, it was hoped, would better survive the West African climate. Four of these recruits actually served as governors

of Sierra Leone. They were John Carr from Trinidad (1841), William Fergusson from Jamaica (1841–1842 and 1844–1845), Robert Dougan (1854, 1855) and Alexander Fitzjames (Trinidadian, 1859–1860). Lawyer William Rainey from Trinidad became a newspaper publisher, like John Russwurm in Liberia and Robert Campbell in Lagos. In 1865 he also authored *The Censor Censured, Or, The Calumnies of Captain Burton on the Africans of Sierra Leone*. This was a rebuttal of racist remarks contained in a book by an Englishman, very much like the celebrated and similarly inspired *Froudacity* by Trinidadian J. J. Thomas in 1887.

Other Caribbean people were recruited to help build and operate railways, especially in Nigeria. Others went as teachers, policemen and middle-rank civil servants. These people were still being sent over up until well into the twentieth century. One such, Amos Shackleford, went from Jamaica to Nigeria to work on the railways in 1913. He later became a prominent businessman in Nigeria and Ghana, especially in the bread industry. He was an important participant in Nigerian nationalist politics and a leader of Marcus Garvey's UNIA in Lagos. John Alexander Barbour-James of British Guiana served in the Gold Coast post office from 1902 to 1917. He was a postal inspector.

During the mid-nineteenth century, the remembrance of Africa was also fed by the thousands of liberated African indentured workers who entered the area (see Chapter 11). In addition, demobilized West India Regiment soldiers, many of course African born, were settled in the Caribbean, especially in Trinidad, throughout the nineteenth century. Others settled in West Africa, especially Sierra Leone, thus fostering the ongoing African–Caribbean cross-fertilization.

There was yet another group of free Africans who settled in the Caribbean, this time even before the end of slavery. These were African American veterans of the War of 1812 between Britain and the United States. These soldiers escaped from enslavement to join the British forces against their American masters. In return they extracted from the British a promise of freedom. The British kept their promise and resettled these troops in Trinidad's famous "Company Villages" at the war's end.

Some of these African American veterans were doubtless African born and in Trinidad they referred to themselves as Africans, even if persons outside their community often called them Americans or "Merikins." The Spiritual Baptist faith is among the legacies of this African American community in Trinidad.

The Europeans had a practice of exiling troublesome African leaders to the Caribbean and this, too, helped to foster interest. King Jaja of Opobo (in modern-day Nigeria) was a merchant who gave the British so much competition in their trade that in 1888 they put him on a ship and sent him off to St. Vincent. He stopped in other islands, too, along the way. Everywhere people demonstrated in solidarity with him. King Jaja later became ill and in 1891 the British put him on a ship back to Africa. He died on his way back. He never saw his native land again. One of his wives was still alive in Trinidad in 1937.

The French did the same thing to King Behanzin of Dahomey, the country that Daaga had sailed from many years before. Behanzin waged a bitter armed struggle against the French (and their Senegalese mercenary troops), but was eventually defeated. In 1894 the French exiled him to a fort in Martinique, installed a puppet ruler in his place and broke his country up into a colony and protectorate. Behanzin was kept in Martinique until 1905 and then transferred to the Algerian town of Blida, where he died in 1906. Half a century later, in that same Algerian town, an African son of Martinique, Frantz Fanon, would join the Algerian revolution and help bestow on France its greatest defeat in Africa. And King Behanzin's nephew, Prince Kojo Tovalou Houénou, in the 1920s became an avid supporter of the Jamaican Pan-Africanist Marcus Garvey. Houénou is even said to have led a Garvey-inspired uprising against the French in Dahomey in 1923.

UN Special Committee Against Apartheid, special session in Kingston, Jamaica, 1979. The meeting honored six historical figures from the Caribbean for their contributions to the struggle against apartheid in South Africa. The honorees were Henry Sylvester Williams (Trinidad), Marcus Garvey (Jamaica), Jose Marti (Cuba), Frantz Fanon (Martinique), Dantes Bellegarde (Haiti) and George Padmore (Trinidad). Dr. John Henrik Clarke is second from left. C. L. R. James is fourth from left.

All of these varied African immigrants—the soldiers, the indentured servants, the liberated Africans, the exiles, and of course, the enslaved—helped keep alive the memory of Africa. And perhaps this may be part of the reason, though not the whole reason, why well into the twentieth century there still existed in the Caribbean communities of Africans who self-consciously preserved their roots in specific African nationalities. The Cuban Congo people previously mentioned were one example. In Trinidad there were Mandingo, Yoruba, Hausa and Congo communities. A Rada community in Belmont, Port of Spain, was still alive and well in the 1950s. It was communities like these, creatively applying their African cultural heritage to new environments, that gave the world calypso, reggae, son and steelband.

By the time that the twentieth century came along, then, Caribbean people had long been manifesting their interest in Africa in all kinds of ways.

Some were going back to Africa physically, some were agitating on behalf of Africa, some were trying to prevent the European scramble for the continent, some were going as civil servants and soldiers, some were living in African communities in the Caribbean. Several of the prominent Pan-Africanists operated in both Europe and North America.

Henry Sylvester Williams was able to usher in the twentieth-century standing on the shoulders of all these African-conscious people who had preceded him. Then in the early twentieth century there appeared the Jamaican Pan-Africanist Marcus Mosiah Garvey, who was able to gather up most of these trends into a movement, the Universal Negro Improvement Association and African Communities League, and was able to have an unprecedented impact on the whole African world and indeed the whole world in general. We will discuss Garvey later.

Further Readings

Blyden, Nemata Amelia. *West Indians in West Africa, 1808–1880: The African Diaspora in Reverse.* Rochester, NY: University of Rochester Press, 2000.

Campbell, Carl. "Mohammedu Sisei of Gambia and Trinidad, c. 1788–1838." *ASAWI Bulletin*, 7, 1974, 29–38.

Cox, Edward. *Rekindling the Ancestral Memory: King Ja Ja of Opobo in St. Vincent and Barbados, 1888–1891.* Bridgetown: University of the West Indies, Cave Hill, History Department and Barbados Museum and Historical Society, 1998.

Hooker, J. Ralph. *Henry Sylvester Williams: Imperial Pan-Africanist.* London: Rex Collings, 1975.

Martin, Tony. *The Pan-African Connection: From Slavery to Garvey and Beyond.* Dover, MA: The Majority Press, 1984. First pub. 1983.

Mathurin, Owen. *Henry Sylvester Williams and the Origins of the Pan-African Movement.* Westport, CT: Greenwood Press, 1976.

13

The United States and the Caribbean to World War II

THE AFRICAN AMERICAN CONNECTION

The Caribbean and African America shared a common experience of enslavement which led to a series of interactions that endured for centuries. The famous Africans who arrived in Jamestown, Virginia, in August 1619 (long thought to be the first) could easily have ended up in the Caribbean rather than North America. They were on a Portuguese slaver bound for Vera Cruz from Angola when they were captured by a pair of pirate ships, one English and one Dutch. This was in the vicinity of Campeche, Mexico, near Cuba. Some of the captured Africans were deposited in Virginia, some in Bermuda.

By this time, Africans had been enslaved in the Caribbean for over 100 years. Most of the main features of slavery had been established. The English North Americans therefore did not have to reinvent the institution. The Caribbean provided a ready-made precedent which they could adopt. Some historians have suggested that there may have been a short period of uncertainty before a fully fledged system of enslavement descended on the Africans of Virginia. Be that as it may, once slavery was unequivocally established it clearly reflected its Caribbean precedent. Slave laws, punishments, attitudes to Christianization among the Protestant nations and much else reflected these similarities.

Europeans travelled back and forth between North America and the Caribbean facilitating mutual knowledge. The major Caribbean colonizing powers operated in both areas resulting in a constant to-ing and fro-ing of administrators, soldiers, merchants, white indentured workers and enslaved Africans. A British official might be posted in Virginia or Massachusetts one year and Barbados the next. An Admiral William Penn might help conquer Jamaica for the British in 1655 and later see his son, William Penn, found the British North American colony of Pennsylvania. George Washington, slaveholder and future first president of the United States, spent two months in Barbados in 1751, his only overseas trip.

The first enslaved Africans in New England were brought from Providence Island in 1638. For some time thereafter many of the enslaved Africans arriving in New England came from the Caribbean, rather than direct from Africa. New England slave ships routinely brought some Africans to the Caribbean on their way back to the United States.

The first enslaved Africans in New Amsterdam (later New York) were introduced in 1626 by the Dutch West India Company. The company brought some Africans directly from West Africa and some, increasingly so as the years went by, from the Caribbean.

The first Africans in South Carolina were brought there by the white Caribbean islanders who helped pioneer the colony from the 1660s. The majority of these whites came from Barbados but others arrived from St. Kitts, Antigua, Montserrat, Nevis, Jamaica, Bermuda and the Bahamas. There were six Barbadian governors of South Carolina between 1670 and 1730. Five more governors to 1737 were the sons of Barbadians. Of the fifteen Barbadians who took out warrants for free land in 1679, thirteen had brought their enslaved Africans with them. It was the islanders who introduced African servitude into South Carolina.

Much earlier, in the sixteenth century, some Africans left the Caribbean with early Spanish explorers of North America. The best known of these is Morocco-born Esteban (also known as Estebanico). He spent some time in Santo Domingo before leaving Cuba in 1528 with the Pánfilo de Narvaez expedition to Florida. He was one of the expedition's only four survivors. He journeyed on foot from Florida to Mexico City. He later helped the Spaniards explore Arizona, Texas and elsewhere in the American Southwest. He was eventually killed by Zuni Native Americans.

Once slavery was established in North America the African American–Caribbean relationship grew. New England slave ships continued to drop off some of their African captives in the Caribbean. Ships sailing out of New England and elsewhere often had African American crew members. This was especially the case for ships sailing to the Caribbean. The converse was also true. The enslaved Olaudah Equiano, as previously noted, sailed out of Montserrat to the southern United States for many years. On one occasion he had to go into hiding in Charleston, South Carolina. He won a fight against an enslaved African American whose owner came looking for Equiano to avenge the destruction of his property.

European wars also facilitated contact between the Caribbean and African America. African American troops fighting for the British during the American Revolutionary War were evacuated to the British Caribbean to save them from re-enslavement by the Americans. Some were stationed initially in Jamaica, where the white populace expressed unease at the introduction of free, battle-tested black veterans. They were not totally averse, however, to using these soldiers

to fight as mercenaries. They therefore relocated them to other islands and formed them into the nucleus of the 1st West India Regiment (WIR).

Five hundred and forty-five black and colored Haitians fought in 1779 with the French force that helped the Americans at the Siege of Savannah, Georgia, during the American War of Independence. Among them were two future rulers of independent Haiti, Henri Christophe and Andre Rigaud. Among the besieged British troops were the South Carolina African American loyalists. One of these, George Lisle, was later evacuated to Jamaica where he became the first Baptist missionary in Jamaica and the first African American missionary to foreign parts.

The Siege of Savannah was practically an extension of British–French fighting in the Caribbean. The French commander Admiral Comte Charles d'Estaing, a former governor of Saint Domingue, arrived in Savannah fresh from conquest of St. Vincent and Grenada from the British. Many of his 41,000 troops had been recruited in the Caribbean, among them the black and colored *Chasseurs-Volontaires de Saint-Domingue*, raised at Cap Français especially for this campaign. This ostensibly voluntary force had been subjected to some coercive recruiting. "Quadroon" militia members (officially so named) refusing to enlist were demoted to "mulatto" units. "Mulattoes" were demoted to "black" units. Nine hundred and forty-one eventually "volunteered," with many later deserting. The white Volunteer Grenadines could manage only 156 members when the time for departure to Savannah arrived.

Haiti impacted African America in many other ways. Jean-Baptiste Pointe du Sable, a colored Haitian fur trapper and merchant, founded what later became Chicago, around 1779. Thousands of white, black and colored Haitians also emigrated during the revolution to escape the fighting. Many took their enslaved people with them. They went to places like Jamaica and Trinidad. Many went to the United States. New Orleans and Philadelphia became centers of Haitian activity. Haitian caterers in Philadelphia were among the most successful African American businessmen in the city.

The Haitian Revolution also had a profound impact, both on white abolitionists and on the African American community at large. Haiti was seen as a "vindication of the race," proof positive that black people were the equal of everybody else and could triumph over oppression given half a chance. The U.S. government actually feared a Haitian invasion to liberate African America. Toussaint had contemplated an expedition to West Africa to end the slave trade. After independence Haiti had provided assistance to Simon Bolívar in his quest to liberate South America. An invasion of the southern United States did not seem so far-fetched in this context. The attempted enslaved revolts of Gabriel Prosser in Richmond, Virginia, in 1800 and Denmark Vesey in Charleston, South Carolina, in 1822 were both inspired by Haiti. Vesey, born in St. Thomas and resident for some time in Haiti, had hoped to sail with his fellow revolutionaries to Haiti after freeing the African Americans of Charleston.

Formal Emancipation in the British Caribbean on August 1, 1834, also had a profound impact on African America. August 1, "West India Emancipation Day," became the major African American celebration, marked by picnics, outings, speeches and sober commemorations. It only began to fade as the major African American observance when President Abraham Lincoln's Emancipation Proclamation of January 1, 1863, introduced a new date for celebration. Yet as late as the 1890s black folk in Roslyn, Washington, successfully advocated a city holiday for West India Emancipation Day.

Frederick Douglass, one of African America's most influential leaders for much of the nineteenth century, made probably his most often-quoted speech on the topic, "The Significance of Emancipation in the West Indies." It was delivered at a West India Emancipation celebration on August 3, 1857, at Canandaigua, New York. There, he famously said,

> If there is no struggle there is no progress. Those who profess to favor freedom and yet depreciate agitation, are men who want crops without plowing up the ground. They want rain without thunder and lightning. They want the ocean without the awful roar of its many waters.
>
> This struggle may be a moral one, or it may be a physical one, and it may be both moral and physical, but it must be a struggle. Power concedes nothing without a demand. It never did, and, it never will. Find out just what any people will quietly submit to and you have found out the exact measure of injustice and wrong which will be imposed upon them, and these will continue till they are resisted with either words or blows, or with both. The limits of tyrants are prescribed by the endurance of those whom they oppress.

Douglass' rapturous embrace of West India Emancipation Day is made even more significant by probably his second most quoted speech, in which he absolutely rejected any need for African Americans to celebrate July 4, the United States' Independence Day. As far as Douglass was concerned August 1 and not July 4 was African America's day of celebration as long as slavery endured in the United States. Douglass delivered this speech, "What to the Slave is the 4th of July?" in Rochester, New York, in 1852. He said,

> What, to the American slave, is your Fourth is July? I answer: a day that reveals to him, more than all other days in the year, the gross injustice and cruelty to which he is the constant victim.

Douglass' sentiments explain why African Americans during slavery had no qualms about fighting for the British or whoever was in conflict with the United States. Many thousands of white loyalist refugees and their enslaved Africans reached several islands at the end of the Revolutionary War. Jamaica experienced a significant increase in population. Some 5,000 enslaved African Americans are thought to have arrived in Jamaica as a result of the 1782 evacuation of Savannah alone. Others went to St. Lucia, Antigua and St. Kitts. The Bahamas gained 6,000–7,000 black and white loyalist Americans, making Americans the majority element in the Bahamian population.

During the war of 1812, in which the British burned down Washington, D.C., enslaved African Americans flocked to the British lines. Like the Maroons of old, they were anxious to fight for whoever was attacking their hated masters. After the war they once again had to be removed from the United States to avoid re-enslavement. Several hundred were sent to Trinidad. They arrived in 1815 and 1816 and were settled in various places including the "company villages," Third Company, Fourth Company, Fifth Company and Sixth Company, named for their military units.

The mercenary West India Regiment also interestingly fought for the British during the War of 1812. They served in Mobile, Alabama and New Orleans. Some members of the WIR were demobilized and settled near Manzanilla, Trinidad, at around the same time as the African American British forces arrived in the island.

The desire of free African Americans to leave the United States brought some to Trinidad in the 1840s as previously noted. Many also emigrated to Haiti. Several Haitian rulers, beginning with Henri Christophe in 1818, shortly before his death, encouraged African American immigration. Free African Americans were looking for somewhere to escape from racism and Haiti needed skilled black people who could contribute to national development.

One of the strongest advocates of African American emigration to Haiti was James Theodore Holly, later (1874) the first African American bishop of the Protestant Episcopal Church (U.S. equivalent of the Anglican Church). In 1861 Holly took 110 African Americans from his hometown of New Haven, Connecticut, to Haiti. Despite many vicissitudes due to climate, yellow fever and the like, Holly remained based in Haiti until his death in 1911. The title of Holly's 1857 work amply summed up his motivation in combining Haitian independence with an African American presence—*Vindication of the Capacity of the Negro Race for Self Governance and Civilized Progress.*

President Fabre Geffrard had in 1860 expressed a willingness to immediately accommodate "at least" 50,000 African American immigrants. "Hayti will soon regain her splendor," he promised. "Hayti is the common country of the black race. Listen . . . all ye Negroes and mulattoes who, in the vast continent of America, suffer from the prejudices of caste, the Republic calls you; she invites you; she invites you to bring to her your arms and your minds." Dr. J. Robert Love, born in the Bahamas and educated in the United States, joined the African

American trek to Haiti in Holly's time. He was later an important journalist and politician in Jamaica.

The same year (1859) that African American emigrationist Martin Delany journeyed to Abeokuta with Jamaican Robert Campbell, he began his serialized novel, *Blake*. The hero was a free-born Afro-Cuban who was kidnapped by Americans and sold into slavery in Mississippi. He was on a mission to rescue his enslaved wife in Cuba and to foment an uprising against slavery. The literary portrayal of the revolutionary Caribbean hero had long antedated *Blake*. New York's African Company, operating out of its African Grove, African America's first professional theatre, staged *The Drama of King Shotaway, Founded on Facts taken from the Insurrection of the Caravs [Caribs] on the Island of St. Vincent, written from Experience by Mr. [William Alexander] Brown*, in 1823. Brown was a retired ship's steward from the Caribbean. *King Shotaway* was the first known play authored by an African American. *Shotaway* was clearly a pun on Chatoyer, Black Carib chief.

The eighteenth and nineteenth centuries also saw a continuing modest movement of free people from the Caribbean to the United States. Some of these made distinguished contributions to North America. "Black Sam" Fraunces, chief steward in President George Washington's executive mansions in New York and Philadelphia, is thought to have been a Caribbean-born black, though some disagree. His daughter, Phoebe, is said by some to have saved Washington's life from poisoning by a British spy who befriended her. Alexander Hamilton, U.S. founding father and first Secretary of the Treasury, was born in Nevis and raised in St. Croix. He is sometimes thought to have been of part African ancestry. Jewish sources sometimes claim him as well, on the speculation that his mother Rachel Fawcett Levien (or Levine) might have been a Jew, perhaps a "Jewish mulatto." Rachel was married to a Jew before having Hamilton with a Scotsman.

In Boston in 1787 Prince Hall received a charter for his Masonic lodge, African Lodge No. 1, the first black lodge. He was born in Barbados possibly in 1748 (though some have offered alternative birthplaces) of an Englishman and a free colored woman. He worked his way on a ship to Boston in 1765, at the age of seventeen. There he eventually became a leading figure in the struggle for civil rights. He led a campaign urging African Americans not to pay taxes if they could not enjoy civil rights. He operated the first school for African American children in Boston out of his home, since the public schools barred black children.

William Leidesdorff of St. Croix is celebrated as African America's first millionaire, though some Jewish sources claim him too, and at least one suggests that he might in fact have been one Wolf Leidesdorfer, a Hungarian-born Jew. He is more generally said to have been born in St. Croix of a Jewish planter father and an enslaved African mother. He was a successful businessman in New York and New Orleans and sailed his own ship from New Orleans, around South America, to California, before its annexation by the United States. There he became American Consul to Mexico (making him the first African American diplomat). Gold was discovered on his land. Among his many firsts was the sailing of the first steamboat on San Francisco Bay. He died at the young age of thirty-eight and was buried in a Roman Catholic cemetery.

Barbadian school principal, Codrington College alumnus and sometime tailor's apprentice, David Augustus Straker, became the highest ranking African American elected official in the Northern United States in 1893, when he was elected judge in Detroit, Michigan. Straker arrived in Kentucky in 1868. This was in response to a call from Episcopalian Bishop B. B. Smith of Kentucky to his counterpart, Rev. Richard R. Rawle, principal of Codrington College, for "any educated colored men in Barbados who are sufficiently interested in the American freedmen" to come over and help in the work of educating the newly emancipated. About 95 percent of the African American population was illiterate in 1865. Straker was not the only Caribbean contributor to African American postenslavement education. William H. Crogman, president of Clark University, Atlanta, was from St. Martin.

In Kentucky Straker became a teacher. In 1871 he obtained a law degree from Howard University, where he was one of six Caribbean students in Howard's professional schools. He practiced law in South Carolina with fellow Caribbean lawyer and member of the U.S. House of Representatives,

Robert B. Elliott. Straker himself became a South Carolina state representative.

Straker was dean and professor of law at Allen University in South Carolina and combined his many activities with a distinguished career in journalism, which culminated in his own newspaper, the *Detroit Advocate*, begun in 1901. (Dr. J. Robert Love's *Jamaica Advocate* was a contemporary of Straker's Detroit namesake.) He wrote several books, including *Reflections on the Life and Times of Toussaint L'Ouverture* (1886). He was a member of several major African American uplift organizations, including T. Thomas Fortune's National Afro-American League and W. E. B. DuBois' Niagara Movement.

Straker's law partner, Robert Brown Elliott (1842–1884) was born in Liverpool, England, of Caribbean parents. Early twentieth-century African American journalist John Edward Bruce suggested that he may have been part educated in Jamaica. Like so many other Caribbean political figures of the period, he was a printer (typesetter) and journalist. After serving in the Royal Navy he came to Boston in 1867, about a year before Straker arrived in Kentucky. He relocated to South Carolina the same year. Elliott was admitted to practice law in South Carolina. He was elected in 1868 to the state constitutional convention, where he advocated compulsory free education but opposed integrated schools. As state adjutant general in 1870 he raised an anti-Ku Klux Klan militia. He was a sometime state representative in South Carolina, being variously speaker of the General Assembly and attorney general. Elliott served in the U.S. House of Representatives as a member from South Carolina. In 1870 he was elected to the U.S. Congress, the first dark-skinned (as opposed to racially mixed) African American so elected. There he was widely praised for his erudition and oratorical ability. He helped pilot anti-KKK legislation in Congress. Elliott died in New Orleans.

Joseph H. Rainey, political contemporary of Straker and Elliott, became the first African American elected to the U.S. House of Representatives in 1870. Though born in South Carolina, he lived in Bermuda for about three years during the U.S. Civil War.

Violette N. Anderson (1882–1937), was, like Elliott, born in England of a Caribbean father. Her mother was German. Her family moved to Chicago during her childhood. She became the first woman of any race to graduate from an Illinois law school and in 1926 became the first woman to argue before the U.S. Supreme Court. Like many Caribbean immigrants she was an active Episcopalian (the American branch of the Anglican Church). Her career calls to mind that of Constance Baker Motley (1921–2005), born in New Haven, Connecticut, of Nevisian parents. Motley was the first woman of any race at Columbia Law School, the first African American woman elected to the New York Senate, the first woman Manhattan Borough President and the first African American female federal district judge. She was the only woman on the legal team that successfully argued the *Brown v. Board of Education* case (1954), which outlawed racial segregation in the United States.

With work winding down on the building of the Panama Canal and eventually ending with the completion of the canal in 1914, the United States supplanted Panama as the major destination for emigrating Caribbean people. George Roberts estimated a net emigration of 30,000 Jamaicans alone to the United States between 1911 and 1921. Most migrants went to New York, Boston and Florida in that order. Boston was the home of the Boston Fruit Company and later the United Fruit Company. The banana boats of these companies also carried passengers, making Boston a convenient port of entry into the United States.

By 1920 one in five of New York City's black residents was born in the Caribbean. About 65 percent of the Caribbean immigrants were concentrated here and they naturally had a significant influence on Harlem, the city's black "capital," and on African America generally.

Caribbean immigrants were well represented among African American radicals. It was from Harlem in 1916 that Jamaican Marcus Garvey catapulted his Universal Negro Improvement Association (UNIA) into prominence as the largest Pan-African and African American mass movement of all time. Garvey had begun the UNIA in Kingston, Jamaica, in 1914 but relocated to Harlem in 1916. Garvey's career will be dealt with more fully in Chapter 14.

The first black cadre in the new Workers Party in 1921 (later the Communist Party of the USA) came from Caribbean immigrants in the African Blood Brotherhood, led by Cyril Briggs from St. Kitts. George Padmore of Trinidad joined the Communist Party in the United States and moved to Moscow to head the "Negro Bureau" of the Red International of Labor Unions (Profintern), making him the highest ranking black person in the world Communist movement. Frank Crosswaith of St. Croix became a principal organizer for the Brotherhood of Sleeping Car Porters (1925), the most important African American affiliate of the American Federation of Labor. In 1935 he also founded the important Negro Labor Committee, a broad-based coalition of labor organizers and activists.

Several of New York's leading intellectuals also came from the Caribbean immigrant community. These included Arthur Schomburg, born in Puerto Rico of a St. Croix mother. He was African America's leading book collector. Hubert H. Harrison of St. Croix was one of the most popular and erudite of Harlem's intellectuals. Joel A. Rogers of Jamaica was an important pioneer historian. W. E. B. DuBois, African America's leading intellectual of the period, was of part Caribbean heritage, although he did not identify with the Caribbean immigrant community and at times showed considerable antipathy toward it. DuBois' father was born in Haiti. His grandfather was born in the Bahamas. His great-grandmother, a near-unknown figure in his life, was a black Bahamian. Similar to DuBois was James Weldon Johnson, of Bahamian parentage but at times hostile to Caribbean immigrants. Johnson was general secretary of the National Association for the Advancement of Colored People (NAACP). He was a poet, civil rights leader and cocomposer, with his brother J. Rosamond Johnson, of "Lift Every Voice and Sing," African America's "Black National Anthem." His mother was Florida's first female black public school teacher.

A fair share of Harlem's professionals—doctors, lawyers, judges, etc.—came from the Caribbean immigrant community. James S. Watson, a Jamaican, became New York State's first black judge in 1931.

Caribbean immigrants were also well represented in African American business. Marcus

Garvey's Negro Factories Corporation employed over 1,000 New Yorkers in the early 1920s. His *Negro World* newspaper, published in Harlem from 1918 to 1933, was the most widely circulated black newspaper in the world. His Black Star Line Steamship Corporation (1919) was the most spectacular and probably the most highly capitalized black business of its time.

In 1933 Cyril Duprey of Trinidad founded the United Mutual Life Insurance Company, the first such African American company to be chartered in the state of New York. Duprey was part of a closely knit Caribbean–African American business and professional group which, under his leadership, helped launch the Colonial Life Insurance Company (CLICO) in Trinidad in 1936. CLICO became the largest conglomerate of any racial group in the Caribbean (see Chapter 14). Among Duprey's Harlem associates was Dr. Philip M. H. Savory of British Guiana, who bought the *New York Amsterdam News*, one of African America's leading newspapers, in 1936.

Caribbean immigrants were also well represented in the entertainment industry. Nassau-born Bert Williams (1874–1922) was a highly successful actor, dancer and comedian. He was the first African American to star in a Hollywood feature film, *A Natural Born Gambler*, in 1916. He wished to be a serious actor but the realities of the time kept him in stereotypical vaudeville roles, including many in blackface. Caribbean artistes were also some of the earliest black performers to make musical recordings. Trinidad's Lovey's String Band journeyed to the Columbia Phonograph Company in New York in 1912 to record "Mango Vert" and other melodies for the Trinidad market. In the process Lovey's musicians seem to have become the first black band to record in the United States, well ahead of James Reece Europe's Society Orchestra and Jamaican-born Dan Kildare's Persian Garden Orchestra, both of which released recordings in 1914. The National Recording Registry of the Library of Congress named a Lovey's record to its first ever listing of the fifty most significant recordings of all time. Lovey's was the only non-American band (or individual) on the list. Trinidad's Sam Manning and other U.S.-based Caribbean artistes were recording regularly from 1924, placing them

among the pioneer African American recording artistes.

The 1920s witnessed the great outpouring of literary and cultural activity known as the Harlem Renaissance. Caribbean immigrants were well represented in this activity. Claude McKay, a former policeman in Jamaica, wrote probably the most famous poem of the Renaissance, "If We Must Die." Novelist Nella Larsen was born in the United States of a St. Croix father. The "Literary Garveyism" aspect of Garvey's UNIA served as a major outlet for the apprentice writing of a huge number of major and minor writers of the Renaissance. Among them were African American Zora Neale Hurston, Eric Walrond of British Guiana and Claude McKay.

Persons of Caribbean descent were also represented among the less radical "mainstream" sections of the African American Civil Rights movement. W. E. B. DuBois and J. Weldon Johnson, both of largely unacknowledged Caribbean ancestry, were respectively the editor of the NAACP's *Crisis* magazine and general secretary of the association. St. Croix-born Casper Holstein was a great benefactor of race-uplift activity. A major object of his largesse was the National Urban League's *Opportunity* magazine, one of the leading magazines of the Renaissance. Holstein, king of the illegal "numbers" gambling game, also doubled as Harlem's major figure in organized crime.

These immigrants to the United States, like similar later generations of immigrants, interested themselves in political affairs back home and were often a catalyst for political advance. Garvey's UNIA, the Jamaican Progressive League of A. M. Wendell Malliet and W. Adolphe Edwards (founded in 1936) and the West Indies National Council of Herman Osborne, C. A. Petioni and others were among those groups contributing significantly to political advance in their Caribbean homelands.

The huge flood of immigration into the United States came to a near-abrupt halt with the Immigration Act of 1924 when the U.S. Congress virtually stopped black immigration. Caribbean immigration went from 10,630 in 1924 to 321 in 1925. In addition the Depression years after 1929 sent many immigrants back home as work became scarce in the United States. Numbers picked up again with the entry of the

Casper Holstein of the Virgin Islands and New York in 1928.

United States into World War II in 1941. Thousands of Caribbean farm and other workers were recruited during this period. The flow was again stemmed by the Immigration and Nationality Act (Walter-McCarran Act) of 1952. Caribbean immigration would not again assume massive proportions until the laws were liberalized in the mid-1960s.

THE COLOSSUS OF THE NORTH

Increasing Caribbean–African American interaction in the nineteenth and early twentieth centuries coincided with the rise of the United States as the dominant power in the Caribbean, the "Colossus of the North," as it became known. Spain dominated the area from the time of Columbus until the seventeenth century. In the late eighteenth century France and Britain were locked in a struggle for Caribbean hegemony. The loss of Haiti, the world's richest colony, caused Napoleon to sell nearby Louisiana cheaply to the United States in 1803. Louisiana and Haiti were the twin pillars

of French western power and with Haiti independent Napoleon was more easily induced to sell.

Simultaneously with these developments Britain in the closing years of the eighteenth century captured several new colonies from France, Spain and Holland—Trinidad, St. Lucia, Grenada, St. Vincent, Berbice, Essequibo and Demerara. (The last three merged in 1831 into British Guiana.) The British returned Martinique to France in 1802. At this point it looked like Britain was home free as the Caribbean superpower. Its preeminence was, however, to be short lived.

From the beginning of British settlement the Caribbean colonies had traded extensively with their North American counterparts. North Americans had long been active participants in the triangular trade. They had supplied the Caribbean with horses, building materials, salt fish and other foods. They had bought sugar and molasses for the many rum distilleries in the United States—eighteen in Boston alone in the eighteenth century.

Now, with the purchase of Louisiana and later Florida, the United States was itself a full-fledged Caribbean power. The southern coastline of the United States was now the northern border of the Caribbean. American foreign policy showed increased interest in the Caribbean. Southern states expressed an intermittent interest in buying Cuba, to increase the number of slave-owning states in the American union.

By 1823 the United States felt strong enough to issue its famous Monroe Doctrine, enunciated by President James Monroe. Monroe undertook to respect existing European colonies in the Americas. Any European efforts to extend their influence to new areas would be viewed "as dangerous to our peace and safety." Any European effort to retake former colonies now recognized as independent by the United States would be seen as "the manifestation of an unfriendly disposition towards the United States."

In 1823 also, John Quincy Adams, Monroe's secretary of state, propounded his "Law of Political Gravitation," setting Cuba up for future U.S. annexation. "There are laws of political as well as of physical gravitation," he said, "and if an apple, severed by a tempest from its native tree, cannot choose not to fall to the ground, Cuba, forcibly disjoined from its own unnatural connection with Spain, and incapable of self-support, can gravitate only towards the North American Union, which, by the same law of nature, cannot cast her off from its bosom."

As early as 1809, when it seemed that Napoleon would overrun Spain, President Thomas Jefferson had proposed buying Cuba from Napoleon. In 1848 President James Polk offered Spain $100 million for the island. In 1854 President Franklin Pierce upped the U.S. offer to $130 million.

In October 1854 a group of American diplomats meeting in Ostend, Belgium, issued the "Ostend Manifesto," threatening to annex Cuba by force if Spain refused to sell. The document's publication led to diplomatic embarrassment and its repudiation by the U.S. government. During the Cuban liberation war of 1868–1878, Secretary of State Hamilton Fish again offered to buy Cuba.

United States' designs in Cuba were finally realized in the Cuban-Spanish-American War of 1895–1898. This was Cuba's second war of independence against Spain in less than twenty years. Throughout the nineteenth century the United States had viewed Cuban independence as problematic. Independence for a largely black state on America's white doorstep conjured up fears of another Haiti. In any event an independent nation made up of Africans, Indians and Spaniards, as one U.S. diplomat characterized it, would surely be incapable if governing itself. This was an expression of "manifest destiny," a notion enjoying wide currency in U.S. domestic and foreign policy since its formal coining in 1845. Manifest destiny was akin to the British "white man's burden" and the French *"mission civilisatrice"* (civilizing mission), all of which saw the white imperialist nations as having a divinely ordained mission to conquer and civilize the world's darker, allegedly inferior peoples. Similar arguments were soon afterward advanced in the U.S. occupations of Haiti and the Dominican Republic.

In the midst of the Cuban–Spanish conflict the United States dispatched a battleship, the *USS Maine*, to Cuba. On February 15, 1898, the *Maine* blew up in Havana harbor, killing 274 U.S. sailors. There were eighty-nine survivors, including most of the ship's officers. President William McKinley declared war on Spain on April 25, 1898. The popular slogan for the war was, "Remember the *Maine*, to hell with Spain."

The question of who sank the *Maine* has never been definitively answered, despite several enquires. A strong suspicion has lingered in some quarters that the United States sank her own ship to provide a pretext for war.

The war ended with a U.S. victory on August 12, 1898. The spoils of war included much of what was left of Spain's empire, namely Puerto Rico, the Philippines, and Guam in the Pacific. Spain gave up the last three for $20 million.

Whatever hopes the Cubans might have entertained for early independence were crushed in the U.S. Congress' Platt Amendment of 1901, forced on the Cuban people and ratified by the U.S. Congress in 1903. Cuban ratification was deemed a condition for the withdrawal of American forces and the establishment of Cuban independence. This treaty prevented Cuba from allowing any foreign powers to obtain control of any part of the island. It gave the United States the right to intervene in Cuban affairs at any time as it saw fit "for the preservation of Cuban independence." It also provided the framework within which the United States could appropriate Guantanamo naval base in perpetuity. The Cubans resisted but eventually had to give in. The Cuban assembly ratified it in 1901 and incorporated it into the 1902 constitution. U.S. troops withdrew in 1902. The United States nevertheless reoccupied Cuba from 1906 to 1909 under the terms of these stipulations. The amendment was abrogated in 1934, except for the Guantanamo base provisions, during the "Good Neighbor Policy" of President Franklin D. Roosevelt.

Seven U.S. warships had shelled Puerto Rico for three hours on May 12, 1898. On July 25, 26,000 U.S. troops landed, under General Nelson Appleton Miles. Miles had been overall commanding officer in 1890 of the U.S. troops responsible for the massacre at Wounded Knee, South Dakota, where 300 Sioux Native American men, women and children perished.

Puerto Rico was put under military rule. The military promptly changed the country's name from "Puerto" to "Porto" Rico, since the latter rolled off American tongues more easily. (The Puerto Ricans got back their original spelling in 1932.) The Organic Act of 1900 ("Foraker Act") established a civilian government under a U.S. governor and an appointed executive council, not unlike the situation in the British colonies. The Jones-Shafroth Act ("Jones Act") of 1917 bestowed U.S. citizenship, just in time to make Puerto Ricans eligible for conscription during World War I and America's subsequent wars.

By the beginning of the twentieth century U.S. power in the Caribbean was also expressing itself in more subtle ways. When St. Vincent's Soufrière volcano erupted in 1902 a U.S. warship was first on the scene with relief supplies, before a British warship arrived from Trinidad. The *U.S.S. Potomac* donated as much as she could spare of her own food supplies. She also transported official government dispatches to the neighboring British island of St. Lucia, for transmission to London. Normal communications had been disrupted by the volcano. The incongruity of sensitive diplomatic correspondence between a British colony and London being transported on a U.S. warship was probably not lost on the British governor. Governor Llewellyn therefore thanked the American commander and assured him, however incongruously, that there was no need for further assistance.

Within days American scientists were clambering up the volcano, to the amazement of still bemused Vincentians, peering over the top of the crater and reporting on the boiling lake within.

When the Jamaican earthquake happened in 1907 three U.S. warships from Guantanamo were again first on the scene with relief supplies for the British colony. This time the result was the "Swettenham incident." Some prison disturbances occurred around this time and U.S citizens appealed to Rear Admiral Davis, commander of the U.S. ships, for protection. Davis landed marines without first seeking the approval of Governor Sir Alexander Swettenham, a former governor of British Guiana. This was technically a hostile act

and a breach of international law as understood by both the British and Americans. Governor Swettenham demanded withdrawal of the U.S. forces and Davis complied.

Two days and another request from Kingston's Americans later, Davis landed a second detachment of armed marines, again without Swettenham's prior knowledge or approval. Swettenham sent him an angry letter which was later published in the American press. The British government ordered Swettenham to apologize. He did so and resigned forthwith from the governorship and from the colonial civil service. Davis, meanwhile, petulantly gathered up his doctors, nurses, tents and food and went home. Anglican Archbishop of Jamaica, Dr. Enos Nuttall, deeply regretted any actions on Swettenham's part which might have made Jamaicans seem ungrateful for American aid. The Rev. Mr. Graham, pastor of a Methodist Church, commented, "This is a British colony, not Cuba or a Spanish American republic." Britain also felt the rising confidence of American power in 1897 when President Grover Cleveland forced Britain to arbitrate the British Guiana and Venezuela boundary dispute.

The U.S. juggernaut rolled on with an invasion of Haiti in 1915 and Haiti remained a U.S. protectorate until 1934. The invasion came at a time of political instability and growing German influence in Haiti's economic affairs. The small German community of about 200 in 1910 controlled about 80 percent of Haiti's international commerce. There were rumors also of German plans to set up a naval coaling station at Mole Saint-Nicholas. The Haitians had turned down a U.S. request for a coaling station there in 1891, despite the presence of African American Frederick Douglass, minister resident and consul general to Haiti, as one of the principal negotiators and despite the presence of seven U.S. warships adding gravity to the proceedings. The United States had actually helped new Haitian ruler General Louis Modestin Florvil Hypolite prevail in his war for the presidency over General F. D. Legitime, who was backed by the French. At one point the U.S. negotiators had contemplated simply seizing the Mole by force and presenting

Haiti with a fait accompli. At the time the United States was contemplating a trans-Central American canal in Nicaragua and the French were already attempting to build one in Panama. The principal U.S. negotiator, Rear Admiral Bancroft Gherardi, commander in chief of the U.S. North Atlantic Fleet, told Haiti's Foreign Secretary Firmin in the course of the negotiations that it was the Mole's "manifest destiny" to come under the control of the U.S. Navy.

Now in 1915 the United States argued, in keeping with the Monroe Doctrine, that Haiti's probable inability to repay German debts might lead to an unacceptable German attempt to intervene in Haiti. The United States again claimed that black people were incapable of self-government.

The United States dissolved the Haitian government and imposed a handpicked alternative. When even that puppet government, under Philippe Dartiguenave, refused in 1917 to change Haiti's law preventing foreign ownership of land, the United States forced him to dissolve the legislature. It did not meet again until 1929. The racism of U.S. troops (mostly from the segregationist U.S. South), coupled with policies of forced labor and the destruction of democratic institutions, led to three peasant "Caco" rebellions between 1915 and 1920.

The most important leader of this guerilla resistance was Charlemagne Peralte, who was not himself a peasant but a former general in the Haitian army. In 1919 Peralte issued a call to the people of Haiti. "Soon," he wrote, "a day like the 1st of January 1804 will rise. For four years the [American] Occupation has been insulting us constantly." He invoked the memory "of the great Dessalines" to "get rid of those savage people, whose beastly character is evident in the person of their President [Woodrow] Wilson—traitor, bandit, trouble maker and thief." Peralte exhorted Haitians—"Die for your country, Long live independence! Long live the Union! Long live the just war! Down with the Americans!" Peralte also wrote the French minister in Haiti seeking French recognition of his provisional government of Haiti. The Americans, he said, were in violation of their own principles agreed to at the 1919 Paris Peace

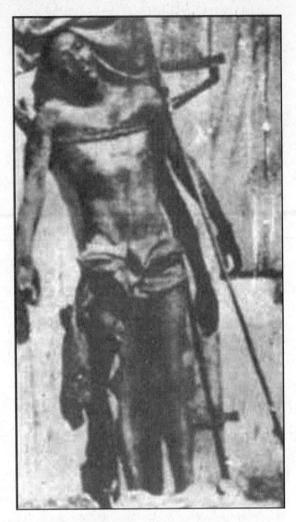

Charlemagne Peralte, leader of the Haitian resistance to the U.S. occupation. Peralte was killed by a U.S. marine in 1919. The American authorities then distributed thousands of copies of a photo of his near-nude corpse affixed to a door, in an attempt to cow the resistance.

Conference after World War I. That conference had affirmed the rights of small countries to freedom from aggression by the strong.

Peralte was betrayed in 1919 by one of his officers who led a disguised U.S. marine to Peralte's camp. The marine shot Peralte through the heart. In an action that could have graced the Maroon wars of earlier centuries, the Americans photographed Peralte's almost nude corpse tied to a door. They distributed the photo all over the country.

The Haitians exhumed Peralte's body in 1935, after the end of the occupation. President Stenio Vincent attended a state funeral in Peralte's honor. In 1994 President Jean-Bertrand Aristide placed Peralte's image on Haitian coins.

One year after the invasion of Haiti, the turn of neighboring Dominican Republic was next. U.S. marines invaded on May 15, 1916 and had overcome most resistance by the end of July. The U.S. set up a military government. As in Haiti, political instability and the threat of intervention by European creditor nations provided the pretext for U.S. invasion. A U.S. customs receivership had existed since 1905, whereby a U.S. receiver collected customs revenues, paid off creditors and then passed on some of the remainder to the Dominican government. As in Haiti there was a popular rural-based resistance movement. The *Gavileros* fought a guerilla campaign for the entire duration of the U.S. occupation.

The United States early on disbanded the Dominican army and replaced it with a National Guard. This unit, renamed the National Police Force, provided the base for the rise to power of Rafael Trujillo, who succeeded the Americans and became one of the Western Hemisphere's most bloody dictators, until he was assassinated in 1961.

The U.S. invasion was staged in the name of the "Roosevelt Corollary" to the Monroe Doctrine, enunciated to Congress by President Theodore Roosevelt in 1904. "Chronic wrongdoing" by any Western Hemisphere nation, he announced, "would ultimately require intervention by some civilized nation." Since the United States adhered to the Monroe Doctrine, he said, it would be impelled in such cases "to the exercise of an international police power." The Roosevelt Corollary was also invoked in Haiti.

The U.S. protectorates over the Dominican Republic and Haiti ended in 1930 and 1934, respectively. In the "Good Neighbor Policy" of 1933, President Franklin D. Roosevelt tried to distance himself from the interventionist Roosevelt Corollary of his namesake.

Shortly after the invasions of Haiti and the Dominican Republic the United States bought the Danish Virgin Islands of St. Thomas, St. Croix and St. John on March 31, 1917, for $25 million. An 1867 treaty to purchase the islands had been ratified by Denmark but failed to pass the U.S. Senate. The United States ratified a 1900 treaty attempt in 1902 but this time the Danish upper house failed to ratify. In 1915, with the United States in full expansionist mode, efforts to buy the islands were rekindled. World War I was raging in Europe and the United States feared that Germany might annex Denmark and thereby obtain the islands for use as a base for submarine warfare.

This time the Danes tried to insist on human rights guarantees, including a local plebiscite and immediate U.S. citizenship for islanders as a safeguard against America's racist practices of the period. The United States executive branch was unwilling to usurp the role of the Congress by making such assurances via treaty. There were hints of a forcible seizure of the islands if Denmark would not sell. Denmark agreed to sell and the islands were formally transferred to the United States on March 31, 1917.

The islands were administered by the U.S. Navy until 1931 when a civil administration was appointed. Virgin Islands "nationals" became full U.S. citizens in 1932. Self-government came in 1936. An elected governor was instituted in 1970.

The United States entered World War I on April 6, 1917. Thanks largely to its recent Caribbean acquisitions, this represented a kind of "coming out" onto the world stage as a fully fledged imperial power.

The Greater Antilles of Cuba, Puerto Rico, Haiti and the Dominican Republic were now all under the U.S. control. Jamaica was the only exception and even there, intermittent voices could be heard advocating U.S. annexation. The U.S. Virgin Islands had been added to the roster. The Panama Canal had been opened in 1914, situated in the U.S. Canal Zone, secured from Panama in perpetuity by the Hay-Bunau Varilla Treaty of 1903. (The Panama Canal Treaty of 1977 gave the area back to Panama.) By this time numerous U.S. military interventions, some still ongoing, had taken place since the 1890s

Two famous Trinidadians (former Prime Ministers George Chambers and Eric Williams), upstaged by an American intruder, Piarco International Airport, Trinidad, 2010.

in Haiti, Nicaragua, Cuba, Puerto Rico, Honduras, the Dominican Republic, Panama and Mexico, together with the "non hostile" landing of troops in Jamaica in 1907. The Caribbean had become the "American Lake."

World War II brought the United States even more deeply into the Caribbean. By the Lend Lease agreement of 1941 the United States gave Britain, in dire straits in its war against Germany, ninety-nine old destroyers. In exchange the United States obtained military bases in the British Caribbean colonies of Bermuda, Trinidad and Tobago, Antigua, British Guiana, Jamaica and St. Lucia, in addition to several in Newfoundland and Labrador, Canada.

Most of the Caribbean bases were closed in 1949. Trinidad's Chaguaramas Naval Base, the largest in the area, was deactivated in 1977 after some contention with the Trinidad and Tobago government, which wanted to locate the capital of the West Indies Federation (1958–1962) there. At its height some 30,000 U.S. troops were stationed at

Chaguaramas. Many of them were African Americans and Puerto Ricans. War had once again facilitated African American–Caribbean contact.

The crowning act in the consolidation of U.S. power was the establishment of the Anglo-American Caribbean Commission (AACC) in 1942. This was a supranational agency which oversaw a wide range of social and economic affairs. It reinforced the reality of the United States as almost a coruler with the British in the British colonies. The United States had grave doubts concerning Britain's ability to control the social unrest which had erupted intermittently throughout the 1930s. U.S. foreign policy officials feared that if things got worse the United States might have to send troops to keep order in the British islands. This was a distraction the United States could do without in the middle of a war with Germany. The AACC was therefore proposed as a device to monitor and control the region while

helping improve social and economic conditions, thereby staving off unrest. The British had sent a commission of enquiry under Lord Moyne to traverse the colonies in 1938–1939 and make recommendations for restoring tranquility. The United States asserted its right to its independent appraisal of the British West Indies when it sent its own version of the Moyne Commission to the area in 1940. President Franklin D. Roosevelt's Caribbean adviser, Frank Taussig, headed a three-man team. Taussig later headed the U.S. section of the AACC.

In 1946 the French and Dutch Caribbean came within the commission's purview and its name was changed to the Caribbean Commission, with headquarters in Trinidad and Eric Williams, future prime minister of Trinidad and Tobago, as its highest ranking Caribbean civil servant. The Caribbean Commission was dissolved in 1955.

Further Readings

Dunn, Richard S. "The Barbados Census of 1680: Profile of the Richest Colony in English America." *The William and Mary Quarterly, Third Series*, 26, 1, January 1969, 3–30.

Dunn, Richard S., Ed. *Shaping Southern Society*. New York: Oxford University Press, 1976.

Elliott, Robert Brown. *Office of History and Preservation, Office of the Clerk, Black Americans in Congress, 1870–2007*. Washington, D.C.: U.S. Government Printing Office, 2008. http://baic.house.gov/member-profiles/profile.html?intID=4 [accessed November 8, 2009].

Frazier, E. Franklin, and Eric Williams, Eds. *The Economic Future of the Caribbean*. Dover, MA: The Majority Press, 2004.

Himelhoch, Myra. "Frederick Douglass and Haiti's Mole St. Nicolas." *Journal of Negro History*, 56, 3, July 1971, 161–180.

James, Winston. *Holding Aloft the Banner of Ethiopia: Caribbean Radicalism in Early Twentieth-Century America*. London: Verso, 1998.

Jordan, Winthrop D. "The Influence of the West Indies on the Origins of New England Slavery." *William and Mary Quarterly, Third Series*, 18, 2, April 1961, 243–250.

Martin, Tony. *Literary Garveyism: Garvey, Black Arts and the Harlem Renaissance*. Dover, MA: The Majority Press, 1983.

Martin, Tony. *Race First: The Ideological and Organizational Struggles of Marcus Garvey and the Universal Negro Improvement Association*. Dover, MA: The Majority Press, 1986. First pub. by Greenwood Press, 1976.

Martin, Tony. "Garvey, Marcus," in Juliet E. K. Walker, Ed., *Encyclopedia of African American Business History*. Westport, CT: Greenwood Press, 1999.

Martin, Tony. *Amy Ashwood Garvey: Pan-Africanist, Feminist and Mrs. Marcus Garvey No. 1, Or, A Tale of Two Amies*. Dover, MA: The Majority Press, 2007.

Phillips, Glenn O. "The Response of a West Indian Activist: D. A. Straker, 1842–1908." *Journal of Negro History*, 66, 2, Summer 1981, 128–139.

Platt Amendment. The full text is at http://www.fordham.edu/halsall/mod/1901platt.html [accessed November 9, 2009].

Reid, Ira DeA. *The Negro Immigrant: His Background, Characteristics and Social Adjustment, 1899–1937*. New York: Arno Press, 1969. First pub. 1939.

Roberts, George. *The Population of Jamaica*. London: Oxford University Press, 1957.

Seraille, William. "Afro-American Emigration to Haiti during the American Civil War." *The Americas*, 35, 2, October 1978, 185–200.

Siebert, Wilbur H. *The Legacy of the American Revolution to the British West Indies and Bahamas.* Columbus: The Ohio State University Press, 1913.

Sluiter, Engel. "New Light on the '20. and Odd Negroes' Arriving in Virginia, August 1619." *The William and Mary Quarterly*, Third Series, 54, 2, April 1997, 395–398.

Turner, Joyce Moore. *Caribbean Crusaders and the Harlem Renaissance.* Urbana: University of Illinois Press, 2005.

14

Twentieth Century to World War II
Turbulent Times

The twentieth century ushered itself in everywhere embroiled in tension and foreboding. There was widespread poverty and suffering, necessitating a visit from a British Royal Commission to the British territories in 1897. The commission recommended helping the poor establish themselves as peasant proprietors. "Potato riots" in Barbados throughout the 1880s and 1890s underscored the desperate poverty. In these riots crowds would assemble to raid fields of food crops for their sustenance.

By 1900 Cuba was about to have the fruits of its independence war snatched away by the Platt Amendment. Haiti and the Dominican Republic were already setting themselves up for an impending fall into U.S. protectorate status. In the British Caribbean activists and reformers were chafing at the bit of an undemocratic society. The first black (as opposed to colored) person on Jamaica's Legislative Council, Alexander Dixon, was elected in 1899, partly through the exertions of Dr. J. Robert Love. Love was born in Nassau and educated in the United States (medical doctor, University of Buffalo), where he was ordained an Episcopal clergyman. He practiced medicine and served as a priest in Haiti from 1881 to 1890. He lived in Jamaica from 1890 to his death in 1914. Love published the weekly *Jamaica Advocate* from 1894 to 1905. He founded the Peoples Convention in 1898 to celebrate the sixtieth anniversary of Emancipation in the British Caribbean. It met annually until 1903. Love himself was elected Jamaica's third black Legislative Council member in 1906.

Jamaica's National Club was founded in 1909 by Sandy Cox and H. A. L. Simpson to press for more democratic government and better conditions for workers. Marcus Garvey was among its more noteworthy assistant secretaries.

In Jamaica, Trinidad and elsewhere black persons remained largely locked out of high-echelon politics by the absence of an elective element or the presence of a very restrictive franchise. In these conditions they found a greater outlet for political activity in municipal councils, where the franchise was generally a bit less exclusionary. In Port of Spain the British government frustrated this avenue of nonwhite participation by disbanding the City Council from 1899 to 1914.

When Trinidad's Henry Sylvester Williams arrived in the Caribbean from London in 1901 to organize branches of his Pan-African Association, he met with a tremendous popular response. People were ready to embrace an organization that seemed to have the potential for uplifting the black masses and securing more democracy. Many of the leaders who threw in their lot with Williams already had or belonged to organizations of their own, mobilized for similar goals.

It was in this period, in 1903, that Port of Spain experienced its Water Riots. Protests by working people and middle class activists against proposed government taxes on water usage were led by a Ratepayers Association, chaired by wealthy veteran black activist, M'zumbo Lazare. A crowd gathered at the Red House, seat of the Legislative Council, on the day the council debated the measure. They burned the Red House down. The police fired on and bayoneted the crowd, killing thirteen and wounding forty-two. In order to mollify the populace, the government in 1904 made C. Prudhomme David, a lawyer, the first black person nominated to the Legislative Council. (Trinidad's crown colony status did not yet allow elected members.) David had been first secretary of a Reform Committee formed in 1893, one of several "reform," "representative government" and "working-men's" associations existing in the British colonies.

NATURAL DISASTERS

In the midst of political turbulence even the elements seemed to strike a blow against the status quo ante. On May 7, 1902, St. Vincent's Soufrière volcano erupted, killing 1,600–2,000 people and devastating approximately 30 square miles of northern St. Vincent. Barbados, 100 miles to the east, was in total darkness for a while and was showered with "pebbles and gritty substances." The noise of the eruptions was heard in islands up to 200 miles away, including Dominica, Antigua, St. Kitts, Guadeloupe and St. Thomas. Fire and smoke were visible from St. Lucia.

Four white people including one Portuguese were among the dead. Remnants of the Black Carib population who had survived deportation and concentration camp decimation in 1797 were among the hardest hit. There was "horrifying" devastation in Carib country, with dead cattle and human corpses decomposing unburied for several days. Refugees fled to Chateau Belair, Chatoyer's old headquarters. Many fled to Dominica in canoes, as their ancestors had journeyed back and forth to St. Lucia in canoes for supplies, during their wars against British incursion.

Some areas, deeply covered in volcanic ash, looked like the Sahara Desert. An American scientist assured survivors that the rest of the island was about to subside. It was "A Weird and Awful

Scene," headlined the *New York Times*; "Every Hour Brings Sadder News":

At midday on Wednesday the craters ejected enormous columns of steamy vapor, rising majestically eight miles high and expanding into wonderful shapes, resembling enormous cauliflowers, gigantic wheels, and beautiful flower ferns, all streaked up and down and cross wise with vivid flashes of lightning, awing the beholder and impressing the mind with fear.

The devastation of St. Vincent was incredibly but a prelude to what has been called the worst volcanic disaster of the twentieth century and the third worst in recorded history. On May 8, 1902, the day after Soufrière, the Mt. Pelée volcano erupted in neighboring Martinique. Almost instantaneously all but two of St. Pierre's 30,000 residents were obliterated. St. Pierre was Martinique's most populous city and the island's capital. One of the survivors lived on the outskirts of the city. The other was a prisoner incarcerated in a dungeon. "As I stood beside the shrunken corpse of St Pierre," wrote a *New York Times* correspondent, "which less than two weeks previously was a splendid city of more than 30,000 inhabitants— the queen of the Lesser Antilles—I gazed upon a panorama which for depressing loneliness and horror must have had a counterpart only when the earth itself was being crushed and molded into shape."

In 1907 the Jamaica earthquake and resulting fire killed over 800 of Kingston's 46,000 population. This completed the trilogy of Caribbean horrors.

EARLY WORKING-CLASS STIRRINGS

The working-class movement meanwhile continued to struggle to its feet. Proto-working-class activity such as strikes had existed for a very long time. Every time an enslaved person escaped from the plantation or revolted, this was a kind of workers' activity. During enslavement there were even, as previously noted, some strike-type work stoppages, where the enslaved walked off the plantation and refused to return until grievances were addressed.

The actions of Damon in British Guiana and others during apprenticeship were akin to strike actions.

In 1842 sugar workers on most of the plantations in British Guiana's Demerara and Essequibo regions struck. The still mostly African workforce was protesting new "Rules and Regulations" by which planters sought to reduce their wages and reduce their provision ground and other benefits. Some Guianese workers struck again in 1846 after renewed attempts to reduce wages. In 1848 a colony-wide strike took place. Strikers burnt several plantations. This time they were protesting reduced wages, unfair taxation which forced them to pay for the importation of immigrant workers and the disbursement of tax revenue on ruling-class projects rather than on the needs of the poorer classes. Strikes occurred in Jamaica in 1863 and 1864, long before the enactment of any trade union legislation.

The earliest formal unions also antedated legislation recognizing unions. Jamaica's earliest union—the Carpenters, Bricklayers and Painters Union (better known as the Artisans' Union)—was established in 1898 and lasted until 1901.

The opening years of the twentieth century saw considerable labor unrest, resulting in substantial fatalities among protesters. Trinidad's 1903 Water Riots were followed by the 1905 waterfront workers' strike in British Guiana for higher wages and better conditions. The police killed eight workers and wounded several. Hubert Nathaniel Critchlow led the waterfront workers. The disturbances spread to several other locations, including Plantation Ruimveldt on the outskirts of Georgetown. It was there that the first police killings took place. After these shootings crowds roamed the city shouting "Kill every white man," and "Kill Lushington" (the English colonel who commanded the police.)

In March 1907 a "Coolie Riot" erupted at the Perseverance Estate in Couva, Trinidad. Indentured Indians killed the senior overseer, one McKenzie. This culminated a period of unrest in which seventy indentured Indians from the Kleinwort estate in Couva had been charged before the Couva police court between January and March 1907.

In April 1907 coal carriers and sugar workers rioted in St. Lucia for higher wages. Authorities brought in 28 Vincentian and 100 Barbadian policemen to reinforce the already largely Barbadian

St. Lucian force. British marines arrived a few days later on the *HMS Indefatigable*. As so often in Caribbean history, inter-imperial cooperation was forthcoming. Dutch marines happened to be on hand and their eagerness to have a go at the workers was warmly applauded by the British. Authorities shot and killed six workers and wounded a further twenty-seven by rifle fire. An undetermined number of people were injured by sticks and stones.

In 1906 the Trinidad Workingmen's Association (TWA), originally founded in 1897, reorganized itself under druggist Alfred Richards. For the next two and a half decades it would provide leadership for much of Trinidad's working class and progressive political activity. Like many other similar organizations of the period, it was a kind of omnibus association, comprising professional and working-class people and interesting itself in a wide range of issues pertaining to workers' rights, anticolonialism and antiracism. It favored a West Indian federation with prior representative government. In 1913 it established a labor/employment bureau with nine offices around the country. It was at the forefront of the campaign for the restoration of an elective Port of Spain City Council. It established a fraternal link with the British Labor Party, with its Labor Party representative asking questions in the British parliament on behalf of the TWA. In 1912 Joseph Pointer, the Labor Party link, visited Trinidad under the auspices of the TWA.

In 1914 there was a split within the TWA, with Richards, now considered too moderate by some, being supplanted first by Grenadian-born John Sydney DeBourg and then by Barbados-born James Braithwaite. DeBourg would later be deported to Grenada after visiting British Guiana on TWA business, as was F. E. M. Hercules earlier. He would later turn up in New York as an important member of Garvey's UNIA. Braithwaite was also a leader of the UNIA in Trinidad.

In 1908 Marcus Garvey led a Printers' Union strike in Jamaica. He and others lost their jobs as a result. In 1908 Jamaica's tobacco workers went on strike. In Guyana, Critchlow led a successful waterfront strike in 1917. This led to the formation, in 1919, of his British Guiana Labor Union (BGLU). Guyanese unions were legalized in 1921 and the BGLU was the first to register, in 1922. Guyanese union legislation was unique in the 1920s British Caribbean for providing protection from tort liability, which exposed workers to lawsuits for damages alleged by employers as a result of strikes.

The BGLU in 1926 hosted the British Guiana and West Indian Labor Congress. This was a pioneering effort, with A. A. Cipriani of Trinidad, Grantley Adams of Barbados and Surinamese delegates in attendance. Critchlow over the years attended several British Commonwealth and international workers' meetings. Among these was the International Trade Union Committee of Negro Workers Conference, organized by Trinidadian George Padmore in Hamburg, Germany and the International Red Aid in Russia, both in 1931. The BGLU published its own *Labour Magazine*.

A slew of thrift, uplift and self-help associations and lodges supplemented this embryonic working-class and political activity. Friendly societies proliferated among the black and colored working and middle classes. Members paid dues and received sickness, death and other benefits. The West African–derived "susu" (*esusu*) allowed people to pool their small savings into a revolving fund to receive a larger lump sum than would normally come into their hands at one time. Indo-Trinidadians had a similar institution, the *chaiteyi*. In 1918 middle-class Afro-Trinidadians (lawyers, doctors, journalists, civil servants) founded the Trinidad Cooperative Bank, affectionately known as the Penny Bank. This was the first nonwhite bank in the country's history. Upon the small savings of its clientele the Penny Bank was able to construct moderate income housing developments. Leaders of Garvey's UNIA and the father of Eric Williams, future prime minister, were among the bank's early directors. The bank's main founder was journalist Charles A. Petioni. He emigrated to New York soon after the bank's founding. There he became, like DeBourg, a prominent member of Garvey's UNIA. He qualified as a medical doctor and spent many decades as a leading figure in Caribbean pressure group politics in New York. The Penny Bank idea was copied in other islands.

An unusual avenue of working-class social and economic uplift was the landship movement, normally associated with Barbados, but not unique to that island. The landships borrowed the trappings of the British Royal Navy. They were replete with "ships," uniformed admirals, crews and the like. They held elaborate balls which even the British governor might condescend to attend. They were also social and economic uplift organizations. Hilary Beckles reports over 60 landships with over 3,800 "crews" in Barbados in the 1920s. Trinidad's best known landship was the Newtown, Port of Spain, based ship of a very influential head stevedore known as Lord Luke. The landship concept bears some comparison with, and may even have been influenced by, the Salvation Army, with its ensigns, majors, divisional commanders and the like.

CUBA: RACIAL MASSACRE

The general pattern of African consciousness described here was true also for Cuba, the Caribbean's largest island and most populous nation. The fact that Afro-Cubans were not in a clear official majority, the reality of U.S. occupation (1898–1902 and 1906–1909) and the grant of universal male adult suffrage in 1902 nevertheless provided Cuba with distinctive features. Cuba formally ended slavery in 1886, the last Caribbean nation to do so, even though most Afro-Cubans had already emancipated themselves by that time. The Afro-Cubans formed themselves into African "societies," published newspapers, maintained a strong practice of African religion and, for thousands of Congoes in Cuba, tried to return to Africa. Inspired by the Afro-Cuban General Antonio Maceo, they constituted the majority of the Liberation Army (whose soldiers were popularly referred to as *Mambis* or *Mambises*) in the 1895–1898 War of Independence against Spain.

Traditional Spanish racism, which existed even within the Liberation Army, and which not even Maceo, Cuba's most successful general, could avoid, intensified during the U.S. occupation of 1898–1902. The United States withdrew in 1902 leaving white Cubans and Spaniards firmly in charge. Afro-Cubans were largely locked out of political power, segregation remained rampant and aspects of African culture, such as the *Santería* religion, were criminalized. In addition, losses in the independence wars of 1868–1878 and 1895–1898, coupled with a deliberate "whitening" policy of massive Spanish immigration, together put the Afro-Cuban population into relative decline.

The enduring Cuban (and Latin American) fiction of a racial democracy made the situation more complex and frustrating. By 1907 a rising conscious-ness had produced several manifestoes and proposals to stem the racist tide. There were calls for the recogni-tion of the inordinate sacrifices made by Afro-Cubans in the recent independence war; there were calls to boycott elections until Afro-Cubans were guaranteed the right, not merely to vote, but to be appointed to high office; there were calls for an independent African political party. Evaristo E. Estenoz, a former Liberation Army officer, tried unsuccessfully to establish an Afro-Cuban caucus within the Liberal Party, the party favored by most Afro-Cubans. Over 200 people attended a 1907 conference in Camaguey to establish a *Directorio de la Raza de Color* (Coordinating Council for People of Color). The group promised to unite Africans and coloreds in a self-reliant organization for "the progress of our race."

It eschewed any intention of forming a race-based political party.

On August 7, 1908, Estenoz formally estab-lished the Independent Party of Color *(Partido de los Independientes de Color)*, which was legally recognized by the U.S. occupation. The total absence of Afro-Cuban winners in the local and provincial elections appeared to be the last straw for Estenoz. The new party condemned the exclusion of Afro-Cubans from the judiciary and diplomatic service, proposed a campaign against illiteracy and for expanded elementary education, demanded admission of Africans into military and naval academies, denounced the death penalty, and advocated prison reform, workmen's compensation and an eight-hour day. It opposed the ban on African immigration. It also opposed the Platt Amendment, under which the United States reserved the right to intervene in Cuban affairs. All of these proposals spoke directly or indirectly to areas of racial discrimination. The party prematurely contested national elections in 1908 and was heavily defeated.

Correspondents to the party's newspaper, *Previsión (Foresight)*, meanwhile exhibited the same racial pride and desire for a strong race that were

Evaristo Estenoz (center, middle row) and members of Cuba's Independent Party of Color.

by now commonplace elsewhere in the Caribbean. "I am a black dot," wrote one reader, quoted by Aline Helg, "one out of the anonymous mass of my race, who longs to see the advance of my people through our own effort, through the compact union and solidarity of our family."

The white Cuban power structure repressed the Independent Party of Color with a ferocity which, while not fundamentally unusual in the context of Caribbean history, nevertheless assumed many of the characteristics of contemporary North American racism. Estenoz was arrested and jailed twice in 1910, as were the top leadership of the party and hundreds of supporters. Many Afro-Cubans were randomly arrested and jailed. The U.S.-type stereotypes of Afro-Cubans as rapists and rumors of a Haitian-type revolution were used as smokescreens to cover the repression. Emulating a common North American tactic, Cuba's white rulers found an Afro-Cuban, Martin Morúa Delgado, the only African in the island's Senate, to introduce a law banning racially based and therefore "racist" political parties. The Morúa Law passed in 1910, by which time Estenoz was claiming 93,000 members. Morúa obligingly died four days afterward, mercifully spared the carnage soon to be visited upon Afro-Cubans in the name of his law.

With the leadership out of jail in 1911 the party continued to mobilize while trying to appease white racism. In 1912, with the party still banned and presidential elections imminent, a few hundred party members staged an "armed protest," in the tradition of similar contemporary protests by veterans and other groups. This provided the pretext for their annihilation. The white structure, always united across party lines in its eagerness to extirpate the Afro-Cuban party, unleashed a reign of terror. Thousands of troops were deployed and the white population was armed. Africans were lynched, shot and beheaded. Afro-Cuban corpses were left to litter the streets. An estimated 2,000 to 5,000 Afro-Cubans, many of them people unconnected to the party, were killed by the military and vigilantes. Thousands were arrested. A large number became refugees. Estenoz and other leaders were slaughtered and their bodies desecrated. A grisly photograph of Estenoz' naked corpse, surrounded by white soldiers and doctors, offers silent testimony to this. In the photo someone is holding Estenoz' head toward the camera, exposing the gaping gunshot wound in the back of his head that killed him at point-blank range. The Cuban massacre of 1912 remains one of the worst reverses suffered by African aspirations in Caribbean history.

The massacre of the Independents of Color underlined a new vulnerability for some post-Emancipation struggles. Marronage and total rebellion aimed at possible state power were usually no longer immediate objectives in the early twentieth century. (This would change later in the century with the Cuban and Grenada revolutions among others.) For the time being, however, the threat to state power could be contained by authorities. State reprisals, as in the Jamaica Rebellion of 1865 and the Cuban massacre of 1912, could be just as savage as in the pre-Emancipation period.

WORLD WAR I

In the midst of all this turmoil came World War I (1914–1918). This conflict represented a kind of coming of age and end of innocence for much of the world. The Caribbean was no exception. This was a period of upsurge for subject peoples everywhere. The Irish Easter Uprising of 1916 struck a bloody blow for Irish independence against Britain. The Russian Revolution took place in 1917.

The world's major imperial powers—Britain, France, Germany, the United States—and a host of lesser powers, with their colonies and vassals pressed into service, devastated the world on a scale unprecedented in human history, though this unimaginable carnage was soon to be but a harbinger of the even greater slaughter of World War II. About 16 million people were killed in the conflict, "the war to end all wars," with a further 21 million wounded. Significantly, as an indication of things to come, civilian deaths (6.8 million) were almost as great as military (9.7 million).

France suffered almost 6,000,000 dead and wounded, out of a population of 39.6 million. This incredible carnage was perpetrated under such slogans as "making the world safe for democracy." The hypocrisy of all this was not lost on oppressed people all over the world. The result was a heightened awareness of the need for real democracy for colonized peoples.

In the British West Indies war propaganda initially excited young men and there was a great desire to enlist. The British War Office was however unwilling to welcome black soldiers into what some officials unabashedly called a "white man's war." It was "against British tradition," said one official, "to employ aboriginal troops against a European enemy."

The British War Office compromised in 1915 out of fear that spurned Caribbean would-be volunteers might become a source of disaffection, with negative consequences for the imperial connection. They therefore formed a special British West Indies Regiment (BWIR) for the conflict. The rank and file were all black (including a few East Indians). Officers had to be white. Three-quarters of them must be British, as opposed to Caribbean white. One-sixteenth or one-thirty-second black persons (according to official stipulations) could qualify as white. And on October 23, 1915, as the BWIR volunteers were arriving in England, King George V issued a statement of unbelievable racial insensitivity, dutifully carried in the Caribbean media, and addressed to the empire. He thanked his "subjects all over the world" for their sacrifices, including life itself, in preserving the "free Empire" which they enjoyed. He promised, however, that now, as in days of yore, "men of *our race* [emphasis added]" would rise to the challenge of defeating the German enemy.

The white sons of merchants and planters, however, refused to join any black regiment, except as officers. White Trinidad merchant George F. Huggins therefore led a two-man delegation to the Colonial Office in London in 1915 to explain the situation and assure London that white boys were not really lacking in patriotism. They just did not want to join a black regiment, that was all. The British authorities consented to having white boys come to England to join British units. Huggins accordingly organized a Merchants and Planters Contingent which dispatched white boys to England for this purpose. Some black volunteers, in their zeal, also made their way to England. There the "lighter colored" of them, as one British official described it, were accepted while the blacker ones often faced rejection.

The BWIR went off to training in England in 1915. Those who remained in Europe were used as laborers. They dug trenches, laid cables, unloaded ships and carried ammunition under heavy fire. On August 6, 1916, a detachment of BWIR troops arrived from Egypt to Tanganyika (Tanzania), where the 2nd Battalion of the old West India Regiment was already stationed. As of June 1917 the 397 men of the BWIR in Egypt were occupied as follows: 101 motor boat drivers, 81 guards, 71 clerks, 23 carpenters, 16 camp police, 12 blacksmiths, 11 fitters, 6 telephone operators and 76 "miscellaneous duties."

A small number from the 1st and 2nd battalions, made up of men from all over the Caribbean, managed to see combat against Turkish troops in Mesopotamia near the end of the war. They fought in Egypt, Palestine, Jordan and Syria. Some now lie buried a long way from home, in military cemeteries in Alexandria, Egypt and Jerusalem. Other BWIR soldiers lie in cemeteries in England, Belgium and France.

The BWIR soldiers were subjected to intense racism and neglect. In one extraordinarily lamentable episode, over 100 Jamaican volunteers were sent home with feet and hands amputated in 1916, without even having reached their training camps in England. These unfortunate youths, many, perhaps most still teenagers, were on board the ship *Verdula* sailing via Halifax, Nova Scotia, whither the Trelawney Maroons had been deported in 1796. They were not provided with warm clothing, blankets or heated accommodations suitable for the wintry voyage, resulting in widespread frostbite. About 200 altogether had to be invalided back to Jamaica.

Many troops died of pneumonia. In England the volunteers were housed in inadequately heated huts near English troops suffering from mumps and other communicable diseases. So many of them became ill or died there that it was long impossible to provide meaningful military training. Several of them now lie buried in military graves in Plymouth, Liverpool and Seaforth, among them two young St. Lucian cousins, Nelson N. Fevrier and Dennis Fevrier, who died on February 2 and January 23, 1916, respectively. They had enlisted together in September 1915 and arrived in England in midwinter to die within days of each other, probably without even receiving military training. It took their family ninety years of cherished remembrance, augmented over the years by family folklore to fill the gaps in information, to find out what really happened to their loved ones.

The few who were able to experience combat in Mesopotamia served with distinction. They also excelled other British empire forces at sports. While stationed in Egypt they ran into some firsthand experience of racism, South African style. White South African troops located down river from them refused to use water that had already passed through the BWIR's area. The BWIR men were appalled at the treatment of the black South Africans and became self-appointed advocates for their less fortunate brethren. They skirmished with white South African troops.

The men of the BWIR finally mutinied in Taranto, Italy, at the end of the war in 1918, when they were ordered to wash the dirty linens and clean the latrines of Italian laborers. Sixty sergeants there formed a Caribbean League. With the commissioned officer ranks barred to black soldiers, the sergeants represented the highest echelon of BWIR troops. They advocated black rule at home and black officers for the BWIR. One of the sergeants was Clennell Wickham, the postwar journalist and political activist in Barbados. The British court-martialled and shot one Jamaican sergeant. The commander of the Taranto camp was a white South African, Brigadier-General Carey Bernard.

Many of the men were shipped home via Britain, where they were caught up in the anti–black race riots of 1919. Wheelchair-bound veterans in an English hospital fought with wounded white fellow patients. The British deployed a warship to cover the return home of some veterans in case they should vent their anger upon arrival. Both during and after the war BWIR soldiers were denied pay raises, adequate pensions and other benefits given to white soldiers or otherwise promised to the BWIR veterans. When World War II rolled around two decades later, BWIR veterans in Jamaica were still lobbying for justice.

Statistics compiled by C. L. Joseph show that the BWIR contained soldiers from the Bahamas, Barbados, British Guiana, British Honduras, Grenada, Jamaica, the "Leewards," St. Lucia, St. Vincent and Trinidad and Tobago. A few were recruited among immigrants in Panama. One hundred and eighty-five were killed or died of wounds, while 1,071 died of the neglect and wanton waste of life inflicted on the soldiers. Six hundred and seventy-seven were wounded.

Nine thousand nine hundred and seventy-seven of the 15,204 soldiers came from Jamaica. Trinidad and Tobago was next with 1,438, followed by Barbados with 811, British Guiana with 686, British Honduras with 528 and the Bahamas with 439. Some British Caribbean soldiers also served with the Canadian Overseas Expeditionary Force and with African American units. These latter followed the same pattern of segregated labor battalions and bad treatment.

AUDREY JEFFERS

The war years with their increase in prices and allegations of profiteering also gave the Workingmen's and similar associations issues to rally around. As in earlier periods, the activities of Caribbean emigrants abroad again helped raise consciousness at home. The British-based Society of Peoples of African Origin (SPAO) brought together Africans, Caribbean residents and African Americans in England. Led by Sierra Leonean J. Eldred Taylor, its membership included prominent Caribbean residents such as F. E. M. Hercules and Audrey Jeffers. Hercules toured the Caribbean in 1919, as seen. Jeffers would return home to Trinidad in 1920 and found the Coterie of Social Workers (1921), for decades the dominant social service and women's organization in the region.

Jeffers (1898–1968) was the daughter of Henry I. Jeffers, prominent lawyer, three-time elected member of the Port of Spain City Council and a very prosperous member of Trinidad's small black elite class. She was sent to England in 1913 to finish her schooling. There she became very active in the Society of Peoples of African Origin, the African Progress Union, the Student Christian Movement and the Union of Students of African Descent. George Padmore said that she cofounded the last mentioned. Concern over the plight of the BWIR and West African soldiers impelled her into social work around their welfare. From her unique position as an independently wealthy black woman who did not have to "work," she was able to devote her full time to social and allied activity.

The Coterie quickly became the preeminent woman's organization in the British Caribbean. It operated hostels for working women, day nurseries in impoverished areas and a home for blind women.

Audrey Jeffers, pioneer woman's rights advocate, politician, philanthropist and social worker, with other members of the Port of Spain City Council, around 1936.

It pioneered school feeding programs in Trinidad and Tobago with its famous "breakfast sheds." The Coterie published a literary magazine edited by Jeffers. It held an annual "Fete de Noel" Christmas fair for children. Its Carnival Monday night dances at Jeffers' exclusive St. Clair home were an institution. It lobbied for a variety of women's causes, including the right of female store clerks to sit when not serving customers, equal pay for male and female teachers, the recruitment of women police and more scholarships for girls.

In 1936 Jeffers and the Coterie hosted, in Trinidad, what was described as Trinidad's and the region's first ever women's conference. Delegates came from British Guiana, St. Kitts, Barbados, Grenada, St. Lucia and Nevis to celebrate the Coterie's fifteenth birthday. Delegates were entertained by an all-female classical orchestra, men were prohibited from speaking (until late in the deliberations) and a new organization was formed, the West Indies and British Guiana Woman Workers Association.

Later in 1936, under the slogan "Vote for a Woman!" Audrey Jeffers became the first woman in the British West Indies to hold elective political office. She ran successfully for the Port of Spain City Council for the same seat previously held by her father for nine years. She defeated A. P. T. Ambard, editor of the *Port of Spain Gazette* and a prominent member of the white French Creole elite. The women of the Coterie, she said during her campaign, had efficiently fed, clothed and cared for the people of Trinidad where men had failed to make any headway. It was time for a woman on the City Council. The City Council's elections coincided with U.S. presidential elections. The next morning's *Trinidad Guardian* accordingly carried two major headlines: "Roosevelt Wins in a 'Landslide'" and "Miss Jeffers Wins in Woodbrook."

In 1946 Jeffers was nominated to the more important Legislative Council, the first woman to serve on that body. In 1956, with the British West Indian federation imminent, the Coterie brought together a Caribbean Women's Association. Audrey Jeffers was Liberian consul in Trinidad and in 1964 attended the fifth inauguration of President W. V. S. Tubman in Monrovia.

Men could not join the Coterie but unofficial "Coterie men," the husbands, sons, brothers and friends of members, hovered on the periphery. Among the Coterie men were C. L. R. James and George Padmore, both later outstanding radical intellectuals and Pan-African activists.

MARCUS GARVEY

The intensified race consciousness of the World War I period became known as the New Negro Movement. The single most important catalyst for the New Negro movement in the Caribbean, in African America and around the world was the Jamaican Marcus Garvey. Garvey's instrument was the Universal Negro Improvement Association and African Communities League (usually abbreviated to UNIA) which he founded in Jamaica in 1914. His perspective was global and the formation of the UNIA came after four years of travel in Central and South America and Europe. In the Americas he had followed the footsteps of Caribbean emigrants to places like Costa Rica and Panama. In England he met with African seamen and intellectuals, the latter at the offices of the *Africa Times* and *Orient Review,* where he worked. His consciousness had already been fed by early reading of Pan-African history, particularly the works of Edward Wilmot Blyden. He was a protégé of Dr. J. Robert Love and corresponded in 1915 with the African American educator, Booker T. Washington.

Garvey had also passed through the crucible of agitation for political reform. In 1910, the year in which the Independent Party of Color was banned in Cuba, he was an assistant secretary of the National Club in Jamaica. Garvey also had intimate experience of the labor movement, having led one of the British Caribbean's earliest strikes, a printers' strike, in 1908.

As a result of his travels and his readings Garvey was struck by the universal suffering of the race, as well as by the possibilities of regeneration inherent in organization. He saw race consciousness in the Caribbean as pivotal to this regeneration and Caribbean people as the instruments of positive

change. Writing in London in 1913 he declared: "As one who knows the people well, I make no apology for prophesying that there will soon be a turning point in the history of the West Indies; and that the people who inhabit that portion of the Western Hemisphere will be the instruments of uniting a scattered race who, before the close of many centuries, will found an Empire on which the sun shall shine as ceaselessly as it shines on the empire of the North today."

Garvey's grand design envisaged a strong African race, with its African homeland reclaimed from European imperialism, strong enough to protect its scattered members and respected in the world comity of nations. In a word, Garvey's was the philosophy of Black or African nationalism (as he himself described it). Its main tenets were race first, self-reliance and nationhood. Race first suggested that persons of the much oppressed African group should put their own uplift first. Garvey advocated the group's writing its own history, controlling its own media, worshipping its own gods and generally interpreting its own reality. Such ideas were widespread among the racial, ethnic and national movements of the time. Mahatma Gandhi of India, for example, advocated racial purity for Indians, as did Garvey for Africans. Unlike some proponents of similar ideas, however, Garvey stopped short of advocating racial supremacy. All he wanted was an end of oppression and equality for the African masses.

For the UNIA's first year and a half in Jamaica it behaved very much like other Caribbean social uplift organizations over the years. It fed the poor, visited the sick and held cultural evenings featuring poetry, recitations, music and elocution contests. Like its contemporary, the Trinidad Workingmen's Association, it tried to find work for the unemployed. Garvey and his fiancé and future first wife, Amy Ashwood, toured the country preaching race pride and recruiting members. In 1916 Garvey left for the United States, where a projected five-month stay lasted eleven years. There, by dint of relentless effort backed by superb promotional and organizational skills, he was well established by 1918. By 1919 the movement had assumed a solidly international character, with branches in Canada and the Caribbean, among other places, in addition to the United States.

Marcus Garvey statue, St. Ann's Bay, Jamaica.

The UNIA's major organ, *The Negro World,* begun in New York in 1918, almost immediately appeared in the Caribbean. One of the earliest British West Indian branches of the new UNIA (the organization having reorganized itself in New York) was in St. Vincent, under the leadership of R. E. M. Jack. The St. Vincent branch helped in the formation of branches in Dominica and other islands.

In the Caribbean, as in many other places, the Garvey Movement found itself preaching to the converted. But the converted lacked a global organization. Both Williams' Pan-African Association and Hercules' Society of Peoples of African Origin had fizzled out. So they flocked to the UNIA with its immense ability to link up local struggles and provide material and moral support in a systematic way. Even before starting a local UNIA chapter, the nucleus of would-be Dominica Garveyites, under J. R. Ralph Casimir and others, formed a Dominica Brotherhood Union in January 1920. One of their first acts was the

drafting of a pledge, "The Negro to Help the Negro." It read :

> We hereby sincerely and truly pledge to give our support, and we are quite ready at any moment to shed our blood and to give our very lives to this cause and shall do all what is in our power to help one and all members of the race who [are] for this good and just cause.
>
> We vow that we are sincerely and truly New Negroes. So help us Good God.

The impact of Garvey's movement on the Caribbean and the world was immense. His "race first" ideology found ready acceptance both among the masses and among substantial sections of the middle classes. There were branches of the UNIA throughout the Greater Caribbean area. Next to the United States, this was the region where the UNIA proliferated most. Cuba led the world outside the United States, with at least fifty-two branches; Panama was next with forty-eight; Trinidad and Tobago was third with thirty-two.

By the mid-1920s the UNIA boasted approximately 1,120 branches in over 40 countries. It had also become one of history's few genuine Pan-Caribbean political movements and doubtless the most successful. For there were UNIA branches in Cuba, Trinidad and Tobago, Jamaica, British Guiana, the Dominican Republic, Barbados, British Honduras, the Bahamas, Antigua, Bermuda, Dominica, Suriname, Grenada, Haiti, Nevis, Puerto Rico, St. Kitts, St. Lucia, St. Thomas and St. Vincent. The UNIA was also heavily represented among Caribbean emigrant communities in Panama, Costa Rica, Honduras, Guatemala and Nicaragua. Many Caribbean people also joined the movement in other countries, especially in such U.S. cities as New York, Boston and Miami, which were major destinations for Caribbean emigrants. Caribbean activists could be found in the leadership of UNIA branches in South Africa, England and Nigeria. Caribbean people, especially emigrants and sailors, were missionaries of Garveyism and helped the movement's rapid dissemination throughout the world.

The rapid spread of Garvey's movement may be attributable to several factors. For one thing, the World War I period was a time of worldwide radicalism. African peoples were also arguably at their most desperate point in history and so needed vigorous leadership. Garvey himself was also a tireless and exceedingly able organizer, in addition to being an exceptional orator and a strongly charismatic figure. His ideological position also appealed to masses of people.

The UNIA's impact on Caribbean affairs was almost immediate. Garvey's agents traversed the area establishing branches and spreading the word of nationalism and anticolonialism. Some were deported from, or refused entry into, certain territories. Several of the British colonial governors banned the *Negro World* illegally in 1919, and from 1920 on by means of hastily introduced Seditious Publications Ordinances. Despite these measures the paper made its way in, sometimes through the mails, sometimes smuggled in by seamen. Copies intercepted by the authorities were destroyed.

By 1919 the UNIA in the Caribbean was firmly entrenched enough to figure prominently in the labor riots and racial unrest that swept the area. The British blamed the *Negro World* for the upsurge in race consciousness which formed a backdrop to the disturbances. In Trinidad, many of the leaders of the Trinidad Workingmen's Association, the major organization involved in the stevedores' strike of December 1919, were also members of the UNIA. It was reported that Garvey's editorials were read aloud at their meetings. In British Honduras, S. A. Haynes, one of the major figures involved in the riots, was a Garveyite. He later became a high-ranking UNIA official in the United States.

After 1919, the UNIA maintained its links with the budding Caribbean labor movement. A. Bain Alves of Jamaica, members of Hubert Critchlow's British Guiana Labor Union and D. Hamilton Jackson, leader of the St. Croix Labor Union, were among those who established contact with the UNIA in the 1920s. Clement O. Payne of Barbados and Trinidad, founder of the Barbados Workers Union, was a Garveyite. He had also been a member of the very Garveyite Trinidad Workingmen's Association (TWA). The connection between the TWA and the UNIA was especially close. There was considerable overlapping between the leadership of the two organizations and the Workingmen's Association held its regular meetings at Liberty Hall, the UNIA's Port of Spain headquarters. Most of the working-class leaders coming into prominence in the 1930s were influenced by involvement at some level in Garvey's UNIA. Garvey himself founded a Jamaican Workers and Laborers Association in 1930, after his deportation from the United States in 1927.

Garvey's impact generally on progressive people and organizations was substantial. Grenada's T. A. Marryshow, "The Father of West Indian Federation," wrote favorably of him in his *West Indian* newspaper. In Trinidad the *Argos* and the *Labour Leader* (organ of the TWA) regularly supported him. In Barbados Clennell W. Wickham endorsed Garveyism in the pages of the *Barbados Weekly Herald*.

By the 1920s the UNIA had become, in several greater Caribbean territories, the virtual representatives of the African population. At a time when most black people in the area were denied the right to vote, and in an age mostly predating mass political parties, the UNIA often performed the function of quasi-political party as well as mutual aid organization. It was a major, sometimes *the* major, organized group looking after the interests of the mass of people. In early twenty-first-century Costa Rica the UNIA still enjoyed a position of importance among the black population.

The massive UNIA presence in Cuba, based primarily on the immigrant Jamaican population, also provided a new source for African consciousness in the wake of the slaughter of 1912. Some Jamaicans and Haitians actually participated in Evaristo Estenoz's armed protest of 1912.

It was into this tropical version of the southern United States that the immigrants massively injected the most powerful African-conscious organization in the world. A mere eight years after the slaughter of 1912 the officers of Garvey's Black Star Line Steamship Corporation were entertained to a banquet by President Menocal. In 1921 Garvey himself visited Cuba and was treated almost as a head of state. He was received by President Menocal and the governor of Oriente province. He addressed various Afro-Cuban groups, including Club Atenas, Havana's most prestigious society of color. So great was the power of the Cuban UNIA by 1923 that the resident British diplomatic representatives agreed to extend its recognition as the quasi-official body representing British Caribbean workers in Cuba. (The Foreign Office in London vetoed the idea after canvassing Caribbean governors). The Machado dictatorship banned the UNIA for a while in the late 1920s and early 1930s.

When mass-based party politics came to the Caribbean, Garvey and the UNIA were again in the vanguard—for Garvey's Peoples Political Party, formed in Jamaica in 1929, was a pioneer in its class. A Caribbean federation with dominion status was among its aims.

The white power structure in the Caribbean feared Garvey's radicalism and his organizing success, but sometimes they showed a grudging respect for his accomplishments. At various times he was refused permission to land in Bermuda, Cuba, the Canal Zone and Trinidad. Yet on other occasions

he was received by such persons as President Mario Garcia Menocal of Cuba, the governor of Oriente province in Cuba, the president of Costa Rica and the governor of British Honduras. His most extensive trip to the British Caribbean came in 1937, three years before his death. On that occasion he was prevented by the British authorities from holding open-air meetings in Trinidad. Nor was he permitted to refer to the labor struggles which had erupted there. Indeed, were it not for the personal intervention of Captain A. A. Cipriani, he may not have been allowed in at all.

Garvey did more than any other single individual to stimulate the anticolonialism, racial pride and working-class consciousness that laid the groundwork for the struggles of the late 1930s and thereafter. No one can equal him in his successful effort to demonstrate the historical and cultural unity of the Caribbean.

W. E. B. DuBois, African American integrationist scholar and activist, was the great Pan-African adversary of Garvey. DuBois convened Pan-African congresses in 1919, 1921, 1923 and 1927. The first three met in a variety of European capitals (Paris, London, Brussels and Lisbon). The fourth, largely the work of African American women, convened in New York. Caribbean delegates were sometimes the majority element at DuBois' congresses. E. F. Fredericks of Guyana served on the executive committee of DuBois' Paris congress in 1919. T. A. Marryshow, an admirer of Garvey, attended DuBois' 1921 congress. Audrey Jeffers of Trinidad was considered as a possible host for one of DuBois' congresses.

POSTWAR UPHEAVAL IN TRINIDAD

The years after World War I were extremely turbulent as workers and race uplift organizations agitated for positive change. There were numerous strikes all over the region. The pioneer trade union laws of British Guiana and Jamaica were attempts to placate the workers. British Honduras and Trinidad and Tobago experienced serious disturbances resulting in the authorities killing several people.

The Trinidad disturbances of December 1919 grew out of a strike by dockworkers in Port of Spain. The unrest was accompanied by widespread manifestations of hostility against whites. Racial tensions had been simmering for some time. A key element in the atmosphere of resentment against the British authorities in particular and white people in general was the returning soldiers of the British West Indies Regiment.

In addition to all their war-related problems, some of the returning soldiers had been involved in riots in Cardiff, Wales, during which British mobs had vented their fury upon the tiny black population. Upon returning home to Trinidad, the veterans immediately organized The Returned Soldiers and Sailors Council and Organization which held public meetings and propagandized their grievances to the people. This organization may have been an offshoot of the Caribbean League formed by BWIR sergeants in Taranto, Italy.

Major (later Lt. Col.) Maxwell Smith, commanding officer of the 8th Battalion, BWIR, at Taranto had leaked the existence of the Caribbean League to the Secretary of State for the Colonies. Now on July 22, 1919, he warned the Commandant of Local Forces in Trinidad that "the feeling of the black man against the white, to which I alluded in [Taranto] and which at that time was limited almost entirely to Jamaican troops, has spread, not only to many of the returned soldiers from this Colony, but also to the black population of Port-of-Spain generally."

In order to appease the veterans, the authorities invited them to participate in a parade marking the peace celebrations, which took place at the Queens Park Savannah on July 19, 1919. They were to be given the privilege of leading the parade. Only 132 fell in. A "considerable number" turned up to watch, and they all booed as their participating colleagues marched past. The reason for the poor turnout, according to the Inspector-General of Constabulary, was that the soldiers were disappointed at not being armed for the parade, since "some who had possessed themselves of ammunition whilst on active service intended to load with ball cartridges during the *feu de joi* and shoot down all the officers."

Meanwhile, other efforts to appease the soldiers were redoubled. Governor Sir John Chancellor appointed a Discharged Soldiers Central Authority to find jobs for unemployed soldiers and administered a land settlement scheme whereby veterans

could be apportioned 5 acres which would assume the character of a free grant when cultivated. (In St. Vincent invalided veterans were given 5 shillings each and the country's destitutes were given 2 shillings as part of the peace celebrations.)

For many months before December workers had also been restive, probing the government with a series of strikes. As early as May the American Consul in Port of Spain, Henry D. Baker, had informed his superiors in the U.S. State Department of serious work stoppages by stevedores, railway workers and tramcar operators. He noted their impoverished condition.

Allied with the veterans and workers was the *Argos*, a local newspaper owned by Chinese Trinidadian Lee Lum, but edited by Afro-Trinidadians, and *The Negro World*, organ of Marcus Garvey's UNIA. Many of the December strikers were Garveyites. The leadership of their organization, the Trinidad Workingmen's Association, was thoroughly Garveyite and maintained close ties with Garveyism until the 1930s.

Yet another factor playing upon the situation in the months preceding December was the question of racism in Britain. On the 17th of July persons involved in the Cardiff riots had returned home and the *Argos* had taken the opportunity to familiarize the populace with the atrocities which had been visited upon the black population in Britain. So that when, during the peace celebrations in July, several British sailors from the *H.M.S. Dartmouth* "were wantonly and severely assaulted, as were several other European members of the community" and "very lewd and disparaging remarks were freely made about the white race and about their women folk," and the Deputy Inspector General and an Inspector Carr of the Constabulary were stoned, the blame was placed on the *Argos*. The offending article had described how a white mob in Cardiff had attacked a black man's funeral, cut off the corpse's head, and used it as a football. It is interesting to note that veterans and others were reacting against the same mix of events at the same time (during the peace celebrations) and in a similar fashion, in Jamaica and in British Honduras.

On the 24th of July, two days after some of the above attacks on whites, a delegation consisting of the mayor of Port of Spain, a city councilor and two black solicitors appealed to the acting governor to ease the tension by releasing the Trinidadians among a batch of military prisoners who had been landed in transit to Jamaica. The prisoners were released. In advocating their release to his superiors in London, the acting governor explained that "a very strong feeling was at once aroused amongst the black section of the community and threats were openly made, not only by the usual idlers and loafers and irresponsible persons, but by black and coloured men of some standing and influence, that the whites should be killed."

On July 30 a committee of Trinidad's most influential white citizens urged the suppression of the *Argos*, "this poisonous organ," the arming of the white population, the establishment of "a body of white regular troops however small," and warned against the emergence of the "creole coolie," as they termed the new Indian who might not be manipulated as a buffer against the African, but who might even join the African in a common cause. After much discussion the authorities in London decided that British troops on the ground were more urgently needed in Belize, but they authorized a warship, the *HMS Cambrian*, to remain in Trinidad for the time being.

On December 1 the fury of the workers and their supporters erupted. For three weeks previously a strike by dockworkers had been successfully broken by workers imported for the purpose from Venezuela, Barbados and rural Trinidad. But now the strikers turned violent. On December 4, Governor Sir John Chancellor confessed how close colonial rule in the colony had come to disaster: the populace had forced the closing of businesses and the halting of traffic in the business and administrative district; the Inspector General of Constabulary had declared that he could no longer ensure the safety of Port of Spain unless concessions were made to the strikers; the authorities were afraid to open fire on rioters in Port of Spain lest there be reprisals against whites living in the country districts; a committee from the Chamber of Commerce had expressed its worry; and a warship, the *HMS Calcutta*, complete with an admiral on board, had arrived.

"I accordingly induced shipping agents on grounds of public policy," the governor explained,

"to meet the representatives of strikers and try to come to an agreement. They reluctantly consented and have granted an advance of wages which has satisfied stevedores who are returning to work." The American Consul, Baker, advised the State Department that the resulting 25 percent wage hike represented "apparently the first instance of any Labor Union in the British West Indies ever having received recognition from employers."

By the end of the first week in December the most precarious point seemed to have been passed, thanks to prompt concessions to the Port of Spain stevedores. By this time, however, the disturbances had spread to rural Trinidad and to Tobago, in which latter place the police fired into a crowd, inflicting several casualties, and killing one Nathaniel Williams, who they identified as the "chief ringleader." The concessions given to the strikers had, of course, brought criticism upon the British administration from local white businessmen. The vice president of the Chamber of Commerce, Edgar Tripp, was vehement in regarding the decision to appease the strikers as "one of the most humiliating surrenders to brute force that had ever been known in a British Colony."

The events of the first few days of December, and especially the apparent reluctance of the black police in Port of Spain to confront the rioters, caused a realization of the fear expressed during the preceding months concerning the scarcity of white troops. As early as December 1 the Mounted Volunteers of Trinidad, composed mostly of white businessmen, were called out. This was followed by the formation of a volunteer force known as the Colonial Vigilantes. By December 11 Baker reported 270 members of this force "composed entirely of white persons, or of those who belong predominantly to the white race, and could be relied upon in the event of any Negro uprising." A few weeks later regular white troops did arrive, in the form of the Royal Sussex Regiment, who were brought in from Jamaica.

There were in Trinidad at this time several American businessmen and supervisory personnel and their dependents. Many of these were concentrated far from Port of Spain in the oil fields in the southern part of the island and in the vicinity of Brighton, where the General Asphalt Company of

Philadelphia operated. U.S. Consul Baker enquired of the State Department whether it would be kind enough to send some American naval vessels. Perhaps mindful of the Swettenham affair in Jamaica in 1907, however, he suggested that American marines should not be landed without the consent of local authorities. The Secretary of the Navy, however, thought that American vessels would not be necessary.

And since Baker traced much of the Trinidad unrest to Marcus Garvey's *Negro World*, he "sincerely" hoped that the State Department would move against this paper, preferably by having the Post Office deny it use of the mails. He once more reminded Washington that the *Negro World*, more than other revolutionary organs, was "responsible for the rapid growth of class and race feeling, and of anarchistic and Bolshevist ideas among the ignorant population" in Trinidad.

In the aftermath of the postwar unrest the British government sent out a Royal Commission in 1921 and 1922, led by Major E. F. C. Wood. They toured the area meeting with a cross section of the population. In St. Lucia a newly formed Representative Government Association formulated demands for more democracy. Based on Wood's recommendations a limited electoral element was introduced into colonies where none existed.

EARLY POLITICAL PARTIES

In the years after Wood the first modern political parties began to appear in the British colonies. Charles Duncan O'Neal, an Edinburgh University–trained medical doctor and member of the Barbados colored elite, founded the Democratic League in 1924. He had come in contact with socialism in Britain and was actually elected to the Sunderland County Council while practicing medicine in Newcastle. He campaigned for women's rights, an end to child labor and universal adult suffrage. O'Neal and some of his colleagues won seats in the Barbados House of Assembly. O'Neal also formed ancillary organizations, including a Workingmen's Association in 1926. This was influenced by the Trinidad Workingmen's Association. (O'Neal had earlier practiced medicine in Trinidad.) O'Neal worked closely with other progressive forces, including the Garveyites of Barbados. He invested in

the *Barbados Herald*, founded by Clement Innis in 1919 and edited by Clennel Wickham.

Upon his deportation from the United States to Jamaica in 1927, Marcus Garvey founded the Peoples Political Party in 1929. His 1929 election platform called for workmen's compensation, an eight-hour work day, free secondary and night school education, public libraries, official court stenographers, public works to absorb the unemployed, prison reform, expanded electrification, "health outreach programs for rural areas," "decent low priced housing, for the peasantry," an end to profiteering in real estate and a 60 percent minimum local labor component for jobs.

He also advocated more self-government, minimum wage legislation, and reforms to force large landowners to give over idle lands to productive use. He would force large foreign corporations to contribute to the country's social and material infrastructure. He advocated the encouragement of local industry, a national theatre to "encourage" black art, impeachment of judges who abused their authority, legal aid, a law against employers obtaining votes through duress, upgrading Montego Bay and Port Antonio to the status of cities and upgrading the Kingston Race Course.

In Trinidad, Arthur Andrew Cipriani converted the Trinidad Workingmen's Association into the Trinidad Labor Party in 1934. In British Guiana, as elsewhere in the British colonies, the first modern political parties were preceded by years of mostly short-lived race uplift, political reform and other organizations. A British Guiana Political Reform Club, a British Guiana Constitutional Reform Association and a British Guiana Progressive Association appeared in the 1880s and 1890s. A short-lived Young Guyanese Party appeared for the general elections of 1916. The British Guiana People's Political Association and the Popular Party were put together for the 1921 and 1926 elections, respectively. The People's Association lasted from 1903 to 1916.

Several nonwhite persons won elections to the representative bodies left over in British Guiana from Dutch rule. In 1928, however, the British government abolished these quasi-representative arrangements and imposed crown colony status, with local representatives nominated by the British, rather than elected by the populace, albeit based on a narrow franchise. This was in a way an overturning of the 1921–1922 Wood Commission's recommendations, which had brought an elective element to such original crown colonies as St. Lucia and Trinidad and Tobago. The British Parliamentary Commission which recommended these retrograde measures argued that British Guiana's elections were marked by bribery and corruption and that the colony comprised "a congeries of races from all parts of the world with different instincts, different standards and different interests," which made elective government, in their view, difficult.

MIDDLE-CLASS RISING

The Caribbean middle class was on the rise in the 1930s. For more recent immigrants like the Indians and Chinese (see Chapter 11) the 1930s saw the continued transition to acceptance of a Caribbean identity and participation in the struggles of the wider community. In most territories, however, it was the numerically dominant and long-established African population whose middle class largely defined the political and social struggles that characterized middle-class advance. A dim light appeared visible at the end of the colonialist tunnel. A superior secondary education awaited the academically gifted. University education abroad followed for the exceptionally brilliant, the wealthy, the fortunate and the ambitious. The result was an African middle class of great erudition, with a confidence tested in successful intellectual competition with the best of Europe and North America.

With a Marcus Garvey rising to preeminence in the Pan-African movement, a George Padmore becoming the major African figure in the Communist International and a C. L. R. James occupying a similar position in the Trotskyist Fourth International, African Caribbean people had no need to doubt their abilities. H. O. B. Wooding of Trinidad topped his law finals at the Inns of Court in London in the 1920s. Eric Williams graduated first among the firsts at Oxford in the 1930s. P. M. H. Savory of British Guiana topped his class at McGill University medical school prior to establishing a practice in New York in November 1919.

Among the middle class, as among the working class, interaction with African Americans and continental Africans overseas continued to help raise racial consciousness. The role of Trinidad's F. E. M. Hercules in post–World War I London has already been noted. At about the same time Audrey Jeffers, later the doyenne of Trinidad's rising African elite and the leader of the Anglophone Caribbean women's movement, was an active participant in London-based Pan-African activities. Jeffers was present at the inaugural dinner of the African Progress Union (APU) in London in 1918. The largely West African and Caribbean membership of the APU were "actuated . . . by intense love for their country and race. . . ." They felt "that only Africans or descendants of African blood can rightly and truly interpret the feelings, aspirations and idiosyncrasies of their kith and kin. . . ."

Jamaica's Amy Ashwood Garvey, first wife of Marcus Garvey, actually founded a West African organization, the Nigerian Progress Union (NPU), in London in 1924. The NPU later evolved into the West African Students' Union (WASU), one of the most important organizations in the history of Pan-Africanism. Future chief justice of Trinidad and Tobago, H. O. B. Wooding, was made an honorary member of WASU while a student in London. Dr. P. M. H. Savory was treasurer of the broad-based United Aid for Ethiopia formed in Harlem in the wake of the Italian fascist invasion of 1935. He served along with Capt. A. L. King of the Universal Negro Improvement Association, Harlem Congressman Rev. Adam Clayton Powell Jr, and others.

People like Jeffers and Wooding, though politically conservative and economically well-to-do, strove for the uplift of their group. The racism which surrounded them and impacted them personally served as a spur to their efforts. There was de facto residential segregation. Unfair legislation and government practices sought to hamper the growth of black business. African religions and culture continued to be repressed. Calypsonians in Trinidad had, under the Theatre and Dance Hall Ordinance of 1934 (repealed in 1951), to obtain police approval of their lyrics every night to sing at their calypso tents. Whole departments in the British colonial civil service were reserved for white employees only.

In 1914 Sir Walter Egerton, governor of British Guiana, articulated a long-lasting policy when he refused to appoint Dr. L. R. Sharples a Government Medical Officer. He denied Sharples the job, he told his Secretary of State in London, because "he was of African descent . . . and white patients object to being treated by a medical officer who is not of their own race."

The nationalism of this middle class found an increasingly important outlet through literature, both scholarly and creative. Garvey helped usher in the "Harlem Renaissance" of the 1920s with an unparalleled promotion of African-conscious literary activity. He defined the aesthetic of his literary offensive in his essay on "African Fundamentalism" in 1924:

> The time has come for the Negro to forget and cast behind him his hero worship and adoration of other races, and to start out immediately to create and emulate heroes of his own. We must canonize our own saints, create our own martyrs, and elevate to positions of fame and honor black men and women who have made their distinct contributions to our racial history. . . . We must inspire a literature and promulgate a doctrine of our own without any apologies to the powers that be. The right is ours and God's. Let contrary sentiment and cross opinions go to the winds.

H. A. Vaughan of Barbados captured the resurgent celebration of blackness in his poem, "Revelation":

> *Turn sideways now and let them see*
> *What loveliness escapes the schools,*
> *Then turn again, and smile, and be*
> *The perfect answer to those fools*
> *Who always prate of Greece and Rome,*
> *"The face that launched a thousand ships,"*
> *And such like things, but keep tight lips*
> *For burnished beauty nearer home.*

Vaughan was a leading figure in the Forum Club of Barbados. Their members kept in close touch with the literary developments of the Harlem Renaissance. In January 1932 a Forum Club committee of Clennell W. Wickham, J. C. Hope and Vaughan, together with two members of the Barbados Elementary Teachers' Association, met with a commission of enquiry into the educational needs of the British West Indies. They requested enhanced Caribbean content and the removal of racially offensive material from the British-imposed textbooks. Garvey's 1920 First International Convention of the Negro Peoples of the World had also called for the teaching of Black History in schools.

Similar developments were taking place in the non-Anglophone Caribbean as well. The indigenist movement of Haiti was ushered in by the journal *La Revue Indigène* (1927–1928). The writers of this movement, among them Jean Price-Mars and Jacques Roumain, rediscovered and treated with a new respect the folkways and religion of their fellow Haitians. They were responding in part to the racially repressive American occupation.

This trend intensified with the Griot movement, led by François Duvalier (later president of Haiti) and Lorimer Denis, whose *L'Essentiel de la Doctrine des Griots* appeared in 1938. They also published the magazine *Les Griots* in 1938–1939. Duvalier and Denis were uncompromising in their advocacy of race first. They urged Haitians to rediscover and respect the African essence of their culture as a means of national regeneration.

The Negritude movement of Francophone Caribbean and African writers, like its Haitian counterpart, took off with the publication of a magazine. *L'Etudiant Noir* was published in Paris in 1934. Its editors were Negritude's best known personalities, the poets Léopold Senghor of Senegal, Léon Damas of French Guiana and Aimé Césaire of Martinique. For over ten years these three oversaw a flourishing movement which tried to combat French cultural imperialism, rejected the European demeaning of African history, sought escape from assimilation into French culture and embraced the Harlem Renaissance. This did not prevent them from adopting some aspects of European radicalism, such as communism and socialism.

The white Puerto Rican Luis Palés Matos' poem "Pueblo Negro" in 1926 launched a "Negrismo" (also called "Negrista") movement in Cuba and Puerto Rico. Its proponents, almost exclusively white, tried to speak for the African masses. The Negrista movement, like Negritude, exoticized African people into sensuous, sinewy, simple-minded, nonambitious, animalistic, drumbeating, dancing children of nature who had somehow preserved the desirable primitive purity which Europeans had lost through what Palés Matos called their "dangerous cerebralisation. . . ." In the Cuban poet Nicolás Guillén, Negrismo found its only nonwhite luminary.

The rising African consciousness of the period was reflected throughout the arts. C. L. R. James' 1936 novel, *Minty Alley,* made a statement by setting itself in an impoverished African Trinidadian environment. Boscoe Holder chose African Caribbean subjects for his paintings. In Trinidad, Holder and Beryl McBurnie took African dance from the countryside and the barrack yards onto the stage, as Olive Walke would later retrieve folk songs from village and hamlet. Nicolás Guillén elevated Afro-Cuban music (the *"son"*) to respectability. To crown it all, working-class Trinidadians would, after years of experimentation, reinvent the banned African drum in the guise of the steelband.

The spirit of a blossoming racial consciousness could also be seen in scholarly writings of the period. Despite (perhaps even because of) the Eurocentric education forced on Caribbean children, there was a long tradition of Afrocentric journalism and scholarly writing. In the interwar years J. A. Rogers of Jamaica and the United States traveled the world in search of obscure information on African history. So, for many years, did his friend Arturo A. Schomburg of Puerto Rico and New York, African America's most celebrated bibliophile. Rogers' books, beginning with *From Superman to Man* in 1917, have remained popular into the twenty-first century. In 1917 Grenada's T. Albert Marryshow wrote *Cycles of Civilization* wherein he chastised the racist utterances of General Jan Christian Smuts of South Africa and asserted the African origins of civilization. Norman Eustace Cameron of Guyana published *The Evolution of the Negro* in two volumes in 1929 and 1934. He advocated race pride, saw no need for massive (as opposed to selective) emigration to Africa and saw economic advance as the way out for African people. "As long as Negroes are poor they will be despised," he wrote. "When they become wealthy as a people all their faults will be overlooked or spoken of in hushed whispers which will not affect them."

In Eric Williams of Trinidad the Caribbean produced a formally trained historian of great brilliance. With an island scholarship from Queen's Royal College and an Oxford first behind him, he moved on to a doctorate at Oxford University in 1938. His dissertation, revised and published as *Capitalism and Slavery* in 1944, combined the race consciousness of the age with brilliance of scholarship. The result was a seminal work.

The brilliance of the nascent Afro-Caribbean middle class in the arts and scholarship had its counterparts in business. William Sewell in the post-Emancipation years, as already noted, had marveled at the commercial drive of the newly freed. He confidently predicted that they were destined to dominate commerce in Trinidad at least. He thought that by 1859 they had already won the battle for commercial success, despite the relentless hostility of the white ruling class to black economic progress. Sewell noted laws against small businesspeople and taxation policies designed to favor sugar planters and hurt the rising black commercial class.

The legislative campaign against black business was reinforced by new stereotypes of a supposed black inability to do business. The lending and employment policies of the major colonial banks (British and Canadian) and quasi-banking institutions reinforced these antiblack business laws and attitudes and tried to convert prejudice into self-fulfilling prophecy. By contrast, when refugees from Hitler's anti-Jewish European campaigns arrived in Trinidad in the 1930s with quite literally nothing, they received instant credit from local merchants to set up as peddlers.

Black business, though under great pressure, nevertheless persisted, although the campaign against it took its toll. Isaiah Morter in British Honduras was able to leave $100,000.00 in 1920s U.S. dollars to Garvey's UNIA for "African redemption." The local British chief justice deemed African redemption "an illegal purpose and contrary to Public Policy" and so voided Morter's gift.

Arnold A. Waterman, "Trinidad's Leading Merchant," and family, around 1905.

In the early twentieth-century Trinidad's A. A. Waterman, "The Hatter, Clothier & Outfitter," was one of several Afro-Trinidadian owners of major department stores. He opened his downtown Port of Spain establishment in 1899. By 1905 the *Colored American* magazine of Boston considered him Trinidad's leading merchant. The Duprey Brothers were said to be Trinidad's most successful commission agents around 1917–1920. They were led by Cyril Duprey who would later make business history in Trinidad and the Caribbean as the founder of the Colonial Life Insurance Company (CLICO).

The father of Trinidad's most famous nurturer of musical talent, "Aunty" Kay (Kathleen Davis), owned a jeweler's shop on Frederick Street, the city's major shopping thoroughfare. Robert McShine, brother of Dr. A. H. McShine, long-standing head of the Trinidad Co-operative Bank, owned a soft drink factory. Henry I. Jeffers, father of Audrey Jeffers, by the 1940s owned probably more real estate in downtown Port of Spain than anybody else, in addition to hundreds of acres of agricultural land. Many of these men had actually immigrated to Trinidad from other

islands. Waterman and Jeffers came to Trinidad as children, from Barbados and Montserrat, respectively. Davis was from St. Vincent and had made money as a gold prospector ("pork knocker") in British Guiana. McShine was the first of his siblings born in Trinidad to St. Vincent immigrant parents. His father-in-law, Carlos Robertson, born in Lagos, Nigeria, arrived in Trinidad around 1847 as a "recaptive" liberated from a foreign slave ship by the British Royal Navy. He emigrated to Venezuela in the 1850s as a protégé of George Numa Dessources, the Trinidadian civil rights activist. He made a fortune in the gold industry. He remained a successful businessman with gold industry holdings and agricultural property in the El Callao region of Venezuela and extensive urban and agricultural property holdings in Trinidad. For some of these people, such as Jeffers and McShine, business was still only an adjunct to their professional lives.

Out of this climate of persistent effort in the face of relentless obstacles emerged, remarkably, Trinidad's Colonial Life Insurance Company Limited (CLICO) which in due course became the wealthiest and most successful indigenous conglomerate of any racial group in the Caribbean. CLICO was founded in 1936, at the height of the labor troubles that were consuming the Caribbean. This was also the period, ironically, when Afro-Trinidadian retail businesses were under severe attack from the imminent Shop Closing Ordinance, discussed earlier. Politicians and labor activists were also, as seen, in the midst of a campaign to stop Lebanese-Syrian, Chinese and Jewish immigrants from entering an already-depressed economic market.

CLICO's roots actually extended to the Caribbean-African American Diaspora. Cyril Duprey (1897–1988) arrived in New York on his third and most important trip on the ship *Mayaro* on May 26, 1924, shortly before the ban on black immigration. At twenty he was already a successful commission agent and had embarked on his first trip to the United States, in search of products to represent in Trinidad. In 1924 Duprey worked first as a bellhop in Detroit and then for insurance companies in Chicago, where his special "beat" was the African American community. His cousin Libert Lezama, who had preceded him to Chicago and encouraged him to try the "windy city," owned a cab company of thirty-three vehicles, though he lost it due to problems with the law.

By 1933, in the midst of the world depression no less, Duprey felt sufficiently experienced to start his own African American company, the United Mutual Life Insurance Company, with headquarters in Harlem, New York, the "capital of the black world."

In subsequent years Duprey was often praised as the first real captain of industry in Caribbean history. Perhaps the most dramatic of the many bold entrepreneurial moves that characterized CLICO over the years was his decision after about two successful years in Harlem, and in the midst of a worldwide depression, to sell United Mutual, relocate to Trinidad and start an insurance company there. He had dreamed of starting an insurance company in Trinidad at least since 1928. Yet following his idea back home was a bold move. He was leaving a large African American population base to venture into a relatively small British colony. Impediments in the way of black business in Trinidad were many. The insurance field was controlled by white British and

Canadian firms which benefitted from various government preferences. One of these, the privilege of arranging automatic premium deductions from civil servants' salaries, was denied to CLICO for several years. Duprey's experience operating in a racially challenging North American environment would however serve him well in Trinidad.

He sold United Mutual to fellow Caribbean-African American entrepreneurs who had been associated with him for some time. Duprey's associates at United Mutual included Attorney Hope Stevens, born in the British Virgin Islands, an important figure in radical Caribbean-focused Harlem politics and Dr. Charles N. Ford, a Trinidadian dentist who, as of 1945, had been practicing in New York for twenty-six years. United Mutual continued to prosper after the sale. When in 1992 the giant white Metropolitan Life Insurance Company absorbed United Mutual, it was the ninth largest black-owned insurance company in the United States and the last remaining one in the Northeast.

Duprey incorporated CLICO in Trinidad on December 15, 1936 and opened its doors for business in 1937. Duprey was actually no rags-to-hoped-for-riches outsider in Trinidad society, as sometimes assumed. His father was a lawyer and his uncle a doctor. He had estate-owning antecedents on both sides of his family. He himself had been a successful businessman in Trinidad before leaving for the United States. He thought he might have been the most affluent of the passengers on the *SS Mayaro* in 1924, where his shipmates included white French Creole, Portuguese, Chinese and African Trinidadians. On his return home he moved immediately into the bosom of the Afro-Trinidadian business elite.

The incorrect stereotype of black Caribbean inability to succeed at business has obscured the fact that there was in fact by the 1930s a powerful black business and professional elite in Trinidad. Trinidad big business then, and to a large extent thereafter, tended to be organized along ethnic lines—French Creole, English Creole, Syrian-Lebanese, Chinese, Portuguese, Indian. Duprey immersed himself in the Afro-Trinidadian leadership group. He quickly appeared on the board of directors of the Trinidad

Duprey and ones that followed actively tried to uplift and organize black

Cooperative Bank, the leading black business before CLICO. The board of directors at CLICO read like a Who's Who of Afro-Trinidadian business leaders. It included J. Haynes-Clarke, the country's premier undertaker; Aldwin Maillard, the department store owner; L. C. Hannays, a leading lawyer; Dr. Simeon A. Hayes, pharmacist and physician and founder, in 1946, of the Champs Elysees Nursing Home; Elliott P. Gibbs, a commission agent; and Garnet J. McCarthy, who invested in real estate. McCarthy was born in Nova Scotia, Canada, and was mayor of Port of Spain in 1937.

When on August 29, 1942, Duprey's closest associate, Cyril Monsanto, married Liris, the daughter of Dr. A. H. McShine of the Cooperative Bank, with Duprey as best man, this was a royal marriage among the Afro-Trinidadian business and professional elite. St. Lucia–born Monsanto was the son of a St. Thomas–born father. As a medical student at McGill University he had aspirations of becoming a medical missionary in Africa.

Monsanto was another veteran of the Caribbean-African American community out of whom CLICO sprang. In Harlem, Monsanto had worked briefly for Guyanese Dr. P. M. H. Savory's Victory Life Insurance Company of Illinois, before moving to Duprey's United Mutual. Savory's multifaceted business interests included purchase, in 1936, of the *New York Amsterdam News,* one of African America's major newspapers. He had worked as a compositor for the *Daily Argosy* and *Daily Chronicle* in Guyana from 1906 to 1909 and also as a printer in Brazil in 1910–1911. Other important members of the Caribbean-African American network were Duprey's brother Gil and a Jamaican lawyer, Eustace Vincent Deuch, who helped Duprey set up United Mutual.

The Caribbean immigrant group were a close-knit business community in the United States. After Duprey returned to Trinidad he maintained close relations with them in a sort of informal Caribbean Diaspora entrepreneurial network. In 1947, Victory Life and CLICO celebrated CLICO's tenth anniversary by staging a competition to see who could sell the most insurance that year. CLICO won. Duprey was a guest of honor at United Mutual's twentieth anniversary celebrations in 1953. United presented him with a plaque. At United Mutual's eighteenth

anniversary celebrations in 1951 the Caribbean–American connection was still evident. Jamaican-born Judge James S. Watson, now president of the Municipal Civil Service Commission of the City of New York, praised the birth and growth of United Mutual in much the same terms that commentators often praised CLICO, as "a striking example of daring, persistence, and imagination in the field of industry and finance."

And once CLICO got going in Trinidad, it was to his Caribbean-African American colleagues that Duprey turned for his most important appointments. He invited Monsanto to join him in Trinidad in 1940. He had already enticed Trinidadian Arthur Donowa home from New York in 1937 to head CLICO's San Fernando operations. Donawa was another veteran of Harlem's United Aid for Ethiopia. Like Monsanto, he had worked with Duprey at United Mutual in Harlem. Both had contributed to CLICO's start-up funds on a purely gentleman's agreement basis. If they lost their money, they said, no questions would be asked. They were simply happy to contribute to this historic venture and they trusted Duprey.

All of CLICO's first directors were recruited from the Afro-Trinidadian business and professional community. Chinese Trinidadian businessman William H. Scott declined an invitation to serve, though he accepted some years later when CLICO had become a major player. The black Trinidad business elite shared important qualities with Duprey's Caribbean associates in Harlem. They represented the same mix of political activism, African consciousness, advocacy of thrift and determination to accumulate wealth. They saw this activity within the context of helping themselves and uplifting their race and wider community at the same time. The Trinidad Cooperative Bank's self-proclaimed mission in 1914 was "to inculcate in the people the virtue of thrift . . . and to provide a quick, easy, safe means for children and poor people to save small sums and put by for the coming of the rainy days." CLICO's early motto was, "Save, brother, save."

Like their Trinidad counterparts, many of the Caribbean-African American entrepreneurs were professional men. Both in African America and the Caribbean these pioneers established their own

[marginal note, left column, vertical] Shows they were reliable despite Diaspora

banks and insurance companies in a bold effort to encourage thrift, mobilize capital and provide for their communities the credit that was not forthcoming from established white sources. The Trinidad Cooperative Bank built Trinidad's first housing developments for persons of moderate means, providing them with mortgages they could not get elsewhere. CLICO ventured into the small mortgage field shortly after its inception. Marcus Garvey's UNIA in the 1920s established the most spectacular of these Caribbean Diaspora businesses in the Black Star Line Shipping Corporation and the Negro Factories Corporation. Garvey considered establishing a bank.

It is often erroneously said that Afro-Caribbean leaders went into education instead of business, as other communities did. In fact black professionals often used their professions as doctors, lawyers, dentists and the like to accumulate the capital not available via other means. A significant number of these entrepreneurs actually ran big businesses while simultaneously practicing their professions. Savory topped his medical school class at McGill University in Canada. McShine, a Trinidad island scholar and Edinburgh University graduate, was Trinidad's most distinguished eye surgeon. Even CLICO's Duprey and Monsanto were one-time medical students, Monsanto at McGill and Duprey in New York.

The Afro-Trinidadian complexion of CLICO's initial directorate was matched by its early focus on the poorer, mostly Afro-Trinidadian community. Their premiums were as low as 6 cents per week. As Duprey and his early salesmen tramped from door to door they must have encountered the Lebanese-Syrian and Jewish peddlers who were simultaneously walking their way to future wealth.

The middle and upper classes and civil servants were still in the hands of the white insurance companies (though CLICO would soon oust its white rivals), thanks in part to government policies discriminating in favor of white insurance providers. The poorest sometimes escaped the safety net provided by the mostly black friendly societies, which became CLICO's main early competitors. These friendly (mutual benefit) societies, 330 of them in Trinidad in 1937, provided

sickness, accident and death benefits to members. They had long been part of the thrift landscape among African Americans and Caribbean people. United Mutual in Harlem started as a sort of quasi-friendly society. Marcus Garvey's UNIA had incorporated some of the features of friendly societies.

Audrey Jeffers' Coterie of Social Workers had as its motto, "Lifting as we climb." This they had evidently adapted from their African American counterpart, the National Council of Negro Women (NCNW), whose motto was "We lift as we climb." In borrowing this African American slogan Audrey Jeffers was symptomatic of much of the African Caribbean activist middle class, which found it easy to see the African American struggle as a kindred one. Thus C. A. Petioni and other founders of the Cooperative Bank were Garveyites and Duprey's early Harlem associate Hope Stevens was for decades a leading radical Caribbean-African American activist. The pantheon of heroes for the Caribbean group based at home included persons such as Booker T. Washington, Marcus Garvey, the NCNW and the writers of the Harlem Renaissance. Many of these African American heroes of course were themselves of Caribbean origin.

Like Eric Williams, who moved freely in radical Caribbean circles in England and the United States, but preferred to take his radical background into more broad-based politics, Duprey seemed to take his radical exposure into a more broad-based business which could make money, while mobilizing local capital on an unprecedented scale, promoting regional development and generally helping uplift his community.

Among CLICO's major achievements was the unprecedented mobilization of indigenous capital for the financing of development projects undertaken by Caribbean governments. By 1969 CLICO had funded governmental projects in Jamaica, Barbados, Grenada, St. Lucia, Guyana and Trinidad and Tobago.

From its life insurance base the company expanded into other forms of insurance, property development, real estate, alcohol distilling, retail shops, methanol, ethanol, oil and gas exploration and other areas. Its banking operations by the 1980s included purchase of Citibank Barbados (1984) and Chase Manhattan Barbados (1986), followed later by majority shareholding in Republic Bank (Trinidad) and substantial holdings in Royal Bank of Trinidad and Tobago. It eventually opened its own CLICO Investment Bank. Its expanded operations, later under the umbrella CL Financial company, ultimately spanned over thirty countries. Possibly the most poignant indicator of its success came in the late twentieth century when Republic Bank of Trinidad and Tobago, successor of the flagship Barclays Bank of colonial times, which would not hire black tellers into the 1960s, appealed to an independent government of Trinidad and Tobago for protection from a CL Financial takeover.

After seven decades of practically uninterrupted growth CLICO ran aground during the U.S.-induced global recession of 2008, said by some to be the worst since the Great Depression of the 1930s. Some of the world's largest corporations, including General Motors, Chrysler and AIG (American International Group), declared bankruptcy and received billions of dollars in governmental bailout support. They typically had to sell off assets as a part of the bailout deals, in order to meet commitments. Financial services giant Lehman Brothers disintegrated all together.

The 2008 recession was characterized everywhere by a liquidity crisis, brought on by reckless lending, real estate speculation followed by a collapse in real estate prices, inflated asset prices and inadequate oversight and regulation by central banks and other government regulators.

CLICO's problems fit squarely into the global pattern. The Trinidad and Tobago government initially followed the standard path of winding up some portions of the CLICO empire, shoring up others with bailout assistance and taking over temporary management of the company. It put the full faith and credit of the government behind a promise to repay policyholders and creditors. In 2010 the new Peoples Partnership replaced the Peoples National Movement as Trinidad's government. They reneged on the previous government's promise of full repayment to CLICO policyholders and depositors, setting off a new crisis. Instead they offered small initial payments followed by twenty-year bonds at zero interest. Many feared that inflation and no interest would significantly wipe out the value of their investments over twenty years. (Cuba had, by coincidence, offered the United States twenty-year bonds instead of immediate compensation for confiscated U.S. property.) As of August 2011 this question remained unresolved.

Some Caribbean countries, including the Bahamas, Barbados, Belize and Guyana, had meanwhile either wound up their local CLICO affiliates, brought them under judicial management, or otherwise sought to resolve the problem.

SPORT

The relentless onward push for equality found expression also in sport, where middle- and working-class people both excelled and struggled against entrenched undemocratic practices. Sport was in fact one of the areas of Caribbean life where racism was most entrenched and obvious. Sports probably ran second to whites-only social clubs and the nonemployment of blacks in white banks and other firms (and in some departments of the Civil Service as well) as an area of nearly unvarnished racism. The exclusion of most black people from voting privileges could be thinly camouflaged behind property qualifications for the franchise. The absence of black residents in exclusive white suburbs could likewise be spun as an economic reality. In sports, an area of often intimate social interaction, racism was often more difficult to pass off as anything other than what it was.

The athletic prowess of Caribbean people was already attracting world attention by the nineteenth century. Pater Jackson, heavyweight boxing champion of Australia and the British empire, has already been mentioned. Joe Walcott, born in Barbados in 1873, emigrated to the United States in 1887 and became the first black welterweight champion of the world (1901–1904). He fought out of Boston. Some consider him the greatest pound for pound fighter of all time. He won several bouts against heavier fighters, including heavyweights. Walcott coined the saying, later popularized by Muhammad Ali, that "The bigger they are, the harder they fall." Jack Johnson, who went on to become the first black heavyweight champion, was a Walcott sparring partner in 1893–1894. In 1913, three years after Johnson had succeeded in being allowed to fight (and beat) the "great white hope" Jim Jeffries in Reno, Nevada, black–white boxing contests were banned in Trinidad. British West Indies Regiment soldiers, as seen, were champions among British empire troops in Egypt.

As cricket and football, the two most popular team sports, developed in the twentieth century they became bastions of segregation and class distinction. Unlike the United States, where black players were simply excluded from major leagues, in most of the Caribbean the small white populations made such a policy less feasible. Instead, black, white and mixed-race teams competed in the same leagues, but on a segregated basis. The old practice of the slavery era which mandated white, colored and free black militias, in addition to manumitted Ranger and still enslaved black conscripts, was now transferred to the playing field. By the 1950s in Port of Spain's first class football league, it was possible to tell a player's color simply by knowing which club he played for. Shamrock and Casuals were white (or whatever passed for white in Trinidad). Notre Dame would probably have qualified as quadroons and octoroons during the days of slavery. Sporting Club would probably have been designated "mulattoes." The darker teams (e.g., Malvern, Maple, Colts, Providence) were organized along class or neighborhood lines or both.

Trinidad's first class cricket league for much of the twentieth century was led, so to speak, by Queens Park, mostly white and owners of the Oval, where international "test" matches were played. They controlled the administration of cricket in the country. Next in the pecking order came Shamrock, "almost exclusively white" and Roman Catholic according to C. L. R. James, in *Beyond a Boundary*. "I would have been more easily elected to the MCC [controlling body in English cricket]," said James, "than to either." The black police Constabulary team had a white police officer as captain. Blacks in the 1920s could not advance beyond the rank of sergeant-major in the police force. Nor could they, it appears, captain a police cricket team.

Then there was Stingo. "They were plebians: the butcher, the tailor, the candlestick maker, the casual labourer, with a sprinkling of unemployed. Totally black and no social status whatever." There was also Maple, "the club of the brown-skinned middle class. Class did not matter so much to them as colour." And there was Shannon, club of the legendary

Learie Constantine, "the club of the black lower-middle class: the teacher, the law clerk, the worker in the printing office and here and there a clerk in a department store." Shannon, said James, "played as if they knew that their club represented the great mass of black people in the island." James opted to play for Maple over the stronger Shannon, to his later remorse.

The Chinese and Indians did not play much football. There were however Chinese men's and women's hockey teams, tennis clubs and women's netball clubs. Many of the Chinese teams were officially named "Chinese." Trinidad and Guianese Chinese teams exchanged visits. Occasionally Jamaican Chinese participated in these friendly matches as well. There was long an East Indian cricket league, with Trinidad Indians playing tournaments against Guyanese Indians. Portuguese women had their own netball teams, though the men assimilated into the white football teams, unless dark skinned. When the Northern Ladies Netball League was founded at the Portuguese Association building in Port of Spain in 1940 it comprised three Portuguese teams, "Chinese," Malvern (a middle-class Afro-Trinidadian multisport powerhouse), Perseverance (a school team) and a team from the Government Teachers' Training College.

Caribbean cricket preceded football into international prominence. St. Vincent beat a touring English team in 1895. The regional West Indies team achieved "test" status in 1928. The effort to keep the captaincy white, somewhat akin to American football's effort to maintain quarter backs as a "whites only" position, became a defining aspect of West Indies cricket. As the pool of black talent overwhelmed the selectors they made extraordinary efforts to keep at least one white player on the team, so that he could be appointed captain. When they ran out of plausible white candidates in the 1950s they selected the next best thing, a light-skinned newcomer to test cricket, who they duly appointed captain in his first test match, over some of the world's most experienced and accomplished players.

C. L. R. James, now editing the *Nation* newspaper of the Peoples National Movement in Trinidad, could take it no longer. He began a journalistic campaign for an end to the white-captains-at-any-cost policy. He dispensed with the polite silence of even those who were victimized by the practice. His campaign bore fruit when Frank Worrell of Barbados was appointed captain in 1960.

White dominance of the administration of sport in the colonial era resulted on occasion in grave injustice to black players. In 1933 the black Everton, Trinidad's most successful football club, was totally banned from Trinidad football forever after a fight with the white Casuals team. During the slavery era a black person might have been deprived of life or limb for hitting a white.

This time around, a white football "court," headed by one F. J. Leotaud, dispensed heavy suspensions to individual players, mostly from Everton. The team was effectively destroyed for good, and this after winning the premier league in 1930, 1931 and 1932. Casuals had won in 1929. They were also the main beneficiaries of the destruction of Everton, for they won the now Everton-less league in 1934 and 1935. With the destruction of Everton, Trinidad was able to field a predominantly white team in its tour of Jamaica in 1936. The Everton captain, Alfred Charles, reputedly the best footballer in Trinidad, was suspended for two years for punching a Casuals player. He found alternative employment in England, where, with the help of Learie Constantine, he became a pioneer black figure in English professional football.

RASTAFARIAN MOVEMENT

A discussion of African consciousness in the interwar years could not be complete without reference to the Rastafarian Movement and the Italian fascist invasion of Ethiopia. Rastafarianism emerged in Jamaica in the early 1930s. Many of its initial adherents came out of the Garvey Movement, with its universal African consciousness and its widespread Ethiopian symbolism. The coronation of Emperor Haile Selassie (formerly Ras Tafari) of Ethiopia in 1930 provided a rare opportunity for an internationally disseminated nonpejorative view of Africa. Out of the Garveyite background and with the stimulus of the coronation came the new movement.

The poor and oppressed Africans of Jamaica who initiated the movement ingeniously constructed an Afrocentric theology, worldview and lifestyle to replace European cultural imperialism. Haile Selassie,

an African, was recognized as God. Africa was the promised land and focal point of repatriation. Africans had been forcibly deposited into exile in the west (Babylon). Africans, as the true Israelites of the Bible, were God's chosen people. Rastafarians embraced Garvey as a prophet, a John the Baptist, second in veneration only to His Imperial Majesty, Haile Selassie.

The movement emerged from intense repression in the colonial and postcolonial Jamaican state to fundamentally impact Jamaican and Pan-African society. Rastafarians practically developed a new language. They gave the world reggae music. They Africanized painting, sculpture, dance, theatre and ceramics in Jamaica. They influenced the culinary arts. They challenged some of the core concepts of Christianity. Their once persecuted dreadlocks in time became commonplace all over the African world among adherents and nonadherents alike. Some non-Africans eventually become attracted to the movement.

The Italian fascist invasion of Ethiopia in 1935 was perhaps the most traumatic event to affect the Caribbean and the rest of scattered Africa since the European scramble for the continent in the late nineteenth and early twentieth centuries. Ethiopia became the only African country to militarily repel European aggression when the Emperor Menelik II routed the Italians at the Battle of Aduwa in 1896. The 1930 coronation of Haile Selassie enhanced this tradition of veneration for Ethiopia. Then in 1935 Benito Mussolini, Italy's dictator, invaded Ethiopia, dropped poison gas on its inhabitants, overran the country and forced the emperor to flee to Europe. The League of Nations declined to come to Ethiopia's aid. In the Caribbean, as elsewhere, the populace was enraged. Young men tried to volunteer for the Ethiopian army; dockworkers refused to unload Italian ships; there were protest rallies and demonstrations.

In Trinidad, calypsonian Inviegler changed his name to Ras Kassa, becoming perhaps the first "Ras" in Caribbean show business. His fellow calypsonian, The Growling Tiger, sang

De gold, de gold, de gold, de gold
De gold in Africa
Mussolini want from the emperor.

The Caribbean Diaspora was equally active. In England, C. L. R. James formed the International African Friends of Ethiopia. Garvey, now also resident in England, criticized the emperor for keeping Ethiopia weak but nevertheless supported the Ethiopian cause. His support often found poetical expression, such as in the following lines from "The Beast of Rome" (1935):

> *The Rome of sin and human hate*
> *Has plagued the world before,*
> *But God will serve their awful fate*
> *On Ethiopia's shore.*
> *Their guns and gas may threaten all*
> *As hymns they sing at home*
> *But ere Adowa's final fall*
> *The fight shall pass from Rome.*

U.S.-based Trinidadian Hubert Fauntleroy Julian, the "Black Eagle," one of the first black people to fly an airplane, went to Ethiopia to train an Ethiopian air force.

LABOR STRUGGLES OF THE 1930s

The 1930s ushered in a renewed period of unrest, this time more firmly concentrated in the labor movement. There were riots in British Honduras in 1934. Several of the leaders were veteran Garveyites. Thousands of Indian sugar workers on several Trinidad estates were also involved in disturbances in 1934. Sugar workers struck in St. Kitts in 1935. The authorities shot and killed three workers and wounded eight in one encounter. Others were wounded in other incidents. Several labor disturbances occurred in British Guiana between 1934 and 1939, culminating in the police killing of four strikers at Plantation Leonora in 1939.

In St. Vincent the same year crowds protested the government's intention to raise prices on essential goods. "We have no work," they chanted. "We are hungry." Crowds broke into a jail and freed prisoners. Sheriff "Selassie" Lewis and Bertha "Mother Selassie" Mutt emerged as popular leaders. The quasi-official and white-edited *St. Vincent Handbook* described the events in a manner suggesting that little had changed in the colonial administrative mind-set since Queen Victoria's famous admonition to workers on the eve of the Jamaica

Rebellion of 1865. Labor where you are directed, she had scolded, "not uncertainly, or capriciously, but steadily and continually." The *Handbook's* take on labor protests may have been hilarious were it not for the fact that people of this ilk exercised the power of life and death over the workers. The *Handbook* saw the protests this way:

> Disquietude developed into rioting in Kingstown on the morning of Monday the 21st of October [1935]. The meeting of the Legislative Council was in progress under the presidency of His Excellency Sir Selwyn Grier, when a crowd gathered at the entrance to the Court House and afterward entered the yard. They comprised the labouring classes and those in the humbler stations of life all of whom lost control of themselves and indulged in a disgraceful conduct which until then was foreign to St. Vincent.
>
> There was no member of the intelligent class anywhere near these frantic persons who could exercise any restraint. . . .

The nickname "Selassie" among two of the Vincentian leaders was of course no accident, and the governor was not amused. "I feel however," he informed the Legislative Council, "that there is another cause [of the riots] and that is the unfortunate spirit of racial antagonism which has been engendered by the Italy/Abyssinian War, a war which we all deplore. . . ." The workers invested Town Councilor George McIntosh with overall leadership of their struggle. The authorities killed one and injured several workers.

In St. Lucia that year coal loaders struck. The British called in a warship. In Barbados in 1937 the authorities killed fourteen people and injured forty-seven during protests caused by the deportation of labor leader Clement Payne. Payne, a Garveyite in Trinidad, had been born there of Barbadian parents. He was surreptitiously deported to Trinidad after winning a court case against deportation. Lightermen and foundry workers also struck at this time.

Trinidad in 1937 saw the "Butler Riots," one of the pivotal occurrences in the country's labor history. Tubal Uriah Buzz Butler immigrated to Trinidad from Grenada in 1921. He was a veteran of the British West Indies Regiment. Back home from the war in 1919 he joined the Grenada Representative Government Association. He also founded the Grenada Union of Returned Soldiers in 1919. In Trinidad Butler joined thousands of Grenadians working in Trinidad's oil belt. He was retired early because of a job-related injury and became a Baptist preacher.

Butler also joined the Trinidad Labor Party (TLP) of Captain Arthur A. Cipriani. Cipriani was a local white officer in the British West Indies Regiment, who had developed a reputation for empathy with his black soldiers. In 1919 Cipriani assumed leadership of the Trinidad Workingmen's Association. In 1934 he converted it into the TLP. He was a member of the Legislative Council and eight times mayor of Port of Spain. Butler led a hunger march in 1935. He broke with Cipriani in 1936 for his "somersaulting and back peddling."

Butler began to organize in Southern Trinidad's oil belt, where he lived. He founded the British Empire Workers and Citizens Home Rule Party in 1936. His demands and concerns can be gleaned from, among other things, several letters he wrote to the governor and other officials. His demands provide an excellent insight into the state of industrial and racial relations in the 1930s.

He wanted British "justice and fair play" for black workers. (Guyana's "Angel Gabriel" and Marcus Garvey had also called for "British justice." The inference was that there was more justice in Britain than in its colonies.) Butler also demanded unemployment relief; "British trade union laws"; health insurance; an end to racial discrimination in the police force (where black officers could not rise above sergeant-major); opening up of the "drillers" and other whites-only job categories on the oilfields; the opportunity for black people "generally to reach the highest positions in every avenue of Thought and Labor"; an end to "blacklisting" of oil industry workers; an end to employer schemes to frustrate access to workmen's compensation benefits; workmen's compensation benefits for agricultural workers; substantial worker representation on workmen's compensation arbitration boards; improved health facilities; exemption for the unemployed from taxes, water rates, court orders, rents and train fares, "with or without the dole"; cheap and easy divorces for poor people; 50 and 100 percent wage increases for the lowest paid; state control of all industries unable to implement these wage increases; "anti-Fascist" and antitrust laws; an end to the "No Bonus for Blacks" policy of the oil industry; and the disciplining of "unfair judges." (A similar demand landed Marcus Garvey in a Jamaican jail, convicted of sedition, in 1929.)

Butler tried both agitational and pacific means in his campaign against injustice. When workers were summarily dismissed from their homes and provision grounds without compensation he sought legal advice on their behalf. Henry Hudson-Phillips, one of Trinidad's leading lawyers, provided free legal advice. Hudson-Phillips had been Butler's schoolmate in Grenada and was a sometime mayor of Port of Spain. This incident illustrates the frequent interconnectedness of the middle- and working-class struggles.

Like many contemporary labor leaders, Butler mixed working-class activity with a racial and Pan-African consciousness. He called himself Butler the Black. One of his meetings sent a resolution to the League of Nations denouncing Germany's demands for a restoration of its former African colonies, lost after World War I. He likened some parts of the Vessigny and Sobo areas in southern Trinidad to "Fascist-destroyed Ethiopia." He also simultaneously reached out to Indian workers and colleagues.

As European governments often did with activists or groups they considered inconvenient, the British authorities considered deporting Butler to Grenada or the United Kingdom, much as they had earlier deported the Black Caribs, the Trelawney Maroons and others. St. Croix had deported General Buddhoe to Trinidad. The Americans had deported Marcus Garvey to Jamaica in 1927. The British in Barbados deported Clement Payne to Trinidad in 1937. British Nigeria had deported King Jaja to St. Vincent. In this case, however, they thought that Butler's early 1921 arrival in Trinidad made deportation problematic. The very recent case of Clement Payne (who was also a Butler associate) probably gave them pause as well. A Butler deportation in

1938 or 1939 would probably have resulted in bloodshed comparable to or greater than that accompanying Payne's case. And Butler's followers had already demonstrated a willingness to kill as well as be killed.

The British therefore charged him with sedition and inciting a riot for alleged remarks he made in May 1937. He failed to appear for the court case and they tried to arrest him at another rally in Fyzabad, his home base, on June 19, 1937. His supporters sprang Butler from the arresting officer. They chased Corporal Charlie King, one of a detail of policemen assigned to harass Butler, into a nearby Chinese shop. King was long an object of great hatred among Butlerites. He jumped through a window and broke his leg. Someone in the crowd, widely believed to be a woman, threw kerosene on him and they burnt him to death. The Butlerites also killed twenty-five-year-old Englishman William Bradburn, sub-inspector of police and the only son of Colonel W. E. H. Bradburn, inspector-general of police in British Guiana.

Butler went into hiding for three months before voluntarily giving himself up. He was acquitted on the sedition change but was sentenced to two years at hard labor on the incitement charge. The British released him in 1939 but re-incarcerated him, this time for six years and without trial, under wartime emergency regulations.

Butler returned to workers' activity and politics after his release from jail at war's end in 1946. He and his party won seats in various Legislative Council elections from 1946 to the 1950s. After the 1950 election he controlled the largest bloc of votes among the elected members in the partly elected council. He was unfairly denied the opportunity to form a government under the new quasi-ministerial system. The governor chose Portuguese Albert Gomes instead. After independence Butler was awarded the Trinity Cross, Trinidad's highest honor. June 19 became Trinidad's Labor Day public holiday.

Jamaica in 1935 and 1936 was rent by strikes, riots and workers' marches, in Falmouth, Kingston, Oracabessa and Port Antonio. Prominent leaders included Hugh Buchanan, a Marxist and former Garveyite, and G. S. Coombs, union leader. In 1937 Robert E. Rumble organized a Poor Man's Improvement and Land Settlement Association. There were strikes in December on the Serge Island estate. In 1938 five workers were killed and over twenty-five wounded at the Frome sugar estate, Jamaica's largest, owned by the British firm Tate and Lyle. Three weeks later in Kingston a dockworkers' strike escalated into a general shutdown of the city, spreading eventually across Jamaica. Eight people were killed and over 200 civilians and police wounded. Further flare-ups continued and there were rumors of a grand uprising for August 1, the centenary of Emancipation.

Alexander Bustamante, a near-white man, began his rise to prominence during the labor struggles of 1937–1938. He wrote a series of letters to the press in support of the workers. Garveyites gave him a platform for direct face-to-face interaction with the black masses. St. William Grant, former president of Marcus Garvey's UNIA in Brooklyn, New York, and, like Bustamante recently returned home, invited Bustamante in 1937 to speak to his regular street meetings. Yet another politically active BWIR veteran, Grant, became a high-ranking aide to Bustamante. The two men spent time in jail together in 1938. In June 1938 Bustamante formed the Bustamante Industrial Trade Union (BITU), composed initially of maritime, transport, factory, municipal and "general" workers. J. A. G. Edwards, general-secretary of the BITU and another top aide, was sometime president of the Kingston branch of Garvey's UNIA.

Bustamante was initially allied with his cousin, Norman Manley, a prominent lawyer. Manley's Peoples National Party, launched in 1938, was the political arm of the BITU. When Bustamante split from Manley in 1942 and formed his Jamaica Labor Party, Manley formed his own union affiliate, the Trade Union Congress.

In the wake of the 1930s disturbances the British government sent out a commission of enquiry under Lord Moyne in 1938. They issued a report in 1939 (but not released until 1945), among other things agreeing on the need for trade unions. Proper trade union legislation, with protection in tort, began to appear in the British Caribbean in the 1930s.

Publication of the Moyne Report was delayed by the onset of World War II in 1939. The British feared that its sympathetic attitude toward the suffering and restive masses might encourage further turmoil. If Britain thought it could contain wartime unrest, however, the United States was not so sure. One of the reasons put forth by American officials for the establishment of the Anglo-American Caribbean Commission in 1942 was the fear of continued trouble in the British colonies. From the American perspective, Britain was weak and preoccupied in war-ridden Europe. In the event of British Caribbean unrest the United States might have to send in troops to keep order. They would rather not have to deal with such a distraction in the middle of a war. The AACC, by encouraging economic and social improvements seemed, to American planners, a better alternative than forced intervention in a weakly held British Caribbean.

WORLD WAR II

As World War II approached (the United States entered the war in December 1941) the Caribbean initially felt many repercussions. Trinidad's oil industry became a vital commodity for the British war effort. The area became a theatre for submarine warfare. Thousands of Jewish refugees from Hitler ended up in Trinidad and the Dominican Republic, with lesser numbers to Barbados, Jamaica and elsewhere. The United States, Britain and world Jewish representatives appeared in 1939 on the brink of appropriating half of British Guiana for a Jewish state (as an alternative to Palestine) when the outbreak of hostilities in 1939 turned their attentions elsewhere.

Lord Moyne did not live to see the publication of his report. He was murdered in Egypt in 1944 by two Zionist Stern Gang assassins. Moyne had been appointed British minister of state in the Middle East. The Stern Gang was upset at what they perceived as British resistance to continued Jewish immigration into Palestine. Palestine was still a British "mandated" territory, placed under British control by the League of Nations after World War I. The troops of the BWIR had helped Britain conquer Palestine.

In the very year that Lord Moyne was murdered a Caribbean regiment arrived in Italy and then Egypt. Their story was a bit like the World War I experience all over again. The British resisted organizing them until 1944, late in the war. They saw no service as combat troops. They were stationed in Egypt, where they spent their time guarding some German prisoners, playing sports, sightseeing and fighting white South African troops. The British Royal Air Force, strapped for manpower, recruited Caribbean men, among them Errol Barrow, future prime minister of Barbadoss and Dudley Thompson, future cabinet minister in Jamaica. Squadron Leader Ulric Cross of Trinidad, later a judge, was probably the most highly decorated. He flew eighty missions over Europe. Several hundred men were recruited as munitions factory workers. Hundreds of Belizeans went to Scotland to do forestry work. Caribbean women were also recruited for work in the Auxiliary Territorial Forces (ATS) in England. The huge number of U.S. military personnel in the Caribbean, especially in Trinidad, ushered in the "Rum and Coca Cola" era and profoundly impacted social relations.

With the war's end came universal adult suffrage in 1944 (Jamaica) and 1946 (Trinidad and Tobago), with other colonies following over several years.

Further Readings

Baptiste, Owen. *Duprey: The Success Story of Cyril L. Duprey and the Colonial Life Insurance Company*. Port of Spain: Inprint Caribbean Ltd., 1986.

Beckles, Hilary McD. *Great House Rules: Landless Emancipation and Workers' Protest in Barbados, 1838–1938*. Kingston, Jamaica: Ian Randle Publishers, 2004.

British West Indies Regiment Graves in Sussex, 1915–1916, http://www.jeffreygreen.co.uk/british-west-indies-regiment-graves-in-sussex-1915-1916 [accessed September 19, 2010.]

DeVerteuil, Anthony. *The McShines of Trinidad*. Port of Spain: The Litho Press, 2006.

Eaton, George. "Trade Union Development in Jamaica." *Caribbean Quarterly*, 8, 1, March 1962, 43–53.

Eaton, George. "Trade Union Development in Jamaica—Part 2." *Caribbean Quarterly*, 8, 2, June 1962, 69–75.

Helg, Aline. *Our Rightful Share: The Afro-Cuban Struggle for Equality, 1886–1912.* Chapel Hill: University of North Carolina Press, 1995.

Jacobs, W. Richard. *Butler versus the King: Riots and Sedition in 1937.* Port of Spain: Key Caribbean Publications, 1976.

James, C. L. R. *Beyond a Boundary.* Durham, NC: Duke University Press, 1993. First pub. 1963.

Joseph, C. L. "The British West Indies Regiment, 1914–1918." *Journal of Caribbean History*, 2, May 1971, 94–124.

Martin, Tony. "Revolutionary Upheaval in Trinidad, 1919: Gleanings from British and American Sources," in *The Pan-African Connection.* Dover, MA: The Majority Press, 1984. First pub. 1983.

Martin, Tony. "Marcus Garvey and the West Indies." *Pan-African Connection*, op. cit., pp. 59–62.

Martin, Tony. "Marcus Garvey and Trinidad, 1912–1947." *Pan-African Connection*, op. cit., pp. 63–94.

Martin, Tony. "Garvey and the Beginnings of Mass-based Party Politics in Jamaica." *Pan-African Connection*, op. cit., pp. 111–132.

Martin, Tony. "Marcus Garvey and Southern Africa." *Pan-African Connection*, op. cit., pp. 133–154.

Martin, Tony. "Benito Sylvain of Haiti on the Pan-African Conference of 1900." *Pan-African Connection*, op. cit., pp. 201–216.

Martin, Tony. *Race First: The Ideological and Organizational Struggles of Marcus Garvey and the Universal Negro Improvement Association.* Dover, MA: The Majority Press, 1986. First pub. by Greenwood Press, 1976.

Martin, Tony. "A Pan-Africanist in Dominica: J.R. Ralph Casimir and the Garvey Movement, 1919–1923." *Journal of Caribbean History*, XXI, 2, 1988; Reprinted in Harry Reed and John Henderson, Eds., *Studies in the African Diaspora* (Dover, MA: The Majority Press, 1989).

Martin, Tony. "Jews to Trinidad." *Journal of Caribbean History*, XXVIII, 2, 1994, 244–257.

Martin, Tony. "Vote for a Woman!!!" in Brian Moore and Swithin Wilmot, Eds., *Before and After 1865.* Kingston, Jamaica: Ian Randle Publishers, 1998.

Martin, Tony. *Amy Ashwood Garvey: Pan-Africanist, Feminist and Mrs. Marcus Garvey No. 1, Or, A Tale of Two Amies.* Dover, MA: The Majority Press 2007.

Metzgen, Humphrey, and John Graham. *Caribbean Wars Untold: A Salute to the British West Indies.* Kingston, Jamaica: University of the West Indies Press, 2007.

Mohamed, Paloma. "The Press, Politics and Race in Guyana." *Journal of Caribbean Studies* 17, 3, Spring 2003, 251–269.

Moitt, Bernard. *Women and Slavery in the French Antilles, 1635–1848.* Bloomington: Indiana University Press, 2001.

Nehusi, Kimani. "The Causes of the Protest of 1905," in Winston F. McGowan, James G. Rose, and David A. Granger, Eds., *Themes in African-Guyanese History.* Georgetown: Free Press, 1998.

Rose, James G. "The Strikes of 1842 and 1848," in Winston F. McGowan et al., *Themes in African Guyanese History,* op. cit., pp. 158–200.

Samaroo, Brinsley. "The Trinidad Workingmen's Association and the Origins of Popular Protest in a Crown Colony." *Social and Economic Studies*, 21, 2, June 1972, 205–222.

Smith, Michael Garfield, Roy Augier, and Rex Nettleford. *The Rastafarian Movement in Kingston, Jamaica.* Kingston, Jamaica: Institute of Social and Economic Research, 1960.

Smith, Richard. *Jamaican Volunteers in the First World War: Race, Masculinity and the Development of National Consciousness.* Manchester: Manchester University Press, 2004.

Vaughan, H. A. *Sandy Lane and Other Poems.* Bridgetown, Barbados: The Book Place, 1985. First pub. 1945.

Whitaker, Mark. "Worrell's Tortured Path to West Indies' Top Job: Politics and Racism Kept Captaincy in White Hands Until Trinidad Journalist's Campaign Changed Game 40 Years Ago." *Independent* (UK), August 24, 2000.

Woolford, Hazel M. "The Origins of the [Guyanese] Labor Movement," in Winston F. McGowan, James G. Rose, and David A. Granger, Eds., *Themes in African-Guyanese History.* Georgetown: Free Press, 1998.

15

World War II to Century's End

CONSTITUTIONAL ADVANCE

In 1944, with the end of World War II in sight, Jamaica became first among the British colonies to receive universal adult suffrage. The British had everywhere conceded political ground incrementally in the face of protracted pressure from the various labor, political and other pressure groups clamoring for constitutional advance.

With the coming of proper trade union laws in the late 1930s and 1940s, union members could now strike and picket without fear of transgressing the law. Powerful unions emerged and in time gave rise to, or allied themselves with, new political parties. Alexander Bustamante, winner of Jamaica's 1944 election, led the Jamaica Labor Party, which was closely allied to his own Bustamante Industrial Trade Union.

Trinidad and Tobago was next with universal adult suffrage, in 1946. Tubal Uriah Buzz Butler's British Empire Citizens' and Workers' Home Rule Party won the largest share of the popular vote (23.7 percent) and three of the ten seats contested in the 1946 elections. In 1950 Butler won six seats, at the head of a successful African-Indian political alliance. Three other parties won two seats each. Six independents were elected. "Butler the Black" (as he sometimes called himself) should have been appointed to head the newly introduced quasi-ministerial system. Instead, the governor appointed the Portuguese-Trinidadian radical Albert Gomes, whom he considered a more congenial collaborator and, if need be, adversary. With the black-led Butler Party outstripping all others at the polls and with Afro-Trinidadians a majority in the country, Governor Sir Hubert Rance somehow managed to appoint a virtually African-free ministerial team comprising Portuguese Gomes, half-Lebanese Roy Joseph, Chinese Norman Tang, colored Victor Bryan and Indian Ajodasingh. The aggrieved Butler is said to have promised to make Rance rancid.

It was only in 1956 that Trinidad and Tobago obtained a dominant political party. This was the Peoples National Movement (PNM), founded by Dr. Eric Williams in 1955, after his acrimonious break with the Caribbean Commission. The PNM proceeded to dominate Trinidad's politics uninterruptedly for the next thirty years and for several of the years thereafter. The PNM was near-unique in the British colonies in not having a labor union affiliate.

Universal adult suffrage came to other colonies in the years following (Barbados in 1950, St. Lucia, St. Vincent and Dominica in 1951, etc.). Jamaica and Trinidad and Tobago again led the colonies into independence, both in 1962. In 1967 Antigua, Dominica, Grenada, Montserrat, St. Kitts-Nevis, St. Lucia and St. Vincent were grouped into the West Indies Associated States. They had internal self-government. In 1981 they became the Organization of Eastern Caribbean States as a prelude to individual independence in the early 1980s, with Montserrat remaining a British colony.

Independence came to Guyana and Barbados in 1966; the Bahamas in 1973; Grenada in 1974; Dominica in 1978; St. Lucia and St. Vincent and the Grenadines in 1979; Antigua and Barbuda in 1980; Belize in 1981; St. Kitts and Nevis in 1983. Montserrat, the British Virgin Islands, Cayman Islands and Turks and Caicos Islands were still crown colonies in 2011.

The final push for independence, though largely uneventful, was nevertheless punctuated by some noteworthy and sometimes turbulent episodes. Unlike Puerto Rico with its anomalous status as a "freely associated" nonindependent entity of the United States, unlike the Netherlands Antilles and Aruba where at times it seemed that the metropolitan power was more pro-independence than the islands themselves, and unlike the French Caribbean islands, where prospects of wringing independence from France seem remote in 2011, the former British colonies increasingly envisioned independence as a realizable goal.

Although the precise dates of constitutional advances varied from colony to colony, broad developments within the British West Indies tended to be in tandem. The reform associations, representative government associations and the like existed all over the British Caribbean.

Overseas-based individuals and organizations in the twentieth century also intervened effectively in the struggle for political advance at home. Among the organizations were Garvey's U.S.-based UNIA, the African Blood Brotherhood of Kittitian Cyril Briggs, the Virgin Islands Association, the Jamaica Progressive League (JPL, usually credited with helping give birth in 1938 to the People's National Party of Norman Manley) and the West Indies National Council (WINC), led by veteran Trinidadian activist C. A. Petioni, together with Herman Osborne of Trinidad, W. A. Domingo of

Jamaica and Hope Stevens of the British Virgin Islands. Both the JPL and the WINC collaborated with Eric Williams in his important conference on the Economic Future of the Caribbean at Howard University in 1943. Petioni said at that conference that "The West Indian abroad is the only hope for those in the Islands."

British-based groups included the Society of Peoples of African Origin, the Pan-African Federation of George Padmore and the League of Colored Peoples, founded in 1931 by Jamaican Dr. Harold Moody. From Paris the *Association Générale des Etudiants Guadeloupéens* (General Association of Guadeloupean Students) had a profound effect on the struggle of the 1960s.

Once independence was achieved the newly emerging nations slid effortlessly into the two-party Westminster arrangements they had inherited. In Jamaica, JLP and PNP governments succeeded each other like clockwork, two terms in office, two terms out, from 1944 to 1983. In 1989 the PNP embarked on a four election winning streak, which finally ended the two terms tradition.

There were however some periods of great turmoil, when the usually placid tenor of political life was broken. One such was the Black Power era of the late 1960s and the early 1970s. This was associated with the parent movement, as it were, emanating from African America.

BRITISH GUIANA DISTURBANCES

British Guiana ran into problems with Britain and the United States over its open espousal of communism. The early 1950s, at the height of the Cold War, was not a good time for the leadership of a small British colony on the southern edge of the "American lake" to openly espouse communism, but this is what Dr. Cheddi Jagan, head of the Peoples Progressive Party (PPP) government, chose to do.

The PPP, founded in 1950, brought together the majority Indian population and the African element. At its first congress in 1951 Jagan (Indian) was elected leader of the legislative group and de facto maximum leader of the party. Burnham (African) was elected party chairman. Janet Jagan became secretary-general, theoretically under the

Forbes Burnham Memorial, Georgetown, Guyana.

chairman but actually a more powerful position. The PPP grew out of a Political Affairs Committee (PAC) which existed from 1946 to 1949.

Prior to the PAC the most influential quasi-political groupings included the Guiana Industrial Workers Union (GIWU), the British Guiana Labor Union (BGLU), the Man-Power Citizens' Association (MPCA), the League of Colored People (LCP) and the British Guiana East Indian Association (BGEIA).

Jagan's Marxism is sometimes attributed to the influence of his American wife. Janet Jagan, née Rosenberg, was from a middle-class Chicago Jewish family. She married Cheddi, a dental student in Chicago, in 1943. The two returned to British Guiana that year and remained politically active for over half a century. The United States stripped Mrs. Jagan of her U.S. citizenship in 1947. She became a Guianese citizen in 1966. After Jagan's death in 1997, Mrs. Jagan was president of Guyana from 1997 to 1999.

The PPP won eighteen of twenty-four elective seats in the elections of 1953, the first under universal adult suffrage. Dr. Jagan became premier. British Prime Minister Winston Churchill sent troops into the colony, jailed the Jagans, suspended the constitution and appointed an interim government later in 1953, because of unease with Dr. Jagan's Marxist rhetoric. Other British Caribbean politicians had espoused socialism before the Jagans, but theirs was one variant or another of "democratic" British Labor Party socialism. When the Jagans spoke of socialism they were talking about the "totalitarian" variant practiced on the wrong side of the Iron Curtain.

The constitution was restored in 1957 and new elections were held. The PPP won nine of fourteen seats. Jagan became chief minister. In 1961, with independence in the offing, U.S. Secretary of State Dean Rusk informed the British foreign minister that accession to power by the Jagans in an independent Guiana "would be a most troublesome setback in this hemisphere."

The British demurred, but as in the British Guiana–Venezuela boundary dispute of 1898,

U.S. power was not to be ignored. Dean Rusk was adamant in June 1963 that Britain must not "wash its hands of British Guiana by granting early independence, leaving the mess on our doorstep." Similar sentiments had preceded the formation of the Anglo-American Caribbean Commission in 1942.

In October 1961 Jagan, fresh from a new election victory which gave him twenty of thirty-five seats, visited President John F. Kennedy at the White House, seeking economic aid. Jagan's effort to allay the apprehensions of U.S. officialdom actually backfired. He was grilled concerning his communist leanings on the popular television program, "Meet the Press." He did not handle himself well and reinforced President Kennedy's earlier decision, as he watched

the program, that Jagan must be removed from power. The Cuban Revolution was now a reality and a Marxist ruler in British Guiana seemed an unnecessary irritant to the Colossus of the North.

Jagan was introduced to the "Meet the Press" audience as the new prime minister of British Guiana, which his hosts ominously described as the gateway to South America. The first question put to him accordingly referenced Senator Thomas Dodd's assertion in the U.S. Senate that Jagan's election victory provided international communism with its first beachhead on the South American continent. Jagan waffled a bit and then admitted that he was indeed a socialist. He believed in a planned economy, he said, but he assured viewers that socialism would in no way threaten the liberties of the Guianese people.

Janet and Cheddi Jagan, 1957.

The "Meet the Press" interviewers ("interrogators" might have been a better word) had done their homework well. Jagan's apparent long-standing tendency to unguarded speech did not help him. They quoted Jagan's 1953 speech to the Legislative Council where he extolled the views of Marx, Engels, Lenin and Stalin that communism and socialism were the same. When Jagan tried to extricate himself from his threats to nationalize major industries, one interviewer reminded him of his 1954 book which contained an explicit promise to nationalize.

Jagan denied the allegations of Afro-Guianese politician Sydney King (later Eusi Kwayana and a former 1953 PPP cabinet minister), in letters written to the UN and to the U.S. authorities, that Jagan's election victory was merely a reflection of the numerical preponderance of Indians over Africans. Since the 1955 split in the PPP, the Jagan government had increasingly pursued policies designed to empower its rural Indian base. The 1969 U.S. *Area Handbook for Guyana* described *apanjaht* (vote for your own) as the PPP's "unofficial slogan." Burnham's defeat at the 1957 polls had likewise brought home to him the necessity to aggressively consolidate his African base.

The final "Meet the Press" question to Jagan, perhaps deliberately left for last, targeted the sensitive issue of Janet Jagan's communism. It was couched in the form of a statement. Mrs. Jagan, said an interviewer, had been a member of a Communist front organization in Chicago. She had been until August 21 a member of Jagan's government. Jagan's response to this final observation suggested that he must have been, by this time, fatigued by the relentless well-researched questions from his panel of interviewers. Backward colonial countries, he said, needed skilled politicians as much as they needed skilled technicians and his party was introducing new faces into governance in order to give them experience. He did not answer the charge of Mrs. Jagan's communism.

President Kennedy, the CIA and American labor unions acting as conduits for the CIA thereafter escalated their campaign against Jagan. The main beneficiary of the American anti-Jagan campaign was Forbes Burnham. Burnham had led a defection from Jagan's wing of the PPP in 1955. In 1957 he formed the Peoples National Congress. He was leader of the opposition in parliament from 1957 to 1964. He was

elected mayor of Georgetown in 1959 and 1964. He became president of the Guyana Bar Association in 1959 and from 1957 to 1964 was president of the Guyana Labor Union. Jagan's PPP and Burnham's PNC became quickly polarized into predominantly Indian and African parties, respectively.

A series of riots erupted in 1962 leaving much of downtown Georgetown devastated. The causes included a proposed PPP budget opposed by urban Guyanese and big business and efforts to replace the pro-Burnham Man-Power Citizens' Association by the new PPP-sponsored Guiana Agricultural Workers' Union (GAWU) as bargaining agent for the Indian sugar workers. In 1963 the PPP introduced a Labor Relations Bill, designed in part to facilitate the GAWU thrust into the sugar arena. The new bill would have appointed Jagan's government final arbiter on who qualified as bargaining agents. The Trade Union Congress led an eighty-day general strike against the bill and Jagan's government. The bill lapsed in the legislature without becoming law.

The worst and most racially polarizing riots took place in 1964 in the wake of a nationwide GAWU strike encouraged by Jagan. The sugar producers brought in mostly African workers to replace the striking Indians. Someone threw a bomb into a bus killing two of the replacement workers and the industrial dispute turned into a racial explosion. The fighting is said to have claimed 176 lives, with 920 injured, 1,400 homes destroyed and about 15,000 persons forced to flee to racially safer neighborhoods. In the signature incident of the 1964 riots a bomb exploded on the *Sun Chapman* passenger boat killing thirty-eight Afro-Guyanese. Mediation efforts by the governments of Ghana and Trinidad and Tobago proved futile.

The 1964 pre-independence elections were fought under a new system of proportional representation which was less favorable to Jagan than the "first past the post" or "winner take all" of traditional British practice. Jagan had surprisingly signed off, together with Burnham and Portuguese-Guyanese businessman Peter D'Aguiar, leader of the third party United Force (UF), on a document giving the British colonial secretary, Duncan Sandys, authority to unilaterally impose new electoral arrangements. This was at a 1963 constitutional conference in

London. Under the new system, parliamentary seats were awarded in proportion to the popular vote obtained. Burnham was able to form a government in coalition with the UF. The UF's support came from the Portuguese, Chinese and Amerindian communities, together with big business, the Roman Catholic Church and the very wealthy of all ethnic groups. For the 1961 elections the UF had actually negotiated an informal arrangement with the PPP whereby the latter withdrew from urban areas in which the UF had a chance of winning if the votes were not split. This did not preclude the later PNC–UF alliance.

Jagan's PPP won 46 percent of the popular vote in 1964, to the PNC's 41 percent and the UF's 12 percent. A record 96.9 percent of the eligible electorate voted. Jagan refused to accept the results, belatedly accusing Sandys of bias. He was forcibly removed as premier by a British executive order. Burnham became premier on December 14, 1964.

British Guiana, renamed Guyana, became independent in 1966. Burnham, though benefitting from U.S. anti-Jagan activity, proved a difficult entity for Washington to handle. He pursued a foreign policy to the left of most of the former British colonies. He resisted American pressure and allowed Cuban planes for a while to land and refuel on their way to defeat South Africa in Angola in the 1970s. "To come and tell me that it is wrong," Burnham is reported to have told the Associated Press, "is like telling me I have no right to feel like a black man." Burnham was also the first to provide arms to the Grenadian revolution in 1979.

On the domestic scene Burnham proved no less a loose cannon for the Americans. He nationalized bauxite in 1971 and sugar in 1975. In the Declaration of Sophia in 1974 he supported socialism. By the end of the 1970s Burnham had nationalized about 80 percent of Guyana's economy. Jagan had been unseated for merely talking about these measures. Now, in opposition he extended "critical support" for Burnham's left policies.

WEST INDIES FEDERATION

While British Guiana was undergoing its turmoil, the rest of the British Caribbean was experiencing a short-lived federation, from 1958 to 1962. Federation

leading to independence seemed a convenient and cost-effective way for Britain to rid herself of these colonies, once jewels in the imperial crown, but now just bothersome anachronisms.

Federation was theoretically good for the Caribbean, too. History had molded the territories into essentially one people. Several official and voluntary associations had already implicitly adopted a federal basis. There was the University of the West Indies, established in Jamaica in 1947, with campuses to follow in Trinidad and Barbados. The West Indies cricket team had been an international institution since the 1890s. Several prominent politicians, including Forbes Burnham of British Guiana and Dudley Thompson of Jamaica, had headed the West Indian Students' Union (WISU), most important affiliate of the Union of West Indian Students in Great Britain and Northern Ireland. Eric Williams had mentored WISU by long distance while teaching at Howard University in the 1940s. He was also faculty adviser to a West Indian students' club at Howard. The British West Indies Regiment of the First World War , and before it the West India Regiment of the late eighteenth century and onward, had all implicitly based themselves on the federal principle. As early as 1913, a West Indian Club at Howard University had urged the establishment of a West Indian National League, to include branches in the United States, and with a possible headquarters in Washington, D.C.

Over the years the British government proposed or implemented various schemes of consolidation or federation. Berbice, Demerara and Essequibo were merged to create British Guiana in 1831. The British placed the Leeward Islands and Dominica under a single governor in 1833, though they retained their separate assemblies until 1871. In 1876 Barbados refused to join a proposed federation with the Windward Islands (St. Lucia, St. Vincent, Grenada and Tobago).

In the twentieth century businesspeople and local politicians took up the call for federation. A West Indian Federal League established in Trinidad in 1917 advocated a loose federation which would nevertheless enable the region to speak with one authoritative voice in international forums.

Edward Davson, chairman of the Federation of Chambers of Commerce of the British Empire and son of a British Guiana sugar baron, reported in 1920 a lukewarm reception among Caribbean businessmen to a political federation, but receptivity to other forms of cooperation. He pointed out that there was already established a tradition of regional conferences. Medical officers had met on quarantine issues, law officers on the formation of a West Indian Court of Appeal and customs officers on harmonizing tariffs. Chambers of Commerce and agricultural departments had also held regional conferences. He proposed to formalize these arrangements into a system of "Federation by Conference." Davson formulated these ideas after meeting in Barbados with the Associated Chambers of Commerce. This body brought regional chambers together in triennial meetings.

Leaders of the democracy and labor movements had also long advocated federation. In 1913, a year before he founded the UNIA, Marcus Garvey said,

> There have been several movements to federate the British West Indian Islands, but owing to parochial feelings nothing definite has been achieved. Ere long this change is sure to come about because the people of these islands are all one. They live under the same conditions, are of the same race and mind and have the same feelings and sentiments regarding the things of the world.

At the British Guiana and West Indies Labor Conference in 1926, Arthur Cipriani, representing the Trinidad Workingmen's Association, introduced a resolution calling for federation with dominion status (that is, the quasi-independent status within the British empire, enjoyed by such white or white ruled "dominions" as Canada, South Africa, New Zealand and Australia). Guianese delegates however expressed some reservations.

Cipriani was a major force behind a West Indian Conference on federation for Trinidad, Barbados, the Leeward and Windward Islands, held in Dominica in 1932. Cecil Rawle of Dominica referred to Caribbean people as "a people of common interest, of common stock, upbringing, tradition and ideas. . . ." The Second Caribbean Labor Congress meeting in Jamaica in 1947 called for federation of all the colonies including British Guiana, British

Honduras and the Bahamas. A British Closer Union Commission recommended in 1933 a federation of the Leeward and Windward Islands. There had also been various schemes to unite varying combinations of islands. In 1947 the British government convened a conference on federation in Montego Bay, Jamaica. The conference set up a Standing Closer Association Committee. The Caribbean Commission of the 1940s and 1950s was in actuality a highly successful experiment in regional integration.

Out of all this came the West Indies Federation of 1958–1962. It comprised the ten units of Antigua and Barbuda, Barbados, Dominica, Grenada, Jamaica, Montserrat, St. Kitts-Nevis-Anguilla, St. Lucia, St. Vincent and the Grenadines and Trinidad and Tobago. British Guiana's Cheddi Jagan opted out, responding to Indo-Guianese reluctance to be part of a majority African entity. Opposition leader Forbes Burnham supported Guianese participation.

Grantley Adams of Barbados became the first federal prime minister. The other big names, Eric Williams of Trinidad and Norman Manley and Alexander Bustamante of Jamaica, preferred to remain in their island bases, rather than contest federal posts. The federation foundered on a variety of unresolved issues. There was no freedom of movement, no federal taxation and no customs union. Jamaica seceded from the federation in 1961 after Bustamante, then in opposition, cajoled Manley into holding a referendum on the issue. Bustamante won. Eric Williams then announced that "One from 10 leaves nought," and withdrew Trinidad, thus ending the experiment. The capital of the federation had been in Port of Spain. Chaguaramas, home of Trinidad's U.S. World War II naval base, was chosen as the capital site but the Americans had not yet given it back as of 1962, despite a spirited campaign by Williams.

The work of Caribbean integration continued after 1962, principally in CARIFTA (Caribbean Free Trade Association) from 1965 and its successor, CARICOM (Caribbean Community) from 1973. CARICOM has expanded beyond the former British territories. The fifteen full members as of 2011 were Antigua and Barbuda, Bahamas, Barbados, Belize, Dominica, Grenada, Guyana, Haiti, Jamaica, Montserrat, St. Kitts and Nevis, St. Lucia, St. Vincent and the Grenadines, Suriname and Trinidad and

Tobago. Associate members (all British overseas territories) are Anguilla, Bermuda, British Virgin Islands, Cayman Islands and Turks and Caicos Islands. There are seven observers—Aruba, Colombia, Dominican Republic, Mexico, Netherlands Antilles, Puerto Rico and Venezuela.

BLACK POWER

The age-old Civil Rights movement in the United States had assumed a new intensity from 1954, when the U.S. Supreme Court in *Brown vs Board of Education of Topeka, Kansas* outlawed segregation. Segregation ("Jim Crow" or the fiction of "separate but equal") had been the official law of the land since the 1896 Supreme Court case of *Plessy vs Ferguson.*

In 1955 the new law was tested in the Montgomery (Alabama) Bus Boycott, when African American seamstress Rosa Parks was arrested and jailed for not giving up her seat on a segregated bus to a white Southern gentleman. The resulting bus boycott by the black community ushered in the national Civil Rights career of the Rev. Martin Luther King Jr. By the 1960s, as the first British Caribbean colonies were becoming independent, the largely nonviolent and integrationist U.S. Civil Rights movement was beginning its transformation into Black Power.

As in the Garvey era after World War I, African American struggles resonated in the Caribbean. For one thing, several of the participants in the North American struggle, then as now, were of Caribbean background. Stokely Carmichael (later Kwame Ture) who first popularized the term "Black Power" in Mississippi in 1966, was a U.S. immigrant from Trinidad. Malcolm X, the "Black shining Prince" of the movement as he was famously eulogized by actor Ossie Davis, was born in the United States of a Grenadian Garveyite mother. When the Black Power movement spread to Canada and Great Britain, it was the Caribbean immigrants and students in both places who largely spearheaded the transfer.

As influential as extra-Caribbean events may have been, however, they were not essential to the growth of Black Power in the area. The Caribbean had been a place of strong African consciousness from the proverbial time immemorial. Two of the more interesting happenings of the 1960s illustrating

this were the Ronald Henry–attempted rebellion in Jamaica in 1959–1960 and the visits of His Imperial Majesty Haile Selassie of Ethiopia to the Caribbean.

Thousands of Jamaicans responded to Rev. Claudius Henry's repatriation activities in 1959. Many bought tickets for a projected trip to Ethiopia. They also expected the Jamaican government to alleviate widespread suffering among the country's poor. When police raided Rev. Henry's headquarters later in 1959 they found extensive quantities of arms and ammunition. Henry was convicted of treason and sentenced to six years' incarceration. In 1960 Ronald Henry, Rev. Claudius' son, entered Jamaica from the United States with a handful of activists comprising the First Africa Corps. They quickly killed and wounded a few of the British troops deployed against them. The rebellion was put down by 1,000 police and troops. Ronald Henry was hanged. These events came after over two decades of repression of the Rastafarian movement. In 1954, for example, police and soldiers had destroyed Pinnacle, the agricultural and residential community of Rastafarian pioneer Leonard Howell.

Emperor Haile Selassie of Ethiopia visited Trinidad, Jamaica and Haiti in that order in 1966. He also visited Bermuda in 1963 and 1967. He was enthusiastically received everywhere, but the Jamaican welcome on April 21 has assumed legendary proportions. Over 100,000 Rastafarians are said to have greeted him at the airport, evoking comparison with the welcome extended to Marcus Garvey on his return home in 1927. Security personnel were unable to prevent the crowd from converging on the aircraft. Ganja smoke thickened the atmosphere. The emperor was gracious, as he had been to the Garvey movement in the 1920s and 1930s, and as he had been in 1948 when he pledged free land from his personal holdings at Sheshemane to Africans repatriating from the West. The first repatriates, from Montserrat, relocated in 1955. The emperor's visit provided Rastafarians with a positive visibility which helped loosen the chains of social proscription still afflicting them. The publicity helped market their religion to the unconverted.

In all the countries visited the emperor appeared on the eve of the Black Power revolution and became another element in the buildup of black consciousness. Jamaica's Walter Rodney riots took place in 1968.

Trinidad's Black Power movement became a mass movement in 1968, with street demonstrations and protests. Bermuda in the 1960s was segregated and racist to a degree no longer obtaining elsewhere in the Anglophone Caribbean. Universal adult suffrage arrived only in 1968. In that year students at the Berkeley Institute demanded Black History courses and shut down the school for two days. There were serious riots in 1968, 1970 and later. In 1969 an international Black Power conference brought major African American Black Power activists to the island. In the early 1970s Bermuda's white police chief, governor, governor's aide and two supermarket owners were assassinated. The white establishment blamed the local Black Beret Cadre.

The fact that from 1962 most of the former British colonies were becoming independent did not diminish the appeal of Black Power. Many youths, students, intellectuals and workers began to argue that

independence had brought with it neocolonialism, where economies were still controlled by white foreign corporations. The quest for Black Power therefore seemed appropriate, despite mostly black politicians ostensibly in power. This generation was also greatly influenced by the Martiniquan Frantz Fanon, whose book, *The Wretched of the Earth*, had become a sort of bible for the Black Power movement in the United States. Fanon argued that colonialism was a violent phenomenon and those opposed to it must at least be prepared to oppose it violently.

The Eric Williams government in Trinidad and Tobago sought, too late, to isolate their country from Black Power influences. Stokely Carmichael/Kwame Ture visited England in 1967 and almost single-handedly ushered in a Black Power movement. (Malcolm X had visited in 1965.) As soon as Stokely left England the British government banned him. As soon as the British banned him Eric Williams

Caribbean students in London protest outside the Trinidad and Tobago High Commission after the banning of Stokely Carmichael (Kwame Ture) in August 1967.

banned him, too. It would be almost twenty years before a government of the National Alliance for Reconstruction, which ended the thirty-year winning streak of Williams' People's National Movement, would remove the Trinidad ban on Stokely.

In Montreal in October 1968, Caribbean student activists convened a Black Writers Conference featuring Carmichael/Ture and C. L. R. James among others. Dr. Walter Rodney, Guyanese African history lecturer at the University of the West Indies, Jamaica, was not allowed to land when he returned to Jamaica after the conference. Student initiated marches and demonstrations followed in Jamaica. Police killed a few people.

The anti–Black Power paranoia of Caribbean governments was now in full swing. Black Power was now increasingly conflated with the dreaded cold war bogey of Marxism, and not without reason. While in African America Marxists made little headway into the Black Power movement, in the Caribbean the lines of demarcation were more murky. Rodney was an avowed Marxist. Veteran Trinidadian Marxist C. L. R. James, earlier expelled from Eric Williams' Peoples' National Movement, was a revered father figure of the movement. Fanon was an anti-Stalinist independent Marxist. Stokely Carmichael, as he increasingly came under the influence of Presidents Kwame Nkrumah of Ghana and Sékou Ture of Guinea, defined his ideology as one of Pan-African socialism.

When in 1966, before the bans on Walter Rodney and Stokely Carmichael, the Jamaican president of the West Indian Students Union in London was offered a free ticket to attend the Fourth Congress of Latin American Students in Havana, he could not go. He was on a Jamaican government scholarship. His place was taken by a Guyanese student. This was the year of Guyanese independence. Forbes Burnham, now firmly in power, was the outstanding exception to the Commonwealth Caribbean's anti-Marxist and anti–Black Power paranoia. Stokely Carmichael was welcome in Guyana after the Trinidad ban.

The Black Power buildup took another leap forward with yet another event in Montreal acting as the springboard. Caribbean students at Sir George Williams University (now Concordia University) had been trying for a year to obtain redress from the racist grading practices of a biology professor.

In February 1969 their patience ran out. They occupied and burned down the university's computer center.

There was tremendous sympathy at home for the students. The Trinidad government provided financial assistance for legal and other expenses. One of the students was the son of Cheddi Jagan, at that time Guyana's leader of the opposition. Students at the University of the West Indies in Trinidad, newly organized as the National Joint Action Committee (NJAC), held marches of solidarity. When Canadian Governor-General Roland Michener paid a courtesy visit to the university in the company of Prime Minister Eric Williams, the students prevented his entry. Dr. Williams and party turned around and abandoned the visit.

NJAC's marches and demonstrations continued. Canadian banks and the country's high commission became targets. Workers, unemployed people, intellectuals and others began to swell the demonstrations. Targets expanded to include other symbols of neocolonialism and of lingering racism in postindependent Trinidad and Tobago. By 1969 Trinidad's home-grown Black Power movement was emerging as possibly the most serious in the Caribbean.

One of the first local targets of the protesters in 1969, as they marched from target to target, was the Trinidad Country Club, a long-established bastion of racial exclusiveness. The club had just found itself in the center of a fire storm concerning its alleged racist practices. Two African American dentists attending a medical conference in Trinidad had forced a reluctant Prime Minister Eric Williams to set up a commission of inquiry into racism at the club.

The commission of inquiry invited local victims of racism at the club to come forward and testify. Only one did, a young lawyer-economist recently returned from studies in England. He had been invited to address a private organization meeting on the Country Club's premises. He testified that he felt like "Alice in a South African [apartheid] Wonderland." The Commission found that there was no racism at the club though, they said, it was possible that they did not treat black people well.

Protests escalated in 1970, with an invasion and desecration of the Roman Catholic cathedral, a symbol to some of anachronistic racial intolerance. By April 1970 the movement had achieved massive proportions. It had also received its first martyr, a young man shot by police. In April 1970, fearing an impending general strike, Eric Williams declared a state of emergency and detained Black Power leaders. The army then mutinied, though the police and Coast Guard remained loyal to the government. Emergency arms were rushed in from the United States and the situation was eventually contained.

The Williams government made concessions to the neocolonialism allegations by forcing banks (including the Royal Bank of Canada and the Bank of Nova Scotia) to sell their assets to locals. In 2009 the Royal Bank of Canada was able to repurchase its former bank, which had become in the interim the Royal Bank of Trinidad and Tobago. The forces of globalization and economic liberalism had forced Trinidad to again open up to foreign acquisitions and ownership.

GRENADA REVOLUTION

At the height of the Trinidad Black Power buildup in 1970 Maurice Bishop stopped briefly in Trinidad. He was on his way home to Grenada after several years of law studies in London. Like thousands of other Caribbean students of the period he had left Grenada (in 1963) somewhat unprepared for the more overt racial discrimination experienced in the metropolis. He had also left Grenada a great admirer of Eric Gairy, the island's populist trade unionist-turned-political leader. Now he was returning home radicalized, receptive to Black Power. He would later overthrow Gairy in the Commonwealth Caribbean's only successful coup in the era of independence.

Back in Grenada, Bishop formed the New Jewel Movement (NJM) in collaboration with other reformist and radical groups. They mobilized against Gairy, who had led the nation to independence in 1974. Gairy had a long history in trade union activism and politics, very much in the mainstream of British Caribbean politicians. He had been a student teacher in Grenada from 1939 to 1941. He worked at a U.S. naval base in Trinidad from 1941 to 1942. From 1943 to 1949 he worked in Aruba, where he became active as a trade unionist. He returned to Grenada in 1949. From 1951 to 1979

he was president-general of the Grenada Manual, Maritime and Intellectual Workers' Union. From 1951 to 1979 he was president of the Grenada United Labor Party (GULP).

Gairy was immensely popular in his early years of Grenada politics. Opposition to him grew, however, in the 1970s. The return of Bishop and other young radicals added impetus to a growing frustration with Gairy, who was increasingly seen as an embarrassing relic of a bygone era. In 1970 Gairy expressed alarm at the Black Power disturbances in Trinidad. In that year he established an informal alternative police force that came to be known as the Mongoose Gang. Demonstrations against Gairy increased in the run-up to independence in 1974. On January 21, shortly before independence on February 7, Maurice Bishop's father, Rupert Bishop, was killed during one such incident.

The NJM seized power in an armed but near-bloodless coup on March 13, 1979. Bishop and several of the new leaders were populists with vague notions of socialism, very much in the Commonwealth Caribbean tradition. There was, however, a hard core of doctrinaire Marxists, led by Bernard Coard, who became deputy prime minister under Bishop. Coard and his clique assumed dominance over the ideological orientation of the NJM in power. They dismantled the New Jewel Movement, a popular mass party in the Caribbean tradition. They reconstituted it as a "Leninist vanguard party," where only a chosen few ideologues could be full members. High-ranking foundation members of the party suddenly found themselves relegated to probationary "applicant members" and "candidate members" on the Soviet pattern. As of September 1983, near the end of the NJM experiment, the party was said to contain only sixty-five full members. Coard even instituted ideological classes within the party leadership, with himself as schoolmaster. Prime Minister Maurice Bishop implausibly found himself a lowly student in these classes, receiving good grades from Coard for relating to the masses and poor grades for his lack of knowledge of Marxism-Leninism.

The upshot of this unseemly situation was a palace coup within the revolution in October 1983. Coard and his clique placed Bishop under arrest. The "masses," who loved Bishop, freed him from

Prime Minister Michael Manley of Jamaica, Prime Minister Maurice Bishop of Grenada,
Secretary-General Kurt Waldheim of the United Nations, and President Fidel Castro of Cuba,
during arrival ceremonies for Non-aligned summit, Havana 1979.

incarceration and marched, thousands strong, to Fort
Rupert (named after Bishop's murdered father). There
the unthinkable happened. Coard's forces fired heavy
weapons and small arms into the crowd, killing a large
but unknown number of persons, possibly a hundred.
Bishop and other officials loyal to him were executed.
Bishop's body was never found. The United States,
under President Ronald Reagan, invaded Grenada on
October 25, 1983, though army and navy special
forces were infiltrated in on the 24th. Reagan had
been looking for an invasion pretext for a long time
and Coard's ultra-left Marxist-Leninist bloodbath
gave him the opportunity. Half of Grenada's approximately 2,000 plus strong army did not show up for
work, being thoroughly demoralized by the savage
killings of Bishop and his supporters.

Yet those who did report to duty, augmented by
members of the militia, gave the invading force quite a
shock. They were reinforced by the 53 Cuban military
instructors and 636 Cuban construction workers who
were in the island. Cuban intelligence was aware of
the impending invasion and on October 24 they sent

in a Col. Comaz from Havana to see what he could do
to organize these few Cubans.

The near-10,000 invaders of "Operation Urgent
Fury," some of them using Barbados as a staging
post, struck in the predawn hours. They were backed
by two aircraft carriers, twenty-three warships,
planes, helicopters and the whole panoply of U.S.
superpower. Against Grenada, then the smallest
independent nation in the Western Hemisphere, the
U.S. assembled a force comparable in size to Great
Britain's in the Falklands War against Argentina in
1982. The U.S. deployed less ships than the British,
but had many more aircraft and helicopters.

The invaders confidently expected to have
Grenada conquered in time for lunch. Instead they
were forced to fight a real war for nearly a week.
Official American figures reported 19 U.S. servicemen
killed and 116 injured. Forty-five members of
Grenada's People's Revolutionary Army were
reported killed, but this figure may include nineteen
civilian fatalities from American bombing of a
psychiatric hospital. Three hundred and forty-eight

Grenadians were reported wounded, though estimates varied. Some sources reported at least twenty-four other civilians killed. Twenty-five Cubans were killed and fifty-nine wounded.

General Norman Schwarzkopf, overall second in command and head of ground forces for the invasion, said that invading forces met some of the most withering antiaircraft fire in America's military history. Schwarzkopf was a veteran of the Vietnam War and later commander of the U.S. forces during "Desert Storm," the first Gulf War of 1990–1991 against Iraq. The old adage of "never underestimate an enemy" was forcibly brought home in Grenada, he said.

The four and a half year Grenadian Revolution had attempted to give the Commonwealth Caribbean its only experiment with a style of government radically different from the Westminster model. Although the NJM promised elections (which they could have won easily in the early years), they never did hold any. They claimed to substitute for parliamentary democracy a system of mass organizations which, it was argued, had the constant ear of the leadership. They ran into trouble with hostile local media, first in the *Torchlight* newspaper of veteran journalist Alister Hughes and part owned by the *Trinidad Express*, and then in the short-lived *Grenada Voice*. The NJM shut down both of these papers.

The revolution's leadership had a close encounter with annihilation on June 19, 1980, when opponents planted bombs at a mass rally. Almost the entire People's Revolutionary Government (PRG) leadership was assembled on the platform where an explosion took place. Three young women were killed and almost a hundred persons injured. Persons sentenced to death in 1982 for this crime were summarily released in the wake of the U.S. invasion.

The PRG allied with some unions, but ran into problems with others. For economic and technical assistance the revolution turned to such nontraditional places as Cuba, the Soviet Union and Eastern Europe. They joined the Non-Aligned Movement, then headquartered in Cuba. Maurice Bishop and Fidel Castro developed an especially warm personal relationship. Cuba sent the corps of construction workers to help build a new airport at Point Salines. The Grenadians nationalized a Canadian bank and a telephone company.

The new airport was seen as a boost for tourism. President Ronald Reagan saw it as an instrument of Cuban military penetration. Why, he asked, did little Grenada need a 9,000 feet runway? Surely it must be to accommodate Cuban warplanes. In vain did the Grenadians show that the Bahamas, Barbados, Curaçao, Guadeloupe, Martinique, Puerto Rico, St. Lucia and Trinidad all had longer runways. Antigua and Aruba also had runways of 9,000 feet. In vain did Plessy, the British firm constructing the airport, point out that it had none of the attributes of a military runway. U.S. forces were nevertheless the first to use it—for the invasion. The airport was much later renamed for Maurice Bishop. Efforts to have it named for Ronald Reagan failed.

Grenada's foreign policy became the most radical of the Commonwealth Caribbean. They were more adventurous than Cheddi Jagan in the 1950s or Forbes Burnham thereafter. At the United Nations, Grenada supported the Soviet adventure in Afghanistan. In 1982 the PRG condemned the killing of over 3,000 refugees by Israel in West Beirut, Lebanon. It called this one of the "century's most bestial crimes against humanity." It placed "moral responsibility for this horrific act of genocide" on the United States who "armed the Zionists and their Falangist puppets. . . ."

For a while it seemed as if Grenada was facilitating a new anti-American axis in the area consisting of Grenada; Cuba; Nicaragua under the Sandinistas; Jamaica, under the newly radicalized Michael Manley; and Suriname, under coup leader Desi Bouterse. Grenada was also becoming a mecca for progressive groups and individuals of all description. The U.S.-based American Indian Movement showed up. So did C. L. R. James and Walter Rodney. Angela Davis, political bureau member of the Communist Party of the USA (CPUSA) paid a two-week "political holiday" visit in 1982, her second visit. She was the CPUSA's vice presidential candidate in the national U.S. elections of 1980 and 1984, both won by Reagan. Twenty-five members of the National Black United Front visited from the United States, the month before the invasion. "Grenada is the victory we need," they said. This must have resonated with the Reagan administration. The last thing Reagan needed was a radical, black, English-speaking nation, no matter how small, on America's doorstep. The revolution had defiantly proclaimed that the Caribbean was not an American lake and "We are in nobody's backyard."

The United States engaged in a campaign of saber rattling against Grenada and staged several military exercises designed as practice runs for an invasion. The United States made no effort to conceal the intent of these maneuvers. A 1981 exercise was code-named "Amber and the Amberines," in provocative allusion to Grenada and the Grenadines.

Grenada also ran into severe hostility from Prime Ministers Eugenia Charles of Dominica and Tom Adams of Barbados. Eric Williams of Trinidad early refused to meet emissaries of the NJM. President Ronald Reagan's 1982 visit to Barbados was viewed with alarm in Grenada.

When Edward Seaga and the Jamaica Labor Party unseated Michael Manley in Jamaica in 1980 another powerful ally came on board the Reagan-Charles-Adams axis. Michael Manley had been second only to Grenada as an object of Reaganite disdain. Manley had announced a turn to "socialism." He had nationalized key industries. He had drawn close to Cuba. Rumors abounded of CIA campaigns to destabilize him. *Playboy* magazine ran a story alleging American plans to kill him. The United States was alleged to have armed Seaga's supporters in the mini civil war that helped unseat Manley. The United States now poured aid into Seaga's Jamaica. Seaga broke off diplomatic relations with Cuba and dismantled the trappings of Manley's socialism.

Charles, Adams and Seaga helped Reagan fabricate the fiction of a joint U.S.-O.E.C.S. (Organization of Eastern Caribbean States) invasion. A token 353 troops from Jamaica, Barbados, Dominica, Antigua, St. Lucia and St. Vincent were brought in after the fact to police areas already secured by U.S. forces. The Trinidad government of George Chambers refused to send troops. Reagan's invasion was officially staged at the "request" of Barbados and Jamaica.

After the invasion Grenada was ruled by an Interim Advisory Council until elections in 1984. Bernard Coard and his accomplices were sentenced to death, later commuted to life in prison. Coard and others still incarcerated were released in September 2009. Coard immediately issued a statement blaming Fidel Castro for the murder of Bishop. He said that Bishop was about to call on Castro for help and Coard feared a Cuban invasion along the lines of Cuba's intervention into the Angolan war against then apartheid South Africa. He also said that Castro advised Bishop, apparently a political innocent in many ways, to make himself maximum leader rather than allow Coard to diminish his power in a collective leadership.

DEATH OF WALTER RODNEY

It was in Forbes Burnham's Guyana, more sympathetic to Black Power than most Caribbean governments, that Rodney met an untimely death in 1980. By this time he was perhaps the most high-profile radical activist in the Anglophone Caribbean. Rodney was a committed Marxist and tried harder than most to turn his intellectual radicalism into concrete revolutionary action. He began teaching at the University of the West Indies, Jamaica, in January 1968, after a year and a half at the University of East Africa in Tanzania (later the University of Dar-es-Salaam). He immediately came under scrutiny from the anti–Black Power government of the Jamaica Labor Party's Hugh Shearer. The Jamaicans shared the results of their Rodney surveillance with American intelligence organizations, who were equally eager to contain the Black Power movement, which was internationalizing itself from its North American base.

Rodney was blown up by what was widely reported to be a malfunctioning (some say booby-trapped) walkie-talkie, while sitting with his brother, Donald, in a car outside Georgetown's main jail. After his expulsion from Jamaica in 1968 Rodney had spent a few months in Cuba before relocating to the University of Dar-es-Salaam, where he taught until 1974. In that year he returned to take up a position as professor of History at the University of Guyana. The Burnham administration, reacting to Rodney's arrival with what C. L. R James thought unwarranted fear, blocked his appointment. Rodney became a coleader of the newly formed independent Marxist Working Peoples Alliance (WPA), a combination of Indo and Afro-Guyanese pressure groups opposed to Burnham.

Rodney's death was seen by many as an assassination. It came at a time of an increasingly violent contest between Burnham's PNC and Rodney's WPA. Rodney was at the time of his death actually free on bail, charged along with two top WPA leaders with arson in the July 1979 torching of two government buildings. Days after the fire the WPA had declared itself a political party. Rodney famously called Burnham "King Kong" and "a King Midas-type whose touch changed everything to shit."

William Gregory Smith, an electronics technician trained at a Naval Weapons, Radio and Electrical School in England and sometime member of the Guyana Defense Force, was widely accused of setting Rodney up on behalf of the Burnham administration. Smith died in exile in Cayenne in 2002 and in 2007 his posthumous account of his connection with Rodney was published. Smith claimed to be one of the people disaffected with the Burnham regime who Rodney recruited for the WPA. Rodney, he said, had by 1980 come to the conclusion that Burnham had to go and constitutional measures would not suffice to achieve this purpose.

In 1980, Smith said, he agreed to Rodney's request to modify Citizen Band (CB) radios (walkie-talkies), to enable them to detonate explosives. On the night of his death, Smith reported, Rodney insisted on testing the devices with real explosives because an unspecified three -hour "window of opportunity" had arisen.

Once Rodney was killed, Smith said, the WPA quickly decided to turn catastrophe into a victory of sorts. They proclaimed Rodney's death to the world as an "assassination." If Smith was telling the truth, then the WPA assassination spin on Rodney's death would not have been difficult to accomplish. Burnham was in the unique position of having a very bad international press, both on the left and the right. In the wake of a hostile anti-government mobilization in New York, the Guyanese consul lamented the ineffectiveness of his government's public relations efforts.

Rodney, by contrast, was a much loved figure in many academic and radical constituencies in many countries. Messages of outrage at his "assassination" and earlier victimization poured in from prominent individuals and groups in many countries.

LEFT-WING GROUPINGS

Radical groupings of all sorts mushroomed during the Black Power era. Their precise ideological formulations varied from near-mainstream Black Power to self-consciously Marxist, but a loose camaraderie existed among most of them. There was a Workers Party of Jamaica, led by Trevor Munroe. Trinidad had its New Beginning Movement. History professor James Millette led Trinidad's Moko. Economist Lloyd Best led Trinidad's Tapia House movement. One of the most radical of these groups, the National United Freedom Fighters (NUFF, 1970–1973) found itself in a small-scale guerilla war with the Trinidad police. Some of its fighters were killed. NUFF was an amalgam of working- and middle-class young men and women radicalized by Trinidad's Black Power movement. Grenada's NJM and other constituent groups that mobilized to make the Grenada revolution were very much in this tradition of small radical formations. Tim Hector's Antigua-Caribbean Liberation Movement was one of the best known. There was a Movement for a New Dominica. Guyana's Working Peoples Alliance (WPA) was an amalgam of some of these organizations, namely the African Society for Cultural Relations with Independent Africa (ASCRIA), led by Eusi Kwayana; the Indian People's Revolutionary Associates (IPRA), led by Moses Bhagwan; RATOON, led by economist Clive Thomas; and the Working People's Vanguard Party (WPVP), led by Brindley Benn.

Many of these groups had in common an affection for such progressive Caribbean intellectuals as C. L. R. James, Walter Rodney, George Lamming and others. Many of the leaders had been activist students in London, New York, Montreal and elsewhere in the metropolis. Hector, Rodney, Walton Look Lai of the New Beginning Movement and others had participated in a study group conducted by James in London. Most of these groups published some combination of newspapers, journals, pamphlets and occasional papers. Several of these groupings evolved into mostly unsuccessful political parties. James himself teamed up with the Workers and Farmers Party which did very poorly at the Trinidad and Tobago general elections of 1966.

MORE COUPS AND ATTEMPTED COUPS

Run Dominica Run, the Ku Klux Klan is Coming!

During 1979 Eric Gairy, newly deposed in Grenada, collaborated with United States and Canadian Ku Klux Klansmen, and a motley crew of other individuals to retake Grenada via invasion from Dominica. He withdrew support over differences in tactics. The Klansmen and their associates then turned in 1980 to Patrick John, recently ousted from the prime ministership of Dominica, after a groundswell of popular upset with his rule. Former members of the Dominica Defense Force joined the conspiracy, as did characters recruited from a soldier of fortune magazine. The North Americans hoped for government positions and various business concessions in return for their restoring John to power. On April 27, 1981, U.S. federal agents and New Orleans policemen arrested ten of the mercenaries as they prepared to set sail in a boat laden with arms, ammunition, explosives and a Nazi flag. Patrick John and local conspirators were arrested in Dominica, as was one Marion Ann McGuire, a North American advance party of one in Dominica.

On August 11, 1981, Prime Minister Maurice Bishop of revolutionary Grenada wrote President Ronald Reagan complaining of this and other mercenary adventures said to be in preparation in the United States against Grenada. On December 19, 1981, John's supporters in the now disbanded Dominica Defense Force tried another coup. It failed once more.

The Abu Bakr Coup in Trinidad and Tobago

In 1990 Trinidad experienced a coup attempt led by Imam Yasin Abu Bakr, leader of the Jamaat Al Muslimeen, This was during the administration of the National Alliance for Reconstruction (NAR). The NAR had in 1986 ended the thirty-year incumbency of the PNM, founded by Eric Williams, with a staggering 33–3 electoral victory. Yet internal squabbling, IMF-imposed belt-tightening and controversial political decisions brought it in four short years to a position of great vulnerability.

On the afternoon of Friday July 27, 1990, the Muslimeen without warning blew up police headquarters, stormed the nearby parliament which was in session and occupied the main television and radio stations. Several people were killed in the initial attack and afterward. One government member of parliament was among those killed. The prime minister, A. N. R. Robinson, was wounded. It took several days of fighting before the insurgents surrendered. By this time Abu Bakr had negotiated an amnesty with the acting president of the republic. This was upheld in the Court of Appeal and he became a free person after a period of incarceration. He remained an influential figure in Trinidad life. Though this coup failed, it was far bloodier and more destructive of property than the NJM coup in Grenada. In the law enforcement vacuum in the immediate aftermath of the coup there was considerable arson and looting.

British Invasion of Anguilla

In the move to independence in the Commonwealth Caribbean five tiny entities remained colonies. They were the British Virgin Islands, Montserrat, the Cayman Islands, the Turks and Caicos Islands and Anguilla. In 1967 Anguilla seceded from the St. Kitts, Nevis, Anguilla federation that the British imposed on it. They asked the United States to take them over, but the United States declined. Anguillans declared themselves independent in 1969 and were invaded by British paratroopers and forty London policemen. By contrast the 1965 "Unilateral Declaration of Independence" by minority white ruler Ian Smith in British Rhodesia, now Zimbabwe, met with no direct British military response. British Labor Party Prime Minister Harold Wilson thought that British troops would not want to invade their white minority "kith and kin." No such considerations had applied to the black troops the British had raised in the Caribbean for hundreds of years for action against Maroons and enslaved insurgents and for British wars of conquest in Africa itself.

In 2009 the Turks and Caicos Islands provided Britain with another latter-day opportunity to flex its colonial muscle. Britain accused the incumbent local leadership of "political amorality and immaturity" compounded by "systemic venality," and proceeded to suspend the executive and legislative branches of government. Britain then reinstituted old-fashioned crown colony undemocratic rule by a British governor. The British also suspended trial by jury.

When Britain threatened Anguilla in 1967 it was left to the Union of West Indian Students in Great Britain and Northern Ireland to censure the colonial power, via a resolution to the International Union of Students congress, meeting in Ulan Bator, Mongolia. By August 19, 2009, the Caribbean governments, via CARICOM, had grown sufficiently self-confident to issue a sharp condemnation of the British action, at least as severe as that of the students in 1967.

CUBAN REVOLUTION

The Cuban Revolution was to the Caribbean of the twentieth century what the Haitian Revolution was to the nineteenth. It was one of the pivotal events in the history of the century. The revolution was ushered in on January 1, 1959, with the hurried departure of Cuban President Fulgencio Batista to the Dominican Republic and the entry of Fidel Castro's revolutionary army into Havana. Fidel himself did not make his triumphant entry until one week later, on January 8, when he was greeted by jubilant crowds.

Castro, a lawyer, was born in Cuba in 1926 into a well-to-do family of Spanish extraction. He had long lived an adventurous and even charmed life as a student activist and radical lawyer. In 1947 he travelled to the Dominican Republic to take part in an abortive coup against dictator Rafael Trujillo.

On July 26, 1953, Fidel and over 100 men and women assaulted the Batista regime's Moncada Barracks in Santiago de Cuba. Most of Castro's party were killed in the assault or murdered afterward in captivity. Castro was tried and sentenced to fifteen years in prison. He used his trial as a platform to deliver one of his most famous speeches, "History Will Absolve Me."

Batista freed Castro in a 1955 amnesty. Castro left for Mexico shortly afterward to resume his struggle. On December 2, 1956, Castro and eighty-one supporters returned to Cuba on the yacht *Granma*. They were intercepted by Batista's forces and almost totally wiped out. Only twelve

survived, including Castro, his brother Raúl and Argentinean revolutionary Ernesto "Che" Guevara. These remnants headed to the Sierra Maestra mountains to launch a guerilla war against Batista.

Batista had ruled Cuba for most of the period since 1933 by a combination of two coups, puppet presidents and elections fair and rigged. He was a close friend of Meyer Lansky and other American gangsters. Like many of his predecessors in office in the twentieth century, he was extremely corrupt.

Castro came to power with much popular support in the United States. The United States quickly recognized the new government on January 7, 1959. Testimony before the U.S. Senate Internal Security Committee in 1961, however, revealed that the United States had earlier tried to thwart Castro's acquisition of power. Three weeks before Castro's forces entered Havana, CIA and State Department personnel had attempted to preempt Castro by setting up an anti-Batista and anti-Castro government.

Castro moved quickly and ruthlessly to consolidate power. A caretaker government of friendly and well-respected mainstream anti-Batista moderates was formed on January 5, 1959. Provisional president was Manuel Urrutia Lleo, a former Supreme Court justice, who returned from exile in Venezuela to take up the appointment. He had long enjoyed the esteem of Castro's July 26 Movement. Urrutia appointed José Miró Cardona prime minister. Cardona was a former law professor at the University of Havana and president of the Cuban College of Lawyers. Castro served in the new twenty-five-member cabinet as Delegate General of the President to the Armed Forces and the Maximum Leader of the July 26 Movement. His control of the armed forces ensured ultimate power. The provisional government barred from political office all who had participated in Batista-organized elections in 1958. It announced that it would rule by decree for eighteen months as a prelude to hoped-for elections. It legalized the Communist Party. It began rewriting school textbooks.

In February 1959 the anti-Batista Federation of University Students, led by its Revolutionary Directorate, seized the University of Havana and expelled pro-Batista professors. They also began rewriting textbooks and revising course content.

The provisional government turned a blind eye. The students later seized the presidential palace. After some conflict with Castro's July 26 Movement, key directorate figures were absorbed into Castro's power apparatus.

When Miró resigned after thirty-nine days as prime minister it was because, he said, he could not run the country from his office while Castro was simultaneously running it from a microphone. Castro accordingly named himself prime minister on February 16, 1959. Castro and Urrutia increasingly disagreed on such issues as the growing influence of the Communist Party, land reform, Urrutia's failure to allow casino gambling to stimulate tourism and the need for elections. He was increasingly sidelined and Castro eventually maneuvered him out of office. On July 18, 1959, Castro resigned as prime minister citing "moral differences" with Urrutia, thereby forcing Urrutia to reluctantly resign as well. Castro then resumed office on July 24. Osvaldo Dorticós became president.

As Castro continued to consolidate his power, there were trials and public executions of Batista's supporters deemed to have committed war and other crimes. Almost 500 were executed. Films of some trials were made available to U.S. television and stimulated considerable anti-Castro sentiment. Urban rents were slashed. Property and businesses were nationalized and many of the middle and wealthier classes went into exile. By the end of 1960 newspapers and television stations, labor unions and other segments of society had been closed down, reorganized or otherwise brought under Castroite control. Afro-Cuban societies, long a part of the Cuban landscape, were disbanded.

Meanwhile, relations between the United States and the revolution deteriorated quickly. Castro's Agrarian Reform Law in 1959 had confiscated large landholdings and redistributed them. Between 1959 and 1961 several U.S.-owned businesses were nationalized, including a telephone company, cattle ranches, hotels and Coca Cola. Cuba and the United States became embroiled in tit for tat reprisals.

Castro had initially declared himself noncommunist, but in the face of U.S.–Cuba tensions he now drew increasingly close to the Cuban Communist Party. In February 1960 the Soviet Union agreed to barter Soviet crude oil for Cuban sugar. The United States was hitherto the most important purchaser of sugar, Cuba's main product. On July 6, 1960, U.S. President Dwight Eisenhower reduced Cuba's sugar quota. He eliminated it altogether in 1961. Cuba nationalized U.S. sugar mills. The Soviet Union and China stepped in to buy Cuba's sugar. U.S. refineries in Cuba refused to refine Soviet oil. Cuba nationalized the refineries. The United States broke off diplomatic ties with Cuba on January 3, 1961. On April 16, 1961, Castro declared the revolution socialist. The Communist Party became officially Cuba's only party. In 1972 Cuba became a full member of the Soviet bloc Council for Mutual Economic Assistance.

Just before midnight on April 16, 1961, the United States launched its most spectacular attack on the Cuban Revolution. This was the Bay of Pigs invasion. This covert CIA operation had been approved by President Eisenhower on March 17, 1960. President John F. Kennedy gave it his enthusiastic support when he succeeded Eisenhower into office.

The CIA had trained a force of Cuban exiles augmented by American advisers and pilots. They were equipped with warships and planes. Their intention was to establish a beachhead in Cuba and fly over a provisional government, the "Revolutionary Council," who were waiting on call in Florida. Once the new "government" arrived on Cuban soil they would call for U.S. assistance. The United States would graciously oblige. Provisional president of the Revolutionary Council was none other than former prime minister of the 1959 caretaker government, José Miró Cardona.

The invaders sailed from Nicaragua in six ships on April 14, 1961. President Luis Somoza was on hand to wish them bon voyage. He asked them to bring back some hairs from Castro's beard. The invaders launched their attack at Playa Girón in the Bay of Pigs. Cuba's well-organized local militia was able to engage the invaders almost immediately and contain them until regular troops arrived. Castro was alerted to the invasion by 3 AM and took personal control of the Cuban defense. Some invading ships were sunk, both by the tiny Cuban air force and by the treacherous coral rocks which the CIA maps had mistaken for seaweed. A few Americans fighting alongside the Cuban exiles were killed, four pilots among them. Within seventy-two hours the Cubans had won a historic victory.

Some of the invading force were executed. These included persons wanted in Cuba for murder and persons infiltrated into the country to commit acts of sabotage ahead of the invasion. Nearly two years later the Cubans exchanged a little under 1,200 prisoners for $53 million in food and medicine.

The defeated and embarrassed President Kennedy tried to get his revenge by authorizing Operation Mongoose on November 3, 1961. "The CIA's outlandish plots to bump off the Cuban dictator would put 007 to shame . . . poison pills, toxic cigars and exploding mollusks," wrote the English *Guardian* newspaper. "As Wayne Smith, former head of the US interest section in Havana, pointed out," the *Guardian* continued, "Cuba had the effect on the US that a full moon has on a werewolf. It seems highly likely that if the CIA had had access to a werewolf, it would have tried smuggling it into the Sierra Maestra. . . ."

Most of the U.S. public became aware of these efforts to kill Castro and other leaders (e.g., Patrice Lumumba of the Congo) via the report of the Church Committee of the U.S. Senate in 1975. Disclosure of these operations led to much speculation as to whether President Kennedy's assassination in 1963 might not have been Castro's response to Kennedy's attempts on his life.

Events leading up to the Bay of Pigs had some interesting similarities to Jagan's experience. When Castro visited the United States in April 1959 at the invitation of the Press Club, President Eisenhower snubbed him. Castro met with Vice President Nixon instead. Nixon's meeting convinced him that Castro was a communist, just as Kennedy's meeting in 1961 with Jagan confirmed his belief in Jagan's Marxist leanings. Kennedy publicly denied any intention of harming Cuba, even as he was preparing covert operations. He had similarly assured Jagan that he really did not care what kind of ideology Jagan subscribed to, even as he was plotting his downfall. Castro addressed a Press Club luncheon. Jagan was interviewed on "Meet the Press."

On February 7, 1962, the United States imposed its full trade embargo on Cuba. In October 1962 President Kennedy instituted his blockade around Cuba, bringing the world to the brink of nuclear war. The Soviet Union had installed nuclear missiles in Cuba capable of hitting U.S. cities. The U.S.S.R. agreed to remove its missiles in exchange for the Americans removing their missiles from Turkey and promising not to invade Cuba.

The CARICOM nations, meanwhile, began to show some independence in nibbling away at the isolation of Cuba. Both Jagan and Burnham had long regarded Cuba with favor. A substantial number of Jagan-affiliated Guyanese were studying and living in Cuba by the mid-1960s. Guyanese students continued to study there under Burnham. When Burnham died on the operating table in Georgetown in 1985, a specially flown-in Cuban doctor was among those ministering to him.

In 1972 Barbados, Jamaica, Guyana and Trinidad and Tobago established diplomatic relations and air and sea links with Cuba. They were apparently emboldened by America's opening up of relations with China. The initiative came from Burnham and Michael Manley, both of whom went on to strengthen ties with Cuba. When Cuba began airlifting troops to Angola in 1975 to save Angola from defeat by invading South African apartheid forces, it was for a time able to use both Barbados and Guyana as refueling stops before both succumbed to U.S. pressure. Trinidad refused Cuba permission to refuel.

Cuba's Angola intervention (1975–1988) confirmed Cuba as a major player on the world political stage, with an impact for a time probably unmatched by any other country in the Americas outside of the United States. Apartheid South Africa (with U.S. encouragement, it later transpired) had invaded Angola from its subject state of Namibia and was poised to win a significant victory. Angola was about to become independent after a long liberation war against the Portuguese colonizers. Of the three major Angolan anti-Portuguese factions the communist-leaning MPLA (Popular Movement for the Liberation of Angola) was poised to control the new independent state. South Africa, supporting UNITA (National Union for the Total Independence of Angola) led by Jonas Savimbi, saw an opportunity in conquering Angola to build a white-controlled *cordon sanitaire* around itself which would have significantly entrenched white minority apartheid rule in Southern Africa. This huge swath of white-controlled Africa would have comprised South Africa, Namibia, Angola,Rhodesia under white apartheid rule and possibly Mozambique. Mozambique had won independence in 1975 but was now, like Angola, threatened by civil war encouraged by South Africa. Swaziland and Lesotho, though African ruled, were enclaves within South Africa. Botswana would have been for all practical purposes enveloped within the new white-controlled Africa.

South Africa invaded Angola in October 1975, a month before formal Angolan independence on November 11. On November 4 Castro decided to launch a full-scale military operation in support of MPLA, at the latter's request. Thirty thousand Cuban troops were in Angola by 1976. By this time Cuba had already intervened militarily on behalf of the Algerian liberation movement in its war against France (1961), the Ethiopians in their struggle with Eritrea and Somalia, in Guinea-Bissau in their liberation struggle against Portugal (1966–1974) and in Zaire, where they fought a proxy war against the United States in 1964–1965.

The Cubans in Angola were eventually able to defeat the South Africans, prevent the establishment of a *cordon sanitaire* around South Africa and, as a result, hasten the end of apartheid in South Africa itself. The crowning Cuban achievement in Angola was the 1987–1988 Battle of Cuito Cuanavale, said to be the biggest in Africa after the Allied-German Battle of El Alamein in North Africa during World War II. The defeated South Africans retreated and sued for peace. Namibian independence ensued and it was only a matter of time before apartheid ended in South Africa itself. Nelson Mandela, great icon of the African struggle against apartheid, was released from jail by white South Africa twenty months after the apartheid regime's retreat from Cuito Cuanavale.

The opening of CARICOM air links had a tragic consequence in 1976 when Cubana Airlines Flight 455 was brought down by terrorist bombs off the coast of Barbados. The plane was on its way from Georgetown to Havana via Port of Spain, Bridgetown and Kingston. All seventy-three people on board were killed. They included fifty-seven Cubans, eleven Guyanese and five North Koreans. The victims

included the entire twenty-four-member Cuban fencing team which was on its way home after winning all the gold medals in the Central American and Caribbean championships. Most of the Guyanese were young students on their way to medical school in Cuba. This tragedy was the most devastating act of aviation terrorism in the Western Hemisphere up to that time.

Two Venezuelan passengers had planted time bombs before exiting the plane in Barbados and flying back to Trinidad, where they were arrested. They had boarded in Trinidad and checked their luggage to Cuba. The two arrested men implicated two other Venezuelans in the plot to blow up the plane.

The four suspects went through a series of trials in Venezuela. They were acquitted in military court and tried again in civilian court. Here the two actual bomb planters received the lowest sentence available to the judge. A third was acquitted on a technicality and a fourth, Luis Posada Carriles, mysteriously escaped and eventually made his way to the United States, where the United States refused to extradite him. In June 2010 President Hugo Chavez of Venezuela addressed a renewed call to President Barack Obama for Posada's extradition. Posada was a Cuban-born naturalized Venezuelan citizen and worked for the CIA. The acquitted terrorist eventually made it to the United States where he was pardoned for all American charges by President George H. W. Bush in 1990. A monument to the crash victims in Barbados was visited by Fidel Castro more than once. Another monument was being promised by the government of Guyana in 2010.

The CARICOM countries have continued to build on the 1972 initiative. Eric Williams in his 1970 book, *From Columbus to Castro,* saw Castro as just another typical Caribbean nationalist. Williams visited Cuba's Isle of Pines in 1975 and Castro praised his commitment to regional integration and Caribbean efforts to diminish Cuba's isolation. Castro and Williams jointly agreed on that occasion to propose that a forthcoming meeting of ECLA (Economic Commission for Latin America) should be held in Cuba. In 1963 on his tour of Africa Williams had been hostile to Castro, but this early hostility was not apparent now.

Cuban medical personnel have been widely utilized in such places as Guyana, Jamaica and

Trinidad and Tobago. Ships regularly take passengers from Jamaica to Cuba. Organizations such as the Association of Caribbean Historians have held conferences in Cuba. Trinidad banks operate there. A few tourists from the Anglophone Caribbean have holidayed in Cuba.

During the Civil Rights and Black Power struggles in the United States in the 1960s and 1970s Cuba became a place of refuge for some high-profile African American revolutionaries, most notably Assata Shakur. Shakur escaped from jail in the United States, where she was serving time for alleged crimes related to her purported membership in the underground Black Liberation Army.

Despite these facts there have been continuing rumblings about a persistence of racial discrimination against Afro-Cubans. The early revolution dismantled the more blatant manifestations of segregation and racism in Cuba, but it also outlawed the Afro-Cuban clubs and societies that had long been part of the Cuban landscape. Education was made available to all. Yet visiting African Americans and Caribbean blacks have often questioned the paucity of black faces in very high places in a country believed to have a sizeable black majority. The expanding tourism industry of the late twentieth century employed few Afro-Cubans.

When a casually dressed black lieutenant colonel in Cuba's military was stopped in Havana by police in an obvious and not unusual case of racial profiling circa 2000, it seemed not very different from similar incidents in the United States. Jamaican American Colin Powell was once racially profiled at the Reagan National Airport in Washington, D.C., while he was national security adviser to President Ronald Reagan. Barbadian American Eric Holder, attorney general to President Barack Obama, admitted to having also experienced racial profiling.

Economic problems due to the fall of the Soviet Union, Cuba's main ally, in 1991 hit Afro-Cubans the hardest. Massive unemployment, very poor living conditions and the recrudescence of prostitution, with an inordinate impact on the Afro-Cuban community, have all testified to this reality.

The election of President Barack Obama as the USA's first African American president in 2008 had the unintended result of further exposing the racial chink in Cuba's armor. Cuba, once an aggressive critic of the United States' racial policies, now found itself facing the inevitable question: "Could a black person have become president in Communist Cuba?" The traditional Cuban position argued that affirmative action was unnecessary in a communist country since the destruction of the economic basis for inequality would automatically extinguish racism. Time and the new equal opportunity would erase past inequalities. This may have seemed a plausible argument to some in the 1960s. It was less convincing in 2008.

In November 2009 an emerging Cuban Civil Rights movement found expression in a document initiated by Afro-Cuban exile Carlos Moore and signed by sixty prominent African Americans, several of them of Caribbean background. It was entitled, "Acting On Our Conscience: A Declaration Of African American Support for the Civil Rights Struggle In Cuba."

The document estimated the Afro-Cuban population at between 62 and 70 percent of Cuba's 11.4 million people. (The official Cuban census of 2002 claimed that 65 percent of Cuba was white.) A related "briefing sheet" asserted that Afro-Cubans constituted 85 percent of the prison population and 60 of the 200 political prisoners, but only 20 percent of Havana University's professors. It supported a letter of October 30, 2009, sent by Abdias do Nascimento, patriarch of the Brazilian Civil Rights movement and long-standing supporter of the Cuban Revolution, to presidents Raúl Castro of Cuba, Luiz Inacio Lula Da Silva of Brazil and Dr. Darsi Ferrer Ramirez, the Afro-Cuban Civil Rights worker whose incarceration on July 21, 2009, brought matters to a head. "[W]e are facing a clear case of political intimidation against those, in Cuba, who raise their voices in protest against racism," Nascimento wrote. Four prominent Jamaican University of the West Indies academics, all former supporters of Cuba and including former Vice-Chancellor Rex Nettleford, later issued a similar statement.

Alberto González, spokesman for Cuba's diplomatic mission in Washington, condemned the African American statement as an "absurd" effort to destabilize Cuba. Fidel Castro's government, he said, had "done more for black Cubans than any other in all areas, including health, education and welfare.'" Various leftist African Americans scrambled to defend Cuba, among them Amiri Baraka, sometime Black Nationalist, sometime advocate of "Marxism-Leninism Mao Tse Tung Thought," and famous playwright and poet.

The new black opposition to Cuba's racial policies initially caught the mostly white and conservative traditional anti-Castro exile lobby by surprise and without a plausible response. It also raised the incongruous possibility of Castro's Cuba and the anti-Castro U.S. exiles finding themselves on the same side in Cuba's racial debate. Even President Obama seemed in danger of involuntarily joining this new unlikely axis. For some now argued that President Obama's new liberal measures permitting exiled Cubans to remit more money home might actually exacerbate the racial situation. Most of these exiles were white, and their remittances would further empower white Cubans.

The "Acting On Our Conscience" declaration took on added significance with the hunger strike–induced death in a Cuban jail of Afro-Cuban "prisoner of conscience" (so described by Amnesty International), Orlando Zapata, on February 23, 2010. U.S. Secretary of State Hillary Clinton expressed deep regret at Zapata's death. President Raúl Castro of Cuba also expressed regret, something unprecedented for the demise of a political prisoner in Cuba. Cuban media was not allowed to report Zapata's death for the first three days after his passing.

Fears were expressed that the Obama administration's moves to initiate a thaw and European Union attempts to soften EU attitudes to Cuba might be early casualties of Zapata's death. Prime Minister Jose Luis Rodriguez Zapatero of Spain, traditionally Cuba's staunchest ally in Europe, and at the time head of the European Union, deplored Zapata's demise. In March 2010 a European Parliament resolution condemned Cuba for Zapata's death. It called on EU agencies to foster dialogue with Cuban civil society with a view to hastening a peaceful transition to democracy.

On March 23, 2010, exactly one month after Zapata's death, President Obama moved to extricate himself from any ambiguity concerning where his overtures to Cuba might have left him in the new circumstances. He issued the following strong written statement:

> Recent events in Cuba, including the tragic death of Orlando Zapata Tamayo, the repression visited upon Las Damas de Blanco [the Ladies in White, wives of Zapata and other political prisoners] and the intensified harassment of those who dare to give voice to the desires of their fellow Cubans, are deeply disturbing. . . .
>
> Today, I join my voice with brave individuals across Cuba and a growing chorus around the world in calling for an end to the repression, for the immediate, unconditional release of all political prisoners in Cuba and for respect for the basic rights of the Cuban people.
>
> During the course of the past year, I have taken steps to reach out to the Cuban people and to signal my desire to seek a new era in relations between the governments of the United States and Cuba. I remain committed to supporting the simple desire of the Cuban people to freely determine their future and to enjoy the rights and freedoms that define the Americas, and that should be universal to all human beings.

Cuba responded by denouncing the U.S. and EU "crusade" against the country. It called for a May Day mobilization against the new "demonization" of Cuba.

CARICOM, long so assertive on pro-Cuban initiatives, remained silent on the allegations of racism in Cuba. One year before Zapata's demise, CARICOM had helped facilitate a major step forward for Cuban reintegration into the inter-American system. This was at the Fifth Summit of the Americas, held in Port of Spain in April 2009. Cuba, expelled at U.S. urging from the Organization of American States (OAS) in 1962, was predictably not invited. Fidel Castro had retired from Cuban leadership in 2008, due to ill health. His brother Raúl Castro was now in charge. Prime Minister Patrick Manning of Trinidad and Tobago (who regularly travelled to Cuba for medical attention) chaired the conference. U.S. President Barack Obama, recently elected and exuding conciliatory gestures not heard since the "Good Neighbor" policy of President Franklin D. Roosevelt in the 1930s, was in attendance. The Soviet Union, whose friendship with Cuba provided pretext for the expulsion of Cuba from the OAS in 1962, was no longer in existence. The summit was being held for the first time in the Commonwealth Caribbean, whose major leaders had broken ranks with the Americans in restoring relations with Cuba in 1972. Several relatively new independent-minded friends of Cuba had emerged in the Americas, among them Presidents Hugo Chavez of Venezuela and Evo Morales of Bolivia. Many of the other hemispheric leaders were simply tired of the isolation of Cuba, which they now viewed as an anachronism and an embarrassment. In these changed circumstances the summit was able to signal optimism concerning the full reintegration of Cuba into hemispheric affairs.

As of November 2010 Cuba, like China, the Soviet Union and Vietnam before it, appeared moving toward some relaxation of its socialist economic system. A widely circulated *Draft Economic and Social Policy Guidelines* document contained 291 proposals to reduce the state labor force, decentralize regional development, eliminate ration books and subsidized food, increase foreign investment, encourage cooperatives, and allow self-employment and private landlords. It was adamant that all of this would still take place within a society where socialist planning would override market forces. The new socialism would connote equal rights and opportunities, not a sterile "egalitarianism." Like Marcus Garvey in his 1920s essay, "Governing the Ideal State," the Cuban proposals promised to prevent any businesses or individuals from accumulating too much economic power.

PUERTO RICO

In 1812 Puerto Rico was made an integral part of Spain. Puerto Ricans were Spanish citizens and sent delegates to the Spanish *Cortés*. A local assembly presided over by a governor was set up. These measures did not end agitation for full home rule. In 1897 came a Charter of Autonomy. Delegates continued to sit in the *Cortés*. A new bicameral legislature was part appointed and part elected. The first cabinet was appointed in February 1898. General elections took place in March 1898. And then along came Uncle Sam. The United States entered the Cuban-Spanish War in April 1898. In June the United States invaded and occupied Puerto Rico.

After a period of U.S. military rule the Foraker Act of 1900 set up a temporary civilian administration. Executive power resided with a U.S. governor. He was assisted by an eleven-member executive council, five of whose members were Puerto Ricans appointed by the United States. The U.S. Congress defined Puerto Rico in 1900 as a "non-incorporated territory" of the United States. This distinguished Puerto Rico from the "incorporated" territories of Oklahoma, New Mexico and Arizona, which were considered integral parts of the United States and became states in 1907 (Oklahoma) and 1912. The Jones Act conferred citizenship in 1917.

Puerto Rico received the right to elect its own governor in 1947. Luis Muñoz Marin became the first elected governor in 1948. In 1950 Puerto Rico was given the right to draw up its own constitution. Governor Muñoz Marin proclaimed a new constitution in 1952. It adopted the term "*Estado Libre Asociado*" ("Free Associated State," officially rendered in English as "Commonwealth").

Under this anomalous designation Puerto Ricans continued to be U.S. citizens but cannot vote in presidential elections while residing in Puerto Rico. (They can vote if they move to the mainland.) Any other U.S. citizens residing in Puerto Rico are equally denied the vote in presidential elections. Puerto Ricans have no representative in the U.S. Senate. They have a representative in the House of Representatives who can vote in committee, but not on the floor.

Around these arrangements has swirled a sometimes violent debate over the preferred status for the island. Plebiscites in 1967, 1993 and 1998 all failed to overturn Commonwealth status. Of the two major political parties the People's Democratic Party favors Commonwealth status while the New Progressive Party favors statehood. The smaller Puerto Rican Independence Party favors independence.

In 1930 the pro-independence movement staged revolts in several Puerto Rican cities. In 1950 two nationalists attacked Blair House in Washington, D.C., where U.S. President Harry Truman was residing temporarily. One policeman and one Puerto Rican attacker were killed. In 1954 Lolita Lebrón and three other nationalists fired thirty shots from a visitors' gallery of the U.S. Capitol, the only armed attack on the U.S. Congress. Five representatives were wounded.

The iconic figure of the independence movement was Dr. Pedro Albizu Campos, a Harvard University–educated lawyer. He interrupted his Harvard studies in 1917 to volunteer for service in World War I. He became a lieutenant in the all-black 275th Infantry Regiment, stationed in Puerto Rico. Like the British West Indies Regiment volunteers and African American soldiers of the World War, black Puerto Ricans served in segregated units. Those in New York served in the 369th Infantry, the famous and much-decorated "Harlem Hell Fighters." (Campos was the son of a prominent white father and a black daughter of former enslaved parents.)

Campos said that his witnessing of racism in the army influenced his future career, which put him in a situation similar to Tubal Uriah Butler of Trinidad, St. William Grant of Jamaica, Clennell Wickham of Barbados and Samuel Haynes who led an uprising in Belize (then British Honduras) in 1919. Haynes later became an important leader in Marcus Garvey's UNIA.

Campos was elected president of Harvard's Cosmopolitan Club and as a club member met such important world nationalist figures as Subhas Chandra Bose of India and Eamon de Valera of Ireland. One year after Campos' graduation from Harvard Law School in 1921, Harvard's African American students' organization, the Nile Club, invited Marcus Garvey to speak. President of the Nile Club was Charles Hamilton Houston, a future major figure in Civil Rights law. One wonders if there was ever any discussion between Houston and

Lolita Lebron is arrested in 1954 after Puerto Rican nationalists fired thirty shots inside the U.S. Capitol.

Campos on the African American and Caribbean nationalism that Garvey articulated. Campos spent most of his adult life in jail, as a result of recurring arrests by the U.S. authorities.

Puerto Rico's anomalous constitutional arrangements have long concerned the United Nations Special Committee on Decolonization, which as of 2009 had passed twenty-seven resolutions on the matter.

On June 15, 2009, a draft resolution brought by Cuba called on the United States to release all Puerto Rican political prisoners, return "occupied land and installations" in Vieques Island (long used for practice bombing runs by U.S. aircraft) and expedite Puerto Rico's achievement of self-determination. Dominica (on behalf of the Non-Aligned Movement) and St. Vincent and the Grenadines addressed the debate. Puerto Rico has observer status with CARICOM.

In the 1950s and 1960s Puerto Rico became of great interest to other Caribbean countries because of its "Operation Bootstrap" economic success. Its Industrial Incentive Act (1947) and related Industrial Development Company (also known as Fomento) were widely seen as models for economic development elsewhere in the region. The policy was one of attracting American industry by a cocktail of tax concessions, unfettered repatriation of profits for a stated number of years, and similar devices.

The hope was that those incentives coupled with lower wage rates than on the mainland, would stimulate jobs and investment. Puerto Rico underwent a period of very high growth as a result. This was helped by some factors not easily replicable in other countries. These included the unrestricted access to the United States of surplus labor and a variety of U.S. federal social programs (e.g., food stamps) to provide an economic cushion.

In time growth stagnated as companies left on the expiry of their tax holidays and other concessions. Wage rates also crept up, making Puerto Rico less competitive with other low wage havens around the world. The benefits of the good years were also unevenly distributed. And the boom still could not curtail the problem of unemployment. The country then moved to high-tech capital-intensive industries, notably pharmaceuticals and new "Section 936" (of the U.S. tax code) incentives, whereby U.S.

corporations with branches in Puerto Rico were able to avoid taxes on profits repatriated to the United States. Interest on profits left in Puerto Rico were also exempted from taxes. In 1996 the U.S. Congress withdrew Section 936 for future undertakings. Tourism helped cushion the blow.

NETHERLANDS ANTILLES, ARUBA AND SURINAME

The Netherlands Antilles prior to October 10, 2010, consisted of two groupings. Curaçao and Bonaire are situated off the coast of Venezuela. St. Eustatius, Saba and St. Martin are not far from the Virgin Islands. The islands received universal adult suffrage in 1948 and internal self-government in 1950. During the 1940s and beyond Aruba (which left the grouping in 1986) and Curaçao derived considerable income from oil refining. Aruba attracted immigration from British islands.

Unlike the British colonies which mostly opted for independence, the Dutch (like the French and Puerto Rico) have been caught in a web of uncertainty. In 1954 Holland officially replaced colonial status with the Kingdom of the Netherlands, which supposedly consisted of the three autonomous areas of Holland, Suriname and the Netherlands Antilles. Suriname opted for independence in 1975 and Aruba seceded from the Antilles in 1986 to a separate "status apart" as an autonomous, but not independent state within the Kingdom of the Netherlands.

Referendums between 2000 and 2005 resulted in a welter of preferences—St. Martin and Curaçao wanted "status apart"; Saba and Bonaire preferred closer ties to Holland; St. Eustatius preferred to stay with the Netherlands Antilles. A Round Table Conference in 2005 tried to sort out these preferences. Curaçao and St. Martin emerged as autonomous (for Curaçao with effect from 2007). In 2006 Saba, Bonaire and St. Eustatius became "special municipalities" of the Netherlands.

On October 10, 2010, the Netherlands Antilles were dissolved, with the constituent elements going their various ways. The tiny entities of Bonaire (population 11,000 in 2000), Saba (1,100) and St. Eustatius (1,861) remained special municipalities of the Netherlands. Curaçao and St. Martin were designated constituent countries, theoretically akin to the relationship between Scotland and the United Kingdom.

Suriname achieved limited internal self-government within the Kingdom of the Netherlands in 1954. It became independent in 1975. Almost one-third of its population emigrated to Holland in the lead-up to independence. In 1980 sixteen noncommissioned military officers led by Desi Bouterse staged a successful coup against the elected government. Bouterse proclaimed his regime socialist and established cordial relations with the revolutionary government in Grenada. The military rulers allowed a resumption of civilian government in 1991. The New Front ethnic coalition of the major Creole (non-Maroon African), Hindustani and Javanese parties came to power. The NF was supplanted by the National Democratic Party of Bouterse in 1996. It returned to power in 2000 and 2005, but lost to Desi Bouterse's Mega Combination coalition in 2010. This represented a remarkable triumph over political problems for Bouterse. In 1982 during his initial military rule fifteen opposition figures were rounded up and murdered by the regime, though Bouterse has denied responsibility. Between 1986 and 1992 his troops fought a bitter war against Maroon insurgents of the Jungle Commando led by Ronnie Brunswijk. In the course of this conflict Surinamese troops killed thirty-five or more innocent persons in the infamous Moiwana Massacre. Bouterse has been tried and convicted in absentia in Holland on drug-related charges.

FRENCH ANTILLES

France has been the most tenacious of colonizers. Despite suffering some of the most crushing defeats in the history of anticolonial struggles (Haiti 1804, Vietnam 1954, Algeria 1962), compounded by devastating defeats by Germany in the Franco-Prussian War (1870–1871) and World Wars I and II, France has continued to be a most reluctant divester of control over colonies.

On February 23, 2005, The Union for a Popular Movement (UMP) government in France went so far as to enact into law a directive that the history of French colonialism be taught only in a "positive" manner. Nicolas Sarkozy, elected later (2007) president of

France, was leader of the UMP at the time of this remarkable law, which directed teachers to "acknowledge and recognize in particular the positive role of the French presence abroad, especially in North Africa. A thousand Martiniquans demonstrated against this law and Sarkozy had to cancel a proposed visit there. Aimé Césaire, mayor of Fort de France for fifty-six years and deputy to the French parliament, refused to meet Sarkozy on the projected visit. The law was repealed in 2006 under pressure from a wide array of sources.

When French ruler General Charles de Gaulle offered France's African colonies the choice in 1958 of voting "Yes" (for integrating into a French-dominated community and receiving various economic benefits) or "No" (opting for immediate independence), only Sékou Ture's Guinea voted "No." The French responded by destroying as much as they could in Guinea, even pulling telephones out of the walls before they left. By 1960 the "Yes" colonies had changed their minds and opted for independence. By then France was locked in a desperate struggle with Algeria and hardly able to contain the rest of its African empire.

The Antilles were not given the "Yes" or "No" option because of their 1946 designation as overseas departments (*Départements d'Outre Mer,* or DOM), under the new constitution of the French Fourth Republic. World War II had highlighted the Antillean connections with France. In June 1940 the Bank of France shipped 286 tons of gold to Martinique for safekeeping. From 1940 to 1943 Martinique and Guadeloupe were under the control of the French Vichy regime, which collaborated with Nazi Germany after the Germans defeated France early in the war. The British and U.S. navies blockaded the islands but agreed not to invade if the Vichy regime would keep its warships in port. The blockade caused near starvation, which was averted by intense efforts to substitute local produce for imported food, and by slight easing of the blockade from time to time.

About 4,000 young Antilleans slipped out of the islands for the Free French recruitment centers in Dominica (for Guadeloupians) and St. Lucia (for Martiniquans). Resistance, sometimes violent, brought down the Antillean Vichy regime in July 1943. In 1940 a committee of Guadeloupians sought help from the U.S. consul in Martinique. They proposed to declare Guadeloupe independent and then request U.S. protection. They requested the presence of three U.S. warships for that purpose. The United States declined. After the war the Free French refused to fully acknowledge Antilleans as integral parts of the much heralded resistance movement. They were supposedly afraid that Antillean mobilization around the question of resistance to Vichy France might stimulate ideas of independence from France. The result was the transformation of Guadeloupe, Martinique, French Guiana and Réunion, into "overseas departments," theoretically integral parts of France. Antilleans were full citizens of France. They could vote in French elections and elected representatives to the French parliament. They were eligible for French welfare subsidies, though these were not fully phased in until the 1970s.

Césaire and others felt that departmentalization would ensure full participation in the benefits of French citizenship. This idea came as a culmination of years of French efforts to "assimilate" the privileged elements within its subject populations. During World War I the French could therefore boast a Senegalese, Blaise Diagne, as a cabinet minister in France. Felix Eboué, a black man born in Cayenne, was governor of French Equatorial Africa during World War II (1940–1944). Frantz Fanon, the Martiniquan who became a leader of the Algerian Revolution, recalled the assimilationist phrase, "our ancestors the Gauls," which assaulted the sensibilities of black schoolchildren in the French Antilles. In 1949 the French enshrined assimilation when they reinterred the remains of Victor Schoelcher, paramount nineteenth-century abolitionist and Felix Eboué in the French Pantheon.

Departmentalization was followed by the decline of sugar and other agricultural mainstays of the Antillean economies. Their place was taken by service industries, notably tourism, a large French bureaucracy and welfare payments. From 1963 to 1981 France ran an official agency, BUMIDOM (Bureau for Migration from the Overseas Departments), to encourage Antillean emigration to France. Some 84,000 Antilleans migrated, artificially relieving Antillean unemployment while providing needed labor for low-end French jobs. Aimé Césaire called the black Antillean exodus and its replacement by white French arrivals, "genocide by substitution."

These developments have been met by a persistent but heavily repressed nationalist movement. Antillean students in France provided an early vanguard for this movement. Out of the *Association Géneralé des Etudiants Guadeloupéens* (General Association of Guadeloupean Students, or AGEG), came the *Front Antillo-Guyanais* (Antilles-Guiana Front) in 1961. The French government destroyed it. In 1963 came the *Groupement des Organisations Nationalistes Guadeloupéennes* (Group of Guadeloupe Nationalist Organizations or GONG), and the *Front Guadeloupéen pour L'Autonomie*).

In 1967, what many Guadeloupeans call "The Repression" brought many of these issues to the fore. In March a white merchant in Basse Terre set his dog on a black shoemaker, resulting in three days of riots and dozens injured. French riot police were flown in. Black protesters were heavily sentenced, but the white man was not prosecuted.

Then on May 26, 1967, French police fired on striking construction workers, triggering three days of upheaval. There is no definitive figure for casualties. Officialdom admitted at least seven deaths. A figure of over 100 killed is commonly put forward in Guadeloupe. Elie Domota, leader of Guadeloupe's 2009 protests, was quoted as supporting this figure.

The 1967 killings were attributed to the CRS (*Compagnies Républicaines de Sécurité*), the infamous national French antiriot police. For years they have been routinely flown in to put down protest in the Antilles. Their trigger-happiness in Guadeloupe contrasted with the May 1968 situation in France, when the worst riots of the century, which ultimately brought the downfall of Charles de Gaulle, resulted in no deaths directly attributed to the riots.

Even outside of riot situations, Antillean realities tend to assume racial overtones. The presence of white rank-and-file gendarmes in Antillean streets has long been a cause of surprise to black visitors, especially from the former British West Indies. Antillean prisoners are often tried and imprisoned in France.

A year after 1967, several Guadeloupian trade unions merged into the *Union Générale des Travailleurs de la Guadeloupe* (General Union of Guadeloupe Workers, or UGTG), making it the country's largest union. In 1978 there appeared a

French riot police confront demonstrators during the Guadeloupe protests of 2009.

closely linked political party, the UPLG (*Union Populaire pour la Libération de la Guadeloupe*—People's Union for the Liberation of Guadeloupe).

In the 1960s clandestine Antillean groups claimed responsibility for over sixty bomb attacks in the Antilles and France. In 2001 the UGTG formed NONM (Créole word for "man" or "humanity") to concentrate on building a consciousness of Afro-Antillean history. They found themselves struggling for an Emancipation Day holiday, something by then existing in most of the former British colonies.

In 2009 Guadeloupe erupted once again. A general strike lasted forty-four days. It was led by a coalition of forty-eight organizations including unions, the pro-independence movement and political, civic and cultural groups. The action threw up a new organization, the *Liyannaj Kont Pwofitasyon* (Alliance Against Profiteering).

The LKP drew up a list of 165 demands reflective of Guadeloupe's situation under department status. Despite well-stocked supermarkets and a veneer of prosperity, average incomes of Antilleans are slightly above half those of metropolitan workers. Guadeloupe suffers from the severest unemployment

in the European Union, despite the fact that about 100,000 of the combined approximately 800,000 people of Martinique and Guadeloupe live in France. Welfare benefits are eroded by high taxes and profiteering. The 2009 demands included an increased minimum wage; lower bank fees; reduced airfares between metropolis and the departments; reduced prices for water, food, gasoline and public transport; and much more. Christiane Taubura, a deputy from French Guiana, characterized the struggle as one against "social apartheid."

The LKP collective did not try to produce a political platform but greater autonomy, if not independence, seemed the logical inference of the struggle. It did eventually propose an enhanced transitional autonomy. The strike spread to Martinique, though calls for major French metropolitan unions to express some solidarity went mostly unheeded. The protests were peaceful until police brutality and the use of racial insults by the French police inflamed passions. Guadeloupe protesters developed a chant, "Guadeloupe belongs to us!" The chant in Martinique was "Martinique is ours, not theirs!" Demonstrations in Guadeloupe brought out as many as 100,000 people, an astonishing quarter of the island's population. Malek Boutih, a national secretary of the French Socialist Party, caused a stir among politically correct French people when he expressed shock at the large numbers of white CRS police sent to confront a black population.

The French government made some wage concessions and temporarily capped prices of certain basic necessities, thereby allowing the strike to end. There was only one fatality this time. Shortly after the upheaval French President Nicolas Sarkozy visited the area. He offered Martinique and French Guiana a referendum on greater autonomy. "Martiniquans will be free to choose in their heart and conscience the road they would like to take," he said. He then immediately rendered his offer largely meaningless by insisting that "The debate is not about independence, but rather of a fair autonomous status. Martinique is French and will remain so."

The referendum, ostensibly on greater autonomy, therefore became in fact another indication of France's reluctance to let go of its overseas territories. When the referendum took place in 2010 participants could vote only for an unspecified increase of local government autonomy. If they voted "Yes," Sarkozy would decide *after the fact* how much autonomy they would get. Moreover the referendum was not extended to Guadeloupe, the most likely of the departments to vote "Yes." Over half of the electorate stayed home in French Guiana (52 percent). Forty-five percent of the Martiniquans did not bother to vote. The Martinique independence movement promised to keep up its campaign. Some of those who voted "No" were afraid of losing their social security benefits in the event of more autonomous departments.

HAITI

Haiti, since the U.S. occupation ended in 1934, has been consumed in a welter of changing governments, deposed presidents, chronic bloodshed, economic problems, a U.S. invasion ordered by President Bill Clinton and aborted at the last minute, UN military occupation, thousands of fleeing "boat people," corrupt politicians, political violence and, in 2010, one of the worst natural disasters in the history of the Caribbean. The ever-changing kaleidoscope is every bit as complicated as the events of the Haitian Revolution. This time, however, the light at the end of the tunnel has been slower in coming. And external forces, namely the United States and the United Nations, have been more influential than Napoleon or the British or other interventionist agencies of the revolutionary period.

The United States appointed three colored puppet presidents during its protectorate over Haiti. It felt free to depose them whenever it needed to. They removed President Sudre Dartigueneve in 1922 when he could not bring himself to sign off on a U.S.-proposed loan from National City Bank (now City Bank) to pay off Haiti's debt. President Louis Borno replaced Dartigueneve. He was in a joint power-sharing relationship with U.S. High Commissioner General John H. Russell. They ruled together until 1930.

The U.S. marines remained the real power in Haiti. Many of these soldiers were from the American deep South, and they inevitably recreated their segregationist society in Haiti. Even President Borno could not enter the American Club, the pinnacle of white social life in occupied Haiti. (Most colonies had such racially exclusionary clubs—the Country Club and Union Club in Trinidad, Liguanea Club in Jamaica, Kingstown Club in St. Vincent, Georgetown Club in British Guiana and others). Sometimes, as in the case of the Trinidad Country Club, racially exclusionary recreation continued as usual well after independence.

The inevitable massacres occurred in this period. During a student protest at Les Cayes in 1929 U.S. marines killed a number of protesters, variously estimated at anywhere from 10 to 264. The main slaughter of Haitians in the interwar years came, however, from the Dominican Republic in 1937. Dictator Rafael Trujillo ordered his army to massacre all Haitians living on the Dominican side of their joint border. Possibly 35,000 Haitians were killed. Some casualty estimates go much higher. The United States arbitrated a Dominican indemnity payment of only $525,000.

There was a steady succession of presidents until the Duvalier era. François "Papa Doc" Duvalier came to power in fair elections in 1957 and remained, as "president for life," until his death in 1971. Several presidents before him had ruled as presidents for life, starting with the colored presidents Petion and Boyer in the early nineteenth century. Duvalier's nineteen-year-old son, Jean-Claude "Baby Doc," carried on to 1986 when popular opposition sent him into exile in France.

A few short-lived administrations later, Jean-Bertrand Aristide, a former Roman Catholic priest, came into power in 1990. His *Operation Lavalas* (Operation Avalanche) promised much though it was blamed for much violence, including many deaths by "necklacing," or burning to death while fastened between a blazing tire, a practice apparently borrowed from apartheid-era South Africa. President Aristide was deposed while visiting the United States in September 1991, after only a few months in office. He spent most of 1991–1994 in the United States, where he was given access to frozen Haitian assets impounded in the United States.

Meanwhile President Bill Clinton of the United States instituted extensive economic and other sanctions against Haiti in an attempt to displace the military junta led by General Raoul Cedras. Clinton's attack armada of sixty-one aircraft was already in the skies on their way to invade when General Cedras acceded to Clinton's demand to leave Haiti. U.S. forces nevertheless landed on September 19, 1994, preparing the way for Aristide's return.

Aristide completed his term, begun in 1991, remaining in office from 1994 to 1996. Haiti's constitution prevented him from running for a second consecutive term. Suggestions that he ought to be allowed to make up the ousted years came to naught. He returned to power from 2001 to 2004, amidst charges of electoral corruption and violence. He was now head of a new party, the Fanmi Lavalas, having left his Lavalas Avalanche. On January 1, 2004, when Aristide presided over Haiti's bicentenary, it was against a backdrop of counterdemonstrations and the sound of hostile gunfire. President Thabo Mbeki of South Africa, Prime Minister Perry Christie of the Bahamas representing CARICOM and Congresswoman Maxine Waters representing the U.S. Congressional

Black Caucus constituted the handful of foreign dignitaries present.

A rebellion against Aristide, begun in the town of Gonaives, was nearing Port au Prince when Aristide flew into exile on February 29, 2004. His destination was Bangui, Central African Republic. Aristide said that U.S. military and diplomatic personnel dismissed his American personal security force, kidnapped him, forced him to sign a document relinquishing power and bundled him aboard a U.S. aircraft bound for parts undisclosed. His dismissed security force reappeared on the same plane and were reportedly later flown back to the United States.

Bill Clinton's United States had restored Aristide to power on the backs of an invasion force in 1994. Ten years later, if Aristide's contention is correct, George W. Bush's United States was forcing him into exile at gunpoint.

Aristide's removal to the Central African Republic was said to have been arranged by the United States, France and President Omar Bongo of Gabon, with Bongo as chief contact with the Central African Republic. Aristide left the Central African Republic on March 15, 2004, for Jamaica, where he was temporarily provided a haven by Prime Minister P. J. Patterson, CARICOM's chairperson at the time. CARICOM's welcome displeased Bush administration officials including National Security adviser Condoleeza Rice and Defense Secretary Donald Rumsfeld, who both voiced opposition to Aristide's return to the Western Hemisphere.

On the same day of Aristide's 2004 departure U.S. troops landed once more, and not for the last time, to be followed later that year by the Brazil-led MINUSTAH (United Nations Stabilization Mission In Haiti) comprising over 9,000 soldiers and police from several countries. Peacekeepers were accused of several incidents of wanton killings of civilians.

U.S. troops, over 10,000 within the first few days, entered Haiti yet again in January 2010 in the aftermath of a catastrophic earthquake on January 12. Described by some as the deadliest natural disaster in modern times, the earthquake destroyed or damaged the presidential palace, the national assembly, the Roman Catholic Cathedral and many other buildings. The minister of justice, opposition leader and Roman

Catholic archbishop were all killed. President Rene Preval, in the presidential palace when the earthquake struck, escaped injury. By mid-March President Preval was reporting 217,000 dead bodies counted, with expectations of a final death toll surpassing 300,000. An estimated 250,000 homes were destroyed, over 3 million people adversely affected and over 1 million rendered homeless. At least half of Haiti's Gross Domestic Product (GDP) was destroyed. The UN headquarters on the island were demolished and the top two UN officials in the country killed. Scores of other UN personnel were killed, injured, or missing. Haiti, already the poorest country in the Western Hemisphere, lacked the infrastructure to effectively address its horrific predicament.

While Venezuela and Cuba were some of the first on the scene with humanitarian relief, it was the massive U.S. effort which quickly filled the administrative vacuum created by the catastrophe. Thousands of troops poured in and took over Port-au-Prince's Toussaint L'Ouverture Airport, where the fast-food chains of McDonald's and Pizza Hut were installed to feed them. U.S. forces decided who must be given priority to land and who would have to wait. Among those prevented from landing were a CARICOM delegation containing two prime ministers. A French plane carrying a field hospital was also turned away but landed the following day.

There were echoes of the Swettenham affair and earlier invasions of Haiti in concerns generated in some quarters at the American role in the devastated country. French Cooperation Minister Alain Joyaudet accused the United States of using the disaster for ulterior political motives. "This is about helping Haiti, not about occupying Haiti," the Associated Press reported Joyaudet as saying. Joyaudet felt passionate enough about the matter to engage in a fistfight with an American commander at the airport over differing ideas concerning the flight plan for a French evacuation flight. President Daniel Ortega of Nicaragua called for a withdrawal of American troops. "It seems that the [United States' Latin American] bases are not sufficient," he commented. Iranian Vice President Mohammad Reza Rahimi, meeting in Tehran with President Bharrat Jagdeo of Guyana, "emphasized," as reported by the Iranian news agency, "that the United States, instead of helping the quake-stricken people of Haiti, has sent thousands of US troops to the Caribbean Island." President Jagdeo endorsed Rahimi's observations. The U.S. forces had nevertheless taken the precaution, this time around, of obtaining official Haitian government acceptance of U.S. control of the airport.

Former President Bill Clinton, whose sixty-one plane armada had pulled up in midair on its way to annihilate Haiti in 1994, now got an opportunity to witness nature's annihilation up close. President Barack Obama appointed former Presidents Clinton and George W. Bush as special coordinators of fundraising for Haiti's recovery. Clinton had by now become something of a Haitian specialist. His Clinton Foundation had been working in Haiti for some years providing social and economic services. The UN had appointed him UN Special Envoy to Haiti in 2008. And when the disaster struck, his wife, Hillary Clinton, visited the nation in her capacity as secretary of state. George Bush was no Haiti neophyte either. It was during his presidency that Aristide was allegedly kidnapped and exiled.

DOMINICAN REPUBLIC

The Dominican Republic has rivaled Haiti in the unsettled nature of its politics. Three men dominated the period after the U.S military intervention ended in 1924. They were Rafael Trujillo, Joachin Balaguer and Juan Bosch.

Trujillo ruled either as president or the power behind the scenes from 1930 to his assassination in 1961. He was a product of the U.S occupation. He enlisted in the new U.S.-created National Police in 1918 and rose rapidly through the ranks. He attended officers' training school in 1921 and had become colonel and commander in chief by 1925. He retained this position when the National Police were transformed into the National Army in 1927. In 1930 he was able to use his influence to ensure that he was the only candidate in presidential elections.

Up until the 1950s high commodity prices for sugar, then the country's major export and other products enabled Trujillo to maintain favorable economic growth and living conditions, despite the persistence of poverty. His massacre of the Haitians in 1937 remains one of the most hideous occurrences in Caribbean history. The U.S. government forced him to pay modest reparations. Possibly 50,000 Haitians had been brought in as cheap labor to ease the effects of the 1930s Depression. In 1952 Trujillo, now himself the private owner of extensive sugar plantations, contracted to bring in more cheap Haitian labor.

Trujillo's grandmother was a Haitian, a fact he attempted to conceal. In 1960 Trujillo had his agents try to assassinate President Romulo Betancourt of Venezuela. Betancourt had allowed anti-Trujillo elements to organize for a possible military attack. The Organization of American States and the United States imposed sanctions. Trujillo was assassinated on May 30, 1961. The assassins reportedly received help from the U.S. Central Intelligence Agency. This was a month and a half after the failed Bay of Pigs invasion of Cuba. The United States was reportedly afraid that Trujillo's despotism might trigger a Castro-style response.

In 1960 Trujillo had appointed Joachin Balaguer as a puppet ruler. The United States now forced Balaguer to share power with a seven-man Council of State. Balaguer resigned a few days later on January 16, 1962. He went into exile. Juan Bosch won the ensuing elections in December 1962. He was overthrown by a military coup in 1963. Many vested interests considered him too "leftist." A military junta came into power.

A pro-Bosch coup against the junta triggered civil war in 1965. The United States invaded once more sending in 23,000 troops, later joined by a token OAS force. Balaguer returned to win elections in 1966. He remained in power until 1978. He ruled again from 1986 to 1996. His 1994 victory brought allegations of fraud. His opponent, Jose Pena Gomez, was black and of Haitian descent, orphaned as a result of the 1937 massacre of Haitians. As the *New York Times* put it in his 1998 obituary, "No politician openly acknowledging African ancestry has ever been elected to any Spanish speaking Latin American nation in this century, though a few mixed race have held power. But Mr. Pena Gomez came extremely close to achieving that feat. . . ." Pena Gomez's race and Haitian ancestry became issues in the 1994 elections. Gomez was a protégé of Juan Bosch and had been elected mayor of Santo Domingo in 1982.

DRUGS

The drug problem has bedeviled the Caribbean for some time. Its thousands of islands and cays (700 islands and 2,000 cays in the Bahamas alone), its geographical location linking South American drug suppliers to North American and other consumers, its often porous and unprotected borders (especially in Suriname and Guyana), the presence of sometimes corrupt officials, the extensive legitimate air and sea traffic which helps camouflage drug boats and planes, the substantial financial gains to be realized, all have contributed to entrenching the problem.

The Caribbean has accordingly become a major transshipment point for cocaine, heroin and marijuana. U.S. agencies such as the Drug Enforcement Agency (DEA) and the U.S. Coast Guard have spread their interdiction and anti–money laundering efforts widely throughout the region. The navies of Britain, France and the Netherlands operate against drug traffickers in the area. There exists a multiplicity of antidrug treaties mandating cooperation between Caribbean governments and U.S. and international agencies.

The drug trade has been blamed for a proliferation of guns, resulting in Jamaica, Trinidad and Tobago, the Dominican Republic and others being among the most murderous states, per capita, in the world. The trade has also touched some high-echelon personalities, in one way or the other. In 1985 Turks and Caicos Islands Chief Minister Norman Saunders and his Minister of Commerce Stafford Missick were arrested by the DEA and jailed in Miami on drug-related charges. In 1988 U.S. authorities were pondering charging Bahamian Prime Minister Lynden O. Pindling with drug conspiracy. Etienne Boerenveen, a member of Suriname's military junta, was arrested by the DEA in Miami in 1986. He was later convicted on drug charges. Ronnie Brunswijk, a Surinamese parliamentarian, was sentenced in absentia to six years' imprisonment in the Netherlands. In 1999 a Dutch court sentenced Desi Bouterse, sometime Surinamese junta leader and president, in absentia, to eleven years for alleged cocaine smuggling.

When U.S. authorities began pressuring Jamaica in 2009 to extradite reputed drug figure Christopher "Dudus" Coke, Prime Minister Bruce Golding initially demurred. The prime minister eventually launched an anti-Coke military operation that left over seventy Jamaicans dead. Coke was extradited in June 2010.

Leaked "WikiLeaks" U.S. diplomatic emails released in 2010 actually showed Cuban officials complaining to U.S. officials (with whom they cooperate on antidrug activity) of Jamaican reluctance to cooperate with Cuba on drug interdiction. Cuba, as vulnerable as elsewhere to unwelcome drug transiting, had the lowest incidence of drug consumption in the region.

U.S. indictments in 2010 against Figueroa Agosto of Puerto Rico and the Dominican Republic, supposedly the Caribbean's biggest drug baron, included allegations of complicity against high-ranking Dominican officials. In Trinidad, Patrick Manning, both before and after the 2010 election that unseated him as prime minister, accused drug operatives of politically harassing him.

Guyanese Shaheed "Roger" Khan was convicted in New York in 2010 for cocaine trafficking into the United States. Testimony during his trial seemed to implicate high government officials, but the questions raised remained unanswered because of plea bargaining arrangements.

In developing societies like the Caribbean the drug trade presents many complexities. One such is the "positive" economic impact. Profits of the trade sustain an informal economy and eventually percolate upward into legitimate business, providing employment and sustenance. It has been suggested that a crackdown on the drug trade in Guyana in 1993 dried up the availability of foreign exchange sufficiently to induce a currency devaluation. Another complexity was illustrated by the U.S. government's pressuring the European Community to abandon subsidies to Caribbean banana producers. It was feared that the result of loss of livelihood caused by the demise of bananas would force farmers to produce drugs, which would in turn make U.S. efforts against the drug trade more difficult.

Yet another complexity comes from the loss of sovereignty, principally to the United States, implicit in the U.S.-sponsored antidrug efforts. The actual or threatened arrest by U.S. authorities of high-ranking Caribbean political figures graphically illustrates this reality. The standard "ship-rider" agreements offered by the United States from 1995 gave the U.S. the right to pursue and apprehend suspicious vessels in the territorial waters of Caribbean nations. Some, such as the Basdeo Panday administration in Trinidad, enthusiastically accepted loss of sovereignty as a price of the war against drugs. Some, such as the James Mitchell administration in St. Vincent, went along with a heavy heart, as it were, feeling powerless to resist U.S. pressure. The Owen Arthur and P. J. Patterson administrations in Barbados and Jamaica, respectively, sought arrangements less offensive to their countries' sovereignty. Several Caribbean nations, including Barbados, Dominica, the Dominican Republic, Grenada, Guyana, Jamaica, St. Lucia and Trinidad and Tobago, have also signed invasive Tax Information Exchange Agreements with the United States. In some cases U.S. personnel have been seconded to local inland revenue departments.

The Caribbean is much more important as a transit region than as producers of illegal drugs. Jamaica, the most important consumer and exporter of ganja in the Caribbean, is an exception. The U.S. Office of National Drug Control Policy identified St. Vincent as the major supplier of ganja to the southern Caribbean market.

EMIGRATION SINCE WORLD WAR II

There has been a massive outflow of Caribbean people since World War II. Most have gone to North America and Europe, but there has been movement also to such places as Africa and Australia. Most of this emigration was initially directly stimulated by the metropolitan countries, though they sometimes tried to stem the flow when the influx of nonwhite people seemed too large.

During the war the United States brought in farm labor from Jamaica and Puerto Rico. The British brought in forestry workers from Belize. With the United States experiencing postwar boom conditions a Migration Division Office was set up in 1948 with the help of the Caribbean Commission to bring Puerto Ricans to the mainland. Headquartered in New York, the Migration Division brought hundreds of thousands of Puerto Ricans north.

Faced with a postwar labor shortage, the British likewise set up a similar Barbados Liaison Service (1948–1963), much as the Panama Canal Company had done earlier. In 1948 the now legendary *Empire Windrush* brought the first large, heavily publicized shipload of Caribbean labor to drive England's buses, staff its underground railways, run its post offices and provide nurses for its hospitals. It sailed from Kingston with 492 emigrants, mostly Jamaicans and Trinidadians. Only two were women. The most famous passengers were the Trinidad calypsonians Lords Kitchener and Beginner. In France BUMIDOM, as seen, encouraged 84,000 Antillean workers to France between 1963 and 1983.

Many migrants were also driven by economic considerations, even without the stimulus of metropolitan recruitment. By the early 1950s 3 percent of the Surinamese population were working in Curaçao and Aruba, primarily in oil refineries. As employment declined there they moved to the Netherlands instead. Netherlands Antilleans migrated as well. The coming of independence precipitated a further rush to lock in the presumed benefits of metropolitan citizenship. About 330,000 Surinamese and their offspring were living in the Netherlands in 2007, compared with about 500,000 in Suriname.

Many Anglophone and Haitian workers emigrated voluntarily, legally or otherwise, to the United States and Canada. Women from the Dominican Republic became the majority of domestic workers in Spain. A huge Dominicano population developed in the United States. The most dramatic example of voluntary economic migration was that of the Haitian "boat people" who sailed, many at the cost of their lives, to the United States.

Caribbean immigrants reach Britain on the *Empire Windrush* in 1948.

The emigrants experienced racial antagonism everywhere. Those in the United States seem to have fared best, possibly because of the presence of a large African American host society to cushion the impact of racism, possibly because the Anglophone arrivals, at least, may have been better educated than their counterparts in Europe, enabling them to achieve upward mobility via America's democratic education system. In Europe the ghettoization of the emigrants quickly created something akin to a traditional American pattern of race relations.

Britain probably presented the greatest challenge for Caribbean immigrants. Politicians, such as Sir Oswald Mosley and his British Union of Fascists and later the British National Party, were quick to incite the flames of British resentment at the rapid transformation of their country into a multiracial state. The Conservative Party parliamentarian Enoch Powell called for the repatriation of Caribbean immigrants.

Racial riots became a recurring part of the British landscape. In Notting Hill in 1958, hundreds of English rioters attacked Caribbean people and murdered Antiguan Kelso Cochrane as he wended his way home. Caribbean people defending themselves were inordinately arrested by the police. Trinidadian Claudia Jones, assisted by Amy Ashwood Garvey (the first Mrs. Marcus Garvey) and others, started the Notting Hill Carnival in 1959 to ease the tension. In time it became the largest street parade in Europe. In New Cross, London, in 1981, someone threw a bomb into a Caribbean house party, killing fourteen.

Allegations of police brutality were a recurring factor in the riots. As earlier in American history, riots evolved from white mobs attacking innocent black people, to pitched battles between black people and the police. Several major riots took place in the 1980s, including 1985 outbreaks in Brixton, South London; the Broadwater Farm in Tottenham, North London; and Handsworth in Birmingham. Television clips of the Broadwater riot resembled medieval warfare. A policeman was decapitated by cutlasses. Leaked "WikiLeaks" U.S. diplomatic cables published in November 2010 showed then U.S. ambassador to Great Britain, Raymond Seitz, very critical of British handling of the 1985 riots.

He found the British authorities complacent in the face of a racialized version of Dickensian England.

Still, the new communities gradually changed the face of their adopted societies, through music and culture, through their excellence in sports, and eventually through political participation and entry into the full range of societal activity. Racism nevertheless remains an unsolved problem.

In August 2011 some of the worst riots in England's history were again sparked by a police encounter with a black person. This time, a young black man, Mark Duggan, was shot dead by police in Tottenham. The police used a hollow point bullet, similar to the "dum-dum" bullets outlawed in warfare by the Hague Convention of 1899. (These bullets expand on impact, causing greater damage to human or animal tissue.) As on previous similar occasions, local black residents marched to the police station demanding answers to the tragedy. A riot ensued. Unlike earlier situations, however, the initial protest against police violence against a black victim quickly transformed itself into nationwide multiracial protests, as white and other youths unleashed an unprecedented fury against English society. The riots largely lost their initial racial character, leaving English society at a loss for adequate analysis. To some it appeared that the youthful English working-class antipathy toward Caribbean immigrants of the 1950s had been replaced by a common multiracial youthful resentment against the police and other symbols of English authority. Eight months earlier, in December 2010, student protesters had attacked the royal Rolls Royce carrying heir to the throne, Prince Charles, in the streets of Central London.

On the positive side, remittances home by Caribbeans abroad represents one of the major sources of income for many Caribbean governments. In the late 1990s, 36 percent of households in Guyana were said to be receiving remittances. Figures were 17 percent for St. Lucia, 13 percent for Trinidad and Tobago and 11 percent for Jamaica. Six percent of the region's Gross National Product (GNP) was said to be derived from remittances. Retirees returning home with accumulated savings and social security benefits are also a great boon to their home economies (and sometimes the targets of the criminals they left behind). On the other hand, however, the United

States has unilaterally deported large numbers of Caribbean-born criminals to their countries of origin, thereby precipitating problems of crime and destitution that the region has not adequately been able to deal with. The burgeoning Diaspora has also provided an opportunity for home-based businesses to market their products to Caribbean communities overseas. It has also provided an opportunity, unfortunately not yet imaginatively embraced, for home governments to reverse the brain drain to the metropolis by enticing back those who have acquired advanced technological and developmental skills and experience aboard.

Further Readings

"Acting on Our Conscience: A Declaration of African American Support for the Civil Rights Struggle In Cuba." http://media.miamiherald.com/smedia/2009/12/01/22/Declaration_of_African-American_support.source.prod_affiliate.56.pdf [accessed December 5, 2009].

Andre, Irving W., and Gabriel J. Christian. *In Search of Eden: Essays on Dominican History.* Brampton, ON: Pond Casse Press, 2002.

Bell, Stewart. *Bayou of Pigs: The True Story of an Audacious Plot to Turn a Tropical Island into a Criminal Paradise.* Mississauga, ON: J. Wiley & Sons Canada, 2008.

Bonilla, Yarimar. "Guadeloupe, Labor Protest," in Immanuel Ness, Ed., *International Encyclopedia of Revolution and Protest.* Hoboken, NJ: WileyBlackwell, 1468–1471.

"Documents from the National United Freedom Fighters of Trinidad." *Pan-African Journal,* 8, 2, 1975.

Frazier, E. Franklin, and Eric Williams, Eds. *The Economic Future of the Caribbean.* Dover, MA: The Majority Press, 2004.

Griffith, Ivelaw L., Ed. *The Political Economy of Drugs in the Caribbean.* New York: Palgrave, 2000.

Ishmael, Odeen. *The Walter Rodney Files.* No Place. GNI Publications, 2007. http://www.guyana.org/govt/rodney_files.html [accessed March 17, 2010].

James, C. L. R. *Walter Rodney and the Question of Power.* London: Race Today Publications, 1983.

Jennings, Eric T. *Vichy in the Tropics: Pétain's National Revolution in Madagascar, Guadeloupe, and Indochina, 1940–44.* Palo Alto, CA: Stanford University Press, 2001.

Lewis, Rupert. *Walter Rodney's Intellectual and Political Thought.* Detroit, MI: Wayne State University Press, 1998.

Marshall, Bill, and Cristina Johnson. *France and the Americas: Culture, Politics, and History,* Vol. 3. Santa Barbara, CA: ABC-CLIO, 2005.

Martin, Tony. *In Nobody's Backyard: The Grenada Revolution in Its Own Words. Vol. I, The Revolution at Home.* Dover, MA: The Majority Press, 1983.

Martin, Tony, Ed. "CLR James and the Race/Class Question," in *The Pan-African Connection: From Slavery to Garvey and Beyond.* Dover, MA: The Majority Press, 1984. First pub. 1983.

Martin, Tony. *In Nobody's Backyard: The Grenada Revolution in Its Own Words. Vol. II, Facing the World.* Dover, MA: The Majority Press, 1985.

Martin, Tony. "African and Indian Consciousness in the 20th Century," in Bridget Brereton, Ed., *UNESCO General History of the Caribbean, Vol. 5.* London: Macmillan and Paris: UNESCO, 2003.

Mitchell, William B., et al. *Area Handbook for Guyana.* Washington, DC: Superintendent of Documents, U.S. Government Printing Office, 1969.

Moore, Carlos. *Castro, the Blacks and Africa.* Los Angeles, CA: University of California Press, 1988.

Robinson, Eugene. "Cuba Begins to Answer Its Race Question." *Washington Post,* November 12, 2000. http://www.hartford-hwp.com/archives/43b/183.html [accessed September 5, 2009].

Rodney, Walter. "Tanzanian Ujamaa and Scientific Socialism." *The African Review,* 2, 1, April 1972, 61–76.

Scheer, Robert, and Maurice Zeitlin. *Cuba: An American Tragedy.* Harmondsworth, Middlesex: Penguin Books, 1964.

Smith, William Gregory, and Anne R. Wagner. *Assassination Cry of a Failed Revolution: The Truth About Dr. Walter Rodney's Death.* N.P.: Xlibris, 2007.

"Special Committee on Decolonization Approves Text Calling on United States to Expedite Self-Determination Process for Puerto Rico." http://www.un.org/News/Press/docs/2009/gacol3193.doc.htm [accessed September 3, 2009].

Spivak, Lawrence E. *Meet the Press: Guest, Dr. Cheddi Jagan, Prime Minister of British Guiana. Vol. 5, Sunday, October 15, 1961. No 40.* Washington, DC: Merkle Press, 1961.

The Grenada Revolution Online. http://www.thegrenadarevolutiononline.com/bishltr2.html [accessed April 20, 2010].

16

Prognosis

*As one who knows the people well, I make no apology for prophesying that
there will soon be a turning point in the history of the West Indies; and that the people who
inhabit that portion of the Western Hemisphere will be the instruments of uniting a scattered
race who, before the close of many centuries, will found an Empire on which the sun shall
shine as ceaselessly as it shines on the empire of the North today.*

—Marcus Garvey, *1913*

When Marcus Garvey made this statement in 1913 he was thinking of an Afro-Caribbean contribution to the Pan-African world. There is no reason why the Caribbean of the twenty-first century cannot rise to a position of world prominence. The "specks on the map" self-perception has tended to obscure both the past achievement and future prospects for the area.

Cuba, the Dominican Republic, Haiti, Jamaica, Puerto Rico and Trinidad and Tobago between them alone contain well over 30 million souls. Even without political integration, this in not a small area to exploit for economic integration, and the effort in this direction is underway.

The forays of the Caribbean into world recognition are already impressive. As C. L. R. James pointed out, the Caribbean was very early a modern quasi-industrial society, though in the unfortunate context of enslavement. The socialized workforce of the sugar plantation had, in sugar processing, an industrial aspect that brought it into early contact with technological innovations such as the steam engine.

The capacity of the Caribbean for revolutionary upheaval in the quest for freedom and justice has probably been underestimated by Caribbean people themselves. The struggles of the Maroons and rebellious enslaved came close to perpetual war, often with impressive success against great odds.

From at least the nineteenth century Caribbean intellectuals and creative artists have significantly impacted the world. Due in part to the absence of advanced educational facilities at home, many of the most outstanding made their mark in the Caribbean Diaspora—Edward Wilmot Blyden in West Africa, Claude McKay in the United States, for example. Others, like Eric Williams and Chief Justice H. O. B. Wooding of Trinidad and Tobago, topped their classes in the metropolis (at Oxford University and the Inns of Court, respectively), and returned home. The Haitian and Cuban Revolutions were truly events that shook the world.

In the area of sport the Caribbean record has been nothing short of spectacular. British Guianese Phil Edwards representing Canada won five Olympic bronze medals in 1928, 1932 and 1936, in the 4 × 400, 800 and 1,500 meters. The Jamaican quartet of Arthur Wint, Leslie Laing, Herb McKenley and George Rhoden won gold in the 4 × 400 men's relay at the Helsinki Olympics in 1952. Jamaica also won gold and silver that year in the men's 400m. This from a relatively small colonized country still ten years away from independence.

At these same 1952 Olympics McDonald Bailey of Trinidad, running for Britain, won bronze in the 100 meters. Edwards and Bailey were pioneers in the genre of Caribbean people competing, either through colonial status or emigration, for such metropolitan nations as Canada, Britain, France and the United States. There have been times in recent Olympics where three or four of the athletes in Canadian or British relay teams have hailed from places such as Jamaica, Haiti, and Trinidad and Tobago.

Jamaica, participating in its own name, despite its initial colonial status, won medals at fourteen of the fifteen Olympics from 1948 to 2008. (In Rome in 1960 Jamaicans won medals as part of the British West Indies team of the short-lived federation.) This contrasts sharply with the situation of athletes in the French Caribbean departments, whose only Olympic option has been to compete for France. Yet two Guadeloupian athletes between them won four gold medals for France at the 1972 Atlanta Olympics. Marie-José Pérec achieved the remarkable feat of gold in the women's 200 and 400m events. Laura Flessel won gold in individual and team fencing.

There has been an unofficial movement in recent years to compile Olympic medal rankings, not by raw numbers of medals won, but by medals won on a per capita basis. For the 2008 Beijing Olympics the Bahamas topped the world, with Jamaica second. The United States came in at No. 46 and China at No. 68.

While Jamaica, the Bahamas, Trinidad and Tobago and some others have concentrated largely on track events, Cuba in the Castro era became an athletic superpower with success over a wide range of sports.

By the 2008 Olympics the Caribbean men and women dominated the shorter track events, eclipsing both their compatriots representing metropolitan countries and everybody else. Five of the six medals in the men's and women's 100m went to four Jamaicans and one Trinidadian. Jamaicans won gold in the men's and women's 100m and 200m, with Usain Bolt winning both the men's 100m and 200m. Jamaica and Trinidad and Tobago took gold and silver, respectively, in the 4 × 100m relay. The Jamaican 4 × 100m women were unfortunately disqualified but won gold at the World Championships in 2009.

Jamaica and Trinidad and Tobago win gold and silver in the men's 4 × 100m relay at the World Athletic Championships in Berlin, 2009.

Caribbean excellence has also been demonstrated in other sports. The West Indies dominated world cricket for longer (1970s to early 1990s) than any other team. Trinidad and Tobago in 2006 became the smallest nation to qualify for the World Cup football finals.

If a per capita measure could be devised for cultural and intellectual achievements the Caribbean performance might well rival that of its athletic counterparts. Just as 3,000 or 4,000 Grenadian fighters and a handful of Cuban workers were able to surprise a much larger full-fledged U.S. invading force, so too the island of St. Lucia has produced two Nobel Prize recipients, in economics and literature. Trinidad and Tobago has produced another. Despite relentless self-criticism at home, Caribbean students continue to excel in North America and wherever else they find themselves.

The fact that Caribbean athletes based overseas performed exceptionally well but were in 2008 decisively eclipsed by those based at home, may provide some indicators of what could happen throughout society.

Port of Spain's new skyline takes shape, 2009.

By the early twenty-first century Caribbean emigrant communities had produced a governor-general of Canada (Haitian-born Michaëlle Jean), a secretary of state of the United States (Colin Powell, born in New York of Jamaican parents) and an attorney general of the United States (Barbadian American Eric Holder). These achievers took whatever positive qualities they could extract from their Caribbean backgrounds and wedded them to whatever enhanced material and educational opportunities they could find in the metropolis. The combination proved irresistible. Even with the material and other drawbacks of colonized and recently independent developing societies, the Caribbean has long managed to produce remarkable examples of real excellence in many fields. As an increasingly improving material base combines with an already sophisticated populace, Caribbean society as a whole may well some day emulate the achievements of its athletes at the 2008 Olympics.

The late twentieth century brought mixed experiences in the quest for economic advancement. There were periods of impressive growth in the Dominican Republic, Puerto Rico, Jamaica, Trinidad and Tobago and the Netherlands territories, among others. These were interspersed everywhere by periods of stagnation. In Grenada in the early twenty-first century a succession of natural disasters damaged most of the country's buildings, destroyed its crops and temporarily wiped out its tourist industry, forcing it into negative economic growth and resort to the International Monetary Fund (IMF).

Spectacular increases in oil prices in the late twentieth and early twenty-first centuries severely set back many countries. Sometimes corruption contributed to economic problems. Perhaps the "most unkindest cut" of all came with the destruction of the banana industry in several small states, due to the action of the United States. In an economic equivalent of President Reagan's invasion of Grenada, President Bill Clinton in 1996 filed a complaint with the World Trade Organization (WTO) on behalf of the U.S. Chiquita banana company (successor to the United Fruit Company). Clinton's target was former European colonies, notably the Windward Islands of Dominica, St. Lucia, St. Vincent and Grenada. These small nations depended overwhelmingly on bananas

1888

1900

1930

1940

Frederick Street, Port of Spain, 1888 to the 21st Century.

for employment (70.7 percent of the workforce in Dominica in the late 1990s), export earnings and Gross Domestic Product. Because of their small size, precarious economies and previous colonial situations they were given tariff concessions by the European Union, via its Lomé Convention.

Chiquita already controlled 50 percent of the EU banana market. The Caribbean producers controlled 8 percent. Chiquita nevertheless wanted to increase its share. Two days after President Clinton filed with the WTO, CEO Carl Lindner of Chiquita gave Clinton's Democratic Party $500,000.00. In 1998 he also gave the Republican National Committee and its Campaign Committee $350,000.00. Republicans in the U.S. Senate one month later introduced a bill imposing retaliatory tariffs on the EU for its banana support to its former colonies. In 2001 the United States and EU reached agreement dismantling the tariffs, forcing the Caribbean producers to seek alternative marketing strategies and alternative economic initiatives, such as tourism and offshore banking. Some feared that illicit drug trafficking might emerge as a new alternative.

The petroleum-based economic downturns faced by most countries worked in a positive way for oil-producing Trinidad and Tobago, providing it with windfall profits. Trinidad is by most indices one of the richest nations in the Americas. It recorded a growth rate of 12.6 percent in 2006 and 5.5 percent in 2007. It has become a regional financial center. It recorded growing trade surpluses in the 2000s. Trinidad possesses a heavy industrial base—oil, natural gas, ammonia, urea, methanol, iron and steel, asphalt, etc.—beyond anything else existing in the Caribbean. On the eve of the U.S.-induced world recession beginning in 2008, Trinidad had achieved full employment and had become an importer of workers from China, India, the Philippines, Africa, the Caribbean and elsewhere. An impressive government-led building boom was transforming the Port of Spain skyline. In this atmosphere the government introduced its "Vision 2020" plan to achieve fully developed country status by 2020. When the government lost power in 2010, this initiative appeared to have receded from public view.

Cuba, once one of the hemisphere's wealthiest nations, may rebound once the U.S. trade embargo is lifted. Some other countries, including Jamaica and Barbados, have demonstrated the potential for substantial growth. Every Caribbean nation will not have to achieve economic success simultaneously, any more than Mississippi needs to match New York economically, for the Caribbean to continue its rise.

CREDITS

PHOTOGRAPHS

Chapter 1: p. 7, The Pierpont Morgan Library/Art Resource, NY.

Chapter 2: p. 11, Wiener, Leo. *Africa and the Discovery of America*, Vol. 2. Philadelphia: Innes and Sons, 1922. p. 21, Bartolomé de Las Casas. *Narratio regionum indicarum per Hispanos*, a 1598 Latin version of his *Devastation of the Indies*, published by his illustrator Theodorus de Bry. Accessed at: http://lcweb2.loc.gov/service/rbc/rbc0001/2008/2008kislak20219/2008kislak20219.pdf. p. 29, Bartolomé de Las Casas. *Narratio regionum indicarum per Hispanos*, a 1598 Latin version of his *Devastation of the Indies*, published by his illustrator Theodorus de Bry. Accessed at: http://lcweb2.loc.gov/service/rbc/rbc0001/2008/2008kislak20219/2008kislak20219.pdf.

Chapter 3: p. 46, John Gabriel Stedman/The Bridgeman Art Library.

Chapter 4: p. 61, Tony Martin; p. 63, Library of Congress Rare Book and Special Collections Division [LC-USZ62-34160]; p. 64, The Library of Congress [LC-USZ62-54026]; p. 75, John Gabriel Stedman/The Bridgeman Art Library; p. 85, The Granger Collection, NYC; p. 88, Michael Graham-Stewart / The Bridgeman Art Library; p. 91, Mather Brown/Private Collection/The Bridgeman Art Library.

Chapter 5: p. 96, The Granger Collection, NYC; p. 103, John Gabriel Steadman/The Bridgeman Art Library.

Chapter 6: p. 126, Pete Pattisson/ZUMA Press/Newscom.

Chapter 7: p. 145, Tony Martin; p. 146, John Gabriel Stedman/The Bridgeman Art Library; p. 148, John Gabriel Stedman/The Bridgeman Art Library; p. 152, North Wind Picture Archives / Alamy.

Chapter 8: p. 176, The New York Public Library; p. 178, Rue des Archives / The Granger Collection, NYC; p. 179, Marcus Rainsford/Private Collection/The Bridgeman Art Library.

Chapter 9: p. 190, Tony Martin; p. 193, Library of Congress. Accessed at: http://www.loc.gov/rr/hispanic/1898/slaves.html

Chapter 10: p. 209, Bettmann/CORBIS.

Chapter 11: p. 219, Courtesy of Yuan Tsung Chen; p. 222, Archive Farms/Getty Images.

Chapter 12: p. 256, Tony Martin; p. 258, Ted Cunningham/Agency for Public Information, Jamaica.

Chapter 13: p. 267, New York Daily News Archive/Getty Images; p. 270, William Rossiter Collection (COLL/147), Folder 1, Archives & Special Collections Branch, Library of the Marine Corps, Quantico, Virginia; p. 272, Tony Martin.

Chapter 14: p. 279, Courtesy of Afro Cuba Web; p. 283, Tony Martin; p. 285, Tony Martin; p. 294, From the *Colored American Magazine*, 1905.

Chapter 15: p. 308, Tony Martin; p. 309, Courtesy of Cheddi Jagan Research Centre; p. 314, Courtesy of Marx Library; p. 317, Bettmann/CORBIS; p. 329, Everett Collection Inc / Alamy; p. 333, Julien Tack/AFP/Getty Images; p. 339, TopFoto/The Image Works.

Chapter 16: p. 343, Oliver Lang/Getty Images; p. 344, Tony Martin; p. 345, **a**, Courtesy of Illustrated London News, 1888, **b**, Archive Farms/Getty Images, **c**, Adrian Camps-Campins, **d**, Adrian Camps-Campins, **e**, Marka / SuperStock.

QUOTATIONS

Chapter 1: p. 8, From CHRISTOPHER COLUMBUS MARINER by Samuel Eliot Morison. Copyright © 1955 by Samuel Eliot Morison. By permission of Little, Brown and Company. Reprinted by permission of Curtis Brown, Ltd. p. 9, From NATURAL HISTORY OF THE WEST INDIES by Gonzalo Fernandez de Oviedo, translated and edited by Sterling A. Stoudemire. NORTH CAROLINA STUDIES IN THE ROMANCE LANGUAGES AND LITERATURES, No 32. Copyright © 1959 by the University of North Carolina Press, renewed 1987 by Sterling A. Stoudemire. Used by permission of the publisher.

Chapter 2: p. 19, From THE HISPANIC AMERICAN HISTORICAL REVIEW, David Henige, "On the Contact Population of Hispanola: History as a Higher Mathematic",

INDEX

A

Abercromby, Ralph, 127, 137–138, 139
Abolitionist movement, 184, 188
Abolition of slavery, 162, 184, 189, 220, 232.
    See also Emancipation
  abolition of slave trade, 106, 184, 186–188,
    212, 222
  ameliorating measures, 187–188
    Dutch ameliorative measures, 188
  Antislavery Society, 186–187
  "apprenticeship" period, 173, 188,
    190–194, 195–199, 202, 203–204,
    222, 277
  Colonial Office suggestions, 187
  "crown colonies," 187
  "fanaticism," 186
  Foreign Slave Act (1806), 187
  Macau law (1845), 188
  Magistracy for Slave Defense, 188
  organized abolitionism, 186–188
  "protectors of slaves," 187
  Society for Effecting the Abolition of the
    Slave Trade (1787), 186
Abrabanel, Isaac, 54
Abubakari II, 12
Abu Bakr, Yasin, 321
  Coup in Trinidad and Tobago, 321
Accidental voyages, 11
Acham, E. Bernard, 250. *See also* Chen,
  Eugene
Achievers from Caribbean, 342–346
Adams, Grantley, 278, 312
Adams, John Quincy, 267
Adams, Tom, 319
Aduwa, 254, 300
Affranchis (free people of color, including
  free blacks), 110. *See also* Free people
  of color
Africa and the Discovery of America
  (Wiener), 11, 18
African American Civil Rights movement,
  266–267
African Blood Brotherhood, 265, 307
African cultural survivals, 105–109
  Andranga's shrine, 108
  bongo and limbo dances, 106
  Calypso music, 106
  Caribbean *susu* (capital mobilization), 107
  Creole Grammar, 107
  Creolesk, 107
  deity worship, 108
  grammatical and linguistic influences,
    106–107
  Haitian Voodoo, 108
  "idolatry" of indigenous people, 105
  love potions, preparation of, 107–108

marimbula (musical instrument), 107
  pagan festivals, 108
  prenuptial *kwe-kwe* ceremony, 107
  recreational activities, 106
  religious practices, 107
African Fundamentalism, 292
"African progress," efforts to thwart after
  Emancipation, 198–202
  Angel Gabriel affair, 201–202, 208, 223,
    226, 257
  Orr's open preaching, 199–200, 201. *See
    also* Orr, John Sayers
  antislavery elements, 200
licenses, huckster, 199
  negative stereotype of indolence, 198
  planter-merchant legislature, 198
  riots, 201
  "tenancy at will" laws, 198
  trade by free people of color, 199
African Progress Union (APU), 256, 282, 291
African Society for Cultural Relations with
  Independent Africa (ASCRIA), 320
Ajodasingh, 306
Akan people, 157, 161
Algerian Revolution, 250, 258, 325, 332
Ali, Muhammad, 298
Al-Qalqashandi, 12
Al-Umari, 12
Alvares, Afonso, 11, 18
Amapaia, 38
Ambard, A. P. T, 283
Ambrose, 181
American Colonization Society, 253
American Jewish Joint Distribution
  Committee, 244
American Revolutionary War. *See* American
  War of Independence
American War of Independence, 52, 55, 135,
  138, 157, 167, 261, 326
Amistad Mutiny (1839), 166
Amy Ashwood Garvey, 256, 284, 291
Anacaona, 9, 20, 175
Anderson, Violette N., 264
"Angel Gabriel" riots (1856), 201–202, 208,
  223, 226, 257
Anglo-American Caribbean Commission
  (AACC, 1942), 273, 304, 309. *See
  also* Caribbean Commission
Angola intervention (1975–1988), 324
Angola, 11, 42, 60, 82, 83, 103, 106, 123,
  150, 161, 167, 260, 311, 319, 324, 325
Anguilla, 13, 47, 70, 221, 312, 313, 321–322
Anticolonialism, 277, 286–287
Antidrug treaties, 337. *See also* Drugs
Antigua, 3, 13, 16, 35, 49, 51, 52, 66, 68, 70,
  76, 78, 82, 83, 99, 101, 104, 119, 126,

  127, 165, 185, 191, 196, 197, 198,
  207, 211, 213, 216, 221, 242, 261,
  262, 272, 276, 286, 307, 312, 318,
  319, 320, 340
Antiguerilla campaigns/strategy, 147, 152,
  156. *See also* Guerilla warfare
Anti-Jewish riots, 55. *See also* Jews
Antiracism, 277
Antislavery, 162, 164, 183–184, 199–200, 207
Anti-Slavery Society, 68, 186–187, 201, 247
Anti-Syrian riots, 245
Antoneli, Juan Bautista, 47
Apanjaht (*appan jaat* or *apan jhaat*), 239,
  241, 310
  "Anti-apanjaht Utopianism," 241
Apartheid, 115, 116, 131, 254, 258, 315, 319,
  324–325, 333, 335
*An Appeal on Behalf of the Negro Slaves of
  the West Indies* (Wilberforce), 187
Appeal to the Coloured Citizens of the World
  (Walker), 164
Apprenticeship: savage interlude, 195–198
  aftermath of Emancipation, Grenada, 196
  continued sexual exploitation of black
    women and girls, 197
  continued whippings, 196
  Demerara rebellion (1823), 196
  Demerara slave trade, 197–198
  post-apprenticeship struggle, 204
    cleanliness of apprentices'
      neighborhoods, 204
  post-emancipation riots/uprisings
    Emancipation Day (August 1)
      commemorations, 204
    Hosay riots/Muhurram massacre, 204
    Jamaica Rebellion (1865), 202–203
    Labor Act (1849), abolition of, 203
    workers' rebellion in Barbados (1876), 204
  treadmill, 197
Arawaks, 4, 5, 12, 14, 15, 16, 18, 19, 20, 21,
  22, 25, 27, 28, 30, 31, 37, 56, 57, 201,
  220
Archaic immigrant group, 4
Arico, 47, 149
Aristide, Jean-Bertrand, 210, 247, 271, 335,
  336
Arthur, Owen, 338
Aruba
  immigration from British islands, 330
  "status apart," 330
Arwacas, 56
Aryans, 230–231
Arya Samaj Association of Trinidad (1936), 233
Ashwood, Amy. *See* Amy Ashwood Garvey
Association of Caribbean Historians, 326
Athletics, 298, 343–344